PENGUIN BOOKS

SCOTLAND'S EMPIRE

'From the Union of the Crowns to the great British victory at Waterloo in 1815 . . . Devine tells a good story – and what is better, he tells it extremely well' Trevor Royle, *Sunday Herald*

'A fascinating account' Paul Riddell, *Mail on Sunday*

'A powerful account of our past. *Scotland's Empire* is a historical record, but also a testimony to the influence of Scots in shaping the world . . . An excellent read'
Jack McConnell, MSP, First Minister of Scotland

'A thorough, convincing account of the myriad parts played by Scots in Britain's overseas expansion and how their activities transformed their homeland . . . a book that will be enjoyed by anyone interested in history, or who simply enjoys a good story well told' Lawrence James, *Herald*

'An incredible work . . . a clear and deep thinker'
Aberdeen Press and Journal

'Tom Devine, Scotland's foremost historian, follows up his majestic *The Scottish Nation* with a forensic analysis of Scotland's central role in the British Empire. Questioning the usual unionist and nationalist framing of our history, Devine creates a book that suits post-devolution Scotland – we only have ourselves to understand'
Frank McAvetty, MSP, *Sunday Herald*, Books of the Year

'The history of the British empire will never look the same after this book' Christopher Bayly, Professor of Imperial and Naval History, Cambridge University

'Professor Devine's new book confirms that the revival of
Scottish history is entering a new phase. Eloquent and
closely-researched . . . With typical originality, Tom Devine
shows that it was no "new class" which built up colonial wealth,
but the lesser members of Scotland's old possessing class'
Neal Ascherson

'An evocative account of Scotland's history, her role in the
world, our association with emigration, the power of the
Enlightenment' John Swinney, *Scotland on Sunday*,
Books of the Year

'Devine describes in absorbing detail the relentless penetration of
Empire by Scots' Ian McIntyre, *The Times*

'Compelling . . . a fascinating and brilliantly written exploration
of Scotland's crucial, and often bloody, contribution to the
creation of the British Empire'
Brian McGeachan, *Scottish Catholic Observer*

'Awe-inspiring . . . essential to better understand the complexities
of the Scottish psyche' Scotland Magazine

ABOUT THE AUTHOR

T. M. Devine is University Research Professor and Director of the
Research Institute of Irish and Scottish Studies at the University of
Aberdeen. He is a Fellow of the British Academy and of the
Royal Society of Edinburgh. Among Professor Devine's previous
publications are *The Tobacco Lords, Conflict and Stability in
Scottish Society, Improvement and Enlightenment, The Great
Highland Famine, Clanship to Crofters' War, Irish Immigrants
and Scottish Society* and *The Scottish Nation: 1700–2000*. In
2001, Professor Devine was awarded the Royal Gold Medal,
regarded as Scotland's highest academic accolade.

T. M. DEVINE

Scotland's Empire
1600–1815

PENGUIN BOOKS

PENGUIN BOOKS

Published by the Penguin Group
Penguin Books Ltd, 80 Strand, London WC2R ORL, England
Penguin Group (USA)Putnam Inc., 375 Hudson Street, New York, New York 10014, USA
Penguin Books Australia Ltd, 250 Camberwell Road, Camberwell, Victoria 3124, Australia
Penguin Books Canada Ltd, 10 Alcorn Avenue, Toronto, Ontario, Canada M4V 3B2
Penguin Books India (P) Ltd, 11 Community Centre, Panchsheel Park, New Delhi – 110 017, India
Penguin Group (NZ), cnr Airborne and Rosedale Roads, Albany, Auckland 1310, New Zealand
Penguin Books (South Africa) (Pty) Ltd, 24 Sturdee Avenue, Rosebank 2196, South Africa

Penguin Books Ltd, Registered Offices: 80 Strand, London WC2R ORL, England

www.penguin.com

Published by Allen Lane 2003
Published in Penguin 2004

Copyright © T. M. Devine, 2003

All rights reserved
The moral right of the author has been asserted

Typeset by Rowland Phototypesetting Ltd, Bury St Edmunds, Suffolk
Printed in England by Clays Ltd, St Ives plc

Except in the United States of America, this book is sold subject
to the condition that it shall not, by way of trade or otherwise, be lent,
re-sold, hired out, or otherwise circulated without the publisher's
prior consent in any form of binding or cover other than that in
which it is published and without a similar condition including this
condition being imposed on the subsequent purchaser

For
Seán David Devine
who was born as this book was completed

Contents

Acknowledgements

Since 1999 I have had the privilege of being Director of the Research Institute of Irish and Scottish Studies (RIISS) in the University of Aberdeen. Among several other themes in literature, history, language and cultural studies, RIISS has developed important research projects in the history of Scottish emigration and empire since the seventeenth century to the present. This programme was given further impetus in 2000 with the award of a major grant from the United Kingdom Arts and Humanities Research Board and the incorporation within RIISS of an AHRB Centre for Irish and Scottish Studies in partnership with Trinity College, Dublin and The Queen's University, Belfast. This book has developed out of this stimulating intellectual environment which seeks to present the Scottish past within an international and comparative context.

All members of RIISS, whether postdoctoral research fellows, associated academic staff or administrators, have contributed in some way to the book. However, I am especially grateful to Margaret Begbie, who not only helped to assemble the material but very efficiently translated my crabbed handwriting into clear typescript. The book would have been impossible without her expertise and reliability. Professor George Watson, Associate Director of RIISS, took on a heavier administrative burden in session 2002–3 to allow this text to be completed. I thank George not only for this vital support but also for his comradeship, loyalty, good sense and humour. Professor Allan Macinnes first had the idea of an advanced research centre in Irish and Scottish Studies at Aberdeen. He has given it enthusiastic support since its foundation. The Principal of the University, Professor C. Duncan Rice, himself a distinguished historian, has been a faithful friend of RIISS, and, through his own writings, a source of key ideas for the sections on slavery in this book. The Dean of the Faculty of Arts and Divinity, Professor Iain Torrance, could not have been more understanding and supportive of the intellectual project of which this volume is a small part.

The following expert colleagues, all with interests in emigration and imperial studies, have lent books and articles, given ideas and stimulus and suggested avenues for further exploration: Professor Don Akenson, David Ditchburn, David Dobson, Paddy Fitzgerald, Professor David Fitzpatrick, Alexia Grosjean, Douglas Hamilton (now of the University of York), Marjory Harper, Dauvit Horsbroch, Angela McCarthy, Professor John MacKenzie, Andrew Mackillop, Esther Mijers, Martin Mitchell, Steve Murdoch, Professor Jane Ohlmeyer, and Bob Tyson.

I have made considerable use of material held at Aberdeen University Library and borrowed via the Library from elsewhere, for which my thanks are due to the Library staff in general but particularly to the team who man the Inter-Library Loan Desk. Their prompt, good-humoured response to my many requests has been much appreciated.

I am very pleased also to acknowledge the small army of historians on whose work I have drawn, much of which is listed in the Bibliography and References. This book is, in essence, an interpretative synthesis. I hope those authors will find something of interest in what I have written, even if they do not always agree with the conclusions I have drawn from their work.

A version of Chapter 4 first appeared in T. M. Devine and G. Jackson, eds., *Glasgow*. Volume I, *Beginnings to 1830*.

My agent, Andrew Lownie, provided wise advice and helped to ensure the successful completion of the project. Simon Winder at Penguin has been a model editor: insightful, fair, supportive and intelligent. I owe a major debt to him and his highly professional production team.

This book and others which have preceded it would not have been possible without the loving support of Catherine and the family. They also put up with me stoically in some difficult times. The volume is very fondly dedicated with much love to the latest addition to the Devines.

Maps

1. KINROSS
2. CLACKMANNAN
3. DUMBARTON
4. To KINROSS
5. WEST LOTHIAN
6. MIDLOTHIAN
7. EAST LOTHIAN
8. RENFREW

50 Miles

80 Km

CAITHNESS

SUTHERLAND

ROSS & CROMARTY

NAIRN MORAY

BANFF ABERDEEN

Aberdeen

INVERNESS

KINCARDINE

ANGUS

PERTH

R. Tay

Dundee

ARGYLL

FIFE

2 1

R. Forth

3 STIRLING

4

5 Edinburgh

8 Glasgow 6 7

R. Clyde

BERWICK

LANARK

PEEBLES

AYR SELKIRK

ROXBURGH

DUMFRIES

KIRKCUDBRIGHT

WIGTOWN

IRELAND

ENGLAND

Belfast

1. Scotland

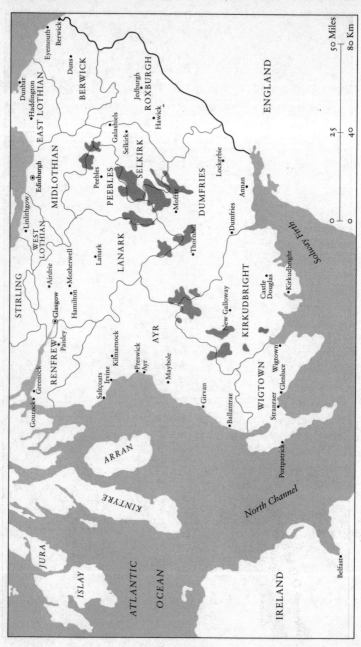

2. The Lowlands

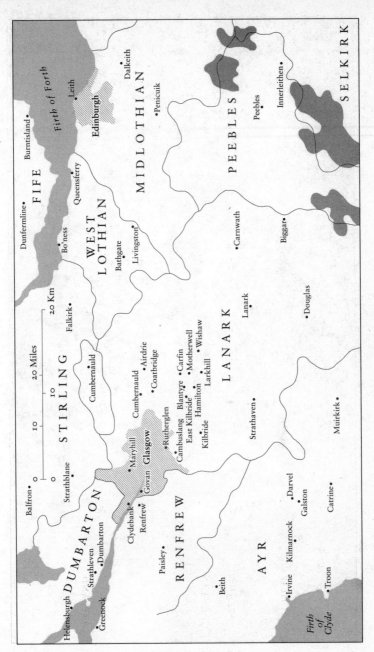

3. Central Scotland

4. The Western Highlands

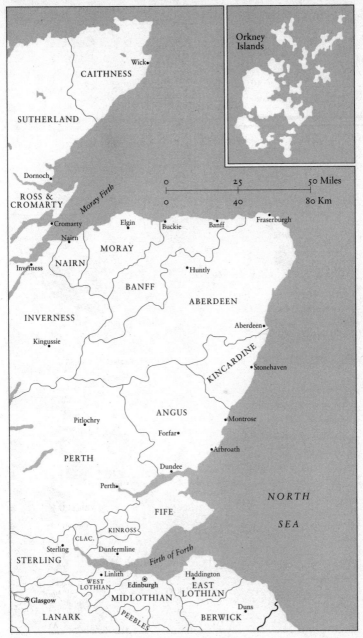

Orkney Islands

CAITHNESS
Wick

SUTHERLAND

Dornoch

ROSS & CROMARTY

Moray Firth

Cromarty
Nairn
NAIRN
MORAY
Elgin
Buckie
Banff
Fraserburgh

Inverness

Huntly

BANFF

INVERNESS

ABERDEEN

Kingussie

Aberdeen

KINCARDINE

Stonehaven

Pitlochry

ANGUS

Forfar

Montrose

PERTH

Dundee

Arbroath

Perth

NORTH

FIFE

SEA

KINROSS
CLAC.
Sterling
Dunfermline

STERLING
Firth of Forth

Linlith
WEST LOTHIAN
Edinburgh
Haddington
EAST LOTHIAN
Glasgow
MIDLOTHIAN
Duns
LANARK
PEEBLES
BERWICK

0   25   50 Miles
0   40   80 Km

5. The Eastern Highlands

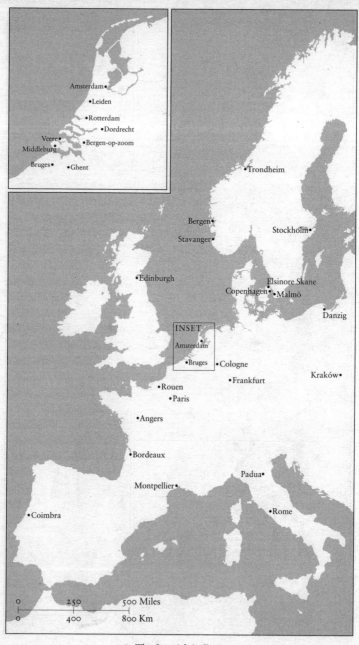

6. The Scottish in Europe

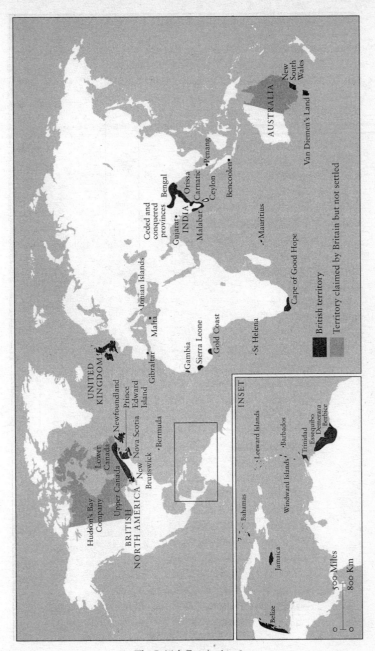

7. The British Empire in 1815

Labels (map):

UNITED KINGDOM

BRITISH NORTH AMERICA
Hudson's Bay Company
Upper Canada
Lower Canada
Newfoundland
Prince Edward Island
Nova Scotia
New Brunswick
Bermuda

Newfoundland

Gibraltar
Malta
Ionian Islands

Gambia
Sierra Leone
Gold Coast
St Helena

Ceded and conquered provinces
Gujarat
INDIA
Malabar
Bengal
Orissa
Carnatic
Ceylon
Penang
Bencoolen

Mauritius
Cape of Good Hope

AUSTRALIA
New South Wales
Van Diemen's Land

British territory
Territory claimed by Britain but not settled

INSET
Bahamas
Jamaica
Belize
Windward Islands
Leeward Islands
Barbados
Trinidad
Essequibo
Demerara
Berbice

0   500 Miles
0   800 Km

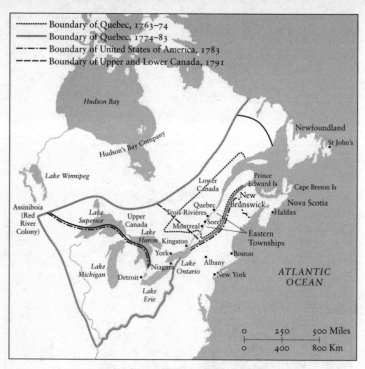

8. Quebec and British North America

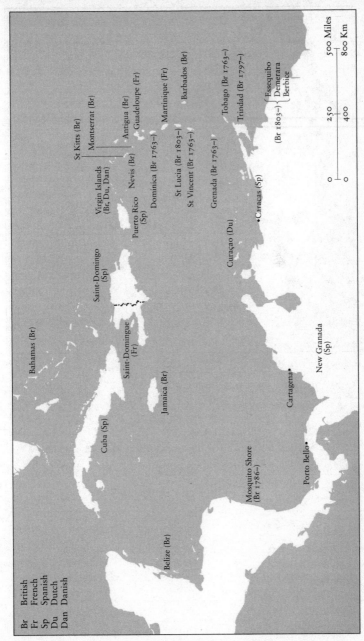

Br   British
Fr   French
Sp   Spanish
Du   Dutch
Dan Danish

Bahamas (Br)

Cuba (Sp)

Saint-Domingue (Fr)

Saint-Domingo (Sp)

Jamaica (Br)

Belize (Br)

Mosquito Shore (Br 1786–)

Porto Bello •

Cartagena •

New Granada (Sp)

Caracas (Sp) •

Puerto Rico (Sp)

Virgin Islands (Br, Du, Dan)

Nevis (Br)

St Kitts (Br)

Montserrat (Br)

Antigua (Br)

Guadeloupe (Fr)

Dominica (Br 1763–)

Martinique (Fr)

St Lucia (Br 1803–)

St Vincent (Br 1763–)

Barbados (Br)

Grenada (Br 1763–)

Curaçao (Du)

Tobago (Br 1763–)

Trinidad (Br 1797–)

Essequibo
Demerara } (Br 1803–)
Berbice

0   250   500 Miles
0   400   800 Km

9. The Caribbean in the Eighteenth Century

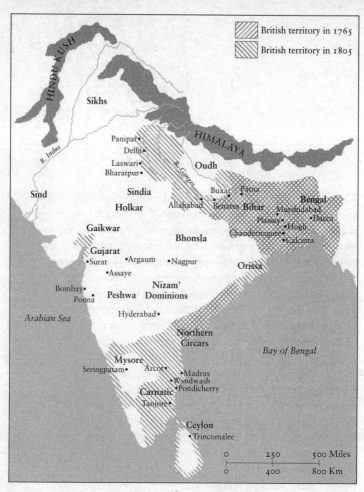

Legend:

▨ British territory in 1765
▨ British territory in 1805

Map labels:

HINDU KUSH

Sikhs

HIMALAYA

R. Indus

Panipat
Delhi
Laswari
Bharatpur

Oudh

R. Ganges

Sind

Sindia

Holkar

Buxar • Patna
Benares • Bihar

Bengal
Murshidabad • Dacca
Plassey • Hugli
Chandernagore • Calcutta

Allahabad

Gaikwar

Bhonsla

Gujarat
• Surat   • Argaum   • Nagpur
   • Assaye

Orissa

Bombay •
Poona •   Peshwa

Nizam'
Dominions

Hyderabad •

Arabian Sea

Northern
Circars

Bay of Bengal

Mysore
Seringpatam •   Arcot •
                 • Madras
               • Wandiwash
Carnatic   • Pondicherry
Tanjore •

Ceylon
• Trincomalee

0   250   500 Miles
0   400   800 Km

10. The Growth of British India

Introduction

The two centuries and more covered by this volume were of fundamental importance in the development of the British Empire whether judged by territorial expansion, size of population, commercial hegemony or global influence. Indeed, it was in the early years of the eighteenth century that the very term 'British Empire' was coined. Only after 1707 and the union between Scotland and England could existing overseas possessions be termed 'British'. Before that, contemporary maps simply described the transatlantic colonies as 'the English Empire in America'. Significantly, a year after the Union of Parliaments, John Oldmixon's two-volume treatise, *The British Empire in America, containing the History of the Discovery, Settlement, Progress and Present State of all the British Colonies on the Continent and Islands of America* (1708), confirmed the new usage.[1] The name would stick. 'England' might still be often used to describe the new union state in Britain. But the term 'the English Empire' was less common. As will become apparent in the course of this book, the widespread acceptance that the developing empire was 'British' and not simply 'English' had a practical rationale which went far beyond mere political symbolism.

Of course, several of the foundations of the later empire had been laid by the end of the seventeenth century. The English presence in North America was particularly well established. The original colonies of Virginia and Maryland were joined by New York, the tiny Scottish settlement at East New Jersey, Pennsylvania and parts of what later became North and South Carolina. Further north, the Hudson's Bay Company was already active in the remote areas which would form part of modern Canada. In the Caribbean, the English held Barbados, Jamaica and the Leeward Islands. Possessions in Africa, however, were limited to a few trading posts on the east of the continent and in the Gold Coast or Gambia. In Asia there was no imperial presence as such but the East India Company had a base on the island of Bombay and grants of some territory in Calcutta and Madras.

In the eighteenth century, and especially after the Seven Years War (1756–63), there were huge territorial gains as a result of conquest and annexation. By c.1770 the population of the North American colonies had grown to around 2.3 million. Georgia, East and West Florida, Quebec and Nova Scotia had all been won from Spain and France. Then came the American Revolution in 1776 and the emergence of an independent United States, born out of the thirteen British colonies. Their departure left only a rump of underpopulated territories in the north of the American mainland. Known as British North America, they would in due course become the Dominion of Canada. Elsewhere, however, the momentum of territorial expansion seemed unstoppable. In the West Indies the Ceded Islands and Trinidad were acquired in 1763, while the most spectacular gains were achieved in India where the whole of the eastern subcontinent and a large part of the Ganges valley were under the administration of the English East India Company by 1815. At that date, it was reckoned that 40 million Indians were now living under British rule which was also fast extending into Ceylon and Mauritius. The Company at the same time was raising some £18 million in taxation within its territories, a sum amounting to around one-third of peacetime revenue in Britain itself.[2] Exploration was also being pursued in the vastness of the Pacific Ocean by the voyages of such famous navigators as Captain James Cook. A permanent British colony was established for the first time in Australia when the First Fleet arrived in New South Wales in 1788.

By 1815 Britain ruled over a global population in America, the Caribbean, Asia and the Antipodes of around 41.4 million people.[3] In 1820, British dominion already encompassed a fifth of the world's population.[4] Contemporaries, such as Sir George Macartney in 1773, revelled in the scale of this vast empire 'on which the sun never sets and whose bounds nature has not yet ascertained'.[5] Patrick Colquhoun's *Treatise on the Wealth, Power and Resources of the British Empire* of 1814 had the revealing subtitle 'in every Quarter of the Globe'. But even these figures underestimated the real extent of British imperial influence. In addition to territories under formal rule there were other areas of 'informal' empire where Britain could, and did, impose its will. At the same time as British dominion was being carved out of the Mughal empire in India, commercial influence was spreading along the Malay coast and as far east as the Chinese port of Canton. Great Indian states such as Awadh (Oudh) and Hyderabad, which were still nominally independent, were nevertheless effectively brought within the sphere of hegemony through Britain's military and naval muscle. Again, in the Caribbean, Dutch or Danish sugar islands became dominated by British planters and capital. It was a similar story in parts of South America, where Britain also began to exercise substantial political influence.

Above all, perhaps, this unprecedented expansion of empire was most significant because it unambiguously confirmed the final victory of Britain over its great national rival, France, in the epic struggle for global dominance. Seven times between 1689 and 1815 the two nations had fought each other in wars which extended well beyond Europe to North America, the West Indies and Asia. The final outcome always remained uncertain. France's population was substantially larger than Britain's and its martial power was formidable. Britain was victorious in the Seven Years War and then annexed much French imperial territory in the Americas and the Caribbean. But the successful revolt of the American colonies after 1776, in alliance with France, was equally a humiliating defeat for the British. Only British success in the Napoleonic Wars and the signal triumphs at Trafalgar and Waterloo finally settled a global contest which had raged for over a century. By 1815 Britain had become Europe's most powerful imperial state. That provided the vital foundation for yet further territorial expansion in India, south-east Asia and Africa in the nineteenth century.

The irony was that as the eighteenth-century empire expanded it steadily became less English and more British. Certainly, English common law continued as the basis of imperial law, and London's dominance as the financial capital of empire remained unchallenged, English politicians for the most part remained the prime influences on imperial policy and the English East India Company's hegemony in Asia was never stronger. Yet, as one historian has put it, by mid-century, 'to all intents and purposes, the English empire had become a fiction ... slowly, almost imperceptibly, the empire had been transformed into a multinational business and military enterprise'.[6] This was partly due to the increasing extent of foreign investment in the English capital markets which were so crucial to the imperial enterprise. It can also be explained by the numbers of Dutch Sephardic Jews and Huguenots who gained greater influence in the eighteenth-century London merchant community. The fact that German immigrants were moving to the American colonies in large numbers after 1750, and that Britain had acquired many French Canadian subjects in the aftermath of her conquests during the Seven Years War, were also significant factors.[7] But, above all, the dilution of an English empire came about because of the enhanced presence within it of Irish and Scots.

Modern Ireland tends sometimes to suffer from acute historical amnesia when the role of the Irish in the British Empire is considered. Yet the Catholic Irish were recruited into the imperial armies in much greater numbers than the English, Scots or Welsh. Indeed, especially after the Act of Union of 1800, 'the Irish of all descriptions entered enthusiastically into the business of empire', as it offered career opportunities which were simply not available in Ireland itself.[8] Nevertheless, from 1700 to 1815, at least, the Scottish factor was immensely more significant. The Scots thoroughly and systematically colonized all areas of the British Empire from commerce to administration, soldiering to medicine, colonial education to the expansion of emigrant settlements. They were also much to the fore in the transformation of the demographic profile of the North American colonies. In the seventeenth century, transatlantic migrants to the plantation economies were overwhelmingly English and Welsh. Between 7,000 and 9,000 Scots can be accounted for in the period 1601 to 1700, compared with over 350,000 English and Welsh emigrants. During the eighteenth century these patterns were transformed. English and Welsh migration fell to less than 100,000 between 1701 and 1780, while Scottish and Irish migration substantially increased, especially from the 1760s. One estimate suggests that down to 1780, perhaps 70 per cent of all British settlers in America were Scots or Irish.[9] It is also the case that for much of the period most of the 'Irish' were in fact 'Ulster Scots', Presbyterian descendants of those who had moved in large numbers from Scotland to the north of Ireland in the seventeenth century. They were part of the Scottish ethnic family, retaining strong Scots cultural affiliations and connections.[10]

In a sense, however, even more important than these mass migrations of Highland Gaels, Lowland farmers and Ulster Scots was the relentless penetration of Empire by Scottish educators, doctors, plantation overseers, army officers, government officials, merchants and clerics. When the statistical record for virtually any area of professional employment in the empire is examined, Scots are seen to be over-represented, and in some cases, like the senior military ranks in India, massively so. In both North America and India after the 1750s, as one writer has put it, they claimed 'not merely a reasonable but a quite indecent share of the spoils'.[11] By mid-century, Scots also dominated the Hudson's Bay Company, which laid claim to the vast expanse of what is now Canada, as well as its great rival in the fur trade, the North West Company. The success of Glaswegian merchants in the transatlantic tobacco trade was such that competitors in London, Bristol and Whitehaven feared by the 1770s that they would monopolize this lucrative branch of imperial commerce. The visibility of the Scots in the imperial project was further confirmed by their own attention to profile. As one of the most literate nations in Europe they publicized their achievements widely in the press and in books.[12] This talent for self-publicity and the *arriviste* triumph in securing many of the glittering prizes of empire goes some way to explaining the rampant Scottophobia which broke out in London and some of the American colonies in the 1770s. The final irony was, of course, that a mere few years before the union with England, Scotland's own ambitious colonial project, the visionary strategy to establish a trading entrepôt at Darien on the isthmus of Panama, had been a catastrophic failure. Penetration of the English empire by stealth after 1707 turned out to be much more effective and profitable.

The Scottish role in the forging and expansion of the eighteenth-century empire is the central theme of this book. It seeks to explain it and evaluate the effects of imperial development both on Scotland itself and the overseas colonies. So intense was the Scottish engagement with empire that it affected almost every nook and cranny of Scottish life: industrialization, intellectual activity, politics, identity, education, popular culture, consumerism, labour markets, demographic trends, Highland social development and much else. In a word, empire was fundamental to the moulding of the modern Scottish nation. The discussion, therefore, needs to maintain a continuous dialogue between domestic Scottish issues and those generated at the global peripheries. Scottish history has always been aware of that broader picture. But one major contention in this book is that the subject in the modern period needs to integrate the national story much more closely with the experience of the Scots overseas. Scotland also impacted profoundly on imperial development. As some of the chapters in this book will argue, Scottish educational traditions and the intellectual achievements of the Scottish Enlightenment had a significant effect on the American colonies, not least in the ferment of political thinking which was one factor in the American Revolution. Governance in India was also affected by a similar intellectual agenda, as was the growing debate on slavery. There is finally the matter of time-frame. The Scottish role in this crucial period of imperial expansion can only really be understood if we move back before the Union of 1707. It is in the seventeenth century, and even earlier, that not only the continuities emerge but also some of the many roots of imperial Scotland.

I

A Nation of Emigrants

I

One of the first references to America in Scottish records appeared in 1597, when one Robert Lindsay, a ship's pilot, presented the council of Aberdeen with a 'haill universal see kart [chart] of Europe, Affrica and Asaia, and new found landes of America'. He received a payment of forty Scots merks for his gift.[1] Around that time there was certainly some Scottish interest in the Newfoundland and Greenland fisheries and occasional references in the early seventeenth century to the odd vessel returning from the Caribbean and the Chesapeake laden with tobacco, sugar and other exotic commodities.[2] Before 1650 or so, however, the connections were fleeting and the few official schemes of settlement unsuccessful. For a nation later celebrated in imperial expansion it seems odd that the Scots came relatively so late to the business of transatlantic commerce and colonization.

One careful estimate suggests that fewer than 200 Scots had settled in the English plantations in America before 1640, with a handful of others in New France and the New Netherlands.[3] And this despite the fact that when James VI of Scotland became James I in the Regal Union of 1603, the *post-nati* Scots (those born after the union) were soon allowed to live, work, trade and own property in all the monarch's dominions including those across the Atlantic. Even the series of official Scottish attempts at trade and colonization were unsuccessful and some ended in complete disaster. A fishing enterprise under Sir James Cunninghame in 1617 off the Greenland coast was short-lived. More ambitious was the plan by Sir William Alexander in 1622 to create a Scottish colony in the territories lying between New England and Newfoundland. Alexander's charter was granted under the crown of Scotland and he hoped that since 'there was a new France, a new Spain and a new England, that they might likewise have a new Scotland'. This was the first serious attempt by Scotland to catch up with the established colonial powers. But enthusiasm at home did not match these aspirations. Indeed, the majority of settlers in what came to be called Nova Scotia may well have been English. Another expedition, this time to Cape Breton Island, under James Stewart, Lord Ochiltree, in 1629, did little to kindle more interest. Of the party of seventy Scots who landed, thirty perished and the remainder surrendered to the French who claimed sovereignty over the area. The Nova Scotia enterprise formally came to an end when the territory was surrendered to France by treaty in 1632. Efforts were also made to trade with Africa.[4] The Guinea Company of Scotland, founded in 1636, was the most notable of these. It brought together both Scottish and London interests but ended badly. In 1637 the Company ship, the *St Andrew of Edinburgh*, was seized by the Portuguese on its return from Africa. The crew was murdered and the cargo of gold, valued at £10,000 sterling, stolen.[5]

Perhaps this train of misfortunes was not entirely unexpected. Even England, which was much more effective than most European powers in encouraging its people to cross the Atlantic in this period, had only recently established its first permanent settlement at Jamestown in Virginia in 1607, though the ventures that followed, such as New England in 1620, and in 1630 at Plymouth colony and Massachusetts Bay colony, did in the end succeed handsomely. Elsewhere the European presence on the eastern coast of America was always fragile, vulnerable and precarious. New Netherlands, for instance, was of limited attraction to the Dutch and was peopled as a result not only by a few emigrants from Holland but also by Germans, Swedes, Jews, Huguenots and English. It has even been suggested that the population of New Sweden at this time probably consisted mainly of Finns.[6] The New World, particularly areas in the northern hemisphere, was simply too distant, inhospitable, alien and wild to entice many Europeans. Significantly both the English and Scottish governments throughout the seventeenth century regarded the colonies as a suitable dumping-ground for convicted felons, vagrants, prostitutes, political prisoners and other undesirables. Transportation to those territories was regarded as an awful punishment and second only to judicial execution as a deterrent.

Nevertheless, Scotland's position on the north-west periphery of Europe meant that it was very well placed for forging American connections. The country also had long experience as a seafaring and trading nation, and an ingrained tradition of migration which for centuries had brought many thousands of Scots to seek opportunities in England, Ireland and throughout western Europe.[7] In addition, the evidence of those colonial enterprises which were attempted in the 1620s and 1630s suggests there were indeed some enterprising spirits among the merchant and landed classes who had the potential to contribute to overseas adventures. Yet, even by comparison with states of similar population size, such as Sweden and Norway-Denmark, Scotland seems an imperial failure in the first half of the seventeenth century.

One explanation for this was the country's anomalous political position within the United Kingdom. Other states, like Portugal, Spain, Sweden and the Netherlands, had strong central executives which pursued aggressive overseas policies as an integral part of their expansionist strategies. Scotland was handicapped in this respect. After 1603 it shared a single monarchy with England. But the Scottish Parliament had never managed to secure much influence over foreign policy before that date when the Scottish King James VI succeeded Elizabeth, and an independent foreign policy therefore disappeared over the Border with James after the Regal Union. At the same time, and crucially, both James and his successor, Charles I, naturally tended to favour the position of England, the senior partner in the dynastic union, especially when any conflict emerged between English and Scottish vital interests. These considerations help to explain why James rescinded the grant made to Sir James Cunninghame in 1618 to establish a Scottish East India Company which might have been in direct competition with the English East India Company. Charles I's decision to hand Nova Scotia back to the French in 1632 confirmed that specifically Scottish interests were also likely to be sacrificed when broader issues of state were concerned.[8]

A similar set of choices was at stake in the 1690s when an even more ambitious Scottish attempt to break into the lucrative East India trade was vehemently opposed by the London government and financial interests. This was the background to the subsequent ill-fated expeditions to Darien on the isthmus of Panama. Several decades earlier, in 1661, the government in London had passed Navigation Acts which treated Scots as foreigners and banned their shipping from the colonies. Without an independent foreign policy or a strong navy, both prerequisites for a successful imperial policy, *formal* Scottish colonization in the Americas was likely to remain an elusive prize. Even with more support coming from the Scottish Privy Council and Parliament during the 1680s schemes for settlement colonies, like Stuart's Town in Carolina in that decade, tended to founder.[9]

But far too much can be read into these failures. The hard lessons of Nova Scotia and the other disappointments of the 1620s and 1630s were absorbed by the next generation. Where English interests were threatened, England's naval and diplomatic might would prevail. There was therefore little point in challenging England directly in the race for colonies. The Scots élites for the most part now adopted a more subtle approach. It was a policy which was pursued from the 1640s and endured even after the union of 1707. The idea was to infiltrate the empires of England and other more powerful European states at the level of the individual merchant, soldier, official and investor. It was in a sense imperialism by stealth. Resources were concentrated in private mercantile syndicates rather than ambitious public schemes. Especially after the passage of the Navigation Acts of 1660, Scottish smuggling in American waters emerged as a growth industry. Scots businessmen used expatriate Scottish communities in the great international entrepôts of London, Rotterdam, Amsterdam and elsewhere to promote transatlantic and Asian ventures. Military, diplomatic and administrative posts in European states and in large foreign enterprises, such as the Dutch East India Company (VOC), also attracted many Scots.[10] Only in the 1680s, with the foundations at Stuart's Town and East New Jersey, and in the Darien scheme the following decade, was the discredited policy of planting Scottish colonies tried once again, with mainly predictable and catastrophic consequences.[11]

However, to stress the political obstacles to a Scottish Atlantic empire in the early seventeenth century is partly to miss the point. Scotland was indeed a nation of emigrants in this period. But that emigration was firmly and overwhelmingly drawn towards the European continent, to Ireland and, to a lesser extent, England. It was these major connections which were the biggest single constraint on Scottish American colonization. Those who wished to seek opportunities elsewhere, and they were numerous, were still able to exploit the old European routes and the more recent opportunities closer to home, across the Irish Sea in Ulster. There was precious little incentive to try one's luck in the far-off wilderness of North America.

Modern research has uncovered some truly astonishing levels of emigration from seventeenth-century Scotland. Several estimates (some of them frankly little more than reasoned guesswork) would suggest a total Scottish population of around 1 million by c.1700. The number of emigrants, whether temporary or permanent, from this total suggests a society where human mobility was an expected and inevitable part of ordinary life. Even given the fragility and ambiguity of the source material, the results of careful scholarship are impressive. 'Rough numbers' indicate a total Scottish migration of between 85,000 and 115,000 from 1600 to 1650. This represents a broad annual loss of around 2,000 people. There was diversity within this emigrant stream. For instance, the movement to Ulster largely consisted of families, while the exodus to Europe was generally of young single men, aged between fifteen and thirty. These were the many soldiers, packmen and small traders who sought opportunities on the Continent. It may be that Scotland lost nearly one in five of its young men during these decades. It was a figure equalled in Europe only by Switzerland in the early modern period.[12] More remarkably, the haemorrhage was proportionately only slightly less than the outflow of young adult males recorded during Scotland's greatest ever emigration in the 1850s. That nineteenth-century diaspora is well remembered. The exodus 200 years previously is largely forgotten. That amnesia is surprising. Few Europeans or English moved to Scotland. The figures which have been collected, therefore, probably represent the highest rate of *net* out-migration in western Europe.[13] As the contemporary statistician G. T. Bissett-Smith remarked in 1909, 'The Scots are notoriously migratory.'[14] Little did he realize that he was describing a crucial part of the nation's heritage which extended back more than six centuries.

It was a tradition which William Lithgow would have easily recognized in his 'explorations' of 'nineteen yeares travayles . . . to the most famous Kingdomes in Europe, Asia and Affrica', published for the first time in 1632. Lithgow was a native of Lanark, and known as 'Cutlugged' or 'Lugless Will' because his ears had been brutally severed by the brothers of a girl he had seduced. He travelled on foot and by ship through England, Ireland, Switzerland, France, Spain, the Low Countries, German-speaking lands, Hungary and Poland, and thence to the Sahara and the Holy Land. There are many striking memories recorded in his *Totall Discourse of the Rare Adventures and Painefull Peregrinations of Long Nineteen Yeares* which climaxed in his being 'cruelly Racked' by the Spanish Inquisition as a heretic Scottish Protestant. The memoir included stories about inordinate drinking and exotic sexual experiences in far-off lands. Lithgow also recorded more mundane episodes. Among these were the number of times he encountered nomadic fellow countrymen in the very heart of Europe. In Cracow he met 'diverse Scottish merchants'. In Lublin, there was an 'abundance of gallant rich Merchants my Countrey-men'. Their congenial meetings were 'sealed with deepe draughts' ended by the toast, 'God be with you'. Lithgow fell ill in Gdańsk after a journey from Warsaw in the company of one William Baillie, who had also been born in the valley of the river Clyde in Scotland. He was so close to death in Gdańsk that his 'country-men there' prepared his 'Grave and Tombe' in readiness. Lithgow, however, survived and lived to tell the tale in his *Painefull Peregrinations*.[15]

Medieval historians argue that significant levels of Scottish emigration began in the later fourteenth century. Scottish soldiers, vagrants, scholars and merchants were soon to be found in France, the Low Countries, Scandinavia and England.[16] As early as 1398 the Scots were deemed to be such a political menace in Northumberland that the London government moved to disperse them south of the river Tyne. In the German states and Poland, Scottish hucksters, pedlars and hawkers during much of the fifteenth century were sufficiently numerous to invite judicial retribution because of their nefarious practices of undercutting and selling cheap goods. But the Scots were also valued for their martial expertise and scholarship. In the fourteenth and fifteenth centuries, the legendary *gaillóglaichs* (gallowglass or foreign warriors), later to be joined by the 'Scottes redshanks', became the shock troops of medieval Irish chieftains. Wielding their favourite weapon, the double-edged axe on a long shaft, these Scottish mercenaries wreaked terrible havoc and were themselves slaughtered in large numbers in the savage conflicts of the time.[17] In due course, they were immortalized in Shakespeare's *Macbeth*. But Scottish soldiers for hire were also to be found in the armies of England and France. In the latter country they formed the Garde Écossais, given the special honour during the reign of Louis XII of protecting the person of the French monarch after dark.

Throughout the entire period covered by this book, Scots trained in the arts of violence were in great demand. But the cerebral Scot was also a feature of European society in the medieval era.[18] Even after the foundation in the fifteenth century of universities at St Andrews, Glasgow and Aberdeen, Scottish students still travelled in significant numbers to European centres of learning. Until the Reformation the favourites were Paris and the Italian universities. But in the later Middle Ages Scots could be found at around thirty European institutions of higher learning, from Copenhagen in the north to Bologna in the south.[19] Not all these students returned immediately. Indeed some of those who stayed on for longer reached positions of high eminence. Between its foundation and the Reformation, seventeen or eighteen rectors at the University of Paris were Scots.[20] John Duns Scotus, trained at Cambridge, Oxford and Paris in the thirteenth century, John Ireland, John Major and James Liddell were all scholars with huge international reputations.

Individual scholars went to Europe for advanced learning but the mass emigrations of medieval times were essentially driven by economic crisis, relative poverty, demographic pressure, constrained opportunity and openings abroad, all of which created a long tradition of searching for betterment. These factors were a constant running through Scottish history from the fourteenth century to the era of the Industrial Revolution and up to more modern times. In 1682, for instance, the Hudson's Bay Company was urged to recruit Scots. The correspondent noted perceptively, 'that countrie is a hard country to live in, and the poore-mens wages is cheap, they are hardy people both to endure hunger and cold, and are subject to obedience'. The reporter continued: 'I am sure that they will serve for 6 pound pr. yeare and be better content with their dyet than Englishmen will be.'[21] John Nixon, who provided this advice, understood much of the force that impelled Scots to look outside their native land, not only in his own era, but in earlier centuries. In most of the first half of the seventeenth century, however, the opportunities in European lands were especially attractive and in consequence the Americas were pretty far down the list of Scottish priorities. In sum, these 'pull' factors included the massive military demands of the Thirty Years War, the attractions of continental trading connections, and the development of the Ulster plantation, Scotland's first great rural migration. These were the constituent parts of an 'informal' Scottish empire which had precious little to do with risky adventuring across the oceans.[22] In this period Scotland was indeed expansionist, but both its emigrations and the ambitions of its people were mainly confined to Europe and the British Isles.

2

There were several good reasons for this. Scotland had the economic advantage of a land frontier with England and the benefit of easy access to the north of Ireland by a short sea crossing. Even more crucially, its long North Sea coastline meant that Scottish merchants had a much shorter sea journey to Scandinavia and the Baltic than to any port in eastern England. This geography was of critical importance because for much of the seventeenth century it meant that Scotland had easier access to the Baltic, Europe's inland sea, and the maritime environment for the development of the Swedish economic renaissance and the thriving trade in grain through the northern Baltic ports like Gdańsk (Danzig), Lübeck and Königsberg (modern Kaliningrad).[23] In time, the centre of gravity shifted south to the London–Amsterdam axis and from there westwards to the wide expanses of the Atlantic. But in the early decades of the seventeenth century the Scots were indeed fortunate in being so close to one of the nerve centres of European economic and military power. Both Sweden and Denmark were aggressively expansionist states in this period and their territorial imperialism was sustained by domestic economic success. Not surprisingly, therefore, Scottish international trade was focused on the North Sea with links to Scandinavia, the southern Baltic, Flanders and northern France.

Scottish customs accounts for 1621–3 suggest that nearly two-thirds of imports originated in the Netherlands (32 per cent), the Baltic and the north German plain (22 per cent) and France (18 per cent). Goods coming from England yielded 22 per cent in revenue and all other destinations a mere 6 per cent.[24] These figures are striking confirmation of Scotland's European commercial orientation at this time: the sea united and the land divided. Thus Orkney, Shetland, the north-east of Scotland, Dundee and the Fife ports had much closer connections with centres in Norway, Denmark, Sweden and Holland than with the Clyde burghs or the Border towns.[25] After all, in fair weather Norway could be reached in less than four days. Along these time-honoured connections came an intermittent flow of emigrants. Virtually every major town (and even a few less famous) had Scottish communities.[26] As early as the 1540s the Scots were second only to the Dutch in Gothenburg in Sweden. Germans and Scots from the Northern Isles vied for hegemony in the Norwegian port of Bergen. In the southern Baltic the Scots were everywhere. They were so competitive in Kedainia in Lithuania that, as elsewhere, the local merchants vigorously protested about their growing power. However, that did not stop the Scottish rise to overall authority in the town by the later seventeenth century.[27]

Ethnic relationships were reinforced by the risks of trade. Scottish merchants shared in the ownership of ships. They also consigned goods in small quantities. Family, friends and trusted associates were much preferred as business partners.[28] Above all, the prudent trader kept to traditional routes where knowledge of the localities and confidence in the people there helped reduce some of the perennial hazards. But maintaining the old ways was not necessarily a conservative strategy. On the contrary, trading from east-coast Scottish burghs through the Sound and then into the Baltic Sea opened up a vast market and a colossal source of supply of goods in demand throughout the Continent. It is well known, for instance, that the Baltic ports were 'Scotland's emergency granary' in times of famine and food shortage. Often less recognized were the abundant commercial opportunities in this huge region provided both by nature and the contemporaneous decline of the monopolistic Hanseatic League.[29] Of the two factors, nature was probably the more important. From the Middle Ages much of the commerce of enormous stretches of northern and eastern Europe was generated through the great river valleys, from the Elbe in the west to the Vistula. The Vistula basin alone had a network of waterways open to navigation which reached more than 400 miles inland. This was an economic cornucopia far greater than anything the Atlantic empire could offer before the eighteenth century.

These opportunities engendered an impressive Scottish connection. By the time of the Wars of Independence which began in the late thirteenth century, Scottish merchant ships were sailing regularly into the area. Famously, the renowned Scottish patriot William Wallace corresponded with the Senate of Lübeck in 1297, in a letter now in the Museum of Scotland, advising that the English invader had been repulsed and so trade could be started again. But it took another three centuries for the relationship to reach full maturity. From the later sixteenth century Scots moved into Poland in unprecedented numbers. As early as 1569, Sir John Skene observed 'ane great multitude' of Scots pedlars in Cracow, while in 1598 Fynes Morrison thought the country was then swarming with these petty Scottish merchants.[30] The exodus must have been very considerable. Debates in the London Parliament after the Regal Union of 1603 used 'the multiplicities of the Scots in Polonia' as a dreadful example of the fate to befall England if the Scots became naturalized subjects. The conclusion was simple: 'we shall be over-run with them'.[31] In a much-quoted passage, William Lithgow thought Poland 'the Mother and the Nurse, for the youth and younglings of Scotland', and asserted that 'thirty thousand Scots families . . . live incorporate in her bowels'.[32]

No one knows for certain the overall numbers of emigrants. Since the majority seem to have been young men, many intermarried and assimilated rapidly into Polish society. Integration accelerated after c.1660 as immigration declined and was virtually complete by the end of the eighteenth century. Not surprisingly, Poland became Scotland's 'forgotten diaspora'. Large numbers stayed. Many converted to Catholicism. They learnt Polish and German. Chalmers became Czamer; Forbes, Frybes; Gordon, Gordonowski; Ramsay, Ramze; Reid, Ridt; Smith, Smizd, and so on as Polonization intensified. Not all traces, however, were removed.[33] Today in the dialect of Polish Pomerania, *Szot* means a commercial traveller, a reminder of the time when the Scots in Poland were mainly pedlars, hucksters and merchants. '*Skapy jak Szkot*' ('as mean as a Scot') remains a Polish saying and a testimony to the pedlars' ability to strike a tough deal. Surviving place-names, such as Nowa Szkocja, Scotna Gòra, Pasas Sjkocki ('Scottish Passage'), Brama Douglasa ('Douglas' Gate') and Stary Szkoty ('Old Scotland', in Gdańsk), among many others, provide a modern link with a distant past. In addition, municipal and national archives in Poland are replete with numerous prohibitions against vagrant Scottish pedlars and itinerant tradesmen. They speak of a country with plenty of Scots hucksters on the make who were destabilizing crown and town commercial regulations governing fair trade and established business practices.[34]

Quantifying the actual impact of all this is much more difficult. One Polish scholar has traced the names of over 7,400 male Scots in no fewer than 420 places throughout Poland. Overwhelmingly, they were either natives of the east of Scotland (140 localities have been indicated in that region) or second-generation migrants. The same researcher is confident, however, that this number represented only a fraction of those who came to seek their fortune or try to escape a life of poverty.[35] Almost certainly, indeed, movement to Poland was the biggest single civilian Scottish emigration of the early seventeenth century, significantly eclipsing movement to England and even to Ulster in this period. The 'rough guess' at the moment by scholars is that 30,000 to 40,000 came between 1600 and 1700. This was a quite massive number, given that the total Scottish population was then under 1 million and the great exodus was concentrated on the eastern counties of the country.[36] The demographic consequences can only be guessed at. But since so many young men left, marriage patterns must have been affected and domestic population increase dramatically cut back.

The emigration took place for a number of reasons. At this time, the vast mass of Scots lived in the countryside, practising husbandry and eking out a living sufficient to pay the rent to the landlord and produce enough for the family to subsist for another year. Yet the scale of urban development, especially along the eastern rim from Inverness to Edinburgh, in the early modern period also has to be acknowledged. In fact, by 1600 the proportion of Scotland's population living in the larger towns probably exceeded that of Switzerland, Scandinavia and most of eastern Europe.[37] The evolution of the smaller towns was more significant because Scotland was *par excellence* a country of tiny urban centres. St Andrews, Cupar, Crail, Dunfermline and Kirkcaldy were much more typical than Edinburgh, Dundee, Aberdeen and Glasgow. The proportion of Scots living in burghs with over 2,000 people in 1639 may actually have been as great or even greater than in England, and this despite that country's precocious urban renaissance in the first half of the seventeenth century.[38] Indeed in the urban clusters around the Forth estuary, town development was probably as intensive as in the urbanized Low Countries.[39] Overwhelmingly, however, these centres were concerned with exchange. On the whole they specialized in marketing, unlike the industrial villages and towns, and dealt in the selling of cattle, skins, wool, fish, grain, salt, coal, linen and woollen goods, while importing many goods from abroad. They were not industrial centres.[40] These urban enclaves were almost like schools of commerce functioning in an underdeveloped economy with limited opportunities.

From them, therefore, came the pedlars who worked their way across Scandinavia, and pre-eminently found their niche in Poland. There they discovered in abundance the opportunities for profit which were scarce at home. The Polish commercial structure was stagnant, with few towns scattered across the countryside. At the same time, the Polish aristocracy were marketing the surplus wheat and rye of their great estates in a period of population increase and urban growth in western Europe. The potential for gain was immense. Scots merchants moved in first from Gdańsk along with the Dutch and other nationalities. Credit was advanced to grain producers, in a manner not unlike the relationship between Glasgow tobacco lords and Virginian planters in the following century. One suggestion is that at the peak of the grain trade's prosperity in the early seventeenth century there were over 400 small Scottish settlements in Poland and along the Prussian coast. The success of these ethnic communities was demonstrated by the rise of the twelve 'Scottish Brotherhoods', each organized by an elected committee of 'Elders' drawn from all the Scottish 'colonies'. It was also confirmed by the ascent of a few Scots to positions of real power in Poland. Perhaps the most famous was Alexander Chalmer (Czamer), born in Dyce near Aberdeen, who made his pile in textiles and then served four terms as Mayor of Warsaw. Some, like Robert Gordon, a wealthy Gdańsk merchant who endowed Robert Gordon's College at Aberdeen, invested part of their riches back home. Yet others, especially those Scottish soldiers who fought under Polish command, sometimes entered the ranks of the nobility.[41] But these were not the typical Scots. The vast majority were packmen, plying their trade on horseback, selling cheap household wares into the remotest parts of the country. In straitened times or when the opportunities presented themselves, they exchanged the role of petty trader for that of professional soldier in the manner of their fellow countrymen in other parts of Europe.

It was not simply in Poland that the fighting Scot was in demand. The high reputation of Scottish soldiers, whether as shock troops or defensive formations, was well attested. Scots companies never made up more than 7 per cent in the Dutch army of the seventeenth century, but their service was chronicled in Holland by pamphlets and verses. Sometimes this was because of the terrible hardships they seemed prepared to endure. At Nieuwpoort in 1600, the carnage was such in the battle against Spanish forces that the Scots levies lost more than half their number. Even the English observers confirmed that they were 'the bulwark of the [Dutch] Republick' and were like 'Beanes and Peas among chaffe ... sure men, hardy and resolute, and their example holds up the Dutch'.[42] The Swedes took a similar view. Chancellor Axel Oxenstierna was the most influential political figure in Sweden during the first few decades of the seventeenth century. He was also a great admirer of the martial nature of the Scots, praising them on many occasions for their fidelity and courage under arms.[43]

Scots had sold their martial expertise to Irish chiefs, English kings and French monarchs since the fourteenth century. The professional soldier was not only an accepted figure but a respected part of the Scottish nation. Before 1600, and in some parts for even longer, warrior societies thrived in most of the Highlands. The *Buannachan*, or mercenary corps, were the Hebridean clans' acknowledged spearhead of ferocity.[44] The landscape of the Scottish Borders was also studded by a remarkable proliferation of tower-houses and other fortifications. The military architecture confirmed the region's notoriety before 1600 as a centre of murder, cattle thieving, assault and vicious family vendettas which were on a par with the Sicily of the Mafia in the twentieth century. Proficient swordsmen were a common breed in early seventeenth-century Scotland. Thus when Europe entered its greatest ever military recruitment boom in the Thirty Years War from 1618, the Scots soldiers were at a premium. One modern estimate suggests that between 1618 and 1648, over 112,000 men from the British Isles were raised for service by different European powers in the mighty conflict between Protestantism and the Catholic Hapsburg empire. Of these, around 60,000 (or 55 per cent of the total) may have been Scots, a figure which does not include female camp-followers.[45] Thus, long before they became British imperialists, the Scottish élites and their family regiments had become a force to be reckoned with in Europe. This was especially the case in Scandinavia, where close relationships were forged with the Protestant powers of Norway-Denmark and Sweden. The Oldenburg and Vasa dynasties relied heavily on Scottish military support. In return, Scottish officers became integral to the Scandinavian state systems as senior military and naval commanders and as regional governors.[46]

To understand the extraordinary levels of military demand at this time we need to broaden the perspective. The armies which fought in the Thirty Years War were enormous by comparison with their predecessors. By 1648, for example, the warring factions in central Europe had 210,000 men under arms.[47] Such massive forces quickly outran the supply of amenable local recruits. The combatant states had to look elsewhere for a ready supply of personnel. The dreadful rate of attrition on muster strength, caused mainly by the toll of disease rather than conflict, ensured a continuous and insatiable appetite for ever more fresh recruits. By 1600 the main sources of supply of military manpower were well defined. They included, in addition to Scotland, the populations of the poorer districts of Flanders, Ireland and the hilly regions on both sides of the Rhine, reaching as far south as the Alps and Switzerland. Military service tended to be the specialist function of regions of poverty. The life of a seventeenth-century soldier was harsh and brutal and the pay uncertain; hence it had little appeal for the peoples of the richer territories of north-west Europe.[48] Yet military service could have significant social effect. Fighting abroad accustomed the inhabitants of remote areas to life beyond familiar horizons, though we shall never know how many returned from foreign wars to tell the tale. In addition, a short-lived career as an army or naval officer could also be the prelude to merchanting in a foreign port.[49] Some Scottish soldiers of fortune in Sweden moved into the ranks of the rural traders, the *landsköp*, who challenged the commercial privileges of the townsman.[50] There is also evidence of wandering packmen joining up for the spoils of war and then going back to huckstering when peace returned.[51] This fluidity partly explains the huge desertion rates experienced by these seventeenth-century armies. It also meant, however, that military service was a powerful force for promoting general mobility. Scotland's high rates of emigration in the first half of the seventeenth century (much greater than the levels achieved in the eighteenth century) were probably shared only by Switzerland in this period.[52] It was hardly a coincidence that both countries had achieved international renown by exporting very large numbers of soldiers to fight on the battlefields of foreign lands.

Economic and social factors in Scotland also helped sustain the great exodus of young men. A combination of geology, marginal agriculture and uncertain weather meant it was a hard country to live in. In the words of Neal Ascherson; 'Much of Scotland's soil is shallow and acid. The rock pokes through the worn sleeve of the turf; erosion gullies fan downwards from the ridges . . . Scottish earth is in most places – even in the more fertile south and east – a skin over bone . . .'[53] Despite these harsh limitations, the early decades of the seventeenth century have been judged years of some economic improvement.[54] Even so, the contemporary political obsession with vagrancy and the evidence of a rise in numbers in the later 1500s, might suggest that Scotland had an emerging problem of over-population. One intriguing confirmation of demographic pressure was the growing trend away from meat-eating in the national diet towards cheaper grains such as oatmeal.[55] Certainly, small tenants, cottars and farm servants were very vulnerable to the consequences of even partial harvest failure which could mean, quite literally, the difference between life and death for them. Thus in 1623 a severe famine struck many parts of Scotland. It killed 10 to 15 per cent of the inhabitants of Dumfries. Dunfermline also lost between a quarter and a third of its population, though some of these people might have been strangers searching for food.[56] A crisis on this scale not only caused heavy levels of internal movement, as small farmers, unable to pay rents, lost their holdings and servants were dismissed by their penniless masters, but also led to emigration from Scotland to both Ireland and Europe. Military recruitment could also more readily take place at such a time when other more desirable options were closed off or markedly reduced.

In good times the reluctance to join the colours was hardly surprising: 'to become an ordinary soldier in the Thirty Years War was to buy a one-way ticket to almost certain death'.[57] Yet huge numbers were still delivered to the recruiters. Landed families used their economic muscle to ensure that their tenants yielded up sons for service. After all, recruitment was an excellent way of ensuring honourable employment for the younger sons and other male dependants of the gentry who then colonized the numerous officer posts in the regiments. Entire military dynasties were established around this tradition. The Munro lineage from Easter Ross was one of the most famous. It was reputed to have had three generals, eight colonels, five lieutenant-colonels and thirty captains all serving in the armies of the Swedish king, Gustavus Adolphus.

For members of this élite, unlike the common soldier, there was a real chance of achieving fame and fortune in foreign fields. Thomas Dalyell of the Binns is best known in Scottish history as the notorious persecutor of the Covenanters in the 1680s, and the man who introduced thumbscrews to Scotland as instruments of torture to be used on unfortunate enemies of the state. But 'Old Tam of Muscovy', as he was often known, had begun life as a soldier, serving the Czar of Russia so loyally that he was created a general before leaving for home in 1665. The story of Patrick Gordon was even more colourful. Born near Ellon in Aberdeenshire, the son of a minor and impoverished laird, Gordon left for Europe in 1651. Throughout the 1650s he served in the Polish and Swedish armies before entering Russian service. There he remained for nearly four decades, punctuated only by a few visits back to Scotland. He ended his highly eventful career as confidant and adviser to the young Peter the Great. These are the names remembered in military chronicles of the time.[58] But they were the tip of a very large iceberg. Over 3,500 Scottish officers have already been identified fighting in Scandinavia and the Baltic states during the Thirty Years War.[59] Several of them were ennobled and became members of the landed aristocracies of Sweden and Denmark. Nor can they always be described simply as mercenaries or fighting only for money. Recent research has shown how many Scots became involved in these religious wars because they saw the Scottish Kirk as having a special role as a champion and defender of Protestantism. Moreover, the original aggression of the House of Hapsburg against Frederick of Bohemia in 1619, which had triggered these long wars, had a special resonance for the Scots. Frederick was married to the Princess Elizabeth of Scotland and an attack on Bohemia was widely perceived as an act of war against the Scottish House of Stuart and not simply an onslaught against European Protestantism.

Certainly in Scandinavia the Protestant powers regarded the Scots as an allied nation rather than simply as soldiers available for hire to the highest bidder.[60] The Danes called them *hjoelptropper* (literally, 'help troops') and distinguished them from German mercenaries who were usually called *lejetropper* (literally, 'rented troops'). Similar distinctions were made by the Swedes. It is difficult to know whether the majority of the rank and file recognized these political nuances. As the records of the Privy Council reveal, some had become soldiers because they were forcibly impressed by recruiting officers. Others perhaps saw the recruiting bounties as a short-term solution to hunger and destitution in bad times. Nonetheless, there is also convincing evidence that loyalty to country and king was strongly felt by many Scottish soldiers in Scandinavia, though its extent and significance in other theatres of war remain matters for future research.[61] Much less debate surrounds the whole issue of recruitment. Few areas in Scotland, with the possible exception of Argyll and parts of the south-western Lowlands, where migration to Ireland was an attractive alternative, escaped the nationwide recruiting net.[62] Between the 1620s and 1640s Scotland had become one of the most militarized countries in Europe and a huge exporter of warriors. It was also in this period that it embarked on its first and most successful attempt at colonization outside the borders of Scotland. This project, however, was not focused on the Americas but on land across the Irish Sea.

3

In medieval times relations between Scotland and Ireland had been close and enduring. Their intimate connection as kindred Celtic peoples was well articulated by the Scottish hero-king, Robert the Bruce, after his famous victory at Bannockburn. In 1315 he addressed the Irish chiefs, asserting that 'the special friendship' should be strengthened in order to recover for '*our nation* . . . her ancient liberty'.[63] Bruce's assumed strategy was to open a second front against the English but he also felt that the Irish and the Scots were one people. It was certainly true that the Gaeltachd did form a single and distinctive culture which stretched from the Ring of Kerry to the Butt of Lewis. Also, as noted earlier, Highland mercenary warriors, the gallowglass and the redshanks, had played a key part in Irish wars for generations. Peaceful migration between the territories of the Irish and Scottish Gaels was also common, especially after the cultural and linguistic ties were forged even stronger by the marriage in 1399 between John Mor MacDonnell of Islay, a brother of the Lord of the Isles, and the heiress to the Glens of Antrim. This incursion of the Clan Ian Mor (or Clan Donald South) into the north of Ireland was the prelude to a further series of marriages between ruling families in Ulster and Scottish Gaeldom.[64] All this facilitated the expansion of Scottish Gaelic settlement in northern Ireland. The disparate gallowglass possessions of earlier times were now supplemented by the extension of Clan Donald territory into north-east Antrim during the fifteenth century. Together these settlements in Ulster could be compared to the Anglo-Norman colony of east and south-east Ireland in the area which came to be known as the Pale.[65] They became even more significant as the Hebridean sea empire of the McDonalds started to crumble under the relentless aggression of the Campbells of Argyll and other hostile clans, like the McLeans and Macleods. As a result the axis of Clan Donald power swung even more emphatically towards Ulster. By 1600 the Irish branch of this immense kinship network, the MacDonnells, had achieved virtual control over the whole of Antrim, sometimes by displacing indigenous Irish lords, like the MacQuillans, in their rise to territorial pre-eminence.[66]

The Scottish presence in Ulster was to change radically in the early seventeenth century in scale, social composition and religious affiliation. Several factors created a completely new context for migration to the north of Ireland. A primary influence was the availability of unprecedented areas of Irish land for purchase and lease. The final defeat of the Gaelic lords, O'Neill and O'Donnell, by the English at the battle of Kinsale in 1601, followed by their escape from Ireland in 1607, led to the forfeiture of their lands to the crown. The subsequent foiled rebellion of Sir Cahir O'Doherty the year after the 'Flight of the Earls' also placed his estates under the control of the state. To these territories could be added the vast tracts of church land, amounting to around a fifth of the entire province. These were technically already confiscated but had still hardly been touched by the end of the sixteenth century. In all, virtually the whole of modern Cavan, Armagh, Tyrone, Fermanagh, Derry and Donegal had now been appropriated and awaited disposal by the crown.[67] Coinciding with these state forfeitures, Scottish private speculators added to the huge supply of land which was available for settlement. In 1605 Sir Hugh Montgomery of Braidstone, an Ayrshire laird, and James Hamilton, another Ayrshire man who was a favourite of James VI, having acted as his emissary in Dublin and London, took advantage of the difficulties of a County Down landowner, Con O'Neill, to force him to grant them large areas of his estates. They soon proceeded to lease much of this property to Lowland Scottish tenants, which produced the most concentrated Scottish settlement in Ulster before 1660, extending from the Belfast Lough to the Ards peninsula.[68] Other Scots sought and obtained grants of land in other parts of Down and Antrim. It was said that within a generation a great proportion of both counties had been transformed in population and way of life into 'a sort of extension of the Scottish Lowlands'.[69] At the same time, in Antrim, Sir Randal MacDonnell was one of the few Catholic Gaelic lords to survive the onslaught of the crown with his power intact. He was untainted by treason, having kept out of the Nine Year War, was favoured by King James (he was soon to become Earl of Antrim) and was a leading courtier who married the widow of the Duke of Buckingham. MacDonnell moved easily between the Gaelic world of Ireland and Highland Scotland, having been fostered on the island of Arran off the coast of Ayrshire. But he was also very much at home within the anglicized power structure. His pragmatism meant that while the Antrim estates remained a haven for migrant Hebridean Catholics, MacDonnell also encouraged some 300 Lowland Scots Protestants to settle on his lands as well.[70]

These historic changes in Irish landownership were vital, but equally important were the political consequences of the Regal Union in establishing the crucial context for large-scale Scottish migration to Ulster. In 1603 the Three Kingdoms of Scotland, Ireland and England were united under the personal monarchy of James VI, I and I. James had for some years pursued a policy of conquest and control in Scottish Gaeldom as an integral part of his overall strategy of extending central authority throughout his realm. The Hebrides were in his eyes a primitive and recalcitrant society which should be brought to heel in order to advance the cause of 'civility' over 'barbarism' throughout his Kingdom of Scotland. He warned his young son, Henry, about those 'that dwelleth in the Iles, and are allutery barbares, without any shew of civilitie'. He advised 'planting Colonies among them of answerable In-lands subjects' who 'may reforme and civilise the best inclined among them; rooting out or transporting the barbarous and stubberne sort and planting civilitie in their roomes'.[71]

The King's policies began in failure. Two attempts in 1598–1600 and 1605–6 to settle the island of Lewis with 'answerable In-lands subjects' from the Lowlands ended disastrously. However, military expeditions to the Hebrides in 1596, 1599, 1605 and 1607 culminated in the Statutes of Icolmkill (Iona, 1609) which provided comprehensive legislation for breaking the power of the semi-autonomous clan chiefs by educating their sons in Lowland 'civilitie', discouraging the keeping of weapons, attacking communal drunkenness, promoting Protestantism and much else besides.[72]

Before the Ulster Plantation, therefore, the Scottish crown had already developed both theory and practice in internal colonialism buttressed by explicit assumptions about the 'barbaric' inferiority of the Gaels and their proper subordination to 'civilised' authority. The year 1603 was catalytic in the strategy which eventually led to the transformation of the history of the north of Ireland. Both the English and Scottish monarchies before the Regal Union had been independently attacking the Gaels of Ireland and Scotland. Now, under James I, a single assault from an enhanced base of power became possible. The aim was to drive an Anglo-Saxon Protestant wedge between the two areas of Gaelic-Catholic civilization. It came to be recognized as an Anglo-Scottish partnership, the first joint 'British' enterprise of the new 'Kingdom of Great Britain'. English intellectuals, like Francis Bacon, hailed the idea as a 'second brother to Union'. Those to be sent to Ulster were designated 'British families', 'British tenants' and of '*British* birth and descent'. It was the start of a historic cooperative project which would eventually reach the ends of the earth in the eighteenth and nineteenth centuries.[73] James intended full union between his realms. For Scotland and England, 'I am the husband and the whole isle is my lawful wife.' He desired that the two nations 'first to shake Hands and, as it were, Kiss each other, and lie under One Roof or rather in One Bed together'. However, the romantic adventure failed because of English indifference and prejudice towards Scotland, 'the barrenest land in existence' whose multitude of beggars and vagrants could overwhelm and 'feed upon our full pastures'.[74] Yet this disappointment merely served to feed James's determination to create a common British enterprise in

Ireland as a preferred alternative to a full British union. Indeed, not only the King himself but also his advisers regarded a project in the north of Ireland to be much more significant for the future of the country as a bastion against foreign Catholic enemies than speculative ventures in the fragile transatlantic colonies.[75] As Sir Arthur Chichester, Lord Deputy of Ireland, declared: 'I had rather labour with my hands . . . in Ulster than dance or play in Virginia.'[76] Through such thinking the seeds of present-day tribal and cultural divisions in northern Ireland were sown.

The mechanism chosen for the distribution of confiscated Irish lands was 'plantation', a strategy tried earlier in the province of Munster with mixed success. Military conquest was the *sine qua non* of British annexation of the territory of Irish lords. But 'plantation' was something more. It would penetrate into the very culture and society of the conquered lands through the transfer there of loyal 'planted' subjects who would, over time, ensure the stability of the territory. In outline, if not in scale, the plan followed James's earlier attempts at Lowland colonization in Lewis and Kintyre. In Ulster the scheme of plantation involved the division of six counties (Donegal, Cavan, Derry, Tyrone, Fermanagh and Armagh) into various categories. A distinguished Irish historian summarizes the consequences:

The plantation scheme involved the division of six counties (Donegal, Londonderry, Tyrone, Fermanagh, Armagh and Cavan) into three categories: first, land to be granted to English and Scottish undertakers; second, land to be granted to servitors (usually English government officials) and 'deserving' Irish; third, land belonging to or to be granted to the established church and Trinity College. The undertakers were required within three to five years to settle English or Scots on their lands at a rate of 24 per 1,000 acres, and to provide defences and build stone houses and bawns, or risk hefty fines. No one who did not conform to Protestantism and no Irish could rent these lands. The other two categories were granted with no condition to plant or conform, and here the Irish inhabitants could remain. In fact, although some displacement did occur, the Irish remained even on undertaker land, for tenants were scarce. The Irish remained likewise on the lands given to the London companies: the new county of Londonderry, encompassing Derry and its immediate Inishowen hinterland, part of north Tyrone, and O'Cahan's lands around Coleraine.

On the whole the Irish remained in occupation of the land. Only the remaining swordsmen of the Irish lords or 'kerne' were totally expelled, some transported to continental service, others taking refuge as outlaws in the woods. But 'occupation' and 'ownership' are quite different things. Those Gaelic lords who had participated in various 'surrender and regrant' schemes recognized as much, and so increasingly did the minor septs. The abundance of Irish families claiming freehold over the land they occupied, even though most such claims would have been untenable, testifies to this. Only a small number were to be satisfied. This and the loss of the top tier of Gaelic lordship (through the Flight of the Earls and death in battle) pushed the gentry of Catholic Ulster down a tier. A new tier of chief lords had been substituted for the old and generally the main undertaker in each barony ended up occupying the residence and demesne land of the former Irish chief.[77]

As a powerful symbol of 'Britishness' and partnership the divisions of land offered to the Scots and English were roughly equal in size – 81,000 acres to the Scots and 81,500 acres to the English. The connections between the Ulster Plantation and earlier punitive expeditions to the Western Isles were confirmed by some of the leading personalities who participated in the Irish project. Andrew Stewart, Lord Ochiltree, had led the 'civilizing' missions to the Isles in 1608–9. He also became a prominent undertaker in Ulster. Similarly, Andrew Knox, the Bishop of the Isles, served as Bishop of Raphoe in Donegal between 1610 and 1633.[78] The majority of the Scottish undertakers were Lowland lairds and aristocrats who brought over their tenants and servants to occupy the confiscated lands. They recruited using the same complex networks of kin, association and friendship which were also deployed to raise men for European service. Scottish settlers in east Ulster came on the whole from the south-west coast (where migration to Europe was less significant) and the counties of Lanark, Renfrew and Stirling. The Borders were also well represented, as were Argyllshire and the southern isles of Bute and Arran. Here, the implacable pressure of the imperialist Clan Campbell on Clan Donald South was a factor in the exodus as the Earl of Argyll carried out sweeping evictions of McDonald tenants and cottars in Kintyre and other parts of the southern Hebrides. In north Kintyre, for instance, the area of waste land rose from 26 per cent to 41 per cent in the first two decades of the seventeenth century.[79] The introduction of more effective royal authority in the

Borders and the islands also promoted movement as the potentially disaffected were cleared from their holdings and loyal tenants installed in their place. Ironically, these migrants then displaced the native Irish in east Ulster.

Fundamentally, however, the exodus to Ireland, as to Europe, was rooted in economic and social factors.[80] The first two decades of the seventeenth century were years of modest economic expansion in Scotland. Some landowners and merchants therefore sought new outlets for their rising incomes. The Scottish land market was sluggish and, by this time, most of the lands of the pre-Reformation church had already been granted to new possessors.[81] There is also evidence of a new commercial spirit abroad among some of the greater land-owners of the south-west, like the Earl of Eglinton and the Earl of Cassillis. Rents were raised, tenancies reorganized and payments in kind converted to cash. All this created a pool of people who had not only lost land but had little prospect of gaining new holdings. They were therefore easily enticed to Ulster where cheap and abundant land was available. It was a route not only to advancement but to security.[82]

This background explains why the composition of the Ulster groups differed from those of the great migrations for military service and petty trade in Europe, which overwhelmingly consisted of single, young males. Some critics argued that only the poor, the vagrants and the criminal classes were tempted to remove to Ireland. The Presbyterian minister of Donaghadee in the 1670s declared that: 'From Scotland came many, and from England not a few, yet all of them generally the scum of both nations, who, for debt or breaking and fleeing from justice, or seeking shelter, came thither . . . Going for Ireland was looked on as a miserable mark of a deplorable person.'[83] The evidence, however, suggests these comments were much exaggerated. The Scots who made the move to Ulster seem to have been a relatively balanced cross-section of the national population. At the upper end of the scale were small landowners and substantial tenants who saw the venture as an unprecedented opportunity for economic advancement. Indeed, by the 1630s so many farmers from the larger south-west estates were contemplating leaving for Ulster that the Scottish Privy Council ruled that no tenant was to move except with his landlord's permission.[84] Below this élite class was a broad social spread which included artisans and labourers as well as farm servants and cottars. Significantly, for every four men, three women moved to Ulster.[85] It was a more balanced ratio of the sexes than in the Scottish communities of the towns and cities of Europe. There, most young Scotsmen had to marry outside their ethnic group.[86] This in turn promoted assimilation and an erosion over time of the Scottish connection. In Ulster, however, though intermarriage with the Catholic Irish was more common than often supposed, the choice of partner from within the Scottish settlements was much more desirable. This was an important influence which helped to maintain the distinctive identity of the Ulster Scots long after traces of the Scottish link had faded from the emigrant communities in Scandinavia and Poland.

Another hugely important factor in promoting ethnic solidarity was religion. During the reign of James VI and I at least sixty-five Scottish ministers served in Ireland. The King also appointed twelve Scots to Irish bishoprics, seven of whom were nominated to Ulster dioceses. The religious ties remained strong and deepened further when Charles I launched his campaign against Presbyterianism in the two countries. A great movement of protest, centred on the National Covenant, involved both Scots and their fellow countrymen in Ulster. The government retaliated by requiring the Ulster Scots to sign the Black Oath, renouncing the Covenant.[87] The settlers also had to contend against the enemy within. The outbreak of the Catholic rebellion in autumn 1641 was soon followed by a series of appalling atrocities. While many fled back to Scotland to escape the horrors, others proved more tenacious. For an embattled community, the ethnic ties with Scotland remained a vital source of moral, religious and political support. By 1622 some 6,520 adults from Scotland were listed as living in the Plantation, together with around 2,500 to 3,000 Scottish adults in 1630 settled in County Down and a further 2,000 to 3,000 in Antrim. Allowing for children, a figure of 16,000 Scottish settlers in Ulster by 1630 is probably the best current estimate.[88] This was between 1 and 1.6 per cent of a Scottish population of around 1 million in the middle decades of the seventeenth century, a figure substantially less than the migrations to Scandinavia and Poland considered earlier. A further influx to Ulster from Scotland took place in the 1630s, but this was more than cancelled out by the impact of the Irish rebellion in 1641 which dragged on for ten years and caused a major exodus from the province back to Scotland. It is reckoned that more than half the original settlers fled, some bearing lurid tales of massacre at the hands of the Papist Irish. Plague in the early 1650s carried off even more. Contemporary reports painted a bleak picture of unpaid rents and untenanted holdings. The future of the Plantation project now hung in the balance.[89]

Only with further migrations in the 1660s, 1680s and, above all, in the 1690s, when acute famine struck Scotland, was a substantial Scottish presence restored. Before the 1650s, however, the exodus to Ulster was still deeply significant. Not only did that influx establish the foundations for much greater migration in the future (the level of movement in the 1690s was between three and four times as great as the entire period 1600–1650) but Ulster also helped to explain why involvement in North America was long delayed. The north of Ireland was simply closer and more convenient. As a result, Scottish enterprise in the Americas fell a good forty years behind that of the English.[90] These constraints in transatlantic activity were not simply caused by demographic factors. Much Scottish capital, mainly from the south-west region, had been invested in the Ulster project through the provision of loans, bonds and mortgages to the principal adventurers.[91] It may well be that in the short term at least there were few resources to spare for even more speculative schemes. The problem was compounded by the economic troubles Scotland endured because of the long wars between 1640 and the early 1650s. In the second half of the seventeenth century, however, the pattern was to change and a new context for transatlantic activity became established.

2

Moving West

For centuries Scottish merchants, soldiers, clerics, and intellectuals had looked to Europe. In 1700, from one perspective, it looked as if little had changed. The Scots still imported Norwegian timber, French salt and claret (the latter in large quantities), and innumerable luxuries such as spices, fine silks and expensive furnishings from the great marts of the Low Countries. For advanced study, they sent their sons for medical and legal training to Leiden, Utrecht and Orleans, while Rome was a veritable mecca for Scottish painters and architects. Those scholars who seek the taproots of Scotland's golden age of enlightenment in the eighteenth century invariably turn to European masters like Grotius, Pufendorf and Boerhaave as seminal influences on the new generation of Scottish scholars.[1] Scots also continued to serve in European armies. The Scots Brigade in Holland and the Garde Ecossais in France maintained their traditional roles for some decades after 1700. Yet continuity was a surface impression. In the later seventeenth century, the ancient European ties, built on commerce, culture and migration, were loosening. Slowly but surely Scotland's external axis was turning away towards England, Ireland, the Atlantic and Asia. The foundations for a pre-eminent role in the British Empire were therefore not laid after 1707 but in the decades before the union. These were the truly defining times. Ironically, however, the old European connection remained very relevant because it was often from the ports of Holland and Scandinavia that Scottish merchants and adventurers infiltrated the Caribbean and Asiatic trades. Denied legal access by the monopolistic privileges of the English East India Company, several adventurers used their overseas networks, notably in the Dutch East India Company, to circumvent the barriers.[2]

The signs of changing orientation were everywhere. When the Thirty Years War ended in 1648 with the Peace of Westphalia, the huge continental demand for Scottish soldiers, which had lasted from the 1620s, was markedly reduced. The major database of Scottish élite migration to Scandinavia and northern Europe, compiled by the Research Institute of Irish and Scottish Studies at Aberdeen University, allows the decline to be plotted in some detail. To date, the biographies of nearly 7,000 Scottish officers, merchants, students and diplomats have been collated. The information confirms the erosion of the military connection. Indeed, the last major migration to Scandinavia took place in the 1650s as many royalists fled from Cromwellian Scotland. Throughout the later seventeenth century small numbers of merchants and others continued to arrive in northern Europe but this was a mere trickle of migrants compared with the huge movements of young men from Scotland in earlier decades.[3]

After 1688 the Scots were once again drawn into large-scale European conflict and the tradition of militarism lived on. But this time, most soldiers joined the armies of the new monarch of the United Kingdom, William III, in his crusade against the French King Louis XIV on the battlefields of Flanders during the War of the Spanish Succession. This was to be the first of the six major conflicts between France and Britain for global supremacy which only ended with decisive victory for the British in 1815. In this first war William created a new British army almost from scratch. To do so, he used Scottish soldiers, which were his by right as king of both England and Scotland, as a single royal force. They fought with the long-standing Scots Brigade in Dutch service against the French. By the union of 1707, both Scots officers and men had had substantial experience in the European service of a British army. They included established formations with distinguished lineages stretching back to the Wars of the Covenanters in the 1640s and before that to the European theatre in Scandinavia. Both old and new regiments, like the Cameronians, Scots Guards, Royal Scots Greys, Royal Scots (1st Regiment of Foot), King's Own Scottish Borderers (Earl of Leven's) and the Royal Scots Fusiliers (Earl of Mar's), were to achieve even greater celebrity in the eighteenth and nineteenth centuries as the military cutting-edge of the British Empire.[4]

Another sign of the re-channelling of Scottish military effort away from European service was already apparent in the English colonies.

27

In the 1650s the Cromwellian government of occupation in Scotland transported many Scottish veterans who had fought in the royal armies to the Americas as prisoners of war. After the catastrophic Scottish defeat at Dunbar in September 1650, more than 10,000 were taken prisoner and many of them marched to England as captives. Cromwell's government then began a process of disposal. One thousand veterans were offered to Cardinal Mazarini in 1651 for the defence of Candia. Another consignment was intended for Venice. The majority, however, were shipped across the Atlantic to work as indentured labour. There they formed the first substantial group of Scottish 'emigrants' in colonial America. Nine hundred prisoners were authorized for Virginia and 150 for New England in the autumn of 1650. A year later the defeat of the largely Scottish Royalist army at Worcester harvested another abundant crop of around 6,000 transportees. A substantial number of them ended their days in Jamaica, Tangiers, Guinea and Barbados as well as New England and Virginia.[5]

Sold into virtual slavery, they were able to purchase their freedom after eight years. The fighting qualities of these Scottish veterans ensured that they were soon reinforcing the colonial militias. Settlers in the Americas had sole responsibility for their own defence and deportees and indentured servants were the backbone of the local militias. Virginia, for instance, had a potential force of 15,000 men, two-thirds of whom were servants in 1665. The role of the Scottish captives in bolstering the militias in the Caribbean and elsewhere was often described. Thus one document, giving 'An Account of the English Sugar Plantations', noted how 'the Colonyis were plentifully supplyed with Negros and Christian servants' who were 'the Nerves and Sinews of a Plantation'. Most servants had come from Scotland '. . . who being excellent Planters and Soldiers . . . kept the Colonists in soe formidable a posture that they neither feared the Insurrection of their Negros, nor any invasion of a forieigne Enemy'.[6]

New civilian emigration networks were also evolving in the later seventeenth century as Scottish movement to Poland and Norway-Denmark was on the ebb by the 1670s and 1680s.[7] In this respect, the impact of the 'lean years' in Scotland of the 1690s is striking. This crisis was arguably the worst Scottish famine of early modern times. Hunger and famine-related diseases caused an estimated decline in population of between 5 and 20 per cent, a figure in the range of relative demographic decline suffered during the great Irish Famine of the nineteenth century.[8] Perhaps Scotland lost somewhere in the region of 160,000 people, about half of this number due directly to hunger and disease, the rest to emigration and a fall in the birth-rate. The most recent calculation suggests that about 40,000 to 50,000 emigrants left Scotland in these crisis years.[9] Europe, England and the Americas certainly accounted for some. But Scandinavia and Poland were no longer the favoured areas. Movement there had dropped to an insubstantial trickle.[10] Instead, Ulster seems to have attracted the overwhelming majority. It was in the 1690s, even more than in earlier decades, that the Scottish identity in whole areas of the province was really established.

One index of this mass Scottish invasion of Ulster was expansion in the number of Presbyterian ministers and congregations by about 50 per cent between 1689 and 1707.[11] In 1700 Presbyterians outnumbered Anglicans in Ulster and their growth did not decline significantly until the 1720s. Acute harvest failure in Scotland, coupled with more clement weather and better seasons in Ulster, were the primary catalysts for the migration. But evidence has also survived of an earlier movement before 1695 which consisted of Scots with capital taking advantage of new economic opportunities in Ireland. The Treaty of Limerick of October 1691, which brought the Williamite war to a close, triggered a substantial increase in Scottish settlement. During the conflict large numbers of Irish tenants had deserted their holdings, forcing landowners during the peace to offer their lands at attractive leases and rentals. Scots families with means took full advantage of these enticements and their capital then became an important factor in the recovery of the Ulster economy in the post-war era. During the period of the famine they were then followed across the Irish Sea by their poorer countrymen.[12]

The Irish factor demonstrates the growing reorientation of Scottish emigration away from Europe. But, as earlier, the preference for Ulster also constrained mass movement to the Americas. During the second half of the seventeenth century some 7,000 Scots crossed the Atlantic. Perhaps two-thirds of this number settled in the Caribbean.[13] The totals did represent a substantial increase over the few hundreds who have been traced to the decades before 1650, but the emigration was still very limited compared with the many thousands who sailed for the colonies from England.[14] Moreover, probably the majority of these migrant Scots ended up across the Atlantic against their will, as deported prisoners of war or felons and vagrants sentenced to transportation. Indeed, the impact of the famine years on Scottish transatlantic emigration was far-reaching in the longer term. Not until the second half of the eighteenth century did Scottish movement to the colonies really take off in a major way. In part, this may be explained by the long-term effects of the high mortality and mass exodus of the 1690s. The natural growth of the population was cut back so dramatically that the demographic pressures which might have made for large-scale emigration were substantially reduced.[15]

It was a different story, however, with Scottish commercial networks overseas. During the second half of the seventeenth century the pattern here was one of dynamic diversification which prefigured many of the key trends in the period after 1707. The European link was not so much severed during these decades as somewhat diminished in significance. Trade with France was badly hit during the wars with Louis XIV between 1688 and 1697 and again from 1701 until 1715.[16] The Scots were also seriously affected by the new 'mercantilist' policies increasingly favoured by some of their key European trading partners. There were two main assumptions behind mercantilism. First, it was believed that military power was ultimately derived from national wealth based on commercial success. As Colbert, the influential French Minister of Finance, put it in 1666: 'Trade is the source of finance and finance is the vital nerve of war.'[17] Second, the world's store of wealth was thought to be finite; hence an expansion of one nation's resources could only take place at the expense of other powers. It was a mindset which legitimized commercial war, economic nationalism and rampant protectionism.

Plainly, a small country like Scotland with little military or naval muscle and few commodities vital to international trade was at grave risk in such a hostile environment. The lucrative trade in coal to the Low Countries was adversely affected by prohibitive duties imposed on coal shipped to the Spanish Netherlands. The Norway trade was hit by Danish corn tariffs imposed in the 1680s, while commerce to France, in addition to the effect of war, was inhibited by absolute prohibitions on Scottish fish and woollen cloth.[18] Ironically, a more stable food supply between 1660 and the famines of the 1690s also helped to undermine traditional connections with the Baltic. Throughout the sixteenth and early seventeenth centuries the great plains of the southern Baltic lands had been Scotland's emergency granary in times of harvest shortage. After $c.$1660 this relationship withered, partly because there was a run of favourable harvests in the 1670s and 1680s, and only one year (1674) of acute shortage before the catastrophes of the 1690s. Yet even in the middle of that decade of crisis, when Scottish merchants desperately searched the international market for scarce grain supplies, they were now more likely to turn to Ireland and England rather than the old sources in the Baltic.[19]

Ulster, England and the transatlantic colonies were therefore becoming the most dynamic elements in the Scottish commercial network. On the eve of the Act of Union, for instance, around one half of the total export trade of Scotland was already directed towards England. Equally importantly, the key commodities involved, linen cloth, black cattle and coal, had been the foundations of a modest Scottish economic renaissance in the 1670s and early 1680s. Ulster also represented a great new consumer market, a mere few hours' sailing time from the Clyde burghs and the towns of the Ayrshire coast, especially as the waves of Scottish emigration built up during the 1660s, 1680s and, especially, in the 1690s. Small boats almost ran a shuttle service across the North Channel, carrying coal, farm tools, consumer goods, and exotics like sugar and tobacco imported from across the Atlantic. Saltcoats in Ayrshire was reckoned in 1705 to have forty or fifty small ships busy on Irish traffic.[20] Ulster was also one vital factor in Glasgow's spectacular rise at this time. Until the 1640s, the burghal tax rolls confirm the continued ascendancy of Edinburgh, Aberdeen, Dundee and Perth, for over three centuries Scotland's leading towns. By 1649 Glasgow had displaced Perth to take fourth place, and by 1670 it has moved clearly ahead of both Aberdeen and Dundee. Edinburgh remained pre-eminent but Glasgow was now a close second.[21] Part of that shift to the west was the result of a measurable increase in transatlantic trade connections. At first this seems puzzling. Scotland stood in an ambiguous relationship to England and its colonies across the ocean. Both countries were joined in a dynastic union but after 1603 were still separate in a fiscal and commercial sense, apart from the brief interlude of the Cromwellian occupation from 1652 to 1660. One consequence of this unusual status came shortly after Charles II's restoration in 1660. A new Navigation Act of that year re-classified

Scotland as a 'foreign' nation and directed that three-quarters of the crew of a ship trading with English colonies had to be of English nationality. Further extensions to this legislation in 1662, 1663 and 1664 confirmed Scotland's legal exclusion from colonial commerce, even asserting that goods intended for the plantation markets must first pass through an English or Welsh port in an 'English' vessel as prescribed by the initial Act of 1660.[22]

However, until at least the final decade of the seventeenth century, Scots adventurers were remarkably adept at circumventing these protectionist barriers. Scottish and English merchants in Whitehaven, Liverpool, Bristol and London became important points of contact in this strategy. One of the most successful traders in the 1680s was John Dunlop from Glasgow. He developed business interests which stretched from New York to Jamaica. All his passages were made on English vessels and his letters home were delivered from English ports.[23] English front-men in Scottish towns were also commonly employed to legitimize direct colonial trading ventures from Scotland itself. The Crown Agent for Customs in Scotland reported that two dozen vessels were trading to the Americas in defiance of the Navigation Acts, a figure which was not far off the number of vessels working the tobacco trade in its great heyday of the mid-eighteenth century.[24] Scottish settlers in the Chesapeake colonies were also key links in this clandestine relationship. Edward Randolph, Surveyor General of Customs for the American Plantations, explained the techniques used in a report to his London superiors in 1696:

The people on the Eastern Shore of Virginia and Maryland and the Delaware River, Scotsmen and others, have great stocks lying by them to purchase tobacco and prepare a loading ready to put aboard any vessel. The master assists to get the goods ashore before the vessel is entered. The vessel lying in some obscure creek 40 or 50 miles from the Collector's office is presently loaded and sails away undisturbed.[25]

Another favourite ploy was to use Newfoundland as an entrepôt as it was not formally considered a colony but an integral part of England. This meant that colonial goods could be landed perfectly legally as if at an English port. Thus vessels carrying sugar, rum and tobacco sailed ostensibly from American and West Indian ports with papers showing Newfoundland as the destination, but then changed course for Scotland as soon as the customs and Royal Navy cruisers had been left behind. Scottish merchants also settled in Newfoundland. In 1701, for instance, one official report noted that 'the Scotch have lately settled a factory there [Newfoundland] and send tobacco etc. to Scotland, Holland and other prohibited places'.[26]

If anything, the pickings were even richer and easier in the Caribbean. The later seventeenth century in the West Indies was the golden age of buccaneering when the lines between legal privateering and illicit activity were often very blurred. Wars between the Dutch and the English in the 1660s and 1670s, between the English and the French after 1688, minor conflicts between islands and sporadic conquests all added to the chaos and created a veritable bonanza for seafarers with nerve, opportunism and limited scruple. It was no coincidence that one of the most notorious pirates of the time was Captain William Kidd, a Scot from Dundee who moved from legitimate privateering against the French in the West Indies and off the African coast to Madagascar where he launched his criminal career. Kidd was eventually condemned for murder and five charges of piracy at the Old Bailey before being hanged at Wapping in 1701. His rotting corpse, publicly displayed in a cage, was kept for some years at Tilbury Point as an awful warning to other malefactors. Immortalized by Robert Louis Stevenson in *Treasure Island*, Kidd's legend lived on.

Three further points are worth making about this colourful phase in Scottish transatlantic activity. First, some inconsistency in London policy helped Scots adventurers to become established in the very heart of the English empire. In time of war (1664–7, 1672–4 and 1678) the prohibitions of the Navigation Acts were temporarily lifted. On a further two occasions royal licences were granted to the Scots to trade. All this diluted for a time the draconian regulations of the Navigation Acts. Second, the Scottish merchant community clearly saw the trade to the Americas as a long-term venture rather than simply a chance to make some quick opportunistic profits. One confirmation of this was the strategy adopted by the Glasgow traders. In 1668 Glasgow bought the estate of Newark and immediately began work on what was called 'Newport Glasgow' (now Port Glasgow) in order to act as a harbour for ocean-going vessels and so head off potential competition in Atlantic commerce from

Dumbarton and the Ayrshire coastal towns. There was heavy investment in the processing of colonial products. Between 1667 and 1700 four sugar refining factories were built in Glasgow, with the capital coming from merchant families already engaged in the Atlantic trades. The search was also on for oceanic competence in seamanship. The city appointed a Professor of Navigation in 1681, navigation schools opened in 1695 and 1707, and one Captain Davis became a burgess of Glasgow gratis 'in respect he is a person qualified to be useful to this burgh in voyages to Africa and America'.[27]

Third, an equally impressive strand at this time was the relevance of the older ties with Europe to the development of the new Atlantic economy. Commercial practices and business habits, refined over many generations in the Scottish trading colonies of Rotterdam, Bergen, Gothenburg, Cracow, Warsaw and a host of other places, were transferred *en bloc* to the Americas. Scottish mercantile communities were now being steadily built up in New York, Boston, Charleston, Jamaica and Barbados, based on the same family and neighbourhood networks of recruitment as in the old continental centres. Scottish ethnicity was used as a resource to enhance business trust and security in unstable frontier areas where the rule of law and government protection was weak or underdeveloped. Another classic technique inherited in the Americas from the European tradition was to seek out opportunities at the periphery where competition from commercial rivals was less intense. It was no coincidence, for instance, that those Scots involved in the Virginia tobacco trade quickly moved into the back country of the Chesapeake, away from the tidewater districts where London interests were already well entrenched.[28]

But the European centres were not simply sources of commercial expertise. They were also platforms from which the Scottish trading empire in the west could be expanded. Here, Scottish expatriates in Holland were to the fore. They were a substantial community. In 1700 the Scottish Kirk in Rotterdam had around 1,000 communicants. The merchants and seafarers who belonged to it were well placed to benefit from Rotterdam's emergence as a vibrant Atlantic and Asian trade centre with global connections to Brazil, the Caribbean, North America and India.[29] The city's main employers were the navy, the Dutch East India Company and innumerable private merchant houses all of whom had need of skilled and experienced sailors. Indeed, Communion in the Scots Kirk tended to be held in spring and autumn because so many members of the church were sailors serving in Dutch merchant service and were away in Arctic waters in summer and in the Mediterranean and elsewhere all winter.[30] According to some reports, the Dutch marine employed as many as 1,500 Scots in 1672. Recent research has also uncovered Scottish involvement in the United Dutch East India Company and some instances where individual Scots rose to high naval and administrative positions within that large organization.[31]

This was one advantage of a close connection with the Dutch empire. Another was the experience gained by being at the heart of one of the world's most sophisticated economies. Rotterdam, for example, had a stock exchange in 1598, a chamber of insurance in 1604 and a bank of exchange by 1635. Sons of Scottish merchants were often sent to commercial academies in the Low Countries to learn accounts and cyphering.[32] The experience of one family, the Livingstons, shows the advantages that could accrue to those Scots schooled in that context. John Livingston was a Covenanting cleric who took refuge in Holland in 1663. One of his sons, Robert, became a leading merchant in Rotterdam before moving back to Scotland and then to Boston. By 1674 he had settled in New York, where his fluent Dutch, Scots and English were a decided asset amid the ethnic diversity of that city. He married Alida Schuyler in 1678, a bond which connected him with three of the most powerful Dutch New York families. Ultimately, Livingston became a successful transatlantic trader, maintaining close ties with both Scotland and Holland, and founding a family which attained eminence in American politics during the revolutionary era.[33]

His story is a classic exemplar of the global reach of the Scottish business community in this era of colonial expansion. It also testifies to the enduring strength of the Scoto-Dutch connection, which continued to flourish when other European ties were starting to wither. The Dutch influence on both Scottish medicine and science remained of paramount importance. About two-fifths of Scotland's senior legal body, the Faculty of Advocates, are reckoned to have studied in the Netherlands in the century after 1660.[34] The influential Dutch civil lawyers, Hugo Grotius, Johannes Voet and Petrus Gudelinus, had a profound impact on the new climate of intellectual scepticism which provided the context for the Scottish Enlightenment of the eighteenth century. It is no accident that Viscount Stair's *Institutions of the*

Laws of Scotland (1681), the key text of the distinctive Scottish legal system, owed much to his sojourn in Holland as a political refugee and his time at Leiden where he enrolled as a very mature student at the age of sixty-three. The bonds were even tighter in the world of medicine. When Alexander Monro *primus* established the first Faculty of Medicine in the English-speaking world in 1782 at Edinburgh University, he and all the other original teaching staff were former students at Leiden: thus when modern medical teaching came to Scotland, 'it was virtually a Dutch organ transplant'.[35] These intellectual links were part of the complex texture of Dutch–Scottish relationships in the later seventeenth century. Perhaps they were symbolized above all by the extraordinary success of one Scots family in the Netherlands. The Hopes of Amsterdam had originally come from Craighall in Fife. Henry, a scion of the family, had settled in Amsterdam in the early 1600s and there laid the foundations of a great fortune. By the eighteenth century the Hopes were arguably the most prominent bankers in the Netherlands, having grown immensely rich by transferring their trading profits to help fund the British National Debt.[36] Yet they were only the most eminent of a number of significant Scots-Dutch families of this period. Against this background it was hardly surprising that in 1706, at the time of the debates over union, some argued that the best deal for Scotland was to unite with the Netherlands rather than England.

2

In the 1680s a new factor entered the Scottish colonial equation. For the first time in a wholly committed way, the Scottish state began to develop a strategy for independent colonization across the Atlantic. Doubtless this was partly inspired by the growing success of informal trading in the Americas which helped to place colonial issues more firmly on the national political agenda. But other influences were also relevant. The 1670s was a decade of unusual levels of prosperity in Scotland. The Baltic trade was more vigorous than at any time since the Covenanting Wars of the 1640s and coal, woollen cloth and grain exports to Scandinavia were all buoyant. But this period of commercial boom was short-lived and came to an abrupt end in 1680–81.[37] After almost ten years of economic success, this drastic slump in national fortunes seemed to crystallize mounting concerns among the Scottish élites about the nation's precarious position in a world of predatory mercantilism. The result was an important meeting of the Committee of Trade of the Privy Council in February 1681 to consider the country's economic future in an increasingly hostile world. The committee of leading merchants met under the presidency of the Duke of York, the future James VII and II, 'to give their advyce anent the causes of the decay of trade and what they would propose for the remeid thereof'. James's presence was a stroke of luck. He had been sent north, partly for his own safety after the Exclusion Crisis of 1679 when Parliament had made an abortive attempt to block his accession to the throne in favour of the Protestant William of Orange and his wife, Mary Stuart. In 1681 James was appointed Royal Commissioner for Scotland, holding the King's warrant. This made him the most powerful figure in the land. Unlike his brother, Charles II, whose attitude to Scotland was an unhappy combination of hostility and indifference, James had a deep interest in improving the weak condition of the Scottish economy. In part, this was doubtless to make friends and influence people in order to secure his own right of accession to the throne. But he also had a long pedigree of enthusiastic support for colonization. In 1664, for instance, he had become proprietor of New York (which was renamed after him) when the colony was taken from the Dutch and had given his personal backing in 1673 to a plan to create a Scots–Dutch trading network based on Albany.[38]

The deliberations of the Committee painted a gloomy picture and concluded that the country had a huge adverse balance of trade which was producing a continuous haemorrhage of bullion. It proposed in response nothing less than a new national strategy of economic regeneration, supported both by leading mercantile figures and Parliament. At its core was the classic mercantilist policy of reducing imports by raising customs duties and, at the same time, aggressively increasing exports. To this end, colonization, which had rarely featured in Scottish public debate over half a century, began to be favoured once again. Indeed, some pointed the way ahead in simple but stark terms. The choice was either to seek a commercial union with England or develop new markets by founding Scottish overseas colonies. As one historian has neatly put it, 'colonial endeavours offered Scots the opportunity not just to break out of the mercantilist dominance of the great European powers, but also to sustain regal union without recourse to political incorporation with England'.[39] Government blessing was now given to Scottish colonial projects in addition to an array of complementary policies, ranging from encouragement of domestic manufactures to legislation to improve agriculture. Two schemes eventually emerged. The first was in South Carolina in 1682; the second, and more successful, in East New Jersey three years later.

The South Carolina settlement has often been dismissed as little more than an ephemeral refuge for persecuted Covenanters from the south-western counties of Scotland. In fact it was a carefully planned business venture, intended to be permanent, and was a direct outcome of the new consensus among the Scottish landed and mercantile classes to improve the national economy.[40] The Carolina Company was an attempt to establish a legitimate trade with the Anglo-American colonies alongside and in parallel with the thriving illicit commerce across the Atlantic. To this end, the promoters were able to purchase some land from the proprietors of South Carolina. They were not a group of fanciful and naive speculators. Many of the subscribers were Glasgow merchants like the Dunlops, Bogles and Cochranes, already well established in the American market and later to achieve fame as some of the richest tobacco lords in the city during the eighteenth century. The cargoes for export were coarse cloth, hats and clothes, exactly the cheap products which were in widespread demand in the colonies and at the time were experiencing difficulty because of rising English tariffs on Scots manufactures. As a Carolina customs official put it in 1685, 'the Scots are evidently able to undersell ye [the English] their Goods being much coarser or slighter, which will serve for servants weare and so will be sure to go off, they being cheap so that an Englishman must go away unfreighthed or sell to vast Disadvantage'.[41] The voyage to Carolina was entrusted to Walter Gibson, one of the most skilled and experienced exponents of the smuggling trade in the Americas and a future Provost of Glasgow. Yet despite the many portents for a successful venture, the Scottish scheme fell victim to the country's anomalous diplomatic status and military weakness. A central flaw in the project was that the settlement was to be founded on territory still claimed by Spain. The English Governor of South Carolina and his officials also proved less than helpful, perhaps predictably since the colonists insisted on an autonomous administration under Scots law. Then in September 1686 the little settlement of Stuart's Town, named in honour of its royal patron, was completely overrun by Spanish forces and the survivors fled to Charleston.[42] The débâcle was a harsh lesson, reminiscent on an infinitely smaller scale of the greater disaster at Darien which was to follow in the next decade. The Carolina failure confirmed the enormous difficulties of independent Scottish colonization in the Americas after a late start and when the great powers had little compunction in using their military might to defend their interests against the petty aspirations of smaller countries.

The East New Jersey scheme fared much better.[43] Partly this was because the colony was born harmoniously through an arrangement between the existing English Quaker proprietors of East New Jersey and their Scottish brethren from the north-east Lowlands. The prime Scottish mover was the Quaker, Robert Barclay of Urie; William Penn himself had first interested him in a colonization project. Barclay was also a noted agricultural improver and his venture reflected the new economic aspirations of his class. The proprietors included important Scottish aristocrats like the Earl of Perth and his brother John Drummond, as well as many Presbyterian and Episcopalian lairds drawn mainly from the north-east and south-east regions of the country. Several of the key members were also close associates of the Duke of York, which was further confirmation of his important role in these ventures. Significantly, too, some were investing in the new manufactories at home at the same time as they were helping to finance overseas projects. It was all part of an élite drive for Scottish economic modernization. Within a few years, nearly 100 prominent Scots had become involved in funding the East New Jersey experiment and nearly 700 had settled there. The colony prospered and soon became a gateway for Scottish emigrants to America, who then fanned out northwards to New York and west to Philadelphia and Trenton. After 1690, emigration to the colony fell away despite the Scottish crises of that decade, a pattern which confirmed again that Ulster, rather than the Americas, remained very much the first choice of most emigrants. In 1702 the Scottish colony was absorbed into the royal colony of New Jersey but, despite this, the ethnic connection survived. Scottish immigration picked up again in the 1720s and by mid-century there were about 3,000 settlers of Scots descent throughout the central Jersey corridor. Moreover, despite the ceding of the settlement in the early eighteenth century, the schemes of the 1680s demonstrated that Scottish colonial strategy was not simply founded on pragmatic economic interest. The thinking was much more ambitious than that. It amounted to nothing less than the assertion of independent Scottish sovereignty in a world of intense global competition for territory and trade. That aspiration was soon to be put to the supreme test in the most ambitious project of all, the attempt in the 1690s to locate a Scottish free port in the very heart of the Spanish empire on the coast of the isthmus of Panama in Central America.

3

In 1693 the Scottish Parliament passed the apparently routine 'Act for Encouraging of Forraign Trade'. The legislation fitted well with the drift of economic policy from the early 1680s and came onto the statute book with little fuss or comment. Nevertheless, from this humdrum initiative grew Scotland's most remarkable global enterprise to that date. The 1693 legislation advised that any organization founded to carry on trade with the East or West Indies, the Mediterranean or Africa would be granted wide privileges under the Great Seal of Scotland. Two years later, the Company of Scotland trading to Africa and the Indies was established by a second Act of Parliament. It was granted unusually wide powers. For thirty-one years the Company was to have the exclusive privilege of trade between Scotland and America and a perpetual monopoly of commerce with Africa and Asia. In America, Africa and Asia the directors were empowered to establish colonies, held by the crown of Scotland, in uninhabited places or in areas where there was no prior European settlement. The Company's ships were to enjoy complete freedom from all customs duties for a period of twenty-one years. Twenty directors were entrusted with the management of its affairs. Half their number were drawn from the London merchant community and the other half from Scotland. In order to maintain the Scottish character of the organization, at least 50 per cent of its capital was reserved for investors living north of the Border.[44]

Several elements had come together to establish the Company. Undeniably, powerful mercantile interests in London saw the opportunity to obtain separate legislation from the Scottish Parliament as an effective way of challenging, and if possible subverting, the monopolistic rights of the English East India Company in Asian trade. From the start, this group was committed to an expanding commerce in the Indian and China seas and had no interest in any more speculative adventures.[45] In addition, however, there was a specific Scottish agenda. To some extent the Company represented the culmination of the strategy, in place since the Duke of York's Council on Trade of 1681, to establish new markets across the Atlantic and in Asia to compensate for shrinking prospects in Europe. But other factors specific to the 1690s gave even greater urgency to the policy. Scotland was a nation in crisis, caught increasingly in a vice fashioned by the impact of European war and rising tariff barriers both in England and on the Continent. Even the lucrative smuggling trade to England's overseas colonies was now at risk. In the reigns of Charles II and James II, the Royal Navy had an obligation to defend the interests of the United Kingdom as a whole. The Revolution of 1688 changed all that. William and Mary came to the throne of Scotland, after the removal of James, not by divine, hereditary right but through the decision and initiation of the Scottish Convention of Estates. At a stroke, the balance of power between executive and legislature was altered. A contractual relationship had replaced a dependent one. The Scottish Parliament was now much more prepared to flex its muscles in order to advance what it saw as the nation's vital interest. The legislation establishing the Company of Scotland was one result. Yet this new assertion of Scottish sovereignty was likely to cause even more friction with London, especially since many influential Scots now saw the promotion of oceanic trade and colonization as the only sure escape from the unequal relationship of the Union of the Crowns.[46]

This was an area in which England was unlikely to yield. Indeed, in the 1690s mercantilist regulations against 'foreign' interlopers were made even tougher.[47] English tariffs escalated to pump out more revenue for William's war with Louis XIV's France. The customs service was also made more efficient. Even more provocatively, English naval vessels began to police Scottish waters, searching with impunity for contraband, Jacobite intriguers and ships engaged in the clandestine trade from the colonies.[48] These actions were not simply irritating but were, by implication, an attack on the independent sovereignty of Scotland, so much so that the hard-pressed Scottish Exchequer was forced to concede some funds to establish a tiny 'Scots Navy' (which numbered three warships by 1703) to counter the threat. The Company of Scotland, and the extraordinary national support it later achieved, was partly born out of the frustrations of these years. After all, the historical record showed that smaller nations in Europe had managed to retain their independence by enriching themselves through overseas trade. The experiences of both Portugal and the Netherlands were testimony to that fact. The Dutch had escaped the impact of Spanish embargoes on their European trade with the founding of the Dutch East India Company. The Portuguese had liberated themselves from the rule of the Spanish monarchy in 1640, largely because their drive for independence was supported by the fruits of colonial empire. In the words of one scholar, 'By the 1690s the Scots believed that it was not too late to win their own economic dependence on the waters of a Scottish Atlantic.'[49] With the help of London financiers who subscribed £300,000 of the £600,000 total, that idea, in 1695, did not look at all like pie in the sky. The privileges of the English East India Company were already attracting vociferous criticism in the Westminster Parliament precisely in the year when its monopoly came up for renewal. Few could have guessed at the time that the colonial dream would end in national nightmare.

Support first crumbled at the London end. Both Commons and Lords petitioned the King, waxing eloquent about the threat to England if Scotland became an alternative route for East India goods into Europe. The London Parliament not only proposed legal sanctions but showed a determination to impede those merchants in the capital who had dared to associate themselves with the Scottish enterprise. William III, absent on the battlefields of Flanders at the time, also angrily distanced himself, stating, 'I have been ill served in Scotland.' Almost immediately, the promised English finance was withdrawn from the Company and the subscription books in London were closed.

But the scheme did not collapse. Far from it; the venture was given a new lease of life. In February 1696, the subscription opened with £400,000 sterling of capital on offer. A mere six months later that figure was reached. It was a remarkable achievement, especially when compared with similar stock schemes of the period. More than that, it represented a huge investment for a poor country.[50] The subscribed capital was nearly two and a half times the estimated value of Scotland's annual exports, and this in a year of harvest failure when the newly-established Bank of Scotland was also seeking a hefty capitalization. The Company of Scotland had caught the national mood. It was no longer simply a business venture but virtually a patriotic crusade. Nearly 1,500 Scots pledged money. The two great burghs of Edinburgh and Glasgow were pre-eminent, subscribing together roughly a third of the total capital. The great and the good were also well represented – indeed, it was the support of the rich, famous and titled which perhaps above all else helped to give credibility to the enterprise. On the morning the books were opened, a throng of subscribers was headed by the flower of the Scottish aristocracy:

Slowly and carefully, in a fair seemly hand, with rounded curves and finely graduated quill-strokes, one of the Company's clerks drew out the opening entry: 'We Anne, Dutches of Hamilton and Chastlerault etc., dow Subscrive for Thrie Thousand Pounts Sterling.' The Duchess of Hamilton, quill in hand, bent over the page and traced her signature. Two other noble ladies followed the Duchess of Hamilton; Margaret, Countess of Rothes, and Lady Margaret Hope of Hopetoun; each became a subscriber for £1,000; in addition, the Countess of Haddington subscribed £1,000 for her son, the Earl of Haddington; Lady Margaret subscribed £2,000 on behalf of her son, Hopetoun. The signatures of this group of noble ladies were followed by that of Sir Robert Chieslie, Lord Provost of Edinburgh, who put down his name for £2,000.[51]

But of most interest was the geographical spread of subscription and its varied social composition. Clergy, tradesmen, farmers, merchants, lawyers, physicians, mariners, soldiers, landowners, professors, as well as labourers, servants and students, all made contributions. In addition, though the suspicion cannot be proven definitively, there was probably also significant 'invisible' subscription from expatriot Scots and other interests both in London and Europe. Otherwise, it is difficult to understand why Scottish interest rates did not soar to unprecedented levels as both the Bank of Scotland and the Company of Scotland competed fiercely for scarce funds. Not only did this not happen, but the rate of interest actually fell slightly in 1696. It was vital that Scottish investors should have responded with such enthusiasm. Efforts to attract alternative funds from Europe, particularly in Amsterdam and Hamburg, had ended in failure. In the Netherlands, the Dutch East India Company was as vehemently opposed as its English counterpart. In Hamburg, where there was more hope, Sir Paul Rycaut, King William's representative in the city, acting on explicit instructions from London, so threatened the German merchants with the displeasure of his royal master that they would have nothing to do with the proposals of the Scots.[52]

In the meantime, plans for the venture had taken a dramatic turn at home. One of the Company's directors, William Paterson, had persuaded his colleagues not to bother with African and Indian trade but instead to concentrate their energies in establishing a Scottish colony and free port to attract the commerce of both hemispheres on the isthmus of Panama in Central America. Paterson was a figure of some substance.[53] Born in Dumfriesshire in 1658, he had travelled widely, especially in the Caribbean, and had a good knowledge of the prospects there. His credibility was also enormously enhanced by his key role in the promotion of the Bank of England in 1694. Paterson had conceived the grandiose plan for Darien much earlier and had apparently discussed his proposals both in Amsterdam and some of the German principalities in the 1680s. The foundation of the Company of Scotland now gave him his great opportunity. As he later put it with passionate eloquence:

The time and expense of navigation to China, Japan, the spice Islands, and the far greatest part of the East Indies will be lessened more than half, and the consumption of European commodities and manufactories will soon be more than doubled. Trade will increase trade, and money will beget money, and the trading world shall need no more to want work for their hands, but rather want hands for their work. Thus, this door of the seas and the key of the universe, with anything of a sort of reasonable management, will of course enable the proprietors to give laws to both oceans and to become arbitrators of the commercial world, without being liable to the fatigues, expenses and dangers or contracting the guilt and blood of Alexander and Caesar.[54]

It was a dazzling vista. Despite the enormous risks and multiple dangers, here indeed was a panacea for all Scotland's economic ills and, at the same time, a means of releasing the country from debilitating dependency on the unsympathetic English. The warnings of the sober and the cautious went unheeded. They rightly argued that the Spaniards would inevitably retaliate to this threat to the very heart of their American empire at a location which, though unoccupied, still lay between the two major bullion-exporting ports of Cartagena and Portobello. The hostility of England was also certain. The succession to the throne of Spain hung in the balance. William had a crucial interest in maintaining good relations with the Spanish court as his major ally in the war against Louis XIV. Scots interlopers making mischief in strategic territory claimed by Spain was hardly likely to promote good relations with a vital ally. Indeed, when word of the Darien scheme leaked out, William angrily denounced the project's promoters as 'raging madmen'.[55] By his command all English colonies in the Americas were to deny succour and support to the Scottish expedition. Even the Pope voiced his opposition at the damage to the Catholic faith that might be done in the region by these upstart Calvinist Scots.[56]

Yet despite the hostility, Paterson's bold plan and charismatic personality did convince his fellow directors. A key determining factor was the widespread belief that Spain was a paper tiger whose great days of imperial and military glory were in the past. The Scots, because of their successful venturing to the West Indies, were familiar with some of the recent stories about its failing powers. Henry Morgan, the legendary buccaneer, had marched across the isthmus with just over 1,000 men and destroyed a much larger Spanish force which attempted to bar his path to Panama. Eight years after the sack of that city, Portobello was taken by a few hundred buccaneers. Again, in 1680, around 300 Brethren of the Coast had successfully fought their way inland through the dense jungle of Darien in the search for gold at Santa Maria. Many who knew the Spaniards on the isthmus were sure they would not put up a resolute defence, especially against a Scottish expedition stiffened by veteran officers and men from the armies in Flanders. As recent research makes clear, underestimating Spanish power at this time was a common mistake, not simply by contemporaries, but on the part of later historians.[57]

Two expeditions set sail from Scotland. The first left in July 1698 with 1,200 settlers and arrived the following October off the mainland of Panama at Caledonia Bay. The settlement was named New Edinburgh, and Fort St Andrew was erected nearby to defend it. After a mere seven months, however, the site was abandoned. Shortage of provisions and a terrible fever epidemic forced the decision. Over 300 of the colonists, including Paterson's wife, had perished, and their bodies were buried in large pits within the settlement. Only one of the four ships made it back to Scotland. All suffered further heavy loss of life. Before news of the disaster reached home, a second expedition had set out in June 1699. It arrived in Caledonia Bay to find a deserted and ruined settlement: 'The site marked out for the proud capital which was to have been the Tyre, the Venice, the Amsterdam of the eighteenth century was overgrown with jungle and inhabited only by the sloth and the baboon.'[58] Against all the odds, however, the new settlers decided to stay. Spirits rose when a Scottish force, under Captain Alexander Campbell of Fonab, routed a Spanish detachment at Toubacanti. Victory in this skirmish merely postponed the inevitable and further enraged the enemy. A week later a Spanish flotilla arrived to take revenge. Hopelessly out-numbered and outgunned, the Scots surrendered after a fortnight and left Darien for good in April 1700. The extraordinary attempt to establish an international emporium without the costs of terri-torial empire had ended in abysmal failure, with catastrophic loss of blood and treasure. Of the thirteen Company ships that had ventured across the Atlantic, only three ever returned to the Clyde.

Bitter recriminations quickly followed. Paterson the visionary was attacked as a 'Pedlar, Tub-Preacher, and . . . Whimsical Projector' who had 'bewich'd' the Scottish nation with his 'Golden Dreams'.[59] But perfidious Albion became the main target of the devastated and humiliated Scots. William's proclamation denying succour from the English colonies to the survivors of the abandoned settlement, which condemned many on the fleeing vessels to death by malnutrition, was long remembered as an act of treachery. In April 1705, five years to the month since the settlers had left Caledonia Bay for the last time, an English ship rumoured to have sunk one of the Darien vessels put into Leith. Its captain, Thomas Green, and his crew were arrested on charges of murder and piracy. The trial and subsequent execution of the unfortunate Green and two of his officers, amid the joyous celebrations of the Edinburgh mob, further embittered Anglo-Scottish relations. This was a bitter time of national soul-searching. Pious Presbyterians saw the Darien fiasco, followed in February 1700 by a major fire in Edinburgh, as a terrible manifestation of divine displeasure. The idea that Scotland was a chosen nation, bound by covenant to the deity, remained a widespread belief in the country and God's wrath had to be assuaged by repentance. The General Assembly of the Church of Scotland called for national days of prayer and fasting.[60]

The significance of Darien has long been debated by historians. Traditionally, the project was usually dismissed as a fantasy or, in the words of one eminent scholar, a 'tragic farce'.[61] More recent opinion has been kinder. The Company of Scotland symbolized as no other initiative could the determination of the Scots to seek their economic future in the New World. This ambition was not realized successfully at the time but was certainly achieved beyond the nation's wildest dreams in the new political context created after 1707. Moreover, if the idea was so crazy, it becomes difficult to explain the vigorous opposition of several European nations to the scheme. In 1697, for instance, the English Board of Trade concluded in a report that it would be 'no very difficult matter for any European Prince or State to make some secure settlement on the Isthmus of Panama'. Action therefore had to be taken urgently to pre-empt the Scots. If they succeeded, the population of the English colonies in the Caribbean would drain away to Darien. The whole issue was a matter 'of the utmost importance to the trade of England'.[62] However, not all was lost. The Darien investors were eventually handsomely compensated under the terms of the 1707 Act of Union by the so-called 'Equivalent' valued at nearly £400,000 sterling, together with the additional sweetener of 5 per cent interest. The mass subscription to the Company of Scotland also helped to spread experience of debt and credit among a much broader section of Scottish society. It has recently been argued that this was a factor in initiating 'a financial revolution' which helped form the development of Scottish banking and Edinburgh's pole position in the nation's management of monetary affairs in the eighteenth century.[63]

But Darien's pivotal significance was, in the final analysis, political rather than economic. The disaster effectively served notice on the Union of the Crowns. It proved conclusively that when the vital interests of Scotland and England were in conflict, the monarch would always opt to support the position of the more powerful kingdom. This was a recipe for continuing tension and crisis. The governance of the United Kingdom needed radical revision if this outcome was to be avoided. At the same time, the Darien fiasco brought home brutally to thinking Scots that their nation was not only in crisis, but was rapidly running out of credible alternatives and could not go it alone in the colonial sphere where massive military and naval resources were now vital to achieve success. All this did not lead inevitably to the Union of the Parliaments. There were still passionate debates to take place on the varied options of federalism, independence, even links with other nations like the Dutch, and full incorporating union. What Darien did, however, was to place the future of the Anglo-Scottish constitutional relationship on the political agenda even more emphatically than ever before.

3

Union and Empire

I

On 5 February 1705 the House of Commons passed legislation which would help to shape the entire future history of the United Kingdom.[1] The Aliens Act recommended to Queen Anne that commissioners be appointed to negotiate for union between England and Scotland and, if the Scots did not comply or discussions were not advanced by Christmas Day 1705, severe penalties would be imposed. All Scots, except those living in England, would be treated as aliens and the major Scottish exports to England of coal, linen and cattle would be suspended. This was a naked piece of economic blackmail, designed to bring the Scottish parliament swiftly to heel and to the negotiating table; north of the border the first response was one of outrage.

In the event, the obnoxious clauses of the Aliens Act were repealed by the new Whig government at Westminster in November 1705 and this took some of the heat out of a growing crisis between the two nations. But the message of the Aliens Act was clear. The historic English opposition to closer union with Scotland had now been abandoned. Instead, many influential politicians and the monarch herself, Queen Anne, now regarded a parliamentary union with the Scots as essential for the future stability of the revolutionary settlement of 1688 and the security of the two kingdoms. Throughout the seventeenth century various schemes for union had been proposed but had foundered mainly on the rock of English indifference or antagonism. James VI and I tried to bring the two countries closer after the Union of the Crowns in 1603, and further attempts were made in 1667, 1670 and 1690. As recently as 1702–3 joint discussions on union had come to nothing. A fundamental sticking-point was always that London saw no reason to concede to the Scots

freedom of trade with her colonies in America. As Sir Edward
Seymour, the Tory Leader in the Commons, proclaimed in 1700,
Scotland was a beggar and 'whoever married a beggar could only
expect a louse for her portion'.[2]

A first step therefore in trying to understand the making of the
union of 1707 is to explain why Westminster's political attitudes to
the prospect of a closer political relationship with the Scots radically
altered in the early eighteenth century. Equally, however, the Scottish
position, and in particular that of the Parliament in Edinburgh,
deserve careful examination. There was nothing inevitable about a
parliamentary union between the two nations. As noted in the last
chapter, serious tensions were emerging within the Union of the
Crowns in the later seventeenth century, but there was scope for
addressing these by amendment and adjustment rather than by more
radical constitutional change. It is also striking how many Scottish
politicians who favoured union in 1705–6 feared that it could not
be delivered through the Edinburgh Parliament. They were conscious
of the deep animosity towards union passionately articulated by the
national Presbyterian church, which was alarmed at the intolerable
prospect of Anglican domination. John Clerk of Penicuik, one of the
treaty negotiators who strongly favoured union, was later to write
that he observed 'a great backwardness in the Parliament of Scotland
for a union with England of any kind whatsoever' and felt that the efforts of himself and his fellow commissioners might come to nought.[3]

The revolution of 1688 had transformed the structure of Scottish
parliamentary politics. In 1690, in a crucial decision, the Lords
of the Articles, the key parliamentary committee for drafting and
initiating legislation, and normally firmly under executive control,
was abolished. In the same year the estate of bishops was removed.
These two developments substantially increased parliamentary
authority while at the same time reducing royal influence. The scenario for conflict now existed between the King's ministers, whom
William still had the right to appoint, and a much stronger legislature.
The Articles had been replaced by a number of *ad hoc* committees
which were not as easily influenced by the executive, and as a result
for the next several years the government of Scotland became increasingly volatile. After 1695 the King's main strategy was to try to build
a stable ministry around such powerful noblemen as Queensberry,
Argyll, Atholl and Hamilton. The theory was that only these mighty

aristocrats could deliver a pro-government majority in Parliament through their personal followings and networks of clientage. This, together with an effective system of 'management', the promise of offices, pensions, fees and jobs in return for toeing the line, would perhaps ensure secure government. The hope proved illusory. The magnates were divided by bitter personal rivalries and by the craving for the spoils of office which were necessary not only for their own personal advantage but, equally crucially, to ensure the loyalty of their own supporters and dependants. Collaboration among these grandees for any length of time was impossible, yet no single great man could dominate Parliament single-handedly. To deliver power to one dynastic grouping was to risk alienating others, who would then promote a destructive opposition in Parliament itself. Not surprisingly, business was often in a state of paralysis for long periods and it was increasingly difficult to extract agreement on financial supply to carry on the administration of the country.

This volatile situation was aggravated by the increasing friction between England and Scotland. Between 1689 and 1697 William's wars with France were having serious effects on Scottish commerce, while the Royal Navy was implementing the Navigation Laws with full rigour against illicit Scottish trade with England's American colonies. Conflict in the economic sphere was intensified by the collapse of the Company of Scotland's ill-fated expedition to Darien. Simmering discontent gave way to strident criticism that Scotland's miseries were all rooted in the Regal Union of 1603.[4] This alienation crystallized in truculent opposition, shown during the parliamentary sessions of 1698 and 1700, which was so alarming that only the lavish use of patronage allowed the Scottish ministry to survive. Indeed, long before the end of his reign William had concluded that Scotland could not be governed within the existing context of the Regal Union, and that a union of the Edinburgh and Westminster parliaments was vital to national stability and security. The King was obsessed with winning the great war against the France of Louis XIV, and political instability in Scotland threatened this grand strategy. This was not only because Scotland was an important source of recruits for his armies but also because support for the exiled House of Stuart was being encouraged by French money and promises of military aid. Nevertheless, while the union project had great appeal for the King personally, it still did not attract much support in

Westminster. This attitude was to change radically after the session of the Scots Parliament which met in 1703 in the reign of William's successor, Queen Anne.

This Parliament now seemed virtually outside the control of the Duke of Queensberry, the Queen's Commissioner, and his ministers and supporters. The resentment which had been building up in earlier sessions boiled over with a vengeance. The Parliament refused to vote the financial supply which was badly needed to maintain the civil government of the land. An Act of Security, passed in open defiance of Queensberry and the Court or governing party, stated that the Scots Parliament had the right to decide on Queen Anne's successor and that England and Scotland could not have the same sovereign in the future unless the London Parliament granted the Scots 'free communication of trade . . . and the liberty of the plantations'. In addition, the Union of the Crowns would be preserved only if in the current parliamentary session 'there be such conditions of government settled and enacted as may secure . . . the freedom, frequency, and the power of Parliament, and the religion, liberty and trade of the nation from English or any foreign influence'. This read like a manifesto for independence and was intended to be deliberately provocative. Not surprisingly, the Queen initially refused to give her assent, although she conceded it, reluctantly, in the following year. The governing ministry was then forced to accept the equally contentious Act anent (concerning) Peace and War, which gave the Scots Parliament the right to declare war and make peace if the two nations continued to share a sovereign after Anne's death. In the vain attempt to extract financial supply in return for these concessions, the ministry allowed this to pass, despite the fact that its whole emphasis suggested a separate and autonomous Scottish foreign policy. A third measure, the Wine Act, formally permitted trade with France during the war. The primary motive came from the governing party, which was keen to raise more revenue by boosting trade, but on the surface it also seemed driven by economic nationalism. Certainly the Wool Act, passed during the session the following year, was regarded as openly hostile by England in allowing the export and prohibiting the import of wool. As such it was viewed as an openly aggressive act against English trade.

The Scottish legislation of 1703 was the catalyst for parliamentary union because it convinced Westminster opinion that Scotland could no longer be governed effectively within the Regal Union at a time when the entire revolutionary settlement of 1688–9 had become uncertain because of Anne's failure to produce a living heir. The London Parliament had attempted to deal with this vexed issue of succession swiftly by settling the crown on the German House of Hanover. But the Scots had failed to follow suit and so were in danger of placing the entire Protestant succession in grave jeopardy. Moreover, the belligerence of the Edinburgh Parliament had come at the worst possible time. England and her allies were locked in armed combat with the might of the French state for dominance of western Europe. The War of the Spanish Succession was resumed in 1702. It was a critical stage and the outcome was far from certain. It was not until August 1704 that the Duke of Marlborough laid to rest the legend of French invincibility with his crushing victory at Blenheim. In the meantime, Louis XIV openly encouraged Scottish Jacobites, followers of the exiled House of Stuart, by recognizing the son of the dying James VII and II, Prince James Edward Stuart (the 'Old Pretender'), as the true heir to the thrones of England and Scotland. By doing so he linked the issue of the English and Scottish successions directly to the European war. The Jacobites in Scotland had done well in the elections to the Parliament of 1703 and had seen their strength in the country grow because of the unpopularity of the government. They were also being sustained by the interest shown by Louis and some of his ministers in an invasion of Scotland which would put even more pressure on the London regime.

The continuing volatility of Scottish politics therefore seemed only to be giving comfort to the mortal enemies of the state both at home and abroad. The source of the problem had to be tackled, and quickly. It was certainly the threat of the French war which finally moved Godolphin, Queen Anne's Lord High Treasurer and Chief Minister, and Marlborough, her Captain-General, to opt for the union solution to the Scottish problem. Marlborough was concerned as so many of the crack troops for his armies were recruited from Scotland. Because the need to safeguard English national security was therefore paramount, only an 'incorporating union' which would both dissolve the Edinburgh Parliament and create a new United Kingdom legislature was ever acceptable to English negotiators. A federal solution, which might have perpetuated weak government, was never on offer.[5]

Events now moved quickly. A joint Anglo-Scottish parliamentary commission met from spring, 1706 and worked out a comprehensive draft Treaty of Union with twenty-five Articles to be presented to the two parliaments. At the heart of the proposal was the cardinal principle of incorporation which, from the English perspective, was absolutely indispensable. Most of the Scots commissioners were hand-picked followers of the Dukes of Queensberry and Argyll, both pre-eminent in the Scottish government and likely supporters of incorporated union. When this central component of the treaty leaked out, however, there was widespread anger and opposition. It would appear that some sort of improved accommodation with England and an improvement to the Regal Union may have appealed, but not 'an entire union'. Initially, the proposed treaty alienated whole sections of Scottish opinion.[6] The Kirk's alarm came from a real fear that by closer association with England, bishops would once again be imposed on the church. The General Assembly and the presbyteries denounced the proposed union and the Kirk became the most formidable opponent of the project. The treaty was also anathema to the Jacobites who rightly saw it as a major obstacle to their hope of one day restoring the Stuarts to the throne. One enthusiastic advocate for union, the Earl of Roxburgh, even argued that it was the most practical way to kill Jacobitism off once and for all since, after the union, English armies would be able to move freely into Scotland and suppress any future Stuart insurrection. Anti-English feelings had reached a brutal climax in the spring of 1705 when Captain Green and his two crewmen were executed in Edinburgh following the trumped-up charge of piracy against a ship of the Darien Company. Rampant anglophobia continued well into 1706 and, as the French spy Nathaniel Hooke reported to his masters, was likely to become more intense as details of the secret treaty negotiations leaked out in the months ahead.

Indeed, as the Scottish Parliament met in October 1706 at the start of the historic session to debate the draft articles of union it is plain that opposition had not subsided. Not all burghs and counties sent in petitions, but those that did were virtually all vehemently anti-union in content. Argyll dismissed these as mere paper kites but it was significant that they were not balanced by any pro-union addresses. Presbyterian ministers remained loud in their denunciations, vigorously condemning the proposed union as a profane threat to Scotland's historic reformed tradition.[7] Clerk of Penicuik from the unionist perspective lamented the yawning gap which he perceived between Parliament and people on the issue. He estimated that 'not even one per cent approved of what the former was doing'.[8] The Kirk was by far the main influence on the opinion of ordinary people and the continual preaching against union was believed in government circles to be a threat to public order. In Edinburgh the crowds cheered the Duke of Hamilton, the recognized leader of the parliamentary opposition against union, and then attacked the house of Sir Patrick Johnstone, a strong union supporter. The Duke of Queensberry, the Queen's Commissioner, needed a military escort to Parliament House. From that point on, anti-union demonstrations became commonplace in the capital. In November rioting spread to the south-west, that stronghold of strict Calvinism and covenanting tradition. The Glasgow mob rose against unionist sympathizers in disturbances which lasted intermittently for over a month, while in the burgh of Dumfries the proposed Articles of Union were ritually burnt before an angry gathering.[9]

It was also rumoured that plans were being laid for an armed uprising. This was to be led by the Cameronians, the militant Presbyterians from the western shires, in an unlikely alliance with the Jacobite Highlanders of the Duke of Atholl in Perthshire. Some believed that a force of about 8,000 men could be mustered which would be enough to break up the parliamentary session and defeat any government army which took the field against it. In the event this great military host never materialized. Nevertheless, the potential for armed opposition was clearly there, as is shown by recent research on the Jacobite conspiracy and threatened invasion in 1708 which was fuelled by strong anti-union feelings and was much better supported than was once thought. The elaborate military precautions taken by government also show anxiety about the threat of insurrection. While the Edinburgh mob was taking to the streets, Queensberry ensured that the Scots standing army, 1,500 men in all, was camped near the capital and troops were also quartered in the city itself. But the Privy Council feared that the Scottish forces at its disposal would not be enough if matters got out of hand. In late October, therefore, Godolphin assured the Scottish commander-in-chief, the Earl of Leven, that a powerful force would be ordered to the border, there to be in readiness in case the 'ferment' should continue to give 'any further disturbance' to the 'publick peace'. By December, the infantry had been reinforced with 800 cavalry. The troops were now available for action on order from Edinburgh. More ominously, detachments were also sent to the north of Ireland from where the south-west Scottish counties, the leading bastion of anti-union sentiment, could more easily be intimidated and, if necessary, subjected to martial law.[10] In the event, an English invasion in support of the Edinburgh regime did not prove necessary. But these very public preparations for war cannot but have fuelled popular fears that a military solution remained a real option if the vote went against union in the Scottish Parliament.

Indeed, as late as 1706 there was no guarantee that those who favoured incorporating union could carry the day. Parliament was a single-chamber assembly, with 147 members representing the nobility, the barons (or county members) and the burgesses of towns. Cutting across these social and occupational lines were a number of informal groupings, not organized and structured 'parties' in the modern sense, but much looser alliances bound together by family connection, traditional affiliation and networks of patronage. The Court Party was the largest. As its name implies, the Court was the party of government, the source of political support for ministers; the group, under its leader the Duke of Queensberry, the Queen's Commissioner, had the responsibility for ensuring acceptance of the Treaty of Union. The mere fact of holding office, and also its access through patronage to public appointments, posts and sinecures, gave the Court cohesion and relative stability. The Country Party, on the other hand, was a fluid confederation of differing and sometimes conflicting interests, uneasily connected mainly by a common antagonism to the governing clique. The Jacobites, usually known as the Cavaliers, were also capable of striking up pragmatic short-term alliances with the Country interest. The 'New Party' of about two dozen members, soon to be known by the more exotic name of 'Squadrone Volante', had emerged out of the Country Party as a splinter group in 1704.

It was impossible to predict how these shifting coalitions, seething with personal vendettas, opportunism and old hatreds, would respond to the issue of incorporating union. After all, the Queen's Scottish ministers had signally failed to deliver majorities in past turbulent parliamentary sessions. The legislation of 1703 seemed to suggest that the Scots were bent on loosening the bonds of the Union of the Crowns rather than on closer association with England, and this appeared to be borne out by the animosity which had built up around the country in the autumn and winter of 1706 as Parliament started its deliberations. There was indeed a lot at stake. The idea of incorporating union went much further than earlier ideas. There were those who broadly approved of a closer relationship with England but firmly rejected incorporation because it meant the end of Scottish sovereignty and transfer of legislative authority to Westminster. To some, the offer in the draft treaty of 45 Scots MPs and 16 elected peers in the proposed new UK Parliament seemed meagre in the extreme, based as it was on the presumed taxable capacity of Scotland within the new constitutional context and not on its share of population. Yet despite these potential obstacles and the vociferous popular opposition, the Act of Union was indeed successfully carried. In a historic decision on 16 January 1707, the Scottish Parliament voted itself out of existence by ratifying the Act of Union by 110 votes to 67, a clear majority of 43. Against all the odds, Queensberry and the Court had triumphed.

2

Basic to their successful strategy was the elimination of the threat posed by the Kirk which had played such an important role in articulating anti-union feeling. By an Act of Security of the Church of Scotland in November 1706, the historic rights of the church and the Presbyterian system of government were guaranteed as a basic condition of union and later accepted as an integral part of the treaty itself. Religious anxieties did not disappear, but the Court had effectively drawn the teeth of the opposition of the Kirk and in particular had placated the Commission of the General Assembly, the highest church court in the land. It was a master stroke which immensely weakened one of the key elements in the anti-union campaign. One pro-union sympathizer noted:

... in the churches, by and large, the trumpets of sedition began to fall silent. Ministers who had formerly meddled over-zealously in politics now learned to leave the direction of government to parliament. This greatly upset the Hamiltonians who saw themselves abandoned by those they most relied on to stir up anti-union sentiment.[11]

Several of the Articles of the treaty also played to the Court Party's advantage. The English commissioners who helped to draft the treaty with Scottish representatives were mainly concerned with the vital issues of security and incorporating union and, to help ensure that these essentials were agreed in the Edinburgh Parliament, were willing to concede ground elsewhere. As a result several of the clauses of the treaty were devoted to safeguarding the vested interests of those social groups who mattered in Scotland. Integration was confined to Parliament, fiscal matters and public law. As well as the rights of the Kirk, the privileges of the royal burghs and their merchant élites were guaranteed. Scottish private law was protected and the heritable jurisdictions (or private courts) of the landed class maintained. The Scottish nobility was a particular target since only sixteen Scottish peers were to sit in the House of Lords. However, the majority who could not aspire to such eminence could draw comfort from being offered in the treaty the privileges enjoyed by their English counterparts. These included exemption from civil actions for debt, a not inconsiderable advantage given the endemic financial embarrassment among some distinguished members of the Scottish aristocracy at the time. Much more significantly, the Scots were granted free trade with England and its colonies, a concession they had craved for some years but which Westminster had always been stubbornly unwilling to yield.

How telling this inducement was in the final voting patterns is difficult to say and has been the subject of vigorous controversy among scholars. However, Article IV of the treaty, which allowed for 'Freedom and Intercourse of Trade and Navigation', attracted the largest single majority with only nineteen votes against. This was not surprising given the long history of resentment against the English Navigation Laws and the fact that so many of the Scottish nobility were deeply involved in the cattle, linen and coal trade to England. On the other hand, the burghs, including Glasgow (later to become one of the great European transatlantic entrepôts), voted mainly against. Possibly they feared the threat of English competition in the proposed common market, and the closure of their lucrative smuggling channels. Perhaps just as crucial in carrying the treaty as a whole was Article XV, which dealt with the 'Equivalent'. This was an attractive inducement to the Squadrone Volante, the small party whose support the Court Party had to retain to achieve ultimate success, so finely balanced was the overall position of Parliament. A sum of £398,000 (almost £26 million in today's values) was allowed to compensate the Scots for their estimated share after the union in repaying England's large national debt, which had been swollen by wartime expenditure. But some of this was also to be used to compensate investors in the ill-fated Darien Company. Among the most significant of these were members of the Squadrone. When the first important vote in consideration of the Articles of Union was taken it cast all its twenty-five votes in favour of the government. It was a spectacular volte-face because in 1704 and 1705 the Squadrone had not shown any commitment to union. Whether the lure of the Equivalent monies was a decisive factor in this swift and comprehensive change of mind cannot of course be absolutely determined.

If the Squadrone was important to the achievement of a pro-union majority, the Court Party itself was the fundamental basis of final victory. Computer-based analysis of the voting patterns in the last Scottish Parliament has demonstrated its overall influence.[12] The Court members, with the Squadrone, were the consistent supporters of the treaty through all of its twenty-five Articles, although this final outcome could not necessarily be foreseen at the start of the session. Moreover, the times were uncertain and the cohesion of the Court Party unpredictable. For this reason political management, which had been employed with varying degrees of success since the later seventeenth century, was now deployed on an unprecedented scale.[13] The promise of favours, sinecures, pensions, offices and straightforward cash bribes became indispensable to ensure successive government majorities. Supporters had to be rewarded if disaffection was to be avoided, especially in such a miscellaneous group as the Court Party comprising the disparate followings of several great noblemen each with their own personal and family agendas. Management which had abysmally failed in previous parliaments was now to achieve resounding success. The influential Duke of Argyll agreed to return from the armies in Flanders in order to support the Court in the crucial session. His personal rewards included promotion to the rank of major-general and an English peerage. The sum of £20,000 sterling (the equivalent of £240,000 Scots, and £1.3 million in today's values) was secretly despatched north from the English treasury. Whether it was disbursed to pay office-holders whose salaries were overdue or as straight money bribes, as some have suspected, is in a sense immaterial. Payment of arrears to selected individuals was just as much part and parcel of effective management as handing over direct cash inducements. Once again, the Squadrone benefited handsomely from the distribution. Modern research has also identified former members of the opposition, such as Alexander Murray, Lord Elibank, Sir Kenneth Mackenzie and the Earl of Glencairn, whose rewards seem to have encouraged a more favourable opinion of union.[14] But not all parliamentarians had to be so favoured. The voting record of at least thirteen members shows they supported the union without either cash inducement or promise of office. Nevertheless, the loyalty of the Court Party as a whole could not be taken for granted because there were allegations that some were unenthusiastic for incorporating union. Support had to be therefore shored up by lavish patronage. In this Parliament there was to be no repeat of the débâcle of 1703.

The formidable political management machine presided over by Queensberry and his acolytes contrasted with the disarray of the parliamentary opposition which signally failed to capitalize on the national resentment to union which, if effectively led, could well have been a potent threat to the government. The anti-union forces suffered from three main weaknesses. Firstly, the Country Party and the Cavaliers could always be relied upon to act together to make political mischief and embarrass the Court. But at a more fundamental level they were irreconcilable. The Cavaliers or Jacobites wanted the return of the Catholic Stuart Pretender which was anathema to the Presbyterian nobility who led the Country Party. Second, the leadership of the Duke of Hamilton was weak and indecisive at key moments which might have been exploited to advantage. So ambiguous was his position that some speculated about which side he was actually on. The opposition tactic of formally withdrawing from Parliament in January 1707, and in effect boycotting proceedings so as to give a clear signal about the sheer extent of opposition to the treaty, came to nothing because of Hamilton.[15] He failed to turn up in the first instance, complaining of being seized of the toothache, and when he eventually appeared he declined to lead the proposed mass withdrawal. The man who had been lionized by the Edinburgh crowds as the only hope for Scottish independence had again let his followers down. He had done it before in September 1705 when Parliament was deciding on whether the Commissioners to treat for union should be appointed by the Queen or Parliament. Hamilton amazingly suggested that they ought to be the Queen's nominees, thus ensuring a pro-unionist majority on the Commission. He was also later blamed for calling off the rising of Cameronians from the south-west and Highlands in November 1706. Hamilton's behaviour demoralized the forces of opposition both in and outside Parliament. Some have explained his hesitations as the result of his personal position. Not only was he heavily in debt but had in addition acquired through marriage large estates in Lancashire which he stood to lose if union did not succeed. His personal circumstances meant he was also vulnerable to favours from government. James Johnstone, Lord Clerk Register and one of the Scottish officers of state, alleged that Hamilton was actively seeking assistance with his debts from London ministers in the winter of 1705.

The third reason for the weakness of the anti-union forces stemmed from the fact that their only real hope lay in an alliance between the parliamentary opposition and the disaffected population in the country, given the numerical strength of the Court and its ally, the Squadrone. But whether the leadership of the Country Party had any real stomach for a popular uprising must be doubted, especially since the Kirk was no longer actively or publicly opposed to the treaty. A civil war could have given comfort only to the Jacobites and would have threatened the restoration of the Stuarts through an invasion from France. The 1688-9 revolution (which the Country leaders strongly supported) and the Protestant succession could have been imperilled. Furthermore, there were grounds for believing that England might impose a military solution in order to safeguard her northern borders if the union project failed. Godolphin made veiled threats to this effect and, as has been seen, troops had been stationed in the north of England and reinforcements also sent to northern Ireland. There was no way of knowing whether these large-scale military preparations were simply sabre-rattling or had a more serious intent. They did, however, help to concentrate the minds of the opposition as they debated the Articles of Union in the last months of 1706. It was abundantly clear that they were playing for high stakes.

The Anglo-Scottish Union became law on May Day, 1707. England wanted it for reasons of national security at a time when she was fighting a major war in Europe. In Scotland there seems to have been overwhelming popular opposition to the loss of the Parliament and angry hostility to the whole idea of an 'incorporating' union. Despite this, the treaty was passed by a clear majority. The powerful opposition of the Church of Scotland was weakened when the rights and privileges of the Kirk were solemnly guaranteed in the event of full union. A much improved system of management ensured the stability of the Court Party, and the treaty itself contained several clauses which were designed to appease key vested interests in Scotland. Freedom of trade was granted and the Equivalent helped to maintain the crucial support of the Squadrone. These were the carrots, but there were also some sticks. The danger of civil war if union failed was feared by some, and there were rumours that Westminster might use military means if the Articles were rejected. In this situation the parliamentary opposition was fatally weakened by internal divisions and inept leadership and was in no position to effectively exploit national disaffection.

3

The imperial factor seems to have played little direct part in the union debates. Even some of those who did gain spectacularly from empire in the course of the eighteenth century, such as the Atlantic merchants of the Clyde, were robustly opposed to the treaty. Empire was not seen by Scots at the time as a consolation prize for the loss of Scottish sovereignty.[16] Those who argue that it was are engaging in retrospective judgement through hindsight which would have been incomprehensible to the contemporary mind. Only later observers could view the extraordinary events around the union between Scotland and England as the constitutional sheet anchor of a global imperial partnership. Indeed, in the early eighteenth century even the survival of the union was doubtful. It was an historic marriage of convenience between two countries with precious little affection for each other and was founded on the pragmatism of *realpolitik*. Not surprisingly, therefore, the early years of the new relationship were pretty rocky and the future of the marriage hung in the balance. In

1713 a motion for repeal of the treaty was only narrowly defeated in the House of Lords. Again, two years later, the Jacobites launched their most popular rebellion ever against the Hanoverian state on a groundswell of anti-union hostility in Scotland.

Nevertheless, some thoughtful commentators at the time saw clearly how the Scottish colonial position had changed fundamentally because of 1707. William Seton of Pitmedden was an advocate of the incorporating union and a Scottish Commissioner during the negotiations to frame the treaty. His speech to the Scottish Parliament during the debate on the first Article in 1706 was an incisive statement of the advantages in terms of overseas trade and colonial acquisition that could flow from an Anglo-Scottish alliance.[17] Seton began by clearly indicating the flawed nature of the Regal Union which would always place Scotland at a grave disadvantage:

Every Monarch, having two or more Kingdoms, will be obliged to prefer the Counsel and Interest of the Stronger to that of the Weaker: and the greater Disparity of Power and Riches there is betwixt these Kingdoms, the greater Influence the more powerful Nation will have on the Sovereign.

He then went on to argue that the association between commercial success and military force was critical. In a dangerous world of competing mercantilist powers, trade provided the funds for war while armies and navies defended vital national commercial interests against aggressors: 'No Money or Things of Value can be purchased in the Course of Commerce, but where's a force to protect it.' The brutal lessons of Darien had clearly been absorbed. Seton then concluded:

This Nation being Poor and without Force to protect it, its Commerce cannot reap great Advantages by it, till it partake of the Trade and Protection of some powerful Neighbour Nation, that can communicate both these . . .

The treaty dealt with several of the issues Seton raised in this assessment and in the process potentially removed some long-standing Scottish grievances. Article IV conceded free access to England's colonial and domestic markets. Article V redefined both Scottish and English shipping as 'British' and hence under the protection of the Royal Navy. The separation in law of the English and Scottish church establishments meant that the Scots were also able legally to establish Presbyterian clerical networks in the colonies.

These underpinned the remarkable influence in America of both Scottish ministers and educators in later decades. Little wonder that the Irish regarded the agreement with deep envy and jealousy. They did not achieve full access to imperial trade until much later in the century. In addition, the Catholic Irish professional and military élites were dogged by religious discrimination in the Empire for many decades to come.[18] In contrast, Protestant Scots were allowed a level playing-field. Even before the end of the War of the Spanish Succession the Royal Navy ensured a significant increase in security in Scottish waters. The Cruiser and Convoy Act was passed in 1708 to establish an effective system of defence for British merchantmen against the foraging wolf packs of French privateers.[19] Twelve cruisers were allocated to Scotland, a naval deployment on a scale which before 1707 would have been out of the question from indigenous sources. Certainly the force was never invincible and not until the end of the Seven Years War in 1763 could it truthfully be said that 'Britannia rules the waves'.[20] Nevertheless, British control in both Caribbean and American waters was being robustly extended and the golden age for the buccaneers in the West Indies soon passed into history. By the 1720s most transatlantic merchantmen no longer fitted deck guns, and insurance rates during peacetime came down significantly.[21]

Naval protection was manifestly of great benefit to the Scottish marine. In a sense, however, it was only one aspect of a much larger and wider set of changes. In 1707 the Scots joined in parliamentary union with a bellicose nation which was already building the fiscal, political and military foundations for imperial expansion. This 'fiscal-military state' has been described as 'the most important transformation in English government between the domestic reforms of the Tudors and the major administrative changes in the first half of the nineteenth century'.[22] Like most European governments of the time, the English state spent most of its resources either in waging war or preparation for conflict. It was reckoned that over most of the eighteenth century between 75 and 80 per cent of annual government expenditure went on current military needs or to service debt accruing from previous conflicts.[23] For Britain, far and away the biggest outlay was on the navy, the 'senior service', vital for the home defence of an island people and for the prosecution of a 'blue water' policy around the globe, safeguarding trade routes and establishing secure overseas bases for protection of colonies: Sir Walter Raleigh's dictum of over a century before still rang true: 'Whosoever commands the sea, commands the trade of the world; whosoever commands the riches of the world, and consequently the world itself.' The problem was, however, that navies were fearsomely expensive. Wooden ships rotted fast, maintenance costs were enormous, and the huge dock-yards and shipyards required for repair and construction were inevitably a major drain on the public purse.[24] Abundant finance rather than military force *per se* was reckoned to be the crucial sinew of war.

The English state had been pursuing a policy of aggressively extending its economic and military resources since *c.*1650 and the process was virtually complete by the time of the Anglo-Scottish Union. It amounted to a financial revolution which made available to both the army and navy vast sums for the prosecution of war. The key components included a huge extension of the National Debt, sharp increases in taxation, a government bank (the Bank of England) and the flotation of long-term loans on the London capital market which also attracted funds from the Continent.[25] No other state in Europe (apart perhaps from the Netherlands, which did not link its mercantile prowess so effectively to war strategy as England) was quite as successful in this financial transformation. The costs of the revolution were borne mainly by taxes, especially customs and excise on imported and home-produced goods. As a result, Scotland was undeniably faced with an increased tax burden after 1707.

Taxes rose on consumer items, most notoriously with the salt and linen taxes of 1711 and the malt tax of 1725. Yet one estimate suggests that, in the half-century after the union, up to 80 per cent of the revenue take was absorbed in Scotland itself to cover the routine costs of the civil administration, rather than being transferred to London.[26] Moreover, before the 1740s the Westminster govern-ment tended to tread carefully in Scotland, conscious of the extent of Jacobite disaffection there and the fury the malt tax increases had provoked in 1725. Some have suggested that revenue burdens on a *per capita* basis were therefore lighter in both Scotland and Wales than in the richer counties of southern England.[27] Certainly, the Scots customs service was much less effective in collecting revenue in the first few decades after union than its counterpart in the south. Underpayment was endemic. A black economy ran through Scottish society from top to bottom. To the fury of their rivals in the English outports, the Clyde tobacco merchants were reckoned to have paid duty on only half their imports in the first two decades after 1707.[28] The records of the Scottish Board of Customs also teem with cases of widespread intimidation, violent assaults on officers and gang attacks on the warehouses of the Revenue.[29]

Tax evasion on this massive scale could not disguise the fact that union with England presented the Scottish élites with a golden opportunity. The benefit of naval protection for merchants engaged in the American trade was obvious. Even more fundamental, however, were the possibilities now opening up for the landed classes, the real masters of Scotland in this period. An historic anxiety for the aristocracy and the lairds was the challenge of achieving gainful employment for younger sons which would not only provide income but an acceptably genteel position in society. Landed estates in Scotland, whether great or small, descended by primogeniture to the eldest male child. His siblings had to make their way in the world, either by the family acquiring some landed property for their remaining progeny, by younger sons achieving army or naval commissions, entering the law or the church, or being apprenticed to a merchant house. This was the basic social dynamic which for centuries had impelled the offspring of the Scottish gentry to seek careers and fortunes in Europe. But the European connection was fading fast in the later seventeenth century and there is some evidence that the decline of career opportunities there was beginning to stoke up anxieties among the laird classes. Something of this came through in the plans for the Scottish colony in East New Jersey in the 1680s.[30] The project was dominated by landowners from the eastern counties of Scotland, especially the north-east region, formerly a major supplier of Scots army officers and merchants to Scandinavia. The projectors envisaged a colony of landed estates and among those who eventually emigrated to the New World was a very high proportion of younger sons of the north-east gentry. Thus three members of the Gordons of Straloch purchased proprietary shares, but only the two younger bothers actually travelled to the colony. Several other emigrants can be identified as sons of minor, cadet branches of landed families. Robert Gordon of Cluny probably spoke for many of his fellow proprietors when he stated that his own reason for being attracted to the project of colonization was to provide land for his younger son, 'since I had not estate whereby to make him a Scotch laird'.[31]

But perhaps even more intense pressures were building up by the early eighteenth century. Scottish landed families were simply having more surviving adult children as infant mortality levels started to fall rapidly at that time. No exact figures exist to prove the point conclusively from a specifically Scottish perspective. However, research on the demography of British ducal families for the period can provide a useful surrogate source of information on changing patterns of population growth among the nation's governing classes.[32] Family size among this élite was relatively stable until the later seventeenth century; then a few decades later rapid growth started among the aristocracy at a rate which was considerably higher than in the general population increase in the country as a whole. The percentage of children of the nobility dying under the age of sixteen was 31.1 between 1480 and 1679; from 1680 to 1779, the figure fell to 25.9 and declined further to 21.1 between 1780 and 1829. There were now many more sons surviving into adulthood. If this pattern was replicated across the Scottish landed classes, the concerns for placing younger sons in employment which was both gainful and socially acceptable must have become even more acute.

But this was not all. Changes in the composition of the Scottish landed structure added to the challenge. In 1700 there were around 9,500 landowners in Scotland, only about half of whom had the right to inherit or sell the land they possessed. The structure was dominated by the great aristocratic landlords and their associated kinship groups.[33] Between the later seventeenth century and the 1770s, this élite was expanding its territorial control at the expense of the lesser lairds. The number of proprietors in Aberdeenshire fell by around a third between c.1670 and c.1770 (621 to 250) and the steepest decline occurred among the smallest group of landowners.[34] The trend was repeated all over Scotland. The total of 9,500 landowners at the beginning of the eighteenth century dropped to 8,500 by the 1750s and fell further to around 8,000 at the start of the nineteenth century.[35] Manifestly, the minor lairds were under considerable economic pressure before the 1750s. Rental income was relatively stagnant and increases in farm productivity did not really encompass most of Scottish agriculture until the 1760s.[36] At the same time, as the number of estates possessed by this class was squeezed, one traditional option adopted to solve the problem of younger sons, namely the purchase of additional properties in their name, became much more difficult. In a sense, then, imperial employment after 1707 in the armed forces, colonial administration, trade and the professions may have come more as a crucial lifeline than as an opportunity. In the decades after union, streams of eager Caledonians from genteel but impoverished backgrounds poured into the British Empire at every point from the Arctic wastes of Canada to the teeming cities of Bengal. The bureaucratic growth of the fiscal–military state ensured that career openings were now much more abundant than before and the Scots were very keen to exploit them.

4

Trade and Profit

One of the key features of Europe's growing connection with the
New World was the consumption of exotic commodities provided
through an unprecedented increase in transatlantic and Asian trade.
By the eighteenth century tobacco, tea, chocolate, sugar and coffee
were all familiar to European populations. Of those, tobacco was
the first to establish itself permanently as a valued commodity in
Britain and the Continent. One speculative estimate suggests that by
c.1670 enough tobacco was already available for at least a quarter
of the English population to enjoy a pipeful once a day.[1] Tobacco
addiction spread rapidly and by the mid-eighteenth century had
entered into mass consumption, especially in Holland, France, Britain
and the Scandinavian states, though few parts of the Continent
remained untouched by the new craze.

Tobacco was not simply popular because of its properties as a
pleasurable recreational drug. It was also widely praised for its
medicinal value. Some seventeenth-century theorists advocated universal smoking not only to cure illness but also to satisfy hunger and
stimulate the brain. But opinion soon drifted. By the eighteenth
century, tobacco was mainly consumed in most European countries
in the form of snuff rather than being smoked through a pipe. 'Far
from being just the fashionable accessory of a few fops, it was the
normal way of taking tobacco in the early industrial age.'[2] In 1775,
for instance, 80 per cent of the tobacco sold in the vast French market
was either in manufactured snuff or in *carottes*, which customers
could use to grate their own snuff.

However, tobacco's significance in this period was not confined to
the changing habits of consumption. It was also a vital element in

the expansion of European colonialism. Often initial settlements in the New World would not have been possible if tobacco had not been available as a cash crop. It had major advantages. The growing cycle was short, normally nine months from planting to being ready for market, and tobacco could grow well in various soils and climates. This had the secondary advantage of differentiating a wide range of quality in the supply for European consumers. Over time, however, as different areas of European settlement specialized in different types of exotic groceries, tobacco cultivation came to centre on two regions. By 1700, and for the following century, Brazil and the English colonies of Virginia and Maryland surrounding Chesapeake Bay accounted for almost the entire output of New World tobacco. Exports from the Chesapeake soared from just over 37 million lb. in 1700 to over 100 million lb. in 1771. This enormous trade was not only basic to the economic prosperity of Virginia and Maryland. The tobacco business also brought an invaluable flow of income to the Exchequer (duties stood at around 8d. per lb. in the 1750s) and held out the opportunity for immense profit for those British merchants who arranged credit for planters, organized their supply of goods and carried out the sale of crops in European markets. Not surprisingly, therefore, competition was intense, with London and the provincial ports each vying for supremacy.

The trade in tobacco became the most remarkable example of Scottish commercial enterprise in the imperial economy during the course of the eighteenth century. The statistical evidence of business success is revealing. In one year, 1758, Scottish tobacco imports from the colonies of Virginia and Maryland exceeded those of London and the English outports of Bristol, Liverpool and Whitehaven combined. Three years later the highest-ever volume of tobacco leaf was landed in Scotland, a staggering 47 million lb., which amounted to a third of all the nation's imports and when sold on to European and Irish markets no less than two-thirds of its exports. On the eve of the American Revolution in 1773–4 the Scots were reckoned to control over half the trade in the key areas of colonial tobacco production. Little wonder that one planter, William Lee, could proclaim: 'I think it self-evident that Glasgow has almost monopolized Virginia and its inhabitants.'[3]

Lee's reference to Glasgow was telling. Although in earlier years other Scottish towns, such as Ayr, Dumfries, Bo'ness, Leith, Dundee and Aberdeen, were actively importing tobacco, the Glasgow merchants, through their two outports of Greenock and Port Glasgow, increasingly established a virtual stranglehold on the trade. As early as the 1710s the Clyde's share of Scottish imports was already around 90 per cent and by the 1760s had climbed further again to 98 per cent. Glasgow was Scotland as far as the tobacco trade was concerned.[4] It was not simply that the city's merchants were adept at crushing competition within the country; they were also formidable opponents within the broader imperial system. Over the middle decades of the century they carved out an ever larger share of the British trade. As late as 1738 the Scots controlled only 10 per cent of UK tobacco imports, but this figure rose to 20 per cent in 1744, stood at 30 per cent by 1758 and topped 40 per cent in 1765. Voices were raised in alarm from London, Bristol and elsewhere that if this trend continued for much longer the Glaswegians would surely possess one of the nation's most lucrative Atlantic trades in its entirety.

In an important sense, however, this dynamic business was much more than the simple acquisition of tobacco leaf from colonial planters followed by sale to the burgeoning consumer markets of France, Scandinavia, Holland and the German states. The tobacco trade was Scotland's first global enterprise. Because of it, Glasgow became a player on the world commercial stage by the 1770s. To establish and refine their competitive position in the international market-place, the city's merchants had to ensure they were able to service the needs of the colonial planter class for domestic articles, plantation equipment, household plenishings, clothing, luxuries and a host of other items. American consumers became increasingly sophisticated purchasers as their material standards rose in the wake of expanding markets in Europe for their sugar, tobacco, timber, rice and indigo. Some sense of the new consumerism comes from the New York press. In the 1720s merchants there described only fifteen different manufactured goods in newspaper articles. By the 1770s they were selling over 9,000 different imported items, many of which had highly specific descriptions. Expanding custom in the tobacco colonies, therefore, increasingly meant that Scottish factors and storekeepers had to offer the widest possible range of goods to satisfy these new demands. That in turn meant that their Glasgow principals had to create secure lines of supply for the vast array of consumer goods needed across the Atlantic. A global business emerged. Wine came from Madeira and the Canary Islands; sugar and rum from the Caribbean; linen from Ireland; luxuries from Holland; and so on. The sources of supply ran from the Mediterranean to Russia and across the Atlantic to the West Indies and Canada: 'the shipping routes stretched out from Glasgow like the ribs of a fan'.[5] And at home, tobacco merchants set up their own centres of production by investing in tanneries, bottleworks, linen, sugar-refining plants, breweries, ironworks and many other enterprises in Glasgow itself and in the counties around.

The scale and complexity of the networks developed by the tobacco business had much wider ramifications than the merely commercial. The Scottish–American link became an important conduit of ideas. As Jacob Price noted of the Scottish mercantile community in the Chesapeake Bay, 'twice a year their ships came from the Clyde – ships as numerous as those from all Britain besides. For many a Virginian, this must have meant that mail, news, reading matter, ideas, religion, politics came to him via Glasgow.'[6] Historians have speculated on the influence of the intellectual principles of the Scottish Enlightenment on American politics in the years before the Revolution. It is not too fanciful to claim that the transtlantic trade was one of the channels through which these ideas percolated to the colonies in the books, pamphlets and newspapers which often formed part of the assorted outgoing cargoes in the holds of the tobacco ships. Equally, the trading link stimulated Scottish interest in America. By c.1750, 'Plantation News' became a regular feature in the columns of the *Scots Magazine*, the most important Scottish periodical of the eighteenth century. The same journal commonly printed extracts from the American press, together with other reports and letters from the colonies. The magazine was also a rich source on the emerging dispute with the mother country and its coverage was notable both for depth and detail as well as impartiality.

These intellectual connections were paralleled in other areas. American commerce did not in itself inevitably lead to rising levels of emigration to the colonies from Scotland after c.1760, which are surveyed elsewhere in this book. But the powerful trading relationship doubtless spread awareness of transatlantic possibilities more widely in Scottish society, as well as creating a much larger merchant fleet to facilitate mass sea migration. As one contemporary put it:

By this intercourse between Scotland and North America, which for more than half a century hath been rapidly increasing, Scotland is in a situation which appeareth to be different from what it was in any former period. It may be considered as being, by means of its navigation and foreign commerce brought nearer to the Western continent than it was before. Good roads, you know, do, as it were, diminish the distance betwixt two cities; a long and continued intercourse, by safe and successful sailings, hath the like effect with respect to distant countries.[7]

But this was not all. The tobacco trade transformed the social and cultural world of Glasgow. A new breed of merchants came on the scene. Their wealth and commercial power were unprecedented in the city's history, so much so that they were dubbed 'tobacco lords' as an acknowledgement of their pre-eminence. They were said to promenade the streets of Glasgow clad in scarlet cloaks, satin suits and cocked hats, with gold-tipped canes in hand and an aloof air. This new aristocracy built splendid mansions, founded banks and industries, and dominated the political and cultural life of the city. The modern street names of Buchanan Street, Glassford Street, Dunlop Street, Oswald Street and Ingram Street celebrate the enduring mark which prominent members of this élite left on Glasgow's history.

Their impact was also deeply felt on the other side of the Atlantic. If the needs of the planter class for consumer goods and agricultural equipment were great, their requirements for credit were even more acute. Especially in the newer areas of tobacco cultivation, such as the back-country of Virginia where the less wealthy planters were concentrated, credit was the lifeblood of the economy. With capital provided by British merchants, planters could purchase slave and indentured labour and the tools necessary to expand cultivation and clear virgin land. In addition, the credit advanced meant that the colonists could work through the months between harvests without denying themselves clothing, food and other items. Credit made it possible to cope with the inevitable differences in timing inherent in the tobacco economy – before the return for one year's crop had been harvested, the planter had to live and plant the next crop. In a sense, then, by extending liberal credit the Glasgow houses provided development capital in many parts of Virginia and Maryland. The resulting level of debt owed to the Scots rose steeply from an estimated

£500,000 in the early 1760s to £1.3 million when the Revolution broke out in 1775.[8] The Glaswegians were therefore a key influence on colonial economic history. Moreover, since so much of the credit was used to purchase slaves, the lie was given to the later Victorian claim that Glasgow, unlike Bristol and Liverpool, played little part in the slave trade. This may be true to some extent in terms of the direct trafficking of negroes from Africa to the Caribbean and the Americas, though even here the Scottish role has been under-estimated. But the suggestion ignores the deep involvement of the Scots in a colonial economy which could not have functioned without an entrenched and expanding system of slave labour.

2

One scholar has described the tobacco trade as 'the most efficient business of the age', while another considered the Glasgow merchants 'cut-throat competitors' who were pursuing 'capitalism in its purest and most dynamic form'.[9] But the accolades sometimes conceal the hard-won nature of the achievement. Before the union of 1707 the Scots were slowly establishing themselves in Atlantic commerce, either illegally through the contraband trade to the English colonies or by their connections in London, Bristol, Liverpool and White-haven. But full commercial union between the two countries was necessary to achieve the huge levels of tobacco imports landed at the Clyde ports by the 1750s. No English government would have tolerated such a potent threat to the imperial economy coming from another country. Ironically, Glasgow itself fought hard against the passage of the Act of Union partly because of Presbyterian fears of Anglican hegemony and partly out of concern that a more vigorous customs service might be established in the aftermath of union which would destroy the lucrative contraband trade. But the commercial provisions of the treaty seemed to hold out the promise of a bright future. The Scots were allowed to trade directly with the colonies in all commodities, a privilege denied the Irish until the 1780s. Their merchant ships were granted the protection of the Royal Navy, an important advantage in a century which saw a series of major wars between Britain and France in the struggle for transatlantic supremacy. In addition, certain 'enumerated commodities', of which tobacco was one, had first to be shipped from the colonies to UK ports and there pay customs duties before being re-exported. This requirement virtually excluded both European and Irish competitors from importing tobacco from British colonies.

Yet these privileges were no guarantee of success. In the first couple of decades after 1707 growth was sluggish. Glasgow did less well in the 1720s than Bristol, Liverpool or Whitehaven, and fell well behind London, the leading tobacco entrepôt in the country. It would seem that the union, while it might have been the necessary *foundation* for growth, could not necessarily *cause* it to happen. The origins of the 'golden age' lay elsewhere. At the time, English mercantile interests complained vociferously that the Scots were taking their business away because of systematic fraud practised on a massive scale. The charges from the English outports cannot simply be written off as 'Scottophobia' or the predictable expression of outraged vested interest. Investigations made by the Scottish customs in the early 1720s confirmed that a high level of fraud existed and that the principal abuse in the Scottish trade involved conspiracies between merchants and officers to under-weigh incoming cargoes on a very large scale. In the years from 1715 to 1717, smuggled imports were estimated at 62 per cent of legal imports; at 47 per cent between 1720 and 1721; at 26 per cent between 1722 and 1731, and still as high as 22 per cent in the period from 1739 to 1748. When Glasgow was in the early phase of the era of unprecedented expansion, almost a quarter of total tobacco imports were probably being smuggled. Such was the scale and duration of these fraudulent practices that it is impossible to ignore them in any account of Glasgow's central role in the trade.[10]

Smuggling did therefore give Glasgow merchants a cost advantage in these early decades, as English commercial interests had complained. Fraud enabled the Glaswegians to establish themselves firmly in the British tobacco trade after the union. Significantly, after the customs reorganization of 1723, when fraud in the Scottish ports was brought under tighter control, Glasgow's rate of growth was much slower and its lead was quickly recaptured by Liverpool and Whitehaven in the later 1720s and 1730s. But this chronology also demonstrates that fraud could not have been in the long run a decisive factor in the explosive growth of Clyde imports in the middle decades of the eighteenth century. When the Glasgow trade was at its peak between 1750 and 1775 fraudulent practices were in decline. The surveillance of the navy, new legislation in 1723 and 1751 and reform of the customs service had all played a part in this process. Smuggling was therefore more characteristic of the decades of relatively slow or stagnant activity than of the years of dazzling success.

In the search for more convincing explanations, the geographical factor must be considered. In his classic article of 1954 on the rise of Glasgow in the Chesapeake tobacco trade, Jacob M. Price noted that the order of importance of the leading western British tobacco ports was their geographic sequence from north to south; Glasgow, Whitehaven, Liverpool and Bristol.[11] He explained this pattern in terms of the fact that the route north of Ireland was the shortest and quickest by two or three weeks. The Glasgow vessels saved on sailing time and hence on freight costs. Quicker transport also meant that commercial intelligence also passed more rapidly. The locational advantage was undeniable. But still the explanation is incomplete. The Scots had an advantage on the transatlantic routes, but the great mass of tobacco leaf imported to the Clyde was quickly re-exported after payment of duty to markets in France, the Low Countries, Scandinavia and the German states. In relation to these outlets, Glasgow ships were at a profound geographical disadvantage which must have considerably eroded any significant savings on the Atlantic crossing itself.

Geography and smuggling were therefore relevant but by no means decisive factors in Glasgow's dominant role in tobacco commerce. The fundamental influences lay elsewhere: in the changing context of trade among British west coast ports, the competitiveness of the Glasgow trading system and the sources of capital for transatlantic commerce.

Competition was less effective from Bristol, Liverpool and Whitehaven from the 1750s. At Bristol, overseas merchants increasingly concentrated on the Caribbean sugar trade, and indeed as early as c.1720 the tobacco re-export trade there stagnated. At Liverpool, though tobacco remained more significant than at Bristol, interest in the sector also declined from the middle decades of the century as resources increasingly moved into the slave trade. The case of Whitehaven is the most interesting of all. In the 1740s the growth of her tobacco imports was even more spectacular than Glasgow's. In addition, the Whitehaven merchants attracted the very valuable business of the French customs monopoly which was eventually to be so critical in Glasgow's success. By the 1750s Whitehaven was the only real rival to Glasgow outside London. Its demise in the 1760s was therefore a key factor in Glasgow's ultimate triumph. It was partly due to short-term influences, such as the bankruptcy of two important merchants, George Fitzgerald (1759) and Peter How (1763), and the withdrawal of the important local landed family, the Lowthers, from vigorous commitment to the trade. But there were probably deeper structural factors. Whitehaven did not have the same depth of capitalization or of infrastructure as Glasgow possessed by the 1750s. It was too easily knocked off course by business crises affecting a small number of leading personalities. In addition, much Whitehaven capital moved into the coal export trade in the eighteenth century.[12]

Both Glasgow and Whitehaven possessed a distinctive advantage over their rivals. The majority of tobacco houses in Bristol, Liverpool and London were commission merchants, taking crops on consignment and disposing of them in domestic and European markets for their planter customers in return for a commission on sales. The central element in the whole process was that the planter retained title of ownership until final sale. The merchant in Britain was his agent, committed to obtaining the highest possible price for each consignment, because on that depended the value of his commission. The consignment system flourished particularly in the later seventeenth and early eighteenth centuries, when tobacco prices in the UK were buoyant and most production in the colonies was still controlled by wealthier planters of the tidewater areas who could afford to shoulder the burden of risks and long credits associated with such a business regime. It was, however, in relative decline from the 1730s and in many inland districts of Maryland and Virginia had been superseded by an alternative: the direct purchase system in which British merchants through their agents in the colonies bought up tobacco for goods, cash or credit in advance of the arrival of their vessels from home. For reasons that will become clear later, direct purchase had very significant commercial advantages over consignment in the middle and later decades of the eighteenth century. As a result, the huge gains in importation from the 1740s were to a large extent absorbed by those who specialized in it. Glasgow's success depended in large part on this basic structural change in the Chesapeake trade, the long-term triumph of purchase over consignment.

Hence stores staffed by Scottish factors began to appear in the valley of the Potomac River as early as the 1680s.[13] The papers of the Dunlop and Bogle merchant families make it clear that there was already a functioning 'store system' in Virginia before 1700, though on a much smaller scale than that which emerged during the period after *c.*1730. By that time, when the commercial structure had matured, the great mercantile syndicates which dominated the trade controlled whole chains of stores in Virginia and Maryland. William Cunninghame and Company, one of the giants but by no means the largest firm, owned fourteen such outlets in Virginia alone in the 1760s.

The concentration on direct purchase was crucial to Glasgow's emergence as the most successful tobacco emporium in Britain.[14] In the first place, purchasing was exceptionally well suited to the needs of the smaller and less wealthy colonial planter classes. After the first quarter of the eighteenth century the frontier of tobacco cultivation began to move westward across the fall lines of the great rivers flowing into Chesapeake Bay to the piedmont country beyond. Here crop cultivation was dominated by poorer planters who, unlike the more powerful interest of older tobacco regions, did not have individual crops of sufficient size to attract the custom of London commission houses. The store or direct purchase system was, nevertheless, ideally suited to their needs and limitations. The metropolitan merchant rather than the planter bore the risk and crops could be easily and quickly disposed of in the back-country through the myriad of Scottish stores far into the interior. Furthermore, goods, and even more importantly, credit, could be brought into the heart of the new tobacco country by the Glasgow factors.

The Scottish stores were vital channels of credit to these planters. The tobacco colonies were geared to satisfying international needs for an important commodity. Yet increasingly production was in the hands of a planter class with little capital in areas which lacked an indigenous merchant group of any size. Investment to increase cultivation had to come from outside, especially since output was mainly increased by acquiring more slave labour than by improving modes of production. Even a single extra field-hand could double the output of a household hitherto entirely dependent on the labour of the planter. So marginal was the financial position of many planters that slave assistance could only be secured by borrowing, and in many areas of the Chesapeake that meant drawing on credit available from Glasgow storekeepers who effectively became the bankers of the new tobacco districts.[15]

At the same time, until the 1770s and in some earlier years of financial crisis, their principals at home advised the constant extension of credit in order to secure more customers. John Glassford and Company, for instance, founded a new store in Occoquam, Virginia, in 1759 but recognized that several years of credit extension would be necessary before satisfactory returns were likely. It was reckoned, indeed, that for every hogshead of tobacco a sum of between £25 and £30 had to be invested in the colonies, exclusive of shipping costs.[16]

Direct purchasing was also suited to European customers and particularly to those in France. The French market was the largest and most important on the Continent. From 1674 to 1791 the buying of tobacco from foreign sources for the French customer was not in the control of independent merchants. Purchasing was controlled by a state monopoly farmed out to private interest. The 'Farmers General of the French Customs' bought mainly in bulk to satisfy national requirements. Before the early eighteenth century they acquired little in Britain, but from the 1720s purchasing increased dramatically because of the cheapness and versatility of British colonial leaf and the decision of the Walpole government in that decade to reduce the fiscal burden on re-exports through UK entrepôts. Consumption within the area of the French monopoly rose sevenfold from 1715 to 1775, and between 1730 and 1744 France overtook Holland to become the prime market for British tobacco.[17]

The French, therefore, became major players in the tobacco trade from the 1720s. However, at that stage their impact on the Glasgow sector was limited as only about 10 per cent of their requirements were obtained there, even as late as 1730. In the three subsequent decades this position was transformed. By 1757–62 no less than 52 per cent of a much greater purchase was acquired from Glasgow, and in the same period 35 per cent of all Scottish exports were destined for France. The French market had become the single most important factor in the Glasgow trades in the years of its golden age. It was not simply that the French absorbed more than a third of all sales on a regular basis. Also critical to Glasgow success was their system of payment. Long credits to European customers were one of the hazards of the business, particularly for merchants who engaged in direct purchase and locked up much of their own capital. But because they bought for the whole of France, the Farmers General purchased in bulk and paid in cash or short-term, easily discountable bills of exchange. It was this predictable flow of liquid capital which lubricated the Glasgow trade in its era of expansion and permitted activity to increase in those other tobacco markets in Holland, Scandinavia and the German states where returns were much more sluggish.[18]

The rapid increase in French purchasing on the Clyde from c.1740 partly depended on short-term factors. Insurance premiums, for instance, were lower in the northern sea lanes during the war of 1744–8 and this may have encouraged movement away from traditional sources in the south. More critical, however, were the basic advantages to the French monopoly of the Glasgow direct purchase system. Because the Scottish firms actually owned the cargoes they imported they could dispose of them, sight unseen, in huge sales to the buyers in Scotland on behalf of the French, who in the 1750s and 1760s were William Alexander and Sons, an Edinburgh house with close personal and matrimonial ties with some leading Glasgow merchant families. Consignment was not adapted to French needs because the interest of the commission agent was to achieve the highest possible price for a limited number of hogsheads from different planters who produced leaf of varied quality and price. Such a system was more geared to sluggish sales though perhaps eventually making significant profits for the merchant. But it was far too expensive and time-consuming for the agents of the French monopoly. The drift northwards of French purchasing, with all its benefits, was therefore probably inevitable. As has been argued, it might have happened much earlier but for the fact that the Glasgow trade was not sufficiently developed to satisfy French needs. However, by the 1750s large integrated partnerships had evolved, each consisting of several wealthy merchant families. This process of concentration of control accelerated in subsequent decades until, in the later 1760s, more than half of all tobacco imports to the Clyde was controlled by three giant syndicates headed by Alexander Speirs, John Glassford and William Cunninghame.[19]

The store system also yielded benefits in commercial efficiency. It was one of the familiar comments made by contemporaries that the Scottish merchants were able to sell tobacco more cheaply and operate at lower costs than their rivals. For example, in 1769 one observer, writing from the colonies to a London merchant, described how the Clydesiders had a 'vast advantage' over the traders of the capital 'by sailing their ships so much cheaper than you can do'.[20] Certainly prices in Glasgow were often lower than elsewhere. The Glasgow firms seem to have been keener to achieve rapid turnover of capital than to extract the last farthing of profit from tobacco sales. Because they owned the leaf they supplied they could not tolerate the risk and time of the lengthy and tortuous bargaining conducted by the consignment houses, who were essentially selling agents so naturally sought to hold out for the highest possible price. Time and again the London men scathingly criticized their counterparts in Scotland for accepting lower offers than the market, in their view, merited. The merchants were able to do this partly because they did not depend exclusively on tobacco wholesaling. The sale of European goods to the colonists via their stores was at least as lucrative. Also they were in a sense compelled to seek quick returns because as tobacco purchasers they locked up their own capital in each transaction. But the relatively low returns were acceptable in the final analysis because the Glasgow trade was conspicuously successful in cutting freight costs over time.

Tobacco was a bulky, low-value commodity. Hence transport costs were around one-third of total operating costs in the trade and easily the biggest single charge after the actual purchase price of tobacco. Direct purchase played a key role in reducing these costs because the primary role of the storekeepers was to ensure the collection of full cargoes in advance of the arrival of the armada from the Clyde. Thus the 'stay in the country' was kept to a minimum. It was partly because of this advantage that many Glasgow vessels were able to achieve quite astonishing levels of efficiency on the 7,000-mile round trip between Scotland and Virginia. Almost uniquely in the British tobacco trade, those who engaged in the direct purchase system were able to achieve two voyages across the Atlantic in a year. The *Jeanie* of John Glassford and Company put in 18 voyages in eleven years and the same firm's *Potomack* 13 in nine. William Cunninghame's *Patuxent* achieved 13 trips in eight years, the

Cunninghame 17 in seven, and the *Triton* 11 in seven. Alexander Speirs and Company's *Bowman* recorded the extraordinary total of 16 round voyages in the eight years 1767–75.[21]

Indeed, the whole Glasgow shipping system was highly efficient by eighteenth-century standards and this competitive edge increased substantially over time.[22] In the period before the union, for example, it was common for Glasgow merchants to charter ships locally or from English ports. But in subsequent decades the number and proportion of 'company ships' which were entirely owned by firms rose rapidly. By the late 1740s nearly 60 per cent of vessels in the Clyde tobacco fleet were in this category. By 1775 the figure had reached 90 per cent. This movement from chartering to ownership allowed for more careful planning of shipping schedules and hence cut turnaround time further. It also produced a pool of crack skippers who were absolutely familiar with the routes and whose skills may well have further reduced passage time. So might other advances. In 1762 the first dry dock in Scotland was opened in Port Glasgow with pumping machinery designed by James Watt to allow for speedier careening of tobacco ships, especially important because of their exposure to the teredo-worm-infested waters of the Chesapeake. Ship design improved. In the tobacco fleet the provision of more fore-and-aft sails, as distinct from square sails, enabled ships to sail closer to the wind and made it easier for them to navigate the shoal-waters of the Chesapeake rivers.

Similarly the carrying capacity of those vessels regularly engaged in the trade rose substantially over time. The average annual volume of tobacco carried per ship in the Clyde fleet increased from 219,800 lb. between 1747 and 1751 to 520,000 lb. between 1762 and 1766, and finally to 530,000 lb. in the years 1770 to 1775. This reflected a notable gain in economies of scale. At the same time, the larger vessels maintained very high levels of efficiency. Outward passages of seven weeks were normal and even this was often surpassed. On the round trip the average voyage lasted for about three months because homeward voyages with the Gulf Stream and prevailing winds normally took around five weeks. Yet despite this some ships made three trips in a year. This feat was accomplished no less than four times in the 1760s and again on four occasions in the early 1770s.

Indeed, an analysis of the performance of the Clyde tobacco fleet does suggest that all the improvements described above contributed to a much more effective utilization of ship capacity and hence led to a continued fall in freight costs. The average turn-round in the Chesapeake was consistently pushed down between 1750 and 1775, from 53 days in 1750 to 48 in 1755, 44 in 1760, 40 in 1765, 36 in 1770 and 33 in 1775. The average 'stay in the country' had therefore almost halved in twenty-five years. In addition, from 1750 to 1775 the average turnaround in the Clyde showed an improvement of 43 per cent. These data demonstrate that Glasgow's competitive edge did not simply derive from the dynamics of the direct purchase system. Clearly a major contribution was also made by those who managed the trade, who enhanced the efficiency of operations and substantially cut freight costs. It was hardly surprising that the Glasgow merchants became feared in Atlantic commerce; they were truly intimidating competitors. At the same time as they drove down transport costs, they were also intent on reducing other expenses and increasing the security of supply of their store goods by establishing a series of workshops and small factories in Glasgow to produce the range of commodities required by their planter customers. Between 1750 and 1780 much capital flowed from trade to industry. It was a further means by which the dominance of the Glasgow firms in the Chesapeake trade was consolidated.

3

In one sense, however, the achievement was paradoxical. It is at first difficult to understand why a port town within a relatively poor economy should achieve such pre-eminence. In simple terms, how could Glasgow afford to fund the tobacco trade? The question is particularly pertinent because the system of direct purchasing which it operated was especially demanding of capital. The goods that merchants bought for export to the Chesapeake were normally acquired on twelve months' credit, although it was not unknown for extensions to be made available. While turnover of tobacco was rapid in the French market, it was much more sluggish elsewhere. The French buyers paid quickly in cash or short-term bills, but in Holland, Scandinavia and the German states it could take as much as four to six months before sales were made and proceeds realized.

It has to be remembered too that the French monopoly took only around one-third of Glasgow-imported tobacco, even during the golden age; the rest was exported to those other markets where returns could be secured much less rapidly. Moreover, since the Glasgow houses specialized in the purchase of crops from new tobacco country in the colonies, they were committed to the extensive provision of credit to planters to enable them to improve land and expand cultivation. In a sense, as argued earlier, they helped to furnish the development capital without which the great boom in tobacco production in Virginia could not have taken place. But such grants of credit were rarely self-liquidating and as trade expanded so planter debt rose inexorably.

In accounting for the successful capitalization of the tobacco trade, some writers have pointed to the emergence of a banking system in the west of Scotland in the middle decades of the eighteenth century which enabled such surplus funds as were available to be channelled into foreign commerce.[23] Formal banking did expand at this time in Glasgow, as it did in other British ports, as overseas merchants in particular sought to mobilize the additional capital which could not easily be obtained from the existing banking structure. Also, the new foundations, the Ship Bank (1752), the Glasgow Arms Bank (1752) and the Thistle Bank (1761), were all dominated by tobacco merchants. It is therefore easy and tempting to make a correlation between their foundation and the capitalization of Atlantic commerce.

Closer scrutiny, however, tends to diminish the significance of formal banking. The new banks were relatively small and could only have catered for a very limited proportion of the financial needs of merchant firms. The Ship Bank never had a capital of more then £15,000 and the larger Arms Bank not more than £26,000 in the 1760s. Such evidence as is available of the credit structures of tobacco houses confirms this suspicion. Only 7 per cent of bonds borrowed by Bogle, Somervell and Company in 1768 were lent by banks and only 15 per cent of the credit of Buchanan, Hastie and Company in 1777.[24] Historians also tend to question the importance of formal banking at this time: 'the key institutions of pre-corporate credit were at work in Britain before anything called a "bank" appeared on the scene: mortgage, bond, note, bill of exchange, discount and ordinary commercial credit, short and long term'.[25] When banks appeared they simply made an existing system more efficient. It is therefore probable that the Glasgow ventures of the 1750s and 1760s were useful but not of decisive importance. For instance, they played a valuable role in oiling the trading mechanism by acting as bill discounters. Bills accepted by the Ship Bank rose in value from £8,854 in 1752 to £54,135 ten years later. In addition, the 'cash accompt', or overdraft, was advantageous when merchants had to meet short-term demands for customs, port and freight charges.

In general, however, capital requirements were met by more traditional methods. The golden age after about 1740 rested on the foundations of at least two generations of activity in Atlantic trade, and some of the capital for the era of expansion came from the savings of established merchant families who had been in the tobacco business for some time. Between 1740 and 1790, 44 per cent of tobacco merchants were sons of Glasgow merchants. Sons, grandsons and great-grandsons succeeded one another and it was common for merchant fathers to direct in their wills that monies left to their descendants should be used in trade. Great merchant dynasties of the 1750s like the Bogles, Dunlops, Buchanans and Murdochs could trace their lineage back to the seventeenth century. Through inheritance, therefore, the fortunes of earlier ages helped to provide the capital of the new era. These wealthy interests also managed to attract credit more easily.[26]

Nevertheless, it is unlikely that inheritance alone could satisfy the enormous demands for credit and capital which took place from the 1740s. To meet these, Glasgow firms responded by carefully re-ploughing profits and borrowing on bond on a large scale.[27] By the middle decades of the eighteenth century the loose mercantile federations of earlier days had been replaced by a formal company structure. The trade was organized around thirty to forty partnerships each structured in law according to agreed bonds of co-partnership. These syndicates proved very flexible in mobilizing capital. They allowed for the recruitment of several partners, some of whom would be inactive but whose rights were fully protected by the copartnery bond. This enabled firms wishing to extend their capital base to attract partners with resources to spare. It was an effective way of pooling funds in a commercial centre with much less disposable wealth than London. Significantly, tobacco houses in the capital and at Liverpool and Bristol commonly had two or three partners. In Glasgow, such small groupings were uncommon. Of twenty-four Clyde companies for which data are available for the period 1764 to 1783, fifteen had more than four partners. Of these, two firms consisted of nine individuals and a further two of seven.

Because in Scotland, unlike England, the partnership was a separate legal entity, the tobacco companies were able to draw up regulations governing the conduct of members' which were binding at law. One of the most vital of these, which existed in virtually every partnership deed, was that only 5 per cent interest was paid annually on the capital credited to the partners. All other profits were retained within the firm. This inevitably meant a huge growth in the capital stock of successful firms over time. It was the means by which the tobacco trade produced its own resources for continued expansion. One example will suffice to illustrate the process. The largest single firm in the years before the American War was Speirs, Bowman and Company, one of the partnerships associated with the merchant Alexander Speirs. In 1744 its total capital was £16,200; by 1773 this had swollen to £152,280.[28] The Speirs case was possibly the most extraordinary example of capital growth but there were many instances on a much smaller scale. Apart from anything else, these enormous levels of capitalization, greater than anything at partnership level in the London tobacco trade, made these organizations even more creditworthy and much more capable of attracting external financial support.

In a striking phrase, an early historian of Glasgow noted that one feature of the tobacco business was that 'the strength of the monied interest of the West of Scotland was embarked in it'.[29] Only in recent years have scholars begun to discover the full significance of this remark, but it is now clear that much of the capital for expansion of the trade was mobilized from the resources of the middling rich in Glasgow and the surrounding districts. The western lowlands of Scotland may not have had the financial resources of London or even of the hinterlands of Bristol and Liverpool, but they had the advantage that before the last quarter of the eighteenth century there were few major areas competing for investment with foreign commerce. Industrial development had indeed occurred but, as will be discussed below, most of it was dominated in Glasgow by colonial merchants; where it was not, as in linen, most concerns had capital of less than £5,000 and were entirely dwarfed by the resources of the great tobacco syndicates. Almost certainly the incomes of middle-class families in the region increased gradually in the middle decades of the eighteenth century. An analysis of bonded loans to merchants in Glasgow shows that their value rose fourfold from the 1720s to the 1760s.[30] This suggests that there was more money about seeking an outlet for secure investment. The pattern was paralleled in other British cities, but there was a significant difference in Glasgow. London interests invested heavily in public funds and the great chartered companies, but the practice was more limited in Scotland. This was partly because government stock was regarded as a volatile investment but also because returns of 3 or 3.5 per cent on public funds were much lower than the expected gains nearer home. The main medium for transmission of credit was the loan secured on bond. The basic advantage of the bonded loan was that it produced a higher return than government stock. Most of the bonded loans studied were for the full legal limit of 5 per cent rate of interest between 1750 and 1775. If necessary, further security for the lender could be obtained by guaranteeing them against heritable property, and although bonds were commonly drawn up for six months or a year, they endured in most cases for much longer periods.[31]

There is little doubt that these bonds provided an essential source of long-term capital for the tobacco trade. All the portfolios of the big companies show heavy reliance on them. The majority of lenders lived in Glasgow or its hinterland. They were from the middle ranks of urban society and consisted mainly of merchants with funds to spare, lawyers, doctors, university professors, artisans and small landowners. The curators of trust funds and the widows and trustees of deceased traders were also particularly prominent. A sample of those who lent on bond to one firm, Buchanan, Hastie and Company, between 1768 and 1777 included William Clavil, landowner; Daniel Baxter, bookseller in Glasgow; the factor for the children of James Glen, goldsmith in Glasgow; Dr William Macfarlane, physician in Edinburgh; and John Wilson, Town Clerk of Glasgow. Although the occasional bonded loan of £1,000 or more was recorded, the majority were for smaller sums. Those with money to lend tended to split their investments in amounts of £100 to £500 among a series of companies. The existence of such a lively financial market in and around the city does, however, suggest that mobilization of capital for both trade and industry may have been less of a problem than some accounts have suggested.[32] The evidence is consistent with the findings of recent research that the Scottish economy was already on the move before the even greater acceleration in the last quarter of the eighteenth century.[33]

4

The considerable capital costs of the tobacco trade help to explain the nature and size of the merchant class who managed it in this period. The colonial traders were a remarkably small part of the city's commercial community as a whole because only a fraction of the burgh's traders had the resources and the personal connections to maintain a presence in Atlantic commerce for very long. Those who obtained a partnership in the companies which dominated the trade by the 1750s formed a tiny minority. Only 163 merchant burgesses of Glasgow were directly and consistently involved in tobacco importation at partnership level between 1740 and 1790, out of a total merchant community in the period of several thousands. Of the 174 individuals who became merchant burgesses in the decade 1740 to 1749 less than 10 per cent could be traced later as American traders, and from 1776 to 1780 around 8 per cent. It was a consistently low figure and confirms the impression from other evidence that the 'tobacco lords' were an élite within an élite.[34] But even this evidence does not provide a complete picture of the extent of concentration of control. Throughout the period, a small group of wealthy merchant families, through their shares in interlocked partnerships, maintained an even more dominant position. They would number about two dozen dynasties, sometimes fewer, and although names did change over time power still lay in the hands of a very small group. Between October and December 1742, for instance, over two-thirds of the tobacco landed were shipped by just four family syndicates, the Dunlops, Bogles, Oswalds and McCalls. The bulk of the remaining cargoes were landed by a further six associations of merchants. Three massive associations led by John Glassford, Alexander Speirs and William Cunninghame handled over 50 per cent of the tobacco in the years before the American War.[35]

These features were characteristic of the commerce in colonial commodities. Tobacco and sugar were high-bulk, low-value trades in which buying and selling in volume conferred distinct advantages in economies of scale. Moreover, larger firms of wealthier merchants were able to attract credit more easily because of their security and reputation and, as seen earlier, the capacity to mobilize capital was critical to success in the Atlantic trades. Perhaps, however, the trend towards concentration was even more evident in Glasgow than in London or the English outports because Scottish partnership law enabled the recruitment of powerful additional 'sleeping' partners whose names, reputations and connections strengthened still further the credibility of core interests.

The backgrounds of the men who made up this élite were varied, although as a broad generalization it can be said that the overwhelming majority came from the 'middling' elements in Scottish society. Throughout the period 1730–90 only four of the fathers of tobacco merchants were craftsmen, while on the other hand not one, as far as is known, was the scion of a noble or aristocratic family. The vast majority were sons of the well-to-do in lowland Scotland below the ranks of the aristocracy. As far as the Glasgow tobacco trade is concerned, the 'rags to riches' story was but a comforting myth.

The biggest single source of recruits was established merchant families in Glasgow itself. Between 1740 and 1790, 44 per cent of the total came into this category. Such men would have obvious

	Number	Percentage
Merchants in Glasgow	71	43.5
Merchants in other Scottish burghs	6	3.6
Craftsmen in Glasgow	4	2.4
Landowners with no direct interest in commerce	8	4.9
Ministers of Presbyterian or Episcopalian churches	12	7.3
Lawyers, notaries and members of the judiciary	6	3.6
Schoolmasters	1	0.6
Physicians	2	1.2
Occupation of fathers unknown but not merchants in Glasgow	53	32.5
Total	163	100.0

Table 1. Occupation of fathers of eighteenth-century Glasgow tobacco merchants

Source: T. M. Devine, *The Tobacco Lords* (Edinburgh, 1990 edn.), p.6.

advantages in financial support, personal association and relevant training. But the group was no self-perpetuating caste. In four of the six decades between 1730 and 1790 more recruits came from outside this circle than from within it (see Table 1). The community was therefore sufficiently 'open-ended' to allow newcomers to play a significant role in its expansion. Indeed, the great names of the golden years after c. 1740 were often not the sons of established merchants in Glasgow. John Glassford's father was a burgess in Paisley; Alexander Speirs was the offspring of an Edinburgh merchant family; William Cunninghame was the scion of a cadet branch of the Cunninghames of Caprington, lairds in Ayrshire; the Oswalds were from clerical stock in Caithness. On the other hand, some other families, such as the Ritchies, Bogles, Dunlops and Murdochs, could trace their connections with the tobacco trade back into the seventeenth century.

Two factors help to explain the degree of mobility within the group. In the first place, commerce with the American colonies was expanding so rapidly during the period that openings were always likely to become available for ambitious young men with suitable connections and financial backing. These two latter elements were well-nigh essential ingredients for success. The newcomer had to have personal contacts in the community and be prepared to spend perhaps several years accumulating capital.[36] A second factor facilitating entry of newcomers was insolvency among established merchants. Tobacco commerce was often profitable but sometimes risky, dependent as it was on the whims of the weather, the London money market and the vicissitudes of demand in continental Europe. In such years of credit crisis as 1762–3, 1772 and 1793 some of the most powerful families in Glasgow experienced the collapse of fortunes carefully built up over generations. One contemporary, for instance, observed in December 1762: 'You cannot imagine the distress people here are in for want of money. Several of our Virginia and West India merchants are lately broke here and several were much suspected which hurts credit.'[37]

The new blood had come through some form of education and training process. In the second half of the eighteenth century there were 'several schools' in Glasgow itself which offered rudimentary instruction in reading and writing while, for the older child, introducing also the mysteries of the classical languages. In the main, however, there was little 'vocational' or 'commercial' education at this level. At the Grammar School, a popular institution for merchants' sons, the curriculum was strictly academic, with the teaching geared to Latin and Greek, Classical Antiquities and Geography. In addition, a high proportion of those bent on a mercantile career spent some time at the University of Glasgow, where the teachers at this time were men of such international renown as Adam Smith (Professor of Moral Philosophy from 1751 to 1763), Robert Simson, William Cullen and Jospeh Black. Alexander Carlyle, a student at Glasgow in the 1740s, noted that 'it was usual for the sons of merchants to attend the College for one or two years', while as late as the 1820s a government commission confirmed that 'young men not intended for any learned profession ... are sent for one or more years to College in order to carry their education farther than that of the schools before they engaged in the pursuits of trade or of commerce'.[38] Between 1728 and 1800, indeed, at least sixty-eight tobacco and West India merchants had been students at Glasgow University.[39] Probably no other British mercantile community of the time could claim such a high proportion of young men exposed, however briefly, to higher education. This background in schooling and study helps to explain the impressive standards of literacy in the personal and business papers of numerous Scottish factors, clerks and store-keepers. Much of their surviving correspondence is marked by clarity and precise use of language. The same tradition perhaps explains why some leading figures were energetic supporters of intellectual and cultural activities in the city. The Literary Society of Glasgow and the Hodge Podge Club, both established by tobacco lords, held debates and discussions and attracted eminent speakers like Adam Smith and Thomas Reid. The famous Foulis Academy of Fine Arts would not have flourished but for their financial backing.

Practical experience 'on the job' across the Atlantic was also regarded as a vital part of the training regime. Thus James Lawson's son Robert followed the conventional route. In 1763 he was almost sixteen and had spent four years at grammar school, two at Glasgow College and 'about one year at Counting, Book-keeping and French'. He was then sent to Maryland under the supervision of his father's partner there.[40] For those not sons or close relatives of established merchants it was more common to serve a term as an indentured apprentice with a Virginia house in its colonial stores. Typical of such an arrangement were the terms of an indenture drawn up in 1758 between Glassford, Ingram and Company and Neil Campbell, son of John Campbell, supervisor of excise at Glasgow. Campbell was to serve the firm for the space of five years 'honestly and diligently' and 'not neglect his said Masters Business night nor day Except in the case of Sickness or Leave'. The penalty for breaking this regulation was 1s. per day or service for a further two days at his master's option. Above all, the apprentice was specifically enjoined 'not to reveal any of his said Master's secrets'. For their part the company undertook to instruct him in trade, to give him board and lodging, free passage to Virginia and a salary which would rise from £5 to £25 by annual increments over the five-year period.[41] The larger tobacco houses were able to develop even more elaborate schemes. The commercial empire of William Cunninghame extended to fourteen stores in Virginia, all run by young men recruited from west of Scotland families known to the company principals. Overseeing the entire business in the colony was James Robinson, son of a Scottish schoolmaster, who held the position of General Superintendent of the Company. One of Robinson's key tasks was to ensure that his young staff, sometimes running stores separated by hundreds of miles across difficult country, loyally and efficiently carried out the firm's instructions. He was a hard taskmaster. One Bennet Price was dismissed the firm's service in 1768. Unfortunately Price had taken a wife, and, 'They cannot agree to be served by a married man, if a single one can be got, thinking the former must often be necessarily call'd from their business by his family affairs.' But even this company's rigorous regime sometimes failed amid the stresses and multiple temptations of frontier life. Thus Francis Hay 'gave loose to dissipation. A purchase was made of a servant girl which he kept for sometime; and gaming to excess soon became common – so much addicted was he to this Vice that he has lost as I have been informed £60 at a sitting . . .' William Johnstone's sins were regarded as unmentionable but his 'behaviour was such that we look on him as totally unworthy of continuing in our service'.[42]

The cultivation of good relationships with planters was deemed particularly desirable by James Robinson. His storekeepers had to develop a 'knowledge of People's disposition' in order to extend the circle of his customers and ascertain their creditworthiness. The supreme combination in attracting a fresh clientele was what he called 'good usage' and 'plenty of money'. The latter as a purchasing medium for tobacco was always limited by the company but was considered a sure means of drawing new customers to the store. 'Good usage' consisted of more subtle techniques to encourage planters to offer their crop to the firm. Robinson counselled one of his storekeepers to use 'drink in abundance' when soliciting custom, and in addition, every effort was to be made to 'conciliate the affection and esteem of the people and to gain their confidence' by showing honesty in every transaction. At the same time, however, there was danger in too much intimacy. 'Secrecy in all your Transactions of Business even to the most simple is what I would strongly recommend.'[43] By means such as these the great Clyde firms advanced their business but also ensured that their factors in the colonies remained a class apart. It was a position which could and did make for uneasy relationships with the American colonial populations, especially when political tensions built up with the mother country from the 1760s.

The crucial result of the operation of these giant firms was a huge inflow of profit to west-central Scotland. The success of the tobacco trade not only transformed Glasgow from a provincial port to an international entrepôt. It also created the richest class of business tycoons in Scotland's history to that date, and cemented economic links both with the Atlantic world and Europe. Even more fundamentally, colonial profits helped prime the engines of Scottish industrialization. That is a story told later in Chapter 14.

5

The Scottish Lowlands and North America to 1775

The peopling of North America by the population of Europe was one of the great sagas of modern history and the crucial demographic foundation for the alteration in the balance of economic and political power from the Old to the New World. Without the great exodus of millions of people across the Atlantic the rise of the United States to the status of global superpower would have been impossible. We know a great deal about the nature and causes of the European diaspora in the nineteenth century, when the international movement reached unprecedented levels. Less studied is transatlantic emigration between 1700 and 1815. But that period too is deeply significant. It encompassed the emergence of an independent USA after 1783 but also saw the establishment of the basic political, economic and legal structures of modern North America. This chapter is especially concerned with the emigration of Lowland Scots to the new continent. It begins, however, with a general overview of the process of British and European movement to provide context and perspective for the specifically Scottish experience.

By 1689 permanent English settlement in North America had grown from the two original nuclei of the New England and the Chesapeake Bay colonies of Virginia and Maryland. Thereafter, further annexations went ahead at a steady pace: the conquest of New York from the Dutch, the founding of Pennsylvania, the occupation of what became known as North and South Carolina and the establishment of fur trading posts around Hudson Bay in the territory which eventually became known as British Canada. The Seven Years

War of 1756 to 1763 gave a dramatic new impetus to this expansionism. The final British victory resulted in a series of spectacular conquests not only in North America but also in the Caribbean and India. At the peace, the area under British rule had extended to include Georgia and East and West Florida in the south, and Nova Scotia and Quebec, formerly known as New France, to the north. An enormous boost was given to land speculation, investment and immigration in the newly-annexed territories. Ironically, however, the euphoria was short-lived. The rebellion of 1776 shattered the North American empire. The thirteen colonies became the independent United States in 1783 and Britain was left with only those possessions in the northern mainland and islands which came together to form the Dominion of Canada in the nineteenth century.

Pre-nineteenth-century population counts for the colonies are notoriously imprecise because of the gaps and ambiguities in the records of emigration. The estimates which exist, while grounded on careful examination of fragmentary and elusive information, mainly represent the overall scale rather than the precise and actual size of emigration. That said, there is a fair amount of agreement that, on the eve of the Anglo-Scottish union of 1707, the white population of English North America was around 265,000. Sustained emigration from Scotland had already begun, especially after 1680, with the efforts to settle East Jersey and Carolina and the activities of Scottish traders in the tobacco colonies around the Chesapeake. In all, it has been estimated that around 7,000 Scots moved to these areas in the course of the seventeenth century. The overwhelming majority were from the Lowlands and most crossed the Atlantic in the decades after c.1660.[1]

The most striking feature of Scottish emigration to North America before 1700 was its relative insignificance. The vast majority of the new settlers were from England, Wales and Ireland. Many thousands came in response to the voracious demands of the plantation colonies for a huge labour force to grow and process tobacco, rice, dyestuffs and sugar. In the seventeenth century it was poor men and women from the British Isles rather than imported slaves or native peoples who served the needs of the planters. They migrated as indentured servants contracted to provide their labour for periods of between four and seven years in return for passage across the Atlantic, food and accommodation. Over a quarter of a million souls made the journey across the Atlantic in the course of the seventeenth century. This was a huge number by the standards of pre-modern migrations. It was truly emigration on a massive scale, proportionally greater indeed in relation to the domestic population of the British Isles than the better-known diaspora of the nineteenth century. But of this great transfer of peoples, the Scottish total of about 7,000 represented a mere fraction, of around 2 per cent. Nor is this difficult to understand against the background of international Scottish mobility discussed in previous chapters. The Scots were a habitually migratory people *par excellence*, but at least until the later seventeenth century they mainly looked to Europe, Ulster and England rather than across the Atlantic for work, sustenance and position. Indeed, the actual *per capita* rate of Scottish emigration in the middle decades of the century to all destinations was more significant than even the great English movements to the Americas. Again, no part of the British Isles could equal the remarkable concentrated settlement of the tens of thousands of Scots in Ulster during the famine-stricken years of the 1690s. These long-established European and Irish channels of mobility would powerfully inhibit emigration to the fledgling American colonies for some years after 1700. Even then, however, the levels of Scottish outward movement in the eighteenth century were still less, in relation to the domestic population of the time, than the remarkable surges of emigration to Europe in the 1620s, 1630s and 1640s, and to Ireland in the 1690s.

It is clear, nonetheless, that the emigration histories of the nations of Britain were transformed in the new century. Table 2 summarizes the current best estimates for emigration to America between 1701 and 1780. Several conclusions emerge from these figures. First, and most obviously, the pattern of emigration was strikingly different from that in the seventeenth century. English movement had fallen dramatically, while the exodus of Scots and Irish across the Atlantic rose to high levels. The English national population in the eighteenth century was around five times the Scottish figure which stood at 1.265 million in 1755 (England's was 8.7 million in 1750). Yet remarkably, these data suggest that both nations were sending approximately the same total numbers across the Atlantic. Before the American Revolution no less than 70 per cent of British settlers arriving in America were from Ireland and Scotland.

Second, closer examination suggests that these raw figures under-

England and Wales	80
Scotland	80
Lowland	60
Highland	20
Ireland	115
Ulster	70
Southern	45
Total	275

Table 2. Emigration from the British Isles to America, 1701–1780 (thousands)
Sources: J. Horn. 'British Diaspora: Emigration from Britain, 1680–1815, in P. J. Marshall, ed., *The Oxford History of the British Empire*. Vol. 2, *The Eighteenth Century* (Oxford, 1998), p. 31; T. C. Smout, N. C. Landsman and T. M. Devine, 'Scottish Emigration in the Seventeenth and Eighteenth Centuries', in N. Canny, ed., *Europeans on the Move* (Oxford, 1994), pp. 90–112.

estimate the full impact of the Scots in the transatlantic diaspora. The exodus from Ireland before 1775 and even more so between 1783 and 1815 was dominated by Ulster Presbyterians. Perhaps as many as two-thirds of all Irish emigrants before the American Revolution belonged to this group. Church of Ireland adherents and members of other dissenting churches were also numbered among the emigrant parties. But Ulster Presbyterians were in the majority and were overwhelmingly either first-generation Scots migrants or the descendants of those who had settled in Ireland in previous decades.[2] It is worth remembering again that the biggest single transfer of peoples between the two nations had occurred in the last decade of the seventeenth century. For many the link to Scotland must have been based on the living memory of parents, grandparents and great-grandparents in the eighteenth century. Thus though increasingly 'Irish' by birth, the settlers retained close relationships with Scotland in language, religion, trade, intellectual connections and the constant movement of peoples between the two countries. As the term has it, they were 'Ulster Scots' who were an integral part of the overall impact of the Scottish people on North America in the eighteenth century. Their story is told in Chapter 7.

In another sense, the simple evidence of numbers does not do full justice to the overall significance of Scottish transatlantic emigration. As Table 2 shows, most emigrant Scots were from the Lowlands.

They may have outnumbered the better-documented Highlanders by a ratio of nearly three to one throughout the period to 1775. Among the emigrating Lowlanders were an important minority of men of status, education, social connection and some financial means. As merchants, teachers, clergymen, tutors, doctors, military officers and imperial officials they soon played a key role throughout the colonial world. Mass emigration from Scotland to the Americas dates from the second half of the eighteenth century. But earlier these middle-rank groups were assiduously making careers in the colonies. They also became important organizing factors in the migration of their fellow countrymen in later decades:

Scots formed prominent commercial cliques in the Chesapeake, the port cities of New York, Philadelphia and Charlestown, and throughout the back country, extending into Canada. More than 150 Scottish doctors emigrated to America during the eighteenth century, and almost the whole of the colonial medical profession was Scottish emigré or Scottish-trained. Scots and Scottish-trained ministers dominated both the Presbyterian and the Episcopal Churches in America. Scottish educators were also predominant not only at Princeton, under Witherspoon, but at the College for Philadelphia, the many Presbyterian academies in the middle and southern states, and as tutors in Carolina and the Chesapeake.[3]

But the vast majority of Scottish emigrants were not of that class but were small tenant farmers, cottars, indentured servants, weavers, craftsmen of all types, agricultural labourers and Highland crofters. Some, albeit a small minority, had been forcibly transported to the colonies after the two Jacobite rebellions of 1715 and 1745 or as criminals condemned to serve out their sentences in a far-off land. But most came for the more mundane reasons of possessing land, better employment and the chances, however remote in most cases, of making a fortune. From the 1760s in particular, they became part of that surge in European inward migration unprecedented in the history of British America which was so great that in the words of one scholar, 'it constituted a social force in itself'. A new population, wholly different from the original native peoples, was rapidly spreading inward from the maritime territories along a great frontier which stretched from Nova Scotia in the north to Florida in the south:

The expansion of settlement began with the movement to the frontiers of isolated family and community groups moving here and there along a thousand-mile perimeter in search of new locations – a few hundred isolated clusters of people, at first, pulling loaded carts and sledges and driving wagons along Indian paths across the foothills and through the gaps in the first mountain barriers to the west, poling rafts loaded with farm equipment, animals, and household goods, and paddling canoes into the interior. Soon these movements of separate groups, which at first left no visible mark on the settlement maps of British North America, began to multiply, flowed together to form substantial human streams, and ended as a flood of migrants pouring west, north and south outward from well-settled areas to form new centers of community life. The accelerating momentum of this postwar migration into the interior of America, its geographical range and ultimate numbers, astonished contemporaries, and they remain astonishing to anyone who sees this phase of frontier expansion in its proper historical context.[4]

In addition to the large numbers of arrivals from Britain, other ethnic groups were also to the fore. Between the 1700s and the 1770s more than 110,000 German-speaking settlers from the Rhineland and Switzerland crossed the Atlantic to the British colonies. They were the first major influx of non-British Europeans to establish themselves in the empire. Pennsylvania, through the port of Philadelphia, was their most popular destination, but clusters of Germans also congregated in New England, Nova Scotia and the back-countries of the Carolinas, Maryland and Virginia.[5] It was also at this time that the demography of the colonies was revolutionized by the mass inward shipment of African slaves. By 1760 around 175,000 slaves had already been settled in the plantations, comprising 40 per cent of the population of Virginia alone. A further 84,000 blacks arrived between the end of the Seven Years War and the outbreak of the American War in 1775.[6] The new America which the emigrants from Scotland experienced was becoming remarkably multi-ethnic in social composition.

Scots and Ulster Scots were to be found across most parts of this expanding frontier (as Table 3 suggests). But before 1775 they tended to cluster in New York, especially in the northern wilderness areas of the state, North Carolina and Virginia. North Carolina, for instance, was dubbed the 'New Scotland'. The important Register of

Region and State	Number	Percentage of Whole Population
New England		
Maine	4,325	4.47
New Hampshire	8,749	4.5
Vermont	4,339	5.1
Massachusetts	16,420	4.4
Rhode Island	3,751	5.8
Connecticut	5,109	2.2
Middle Atlantic		
New York	22,006	7.0
New Jersey	13,087	7.7
Pennsylvania	36,410	8.6
Delaware	3,705	8.0
The South		
Maryland	15,857	7.6
Virginia	45,096	10.2
North Carolina	42,799	14.8
South Carolina	21,167	15.1
Georgia	8,197	15.5

Table 3. Distribution of Scots-born in USA, 1790
Source: W. R. Brock, *Scotus Americanus* (Edinburgh, 1982), p.13.

Emigrants, which covers the years 1773 to 1776 and supplies the fullest detail of any contemporary source dealing with this topic, suggests that over two-thirds of Scots made for New York and North Carolina (though one of the key features of this diaspora was its inherent restlessness, flux and continued mobility long after initial settlement). Likewise, the Ulster Scots flocked to the south-western Pennsylvania wilderness, Georgia, South Carolina and West Florida. But they were also ubiquitous across the whole frontier, with small towns and counties named Armagh, Derry and Donegal dotted throughout the back-country: 'A map of their main settlements is almost a map of the pre-revolutionary frontier.'[7]

On the other hand, the northernmost region of the British colonies received comparatively few Scots emigrants before the American Revolution. The great Scottish influx to Canada, in time making the Scots the third largest ethnic group in the country after the English and French, was more a development of the nineteenth and twentieth centuries. Before 1763 the British northern region consisted of one colony – Nova Scotia – and two 'factories', the fur trade in Hudson Bay and the Newfoundland fishery. The conquest of French America during the Seven Years War did give them access to vast new territories. But it was only after 1783, with the mass movement of American Loyalists to the St Lawrence valley and elsewhere, the increase in Highland emigration to Canada which then followed, and the dynamic development of trade from the Clyde to Quebec, Montreal and Toronto, that the Scottish presence really became significant. By 1815 there were an estimated 15,000 Scots in Canada, most of them Gaelic-speakers.[8]

2

The vibrant expansion of British North America was confirmed by its dramatic population growth in the decades after 1750. Numbers of blacks and whites rose from 210,000 in 1690 to 445,000 by 1720 and then to 1,200,000 in 1750. Though perhaps two-thirds of this growth was due to natural increase, the immigration of African slaves and Europeans clearly also made a major contribution. The colonial staples of wheat, timber, tobacco, rice, sugar and dyestuffs depended above all else on labour. Technology was almost non-existent. The universal tools were the spade, axe, hammer and hoe. Without additional hands the entire colonial economic system would have ground to a halt.

By the second half of the eighteenth century the huge importation of African slaves helped to solve the problem. In the Chesapeake alone their numbers swelled twentyfold, from 7,000 in 1690 to 150,000 by 1750. But over much of the period, most plantation owners still had to rely also on immigrant labour from Europe, not least for the many skilled and semi-skilled jobs and the tasks of overseeing and supervision which could not be carried out by slaves. Indeed, so significant were labour shortages in the 1720s that they were reckoned to be a prime cause of the stagnation in the tobacco trade to Europe in that decade. Furthermore, the problem in some colonies was so acute that wars against the Indian tribes were often followed by the enslavement of those natives who had not been killed or dispersed. This, for instance, was the fate of the Yamasee people and many of the Creeks living on the coast south of Charleston when their alliance against the whites was broken in bloody slaughter between 1715 and 1717.[9]

The trade in indentured servants from Europe was one of the main pragmatic answers to this shortage of labour. Indenture involved the legal binding of a servant to a colonial master for an agreed period of four to five years. The servant obtained free passage across the Atlantic plus board and lodging in the colonies. The master then had the right to the servant's labour during the term of indenture. One estimate suggests that at least a half of all white persons who emigrated to the British plantations first came as servants.[10] Almost certainly the vast majority of Scots who settled in the colonies between the union and the 1760s also travelled as indentured servants. Essentially the system meant that poverty was no bar to emigration as both the costs of passage and initial settlement were covered.

The procedure was also very flexible. It could include young men of good family who took out indentures with prestigious merchant houses as clerks, book-keepers or factors with the hope one day of making their mark as key figures in the company's employ. Skilled craftsmen, such as blacksmiths, coopers, masons and gardeners, were also lured at good wages through these contracts and often returned home when their indenture lapsed. But the system was also widely used by men and women at the bottom of the social ladder who virtually sold themselves to ships' captains in return for passage and were in turn auctioned in the colonies to the highest bidder. Jacobite prisoners, prostitutes and vagrants also came into this category. They were bound by law to do their master's bidding for the period of the indenture, could be sold against their wishes, forced to remain unmarried during their contract and required to remain within a specified area of their master's home. Their lives could also be hazardous. It may seem surprising, against this background, that Daniel Defoe could list servants as one of Glasgow's major exports in the early 1720s:

Another article, which is very considerable here, is servants, and these they have in greater Plenty, and upon better terms than the English, without the scandalous Art of Kidnapping, making Drunk, Wheadling, Betryaing, and the like; the Poor People offering themselves fast enough, and thinking it their Advantage to go; as indeed it is, to those who go with sober Resolutions, namely to serve out their Times, and then become diligent Planters for themselves ... if it goes on for many Years more Virginia may be rather call'd a Scots than an English Plantation.[11]

Defoe's enthusiasm for emigration may not have been shared by everyone. Nevertheless, for a number of reasons a substantial Scottish exodus to the New World might well have been expected in the first half of the eighteenth century. As earlier chapters have shown, the Scots were a habitually mobile people who, in the later seventeenth century, were already moving towards the Atlantic and away from the traditional migration routes to Europe. Again, by the early 1700s the influx of Lowland Scots to Ulster had declined to a trickle as the opportunities for acquiring land in the north of Ireland virtually dried up.[12] The Anglo-Scottish union of 1707 officially brought the Scots within the ambit of the British imperial system and so provided the context for even closer association with the American colonies. The opportunities for some land and higher wages across the Atlantic must also have had special appeal in Scotland. Several parishes in the 1720s complained about the 'infestation' of vagrants and vagabonds, a sure sign of a labour surplus in the countryside. The absence of international conflict between 1711 (when hostilities mainly ceased in the War of the Spanish Succession) and 1739 also dramatically cut back a major military employment for young Scotsmen.

Bridging the thousands of miles of ocean between Scotland and America had also become more efficient. Like the Irish and English, but unlike many Europeans, the Scots did not have to endure long and costly journeys to ports of transatlantic embarkation. Instead, by this period, shipping to the colonies was regular and dependable, not simply from the Clyde towns but from the east coast burghs as well. Many merchants had a vested interest in embarking small parties of a dozen or so servants because those working the bulk import trades in sugar, tobacco and rice had difficulty filling their vessels completely with outgoing cargoes. It soon became an integral part of their service for Scottish merchant houses to provide indentured servants to colonial customers. Advertisements like the following were common in the Scottish press:

That any young man who is bred a Taylor, who is good at his Business and can cut and shape well, who will engage for 3 or 4 years, and go over to

Virginia, let them apply to John Elphinstone, merchant in Aberdeen, who will enter into an Indenture with them, and oblige himself to pay £10 sterling yearly, with Bed, Board and Washing.[13]

Some merchants and skippers hired recruiters, who would tour the country fairs, inns and town lodgings, often preceded by a piper and drummer eager to initiate the naive, the vulnerable and the desperate into the delights of the colonial adventure. The correspondence homewards of Scots traders, plantation owners, doctors and clergy is stuffed with requests to their fellow countrymen for gardeners, weavers, clerks, tutors and overseers. It was even suggested that the Scots as an ethnic group had a competitive edge in the market for indentured servants. Scots craftsmen, with the Germans, were considered the hardest workers and because of their Protestantism were also seen as a very desirable addition to the colonial population.

The basic issue, then, is whether all these influences did indeed prompt a significant acceleration of Scottish transatlantic emigration before c.1750. The evidence, unfortunately, does not allow a definitive answer to that question. No systematic data on emigration from Scotland exists for the period. Customs officials only compiled records of overseas trade in summary from 1740 and did not produce full and detailed commercial information until 1755. We know that before the 1760s emigrants normally sailed as passengers on merchant vessels rather than on specialist emigrant ships. Even then their presence was rarely recorded. Moreover, transatlantic movement in this period mainly consisted of the steady if unremarkable exodus of a stream of single young men in their late teens and early twenties and a minority of women of the same age. For the most part the process was shadowy, leaving a meagre imprint on contemporary documentation. There was little at this time of the drama and public interest of the 1760s and 1770s when the emigration of large groups from the Highlands and Lowlands did concentrate the minds of many observers and in so doing generated a great deal of material for later historians to consider.

There is no denying, however, the increase in the emigration of educated Scots of middling status and above. Merchants, soldiers, teachers, clergy, imperial officials and medical men now sought their fortunes in the American empire in much larger numbers than ever before. Scottish traders were also seemingly ubiquitous in the ports.

This was one form of Scottish emigration which did attract contemporary interest, especially in the colonies, where the movement of prominent Scots did much to spread the commercial, religious and cultural influences of their native land and feed the perception among Americans of Scottish presence and power. In these decades, the axis of middle- and upper-class emigration had indeed swung decisively away from traditional opportunities in Europe to the New World.

In volume terms, however, the adventurers, officials and military élites must have represented but a fraction of the common mass of emigrants. Occasionally this majority does surface tantalizingly in the sources. Colonial newspapers sometimes recorded the sale of Scottish servants, as in 1736 when the following advertisement was placed in Pennsylvania:

Just arrived from Aberdeen. A parcel of likely Scotch servant men, some Tradesmen, but all accustomed to Husbandry and Country Work; whose times are to be disposed of by Alexander Gordon, Master of the Brig, *Diligence*, now lying at Mr Fishbourn's wharf.[14]

The numerous notices posted for runaway servants in the *Maryland Gazette* are also an indication of the presence of ordinary Scots in the colony. During the ten-year period from 1745 to 1755, 10 per cent of the servants reported missing and of certifiable nationality were Scots.[15] In the far north, the Hudson's Bay Company had already started the regular recruitment of young lads from the Orkney Islands for work in the fur trade. The route by Stromness in the Orkneys afforded the Company's skippers a direct passage to Hudson's Strait in Canada. There was also the advantage of securing servants experienced in work on land and at sea and accustomed to a harsh climate and demanding environment. In time the Orcadians became the backbone of the Company. Some returned home with their savings after years of labour in the wilderness. Others stayed on, married Indian women and established family dynasties in the service of the Hudson's Bay Company. It was reckoned that in the early eighteenth century around seventy men were enlisted annually. By 1800 four out of five of the Company's servants were Orcadians.[16]

Not all emigrants, however, were fired by the dream of better wages, the right to land or more opportunity. Coercion was also part of the trade in servants. The Scottish courts sentenced around 700 persons to be transported between 1718 and 1775, a significantly lower number than the 35,000 unfortunates banished from England to the colonies in the same period. Transportation was an effective method of saving on the public costs of long-term incarceration. Interestingly, though, defenders before the High Court of Justiciary enjoyed the right to petition for banishment before their cases came to trial. Nearly always these requests were granted, especially if the victims of their supposed crimes were in agreement with the petition. Indeed, most of those sentenced to be transported by the decision of the High Court were petitioners rather than convicted criminals. At a lower level of authority, too, transportation was used by Justices of the Peace and town councils as a common means of getting rid of vagrants, petty offenders and prostitutes. Scottish Houses of Correction were often plentiful sources of supply for merchants and skippers plying the servant trade to the plantation colonies. In 1745, for instance, whores were listed as one of Glasgow's more colourful exports. Andrew Fletcher of Saltoun, who was most renowned for his articulate and robust opposition to the Union of 1707, was among those who advocated transportation as a panacea for the endemic social problem of vagrancy:

In years of plenty many thousands of them meet together in the mountains, where they feast and riot for many days; and at country weddings, markets, burials and other like public occasions, they are to be seen, both men and women, perpetually drunk, cursing, blaspheming, and fighting together. These are such outrageous disorders, that it were better for the nation they were sold to the gallies (*sic*) or West Indies, than that they should continue any longer to be a burden and like upon us.[17]

However, there is little confirmation in the scattered evidence of a major upswing in Scottish emigration to North America in the five decades after the Union. Probably there were under 30,000 Lowland emigrants between 1700 and 1760, of whom some would have been 'sojourners' who returned home after a spell abroad.[18] The Highland figure was also modest: below 3,000 for the same period. The Scots were vastly outnumbered by the Irish and the Ulster Scots before 1760, and even by Germans who accounted for nearly 100,000 migrants in the decades between 1700 and the outbreak of the Seven Years War in 1763.[19] The relatively small scale of the Scottish exodus before the 1760s can also be confirmed by the paucity of contemporary comment or concern about it and by the telling fact that few merchant houses thought it worth their while to specialize in the servant trade. In relation to the remarkable levels of movement to Europe and Ulster in the seventeenth century the global number of emigrants from Scotland had actually fallen substantially after 1700. Why?

A recent careful study has outlined the numbers of Irish immigrants to the Delaware valley ports over the shorter period from 1730 to 1760. Even given this contracted time frame and the fact that the Irish also sailed to other ports such as New York and Baltimore, their migration based on these figures alone comfortably exceeded that of the Scots. At least 30,000 Irish had made the Atlantic crossing during this three-decade period.[20] One approach, therefore, is to look briefly at the two emigrations from a comparative perspective.

Several differences can be noted between the two countries. The pressures of population on resources, land and employment were probably less in Scotland. The terrible famine years of the 1690s and the vast exodus to Ireland had had a lethal effect, cutting the national population back by an estimated 13 per cent, and in the worst-hit areas, such as the north-eastern counties and the Highlands, by even more. So great was the disaster that some regions had not recovered their 1690s population levels half a century later. Thereafter food prices in most parts of Scotland remained stable for several years. There was no serious dearth again until 1740–41, but even then the Scots got off lightly compared with the Irish. In Ireland that crisis is reckoned to have caused even more deaths per head of population than the Great Famine a century later. A key advantage in Scotland, but denied the Irish, was the existence of a Poor Law which provided a basic safety net in times of crisis, especially through local authorities buying meal and selling it at subsidized rates.[21]

It is also possible that the Scots had more alternatives to emigration than the Irish. A striking feature of Scottish society in this period was urban growth. The percentage of the total population in towns of over 10,000 inhabitants rose from around 3 per cent in 1650 to nearly 10 per cent in 1750. Edinburgh and Aberdeen grew moderately between 1700 and 1750 but Glasgow doubled in size of population while Dundee increased its numbers by 50 per cent. Servants and apprentices, the very groups from which many emigrants were drawn, made up a significant proportion of these growing town populations.[22]

Both the Irish and Scots migrated in numbers to England but again the overland route may have given the Scots an advantage. Substantial communities of Lowlanders could be found in London and the northern towns, especially in Newcastle. Itinerant Scottish traders were also common. Over half the keelmen in Newcastle were said to be of Scottish origin and mainly hailed from the eastern Lowlands, especially the communities around the river Forth.[23] It is significant too that large-scale enclosure of lands for sheep and cattle farming first occurred in the Scottish Borders from the 1680s. The consolidation of tenancies and the dispossession of small farmers and cottars to create huge parklands for pastoral husbandry were taking place here a generation or so before the notorious Highland Clearances. The response, however, was not so much transatlantic emigration but the search for employment in spinning, knitting and weaving in the growing Border mill towns of Hawick, Moffat, Selkirk and Peebles, or following the time-honoured route south to England.[24]

3

This pattern of a steady seepage of people from Scotland to the American colonies changed abruptly in the years following the end of the Seven Years War in 1763. The age of mass Atlantic migration can be traced back to this period. For the first time the exodus to the Americas became a truly national phenomenon drawing from all classes of society and most regions of the country. Current estimates suggest that 90,000 to 100,000 Scots left for North America between 1700 and 1815. Remarkably, around half of this total (45,000) emigrated over the few years between 1763 and 1775, with around 30,000 coming from the Lowlands alone.[25] The scale and speed of the diaspora caused widespread alarm among a governing class which believed that a large and growing population was vital both to the nation's prosperity and military power. Fears were voiced especially about the loss of Highlanders now regarded as vital to the imperial war machine. Dr Samuel Johnson's anxieties after his famous tour of the Highlands with James Boswell in 1773 are well known. He talked eloquently of the 'epidemick disease of wandering' which threatened 'a total secession' of Highlanders. But there was also a common belief that emigration would also depopulate parts of the Lowlands as well. The *Scots Magazine* in June 1774 declared that continued emigration would convert the west of Scotland into a grass park.

One important bi-product of this 'emigration mania' was the compilation by the state of a Register of Emigrants for the years 1773 to 1776. Despite its inevitable imperfections, the Register is by far the best guide we have to transatlantic migration in the eighteenth century, casting a fascinating light on such diverse topics as the origin, social structure, occupational background and gender balance of the emigrant parties. The material, which has been exhaustively reviewed by Bernard Bailyn and his associates, yields some arresting conclusions.[26]

First, Scots had a very prominent role in the exodus, comprising 40 per cent of the 9,808 men, women and children who left for the western hemisphere between December 1773 and March 1776 from the ports of mainland Britain. Second, the Scots were overwhelmingly drawn to the thirteen mainland colonies. Over 92 per cent of the emigrants gave them as their planned destination, with the remaining small portion split more or less evenly between Canada and the West Indies. Third, almost all of Scotland from the Orkneys to the Borders, with the exception of parts of the north-east region, was involved in the emigration. Despite the prominence given then and since to the Highland exodus, this was a pan-Scottish movement with the majority leaving from the towns, villages and rural parishes which were in the van of Lowland modernization. This is an apparent paradox which will be considered below.[27] Fourth, as revealed in Table 4, this was not primarily a flight of the rootless poor or of the mass of unskilled labour. Servants and labourers comprised less than a third of the emigrants. The vast majority were farmers and artisans with a range of skills. A particularly striking feature was that there were many more textile workers among the Scots than the English. Most of these came from the western Lowlands, the dynamic heartland of the nascent Scottish Industrial Revolution. These were emigrants with some means. Interestingly, too, only a minority sailed as indentured servants, the common status of the very poor. Fifth, the Scots – especially those from a rural background – were more likely to travel in family groups. Thus although the Scottish movement like the English was concentrated in the pre-forty age group, it was more evenly balanced with respect to both age and sex than the emigrations from London and the neighbouring southern counties. The typical migrants from these latter areas were young, single men. On the other hand, the vessels leaving Scottish ports also contained large numbers of women and children as part of family groups. This was another break with the past. Earlier in the century few women and even fewer children crossed the Atlantic. From the 1760s a new form of emigration had developed which anticipated the even greater movements of the nineteenth century.

In trying to account for this it is important to integrate the ways in which conditions on both sides of the Atlantic operated simultaneously to move large numbers 3,000 miles across the ocean. Too often Scottish historians have studied the 'push' elements at home while their American colleagues have focused on the 'pull' forces in the colonies. A full analysis, however, requires the combination of both approaches and the vital addition of the third influence, how these 'expulsive' and 'attractive' factors were effectively linked by transport connections, information flows and personal networks which then helped to drive movement over long distances.

The end of the Seven Years War and the acquisition of new, unexploited imperial territories was followed by a veritable orgy of land purchase and speculation in British North America. Many groups were involved. They included army officers who during service abroad had seen for themselves the opportunities for getting rich. Members of the political classes and officials from the Board of Trade, the Admiralty and the customs service, who were now more aware of the colonial possibilities during the war, were also to the fore, as were leading American landowners, merchants, government contractors and assorted 'hangers-on', united only in their quest for huge gains from the vast new territory made available for settlement when peace was finally agreed with France in 1763.

Scottish speculators were among them. Richard Oswald, scion of a famous Glasgow merchant family, had made a fortune as a government contractor during the war, and was deeply involved in several land syndicates in East Florida. Sir Archibald Grant of Monymusk in Aberdeenshire saw the potential of selling colonial land to 'the ambitious and avaricious' and enthusiastically joined in the Florida boom. Among the most influential figures was the Reverend John Witherspoon, Presbyterian minister and President of the

Occupation	England Number	England Per cent	Scotland Number	Scotland Per cent
Gentle Occupation or Status	107	2.5	20	1.2
Public Official	1	0	1	0.1
Gentleman or gentlewoman	89	2.1	16	0.9
Professional	17	0.4	3	0.2
Clergyman	5	0.1	1	0.1
Lawyer or physician	9	0.2	1	0.1
Other	3	0.1	1	0.1
Merchandising	226	5.2	84	5.2
Wholesale trade or factorage	63	1.5	40	2.5
Shopkeeping	163	3.7	44	2.7
Agriculture	777	17.8	391	24.0
Independent or semi-independent	671	15.4	373	22.9
Dependent	106	2.4	18	1.1
Trades or Crafts (Artisans)	2368	54.2	614	37.7
Highly skilled	454	10.4	68	4.2
Ordinary skill level	1914	43.8	546	33.5
Metal trades	235	5.4	50	3.1
Food processing or marketing	209	4.8	18	1.1
Construction	370	8.4	106	6.5
Textile manufacturing or trade	773	17.7	333	20.4
Service trades	196	4.5	19	1.2
Other	131	3.0	20	1.2
Labour	888	20.3	520	31.9
Servant – domestic	145	3.3	22	1.3
Servant – unspecified	176	4.0	325	20.0
Labourer – maritime	19	0.4	14	0.8
Labourer – unspecified	548	12.6	159	9.8
Total Known Occupations	4366	100.0	1629	100.0
Unknown Occupations	830		2243	
Spinster	40		11	
Other	790		2232	
Combined Total (known and unknown occupations)	5196		3872	

Table 4. Occupations of emigrants to North America, 1773–6

Source: B. Bailyn, *Voyagers to the West: Emigration from Britain to America on the Eve of the Revolution* (London, 1986), pp. 150–51.

College of New Jersey (later Princeton) from 1768 to 1794. He invested heavily in land purchase along the upper Connecticut River and Nova Scotia and became a vigorous promoter of Scottish settlement in the New World. Indeed, it was partly because of the Witherspoon influence that his former neighbourhood in Paisley became such a fertile source of emigrants. These men recognized that lands without settlers were of little value and so, before too long, the frenzy for territorial acquisition and speculation fed back into publicity for and encouragement to emigration. By the early 1770s notices advertising the many opportunities for cheap land on the periphery of British North America had become commonplace in the Scottish press. It was not simply land which was used as inducement. The expansion of settlement also demanded skilled labour, especially in the building trades. Artisans had always been at a premium in the colonies but now they were needed more than ever before.

The entire enterprise of transporting many thousands of people across the Atlantic was also becoming much more sophisticated. A key factor was the boycott of British goods in the colonies signalled by the non-importation agreements of 1770 and 1775. Scottish merchants specializing in the American trade now actively sought alternative human cargoes to the banned commodities on the outward voyage. Some firms started to specialize in the emigrant traffic. The famous Buchanan family of tobacco merchants entered into the servant trade full-time, with eight voyages to New York and Philadelphia between 1773 and 1775 carrying emigrants. Their advertisements focused on comfort and security during the long voyage, the competence and experience of the captain and the cheapness of the fares. Emigration was increasingly becoming a specialist business.[28]

This context facilitated large-scale overseas movement but in itself could not directly cause it to happen. To understand why emigration levels rocketed in the 1760s and early 1770s we need also to consider the contemporary circumstances in Scotland. At first sight, these present a puzzle. On the whole the period was one of growing prosperity in Scotland. The economic prospects were brighter than at any time since 1707. The Scots had already carved out a major share of the transatlantic tobacco trade. Linen, Scotland's staple manufacture, was also doing well, with official output quadrupling between the years 1736–40 and 1768–72. More efficient practices in agriculture were adopted from the later seventeenth century but it is really only from the 1760s that the pace of change picked up, with improved methods becoming much more widespread in many parts of the Lowlands. The response of agriculture reflected the burgeoning demand from the growing towns and cities for food and raw materials. Glasgow, for instance, in these decades was expanding at a faster rate than any city of comparable size in western Europe. Not all the gains from this new economic momentum were appropriated by the élites. There is evidence that after many years of relative stagnation real wages for farm servants and labourers in agriculture were beginning to creep up. With the wisdom of hindsight we can see that Scotland was moving towards the great watershed of the Industrial Revolution. It is strange indeed that this period of material amelioration also witnessed the largest exodus of Scots to North America of the entire eighteenth century.[29]

To understand the dynamics of emigration two groups need to be considered: first, the artisan classes and especially those from the textile trades who made up a significant proportion of those leaving in the early 1770s; second, the small farmers, their dependants and servants who were also prominent among the emigrant parties. The textile boom brought social costs as well as benefits. As Scottish industry became ever more linked to international markets, so volatility and cyclical fluctuation in some years became a potent factor. One such crisis broke in 1771–3, triggered by poor harvests and financial panic among Scottish houses in London and the spectacular collapse in August 1773 of Douglas, Heron and Company, the Ayr Bank. This was described by some as the worst Scottish economic catastrophe since the Darien disaster of the 1690s. One result was a sharp rise in unemployment among thousands of weavers and other artisans, especially in Paisley and Glasgow. This then triggered a huge wave of emigration. The personal connections and transportation systems with North America were now so well developed that transatlantic emigration presented a real alternative to the Poor Law and social destitution. As the volume of linen manufactures for sale dropped by a quarter between 1772 and 1773 a gentleman in Glasgow writing to an associate in Philadelphia observed:

The distress of the common people here is deeper and more general than you can imagine. There is an almost total stagnation in our manufactures, and grain is dear; many hundreds of labourers and mechanics, especially weavers in this neighbourhood, have lately indented and gone to America . . . If any of your colonies desire to set up manufactures of linen, of stamping, etc. . . . they have now an opportunity as favourable as they could wish for.[30]

But deeper forces were also working in parallel with this temporary economic crisis. The eighteenth century brought a massive transformation in the lives of many urban craftsmen. Numbers rose in dramatic fashion so that in the textile sector alone there were 25,000 handloom weavers in Scotland by the 1780s. Some of the old craftsman controls on entry to the trade weakened. Divisions between masters and men became more marked. Above all, the drive towards higher levels of output undermined the traditional independence of many artisans. The old image of the master weavers buying their own yarn and working it up in their own cottages was being replaced by a new system. Merchant manufacturers in Glasgow, Paisley and Dundee and other centres supplied yarn to weavers working at home or in small factories.[31] They provided credit and advance payments and it was easy to become enmeshed in a circle of debt which brought with it growing dependency. As one contemporary observer noted in 1747:

The people who deal in this way keep the poorer sort very dependent on them. They got or give them Credite for Meal Butter Cheese Hardfish Coals Lint Lintseed and such like things And take their payments in Small Sums of every Web or small parcell of Yarn they bring them. By this means the poorer Sort are Thirled perhaps for Life to the Richer Sort And have Dispose of nothing they have to Sell but to them only.[32]

In the returns made to customs officials on the Clyde between 1773 and 1776 many artisans, especially those in the depressed textile trades, cited poverty and hardship as the main reasons for emigrating. But some also sought in the colonies the independence and opportunity for personal betterment increasingly denied them in the new market economy at home.

The dramatic transformation in the rural world also provides the essential context for understanding emigration from the Scottish countryside. The core of the traditional world was the *ferm-touns*, small settlements of little more than twenty households dispersed across a landscape virtually bereft of the hedges, ditches, dikes, roads or any of the other man-made constructions that cover the countryside today. The touns varied in size. In more developed arable areas such as the south-east, the touns in Lothians and Berwickshire were almost the size of villages. Elsewhere, as few as half-a-dozen families lived in settlements, apparently scattered at random across the land. The names of these old places live on, either as hamlets which have survived down to the present day or in the numerous place names ending in '-ton' which are familiar references in Ordnance Survey maps. These clusters of people all had their own internal hierarchies. Rent-paying tenants were at the top and ranked below them were the cottars, provided with a patch of land in return for labour, the full-time farm servants and the assorted tradesmen, the blacksmiths, wrights, saddlers and weavers, who also possessed a smallholding.[33]

By the 1760s this old world was crumbling rapidly. One factor was the growth in population. Even the relatively slow Scottish rate – only 0.6 per annum in the later eighteenth century – could cause strain in a rural society of inherited rank and set position. Much more significant, however, was actual displacement from the land as the enlarged single tenancies, thought to be essential to the improved agronomy, were carved out of the old *ferm-touns*. Only now can historians appreciate the full significance of these changes. People were on the move everywhere. Some were relocated in new villages, others lost land. In the hill country of Ayrshire, Lanarkshire, Angus and elsewhere the drastic falls in local population suggest levels of eviction reminiscent of the better-known Highland Clearances in order to accommodate the big cattle and sheep ranches. Elsewhere tenants and cottars were squeezed out more gradually. But the net result was the same: a growth in landlessness and the evolution of a smaller farming class than ever before.[34]

All this did not necessarily lead directly to emigration. There was always the alternative of town and village work. Indeed, all the evidence suggests that in the later eighteenth century, the new agriculture needed more rather than less labour for the many tasks of building, ditching, ploughing, weeding and processing. But for some men of modest substance the availability of cheap land in the New World must have promised not only escape from a threatened fall in status but the opportunity for more independence. This was particularly the case in 1772–3. Up till then Scottish agriculture had benefited from good harvests from 1757 and rising prices from the 1760s. The good times abruptly came to an end in 1772, when harvests were poor and market demand stagnant because of industrial crisis. Landlords who had jacked up rents in previous years were now confronted with spiralling arrears. On the vast estates of the Dukes of Hamilton in Lanarkshire 'shakeing winds' were accompanied by 'Rotting Rains' in 1771 and 1772, followed by 'parching Drought' in 1773. This run of climatic calamities caused a 'General Devastation' throughout the estates, a halt to all schemes of improvement, a huge increase in arrears and, ominously, a significant escalation in the eviction of indebted tenants.[35]

But potential emigrants were not simply the passive victims of historical forces. A striking feature of the emigrations from the rural Lowlands was the proactive response of farming societies who came together to plan in a careful fashion the move across the Atlantic. One such was the United Company of Farmers for the shires of Perth and Stirling which sent agents to search for good land on the American frontier, subscribed monies for its purchase, despatched emigrants in a vessel organized for the purpose and eventually settled them in 7,000 acres along the Connecticut River in the colony of New York. A similar and even better-documented example of collective enterprise in the emigrant business was the Scots-American Company of Farmers, which was formed from a group of 138 leading farmers and artisans in 1773 and was drawn from communities in Renfrewshire, western Lanarkshire and Dumbartonshire. Their plans were to contribute to a joint sum which would allow them to acquire 100,000 acres of land in North America. They complained of high rentals, a more rigorous approach to tenure of land by their landlords, Lords Blantyre and Douglas, and, above all, the threat of loss of tenancy. In the parish of Erskine, where many of the subscribers lived, the leases of twelve families fell due in 1771. The following year the entire tract was laid down in one farm for grazing.[36]

The Company sent two of their members across the Atlantic to survey possible lands on the frontier. The journey of these men, James Whitelaw, a land surveyor, and David Allan, a farmer from the parish of Inchinnan, eight miles from Glasgow, became a veritable odyssey. In four months they covered 2,700 miles from upcountry New York to North Carolina before eventually deciding on the

20,000-acre township of Ryegate, far up the west bank of the Connecticut River in New York colony. But theirs was not a journey through an entirely alien land. They seem to have had contacts everywhere, together with letters of introduction to influential expatriate Scots. From the start they worked closely with the Reverend John Witherspoon of the College of New Jersey and William Semple, a Philadelphia merchant, who was related to four of the subscribers of the Company. The final purchase of Ryegate was from Witherspoon himself and the Pagan family of Glasgow merchants who were both deeply involved in land deals in Nova Scotia and New York. It was a telling illustration of the key importance of intimate links between the Scots élite in America, the homeland and transatlantic emigration.[37]

In this regard, the powerful influence of religious belief in the process of Lowland emigration should not be ignored. The political and social attitudes of the evangelical wing of the Church of Scotland were particularly important. The evangelicals had a special concept of civil and religious liberty. It had been won against the forces of arbitrary authority in both church and state after a full century of struggle. The evangelicals of the 1760s and 1770s saw these hard-earned liberties threatened by the hegemony of Moderatism in the governance of the church. The Moderates accepted the legitimacy of patronage (the power of clerical appointment held by local landowners) and advocated both tolerance of doctrinal differences and accommodation with the political system of the day. All this was anathema to the evangelicals, who had come increasingly to view the Scottish church as corrupt and despotic. Several of them now argued that America represented an alternative for those seeking liberty and true religion. That was one reason why evangelical associates urged John Witherspoon to leave Scotland to take up the presidency of the College of New Jersey where he and others would eventually undertake a vigorous campaign to promote Scottish emigration.

These publicists became especially active in the commercial crisis of the early 1770s because it was the rural and artisan population of evangelical sympathies in the west of Scotland who suffered the most acute distress in these years. Several of those at the centre of emigration promotion, Witherspoon himself, the Glasgow merchant families of Buchanan and Pagan, and William Thom of Govan, were all evangelicals. Thom, who authored five extensive tracts on the subject, was the most articulate advocate of emigration. He linked the decay of liberty in religion to the cancer of oppressive landlordism and a diseased economic system:

Where Thom differed from other writers was in his espousal of a remedy, not in the renewal of virtue, but in emigration to America, where provincial liberty still flourished. If tenants and tradesmen in Scotland were impoverished by oppressive landlords and artificially distorted markets, the economic liberty of America would allow them to raise their families in prosperity and independence. If piety and virtue were threatened ... in America they would experience complete liberty in matters civil and religious. Moreover escape to America was no mere retreat from civility and culture. Rather the colonies were 'daily gaining in power, wealth, and science and all the improvements that civilise and polish mankind'. In Thom's America, liberty, piety and prosperity went hand in hand.[38]

Of course, we cannot be certain about the precise influence of these ideas. In large part, as has been seen, the emigrations were one response to epochal material changes in Scottish society. Yet customs officials also recorded the view of some emigrants who did have a vision of a new world of religion and liberty within the protected environment of the British Empire. It is also noteworthy how some interpreted this journey to a new land as a liberating experience. Settling on the far frontiers enabled them to make a fresh start remote from metropolitan decadence and degeneracy.

6

Exodus from Gaeldom

I

Emigration from the Highlands can only be understood against the dramatic background of the momentous social, cultural and economic changes which transformed Gaelic society in the second half of the eighteenth century. Many traditional accounts assert that clan-based society perished in the bloody carnage of Culloden Moor in April 1746 and was finally buried by the systematic repression and punitive legislation following the final defeat of Jacobitism. Certainly no one can deny the uninhibited ferocity of the Whig onslaught in these years. Charles Edward Stuart's forces had come too close to success in the '45. The British state was therefore resolute in its determination to root out disaffection once and for all. With a huge regular army, supported by naval units now drawn into the very heart of the Highlands, government had the military muscle to impose a comprehensive policy of intimidation, terror and revenge. At first, indeed, the victorious Duke of Cumberland contemplated the wholesale transportation to the colonies of such recalcitrant clans as the Camerons, Mackintoshes and Appin Stewarts. Instead, the brutal purging of areas of Jacobite loyalty was followed by an attack on the culture of the Gael, with the proscription of Highland dress and the carrying of weapons, the abolition of 'heritable jurisdictions' (the private courts of the clan élites) and the forfeiture of rebel estates. At this point, the strategy moved from 'punishing' to 'civilizing'. When the Board of Annexed Forfeited Estates was established in 1752 to manage some of these properties the aim was to inculcate 'the Protestant Religion, good Government, Industry and Manufactures, and the Principles of Duty, and Loyalty to His Majesty'. Protestantism would induce ideological conformity and ideological loyalty, while material improvement would remove the alienation which might foster disaffection.[1]

Modern research, however, suggests that the convulsion of the '45 and its bitter aftermath was a part, albeit an important one, in a much broader drama.[2] On the one hand, clanship was already dying before the 1740s; while on the other, Gaeldom could not have remained insulated from the powerful economic, cultural and demographic forces sweeping across western Europe in the eighteenth century. These long-term factors, rather than Cumberland's bayonets and grapeshot, ultimately destroyed the old Highlands. Britain was the first industrial nation and the demands on the rural economy for more food and raw materials were insatiable. Yet in Scotland rapid economic change came later than in England and agrarian modernization took place within a shorter time scale. In the early eighteenth century around one Scot in eight lived in a town with a population of more than 5,000. By the 1820s the figure was more like one in three. This rapid pattern of urban expansion suggests an economy experiencing massive structural change, with inevitable results for agricultural producers. In simple terms the depth and extent of the markets for all that the Highlands could export was transformed and the commercial forces were so powerful that social change in Gaeldom became irresistible.[3]

Demand for traditional staples boomed. Cattle prices quadrupled in the course of the eighteenth century and total exports of black cattle from the region probably quintupled. In Argyll, albeit to a lesser extent further north, commercial fishing of herring became even more significant with, for example, some 600 to 800 boats engaged annually in Loch Fyne alone. Due to changes in government revenue legislation and enhanced Lowland markets, demand increased persistently for illicit whisky, and the exploitation of Highland slate quarries at Easdale, Ballachuilish and elsewhere, and of woodland on many estates, continued apace. Textile production began to expand in Highland Perthshire, Argyll and eastern Inverness and in parts of Ross and Cromarty and Sutherland, and the manufacture in the Highland counties of linen cloth stamped for sale rose steadily from 21,972 yards in 1727/8 to 202,006 yards by 1778.[4]

Southern industrialization had an insatiable and voracious appetite for Highland raw materials in the later eighteenth century and thereafter, with wool being in special demand. The Lowland cotton industry quickly achieved abundant supplies of raw fibre from the Caribbean and then from the southern USA, but it was more difficult for the woollen manufacturers. Overseas supply from Europe was limited and erratic during the Napoleonic Wars and it was only when Australia started to export in volume from the 1820s that overseas sources became really significant. In the interim, the gap was partly filled by Highland sheep-farmers and by 1828 Scottish wool accounted for just under 10 per cent of UK output. Behind these statistics lay the convulsion in Highland society unleashed by the unrelenting advance of the sheep farms. Equally significant for a time, though in different ways, was the manufacture of kelp, an alkali seaweed extract used in the manufacture of soap and glass. Industrial demand for it was on the increase, not least because cheaper and richer sources of foreign alkali were curtailed during the French Wars, and kelp production seemed well suited to the western Highlands and islands where the raw material was abundant. A cheap and plentiful supply of labour was vital since the process of production, though essentially a simple one, was very arduous, with a ratio of one ton of refined kelp to twenty tons of collected seaweed. Kelp manufacture began in the west in the 1730s but not until after 1750 did it begin to take hold: an output of 2,000 tons per annum was reached in the 1770s and 5,000 in 1790. Thereafter the industry boomed, achieving a peak production in 1810 of about 7,000 tons. By that date its main centres had become clearly established as the Uists, Barra, Harris, Lewis, Skye, Tiree and Mull, and on the mainland there was also considerable activity in Ardnamurchan and Morvern. But to a considerable extent kelp production was concentrated in the Hebrides, especially in the Long Island, and there, as will be seen in more detail below, it had profound social consequences.

British demand was not simply confined to the foodstuffs and raw materials of the Highlands. The market for human beings was also expanding, as young adult Gaels, especially from Argyll, had taken up seasonal harvest work in Lowland farms earlier in the eighteenth century. After the 1770s opportunities increased, as output rose in southern agriculture and the old Lowland cottar class, which had been the main source of harvest labour in the past, was steadily reduced in size. Highland migrants also took up seasonal employment in the herring fishery of the Clyde and in the bleachfields around the textile towns and villages. An even more spectacular growth industry was the recruitment of Gaels into the British army and navy in the later eighteenth century. Beginning on a small scale during the Seven Years War (1756–63) and increasing during the American War, recruitment multiplied to extraordinary levels during the Napoleonic Wars when, on one estimate, the Highlands supplied between 37,000 to 48,000 men for regiments of the line, the Militia, Fencibles and Volunteers out of a total regional population of about 300,000. This remarkable figure represents a *per capita* rate of military recruitment which was probably unequalled in any other region of Europe – eloquent testimony to the impact of population pressures at the time and of the ability of the landlords to maximize recruitment to their family regiments through the threat of eviction coupled with the promise of land in return for service.[5]

On a much broader scale the role of the landed classes was fundamental in accelerating social change. They were in a position of virtual omnipotence over their people, with full legal authority to transform their estates when they willed it. In theory, however, the hereditary duties attached to their position in the clan structure were a powerful impediment. The roles of patriarchal chief and capitalist landlord were incompatible and there is evidence in the historical record of landed families agonizing over the conflicts between these two functions. However, the forces making for the victory of landlordism over tribalism were eventually triumphant.

First, many Highland proprietors were increasingly acting in their own commercial interest rather than that of their clansmen long before the 1750s. Second, if chiefs were becoming an integral part of the British landed élite, they could hardly remain immune from the material, intellectual and cultural goals of that class. For the aristocracy and gentry the eighteenth century was an era of conspicuous consumption, of ornate and expensive building, foreign travel and a more opulent style of life. The atmosphere in élite circles was one of competitive display where a family's place was defined by the grandeur of its physical surroundings. This was the world now inhabited by the Highland landowners, one which was a constant drain on the purse and in which they could not easily survive on the paltry returns of traditional agriculture. Third, clearance and dispossession could be and were given intellectual justification. The Highland élites, through education in southern schools and universities and travel elsewhere, had absorbed non-Gaelic values and objectives long before the '45. Alien forces were partly responsible for the destruction of the traditional society through the post-Culloden pacification and the activities in certain districts of the Commissioners for the Annexed Forfeited Estates. Fundamentally, however, the revolution was achieved by the indigenous leaders of Gaeldom who had absorbed and accepted the ideas current among their class elsewhere in Britain. These included a view of the existing social order as 'primitive' and urgently in need of reform, an uncritical belief in the values of individualism, and a contempt for the traditional patterns of life and work as demonstrating the indolence, fecklessness and inefficiency of the people. These assumptions made it much easier to reorganize their estates along more rational and profitable lines. The landlords were not simply making more money but they could also justify the abrogation of their traditional responsibilities by claiming that it was a necessary evil in order to 'civilize' and 'improve' their estates.[6]

Fourth, the sheer force of market pressure was fundamental. Demand for Highland commodities was advancing on all fronts at such a pace that few could resist the rewards. Indeed, it was the combination of the growing financial demands on the landlord class with the emergence in the later eighteenth century of huge new opportunities to satisfy them which was the basic catalyst for accelerated change. Highland rents may even have been rising at a faster rate than those elsewhere in Britain. Indeed, most proprietors achieved what were essentially windfall gains because many significant sources of profit – kelp, cattle, wool, mutton and regimental recruitment – did not require significant investment but accrued to the landlord simply because of his rights of ownership. Little wonder that the period c.1760 to 1815 seemed a bonanza for many Highland landowners and it is scarcely surprising that the majority were tempted to remove the traditional society quickly and completely rather than embark on the more complex and difficult task of patiently developing a fusion between the old and the new.

In the long run, however, an even more potent threat to the traditional ways was the steady rise in regional population which was becoming apparent in the eighteenth and accelerated in the nineteenth century. This was part of a Europe-wide demographic revolution in which traditional levels of population rise were not only sustained but the rate of increase became greater over time. Demographers are still divided about the origins of this historic change of direction but it seems to have been based mainly on increasing food supply (primarily through the potato), rising employment opportunities as a consequence of industrialization and some key medical advances such as inoculation and vaccination against smallpox.

More important, however, than the causes were the social consequences for the Highlands, and closer scrutiny reveals that an explosive demographic problem was emerging. The southern and eastern rim of the Highlands experienced very modest growth because of high levels of migration to the Lowlands, whereas along the western seaboard from north Argyll and in most of the Hebrides increase was more pronounced. Between 1801 and 1841 population in this region increased by 53 per cent. In 1755 the population of the island of Tiree was 1,509, but it had risen to 1,676 by 1768 and to 2,443 by 1792. The average population of each township on the island stood at 56 in 1768 but had reached 90 by 1800.[7] Increases of this order could not have come about except through repeated divisions of tenancies and rampant subdivision, much of it abetted by landlords eager to swell the ranks of kelpers and fishermen and made possible only by the rapid spread of potato cultivation. A major demographic result in the short term was to anchor population on the land on splintered and insecure holdings. There can be little doubt either that population growth outstripped traditional levels of agricultural productivity and the methods evolved over centuries for ensuring a basic living from a poor land and a hostile climate. All detailed studies show that the old agrarian economy was delicately and precariously balanced between a meagre sufficiency and occasional shortage. It could not easily have survived the population upsurge of the eighteenth century without substantial change.[8]

This combination of forces caused a revolution in the peasant way of life. A sustained and widespread assault was mounted on the traditional township or *baile*, group settlements of multiple tenant farmers, cottars and servants which had formed the basic communities of Gaeldom from time immemorial. Over the space of two to three generations, starting in Argyll and Highland Perthshire in the 1760s and quickly spreading north and west in subsequent decades, the *baile* was broken up and virtually eliminated. By the 1830s only a few remnants of a once universal pattern of settlement and cultivation remained. But the new structure that emerged to take its place was far from simple and reflected not only the strategies of individual landowners but varying natural endowment, climatic advantage and market potential. Thus in much of Argyll, Highland Perthshire and the eastern parishes of Inverness, lands were often consolidated into single tenant farms, some pastoral but many arable, with their dependent servants and labourers. In this region too were the crofts or smallholdings that were more typical of the north and west.[9] The heartland of the new 'crofting' society, however, was the western seaboard to the north of Fort William and extending to all the Inner and Outer Hebrides. In this region the communal townships were steadily replaced by individual smallholdings or crofts with the arable land possessed by single small tenants and the grazing land still held in common. The core of the new structure, however, was division of the scattered strips or rigs of arable, which were the basis of the old system of joint farming, into separate holdings of only a few acres. In addition, throughout the whole Highland area, but especially before 1815 in the central and western mainland, commercial pastoral farms were gaining ground. The coming of the *Na Caoraidh Mora* or 'big sheep' posed a particular threat to the old society. Before the 1750s there were few commercial or specialist sheep ranches anywhere in the Highlands. Yet as early as 1802, an official report of the Highland Society described how the hill country of Perth, Dumbarton and Argyll and the entire west coast from Oban to Loch Broom were already under sheep. Most of Mull had been invaded, and the sheep frontier was also starting to advance in Skye. The report concluded ominously, 'In Ross and northwards all parts capable of sheep are or soon will be occupied.'

There were also important effects on social structure partly to do with the impact of the crofting revolution. The delicate and graduated social hierarchies of the *baile* were shattered and replaced by the virtually uniform small tenancies of the new crofting townships. Equally significantly, the traditional tacksman or gentry class was gradually reduced in number and social significance as the deliberate destruction of subtenure became a central theme of landlord policy from the 1770s. The action of the Duke of Argyll against the *daoine-uaisle* (clan gentry) of his estate had been unusual in the 1730s, but fifty years later it was commonplace as the landed classes sought to absorb the middlemen rentals. The demise of the tacksmen varied in speed and extent from estate to estate. Some who were wadsetters (that is, gentlemen who had received lands from their chief as security in return for proving loans) were bought out; others were placed in difficulty by having their rights to subletting reduced. Sharp increases in rental also put acute pressure on many, as in the 1750s much of the rent on many Highland estates would be directly paid by the tacksmen. A century later they were but a minor part of the social structure. Their demise was one of the most unequivocal signs of the death knell of the old Gaelic society. The new middle class in many areas invariably comprised southern sheep farmers and cattle ranchers with little hereditary or ethnic connection with the people.

The new landlord priorities and incessant market pressures soon generated a massive and relentless displacement of population. Eviction and forced removal became an integral part of the destruction of the traditional settlements througout the Highlands. This was the most direct violation of *duthchas*, the core obligation on clan élites to provide protection and security of possession for their people within their lands. 'Clearance', as the process of dispossession became known to later generations, was far from simple.[10] Too often it is equated only with the removals resulting from the creation of large sheep farms. But displacement took place by other means and for other reasons. The carving-out of the monotonous lines of crofts from the scattered rigs of the *baile* sometimes led to the eviction of entire communities. It also became almost routine for estates in the north-west and the islands to move people from inland glens to the sea and to areas of moorland where new crofts were planted in the waste and the settlers encouraged to reclaim it by potato cultivation. Large cattle ranches were as much a threat as big sheep farms. Removal of the *baile* to create larger arable holdings was a marked feature of the southern Highlands. Today at Auchindrain in Argyllshire there still survive many of the buildings of an old farming township in a marvellous open-air museum. But in the 1760s in the half-dozen miles between Auchindrain and Inveraray, the Campbell capital in Argyll, there were no fewer than a further six settlements. By the early nineteenth century they had all disappeared.

Here was a vivid illustration of the subordination of the human factor to the new needs of productive efficiency. Possession of individual areas of land had never been permanent in the old society, when clan territory had been lost by conquest, annexation and insolvency. It was common for subtenants and cottars, and even principal tenants, to be moved from one farm to another. The later eighteenth century, however, brought dispossession on a truly unprecedented scale all over Gaeldom, with people on the move everywhere. Sometimes the pressures did not come by direct removal. The jacking up of rentals in a peasant economy in which the balance between sufficiency and failure was a fine and precarious one also caused immense strain. Often rent increases were pushed above the rise in cattle prices and when the markets collapsed, as they did in 1772–3 and again in 1783–4, rent arrears spiralled and small tenants came under great pressure to surrender their holdings. Similarly, when farms were offered for letting at higher rents, reflecting the new commercial realities of the time, the poorer men had profound difficulty in competing. Loss of land was an inevitable result.[11]

Undoubtedly, however, it was large-scale pastoral husbandry that led to the greatest social dislocation. The new order and the old pastoral economy were essentially incompatible as not only was there intense competition for scarce land but the rental from sheep was significantly higher than that from cattle. This was not only because of price differences in the market resulting from the new industrial demand for wool, but also because sheep used land more intensively and extensively than cattle. They were able to graze in areas formerly under-utilized in the old pastoral economy. Landlords also stood to gain from more secure returns. Sheep farms were normally run by big graziers who could guarantee the proprietor a regular and rising income in most years, whereas small tenants were much less dependable: their rent payments fluctuated with the weather and the state of the cattle markets. Nor could the indigenous tenantry hope to participate in the sheep economy in large numbers, as pastoralism was most efficient when practised on a large scale and this created an insurmountable financial barrier for most Highland tenants. There is evidence, for example on the estates of MacDonnell of Glengarry and Cameron of Lochiel in Inverness-shire, of some townships building up small flocks of Blackface in the 1770s; but most landlords were too impatient for the massive profits to be obtained from grazing on a much larger scale, especially since there were now plenty of ambitious and enterprising farmers from the pastoral districts of Ayrshire, the Borders and Northumberland eager for Highland leases.[12] The unexploited lands of the north had become too valuable to be let to inexperienced native tenantry.

As the sheep frontier advanced, so also did clearance.[13] The most notorious removals took place on the Sutherland estate where, between 1807 and 1821, the factors of the Countess of Sutherland and her husband Lord Stafford removed between 6,000 and 10,000 people from the inner parishes to new crofting settlements on the coast in the most extraordinary example of social engineering undertaken in early nineteenth-century Britain. Old men looking back from the 1880s could still give to a Royal Commission the names of forty-eight cleared townships in the parish of Assynt alone. In its scale and level of organization no other clearance matched that of Sutherland. Indeed, the vast majority of removals probably involved only a few people at a time until the more draconian episodes of the 1840s and 1850s during the potato famine. Gradual and relentless displacement rather than mass eviction was the norm but, taken together, the numbers involved were very great and suggest a systematic process of enforced movement on an unprecedented scale.

What is clear, nevertheless, is that most clearances before 1815 were not designed to expel the people. The conventional eighteenth-century assumption that a rising population was an economic benefit was only slowly being questioned, most landowners and theorists of improvement taking the view that the evicted represented an important resource that should not simply be discarded. A dual economy was envisaged, each part of which would in time be a source of increasing revenue. Thus the people from the inner straths and glens should be moved to the coast where they might find employment in kelp or fishing, and the interior districts would then become extensive sheep farms. This became the pattern along the whole west coast north of Fort William as the entire traditional settlement structure was dismantled in the later eighteenth and early nineteenth centuries. On the Reay estate in north-west Sutherland the inland population was settled on the coast in the 1810s and further south in Wester Ross and western Inverness similar forced movements from the inland areas were imposed in Glensheil, Glenelg, Morvern and other districts. The people no longer had traditional guarantees of land. The old social order was destroyed for ever.

2

This survey of social transformation is the essential context for understanding mass emigration from Gaeldom. When it comes, however, to explaining the Highland exodus itself there is little scholarly consensus. On the contrary, the subject has often generated more heat than light. Mired in historical controversy, some of the key issues remain under-researched or constrained by ideological polemic rather than scholarly analysis. Fortunately, however, there is a tolerable level of agreement on the overall trends and patterns of movement. These will be considered first, before attention is focused on the much more contentious questions of causation.

Table 5, based on customs accounts and the contemporary press, sets out current estimates of Highland emigration to North America in the eighteenth century. It suggests several patterns. Movement across the Atlantic had started early. In 1739 Gaels from the central and northern Highlands were settled on the Georgian frontier. They had been recruited by the Trustees for Establishing the Colony of Georgia in America to help defend the territory against the hostile claims of France and Spain. As the *Caledonian Mercury* put it, the Highlanders were to form 'a gallant barrier' against enemy powers, a telling early recognition of their military role in the expansion of the British Empire.[14] The settlement was soon followed by another in North Carolina. This 'Argyll Colony' reflected the commercial ambitions of lairds from Kintyre and mid-Argyll to exploit the

Period	Estimated number of Highland emigrants to North America
1700–1760	Below 3,000
1760–1775	c.10,000
1775–1801	3–4,000
1801–1803	c.5,000
1803–1815	c.3,000

Table 5. Highland emigration, 1700–1815
Source: T. M. Devine, *Clanship to Crofters' War. The Social Transformation of the Scottish Highlands* (Manchester, 1994), p. 179.

plantation land around the Cape Fear River for such lucrative commodities as tobacco, tar, turpentine, flax and timber. Several Highland landowners were as keen on gaining access to imperial profits as city merchants, and so some emigration from the Highlands was the result of proactive entrepreneurship rather than despairing exile.[15] Equally, the persistent myth that early Highland emigration was mainly caused by the catastrophic failure of the Jacobite risings can easily be scotched. After the '15 most of the prisoners sentenced to transportation were sent to the Caribbean. An estimated 600 may finally have been transported to America with the collapse of the '45 but they were scattered among the several colonies and the effect in any one of them must have been slight.[16]

Significant levels of migration were not reached until the 1760s, coinciding with the quickening pace of social and economic change in the Highlands and the huge increase in general British movement to the colonies in the decade after the Seven Years War of 1756–63. This was the period of the 'emigration mania' when the exodus soared to unprecedented levels. Detailed analysis of the years 1773–5 indicates that the Highlands were second only to London as the emigration capital of Britain, accounting for around one in five of all UK migrants on the eve of the American Revolution.[17]

But the exodus did not increase irresistibly on a rising tide. The levels of 1763 to 1775 were never again attained in the later eighteenth century. The pattern was rather one of dramatic fluctuation. Official figures suggest that emigration all but ceased during the American War and, after the outbreak of war with France, slowed to a trickle until the Peace of Amiens from 1801 to 1803 when the scale of the outward movement was reminiscent of the early 1770s. It was rumoured at the time that as many as 20,000 Highlanders from several estates were making preparations to leave for the New World.[18] The magnitude of the planned emigration shook both landowners and government. Some lairds were alarmed at the loss of a labour force at a time of booming profits for kelp and fishing. The British state was equally concerned about the haemorrhage of a population which had already demonstrated its martial qualities in the imperial armies. The demographic integrity of the military reservoir had to be defended at all costs. One immediate consequence was the passing of the Passenger Vessels Act in 1803. Its purpose was overtly humanitarian, to address some of the problems of overcrowding and safety on emigrant vessels. The real aim was to inflate the costs of the transatlantic voyage and hence make emigration more difficult.

The incidence of imperial war had a varied and complex effect on the emigration process. On the one hand, hostilities markedly reduced the rate of departure by raising the costs of sea transport and severing the link with emigrant communities overseas. Before 1776, the favoured Highland destinations were New York and North Carolina. The loyalism of these Highland migrants during the American War and the later movement of many communities to Canada in the years of peace help to explain why there was negligible movement in the 1780s. It took time to renew the 'chain of migration' and once again forge family relationships with the 'new' post-war settlement areas of Quebec, Upper Canada (Ontario), Nova Scotia and Prince Edward Island.

On the other hand, the connection between recruiting and fluctuations in the trends of emigration is more ambiguous. As already shown, military employment in the Highlands during the two great wars of the later eighteenth century took place on a truly remarkable scale. The temporary removal of thousands of young men must have eased pressures within family economies while also lending them support through remittances sent home by relatives. Again, research on several western Inverness estates has suggested that some lairds cynically delayed the eviction of smallholders in the 1790s in order better to recruit to family regiments. All this may have made emigration less likely at the time. On the other hand, recruitment also generated 'invisible' emigration. Unknown numbers of soldiers did not return in peacetime even if they survived the conflict. The 'official' estimates therefore probably significantly underestimate the real levels of movement. Strategic interests also encouraged the British state to become involved in managing settlement in North America as an integral part of the imperial struggle with France. Tracts of land were offered at public expense to discharged soldiers in the colonies. As a result, thousands of Scots who had served in the campaigns of 1756–63 and 1776–83 were settled in the American South, along the New York frontier and in Canada. In time many of these settlements would themselves become powerful magnets, drawing kindred and friends across the ocean to the New World. Colonial land had been granted in return for army service as a traditional contract in the Highlands which dated back to the Georgia emigration of the 1730s. One could therefore reasonably speculate that the extraordinary success of military recruitment in Gaeldom was partly because it promised 'a free ticket across the Atlantic'. Colonial land offered as a reward for service was often an informal state subsidy for emigration.[19]

3

Accounting for the Highland exodus is a more challenging task than describing the patterns of movement. Certainly, by the 1770s the attractions of America were familiar throughout the Highlands and were well reported in an analysis of the motivations of one group of emigrants who left in 1773:

1. The price of land is so low in some of the British colonies that forty or fifty pounds will purchase as much ground there as one thousand in this country. 2. There are few or no taxes at present in the colonies, most of their public debt being paid off since the last peace. 3. The climate in general is very healthy and provisions of all kinds are extraordinarily good and so cheap that a shilling will go as far in America as four shillings in Scotland. 4. The price of labour . . . is high in the colonies: a day labourer can gain there thrice the wages he can in this country. 5. There are no beggars in North-America, the poor, when they appear, are amply provided for. Lastly, there are no titled, proud lords to tyrannize over the lower sort of people, men there being upon a level and more valued, in proportion to their abilities, than they are in Scotland.[20]

Yet while North America might be regarded by some as 'the best poor man's country in the world', there were other and much less attractive features of emigration which were also given wide publicity at the time. The colonies were 4,000 miles away across the Atlantic Ocean on the very periphery of European civilization. The sea voyage was long and arduous (around six to eight weeks) and, in the pre-steamship age, was tantamount to virtually permanent exile for most migrants:

. . . for many the voyages were a terrible experience. At best they were a severe test of endurance, at worst a six weeks or longer endurance test of indescribable suffering; cramped claustrophobic conditions in airless holds with battened down hatches, water in the holds so that lying down became an impossibility, food turning rotten, stale water and the misery of days of North Atlantic gales in a small sailing vessel continually heeling over.[21]

It may be that most voyages were painfully uneventful but there were also plenty of horror stories which brought into stark focus the daunting perils of the sea passage. Notices of ships 'lost at sea' and passengers killed in storms abounded in the home and colonial press. Infectious disease, smallpox, typhus, influenza and assorted 'fevers' were a constant threat. Once an epidemic broke out almost nothing could be done to contain it. As one historian has put it, 'death stalked these voyages.'[22]

In the most detailed account we have of a vessel carrying migrants through a severe Atlantic storm, Janet Schaw's *Journal* of 1774, the waves are described as running 'mountains high' and crashing into the ship in floods that filled the cabins to the upper bunks. As the vessel, overloaded and sailing heavily, alternately swept upward to the crests of the waves and then crashed down into the troughs, Janet and her maid hung on to anything they could grab to keep from drowning. The hogsheads of water fastened on deck came loose and went overboard, followed by all the poultry in their 'hen coops', the kitchen utensils, and barrels of pickled tongues and hams. Four men struggled with the helm in the roaring gale but failed to control it. After fifty hours of constant high winds and drenching rain the crew lapsed into extreme fatigue. Their hands were 'torn to pieces by the wet ropes' which were constantly snapping, causing the ship to convulse violently with each snap. The sails ripped off, and the foremast finally split. And then, in 'a sudden and violent heel over', the ship 'broached to' – turned over on its side – an accident that was usually fatal. Everything came loose – chests, beds, tables, stools, plates, lamps – all of which, together with the passengers, crashed 'heels over head to the side the vessel had laid down on' and water poured in, in 'a perfect deluge'. The only thing that saved the ship was the loss of the masts, which went overboard; as a result the vessel righted itself, with a jolt as violent as the first. The passengers and all the gear were then 'shoved with equal violence to the other side, and were overwhelmed by a second deluge of sea water'.

All this was the experience of a cabin passenger, with the best accommodations aboard the ship. For the twenty-two or more below the hatches the scene was an indescribable nightmare. Water beat down through the cracks constantly and flooded the dark, airless room. To keep from drowning in the deep pools, the emigrants were forced to sit up or stand, soaking wet, clutching their children, for days on end. 'No victuals could be dressed', Janet Schaw reported, 'nor fire got on, so that all they had to subsist on was some raw potatoes and a very small proportion of mouldy brisket [biscuit]'. A young woman miscarried and passed into unconsciousness; her 'absolutely distracted' husband broke 'thro' all restraint, forced up the hatch, and carried her in his arms on deck, which saved her life, as the fresh air recalled her senses'. The husband begged the cabin passengers for help. 'But what could we do for her?' Janet Schaw wrote, 'her cloaths all wet, not a dry spot to lay her on, nor a fire to warm her a drink.'

The storm lasted twelve days, and when it subsided the ship was a wreck. The masts were gone, and the sails and rigging lay on the deck. Emergency masts had to be erected. Only then, the indentured servants having been confined for nine days 'without light, meat, or air, with the immediate prospect of death before them', were allowed to open the hatches and come up into the fresh air. The scene they left behind in the steerage must have been horrendous. Even in normal times, Miss Schaw reported, 'the smell which came from the hole where they had been confined was sufficient to raise a plague aboard'. And once on deck, shivering and half-starved, they discovered themselves dispossessed. All of their belongings had been stored in chests in the long boat. After a fortnight under water the chests had become unglued and their contents had been swept into the sea.[23]

By 1800 America had not yet established itself unambiguously as 'the land of opportunity' in the contemporary mind. In addition to the positive attractions, lurid tales were also widely published of the savage frontier lands of colonies which were inhabited by barbarous tribes and wild animals dwelling among dense and dark forests. The Highlanders had a reputation for intense attachment to their native glens and hills; it therefore puzzled many observers at the time that the Gaels were prepared to leave Scotland *en masse* for an uncertain existence in a far-off wilderness.

But this was only a part of the conundrum. On the face of it, the familiar 'push' forces which impelled Highland emigration in the decades after *c.*1820 were absent in the later eighteenth century. In the period *c.*1820–60 landlords enforced mass eviction, often supported by emigration schemes, to rid their estates of what was increasingly seen as a 'redundant' population. Clearances became more draconian, especially during the Great Famine of 1846–56, and were pursued in a resolute and undisguised attempt to force the people out. It was different in the period under consideration here. The eighteenth-century mind considered population as an invaluable military and economic resource. For north-west mainland and Hebridean landlords in particular, more people were needed for kelping and fishing and to man the family regiments. There were a few exceptions, but, for the most part, landlords regarded emigration as anathema. Some were even prepared to consider rent abatements and the breaking up of land to accommodate smaller tenants tempted to move away. But such policies of appeasement did not always work.

The British state was equally opposed to Highland emigration. Before 1775 there was increasing concern that an empire of colonization would cost Britain dearly because it would lead inevitably to huge increases in expenditure on army and naval resources. The American Revolutionary War and the emergence of an independent United States of America confirmed the criticisms of the sceptics that colonial expansion could only end in disaster. Thus government continued to enforce an anti-emigration strategy from 1775, when emigration to America was banned during hostilities, until the 1810s. This was the political background to the Passenger Vessels Act of 1803 and the attempt by Henry Dundas, Scotland's most powerful political figure, to introduce yet another prohibition on emigration in 1786. As already noted, Highland emigration fell to a low level in the 1780s in large part because the loss of the old empire broke the transatlantic connection built up over earlier decades. During the Napoleonic Wars, however, especially when Highland emigration once again reached significant levels in 1801–3, the state became even more alarmed about the potential loss of a militarily valuable population. Parliament was even prepared to vote vast amounts of money (over £½ million for roads and bridges alone) to promote communications development in the Highlands, including the construction of the Caledonian Canal, which through the release of enlisted men would help check 'the present Rage for Emigration and prevent its future Progress'.[24]

Scholars are divided on the precise causes of the exodus before 1815. Some contend that emigration was a consequence of a rising population in an impoverished society which could not easily support many extra numbers. But although the population of the Highlands was rising fast, especially in the north-west and the islands, so too were economic opportunities in cattle farming, fishing, kelping, distilling, seasonal work in the Lowlands and military employment. This was the so-called 'Age of Optimism' in Highland history when a new crop, the potato, was widely cultivated and transformed the food supply in the region. It was reckoned, for instance, that an acre of potatoes could support four times as many people as an acre of oats.

Nor is the 'Malthusian' explanation consistent with the evidence of the social composition of the emigrant parties. In general terms it was not a flight of the very poor or of the marginal people in Highland society. Without some assistance sea migration would have been out of the reach of the impoverished. One historian reckons that 'even for indigent emigrants travelling to a wilderness totally supported by charity £10 was a minimum cost per adult'.[25] With the majority of the landlord class firmly opposed in this period, the only evidence of substantial 'assisted' emigration was that which took place from South Uist. This was enthusiastically supported by the Catholic church in Scotland for a time because it feared Protestant proselytism in this period, and partly explains why the Roman Catholic islands and the enclaves of the western mainland tended to generate more emigrants than many other areas.[26]

The alternative for the poor and distressed was to obtain passage as indentured servants by which their travel costs were paid in advance in return for a period of bonded service in the colonies. But only a small number of all Highland emigrants at this time seem to have travelled in this fashion. Of the Scots emigrants documented in the customs return for 1774–5, 150 were indentured and most of these were Lowlanders. The vast majority of those who left the Highlands for North America in the period did so by using their own resources; they belonged overwhelmingly to the tenant group, the middle rank in Highland society, those with some surplus above subsistence, with sufficient stock of cattle, sheep, goats and household goods which, when sold, could raise money for passage and resettlement for themselves and their kinsfolk. Examinations of passenger lists have shown that the movement was led by married tenant farmers of mature years, with their wives, children, other relatives, servants and subtenants. The emigration parties were well organized, usually had close links with established emigrant communities across the Atlantic, carried with them substantial sums of money and consisted of large numbers of related families from specific estates, communities or districts of the Highlands. This was not an exodus born of the stress of hunger and destitution. Rather it was a movement which involved a degree of calculation and a careful weighing of prospects on the part of social groups who were able to exert some choice and could exploit favourable circumstances. One reason for the surge in emigration in 1802–3 was that cattle prices peaked in these years, thus yielding good returns in the sale of stock to help defray the costs of transport and resettlement. At the same time, on some estates tenants employed the threat of emigration as a means of thwarting or delaying landlord plans for the reorganization of their holdings. All this hardly suggests a people driven by the inexorable pressure of demographic forces from their native land.

Another perspective suggests that 'the Highlander chose to come to America of his own free will and usually to improve his situation rather than escape grinding depression. This emigration was one of rising expectations.'[27] The explanation recognizes the lure of cheap land and freedom from 'feudal' oppression that was clearly significant in promoting emigration; it contends that there were no fundamental coercive 'push' forces which could reasonably account for emigration on this scale; and it suggests that the clearance of peasant communities in order to establish large sheep farms, a pivotal factor in post-1815 emigration, was not significant in the earlier period, especially in the western Highlands and islands where it was most apparent. This was, then, a so-called 'People's Clearance' rather than one directly inspired by landlord action.

Mass clearance was certainly more limited before 1815 in most of the Outer and Inner Hebrides where the landed class was creating a labour-intensive economic structure based on kelp, fishing and military employment. But, even in this earlier period, the impact of commercial pastoralism on emigration cannot be underestimated. Close direct links can be identified between sheep clearances and emigration in mainland Argyll, several parishes in mainland western Inverness, some parts of Sutherland and at least one estate in Skye. Moreover, it is clear that the inexorable expansion of the sheep frontier was spreading deep alarm and anxiety throughout the western Highlands and preparation for emigration was often a prudent precaution taken to avoid the expected future catastrophe of complete dispossession. Fear of clearance in the future may have been as potent a factor as actual eviction in promoting emigration.[28]

Nor does the notion of a 'People's Clearance' fully take into account the extraordinary scale and intensity of the broader social and economic changes which were sweeping across the Highland region. Powerful forces of coercion were at work, quite apart from the familiar expansion of sheep-ranching. Long before the ill-fated '45 rebellion, commercialization of the society was well under way. Only from the later 1760s, however, did the real magnitude of the changes become apparent because only then did southern markets for Highland produce start to expand on a revolutionary scale. In the next few years many landowners systematically subordinated their estates to the pursuit of profit. The methods varied from area to area but the general strategy was to extract more income from the land and to transform the traditional social structure in ways consistent with this new priority. The joint tenancy settlement on many Hebridean estates were broken up and replaced by small single-croft holdings. This may not seem as dramatic a step as the execution of sheep clearances, but the strategy nevertheless represented a radical attack on the delicate social hierarchy of the old order as it involved both dispossession and the squeezing of people into less land. Often the allocation of the new crofts was also designed to compel greater dependence on the highly laborious manufacture of kelp to pay rental. The croft system therefore posed a mortal threat to the middle tenantry whose larger holdings were likely to be divided to support the augmented labour force required for kelping and commercial fishing. Modern research has established that the regular harvesting of recruits to the army had a similar effect, as several estates redistributed the holdings of established tenants into minute crofts for soldiers and their dependants.[29]

Against this background of tumultuous and massive social change, the Highland exodus of the period 1760 to 1815 cannot therefore be seen as 'voluntary'. These waves of emigration, consisting mainly of small tenants with some means, were a reaction to the radical changes in land settlement, rentals and tenure which were destroying the old way of life. Dispossession, insecurities and commercial pressures were all intensifying as the new market economy was established. Protest was pointless and would inevitably have invited judicial and landlord retribution. Emigration was a much more rational choice for those who could afford it. Indeed the eighteenth-century emigrations are testimony to the organizing capacities and enterprising qualities of the Gael. Highland peasant society often attracted bitter condemnation from Lowland 'improvers' for its supposed indolence, social inertia and conservatism.[30] The history of transatlantic emigration before 1815 tells a different story. The organization of large groups of emigrants and their successful transportation to the New World, often achieved against landlord opposition, demonstrates initiative and skill of a high order. It was not therefore surprising that new communities were successfully established across the Atlantic, confirming the endurance and the resilience of these pioneers.

7

Ulster Scots and the
Transatlantic Connection

I

Analysis of emigration from the British Isles to the Americas in the seventeenth and eighteenth centuries reveals two contrasting trends. Between 1600 and 1700 the movement to the transatlantic colonies was overwhelmingly English in composition. Nearly three-quarters of the one million people who emigrated to Ireland and the American colonies over the course of the century may have been English. After 1700, but more especially after c.1750, there was a radical change in the ethnic composition of the emigrant flow. The pattern of earlier decades was reversed. Now, between 1700 and 1780, around 70 per cent of all British settlers arriving in America were from Ireland and Scotland: 'whereas seventeenth-century settlement had been mainly English, eighteenth-century migration was emphatically British'.[1]

Earlier chapters have described the major Scottish contribution to the formation of this new British Atlantic. If anything, however, the exodus from Ireland was even greater. One of the most recent conclusions suggests that from 1700 to 1820 between a quarter of a million and half a million emigrants came from Ireland to America. They accounted for 30 per cent of all European immigrants in the period and constituted the largest single nationality group from Europe to cross the Atlantic up to c.1800.[2] By way of comparison, and even by the most generous estimates, Scotland was probably able to muster around 90,000 emigrants to America between 1700 and 1815. Even when Ireland's greater national population is taken into account it is still clear that the Irish rate of emigration was significantly higher than that of the Scots. At certain periods the differences were palpable. For instance, in the period after the American War of Independence when Scottish levels of emigration were in the doldrums, the Irish outflow surged ahead. From 1783 to 1814 perhaps as many as 100,000 to 150,000 Irish men, women and children left for the United States during those few decades.[3]

Apart from scale, the other main distinguishing feature of Irish emigration at this time was its remarkable regional diversity. The largest element between 1700 and the 1790s were Protestants from Ulster. Indeed, from 1717 to 1776 perhaps two out of every three Irish emigrants came from that province.[4] Not surprisingly, given the ethnic and religious structure of the eastern areas of the region, the majority of these Ulster emigrants were Protestant. They came from different faith traditions. Some were of English descent and adherents of the Church of Ireland. Most, however, were Presbyterians, many of whom could directly trace their ancestry back to the seventeenth-century migrations of Lowland Scots to Ulster.[5] They can be seen as an identifiable ethnic group, a hybrid people with their territorial roots in Ireland but also Scottish in terms of religious loyalties, culture, speech and intellectual heritage. They are variously known as the 'Scots Irish', 'Scotch-Irish' and 'Ulster Scots'. No history which claims to examine the Scottish impact on Empire in the eighteenth century would be complete without examining their extraordinary and controversial story. Partly this is because the Ulster Scots can be seen as an important conduit through which Scottish ideas and institutions spread to the Americas. In addition, however, the sheer magnitude of the Ulster Scots diaspora and its widespread geographical impact across the American colonies commands attention. In 1790 something like 14 to 17 per cent of the white population of the United States were of identifiable Irish origin. This was around 440,000 to 520,000 individuals out of 3.17 million whites. Upwards of 350,000 are reckoned to have been first-generation Ulster Scots immigrants or the descendants of earlier arrivals.[6] Their diffusion within the American colonies, and after 1783 throughout the USA, was remarkable. New England was the magnet for many of the first emigrants. Soon, however, they were also moving into Maine, New Hampshire, present-day Vermont and then western Massachusetts, where for the first time they acted as human buffers between the regions of British influence and areas populated by American Indians. The Ulster Scots were to become famous (and notorious) in this frontier role in the back-country from Pennsylvania to Georgia.

Pennsylvania in fact became their first capital, with 100,000 people of Ulster origin or descent living there in 1790. As immigration accelerated, waves of land-hungry Ulster Scots crossed the Allegheny Mountains, settling first in the area where Pittsburgh now stands, then across the Potomac River in western Maryland and the Shenandoah Valley. From there they pressed on to the Carolinas and Georgia. At the same time many thousands of their compatriots penetrated westward through the Cumberland Gap into the territories that became the states of Kentucky (1789) and Tennessee (1790).[7] More than any other ethnic group the Ulster Scots were responsible for the expansion of European settlement on the American frontier. Already on the eve of the Revolution in 1776 they had managed to colonize much of the southern back-country.

Before exploring the impact of the Ulster Scots in detail, two preliminary issues must be considered. The first question is to consider how 'Scottish' they really were, given that many Presbyterian emigrants must have come from families which had lived in Ireland for several generations. The second task is to explore the reasons why so many crossed the Atlantic in the eighteenth century and, where appropriate, to draw comparisons and contrasts with the emigration of the Scots already considered in previous chapters.

One of the key texts for an understanding of the Ulster Scots is James G. Leyburn's study, *The Scotch-Irish. A Social History* (1962). Leyburn's book is a wide-ranging survey of their migrations and adaptation to life in America. He is confident, however, that the 'Scottish' aspects of the Ulster Presbyterian experience across the Atlantic have been much exaggerated. Most of the emigrants had never seen Scotland. The land of their forebears was a distant folk memory and little else. They were Irish but 'with a difference', a different people from their ancestors 'and every year separated them more and more from the country across the Channel'. Moreover, surrounded by the native Irish for generations, they inevitably took on aspects of Irish culture. Leyburn conceded, however, that the fundamental religious divisions between Protestantism and Catholicisim meant that the descendants of the Scots immigrants to Ulster maintained a continuing separate identity. But they were no longer Scots. Instead, 'in their own minds, the Ulstermen were . . . Irish of the North'.[8]

In one sense Leyburn's scholarly scepticism is to be applauded.

Few ethnic groups in colonial history have been so encrusted with myth as the 'Scotch-Irish'. The term itself is an Americanism coined in the New World, not the Old. When the first waves of Ulster colonists arrived across the Atlantic, officials commonly referred to them as 'Irish Presbyterians' or 'Northern Irish', but most often simply as 'Irish'.[9] The label 'Scotch-Irish' was indeed eventually to be found in the thickly settled Ulster areas of western Virginia, the Shenandoah Valley and the back-country of Georgia and the Carolinas. Yet the immigrants were still generally known as 'Irish'. Indeed, it was only after the massive increase in Irish Catholic emigration to the United States during and after the Great Famine of the 1840s that the term 'Scotch-Irish' started to enter the common currency. Irish-Americans of Protestant ancestry wished to separate themselves from the poor Catholic masses from Ireland who increasingly generated violent nativist hostility in some US cities. In 1889 the Scotch-Irish Society of America was formed with the aim 'to preserve the history and perpetuate the achievements of the Scotch-Irish race in America'. The Society's prolific publications not only distanced the Ulster Scots from the Celtic Irish, 'the most undesirable, the most mischievous, the most damnable element of population that could have been scraped out of the corners of the earth', but invented a whole new 'Scotch-Irish' story based on half-truths, misconceptions and inherited myth.[10] The genre continues to flourish down to the present day in such pseudo-epics as Rory Fitzpatrick's best-selling *God's Frontiersmen* (1989) and Billy Kennedy's *The Scots-Irish in the Hills of Tennessee* (1995). The new American interest in ethnic identities and origins since Alex Haley's *Roots* and the more recent flowering in Northern Ireland of Ulster Scots language and cultural issues has given such publications a fresh momentum and a new audience.[11]

Recent scholarly research has also supported parts of Leyburn's thesis. Presbyterians of Scottish origin may have formed the largest element within Ulster emigration to colonial America, but Anglicans and Quakers of English stock were an integral part of the diaspora as well. It is reckoned that around one in three of those leaving Ulster for America before 1776 were Protestant but not Presbyterian.[12] In addition, the collective sense of descent from Scotland may have been weaker than sometimes supposed. Thus, Ulster genealogies in the mid-eighteenth century were invariably traced to the time of settlement in Ireland.[13] Place-names across the colonial frontier also often reflect Irish rather than Scottish origins. The new territories abounded with Derrys, Tyrones, Armaghs, Antrims and Donegals. Some Ulster Protestants at least preferred St Patrick to St Andrew. In 1737 Ulstermen met with other Irishmen in Boston to celebrate St Patrick's Day, organizing themselves in the process into a benevolent association known as the Irish Society. The second Masonic Lodge formed in the state of New Hampshire, consisting mainly of Presbyterians from Ulster, called itself St Patrick's Lodge.[14] Nor is the notion of a clear ethnic and religious separation in Ulster between Scots Protestants and Irish Catholics in the century before mass emigration any longer tenable. This myth, so vital to the assumption of a pure Ulster Scots bloodline stretching from the Scottish Lowlands to the north of Ireland and thence the American colonies, has been at least partly laid to rest some time ago by the work of Estyn Evans. He noted that 'there was much more intermarriage with or without the benefit of clergy than the conventional histories make allowance for. Many planters became Catholics and many natives became Protestants.'[15] Even in the colonies, native Irish names were often to be found in areas of Ulster Scots settlement. Surnames such as Boyle, Devlin, Docherty, Gallagher, Heaney, McArdle, McCann and Mulholland were commonplace.[16]

Despite all this, however, a case for the continuing validity of the term 'Ulster Scot' in the colonial context can still be advanced. The proposition rests on a number of arguments. To begin with, the cycle of migration from Scotland to Ulster needs to be restated. Contrary to later Ulster Scots folklore, most migrants did not settle in the north of Ireland within the classic period of the foundation of the Plantation between 1608 and 1618. In fact, many more Scots moved to Ulster outside the plantation decade than during it.[17] The Scottish connection was constantly renewed by successive waves of migration and return migration. Separated by a mere thirteen miles of water between the Mull of Kintyre and the Antrim coast, constant communication between the two countries was the norm. Thousands of Scots came back to their native land as a result of the ferocious sectarian violence of the 1640s.[18] But migration to Ulster picked up again during the Cromwellian decade of the 1650s and again in the 1670s and early 1680s.[19] This was but the prelude to the unprecedented influx of the 1690s and the early years of the eighteenth century. Current estimates suggest that some 40,000 to 70,000 Scots crossed the North Channel to Ulster due to the sustained harvest failures of the 1690s in Scotland and the availability of land at low prices in Ireland in the wake of the Williamite war. In all, between 1650 and 1700 some 60,000 to 100,000 people moved to Ulster.[20] One key indicator of the vastly increased Scottish presence was the rapid rise in the number of Presbyterian ministers in the province. In 1689, Ireland had 86 Presbyterian ministers, most of whom lived in Ulster. Three years later the number had swollen to 130.[21] It follows, therefore, that the majority of those taking ship for the colonies in the first few decades of the eighteenth century had a more recent and closer connection with Scotland than has often been suggested. In addition, the evidence shows that those Scots who arrived in Ulster in the 1690s were significantly poorer than earlier migrants.[22] They were fleeing a country in the grip of severe famine. Those migrants were often far removed from the image of the sturdy, independent planters of 'Scotch-Irish' tradition. Ironically, it was not only the Catholic Irish of the nineteenth century who can be regarded as famine migrants. Famine was also a vital factor in the colourful history of the Presbyterian Ulster Scots as well.

It is equally plain that Scottish influences continued to pervade the emigrant community in the north of Ireland both before and during the great transatlantic exodus of the eighteenth century. These were especially significant in religion. The Presbyterianism of the Ulster Scots, which defined their sense of themselves more than any other single factor, was imported directly from Scotland. The formal organization of the church was founded on the Army Presbytery, the institution created by the chaplains who had accompanied the Scottish army in 1641. Furthermore, the entire system of church discipline and government which was adopted by the Synod of Ulster in 1690 was modelled on that of the mother church.[23] Nonetheless, Ulster Presbyterianism was never simply a 'mirror image' of the Church of Scotland.[24] The monosubscription controversy of 1720 to 1727, the most divisive religious schism in eighteenth-century Ulster, was of indigenous rather than of Scottish origin. Moreover, by the 1750s the two religious polities had begun to diverge in important ways. The Church of Scotland was the established state church confirmed in its status by the Act of Settlement of 1706 which was later incorporated in the Treaty of Union of 1707. Ulster Presbyterianism remained an unestablished voluntary church which for a time suffered under some disabilities. In consequence, it became less hierarchical, more responsive to lay preferences, more committed to pure Scripture and, above all, suffused with a powerful emotional evangelicalism.[25] Nevertheless, the bonds with the Scottish Kirk remained strong. A very high proportion of Ulster ministers were educated at Scottish universities, especially Glasgow and Edinburgh, and held licentiates from the parent church. In addition, two breakaway communions in Scotland, the Reformed Church and the Secession Church, attracted large followings across the Irish Sea.[26] Presbyterianism also gave the Ulster Scots a well-defined separate identity which, even though changing over time, became the most enduring and visible aspect of their culture as they dispersed across many frontiers.[27] Many features from Lowland Scotland persisted to some degree: 'a fierce spirit of independence and the "dour incivility" that accompanied it, religious revivalism and superstitious beliefs and a tradition of political radicalism' inherited from Scottish Covenanting tradition.[28]

But the relationship went even deeper than this. In the eighteenth century an 'ideological community' could be said to exist between the Scots and the Ulster Presbyterians.[29] The connection was firmly anchored in religion but spread further into the common ground of ideas, education, popular culture and literature. Nor was it a one-way process with Scotland as the source of inspiration and the Ulster Scots mere passive recipients. Irish theorists such as Bishop George Berkeley and Robert Molesworth were read by the Scottish literati and their ideas influenced teaching in the universities of the Scottish Enlightenment.[30] Later, in the radical decade of the 1790s, Irish political militancy had an important effect on Scottish organizations like the Friends of the People Associations and the United Scotsmen.[31] Both Ulster and Scottish Presbyterians had a strong zeal for education not for the sake of intellectual liberation but because it was necessary for the reading of the sacred texts. Informal teaching in both Scottish and Ulster homes had the Bible and catechisms as the key books. The high levels of reading literacy in many parts of Lowland Scotland in the eighteenth century are well known. But many in the Presbyterian communities of Ulster could easily equal these standards. A remarkable testimony to this comes from an address to the Governor of Massachusetts in 1718 in which 319 members of an Ulster community sought permission to settle in the Puritan colony. All but 13 of the 319 appended their names 'in fair and vigorous autograph'.[32]

The intimacy of the relationship was based on the very practical foundation of excellent transport links. The first regular cross-Channel ferry service between Antrim and Wigtownshire was established in 1662. By the end of the seventeenth century a weekly service was in place. Daily crossings advertised in the *Belfast Newsletter* became available from the 1780s. Increased migration between the two countries was both cause and effect of these improvements in communications.[33] Ulster weavers and bleachers were recruited for the Scottish linen industry, while by the 1790s the first significant increase in permanent labour migration from the north of Ireland to western Scotland had taken place, the early phase of the movement which was to have such momentous social, religious and cultural consequences for Scottish towns and cities in the nineteenth century. Among the most significant groups who took advantage of the new transport connections were Irish Presbyterian students attending Glasgow and Edinburgh Universities. Between 1690 and 1809, 1,846 Irish students matriculated at Glasgow. These 'Scoto-Hiberni' or 'Scotch-Irish', as they were designated in the university's records, made up as much as a fifth of matriculants between 1750 and 1779.[34] Most of the Ulstermen studied at Glasgow but the world-renowned medical courses at Edinburgh also proved very attractive. From 1740 to 1800, a quarter of the university's MD graduates were from Ireland.[35] The Scottish universities had several advantages. Presbyterians avoided Trinity College, Dublin because of its general Anglican ethos and the requirement that the Oath of Supremacy had to be taken for graduation. The Scottish institutions were also cheaper than the continental universities, were imbued with a strong Presbyterian tradition and, by the 1730s, had become the cradles of the great age of intellectual achievement later called the Scottish Enlightenment.[36]

This intellectual migration between Ireland and Scotland was critical for deepening the Scottish influence on Ulster. The men educated in the Scottish universities were destined to become influential ministers and teachers within their own communities. Scottish-educated clergy were central to such fundamental developments in Ulster as 'New Light' Presbyterianism, which stressed individual conscience and personal conviction in religion rather than human-made structures or texts.[37] Above all, they became the main channel through which some of the seminal ideas of the Scottish Enlightenment fed through into Ulster society. One key figure was Francis Hutcheson, Professor of Moral Philosophy at Glasgow from 1729 to 1746. Hutcheson himself was the very incarnation of the Scots–Ulster intellectual association.[38] His grandfather was an Ayrshire minister who had left for Ulster in the seventeenth century. Hutcheson was born in Armagh, studied at Glasgow University, spent some time as a minister back in Ireland and then was elected to the Chair of Moral Philosophy at Glasgow in 1729. Hutcheson and his associates are credited with significant influence in Irish radicalism, with his stress on freedom of opinion, religious tolerance and the right of resistance to tyranny. Of course, not all Ulstermen trained in Scottish universities developed political interests. Many were rigidly orthodox adherents of existing values. But 'Scotch ideas' did help to fashion the outlook of such prominent United Irishmen as William Steel Dickson, William Drennan and Thomas Addis Emmet, all of whom had been students at either Glasgow or Edinburgh.[39] They also crossed the Atlantic with the Ulster Scots emigrants and contributed powerfully to political discourse in the period before the American Revolution.[40]

The connections were equally well developed in the literary sphere. The popular poetry books in eighteenth-century Ulster were Scottish vernacular classics such as Blind Harry's *Wallace* and David Lindsay's writings, both of which were also published in Belfast.[41] Until Robert Burns made his massive impact, Allan Ramsay was by far the most popular author among Ulster Scots readers. Indeed, it was because of these shared vernacular traditions that Burns's work had such an immediate effect. As one Belfast writer put it, he was 'Burns, Our Bard', a poet who wrote in the same linguistic tradition as so many others who had gone before.[42] Burns not only became a model for many Ulster Scots poets but was an inspirational figure for Irish radical writers who often composed in vernacular Scots, and who were involved in the United Irish movement: 'He [Burns] was, in many respects, the tutelary poet of radical Ulster.'[43]

On the basis, then, of this range of demographic, religious and cultural evidence, the Ulster Scots emigrants to America deserve to be considered as one distinctive element in the more general Scottish diaspora of the eighteenth century. Plainly Ulster was not simply another Scotland. 'Scottishness' varied between areas of heavy Scots settlement, such as north Down and south Antrim, and those of lighter concentration, like south Armagh, west Derry and east Donegal. Equally, the depth of the Scottish link naturally might vary between recent immigrants and those of much earlier periods. That, too, would alter after movement to America. The Ulster Scots had 'a restless, hybrid, continuously evolving culture' reflecting a mobile people who had migrated first to Ireland and thereafter across the Atlantic.[44] However, an integral factor in their distinctive subculture was their Scottish roots.

2

Historians have long debated the reasons for the mass emigration of the Ulster Scots across the Atlantic. Whig scholars like W. E. H. Lecky and James Anthony Froude in the nineteenth century were keen to show that the Ulster Scots, involvement in the American Revolution was a direct consequence of the resentment they felt at their treatment by the British government in Ireland.[45] They emigrated, so the argument ran, because of religious persecution and political disability. The state had treated them disgracefully after their loyal and courageous support for Protestantism and the British cause in Ireland during the Williamite wars of the 1690s. Their reward for such fidelity was discriminatory legislation and religious intolerance, hence their enthusiastic support for the Revolution in 1776. It was their way of paying off old scores with a vengeance. As Froude put it, 'The resentment which they carried with them continued to burn in their new homes; and in the War of Independence England had no fiercer enemies than the grandsons and great-grandsons of the Presbyterians who had held Ulster against Tyrconnell.'[46]

Whether or not the Ulster Scots supported the Revolution with such force and enthusiasm is a subject to be examined in Chapter 8. The basic premise of the thesis has been convincingly challenged by more recent scholarship. Certainly, like other non-Anglicans, Presbyterians in Ulster were indeed subject to statutory disabilities.[47] The Test Act of 1704 barred them from holding office, they had to pay tithes to help fund the Anglican establishment and even the validity of their marriages could be challenged in the ecclesiastical courts. By the 1720s, however, these burdens were largely nominal. In 1719 toleration was legally extended to Presbyterians, but in any case they had enjoyed this in practice for many years. In addition, on the accession of George I in 1714 the royal grant in support of ministers' stipends was restored, thus renewing 'the quasi-establishment of Presbyterianism alongside Episcopalianism'.[48] Alienation from the Anglican establishment coupled with the insecurities founded on the menace of the Catholic Irish did undeniably contribute to the Ulster Scots' identity and mindset and helped shape their political ethos in the colonies.[49] But despite the best efforts of 'Scotch-Irish' apologists in the later nineteenth-century United States, the Ulster emigrants were not some latter-day Pilgrim Fathers, refugees from persecution, a chosen people searching for freedom of conscience in a new Israel. The basic point was that there was little correlation in time between the period of discrimination from c.1690 to the 1710s and the major waves of mass emigration. The exodus from Ulster did start earlier than is often thought but it did not gather real momentum until the decades after c.1720.[50] By that time both state and religious 'oppression' was a thing of the past.

The more fundamental forces identified by modern writers functioned differently over the course of the eighteenth century. In particular, the period before c.1750 stands out from later decades. For much of the first half of the eighteenth century the Irish economy experienced long-term stagnation in exports and imports and vulnerability to famine. The marked peaks in the transatlantic movement, in 1718–19, 1727–9, 1735–6, 1740–41 and 1745–6, were all years of dearth, and subsistence crisis was often at the heart of these early migrations.[51] But other factors also contributed because the Ulster Scots seem to have been prepared to escape the hard times in greater numbers than the native Catholic Irish. It may be that many did not have the same deep roots in Ireland, having settled there as recently as the later seventeenth century. Further, on arrival in the 1690s Ulster landlords had offered them advantageous rent and tenurial terms. There is evidence that many of these leases ended in the 1720s and this led to the imposition of higher rentals at a time of grave economic insecurity for a large number of tenants. Many responded through realizing their farm capital by selling their interests in the holding, which then produced funds for emigration.[52] Even in the years of acute harvest failure, for instance, the majority of emigrants from Ulster ports were able to pay their own fares. A clear contrast emerges with patterns of emigration from Scotland. Only in the

second half of the eighteenth century did Scottish transatlantic movement reach significant levels. Ulster Scots emigration began much
earlier and was consistently greater in scale. One explanation was
that between c. 1700 and 1750 there were some years of food shortage
in Scotland but no epic crisis of Irish magnitude.[53] Again, demographic pressures in Scotland may have been much less intense. After
all, the country had lost many thousands of its inhabitants through
death or emigration to Ulster in the 'lean years' of the 1690s.[54] It
would take time to recover. The demographic safety-valve of mass
emigration was therefore less relevant. An increase in movement was
less likely because rent increases remained sluggish and did not
provide the same spur to movement that they seem to have done
across the Irish Sea.

Like Scotland's, the Ulster economy was on the move from the
middle decades of the century.[55] From 1700 to 1775 Irish exports
increased in value by almost five times, with cattle and their products
tripling in value. Hemp, flax and linen multiplied almost thirty times
in value until they made up just over half of all Irish exports. The
industrial core of this economic renaissance was linen and linen
manufacture centred north of a line from Drogheda to Sligo. The
centres of excellence were nearly all located in east and mid-Ulster,
the areas of concentration of Ulster Scots settlement. The marked
gains in living standards were visible everywhere: a sharp rise in
population which far outran the increase in numbers in Scotland;
taxable homes expanded even faster than population, suggesting a
movement away from poorer, untaxed dwellings; and consumer
goods became more abundant.[56] The 1760s and 1770s were the
classic period of economic boom with unprecedented peaks in the
Atlantic business world in 1771 and 1776–7. Yet it was precisely in
those very decades that Ulster Scots emigration surged to levels not
seen earlier in the eighteenth century. Nor was this a temporary
feature; it was sustained in the years of peace after 1783. Between
1783 and 1794, for instance, Irish immigration to Philadelphia aver-
aged over 5,600 per annum and many more travellers paid their own
passage than before 1760.[57] Indentured servants were now few and
far between, making up less than one in ten of the emigrant parties
on the eve of the American War of Independence. It seemed that this
was a new form of emigration, different from that of the crisis-driven
movement of the 1720s and 1730s.[58] The poor, the destitute and the

marginal were still involved but most of these emigrants were more skilled and better-off. They were driven by the desire to exploit opportunities across the Atlantic at a time of massive economic expansion in North America and spectacular growth in Ireland's Atlantic trades and linen manufacture. Again, similarities with the Scottish experience come to mind. In the Lowlands and Highlands emigration also started to climb rapidly from the 1760s. There too, though 'push' factors were certainly present, the major driver was the widespread urge to grasp opportunity in the New World. In Ireland, the government was alarmed at the loss of the Protestant people who formed its main ethnic bastion against the Catholic Irish.[59] Equally in Scotland, the state was anxious about the emigration of the Gaels who had already proved themselves invaluable imperial soldiers in the Seven Years War. In both Ulster and Scotland emigration on this scale puzzled some contemporaries because it expanded as living standards in the home country were becoming better. As the patterns in the north of Ireland showed, however, material amelioration was often a key factor in the whole process of movement.

For a start, the improving economy fashioned a much more efficient infrastructure for emigration. The Irish ports towns linked virtually the whole of Ireland with the American colonies through the constant traffic of merchants, ships, soldiers, officials and servants which acted as a vital network of communication in directing migration. The boom in the linen industry transformed these networks. The flax seed trade vital to its success became the more important link between Ireland and the colonies. It was from the hinterland of Philadelphia that most of the seed came and the great flax seed fleets which assembled there in early autumn made possible mass sea migration from Ulster. The ships on the return voyage loaded emigrants as well as goods. The regularity and frequency of the sailings made it easy for prospective migrants to plan their departures in advance. German migrants, on the other hand, often had to travel over long distances to the Atlantic ports and there face uncertainty and complexity in arranging passage.[60] In addition, the cost of the Atlantic passage halved between the 1720s and 1770s as specialization and competition among larger ships in the emigrant trade intensified.[61] Indeed, the normal term for indentured servants fell from 4–7 years to 2–4 years between these decades. This telling fact suggested that potential emigrants were increasingly in a buyer's market and that more inducements were necessary to attract them. Certainly, press advertisements and emigrant agents were both on the increase during this period, extolling the easy availability of transport and the cheapness of American land. Of more fundamental importance, however, was the stream of letters to relatives and friends at home which came back with the ships. A substantial collection now exists in the Public Record Office of Northern Ireland. Many are remarkably detailed and come from family members trusted by the recipients. The very fact that those earlier voyagers had not simply disappeared into oblivion once they took ship must have made the prospect of a similar journey seem much less risky for those they had left behind.[62] The process must also have been helped by the activities of land promoters and speculators. Most of the 33,000 Ulster folk who left for the colonies between 1760 and 1775 travelled in schemes organized by these agents.[63] Arthur Dobbs, a native of County Antrim and Governor of North Carolina, was especially prominent in organizing the emigration of his fellow countrymen. Other land speculators of note included William Johnson in Upper New York and William Beverly and Benjamin Borden in Virginia. Many were also deeply involved in the settlement of Georgia and South Carolina.

Conditions in Ulster also gave transatlantic movement a new and vigorous impetus. Three crucial factors can be noted. First, population in eighteenth-century Ulster was growing at an unprecedented rate and faster than in any other part of Ireland. Recent revisions cast new light on this demographic expansion.[64] Ulster's population grew annually between 1753 and 1791 at between 1.3 to 1.9 per cent and 1.3 to 1.4 per cent from 1791 to 1821 – and this despite the great and sustained haemorrhage to North America. This was more than two and a half times the Scottish rate of increase in the second half of the eighteenth century. The explanation seems to lie in Ulster's economic miracle which helped to cut drastically very heavy rates of child mortality because of more regular family employment in linen, a stable food supply and the absence of famine. But demographic increases and emigration were linked. Unlike Scotland, Irish urban growth in these decades was limited.[65] Many of the new generations in rural society would have to look beyond Ireland for work, land and security. Not all the increasing numbers of younger sons could be accommodated within the family holdings. The emigration of at least some of the numerous offspring was encouraged. Some tenants anticipated the problem by choosing to move and hence avoid downward mobility of their progeny. Population increase was also a potent influence on rising rents, which contemporaries often argued were an important factor in the Ulster exodus.[66]

Second, the long-term trend in the linen industry was one of buoyant and dynamic growth. But not every year was one of rosy prosperity. In fact, in the early 1770s, as in Scotland, the manufacture was badly hit by an acute crisis which opened the floodgates of emigration. A fall in foreign demand ushered in a severe recession and near collapse in the industry. Independent craftsmen who faced financial ruin, as well as cotton weavers and smallholders on the brink of starvation, were numbered among the emigrant parties.[67] Third, the economic success of linen came at considerable social cost. Women especially were placed under great burdens, not only carrying out the tasks of house and family but working in the fields and, increasingly, over the spinning-wheel. The regime was one of unrelenting toil. There is some evidence, therefore, that women were often among the keenest to go.[68] Yet the insecurities of the new market economy and its ethos of labour-intensive rigour also increased the attractions of American land and the frontier lifestyle of the colonies for many more members of the community.

3

These settlers had a marked impact on the transatlantic empire partly because of the remarkable number of Ulster Scots who came to America.[69] They massively outnumbered direct migrants from Scotland not only because of their much higher and earlier rate of emigration but also because many Scots remained loyal to the crown in the American War and after 1783 left the USA for British North America. Significant numbers of Ulster Scots not only supported American independence but continued to pour into the United States in even greater numbers in the 1780s and 1790s.[70] But the impact they made was not a matter of demography alone. The Ulster Scots also had a distinctive pattern of settlement and culture in the New World. Contrary to popular belief many immigrants moved to the cities of New York, Boston and Philadelphia. But the vast majority settled further west. After first seeking refuge in New England, from the 1720s they started to land in large numbers at the Delaware ports. Finding the coastal strip mainly taken over by William Penn's English and Welsh followers and parts of the interior already settled by German Rhinelanders, they struck out across the Susquehanna River and into Cumberland County. Though there were hostile Indians and French to the west they pressed on into the back-country across the Alleghenies, traversing that 'great swathe of rolling and timbered country stretching from western Maryland and central Pennsylvania to the Carolinas'.[71] In this wilderness the Ulster Scots made up a high proportion of the first European farmers. They soon became typecast as the archetypal American pioneers who won the West for future generations. Legendary figures such as Davy Crockett and Jim Bowie, both of Ulster Scots stock, came to personify this story. Frederick Jackson Turner, in his classic frontier thesis, had them in mind when he talked of the backwoodsmen who were in the vanguard of the making of the new nation:

For many Americans there exists a mental image of a 'typical pioneer' living with his large family in a log cabin set in a space he had cleared in the forest. There he led a rough but simple life, hunting and trapping, farming with crude implements and wasteful methods, and occasionally having to fight Indians. He drank a great deal of corn whisky, scorned refinement, loved practical jokes, danced vigorous reels and hoedowns to a scraping fiddle, and enjoyed such rough sports as fights with bare fists. Yet at bottom his character was sound and his impulses were right. He and his kind, according to this image of pioneer life, conquered the wilderness and laid the foundations of democratic faith and practice.[72]

Theodore Roosevelt, in his *The Winning of the West*, further burnished the myth and set the Ulster Scots epic against their ethnic and religious background in Scotland and Ireland:

That these Irish Presbyterians were a bold and hardy race is proved by their at once pushing past the settled regions, and plunging into the wilderness as the leaders of the white advance. They were the first and last set of immigrants to do this; all others have merely followed in the wake of their predecessors. But, indeed, they were fitted to be Americans from the very start; they were kinsfolk of the Covenanters; they deemed it a religious duty to interpret their own Bible, and held for a divine right the election of their own clergy. For generations their whole ecclesiastic and scholastic systems had been fundamentally democratic. In the hard life of the frontier they had lost much of their religion, and they had but scant opportunity to give their children the schooling in which they believed; but what few meeting-houses and school-houses there were on the border were theirs.[73]

In this semi-mythical tradition they were not only seen as brave, God-fearing pioneers who 'settled the frontier . . . founded the Kirk and . . . built the school'.[74] They are depicted as the nation-builders *par excellence* of the United States. For one author the Ulster Scots formed 'the very backbone of Washington's army'.[75] Others quote with approval the contemporary comment that the American War of Independence was 'nothing more or less than a Scotch Irish Presbyterian rebellion'.[76]

It is intriguing to turn from this later legend to contemporary eighteenth-century attitudes to the Ulster Scots. Here the commentaries were much less favourable. One writer described them as 'the scum of two nations'. An Anglican cleric went even further and called them 'the scum of the universe'.[77] Charles Woodmason, 'Anglican Itinerant' in North Carolina, referred to 'the herd of vile Irish presbyterians'.[78] Even the tolerant Quakers of Philadelphia found the Ulstermen subversive and uncouth, and 'a pernicious and pugnacious people'.[79] In Pennsylvania they were constantly at odds with the neighbouring German settlers. Indeed, disturbances became so frequent that the Quaker authorities instructed their agents not to sell any more land to Ulster Scots in areas of German settlement and even to offer them generous relocation terms to move further west. One scholar has suggested that their assertiveness, not to say aggressiveness, which many contemporaries saw as their distinguishing characteristic, may well have been the product of their embattled religious position in Ulster.[80]

The truculence of their identity also marked the Ulster Scots out as a well-defined and coherent ethnic group. It was fashioned in part by their dense concentration in certain regions, a pattern different from that of Scots migrants who were widely scattered along the Atlantic seaboard. Their militant Presbyterianism also gave them a shared belief that they were a chosen people whose many tribulations were simply predictable sufferings on the hard road to final deliverance from their enemies. The roots of emigration may have been primarily economic, but both the message from their clerical leaders and from their own folk tradition implied that the Ulster Scots had come to America through 'a communal exodus compelled by religious and political oppression'.[81] These assumptions in turn cemented the mutuality of the ethnic group. The Ulster Scots were often applauded in their hagiography for rugged individualism. In fact they possessed a strong communal ethos deepened not only by their Presbyterianism but by events such as harvest gatherings, festivals, funerals and weddings.[82] Demography helped too. A large part of the emigrant parties consisted of entire families with significant numbers of unmarried women and girls. This enabled marriage to take place more easily within ethnic boundaries.

Identity is a slippery concept. Plainly third- and fourth-generation migrants would probably have had their attitudes more shaped by American circumstances than by their cultural origins. Again, the acute shortage of Presbyterian ministers and churches in some areas meant that Ulster Scots often shifted their loyalties to Baptistry, Methodism and Congregationalism.[83] In the larger towns such as Philadelphia and Boston, ethnic allegiances were also likely to be abandoned more quickly. Nor were the Ulster Scots monolithic in political belief. This is confirmed by their much misunderstood role in the American Revolution (which will be discussed in the next chapter). Many claim that to a man they were on the American side because of bitter memories of suffering English race and religious oppression in Ulster. In fact, they were often divided in their allegiances. Some were neutral and others were loyalist.[84] All this diversity needs to be taken into account. But to deny an identifiable Ulster Scots culture in the colonies would be disingenuous. It was particularly strong in those regions where they were concentrated – central Pennsylvania and the back-country South – and it is in these areas that their impact on America can best be examined.

At the most basic level they left a bold imprint on the American landscape as farmers on the frontier. The Ulster Scots pioneered the classic human topography of the rural United States, the single homestead, the small scattered hamlets, the livestock and corn economy. The trails they created or inherited from the Indians became roads. The family farm of the Old West surrounded by an extensive 'outfield' of woodland was 'an Atlantic heritage', distinct from the village system of New England and the mansions of the rich tidewater areas of Virginia.[85] The Ulster Scots invited opprobrium at the time. While their German neighbours thoroughly cleared their holdings out of the forest and turned them into neat ploughed fields, they moved on when they had taken the best out of the land. It is not too fanciful to suggest that here was the working of the Scottish 'outfield' system of agriculture adapted, in the words of one scholar, 'to a forest landscape of limitless extent'.[86] One other tradition which crossed the Atlantic was the distilling of whisky in prodigious quantities using American corn and rye rather than barley. It was this hard liquor which fuelled a boisterous and rumbustious social life and helped soften some of the many hardships of frontier life. The log cabin, another frontier icon, was an invention of Swedish and German immigrants but it was soon adopted by the Ulster Scots. Here, too, the influence of the old country was apparent. The ground plan with two opposite doors was not only identical with that of the traditional small Ulster farmhouse, but the overall structure was derived from the cruck-roofed house previously imported to Ireland from Scotland.[87] Even some towns in the Appalachians bore the mark of Ulster urban tradition in the elongated market-place known as 'the Diamond' which is found to this day in several places in Northern Ireland.

The pattern seems to have been one of cultural inheritance and adaptation. Nowhere was this more obvious than in the relationships between the Ulster Scots and the Indian peoples. In large part this is a dark and brutal story. But the immigrants also borrowed much from the native inhabitants, including Indian corn, a prolific substitute for oats and barley, their vast store of knowledge of animals, plants and forest lore and, not least, their skills in hunting: 'The Indian fighters took on many of the attributes of the Indian brave and the strong silent hero of American folklore was surely born in the old frontier.'[88]

It was indeed as implacable enemies of the red men that the Ulster Scots made their bloodiest and most notorious impact on the West. Yet the cruelty and ferocity of the Indian wars came relatively late. In the first half of the eighteenth century, despite the progress westwards of Ulster Scots and German settlers, few major incidents occurred. This was partly due to the absence of significant Indian settlement in the Shenandoah Valley. As the white man steadily migrated to their lands, most natives quietly moved further into the interior. Again, in Pennsylvania the policy of the Quaker government was crucial. Their religious convictions ensured that they treated the Indians as equals, giving a fair price when their land was purchased and avoiding the building of forts and the creation of armed militias.[89] But trouble was inevitable. The insatiable land hunger of the Ulster Scots would brook no interference from those they regarded as pagan savages. They could easily justify the subjugation of the red men as a Christian crusade, the 'smiting of the enemies of the Lord'. In Ulster, the occupation of the lands of dispossessed natives had been an integral part of their history. On the American frontier too the existing inhabitants were deemed an obstacle to the advance of civilization. Official complaints against their ruthless encroachment on Indian territory elicited the response that 'it was against the laws of God and nature that so much land should be idle while so many Christians wanted it to labour on and to raise their bread'.[90] Colonial officials recognized the aggressive Ulster Scots ethos. Massachusetts and South Carolina recruited them as a human shield against the threat of Indian attack. In 1756, for instance, the colony of South Carolina offered Ulster Scots inducements to settle in the back-country after the Cherokee uprising of that year to provide a defence against the Indians and their French and Spanish allies.[91] It was, therefore, probably only a matter of time before armed conflict broke out between land-hungry pioneers and the native peoples.

In the end the catalyst was the start in 1756 of the Seven Years War between France and Britain. Significantly, this is known in American history as the 'French and Indian War'. The French had no difficulty in persuading the Indian tribes to be their allies. After victory against the British, the Shawnees, Cherokees, Tuscaroras, Creeks, Choctaws and Chickasaws were promised restoration to their former territories while the white men would be driven back to the sea. The rout of General Braddock's redcoats at the battle of Monongahela River by a joint French and Indian force in the summer of 1755 unleashed a furious Indian assault on frontier settlements from southern Virginia to Canada. One French officer wrote: 'It is incredible what a quantity of scalps they bring us . . . These miserable English are in the extremity of distress.'[92]

This was a new kind of war, far removed from the codes of honour and chivalry which still governed set-piece battles in eighteenth-century Europe. Civilians were fair game. Houses were burnt, women and children were slaughtered without mercy and hideous torture employed routinely against the enemy. In 1760, a party of some 250 Ulster Scots left their homes to seek refuge in Augusta, Georgia. They were ambushed by over 100 mounted Cherokee and lost about forty killed or captured. One of those who died was the grandmother of John C. Calhoun, the most famous spokesman for the south in the years before the Civil War. In all, the Calhouns lost twenty-three of their number in the Cherokee attack.[93] Indian raids became endemic across the frontier during the Seven Years War and then continued after 1763 in the uprising known as Pontiac's War. During this, over 2,000 settlers were killed in Pennsylvania alone.[94]

The Ulster Scots retaliated with equal ferocity and in the process enthusiastically adopted the Indian methods of butchering women and children, the firing of villages and ritual scalping of the fallen enemy. They carried the war far into Indian territory and wrought extensive devastation in the tribal heartlands. In the set battles of the Seven Years War the regular British line regiments did most of the fighting. But the brunt of the brutal guerrilla warfare against the Indian allies of the French was borne by the Ulster Scots levies. German settlers, especially in Pennsylvania, mainly retreated eastwards rather than fight. The Quaker-dominated authority in Philadelphia refused for reasons of conscience to take up arms. The British army was fully stretched against the French. The Ulster Scots had, on the whole, to defend themselves:

The importance of their military contribution can hardly be exaggerated. In 1756 a Scotch-Irish force captured Kittaning on the Allegheny, one of the two chief Indian strongholds in Pennsylvania. The Scotch-Irish also furnished most of the Pennsylvania militia who helped British regulars capture Fort Duquesne, the key to the French defenses in the Ohio Valley. Then, during Pontiac's rising of 1763–1764, it was again the Scotch-Irish who offered the only effective resistance. But while there can be no doubting their courage and steadfastness when facing the horrors of Indian border warfare, it should not be forgotten that they were not averse to adopting the ruthless methods of their adversaries. They were guilty, for example, of the Conestoga massacre of 1763, when a group of young Scotch-Irishmen in Dauphin County, Pennsylvania, barbarously slaughtered twenty Conestoga Indians whom they suspected of having aided Indian marauders. Although no proof of Conestoga complicity was ever forthcoming, many Scotch-

Irishmen, including some clergymen, clung to the view that the action had been justified.[95]

The Indian Wars further consolidated the Ulster Scots' identity of collective assertiveness, communal cohesion and contempt for the eastern authorities who had failed to provide their families with protection against the savage. It was a short step from self-defence to taking the law into their own hands on other issues. Bitter resentment against the peace-loving Quaker oligarchy in Philadelphia spilt over in 1764 with the march of the 'Paxton Boys'. Five or six hundred armed men advanced on the capital. British regulars were called to stand against them until they were halted a mere six miles from Philadelphia. There they presented 'A Declaration and Remonstrance', defending the massacre at Conestoga, calling for more aggressive action against the Indians and greater representation for western Pennsylvania in the colonial assembly. Frustration also boiled over in North Carolina where the Ulster Scots faced something of the same kind of discrimination which their ancestors had suffered in Ireland. They had to pay tithes to the Anglican Church and their marriages were not officially recognized by the colony until 1766. The Ulster Scots of the western areas combined in a protest movement called 'the Regulators' in the mid-1760s. Until the early 1770s they virtually controlled the back-country, but their power was broken at the battle of Almanac in 1771 and the public hanging by the authorities of several of the leaders.

The Regulators are open to many interpretations. For some Ulster Scots apologists they represented a movement for popular justice against uncaring and tyrannical government. For other writers, they were much more sinister; an example of ruthless vigilantes in action and the forerunners of later lynch mobs and even the Ku Klux Klan.[96] From another perspective, however, the Regulators were yet another manifestation of cultural transfer from the Old World to the New. The tactics they adopted of secrecy, violence and intimidation had all been refined in such Ulster agrarian movements as the Oakboys of the 1760s and the Steelboys of the 1770s.[97] Moreover, the Indian Wars and the later campaigns against eastern colonial governments inbred a warrior ethos in the culture. Boys, and sometimes girls, were brought up to defend themselves with guns, knives and fists. Duelling and its associated code of honour became deeply embedded in the culture. Andrew Jackson, one of the most eminent of the Ulster Scots community and a future President of the USA, was the very incarnation of this ethos. He spent much of his life fighting wars but also killed two opponents in duels.[98] Bloody feuds between back-country families were also common, later to be made infamous in such notorious range wars as those between the McCoys and the Hatfields.[99] All this had two important effects on American history. First, the warrior traditions and expertise of the Ulster Scots explain why those who joined the patriot cause in 1776 became such feared soldiers in Washington's armies. Second, the experience during the Indian Wars, together with their struggle with eastern élites, helped radicalize many communities and bring them into the political process. This, rather than any idealized commitment to freedom from the British oppressor, explains the high-profile role of some Ulster Scots in the American Revolution.[100]

The warrior ethos and the frontier experience were second only to Presbyterianism in forming their character. As early as 1698 the Ulster-born 'father of American Presbyterianism', Francis Makemie, had settled in Virginia. In 1706, together with fellow ministers drawn from Pennsylvania, Delaware and Maryland, he formed the first presbytery in America at Philadelphia. The Presbyterian Church became the most significant Ulster Scots institution. It was not only the basis of religious loyalty but a focus for community life of immense significance. In frontier areas where the civil law was weak or non-existent, the Kirk sessions, as in Scotland and Ulster, dealt with moral offences from fornication to Sabbath-breaking. But they were also concerned with public order and property rights. The clergy were not only religious figures but secular leaders and it was common for the colonial authorities to appeal to them in controlling their often truculent followers.[101] At the same time, the practical impact of the church was often circumscribed by an acute shortage of ministers in the back-country, the huge surges of immigration from Ulster and the habitual movement of the immigrants within the frontier territories. Over time, many fell away from the faith and others converted to Methodism and Baptistry.

Nevertheless, Presbyterianism was still a force to be reckoned with. It was a vital catalyst in provoking tensions both with Anglican-dominated oligarchies and Quaker authorities. The potent evangelicalism of Ulster Presbyterianism – the love of prayer meetings and field gatherings, hellfire and damnation Christianity, a belief in personal salvation – was a key factor in that period of intense Protestant revivalism known as 'the Great Awakening' which swept across the colonies in the 1730s and 1740s. The core factors in this were an emotionally charged religiosity, a deep and direct sense of the agony of hell and the bliss of heaven, and a millennial belief that the second coming of Christ's kingdom would take place in America.[102] The past had gone; only in the land of the future could God's glory be truly celebrated. Some historians have seen the Great Awakening as creating the religious context for the American Revolution.[103] At the very least, it was a transformational force in colonial American religious culture which placed more stress on a personal relationship with God and challenged existing orthodoxies. It was a new way which has powerfully influenced the nature of Protestant Christianity in the United States down to the present day.

The Presbyterian emphasis on an educated ministry as its cornerstone and on elementary learning to enable reading of the Bible by the laity also had remarkable cultural and political effects on American development. One of the key advances was the foundation of the famous Log College at Neshaminy near Philadelphia in 1726 by the Reverend William Tennant, graduate of Edinburgh and native of Antrim, to train young men for the ministry.[104] Equally significant was the work of another Ulsterman, Francis Alison, professor of moral philosophy at the College of Philadelphia and probably the most distinguished classical scholar in colonial America. He began the New London Academy in Pennsylvania in 1735 using the texts and lecture materials from his own education at the University of Glasgow. Alison's foundation established a bridge between the critical thought (especially that of Francis Hutcheson) of the Scottish Enlightenment which he had imbibed as a student and the American Revolution. Three of the New London alumni, Thomas McKean, James Smith and George Read, were signatories to the Declaration of Independence.[105] By the end of the eighteenth century Presbyterian ministers had founded some 100 schools in the colonies.[106]

8

Cultural Relationships and the American Revolution

I

Bernard Bailyn, the leading American historian, has argued persuasively that in the eighteenth century the Atlantic became a highway, a vast ocean thoroughfare across which human beings, commodities and ideas flowed constantly back and forth between the Old World and the New.[1] Scotland, by its location on the European periphery and position within the expanding British Empire, was immersed in these innumerable transactions. The personal, business, intellectual and religious links which were built up over the course of time were vast, intricate and complex. Naturally a primary engine of growth was the unprecedented development of the colonial trades. The great shipping fleets not only became the carriers of tobacco, linen, cotton and sugar, but of people, correspondence teeming with information, books and pamphlets. But the world of commerce penetrated even deeper and wider than this. Members of mercantile families both in the colonies and at home were also clergymen, educators, officials and politicians. Prominent tobacco lords, for instance, had brothers, cousins, nephews and other kinsmen keen to obtain colonial appointments. The big Glasgow firms which dominated the tobacco business were therefore, *inter alia*, a source of labour market intelligence for needy but qualified kinsmen in Scotland. When information on potential openings became available, news could be quickly conveyed in ships returning to the Clyde by the scores of resident factors whose stores were to be found along every other navigable creek along the Chesapeake.[2]

This was one reason among many for the remarkable migration of middle-class and professional Scots to the colonies in the eighteenth century. As seen in Chapter 5, mass Scottish movement across the

Atlantic came relatively late and only reached substantial proportions from the later 1760s. Much earlier, however, a growing legion of merchants, clerics, educators, imperial officials and physicians made their careers in America. They conformed on the whole to the classic Scottish pattern. Many were from families of some social standing but modest means. A large number were well educated, including significant groups who had had the benefit of some university instruction. They were migrants from a society which produced too many trained professionals for too few jobs at home. Thus the number of Scottish physicians in the mainland colonies in the eighteenth century approached two hundred. This was at a time when, in one estimate, Scotland was able to retain no more than a third of the physicians it trained.[3] Increasingly, the fairest prospect in all of Scotland was not, as Dr Johnson famously alleged, the road to London, but rather the way to the Clyde ports and the chance there of taking ship for America.[4]

The hard data for assessing this intellectual migration and its effects have now been assembled.[5] Over the century between 1680 and 1780 some 818 college- or university-educated men came to the American colonies from Britain and Europe. About one third of this total (211) had been educated at three Scottish universities, Glasgow, Edinburgh and Aberdeen. There were several intriguing features to this figure, in addition to the disproportionate Scottish presence. First, most of these university men (about 75 per cent) went to the Chesapeake colonies of Virginia and Maryland and only a minority to New England. New England was well supplied with educational institutions of quality, including Harvard and Yale, Dartmouth and the College of Rhode Island (now Brown). The Chesapeake, however, was attractive to Scots not only because of the tobacco connection but because, despite the best efforts of the College of William and Mary, demand for higher education significantly exceeded supply. At one point in the seventeenth century, for example, the Virginia legislature was forced to offer ships' captains a bounty of £25 on the delivery of a live minister of religion to the colony. The geographical skew of 'learned' Scottish migration meant that the Scottish intellectual influence was mainly confined to the middle colonies and had less effect on New England. Between 1680 and 1780 some 443 college- or university-educated men settled in the Chesapeake, recruited from institutions in Scotland, England, Ireland and Europe.

Nearly 40 per cent were Scottish-trained, by far the largest group. Oxford and Cambridge together sent 153.

Second, although many of these 'academic' migrants were involved in imperial service, medicine, education and trade, the vast majority were clergymen. They made up four out of five of those who came out with some form of university training. Curiously, Presbyterians were in the minority, numbering about a third of the total. Most clergymen were Scottish Episcopalians. Presbyterian ministers had opportunities in the church at home. Scottish Episcopalianism, however, had lost out to Presbyterianism in the Revolution of 1688–9 and the successive defeats of Jacobitism culminating in the catastrophe of 1746. To some extent, the colonies became a haven of refuge for Scottish Episcopalian clergy who had suffered humiliation and removal from parishes after 1688 and been denied advancement thereafter.[6]

Third, this intellectual migration was not only a movement from east to west. Several hundred Americans attended European universities in the course of the eighteenth century. Most were Catholics, forbidden to maintain institutions in their homeland and who therefore travelled for education at the English Catholic colleges scattered across the Continent. But of the remaining non-Catholic Americans, an estimated 44 per cent (191) studied at the Scottish universities of Glasgow, Edinburgh, Aberdeen and St Andrews. The majority were from the Chesapeake. Some were of Scottish ancestry but many were not. They were drawn by the increasing fame of the Scottish institutions in the Age of Enlightenment. Precious few, for instance, came across the Atlantic before c. 1750. Medical education of high quality was also a magnet. Perhaps as many as two-thirds subsequently became physicians and surgeons in the colonies. The Scottish universities had built a world-wide reputation in the medical field for instruction linked to rigorous scientific study, which moved instruction away from the traditional apprenticeship approach, at a fraction of the fees charged by some European institutions.[7] The network of Scottish connections in the Chesapeake must also have facilitated and encouraged American interest in Scottish higher education.

The numbers which have been analysed are the statistical outline of a deep and enduring intellectual relationship between colonial America and Scotland. This was much broader than the exchange of university-trained men, although the signal importance of that process cannot be underestimated, as will be seen below. Modern research has also uncovered a veritable cornucopia of Scottish intellectual interest in American geography, nature, Indian civilization, religion, and much else besides.[8] Again, as the crisis between mother country and colonies intensified before 1776 so American political news became a dominant theme in the Scottish newspapers, magazines and periodical literature. Long extracts from the colonial press were standard items in the public prints.[9] Intellectual coteries on both sides of the Atlantic were in regular contact, not only through correspondence but also by exchanging books.[10] It was through these channels that distinguished Americans visited Scotland as guests of the Enlightenment élite. Benjamin Franklin came twice, in 1759 and 1771. On his first visit he was honoured with the freedom of the city of Edinburgh and was entertained by figures like Smith, Hume, Ferguson, Kaimes, Black and Robertson. Scotland made a deep impression on Franklin. As he said on his return to America:

On the whole, I must say, I think the Time we spent there, was Six Weeks of the *densest* Happiness I have met with in any Part of my Life. And the agreeable and instructive Society we found there in such Plenty, has left so pleasing an Impression on my Memory, that did not strong Connections draw me elsewhere, I believe Scotland would be the Country, I should chuse to spend the Remainder of my Days in.[11]

It was not simply educators who added to the sum of intellectual exchange. During the eighteenth century around thirty Scottish-born governors and lieutenant-governors served in the American colonies.[12] A few had intellectual interests in their own right. One of the most renowned was Cadwallader Colden, Edinburgh University graduate and trained physician, who was Lieutenant-Governor of New York from 1760 to 1775. He ventured into physics, even trying to explain the causes of gravity. But he was also something of a polymath with works such as A History of the Five Indian Nations (1727–44) among his lengthy list of publications.[13] Not quite as intellectually distinguished was Gabriel Johnstone, Governor of North Carolina, who had studied medicine and oriental languages at St Andrews. Nevertheless, Johnstone was an enthusiastic champion of the foundation of schools in the colony. It was also common for significant imperial figures such as these to act as patrons of minor officials, military men and physicians from Scotland. In some cases, this could have an intellectual impact. The best-known example comes from the governorship of New York and New Jersey of Robert Hunter, a native of Ayrshire, in the 1710s. He gathered around him a talented group of Scottish university men with wide interests spanning law, science and imperial administration.[14] Similarly, Scottish physicians often had a broad perspective by dint of their education within a university setting where pure science as well as medical practice were combined. Scholars have identified significant groups of these doctor-scientists, with interests in natural history, politics and natural philosophy as well as medicine, who crossed the Atlantic.[15]

However, it was religion more than any other single factor which forged and formed this international intellectual connection. This was partly because, as already noted, the overwhelming majority of university-educated Scots who migrated to the colonies were clergymen. But it was also a consequence of their status in contemporary society. The clergy were the key cultural figures of the age with wide influence not only in the spiritual world but on values and ideas as well. They expounded on many issues, both sacred and profane, and often also served as schoolmasters and university teachers. In the eighteenth century religion pervaded most areas of life. Scottish clerics, like the renowned John Witherspoon of Paisley, Charles Nisbet, James Blair and many others, spoke and published on topics as varied as imperial politics, government abuses, emigration and education.[16] Over time a distinct community of interest emerged between Scottish and American Presbyterians. This was not necessarily because there were large numbers of Scots ministers preaching from colonial pulpits. As noted above, the Episcopalian clergy far outnumbered their Scottish Presbyterian rivals. Rather, the close connection came about because of a growing dialogue and network of correspondence which developed from the 1740s between the Evangelical wing of the Church of Scotland and their brethren in American Presbyterianism.[17] One foundation of this new rapprochement was migration. Seceders from the Kirk in 1733 and 1744 organized churches in small towns in New Hampshire and Pennsylvania. Scots sects, such as the Glassites, came to Connecticut. By 1730 missionary action in the colonies was also in place. The grandiosely titled 'Society in Scotland for the Propagation of Christian

Knowledge in the Highlands and Islands and the Foreign Parts of the World' was established in 1709. By the 1730s one of the organization's prime concerns was the spiritual welfare of the American Indians. Missionaries were despatched to the frontier who, according to the *Scots Magazine*, had considerable success in spreading knowledge of the Christian gospel 'in those dark corners of the world'.[18] Their most celebrated coup was the conversion of Samson Occom, a Mohegan Indian, who not only became a preacher himself but came to Britain and addressed the General Assembly of the Church of Scotland.[19]

A catalytic force in all of this was the evangelical revivals of the 1740s. They appeared to have been international both in incidence and effect. The 'Great Awakening' in the colonies which had such a huge impact on American Presbyterianism was paralleled by the 'Cambuslang Wark' in Scotland.[20] The coincidence in time of the two 'Awakenings', separated by thousands of miles of ocean, was explained by the fact that God had intervened directly in human affairs. Almost immediately, there was a publication boom on each side of the Atlantic. Scots showed fascinated interest in the 'Great Awakening' while colonial Presbyterians were intrigued by the news of the religious enthusiasm in Scotland. Jonathan Edwards's *Distinguishing Marks of a Work of the Spirit of God* was originally published in Boston in 1741 and then republished, a year later, in Scotland. James Robe's *A Short Narrative of the Extraordinary Work at Cambuslang* came out in America in 1742.

These events did much to establish new loyalties between evangelical groups in both countries. Correspondence quickened, Scots raised funds for their co-religionaries, books were exchanged and publishing and republishing of works for both home and colonial audiences became more common. The Ulster Scots communities were also brought more into association with their sister churches. Indeed, as the grip of the Moderates on the Church of Scotland tightened, the Evangelicals, or the 'Popular Party' in Scottish Presbyterianism, came to see America as the citadel of 'true religion' where it could be freely practised without state interference or the machinations of corrupt lay patrons.[21] This growing belief was to have significant implications for Scottish church attitudes to the American Revolution.

2

Above the entrance to the Medical School of the University of Pennsylvania is carved the Scottish thistle. It is a tribute in stone to the seminal influence of Scotland on the Philadelphia Medical School and of the entire development of Scottish academic medicine on North America. In New Jersey, at Princeton, known in the eighteenth century as the College of New Jersey, there is a similar commemoration of the Scottish impact. In the place of honour on the right-hand nave of the magnificent chapel stands the flag of St Andrew alongside the armorial bearings of the University of Glasgow with the motto *Via, Veritas, Vita*, 'The Way, the Truth and the Life'. Thus the modern university honours and remembers its Scottish antecedents.

With evidence like this it is easy to be seduced into the trap of what has been called 'the Burns Supper school of Scottish-American historians', which uncritically celebrated in a spirit of chauvinistic triumphalism the great deeds of the Scots who were held to be responsible for all that was best in American development, from constitutional government to rugged individualism, and from technological genius to the successful promotion of Protestant values in the young nation.[22] For Woodrow Wilson, as for so many other writers, American history 'is a line colored with Scottish blood'.[23] In the early twentieth century the genre was very much alive and well. Classic studies included G. F. Black's *Scotland's Mark on America* (1921) and Wallace Notestein's somewhat more sophisticated *The Scot in History* (1946). Later, however, the Scottish contribution was marginalized and even forgotten. Books continued to appear but made little general impact. Thus in 1999 one authority could conclude: 'American historians ... have remained largely unaware of the Scottish dimension to the origins of their national identity and culture ... for most Americans today Scotland means, if anything, Brigadoon and golf, rather than the thinkers of the Scottish Enlightenment.'[24]

A worthy desire to respond to this ignorance has been one reason for the remarkable resurgence of the chauvinistic writing of the past decade or so. Thus we have Duncan Bruce's *The Mark of the Scots. Their Astonishing Contributions to History, Science, Democracy, Literature and the Arts* (1996), and *The Scottish Enlightenment*

(2002) by Arthur Herman, subtitled in the British edition 'The Scots' Invention of the Modern World'. Even the hagiographers of earlier decades were not prepared to go quite as far as this. Such works fructify and feed the collective ego of a small nation which, while taking on challenging responsibilities in the post-devolution era, is still somewhat lacking in confidence.[25] As one Scottish scholar put it some years ago, 'most of us still seem to be driven by an unconscious conviction that if we could once and for all demonstrate the scale and importance of Scottish contributions to other nations, we would redeem our country from the historical stigmas of size, poverty and its undignified status as a province to an English metropolis'.[26]

Of course, it ill befits any historian to feel superior about all this. Ethnic or national histories are all vulnerable to accusations of exceptionalism and chauvinism. In order at least to reduce these dangers, contexts, comparisons and the critical use of evidence are all vital. Even then, a full escape from the dangers is difficult. To a large extent much professional historical research on American–Scottish interactions is still devoted to the accumulation of detailed evidence of the interconnections. It is as if 'he who finds the greatest number of Scottish bricks in the fabric of the American building will be the most successful historian'.[27]

Equally, however, to dilute the impact of Scottish intellectuals and academic traditions during the colonial era would be myopic in the extreme. Of course, it was not all one way. American religiosity had a deep influence on evangelical thinking in the west of Scotland.[28] Contemplation of massive American expansionism also had a profound effect on the philosophical thinking of some of the great figures of the Scottish Enlightenment, including Hume, Smith and Robertson.[29] Furthermore, the rancorous debate on the American War itself fanned the flames of popular radicalism in Scotland which culminated in the short-lived attempts at burghal and parliamentary reform in the 1780s and 1790s.[30]

But the lines of influence from east to west across the Atlantic were even more potent. The movement of university-trained Scottish professionals to the American colonies meant that the Scottish model of higher education often became the template there for college development. Even before the union of 1707 this process had started. James Blair, an Episcopalian clergyman, graduate of Marischal College, Aberdeen and former student at Edinburgh University, was the representative of the Bishop of London in Virginia from 1685 and a powerful figure in the politics of the colony. He became a leading promoter, and then long-time president, of William and Mary College in Williamsburg from 1693. From the start, despite being an Anglican foundation, it was the Scottish system of lectures, examinations and compulsory education in moral philosophy rather than the Oxbridge tutorial tradition which dominated teaching in the new college. Even more importantly, the Blair regime laid the foundations of an enduring connection between the Aberdeen colleges and William and Mary.

Of greater fame and influence was that of John Witherspoon at the College of New Jersey.[31] It had gone through five presidents since its foundation and badly needed an academic leader who could bring both stability and vision. The College's trustees believed Witherspoon was the man for the job. A Scottish cleric of orthodox evangelical views he also had wide respect from different factions in American Presbyterianism still suffering the effects of the split between the 'New Side' and 'Old Side' supporters. Despite being a successful parish minister in Paisley, Witherspoon was tempted by the American offer when it came to him in 1766. Like so many other Scottish evangelicals he had become disenchanted with the Kirk under the hegemony of Moderatism. He and several of his associates in the west of Scotland now regarded America as the hope for the future where the 'Great Awakening' had inspired a new religious intensity uncontaminated by secular authority. The colonies, it seemed, rather than Scotland might be the new cradle of a covenanted chosen people. That Witherspoon became an enthusiastic convert to this view is confirmed by his public advocacy of emigration to the New World in the 1770s.

Once in place as President of the New Jersey College, Witherspoon set to work with almost messianic energy. In addition to his administrative role, he served as orator of the College, taught philosophy, Hebrew, history and French and also became headmaster of the College-sponsored grammar school where he carried out a root-and-branch reform of the curriculum. The model for the university curriculum was Glasgow, his *alma mater*. The emphasis was on the development of critical thought, tolerance of different views (even such Moderate Witherspoonian opponents as Robertson, Ferguson and the unorthodox David Hume were on the reading lists), free enquiry and a broad-based education which would attract lay people as well as those destined for the ministry.[32] This ensured that the College's student body would replicate that of the Scottish universities. At Oxford and Cambridge the majority of students went there in preparation for holy orders. At Glasgow, Edinburgh and Aberdeen colleges the student mix was broader, both in terms of social class and later careers.[33] Like its Scottish sisters the College of New Jersey drew students from across the colonies and not simply from the neighbouring districts. Even the occasional black and Native American attended classes. One result was that the College became 'a seminary of statesmen' during Witherspoon's presidency:

Of the young men who studied under [Witherspoon] James Madison became President of the United States, one became Vice-President, ten became cabinet members, six were elected to the Continental Congress, twenty-one entered the United States Senate and thirty-nine the House of Representatives, twelve became governors of states, three were appointed to the United States Supreme Court, six attended the Federal Constitutional Convention.[34]

A key factor in this success story was Witherspoon's public support for the American cause and his signature on the Declaration of Independence – the only clergyman to sign. This assured his personal standing and that of his College after 1783. In this way Scottish educational principles continued to influence the infant Republic despite the vigorous resistance of so many Scots to its conception.

In a sense, William Smith was to the College of Philadelphia (later the University of Pennsylvania) what Witherspoon was to the institution which became Princeton. Born near Aberdeen in 1727, Smith was an Episcopalian who attended the city's colleges and migrated to the colonies in 1757. Three years later he was appointed to teach logic, rhetoric, ethic and natural philosophy at Benjamin Franklin's new College of Philadelphia. He soon rose to become provost of the institution.[35] His reformed curriculum at Philadelphia, which involved a decisive departure from the traditional structure of classical learning and formal philosophy, embraced the science of chemistry, natural history and astronomy. This was a seminal development in liberal education which thereafter had both an arts and a science base in the advanced curriculum.[36]

There were three other reasons why Scottish university education made an important impact on the middle colonies. In the first place, the returning flow of American scholars trained in Scotland, and especially in medicine, had a formative influence on the development of colonial institutions along Scottish lines. While in Scotland, a young American student at Edinburgh named Benjamin Rush acted as one of the intermediaries who persuaded John Witherspoon to accept the post in New Jersey.[37] On his own return home in 1765 he and his associates urged the trustees of the College of Philadelphia to establish the first medical school in North America. When it opened in 1765 it was modelled in large part on Rush's *alma mater*, the University of Edinburgh. Until the end of the eighteenth century virtually all the professors were also Edinburgh-trained. Again, like Edinburgh, Philadelphia established a hospital to help link academic teaching to practical medicine. More crucially, Philadelphia in turn became a model for other foundations such as medical schools in New York (1767) and Boston (1782).[38] Second, Scottish science found favour because it did not carry the stigma of atheism frequently associated with French materialism. Instead, in the Scottish tradition science and religion were usually reconciled, not least because the Enlightenment in Scotland was not anti-clerical or anti-establishment and was built upon a close intellectual association between leading clergy like Francis Hutcheson, William Robertson and Adam Ferguson and their lay confrères. This was a key advantage because in the new American colleges churchmen were often dominant in governing bodies: 'the close alliance between the Church of Scotland and men of culture . . . gave to Scottish thought an added element of religious respectability'.[39]

Third, and above all else, the Scottish Enlightenment became the dynamic engine for the transoceanic transmission of ideas. Here again, however, we enter a minefield. The issue bristles with questions. There is the problem of identifying what is 'enlightened' from what is 'Scottish'. Some argue that 'enlightened' ideas were a common international currency in the eighteenth century across Europe, Britain and America. Hence the hunt for 'origins' can be deemed not simply thankless but pointless.[40] Then there was the extraordinary scholarly uproar in the United States in the late 1970s after the publication of Garry Wills's 'historical bombshell', *Inventing America*.[41] Wills had dared to claim that the primary influences on Thomas Jefferson's draft of the Declaration of Independence were the Scottish philosophers Hutcheson, Kames and Reid, rather than the Englishman, John Locke. Right-wing thinkers were not the only transatlantic intellectuals to be dismayed by Wills's contentious thesis that Lockean individualism should take second place to the Scottish literati's emphasis on communal responsibilities and the virtues of social cohesion. The irony was that Wills's own arguments were not original. A number of American intellectual historians had already drawn attention to the significance of the Scottish school long before him. Wills merely made the point much more forcefully and with greater eloquence and forensic skill, and so triggered a furious scholarly battle.[42] Finally, the perennial difficulty of 'Scottish hype' once again assumes its ugly face. As a distinguished historian of empire has noted, the Scots certainly punched above their weight; but they were also superb propagandists. The Scots were both 'literate and noisy. We know a lot about them because they were usually at great pains to tell us.'[43] Nowhere is this prudent warning more relevant than in the assessment of the purported relationship between the Scottish Enlightenment, the American Revolution and the foundation of the United States.

In order to make some sense of this matter we must begin with a brief examination of the Scottish Enlightenment itself and then proceed to look at its impact on the colonies with special reference to the intellectual roots of American Independence.

3

It was in 1900 that William Robert Scott first introduced the term 'Scottish Enlightenment' to describe the period between the 1730s and 1790s when Scotland became one of the intellectual powerhouses of Europe. At one level there was little surprising in this. Throughout the continent great surges of creative and critical enquiry were taking place at the same time. Different countries had different names for the same phenomenon. It was *Lumièries* in France, *Ilustración* in Spain and *Illuminismo* in Italy.[44] In many parts of Europe thinkers were congratulating themselves for living in an era lit by reason. Each country had different intellectual traditions but they all shared the twin characteristics of Enlightenment.[45] The first was the congratulatory sense of emerging from the darkness of a past constrained by the slavery of passive acceptance of authority, precedent and tradition. The men and women of Enlightened Europe saw great virtue in thinking for themselves. The second essential element was tolerance, the belief that intellectual discourse could take place with a degree of freedom and mutual respect between scholars and the governors of those societies where they were citizens.

The Scottish Enlightenment was, however, something more than a simple territorial manifestation of a general European process. What happened in Scotland in the eighteenth century had distinctive features. One aspect was the depth and range of the creative dynamic which spanned philosophy, poetry, chemistry, architecture, painting, technology, geology, economics, sociology, history and painting. A second characteristic was the sheer quality of these endeavours. New intellectual disciplines were put together. Adam Smith is recognized as the father of economics, Adam Ferguson and John Millar as the seminal influences on what became sociology, and James Hutton can be seen as a master figure in geology. David Hume was hailed as the greatest philosopher of the age writing in the English language. Even thinkers of world distinction like Voltaire believed that Scotland was now the leader in progressive thought in this era.[46] Another, and fundamentally significant factor, was the intimate relationship between Scotland as a particular society and its men of genius. It is true that for centuries intellectual connections between Europe, England and Scotland were continuous and important. Indeed, it was this very exposure to high culture elsewhere over long periods of time which was a critical factor in the Scottish Enlightenment. The thinking of Locke, Newton, Leibniz, Grotius, Pufendorf and the legal and medical training available at Leiden, Utrecht, Paris and Bourges were essential elements in the intellectual brew of the Scottish Enlightenment.[47] But the indigenous strains in the cultural process were also central. We now know that the achievements of the eighteenth century did not come like a bolt from the blue. They depended on context. That in turn was formed by the virtuosi of the later seventeenth century, the medieval universities at Glasgow, Aberdeen, St Andrews, the later foundation of Edinburgh, and a vibrant tradition which stretched back to the Renaissance and the learned élites of pre-Reformation Scotland.[48]

But the Scottish Enlightenment was also bound up with the country's contemporary identity. As the leading authority on the subject has noted:

It is in any case plain that Scots who think about politics, economics, social structures, education, law or religion are bound to have in mind the politics, economics, society, education, law or religious life of Scotland, and these national considerations are bound to influence what they write. It is not simply that Scottish models are the ones that the Scottish thinkers naturally light upon as a starting point for their reflections. The point is that Scottish thinkers write as Scots, that is, as people who have lived in, worked with, and in substantial measure been formed by, these same institutions. Hence, in so far as there is something distinctively Scottish about the institutions on which the thinkers reflect (and demonstrably there is), there will also be something distinctively Scottish about those reflections upon the concepts embodied in the institutions, and upon the values that the institutions were created to serve.[49]

There are a number of reasons why the Enlightenment in Scotland was likely to have a marked impact on the other side of the Atlantic. Some factors are obvious and have already been rehearsed in this chapter. The Scots were at the cutting edge of so much humane enquiry, science and medicine that the colonial intelligentsia simply could not avoid reading their works. Again, unlike the pattern in other European countries such as France, much of the new thinking was delivered by university teachers. There are the famous examples of Smith's *Inquiry into the Nature and Causes of the Wealth of Nations* (1776) and John Millar's *Origins of the Distinction of Ranks* (1771), both of which began life as lecture notes. Perhaps even more influential was Francis Hutcheson during his tenure as Professor of Moral Philosophy at Glasgow from 1729 to his death in 1746. Hutcheson was said to have moulded the thinking of a whole generation of students. His most illustrious pupil was Adam Smith, who described him as 'the never to be forgotten Dr Hutcheson'.[50] His eloquent lectures were delivered in English rather than the traditional Latin. Enlightenment thought was disseminated as part of the Scottish universities' teaching process and so was inevitably exported by university-trained Scots and those returning Americans who were likely to form part of the political and professional élites across the Atlantic.[51] This was rendered even more probable by the Scottish and Ulster Scots' impact on American higher education which has already been examined.

Another key element in the Scottish Enlightenment which ensured widespread appeal in the colonies was its intrinsic religious and political conservatism. Scottish thought for the most part advocated moderation and cautious reform and regarded social revolution as anathema. Only Hutcheson approved of the right of resistance to tyranny, though even he stopped short of supporting such unortho-doxies as government by popular consent. These notions were attrac-tive to the colonial oligarchies who resented imperial interference but had no time for the kind of revolution from below which would threaten their own power. The preference of the Scottish literati for inherited order, the liberties won in 1688, ancient hierarchy and the sacred rights of private property were music to their ears. The Scots intellectuals offered instead a belief in autonomous reason which would enable people to break out of the inertia of old ideas. There was a sense in their writings of basic optimism for a future which could be both materially progressive and grounded in coherent moral values. Unlike the strident anti-Christian tones of French thinkers like Charles-Louis Montesquieu, Voltaire and Denis Diderot, the Scots were comfortable with religious values.[52] After all, the Moder-ate Party in the Kirk had supplied the Enlightenment with many men of distinction. All this was meat and drink to the Christian gentlemen who after 1776 were intent on establishing a new nation in the New World.

Yet specifying the particular relations between the Scottish Enlight-enment and the American Revolution in a rigorous fashion is more difficult, especially since some recent views have gone dramatically over the top in teasing out the possible connections.[53] It is therefore perhaps better to begin by outlining some important qualifications. The most obvious point is also the most significant. This remarkable revolution was the consequence of a complex mix of political, fiscal, ideological, economic and religious forces which a highly sophisti-cated historiography is still refining. To see the 'Scottish variable' as especially catalytic in this dense process of causation is to be judged not only chauvinistic but naive. Equally, however, as will be argued below, to ignore the Scottish philosophical dimension is to omit an important factor in the intellectual landscape of the revolution. That map was constructed by several other thinkers in addition to the Scottish literati. They included the English dissenting ideas of Locke and Milton, Sidney and Harrington, the products of the English Revolution of the seventeenth century, which not only impacted on America, but also influenced the seminal analyses of Francis Hutcheson in Glasgow and those of other Scottish intellectuals.[54] Even more antique elements were part of the intellectual discourse in the America of Jefferson, Hamilton and Madison. They included the Reformation and even the Italian Renaissance.[55] We also need to remember the uneven effect of the Scottish Enlightenment. Due attention must, and will, be given to the moral philosophers. But Scottish science, outside the medical schools, was less significant. A magisterial study, *Science in the British Colonies of America* (1970), shows the rich tapestry of scientific ideas both from Europe and within the colonies which shaped the American discourse. Scottish personalities, such as the redoubtable Cadwallader Colden, are certainly there, but are by no means hegemonic.[56] There is the final and further problem that, whatever the intellectual influence of Scottish thought on the Revolution, the Scots in America were overwhelmingly loyal to the crown and thus reviled for their unyielding attachment to the mother country as 'a lawless and unprincipled faction'.[57]

Having given some disclaimers, the practical linkages which did exist can be considered. The impact of Francis Hutcheson's philosophy on the revolutionary generation is now widely acknowledged.[58] His thinking was the product of Scottish covenanting tradition, Locke's theories, and the circle of Dublin critics of British misgovernment in Ireland in the 1720s which included such luminaries as Jonathan Swift and Robert Molesworth.[59] He argued that all government exists for the good of the governed. A posthumous summary of his political views shows his belief in the right of colonies to resist unjust governance:

If the plan of the mother country is changed by force, or degenerate by degrees from a safe, mild and gentle limited power, to a severe and absolute one or if under the same plan of polity, oppressive laws are made with respect to the colonies or provinces; and any colony is so increased in numbers and strength that they are sufficient by themselves: for all the good ends of a political union: they are not bound to continue in their subjection . . . There is something unnatural in supposing a large society . . . remaining subject to the direction of and government of a distant body of men . . . it is not easy to imagine there can be any foundation for it in justice or equity.[60]

Hutcheson's philosophy became an educational staple in the new colleges of the middle colonies. Francis Alison, an Ulster Scot who attended his lectures in Glasgow, became a leading teacher at Benjamin Franklin's College of Philadelphia for a quarter of a century after 1752. His surviving lecture notes show his significance as a conduit for Hutcheson's views. Alison put a blunter Ulster gloss on them: 'The end of all civil power is the public happiness and any power not conducive to this is unjust and the People who gave it may justly abolish it.'[61] Alison taught such key leaders of the revolution in the middle colonies as Thomas McKean, Charles Thomson and George Read. He also preached to the Continental Congress during its revolutionary deliberations. Alison was not alone in spreading knowledge of Hutcheson's thought. In the order of study at Philadelphia, works by Hutcheson featured in two successive years. At the College of New Jersey, under Witherspoon, his philosophy was also required reading. Witherspoon trained such famous American patriots as James Madison, Hugh Henry Brackenridge and Philip Freneau. Hutcheson was also included in the curriculum at King's College in New York (later Columbia University) and at William and Mary College in Virginia, where Thomas Jefferson was probably introduced to his works by William Small, the Aberdeen alumnus who had such a powerful educational influence on him.[62]

Generations of young Americans 'were trained to think in Hutchesonian categories' and his ringing phrase about the need for 'the consent of the people' anticipated a famous passage in the Declaration of Independence itself.[63] Hutcheson's *Short Introduction to Moral Philosophy* (1742) or *Compend* was also widely circulated and was to be found on the shelves of both college and private libraries.

If any citizens, with permission of the government, and at their own expense find new habitations, they may justly constitute themselves into an independent state in unity with their mother country. If any are sent off at the publick charge as a colony to make settlements subject to the state, for augmenting its commerce and power, such persons should hold all of the rights of other subjects; and whatever grants are made to them should be faithfully observed. If the mother country attempts anything oppressive toward a colony, and the colony be able to subsist as a sovereign state by itself; or if the mother country lose its liberty, or have its plan of polity miserably changed to the worse; the colony is not bound to remain subject any longer; 'tis enough that it remains a friendly state.[64]

Intellectual historians will argue for a very long time about the precise effect of these ideas. Any suggestion that their influence was fundamental must depend on inference rather than positive proof. At the very least, however, Hutchesonian thought had become a vital part of American political theory and vocabulary by the eve of the Revolution.[65] But Hutcheson was not alone. As long ago as 1947, Herbert W. Schneider declared 'the Scottish Enlightenment was probably the most potent single tradition in the American Enlightenment'.[66] For Garry Wills in *Inventing America*, Thomas Reid's 'common philosophy' was the origin of the 'self-evident truths' in the Declaration of Independence. David Hume, alongside Hobbes and Blackstone, is now seen as a seminal influence on the political ideology of Alexander Hamilton.[67] James Madison was another follower of Hume. The vigorous debate over the new American constitution and the balance to be struck between a loose confederation and a strong central authority was triggered by the draft proposals composed by Madison and James Wilson. The latter was a Philadelphia lawyer, graduate of St Andrews and the only native-born Scot, apart from Witherspoon, to sign the Declaration of Independence. When the draft constitution was approved by the Convention it was sent to the states for ratification. Madison's contributions to the discussions, notably through his published *Federalist Papers*, were seminal, and the evidence shows plainly that much of his argument rests on Hume's moral philosophy. Indeed, Madison had the same world view as the great men of the Scottish Enlightenment. For him, like them, the best government was delivered by an élite of the virtuous and wise managing power for the greater good of all.[68]

4

Given the intellectual debt owed Scotland by the American revolutionaries it does seem odd that the Scots came to be so reviled by the colonial patriots as a nation of unreconstructed loyalists and the treacherous allies of the imperial state. The Ulster Scots, on the other hand, escaped opprobrium. Indeed, they were so warmly regarded as key political and military supporters of the revolutionary cause that their contribution quickly became exaggerated and mythologized. It is said that the skill they had acquired with firearms in the savage Indian wars of the frontier made them the backbone of George Washington's Continental Army. Another belief has it that the Ulster Scots with their 'long-standing hatred of the English' were driven *en masse* 'into the arms of the Sons of Liberty and the rebel cause'.[69]

Modern research has uncovered a more complex and less romantic picture.[70] The Ulster Scots, like many other Americans, were divided in their loyalties. In Pennsylvania they overwhelmingly supported the Revolution. That was crucial, because Pennsylvania was the key link in the north–south axis of the colonies with Philadelphia the home to the two continental Congresses and first capital of the United States. There were also strong blocs of patriot support among the Ulster Scots in New Jersey and Delaware. Even where they strongly championed independence, however, their fiercely intolerant religious beliefs meant that the more liberal and humanitarian ideals of the revolutionary movement left them cold. In North and South Carolina they were much less sympathetic, except in the back-country borderland between the two colonies. Parts of these territories even contained pools of Ulster Scots loyalism. What can be said, nonetheless, is that their enthusiasm for the Revolution ran much deeper and wider than that of the Scots, who were generally regarded as the hated enemies of the cause of independence. Indeed, in some areas, the War of Independence could easily be depicted as a vicious fratricidal dispute within the Scottish ethnic family. The battle of King's Mountain, which is located between North and South Carolina, fits this image well. Around 3,000 Ulster Scots from the upper Tennessee Valley mustered to confront a battalion of loyalist militia led by Major Patrick Ferguson from Scotland. It was to be the bloody climax of a guerrilla war of murder and assassination in which loyalist Scots were well to the fore. The confrontation ended in carnage. The triumphant rebels ran amok and butchered a quarter of the loyalists as they offered to surrender: 'Many were doubtless loyal Scots, falling to the blades and bullets of disloyal Scots.'[71] A further nine prisoners, followers of the hated Ferguson, were summarily executed – such was the ferocity of internecine conflict in the back-country.[72]

The dislike for the Scots was also voiced across the colonies in less murderous fashion. In some areas it endured as long as the War of Independence itself. Thus a statute of the Assembly of Georgia of

August 1782 banned Scots from settling or trading in the colony unless they were declared patriots. The reason was simple. They were acknowledged to be the enemies of the Revolution: 'the People of Scotland have in General Manifested a decided inimicality to the Civil Liberties of America and have contributed Principally to promote and Continue a Ruinous War, for the Purpose of Subjugating this and another Confederated State'.[73] The flight of innumerable Scottish loyalists from Upper New York and the Cape Fear territory in the Carolinas during the latter stages of the war for refuge in places as far apart as Canada and the Caribbean told a similar story. They feared retribution for themselves and their families in the aftermath of an American victory.[74] After all, Thomas Jefferson's first draft of the Declaration of Independence contained his notorious reference to 'Scotch and other foreign mercenaries who were being sent by the British government to invade and destroy us'.[75] John Witherspoon secured the deletion of this insult to his fellow countrymen. But the implication in the statement of the Scots as an alien and hostile race is puzzling, coming as it did from a distinguished American educated by Scots and well aware of the intricate and close associations between them and his own country. 'A free exportation to Scotchmen and Tories' became a favourite revolutionary toast.[76] Even the master works of the Scottish Enlightenment did not escape censure. The Library Society of Charleston proposed in 1778 that Adam Ferguson's book *Essay on Civil Society* (1766), written by one 'of the Kingdom of Scotland', should be condemned and burnt.[77] It was an extraordinary outcome. As already seen, Scottish moral philosophy had supplied a whole range of powerful arguments for resistance to British authority. Indeed, some would go so far as to suggest that the American Revolution, in the intellectual sphere at least, was a child of the Scottish Enlightenment. But that debt did not prevent wholesale repudiation of the Scottish connection and denunciation of all its works.

The loyalist sympathies of most colonial Scots partly helps to explain these xenophobic reactions. The fact that John Witherspoon from Paisley was one of the most eloquent speakers favouring American resistance to imperial authority or that John Paul Jones from Kircudbright became America's first naval war hero hardly weighed much in the overall balance. The leading historian of colonial loyalism notes that more loyalists were born in Scotland than in any other country outside America.[78] In Virginia the Scots were the backbone of loyalism and were also significant in the Carolinas, Maryland and parts of New York. A fascinating analysis of loyalist claims on the British government after the war shows that Scottish claimants accounted for nearly 37 per cent of all those made by persons born outside America.[79] This was a much higher proportion than the Scottish share of the colonial population. In a few areas the Scots were divided. In Georgia, for instance, some Highlanders supported the Revolution. In the Carolinas most, but not all, were loyalist.[80] But many Scots also engaged in proactive loyalism. Their role in the notorious loyalist militias of the back-countries of North Carolina and New York is well documented. Others joined the North Carolina Highlanders or the Queen's Own Loyal Virginians and died in battle defending King and Country against the rebels.

At home, the 'Popular Party' within the Church of Scotland often sympathized with the right of their fellow American evangelicals to resist the unjust exactions of the state.[81] Several Scottish intellectuals, like David Hume, opposed the war; others, such as Adam Ferguson and William Robertson, after showing earlier sympathy with the American cause, supported the British government.[82] In the early stages of the dispute this loyalism was less in evidence. There were many Scottish critics of the American policies of Lord North's cabinet, not least because they disturbed the stability of Scotland's lucrative trade with the colonies.[83] However, when hostilities broke out attitudes quickly hardened. In the winter of 1775–6 the Scottish counties and burghs sent more than seventy loyal addresses to London demanding the use of armed force against the recalcitrant colonials. This was as many as those sent in from England, which had a population more than five times the size of Scotland's.[84] This hard line was strengthened further when news filtered through of the confiscation of the assets of Scottish tobacco firms in the Chesapeake and, above all, when the Americans allied with France in 1778. Now the struggle was not simply the result of a colonial rebellion but an imperial war fought against Britain's mortal enemy. Only when defeat followed defeat did the bellicose mood change. Attacks on the ministry and incompetent generals now became more frequent in the Scottish press. As peace approached a kind of apathy set in. By then the country seemed resigned to the loss of the American empire.[85]

Yet the Scots could at least take heart from the fact that they had fully demonstrated their fidelity to Britain at a time of imperial crisis. Their position as partners in empire was now assured. All doubts that England may have had about Scottish loyalties in the wake of the '45 rebellion had been well and truly laid to rest.

Scottish loyalism rested on a number of foundations. The American Revolution jeopardized the remarkable success of Scottish transatlantic trade and emigration. The structure of Atlantic commerce rested on the Navigation Laws which ensured that American commodities should first be shipped to British ports. An independent America could deal directly with Europe. Imperial law also secured the whole superstructure of credit and debt on which commerce depended. On the face of it, therefore, freedom for the Americans threatened a catastrophe for the Scottish economy.

In addition, many Scots factors and merchants had come to the colonies as sojourners to make money and establish their careers. They never intended to settle permanently and remained more Scottish than American. These temporary residents had an obvious vested interest in British victory. They were often unpopular, condemned as 'clannish' because of the networks of ethnicity, kinship and business which supported their commercial activities. In the 1770s many Scottish merchant houses were owed large sums by colonial debtors, especially in Virginia and Maryland. It did not help that the great economic crisis of 1772–3 had forced them to call these in. The Scots factors were therefore easily stereotyped as a collective conspiracy of unyielding and grasping creditors.[86] Scottish imperial officials could be placed in the same sinister category. Scots filled a remarkable number of governorships in the colonies. All attracted a considerable number of their fellow countrymen to fill more junior positions in local courts and in the regulation of trade and customs. This was especially so in the southern colonies of Georgia, Virginia, South Carolina and North Carolina. It was easy for the patriot tendency to label these functionaries as imperial lackeys. Certainly, men like Henry McCulloch, James Glen, Alexander Spotswood and James Abercromby were uncompromising administrators who were determined to strengthen imperial authority. It has been argued that several of them worked for the good of the empire in general rather than the mother country in particular. This may have been the case but it did little to gain these officials the sympathy of dissident colonials.[87] Scots settlers were more committed to life in the New World but they too were loyalist for the most part. In this respect they might fit the patterns outlined in general studies of American loyalism. Immigrants were more likely to be loyalist than the native-born and the more recent the immigrant, the greater the chances of loyalty. Mass Scottish emigration to America came relatively late. Those who came in larger numbers between the end of the Seven Years War in 1763 and the beginning of the American War in 1775 were perhaps still likely to feel closer emotional ties with the home country rather than with their adopted land.

A case in point was the well-known response of the Highland emigrants in North Carolina and New York. Their loyalism is bewildering for some. After all, they were popularly associated with Jacobite opposition to the House of Hanover. Why, therefore, in the words of a distinguished historian of loyalism, 'did they fight for their erstwhile enemy?'[88] The question is partly based on a false premise. Highland society was divided during the '45. Some clans fought for Bonnie Prince Charlie, others for the Hanoverians, and most were neutral.[89] The Jacobite connection in the colonies attracted interest because the legendary Flora MacDonald, heroic companion of the transvestite 'Prince in the Heather', and her husband, Allan, were prominent loyalists. Allan became second-in-command of the loyalist militia raised by his cousin, Brigadier Donald MacDonald, which consisted of emigrant Gaels from the Cape Fear region of North Carolina. The Highlanders met a force of rebels at Moore's Creek in February 1776 and were defeated with heavy loss. But Highland loyalism is not so puzzling. The Gaels were very recent emigrants, led by clan gentry to whom they owed traditional loyalty. They had benefited from generous and substantial land grants from the imperial government. Some had served at officer level in the British army between 1756 and 1763. The opportunities now flowing from emigration depended on political stability and strong government. Revolution not only threatened all this but was instinctively hateful to an old gentry class imbued with strong hereditary feelings of social hierarchy.[90]

Yet the public loyalism of so many Scots was not in itself sufficient to account for the rampant Scottophobia which manifested itself in America in the early 1770s. Anti-Scots feeling became a marked strain in colonial popular culture. It could be seen in such popular stage successes as Robert Munford's *The Patriot*, with starring roles for Scottish mercantile stereotypes like McSqueeze, McFlint and McGripe. Another example would be the mock dedication of John Leacock's *The Fall of British Tyranny* (1776) to 'Lord Kidnapper, and the rest of the Pirates and Buccaneers, and the innumerable and never-ending clan of Macs and Donalds upon Donalds in America'.[91] These popular manifestations of prejudice suggest that in some quarters Scots were perceived as natural supporters of tyranny, a charge apparently confirmed by their support for the exiled Stuarts in 1745, a dynasty which was bent on imposing absolute monarchy and popery on Britain and its colonies. The plot was then orchestrated, so it was believed, under the guidance of the Earl of Bute, the first Scottish Prime Minister, and (more importantly) a man with the family name of Stuart, the royal house associated by Whigs with tyranny and popery. Even when he left office, Bute and his Scottish accomplices were apparently still seen as the real powers behind the throne. The principal authors of the injustices done to the American colonies since the Stamp Act were laid at their door. Apart from Bute's guiding hand, the other suspects were the King's mother, widely believed to be Bute's mistress, and another Scot, Lord Mansfield, Lord Chief Justice of the King's Bench. These beliefs, however bizarre, were given added power by the venomous anti-Scottish rhetoric of John Wilkes, whose views were widely reported in the colonial press. The American Benjamin Rush, who had studied medicine at Edinburgh, met Wilkes in 1769: 'He spoke with as much virulence as ever against Scotland, for . . . all the Scotch members of Parliament in both Houses, are against America.'[92] Xenophobia was only one part of the rich tapestry of Scottish and American connections in the colonial era. It was not by any means the most important. Nevertheless, such racial antagonisms should be remembered, not only as evidence of the angry passions of the revolutionary years but as a bracing antidote to the new vogue of uncritical celebratory writing on the Scottish–American relationship.

9

Scotch Canada

In few of the many areas that the Scots settled across the globe has their story produced more interest, sentimentalization, myth-making and controversy than in Canada. In part, this is explained by the scale of Scottish emigration there. Up to the early 1840s, British North America (which became the Dominion of Canada in 1867) attracted most Scots, with particularly well-established communities in Ontario and the maritime provinces. Canada was also the most favoured choice of Scottish emigrants in the years immediately before the Great War. Partly as a result, a veritable publishing industry grew up in late Victorian times, loudly celebrating the deeds of the Scots and their seminal contributions to Canadian life in all its forms. W. J. Rattray's four-volume work, *The Scot in British North America* (1880–84), John M. Gibbon's *Scots in Canada* (1911) and W. W. Campbell's *The Scotsmen in Canada* (1911) were only the best known of an unending series of books which catalogued Scottish success stories in every conceivable field. Compared with this publication flood, studies of the Scots in Australia, New Zealand and the USA were, at that time, notable by their relative absence.

Typically, the hagiographies which crowd these works construct the same self-myth of the Scot as hardworking, able, thrifty, sober and reliable:

Many biographies of prominent Scots-Canadians seem to share the same stereotypical introductory chapter in which the hero is born in poor circumstances, has the essential Scottish values dinned into him, acquires a modicum of education and a hefty dose of religion, usually of the Presbyterian variety, emigrates (preferably in strained and uncomfortable circumstances), obtains a humble position on the shop floor, usually through the patronage of a fellow Scot, works his way up to the presidency of the company and then launches into a career as one of Canada's luminaries in politics or whatever else.[1]

Running through the genre into the twentieth century is also an overweening ethnic pride which can often verge on naked racism. Even a scholarly volume such as *The Scottish Tradition in Canada* (1976), which contains a wealth of useful information, can assert that 'the history of Canada is to a certain extent the history of the Scots in Canada'.[2] The volume then proceeds to regale the reader with over 300 pages of largely uncritical text about the great Scots who made Canada what it is today.

Undeniably the Scots did make an immense contribution to the Canadian economy, education, religious life, politics and cultural development over the last two centuries or more. The problem is, however, that the story has been so mythologized and exaggerated that it becomes remarkably difficult to separate realities from ethnic conceit. The absence of comparative studies with other ethnicities, such as the Irish, French and English, also makes it very difficult to evaluate the distinctive Scottish role. There are other competing narratives alongside that of the Great Scot which further complicate the problem. Even in the nineteenth century the Scottish self-publicists did not always have it their own way. In some quarters, rampant Scottophobia flourished. W. J. Rattray notes in the course of his four-volume paean of praise to the Canadian Scot that they also provoked virulent criticism for their perceived thrift and clannishness. This tradition reached its low point with T. W. H. Crosland's *The Unspeakable Scot* (1902) which concluded that 'the Scotch are in point of fact quite the dullest race of white men in the world and that they "knock along" simply by virtue of Scottish superstition, coupled with plod, thrift, a gravid manner and the ordinary endowments of mediocrity'.[3] Some modern critics have also seen through the Scotch mist towards a more bitterly jaundiced perspective. The Scottish hero, Mackay, in Wayland Drew's novel *The Wabeno Feast* (1973) is made to utter a memorable judgement on his fellow countrymen: 'We have skewered this country like a fat ham.' Around the same period, an enraged reviewer of Marjorie W. Campbell's *Northwest to the Sea*, a celebratory biography of William

McGillivray, one of the Scottish 'heroes' of the North West Company's exploits in the fur trade, had this to say:

What follows is another astonishing exercise in Canadian double-think, another failed attempt to manufacture a Canadian hero out of a greedy, selfish, small-minded, unimaginative, disagreeable Scots clerk ... Tough, intrepid, phooey. The fur traders who rose to become robber barons were distinguished primarily by their ability to rob the Indians, cheat their competitors, and shaft their friends. A more reprehensible lot would be hard to find in any nation's iconography. [McGillivray] ... owed his success to nepotism, the North West Company owed its success primarily to rum.[4]

Another tradition flourishes in direct conflict with this image of the grasping, greedy and relentlessly ambitious Scot. This is the stereotype of the immigrant as victim. Probably this particular permutation of the Scottish myth has had an even more potent and enduring influence both in the homeland and the emigrant territories than the self-aggrandizing narratives of the Victorian era. It is rooted in three popular assumptions. First, the notion persists that Scottish emigration to Canada was exclusively Highland in origin. This was probably the case down to 1815, but thereafter – and especially after c. 1850 – migration from the Lowlands became much more significant. In this tradition, however, the story of Lowland business élites, artisans, farmers and agricultural labourers is marginalized to the point of being largely forgotten.

The Highland exodus itself is portrayed in terms of tragedy, pathos and involuntary exile. The Scots were forced to emigrate because of the notorious Highland Clearances. They are depicted as the victims of landlord greed and of economic forces outside their own control. In this narrative, any voluntary quest for self-improvement is rarely mentioned. The emotions are those of nostalgia, loss and yearning for the old country. It is no coincidence then that one of the most influential and popular poems associated with Scottish migration to British North America is the famous 'Canadian Boat Song':

> From the lone sheiling of the misty island
> Mountains divide us, and the waste of seas,
> Yet still the blood is strong, the heart is Highland
> And we in dreams behold the Hebrides.

Also to be noted is the powerful impact of the invention of Highland tradition within Scotland which was later exported and embroidered within the expatriate Highland communities. It was mainly in the first half of the nineteenth century that 'Highlandism' became an integral but manufactured part of Scottish identity. Tartan, bagpipes, kilts and the bens and glens of the Highland landscape became the instantly recognizable symbols of Scottishness in the Victorian period. In essence, Scotland, through an extraordinary alchemy, became a 'Highland' country. Clan associations and Highland games, which soon proliferated in many parts of Canada, then helped to embed this link between Highlandism, Scottishness and heritage deep within the consciousness of the descendants of the emigrants and the wider community. Today, not surprisingly, less than a third of those taking part in such Scottish pastimes as piping or Highland dancing have Scottish surnames.

Consideration of the period 1763–1815 in this chapter does serve to confirm, deny, refine and help interpret some of the mythology of 'Scotch Canada'. To a much greater extent than in later times, emigration from Scotland before 1815 was dominated by Highlanders who, especially from the 1770s, established strong enclaves of Gaelic culture in Upper Canada, Prince Edward Island, Nova Scotia and Cape Breton. But, although in a minority, the Lowland Scots of some means and education were already making their mark. The merchants and fur traders (by no means all from Lowland backgrounds), who will be discussed later, were prominent and successful. But of almost equal significance were those involved in medicine, law, the ministry and journalism. These professions gave them an advantage in achieving access to positions of political authority. The Scots were significantly over-represented among elected politicians and holders of official appointments in Upper Canada between 1791 and 1841. The pattern became even more apparent in the higher rungs of the ladder of preferment.[5]

This conclusion is intriguing given that until the Reform Act of 1832 only a small element of the élite in Scotland itself was included in parliamentary politics. Before 1832, even middle-class emigrants would have been excluded from political authority in the country of their birth. Despite this, the most notable leaders of the early reform movements in almost every colony were Scots: William Carson in Newfoundland, James Glennie in New Brunswick, Thomas

McCulloch in Nova Scotia, Robert Gourlay in Upper Canada and Angus Macaulay in Prince Edward Island.[6] They had other advantages which more than made up for their lack of formal political experience in Scotland. All five men were highly educated and had attended Scottish universities. Glennie, indeed, had won mathematics prizes while at St Andrews. This was a cut above the educational background of most other ethnic groups in Canada at the time.

The early over-representation of Scots in the ranks of the politically powerful partly also reflected their loyalism during the American War of Independence. Loyalty to the crown had often been achieved at great personal sacrifice between 1775 and 1783 in the embattled thirteen colonies. Many thousands of Scots paid for their loyalism by losing both land and position in an independent USA, and were forced to flee as refugees across the border to Canada. At least this steadfastness earned them the gratitude of the imperial government and ensured that many Scots of education and standing quickly rose to prominence in both local government and public office. Through these positions of influence they were also able to introduce Scottish institutions to the fabric of early colonial society. Most often this meant foundations in both the religious sphere and in education. Scots established some of the first major schools, academies and colleges in Canada. It was a tradition which lived on:

Nearly half of the institutions of higher learning created in British North America/Canada before World War I had Scots – often clergymen – intimately involved in their foundation. Scottish moral philosophy, usually in its empirically oriented 'Common Sense' variety, had been one of the pillars of the Scottish Enlightenment. It would certainly be perpetuated in nineteenth-century Canadian institutions of higher learning. The curricula of the leading Canadian universities of the century – Dalhousie, McGill, Queen's and Toronto – were all built around moral philosophy.[7]

Yet in some important respects the historical experience of the years 1760 to 1815 is also in conflict with the assumptions about 'Scotch Canada' which were popular at the end of the nineteenth century. One of these was that Scottish success reflected the overwhelming importance of the Protestant ethic. By 1914, most emigrant Scots were indeed Lowland Presbyterians. But in the early period a major Roman Catholic dimension must be acknowledged as well as that of Protestant dissent, such as the Baptists and Congregationalists. Indeed, Catholics were probably the largest single Scottish denomination in British North America during the eighteenth century. The vast majority of emigrants were from the loyal enclaves of Catholicism in western Inverness-shire and the Outer Hebrides which had survived the Reformation. Until 1793 Catholics in Scotland had languished under civil disabilities and political constraints for even longer. But this seems not to have been the case in Canada. For Highland Catholics, then, emigration promised not simply better economic opportunities but also political and social liberation. They became loyal supporters of the Tories, with Alexander Macdonnell, the Roman Catholic Bishop of Upper Canada, emerging as one of the party's most formidable leaders. The Catholic hierarchy in Upper Canada, Prince Edward Island and Nova Scotia were also active in the creation of denomination colleges, academies and seminaries. Out of this enthusiastic support eventually emerged the first-ever Scottish Catholic foundation of higher education in Canada, St Francis Xavier University, established in 1853.

Again, nineteenth-century propagandists liked to give the impression of a monolithic Scottish-Canadian community held together by a shared sense of Scottish values. There was, of course, much evidence of mutuality in business, in the promotion of schooling and in the tight personal and kin networks of the Gaelic settlements to justify the common criticism of Scottish clannishness and nepotism. In Upper Canada, for instance, in the early nineteenth century, the ruling political grouping was labelled 'the clan' or 'the Scotch faction'. But in other respects there was precious little sign of ethnic solidarity. Religious divisions and territorial allegiances in the Old World were often carried over to the New. Catholic Highlanders, who mainly supported Toryism, confronted Protestant Lowlanders, many of whom were committed to a more reforming agenda, across the political divide. The famous North West Company, which for a time not only seriously threatened the hegemony of the mighty Hudson's Bay Company (HBC) in the fur trade, but nearly drove it to the brink of ruin, was itself almost torn apart by savage vendettas between members of its governing Highland families. The bitter war between the HBC and the Nor'Westers was a ferocious struggle between different groups of Scots: the Orcadian servants of the Bay and the Gaels who led the North West Company. Ethnic loyalties in the wild frontier of British North America were easily fractured by the naked greed which fuelled the savage battle for trading supremacy.

2

Even after the emigrations of Scottish Highlanders and loyalists from the former thirteen colonies reached significant levels after 1783, British North America was regarded by the metropolis more as an exclusive field for trade rather than settlement. The Hudson's Bay Company had shown the way. Since its foundation in 1669, it had conclusively demonstrated through its network of posts west of the Great Lakes the value of concentrating on trade and profit rather than territory. Indeed, the two great staples of this colonial economy, the fish of Newfoundland and the furs of the far west, demanded the absence of people rather than the presence of settlers. In the plantation economies to the south ever growing armies of labour were essential to grow, harvest and process the sugar, tobacco, rice and indigo exports. In the northern territories, however, people were regarded as anathema, a real threat to the wildlife which sustained the booming commerce of the area. And in the final analysis this view was strongly supported by the imperial state. It had its own reasons for opposing another empire of colonization on the American mainland after the humiliation of the disasters of 1775 to 1783.

Vast stretches of land to the north and west, far from the semi-populated areas along the St Lawrence River and the fringes of the lower Great Lakes, were virtually empty and, for the most part, still an unexplored wilderness in 1763. At that date, too, the number of inhabitants even in the settled parts was minuscule compared with the immensity of half a continent. In 1763 the population of all the territories amounted to under 100,000 British and French subjects, with a further 200,000 Indians and Inuits spread across the land mass of what is present-day Canada. As late as 1815, colonists of French birth or descent, the *Canadiens*, constituted the majority of all the settlers and the territory where they concentrated, Quebec (Lower Canada after 1791), the main European centre of British North America.

Long before Canada became synonymous with Scottish emigration, therefore, it was seen above all else as an area of opportunity for trade and profit. Mercantile interests, rather than statesmen and armies, were in the vanguard of imperial expansion. And from the Scottish commercial perspective, Canada had several attractions. The country was open to direct trade in a way that India was not. There, the statutory monopoly ensured that all goods were channelled through London via the East India Company. In contrast, Canada offered a level playing-field. Its annexation in 1763 had also come at a convenient time. Scotland was experiencing the early stages of economic expansion which in time would become a fully-fledged Industrial Revolution. The search was on for ever more market outlets for the massive increase in volume output of linen, iron goods, woollens and a host of other consumer commodities. As a letter to the *Glasgow Journal* noted in 1760, three years before the war was finally won against the French,

of all our acquisitions the conquest of Quebec, and consequently of the country of Canada, is the most important and most beneficial to this Kingdom . . . and also such a source of trade and commerce opened to us here, as will be fully significant, had we no other, to employ all our trading and commercial people; *and find a vent or constant consumption for all our goods, products and manufactures* [my italics].[8]

The editor of the same paper was positively euphoric at the prospects. To him Canada was much, much more than 'a few acres of snow':

An exclusive fishery! A boundless territory! The fur trade engrossed and innumerable tribes of savages contributing to the consumption of our staple!

These are sources of exhaustless wealth. Ignorant and despairing men have called this a quarrel for a few dirty lands or acres of snow, but the British public will soon have feeling (*sic*) proofs that Great Britain must sink or swim by her colonies.[9]

If anything, Canada became even more attractive a decade later. As relations between the old colonies and the mother country deteriorated into armed conflict, merchants in a number of Scottish ports began a feverish search for alternative trades and markets. Thus during the last twenty years of the eighteenth century a veritable frenzy of Scottish mercantile activity was concentrated in the Canadian centres of Montreal, St John and Halifax. The Scots took advantage of the shorter sailing time to Canada from the Clyde than from the Thames and the relative indifference of the larger London firms to a trade that was still in its infancy.[10] Greenock and Glasgow merchants were already well established in this commerce in the late 1760s after the conquest of the French. Both the Hudson's Bay Company and the North West Company had already made fortunes in the fur trade. Overwhelmingly, both were staffed by Scots. This undoubtedly spread knowledge of Canada across the nation's business classes. Others also saw the profit potential of the increasing emigrant trade to British North America after 1783. In the same period Scottish exiles from the former American colonies, such as James McGill and John Dunlop, helped to make Montreal something of a Scottish business enclave as they established control over the export trades in grain, potash and timber to Europe.[11]

But this commercial invasion represented an extension rather than the start of Scottish connections with British North America before 1815. It was primarily in the great staple trade of fur that the Scots had made an early mark, first by infiltrating and eventually dominating the London-based Hudson's Bay Company and then in their leadership of the North West Company. The Governor and Company of Adventurers of England Trading into Hudson's Bay (to give the HBC its full title) was established to wrest some of the lucrative fur trade from the intrepid French *coureurs de bois* who had controlled it for much of the seventeenth century. Although the trade itself dates back to the earliest days of the discovery of Canada, it only became especially profitable from the 1650s. The discovery by European hatmakers of the value of beaver skin for the manufacture of felt hats set off a consumer boom which lasted for generations. So valued did beaver become that it was literally turned into money. 'Made-beaver' rather than cash became the standard unit of currency in the trade for over a century and a half:

'Made beaver' (M–B), a prime quality of skin from an adult beaver or its equivalent in other furs or goods, was the fixed unit of barter. At the fur-gathering end of the commerce, all goods were quoted in terms of their beaver equivalents, so that two other skins, eight pair of moose hooves or ten pound of goose feathers each equalled one made-beaver. A moose hide or the fur of a black bear would fetch the equivalent of two made-beavers.[12]

While fur was the enduring core of the business, other items such as buffalo wool and tongues, walrus tusks, bear grease, whale oil, sealskins, dried, smoked and balled salmon and eiderdown from ducks were also exported. Virtually all the commodities had one thing in common: they depended on the systematic slaughter of countless animals. No one can tell how many beavers became fashionable hats. What is certain, however, is that there were plenty of them to fall prey to Indian and European hunters. One modern estimate suggests that *c.* 1670 there were at least 10 million beavers within the boundaries of present-day Canada.[13] But it was not simply skins which could make a man's fortune. Also much in demand was castoreum, an alkaloid substance contained within the scent glands around the anal region of the animals. Europeans craved castoreum because of its supposed magical properties for treating headaches, fever, madness and other ailments. One late-seventeenth-century enthusiast, the medicinar Joanne Franco, thought the value of the substance was boundless, a virtual panacea for pleurisy, infestation of fleas, stomach ache, hiccups and sleeplessness. He had also learnt that 'in order to acquire a prodigious memory and never to forget what one had once read, it was only necessary to wear a hat of the beaver's skin, to rub the head and spine every month with that animal's oil, and to take, twice a year, the weight of a gold crown-piece of castoreum'.[14]

By the eighteenth century the Hudson's Bay Company had established a commanding presence in the Canadian fur trade. It became more like 'an independent beaver republic' than a business firm trading across 3 million square miles of territory, with an eventual domain which encompassed over a twelfth of the earth's surface – ten times the circumference of the Holy Roman Empire at its height. One of its historians recalls the visit of the HBC's overseas Governor, the Scot Sir George Simpson, to Norway in 1838 when he was toasted as the head of the most extended dominion in the world, 'the Emperor of Russia, the Queen of England and the President of the United States excepted'.[15] So enormous was its power that the HBC became the main obstacle to any significant westward movement of population from the St Lawrence core until the sale of its territories in 1870 to the new confederated nation of Canada. The HBC even shaped Canadian identity, endowing the country with the stamp of 'nordicity':

The shape of the indigenous Canadian imagination took root in the experiences of the fur trade, both for the French period and after the Conquest.

Voyageurs, rapids, the outlying frontier, courageous exploration of rivers, long portages, relations with distant Indian tribes, these and other features of the fur trade are echoed today in the Canadian self-image. The vivid response in Canadian public opinion to such issues as pipelines and northern development bears the stamp of this legacy of 'nordicity' . . . The fur trade, in short, more than virtually any other single experience, is the primary matrix out of which modern Canada emerged.[16]

The reasons for this remarkable success story are many. By deciding to settle the deserted shores of Hudson Bay, the Company's officers were able to deliver goods and seek out beaver pelts in the very heart of the fur-rich environment of the new continent. This route from Europe also bypassed the St Lawrence River system which was controlled by the French until 1763 and had access to an extraordinary natural transportation system. The numerous rivers flowing into the Bay (forty-three of which in Canada's entire territory drain into it) and the great lakes of Athabasca, Superior and Winnipeg, Huron, Great Bear and Great Slave, make for a superb, naturally formed waterway. Apart from the nine-mile Grand Portage, west of Lake Superior, and the twelve-mile Methy Portage into the basin of the Mackenzie River, the upper half of the continent east of the Rockies can be traversed by canoe:

Nature could hardly have planned to meet the Company's corporate objectives more effectively: here was a huge subcontinent for the taking with a ready-made, free transportation system; frigid enough that its animals grew thick pelts; fertile enough to sprout an immense boreal forest that provided those animals with shelter; rugged enough to keep out permanent settlers.[17]

But given the internecine rivalries and competition in the fur trade, the HBC's success crucially depended also on the quality of its human capital, the directors and the servants who represented the Company in the far wastes of Canada. The HBC was managed from London because the city was the undisputed prime market for fur products and the manufacture of hats in Britain. The Company was, however, plagued by the acute problem of staffing its isolated trading posts in a subarctic region half-way across the world. Curiously, for such a colossal enterprise, the staffing needs of the HBC were surprisingly small. As late as 1811 it had only 320 employees manning its seventy-six Canadian posts. But reliability, steadiness and loyalty were vital.

Many of the ordinary early recruits had come from the slums of London and the Company's managers were soon vociferous in their complaints of their outrageous levels of promiscuity with Indian women and inordinate indulgence in alcohol. They therefore anxiously sought men 'not debauched with the voluptuousness of the city'.[18] The search brought them north, to Scotland. Scots were being appointed as factors from the first decade of the existence of the HBC and they were also active in the fur trade outside the Company's ambit from an equally early date. Soon, however, the Orkney Islands became the principal recruiting ground for most of the eighteenth century. The Company's vessels sailing northwards from the Thames put in annually at the tiny town of Stromness to take on fresh water and supplies before embarking on the great circle route to Canada. From the later seventeenth century, Orkney lads from the neighbourhood were recruited as Company servants so that by 1800 the HBC had become almost an Orcadian dominion. In 1799, of the 530 on the overseas payroll no less than 78 per cent were from Orkney.[19] It was a marriage of convenience. For the Orcadians, even the wilderness of North America promised a better return than scratching a living from subsistence farming and fishing in the Northern Isles. Temporary migration was nothing new to them. For centuries their ancestors had gone south to the Scottish mainland and east to Europe in search of work. Many also had worked in the icy waters of the Greenland fisheries before the days of the HBC. For the Company, Orkney was a fruitful source of more loyal and dependable servants than it was accustomed to – servants who also, in the Scottish tradition, had a basic education and experience of labouring on both sea and land. One writer summed up the attractions of the Orkneymen thus:

The characteristics that made the island lads so sought after as HBC labourers were their natural frugality, adaptability and inbred obedience to authority which made them docile without being servile. If not particularly imaginative or enterprising, they were possessed of a strong sense of self-sufficiency. Authenticity mattered to them more than originality, and they felt instinctively mistrustful of self-aggrandizement or virtuosity ... The islanders' linguistic ability and a parish school system that encouraged Orcadians to master the rudiments of reading, writing and arithmetic produced recruits with skills particularly suited to the dogged ledgerkeeping of the fur trade. The austere and highly structured life at the little log outposts on Hudson Bay required their inhabitants to practise a system of working relationships based on the mutually acceptable interplay of discipline and deference between Company officers and servants. Unlike the independent-minded Highlanders or the orphaned exiles from London (where tension between social classes was beginning to foster egalitarian demands), the Orcadians did not feel uncomfortable 'knowing their place' – providing, of course, that the bounds of obligation and service were well respected and annual salaries were credited on time . . . Another quality highly appreciated by early bayside governors was the Orcadian affinity for the sea. Patient fisherfolk, splendid boatmen and wise sailors, they knew how to read the wind, estimate a tide or ride out a storm. Latter-day Vikings, they manned the sloops that connected the HBC's early posts and headed north to hunt for whales and Eskimo customers.[20]

The Orcadians' habit of uncomplaining servitude and their own life experience of arduous climatic and economic conditions at home prepared them well for the challenges of Hudson Bay. But in addition to guaranteed food and a regular income which could be hoarded away as a nest egg, there were other compensations in the frozen north. There had to be. The seasons were short and only two in number – a long, harsh winter and a brief spring. Men could be entombed in their rooms for weeks on end at the very edge of a vast and unknown world. The only recognized cure for cabin fever was alcohol and plenty of it. The Company despaired at the extraordinary levels of liquor consumption among its servants, which threatened to devastate its trade. Stern prohibitions flowed continuously from London and a network of informers was recruited to catch habitual offenders, but all to no avail. By the middle of the eighteenth century, the whole Canadian fur trade was not only lubricated by alcoholic liquor but could not have been conducted without it. Over many decades the Indians who supplied the furs had gradually become addicted to strong drink, consciously and systematically fed to them by Europeans in return for pelts. Soon trade was impossible without copious supplies of brandy and rum. The HBC eventually introduced its own cheap mixture called 'English Brandy', consisting of London gin with iodine added to duplicate the colouring of real brandy. Home-brewing was also routine in most trading posts by 1800. The recipe for one of the most lethal and popular concoctions, spruce beer, was quite literally explosive, as gunpowder was used to speed up the ageing process. Even more widely consumed was 'bumbo', the classic cocktail of the fur trade, a potent mix of rum, water, sugar and nutmeg.

In other ways too the Orcadians behaved with a truculent independence which belied the image of servility and dependable loyalty. The HBC always decreed until the early nineteenth century that sexual liaisons between its staff and Indian women should never take place because they might prove a threat to the security of the frontier forts. No edict, however, was more widely ignored. Prostitution was as rife around the Bay as venereal disease. But taking 'country wives' was even more common. The men would marry Indian women in an informal ceremony à la façon du pays. For leaders of the tribes it was an ideal arrangement. In their kin-based society it was a means of extending family allegiances and networks into the world of the white man with the possible promise of more favours in trade and goods. The original Orcadians, especially the Swampies, had long married into the Cree tribes who lived around the Bay. Half-breed daughters of these early unions across cultures then became wives of the next generation of servants. A limited slave trade in Indian women also took place. They were normally captives of war who were then sold on by western tribes to the Cree or Assimboin around the Bay where they were bartered to the white men for bear meat, clothing, trinkets or drink. Sterile women were in most demand because they would not burden either the Company or their mates with unwanted children.

The odds were firmly stacked against these Indian women. Regarded by their own people as expendable commodities in the expansion of trade, many were simply abandoned when the Orcadians, their period of service ended, left for home and 'turned off', as the term had it, their 'country wives'. But the relationships were often more complex than this. The HBC itself formally recognized the commercial value of sex. Sir George Simpson, its Governor, affirmed this explicitly in 1821:

Connubial alliances are the best security we can have of the good will of the natives. I have therefore recommended the Gentlemen to form connections with the principal Families immediately on their arrival, which is no difficult matter, as the offer of their Wives and Daughters is the first token of their friendship and hospitality.[21]

Simpson's analysis was that the women, far from being a threat, were vital to the Company's interest. They could provide the HBC servants with 'cheap scalp insurance', a deep knowledge of the wilderness, and entry into Indian society, which helped to promote trade as well as give sexual pleasure in the long subarctic months. Such unions were more enduring than sometimes believed. Especially after the Earl of Selkirk's Red River settlement was founded in what is now Manitoba, Company servants often retired in the New World. Fur-trading dynasties were founded, with sons and grandsons of mixed parentage following each other in the trade. It was an important factor in the Company's *esprit de corps*. Such intermarriage went up to the highest levels of the Company. Alexander Christie, twice Governor of Assiniboine, established a famous extended clan and took his 'country wife' to settle in Edinburgh. It was acknowledged that the progeny of such marriages made the best traders because they possessed an enviable understanding of Indian speech, lore and customs. Ironically, however, for almost the whole of the eighteenth century the archives of the HBC are silent on the critical role of sex in the ongoing expansion of its business.

Only recently has the position of these native women, who are voiceless in historical terms, been exposed to serious scrutiny:

Generally, the women agreed to being offered to the white men and should they be refused, they could become very indignant at this insult . . . the norm for sexual relationships in fur trade society was not casual, promiscuous encounters but the development of marital unions which gave rise to distinct family units . . . The marriage of a fur trader and an Indian woman was not just a 'private' affair; the bond thus created helped to advance trade relations with a new tribe, placing the Indian wife in the role of cultural liaison between the traders and her kin. In Indian societies, the division of labour was such that the women had an essential economic role to play. This role, although somewhat modified, was carried over into the fur trade where the work of native women constituted an important contribution to the functioning of the trade.[22]

This considered analysis also begs the question of the whole relationship between the Scots incomers and the native peoples. They, with the Orcadians, and later the Gaels of the North West Company, were the labourers of the great fur trade. Yet the Indian responses remain under-researched. As one author has put it, 'they are the

ghosts of Canadian history'.[23] Their story is undeniably different
from that of the extermination of the Andean Incas or the subjugation
of the Plains Indians. Yet their traditional way of life was also
irrevocably destroyed by the arrival of the white man. It was not
simply a matter of seducing the tribes by pressing alcohol addiction
on them in order to push up profits in the fur business. The whole
economic, religious and ideological weight of British and European
civilization made for unprecedented change.

That there was routine abuse and systematic exploitation on a
massive scale cannot be doubted. Disease imported from beyond
the seas was also devastating to peoples who had no resistance
whatsoever. Yet some Scots behaved differently.[24] Robert Dickson
from Dumfries, husband of To-to-Win, sister of a Sioux chief, saw
merit in an aboriginal republic stretching from Lake Superior to the
Pacific. An Orcadian, William Thomson, the HBC Chief Factor on
the Saskatchewan for nearly two decades, gained the gratitude of the
local tribes for his courage in caring for Indians in the terrible smallpox
epidemic in 1781–2. Some of the most famous Scottish explorers, such
as Alexander Mackenzie, who was the first European to discover an
overland route to the Pacific Ocean, and John Rae from Orkney,
who survived four epic journeys to the Arctic, both recorded that
without the assistance and support of the native peoples their journeys would have ended in catastrophe. But Mackenzie, in particular,
was not blind to the broader picture. Perhaps as a Gael he was
especially sensitive to the inevitable death of traditional societies
when gripped by external economic and ideological forces. For him,
even the good deeds of a few could not conceal the broader calamities
which were inexorably destroying native culture. He described the
criminal behaviour of some fur traders which had poisoned relations
with the tribes; already much of the land of the Great Lakes was
already hunted out; greed had also driven the white men to seduce
the Indians into alcohol addiction to secure their custom and the
promise of beaver skins. Mackenzie also believed that even Christian
missionaries had had a disastrous effect on native culture. The great
trading companies, led by the HBC, bore most of the guilt.

As for the Orkneymen themselves, opinion was divided in the long
term. They earned praise from some Company officers for their
seafaring and canoe skills, their fidelity and steadfastness in adversity.
To others they were 'sordidly avaricious' though 'a close, prudent,

quiet people' who were also 'strictly faithful to their employers'.[25]
They were also condemned as dour, stubborn, unimaginative and
unadventurous and the source of a profound structural weakness
which brought the HBC almost to ruin when confronted by the
ruthless competition of the North West Company in the later eighteenth century. It is true that only a handful of Orcadians made it up
the company ladder from the lowly ranks of labourers, apprentices,
tradesmen and clerks to the more elevated status of Chief Traders
and Chief Factors. Even fewer came to be numbered among the great
names of the HBC's legendary élite, most of whom grew up in
Scotland: Sir George Simpson, known as 'the Emperor of the Plains';
Sir James Douglas and Donald Smith, who ruled the Company in
Victorian times; the explorers Robert Campbell and John McLean,
who unlocked and mapped the Yukon and the Ungaya respectively;
John Stuart from Strathspey, who first traversed the distant wilderness of what is now northern British Columbia; and James Leith, a
native of Aberdeenshire, who left half his fortune to spread the
Protestant faith among the Indian tribes. By the early nineteenth
century, the hegemonic days of the Orcadians had passed away. The
HBC diversified its recruitment policy, now searching out likely
servants from Lewis in the Hebrides, Shetland and the Scottish
mainland. It had been forced away from its favourite source in order
to compete against a new and formidable adversary, the North
West Company, which also happened to be dominated by Scottish
interests.

3

The North West Company (NWC) was never a 'company' in the
modern sense. Its first partnership was formed in 1783 in Montreal
but it always remained a loose confederation of small individual
firms each consisting of a few promoters, merchants and fur trader
explorers. Unlike the mighty HBC, the Nor'Westers had no charter
or other privileges, only, in the words of the contemporary observer,
David Macpherson, in 1805, 'what they derive from their capital,
credit, and knowledge of the business, their prudent regulations
and judicious liberality to their clerks, and servants of all kinds'.[26]
Macpherson's formal language, however, concealed the colourful

reality of the NWC. Its members were adventurers and gamblers, devoted to free-market capitalism in its most ruthless and purest form. Its expansion in 1787 to include other syndicates came about because of the murder of a Scottish merchant, John Ross, caught up in the bitter rivalries of the fur trade in the north-west. Fearing that Ross's death would lead to bloody reprisals and all-out war, the principals of several firms decided to unite rather than fight.

There were other similarities between the two organizations. From the start the NWC was dominated by Highland Scots, their sons and grandsons. The prime mover was Simon McTavish, who with his nephew William McGillivray controlled the concern from the beginning. The other great names in the Company's history, such as the two famous explorers, Alexander Mackenzie and Simon Fraser, were from the same background. They looked to Scotland to recruit clerks and servants. As one scholar has put it, 'the names of the North West Company partners sound like a roll-call of the clans at Culloden'.[27] Of the 225 men active in the firm, 62 per cent were Scots from Inverness, Banff or Aberdeenshire, normally from military, farming or small landed backgrounds. The ethnic invasion changed the character of Montreal: 'the country is overrun with Scotchmen,' complained one Englishman.[28] The NWC was also notorious for rampant factionalism and bitter personality conflicts. Alexander Mackenzie, after his epic trek to the Pacific, fell out with Simon McTavish and left in 1800 for a rival organization which named itself the New North West Company. The two syndicates were only saved from certain ruin through suicidal competition by McTavish's death in 1804 and a fresh merger with the Mackenzie group orchestrated by William McGillivray.

Despite these rancorous disputes, however, there is no denying the extraordinary commercial success of the Nor'Westers. They became a legend in their own time. For a while they threatened to drive the Hudson's Bay Company completely out of business. By the 1770s the Highlanders had displaced *Canadiens* in the Montreal-based trade. Three decades later they controlled the bulk of the fur trade in the HBC's heartland of the Hudson Bay drainage basin and Simon McTavish boasted that the entire Canadian trade would soon be ruled by himself and his associates. Even contemporary critics, such as Washington Irvine who condemned the swelling and braggart style of those 'Hyperborean Nabobs', accusing them of behaving like latter-day Highland chieftains attended by scores of retainers in the wilderness, could still acknowledge them as 'the lords of the lakes and the forests'.

In a number of other ways the employees of NWC resembled those of the HBC. They also took Indian wives and sold alcohol in large quantities to the natives. Only when a tribe became addicted to rum (or 'Blackfoot Milk' as it was called when diluted with water) could a sound partnership in the regular supply of pelts be expected. But there were also crucial differences. The NWC was a loose consortium emphasizing individual enterprise and adventuring in contrast to the hierarchical command structure of its rivals. Moreover, by common consent the Orcadians of the Hudson's Bay Company were no match for the boldness, daring and utter ruthlessness of the Nor'Westers. They were a fusion of two ethnic groups, the *Canadiens* of French extraction, highly experienced and skilled in wilderness trade, and the Highland Scots with whom they often intermarried. The fabled clannishness of the Highlanders was a crucial support in the wilds of North America where trust, solidarity and the ability to work together in terrible conditions were vital. A modern scholar has described their other advantages:

The second feature of Highland culture that made these Highlanders such successful fur traders was their familiarity with hunting, the bush, rough living, and the social system of the natives which had many parallels with the clan system of the Highlands. The men who succeeded in the fur trade were not simple crofters, of course, but the sons of Highland tacksmen who had entered the British army as officers or had migrated because of the disruptions in the clan system . . . For such men the wilderness of western Canada was nothing new or intimidating. Highlanders were accustomed to difficult physical conditions and were highly adaptable under them. Most of them were surprisingly well educated and multi-lingual; some had been to schools on the Continent. They soon added native languages to their store of skills, introducing some aspect of Gaelic into fur trade patois in the process.[29]

Here again is further proof of the commercial dynamism of the gentleman class of the Highlands in overseas territories. They were no novices in trade, their families having long dealt in the black cattle business and the shipping commerce between the Western Isles, Glasgow, Ireland and the Continent in coarse cloth, hides and skins in exchange for grain and consumer goods. By the 1770s, however, most had left for the New World and their departure signalled what one scholar had called an 'irreplaceable loss of entrepreneurial flair in Gaeldom'.[30] The colourful histories of these descendants of the clan gentry hardly confirm the usual tale of the emigrant Gael as tragic victim.

Two other factors contributed to the NWC success story. First, the Company was wholly committed to territorial expansionism. It pushed further and further into the interior in the belief that for the trade to grow it had to explore. It is no accident, then, that the NWC's staff were associated with some of the greatest epics of Canadian discovery, most notably that of Sir Alexander Mackenzie, who was the first European to reach both the Pacific and Atlantic Oceans by overland routes, and Simon Fraser, who in 1808 first conquered the great river which now bears his name. The second element was less heroic and more sinister. The Nor'Westers simply outmanoeuvred the competition by ensuring that they always had more alcohol supplies to trade with the Indians than any of their rivals. The story is told of one incident in 1785 concerning an independent firm, Gregory, McLeod and Company, which was outside the ambit both of the NWC and the Hudson's Bay Company. They had in the north-west that year only eight canoe-loads of rum (8,000 gallons) and ninety men. In retaliation the NWC despatched twenty-five canoes, 260 experienced men and 60,000 gallons of rum to crush the competition. The Nor'Westers may have left their mark on early Canadian history by their daring exploits and extraordinary journeys. Not the least of their legacies, however, was the debauching of several Indian nations in the rough, lucrative trade in hard liquor. It was indeed ironic that it was members of one dying culture from the Scottish Highlands who undermined another ancient way of life in the wilderness of a distant continent.

As it turned out, the era of the Company's dazzling success was short-lived. The row between McTavish and Mackenzie before 1804 was simply one sign of the fissure-like tendencies of a loose partnership of uncompromising and egocentric individualists. The war with the USA in 1812 caused further problems by interfering with the NWC's main transport route by way of the Great Lakes. Then came the threat of European settlement, anathema to all in the fur trade. Thomas Douglas, Earl of Selkirk, the aristocratic enthusiast for settling parties of displaced Highlanders in British North America, had acquired shares in the Hudson's Bay Company through a second marriage. Selkirk bought further holdings in the ailing giant until in 1810 he and his family had a controlling interest in the HBC empire. The following year his fellow directors granted him a huge tract of land of some 116,000 square miles for the nominal sum of twelve shillings. The territory was five times the size of Scotland and included much of the modern Canadian province of Manitoba as well as large areas of the present-day US states of North Dakota and Minnesota. The deal was that in return Selkirk would furnish the HBC with servants and clerks mainly recruited in the Highlands. He could in addition recruit crofter settlers and have them transported to the Bay in Company ships.[31]

In 1812, the Red River colony was founded at the fork of the Red and Assiniboine Rivers and was immediately perceived as a grave threat to the Nor'Westers. This was the source of their pemmican, a highly nutritious and easily portable food, made from dried buffalo meat, berries and grease, which was the principal diet for all the NWC brigades in the interior. The Governor of the colony prohibited the export of pemmican from the settlement, provoking a predictably aggressive response from the NWC and ushering in a policy of intimidation which led to the notorious massacre of Seven Oaks in June 1816, when over two dozen colonists were killed, stripped and scalped by a band of Métis hunters (of mixed Indian, Scots and French blood) working for the Nor'Westers. The incident triggered a virtual state of war and a long series of legal cases which were only concluded when the two great rivals united in 1821. But this was not so much a merger as confirmation of the final victory of the HBC. The tortoise in the end had won against the hare by exploiting to the full its key advantage of a shorter and less costly supply route through the Bay, by changing its recruitment policies and by adopting some of the bolder tactics of its old adversary. The HBC now had a monopoly of the trade. But the hegemony of the Scots endured for many decades more, as confirmed by Sir George Simpson, Governor of all the Company's territories during its years of greatest prosperity and enthusiastic promoter of the interests of his fellow countrymen.

4

The period covered by this chapter saw the transformation of the northerly region of British North America from a scattering of marginal settlements to the growth of a new British Empire. By 1815, what remained of the American colonies after the emergence of the USA had started to become recognized as the coherent unit which over time developed into the Dominion of Canada.

This process of growth occurred against a background of hostility by the British state to the expansion of new settlement colonies on the American continent. The conquest of New France in 1763 did not excite fresh ambitions for empire. Canada had been annexed primarily to afford more security to the thirteen colonies to the south and also to consolidate British hegemony of the lucrative fishing grounds of the St Lawrence estuary and the Grand Banks. Yet even then, as one commentator has put it, 'it was with but grudging and indifferent recognition that Canada was received within the imperial circle'.[32] The American Revolution provoked further scepticism by comprehensively discrediting imperial policy as likely in the long run to end in disaster for the mother country. Even the Canadian staples of fish and fur were not regarded as essential to British economic interests. Indeed, it was only in the latter stages of the Napoleonic Wars, and especially during and after the conflict with the USA, that British North America began to assume a new economic and political importance in the view of government.

In the final decades of the eighteenth century, however, London tried hard to contain population loss to the colonies, not least from the militarily valuable areas of the Scottish Highlands. The authorities in Prince Edward Island, Cape Breton and Nova Scotia in 1773, 1786 and 1784 respectively were warned in no uncertain terms not to encourage emigration to their territories. The most powerful Scottish political figure of the day, Henry Dundas, was one of the vociferous critics of colonies of settlement, trying in 1786 to impose an outright ban on emigration. The prohibition of emigration in 1775 and the Passenger Vessels Act of 1803 confirmed that government was also capable of pressing its antagonism to the point of practical action. Of course, in this sense, state policy ran in tandem with the vested interests of both the Hudson's Bay Company and the

North West Company. They regarded Canada above all else as a field for trade and the systematic exploitation of its animal populations and natural resources. Importing more people was to be avoided at all costs. Canada had to remain empty if the fur trade were to flourish; settlement and agriculture could only threaten the wild places where the beaver roamed. These great mercantile empires were therefore determined to bar colonization in the vast lands to the north and west of the areas already settled around the lower Great Lakes and the St Lawrence River. Only in 1817 was this strategy partly undermined when Lord Selkirk settled the Red River.

While the obstacles of state opposition and commercial obstruction may have diminished immigration, they could not prevent it altogether. Two factors worked to fuel the growth in new populations. First, defeat in 1783 generated a great influx of refugee loyalists and others to Quebec, Nova Scotia and other areas which remained under British rule. The precise numbers are difficult to define. As one scholar has asked: 'Should a distinction be drawn between a Loyalist and a disbanded soldier? Were blacks and Indians to be included? How late on arrival could a late Loyalist be? What of the many who, either immediately or after some years, would decide that it was preferable to return to the world they had lost than to remain in this new one?'[33]

The uncertainties mean that modern estimates of these migrations vary between 60,000 and 100,000. Even at the lower end, however, these were still substantial numbers. The 15,000 exiles who arrived in Nova Scotia threatened to outnumber the existing population; some 40,000 settled in the Maritimes; 7,000 made their way to Quebec. As Chapter 8 has shown, Scots, and especially Highlanders, were over-represented among the ranks of the loyalists. One estimate suggests that the Scots who left for Canada may have comprised one in five of the loyalist refugees, or around 10,000 of the total.[34] Nova Scotia was a favoured area of resettlement for Highlanders from North Carolina. The Scottish refugees from New York, many of them recently arrived Gaels from Glengarry in western Inverness-shire, tended to make for what would become eastern Ontario. Even during the war, families from the Mohawk Valley in New York had fled to avoid the vengeance of the American patriots. The conflict in that area was essentially a bloody guerrilla war with savage reprisals and counter-reprisals. The Highlanders had established a fearsome reputation for ferocity and as first-rate frontier guerrillas. It was out of the question that they should remain among their former neighbours when peace came. Instead, they and the disbanded soldiers of the King's Royal Regiment of New York and the Royal Highland Emigrant Regiments sought refuge across the border in Canada. The Roman Catholic Macdonnels and their kinfolk formed a new community on the north bank of the St Lawrence River west of Montreal. A migrant wrote to her family back in Scotland that the 'McDonalds . . . hope to found in the new land a new Glengarry'.[35] The name stuck and, over the following decades attracted numerous emigrants from the Highlands.

The second factor boosting the European population of Canada was the resumption of immigration some years after hostilities ceased in 1783. Here Gaelic-speaking Highland Scots were to the fore. Their destinations had now radically altered from those of the years before 1776. Canada and the maritime colonies virtually completely supplanted the now independent USA. Scottish transatlantic emigration after 1783 was very much Highland in origin, though the individualized and almost invisible movement to the USA has left little record and hence has probably been undervalued. An estimated 14,000 emigrants left Scotland for British North America between 1776 and 1815. As many as nine out of ten may have been Gaels. The annual emigration was significantly lower than in the early 1770s, almost certainly due to the immense disruption caused to the traditional migrant routes by war and the subsequent loyalist diaspora. Remarkably, however, the connections with the Canadian areas of settlement were soon renewed: powerful evidence of the dense network of communications which spanned the Atlantic and linked communities in the wilderness areas of the New World with those of their kindred and friends in remote parts of the Highlands.[36]

Each of the new settlements became a strong magnet attracting people from estates, glens and parishes in Gaeldom. Prince Edward Island had small colonies from Uist and Glenfinnan, while Pictou, Nova Scotia, was settled mainly from Ross-shire. In five large emigrations between 1785 and 1793, people from Glengarry, Knoydart, Morar and Glenelg in western Inverness sailed to join their friends in the new Highland settlement of Glengarry County in western Quebec. Over 1,200 made the transatlantic crossing in these years, around 40 per cent of the entire migrant stream from the Highlands as a whole over the period. It was inevitable, therefore, that these concentrated settlements, often located in very isolated situations, would become enduring outposts of Gaelic culture over several generations.

The complex influences in the homeland of commercialization, demography and landlordism which drove on these migrations are not the primary interest of this section. They have been considered at length in Chapter 6. Here, the experience in the areas of settlement is the main focus and, in particular, the mental and emotional world of the emigrants in their new lives. The popular conception is to see these movements in terms of 'emigration as tragedy', an assumption which lies deeply embedded not only in some aspects of the historiography but even more significantly in Scottish culture and its relationship with the past. Highland emigration is depicted essentially as a forced exodus. This is the governing assumption behind the immensely popular books of John Prebble, more especially *Culloden* (1961) and *The Highland Clearances* (1963). It also resonates in the works of such influential painters as Thomas Faed in *The Last of the Clan* and *Oh, Why Left I my Hame?*. Popular song conveys the image of loss and exile particularly effectively. 'The Canadian Boat Song', first published in *Blackwood's Edinburgh Magazine* in 1829 and ostensibly from the Gaelic, has become the single most influential popular commentary on the Highland immigrant experience in Canada despite its entirely bogus origins as the invention of a non-Gael who was not even an emigrant:

> I've looked at the ocean
> Tried hard to imagine
> The way you felt the day you sailed
> From Wester Ross to Nova Scotia
> We should have held you
> We should have told you
> But you know our sense of timing
> We always wait too long.

A sentimental version of Scottish emigration is also flourishing within the current renaissance in folk music in the Maritimes, while in Scotland the Proclaimers vocal group's 'Letter from America' (1987) links the forced Highland diaspora of the past with Lowland de-industrialization in the modern era: the chorus of the song then follows 'Lochaber no more' with a melancholy litany of industrial closures in the 1980s: 'Methil no more', 'Bathgate no more', 'Linwood no more' and 'Irvine no more'.[37]

The complex history of Gaeldom during the era of the Clearances is, of course, replete with the evidence of mass evictions and coerced emigrations. In the decades after *c.* 1820, as the hopes for a new economy built around kelp and fishing disintegrated, landowner policy radically altered to one based on the expulsion of a 'redundant' population. This unrelenting strategy of 'compulsory' emigration reached its tragic human climax during the Great Famine between 1846 and 1856.

The problem is, however, that this later era is conflated in the popular historical consciousness with the earlier period up to 1815 which is examined in this chapter. The experience of the Gael at this time is often in conflict with many aspects of the traditional narrative derived from a later and gloomier set of circumstances. Between 1763 and 1815 several points of difference can be noted to contrast with the disasters after the Napoleonic Wars. For a start, the emigration parties left in the teeth of opposition from both the state and the overwhelming majority of landowners. The emigrations for the most part were also a success. Virgin forest was cleared and even by the end of the 1780s the settlements in Glengarry were already dotted with small log buildings in tiny clearings. The emigrants had achieved what they sought: land, freedom from landlord oppression, and the reconstitution of networks of family and friends and the traditional culture in the New World. The potential catastrophic loss of land and social disruption in Scotland had in fact been avoided through the decision to emigrate. Several of the new Gaelic colonies flourished. By 1832 the population of Glengarry in Ontario had climbed to 8,500 and doubled again to 17,596 twenty years later. The vast majority of these people were Scottish Gaels or their descendants.

More highly publicized was the Earl of Selkirk's settlement at Baldoon (called after his family estate in Wigtownshire) on Prince Edward Island. Nearly 1,000 Highlanders left for the area in 1803–4. But the territory for colonization had been selected unwisely. The marshlands bred malarial mosquitoes which soon spread disease to epidemic proportions. Baldoon languished until 1812 when it was finally destroyed by invading American forces.[38] Selkirk's Red River settlement in Upper Canada did much better. Colonization did not bring easy or sudden riches. The Highland districts were often too isolated and located on marginal arable land. But they did provide a new security and a modest standard of living, which for the most part were accepted by communities habituated in the old country to even lower levels of comfort.

Only through exploring the scattered evidence of correspondence, oral tradition, song and poetry can we obtain a more realistic picture of the actual mindset of the emigrant parties. The very fact of the continuous stream of people who left for the new settlements over many years suggests an optimism and a strong faith in the benefits of emigration. Surviving poetry is equally positive.[39] A strong theme is that of liberation from servility akin to the exodus from Egypt under Moses. Some songs do reveal the sorrow at leaving home and the fracturing of ancient connection with a beloved landscape, family and friends. But linked with this is often a sense of excitement as the bard contemplated the new life across the ocean. The mood is captured well in *Fair is the Place* by Micheil Mór MacDhómhnaill (Michael McDonald, *c.* 1745–1815) after his arrival in Prince Edward Island in 1772:

O, 'S àlainn an T-àite	*Fair is the Place*
A, 's àlainn an t-àite	Fair is the place
Th' agam 'n cois na tràghad	I have here by the sea,
'N uair thig e gu bhith 'g àiteach ann	when it comes time to till it
Leis a' chrann, leis a' chrann, O.	with the plough.
Ni mi 'n t-aran leis na gearrain	I shall make bread-land with horses
'S an crodh-bainne chuir mu'n bhaile;	and put the cows to graze;
'S cha bhi annas oirnn 's an earrach,	we shall not be in want in spring,
Chuirinn geall, chuirinn geall.	I wager.
O, 's fraoidhneasach, daoimeanach,	Sparklng, diamond-like,
Glan mar sholus choinnlean,	clear as candle-light,
Am gradan le chuid shoillseanach	is the salmon with his brilliance,
Annas gach allt, anns gach allt, O.	in every stream,
Mear ri mire, leum na linne.	Merrily sporting, leaping from the pool.

Rory Roy Mackenzie (1755–?) was one of the Earl of Selkirk's colonists who first owned land in Prince Edward Island before migrating subsequently to Pictou. *An Imrich (The Emigration)*, was composed as he prepared to leave Scotland. He laments the new economic order in the Highlands but looks forward to better times across the Atlantic:

An Imrich	*The Emigration*
Ma 's e Selkirk na bàighe	If it be the benign Selkirk
Tha ri àite thoirt dhuinn,	who will grant us a place,
Tha mi deònach, le m' phàisdean,	with my children I am eager
Dhol gun dàil air na tuinn.	to sail without delay.
Siud an imrich tha feumail	It is necessary to emigrate,
Dhol 'nar leum as an tir s'	to leave this land immediately,
Do dh'America chraobhach,	and go to wooded America
'S am bi saors' agus sìth.	where there will be freedom and peace.
Faigh an nall dhuinn am botul,	Bring us the bottle,
Thoir dhuinn deoch as mu'n cuairt;	pass a drink around to us;
'S mise a' fear a tha deònach	I am most eager
A'dhol a sheòladh a' chuain;	to set sail across the sea,
A'dhol a dh'ionnsaidh an àite	and to go to the place
Gus 'n do bhard am mòr-shluagh;	from which many have embarked;
A'dhol gu Eilein Naomh Màiri,	to go to St Mary's Isle,
'S cha bhi màl 'ga thoirt bhuainn.	and no rents will be exacted from us.
A dheagh Aonghais Mhic-Amhlaidh,	Now, worthy Angus Macaulay,
Tha mi 'n geall ort ro mhòr,	I will wager
Bho'n a sgrìobh thu na briathran	that since you wrote the instructions
'Us an gnìomh le do mheòir,	and their terms with your own hands,
Gu'n grad chuir thu gu'r n-ionnsaidh	you will soon send us

Long Ghallda nan seòl,   a foreign vessel,
'Us ruith-chuip air a clàraibh   foam on her deck,
Thar nam bàrc-thonn le treòir.   rushing powerfully over the waves.
Seo a' bhliadhna tha sàraicht'   This is a taxing year
Do dh'fhear gun àiteach, gun   for one without a dwelling, without
   sunnd,   cheer,
'N uair théid càch 's a' mhìos   when in March others go
   Mhàrta
Ris an àiteach le sùrd.   to their ploughing eagerly.
Tha luchd-riaghlaidh an àite   The overlords here
Nis 'gar n-àicheadh gu dlùth,   reject us completely.
'S gur h-e an stiùuir a thoirt an iar   To turn the rudder westward
   dhi
Nì as ciataiche dhuinn.   is the most sensible course for us.

Ma 's e réiteachan chaorach   If it be sheep-walks
'N àite dhaoine bhios ann,   which will replace men,
Gu'm bi Albainn an tràth sin   Scotland will then
'S i 'na fàsaich do 'n Fhraing.   become a wasteland for France.
'N uair thig *Bonipart'* stràiceil   When the arrogant Bonaparte
   comes
Le làimh làidir an nall,   with his heavy hand,
Bidh na cìobairean truagh dheth   the shepherds will be badly off,
'Us cha chruaidh leinn an call.   and we will not grieve for them.

'S mo ghuidhe ma sheòlas sinn   It is my wish, if we sail,
Gu'n deònaichear dhuinn   that it may be granted us
Gu'm bi 'n Tì uile ghràs-mhor   that the all merciful one
Dh' oidhch' 's a' là air ar stiùir,   guide us night and day,
Gu ar gleidheadh 's ar teàrnadh   to save us and protect us
Bho gach gàbhadh 'us cùis,   from every peril and need,
'S gu ar tabhairt làn sàbhailt   and to bring us safely
Do thir àghmhor na mùirn.   to the land of good cheer.

Gheibh sinn fearann 'us àiteach   We shall get land and a home
Anns no fàsaichean thall;   in the wilderness yonder;
Bidh na coillteau 'gan rùsgadh   the forests will be cleared
Ged bhiodh cùinneadh orinn gann.   though money will be scarce.
'N dràsd s' ann tha sinn 'nar   Now we are cramped
   crùban

'M bothain ùdlaidh gun taing,

'Us na bailtean fo chaoraich
Aig luchd-maoine gun dàimh.

in gloomy huts without
   recompense,

and the fields are occupied by sheep
owned by the unfriendly rich.

The final song comes from Anna Gillis of Morar, who sailed from Greenock to Quebec in 1786 with 500 others to settle eventually in Glengarry County. *Canada Ard* or *Upper Canada* reflects her views of the new colony and contains a tribute to Father Alexander (Scotus) MacDonnell, who accompanied the Knoydart emigrants of 1786 and continued to act as their pastor, leader and counsellor in Glengarry:

Canada Ard

Ann an Canada Ard
Tha gach sonas 'us àgh;
Bidh gach maoin ann a' fas ri
   chéile.

Gu bheil cruithneachd a' fàs,
Luchdmhor, lìonte gu' bhàrr,
Ach trì mìosan thoirt dha de
   thearmunn.

Gheibhear siùcar à craobh
Ach an goc chur 'na taobh,
'Us cha dochair sin a h-aon de
   geugan.

Gheibh sinn mil agus fion,
'S gach ni eile gu'r miann;
Cha bhi uireasbhuidh sìon fo'n
   ghréin oirnn.

Maighstir Alasdair òg,
Mac Fear Scotais na sròil,
Sagart beannaicht' bha mór le
   éibhneas.

Dh'fhalbh e leinne mar naomh
Gus ar beatha bhi saor,

Upper Canada

In Upper Canada
there is every joy and delight;
all requirements will prosper
   together.

Wheat grows
abundantly, ready to harvest,
with only three months to bring it
   to full season.

Sugar may be gotten from a tree
if a tap be inserted in its side,
and not one of its branches
   damaged.

We shall have berries and wine
and all else that we desire;
we shall lack nothing under the
   sun.

Young Father Alexander,
son of Scotus of the banners,
the holy priest, was full of
   kindness.

Like a saint he brought us out
so that we would be free

Mar dh'fhalbh iad le Maois Eipheit.	as were those who followed Moses out of Egypt.
Fhuair sinn bailtean dhuinn fhìn, Le còir dhainginn o'n rìgh,	We got farms of our own with proprietory rights from the king,
'S cha bhi uachdrain a chaoidh 'gar léireadh.	and landlords will no more oppress us.

The task of carving out new communities from wilderness must have been hard, demanding, exhausting and terribly discouraging. But the Highland pioneer of this era had a number of advantages which at least aided the progress of successful settlement in British North America.[40] It was areas where the loyalist Gaels had concentrated after 1783 which acted as the great magnets of future colonization. The imperial state may have been hostile to the idea of populating Canada, but it did recognize the responsibility to families who had sacrificed much in their loyalty to the crown. Thus in June 1784 government bateaux carried the loyalists from their refugee camps in Quebec to the new townships where they not only received land in the best areas but also provisions for two years, clothing, tools, some livestock and household plenishing, enabling a good start to be made in building homes and clearing land. All this lowered the threshold of risk for later migrants, who could hope for food and help in the crucial early years of resettlement. Moreover, the provincial governments had a different agenda from London. They saw colonization as a means of expansion and development. Some governors also took the view that the martial reputation of the Gaels would also make them a robust defensive barrier against attempted armed incursions from the USA. The result was that the local governments were often more than willing to assist with provisions and transport within Canada from the port of disembarkation to the area of resettlement. This was done in Quebec for emigrants from the island of Eigg in 1790, in Nova Scotia in 1791, and again in Quebec in 1794.

In cases where such support was not forthcoming, Scottish merchant houses in Montreal, Halifax and Quebec regularly subscribed substantial sums to assist indigent passengers on arrival. Eventually even the British government conceded that emigration could not be prevented and so should be directed towards the British colonies. The outbreak of war with the USA and the attempted American invasion of Canada concentrated the minds of London politicians and encouraged them to support the settlement of loyal Highlanders to bolster the colony's defences. So in 1815 a scheme was established to offer 2,000 free passages to Canada, with bedding and rations. In a sense the state had been at the heart of the emigration process long before this. It was government which dispensed land, the vital basis of settlement. For the period of this chapter, crown land was available, in theory at least, as a free grant. Concessions were usually 200 acres per recipient and, in the early years to 1797, even survey fees were covered by the state. Thereafter, however, full fees were levied on new settlers, who often had to rent land initially or even share land for a time with relatives who already possessed holdings.

The social composition of the emigrant parties was also a critical factor in adaptation to the colonial environment. This was a movement of entire communities, often several hundred strong. The people moved as families containing those who had lived together for generations in the same Highland townships. There were large numbers of women and children whose inclusion was vital if the new communities overseas were to grow and reproduce. For instance, the emigration led by Archibald McMillan of Murlaggan from the Cameron country along Loch Arkaig in 1802 included some 448 people. Young children made up 32 per cent of the group and women over twelve years of age no less than 51 per cent. Similarly, three vessels sailed from the small Scottish outport of Duchainas in 1790 carrying 405 passengers from adjacent areas of Roman Catholic loyalty on the coastal mainland of Inverness-shire and the neighbouring islands. There were 111 heads of families and only twenty-five passengers travelled independently. Most crucially of all, family heads in virtually all the groups analysed were rent-paying tenants, the middle rank of Highland society. As long as they could keep their holdings until leaving, they might hope to gain by selling their cattle stocks as prices rose, cover the costs of the voyage and still have enough left to help with resettlement in Canada.

Leadership was also vital to plan the ventures, hire the ships and then manage the complexities of land allocation in the colonies. For all this, the emigrants relied on their traditional leaders. In the Catholic districts, some were priests, such as the aforementioned

Father Alexander MacDonnell, *Maighstir Alasdair*. More generally, the leadership class was drawn from the gentlemen of the clans, the *Daoine-Uaisle* (clan gentry), *Fir-Tacsa* (tacksmen) and prominent tenants. They possessed the contacts, financial resources and often knowledge of colonial conditions. Several were half-pay army officers who had seen active service in the colonies. Above all, they were held in respect by the people – an important advantage when difficult decisions had to be made. Their responsibilities did not end when the emigrants landed. In some districts, such as Glengarry County, they managed to gain positions as land surveyors and as members of the land boards where they were able to act as mediators between local crown officers and the people. Like the mass of emigrants they too had a basic stake in the success of colonization. The gentry of the clans were being squeezed out by the loss of favourable leases, the splitting of their holdings to accommodate crofting townships and the loss of traditional status in the community. Emigration not only offered them economic independence through landownership but perpetuated their social leadership. It also held out the promise of financial gain through populating their colonial properties with subtenants in the familiar manner practised in the Highlands for generations. Against this background, it is hardly surprising that the survival of these new settlements depended on the maintenance of conservative values and traditional social hierarchies.

10

The Caribbean World

I

In the eighteenth century Britain's West Indian colonies were universally regarded as crucial to the imperial economy. Even Adam Smith, the most eminent contemporary critic of the colonial system, waxed eloquent about their immense value: the profits of a sugar plantation in the Caribbean, he noted, 'were generally much greater than those of any other cultivation that is known either in Europe or America'.[1] Edmund and William Burke also asserted in 1757 that nowhere in the world could great fortunes be made so quickly as in the West Indies. Their importance to the British state and economy was widely acknowledged. In 1700 the British islands accounted for about 40 per cent of all transatlantic sugar consignments. By 1815 the figure had reached 60 per cent. At the end of the eighteenth century the Caribbean colonies employed, directly or indirectly, half the nation's long-distance shipping, their fixed and movable wealth was reckoned at more than £30 million sterling, duties on West Indian produce accounted for an eighth of Exchequer revenues and the credit structures linked to the plantation economy were crucial elements in UK financial markets:[2]

Situated in a tropical island world easily accessible to sea-going vessels, the sugar colonies supplied Europeans with a variety of exotics in growing demand, took off European manufactures, gave employment to ships and seamen, provided raw materials for processing and manufacturing industries, generated a variety of auxiliary trades ranging from African slaves to Newfoundland codfish, were favourably situated for a lucrative entrepôt trade with Spanish America, provided a field for fortune hunters, yielded revenue to governments, and gave rise to wealth and income which revived the image of the Indies as a source of fabulous riches after the precious metal mines of New Spain began to falter.[3]

The expansion of the British West Indian colonies was forged in the violent crucible of the titanic conflicts with France over transatlantic hegemony. By 1750, Barbados, the Leeward Islands (Antigua, St Kitts, Nevis, Montserrat), and Jamaica had all been conquered or annexed. Further large-scale territorial gains took place after both the Seven Years War (ending in 1763) and the Napoleonic Wars (ending in 1815). As a result of the first, Britain added Grenada, Dominica, St Vincent and Tobago (the Ceded Islands). By the second, the empire absorbed Trinidad, Demerara and St Lucia. Development of these new colonies depended on a number of factors. The British laws of Trade and Navigation gave the islands a virtual monopoly of the protected home market for the products of tropical agriculture, where by the 1750s commodities such as sugar were selling at prices some 50 per cent higher than in continental Europe. The West Indies at that time also exported rum and molasses, and, especially after c. 1760, fed the factories of the early Industrial Revolution with cargoes of raw cotton. But sugar was king. It is reckoned that sugar consumption in England and Wales alone increased about twentyfold in the period from 1663 to 1775. Between 1771 and 1775 colonial imports topped 1.8 million cwt. Consumption per head in Britain rose irresistibly from about 4 lb. in 1700, to 10 lb. by 1748 and then to 20 lb. in 1800.

Britons seem to have had a uniquely sweet tooth. As late as the 1780s, for instance, the French were only consuming about 2 lb. per head. The national appetite for sugar was intimately linked to the new enthusiasm for drinking tea. Consumption per head of tea quintupled in the UK, from 0.32 lb. per head in 1730–39 to 1.78 lb. in 1804–6. This was partly related to the much faster rise of real incomes in Britain in the eighteenth century compared with the countries of continental Europe. But an even more fundamental influence was the British rate of urbanization. Under conditions in town and city, tea was more convenient than milk. Until Indian leaf displaced the Chinese after 1865 tea was usually taken without milk. In Britain as a whole there was a very close correlation between the spread of tea-drinking and the spread of urbanism. In Scotland, in particular, tea was most commonly consumed in cities and towns before 1800.

The Caribbean response to the burgeoning sugar markets in Europe was built on two key foundations – the evolution of the plantation system and the massive use of black slave labour. The Caribbean plantation economy has been described as a revolutionary social, economic and political institution and much more than an innovate organization for agricultural production:

The New World plantation represented a combination of African labour, European technology and management, Asiatic and American plants, European animal husbandry, and American soil and climate . . . animate sources of energy, such as plants, domesticated animals, and black slaves were combined with inanimate energy captured by windmills, water wheels and sailing vessels. Plantations were at once ecosystems, farming and industrial systems, economic systems and social systems . . . They established new trade routes and shipping lanes, shifted millions of African hoe cultivators from one side of the Atlantic to the other, determined the movement and direction of capital, induced the growth of temperate-zone colonies to supply intermediate producers, produced a class of *nouveau riche* planters and merchants, and became a prize in the contest for power and plenty among the mercantile nations of Europe.[4]

This economic revolution in the Caribbean reached its apotheosis in the later eighteenth century. Conceivably, given the vital dependency on negro slaves, the plantations ought to have located in West Africa close to plentiful supplies of labour. But tropical Africa had a notorious reputation as the white man's grave – and also, slaves might more easily escape to their tribal homelands. Transporting Africans half-way across the world, on the other hand, had several advantages. The Caribbean islands were certainly hosts to such virulent pestilences as cholera, smallpox, yellow fever and dysentery. But they were not only relatively free from malaria but also were regarded as less lethal than the deadly shores and jungles of Africa. Moreover, European settlement in the West Indies was facilitated by the trade winds which tempered the unrelenting heat of the tropics. The Caribbean had easy access to cheap sources of provisions in North America, while the prevailing winds were helpful to oceanic commerce and powered the sugar mills which processed the canes.[5] Indeed, such was the capacity in the islands to service the booming markets in Europe that some colonies became little more than vast sugar plantations. It was said, for instance of Antigua in 1751, that the land was 'improved to the utmost, there being hardly one Acre of Ground, even to the Top of the Mountains, fit for Sugar Canes and other necessary Produce, but what is taken and cultivated'.[6]

These were also 'slave societies', in the sense of human communities which depended above all else on unfree, forced labour for their very existence. Without the slave, the sugar economies of the Caribbean would have been impossible. By 1750 black Africans comprised about 85 per cent of the population of the British West Indies. It was scarcely surprising that the contemporary commentator, Malachy Postlethwayt, writing in 1745 in *The African Trade, the Great Pillar and Support of the British Plantation Trade in America*, could report that the nation's transatlantic commercial empire ultimately rested on an African foundation. Slaves outnumbered whites by six to one in 1748 and by twelve to one in 1815. Most whites were transients, hoping to make a quick fortune and return home as quickly as possible with their profits. Despite the fabled riches of the Caribbean few actually managed it. But one consequence was that British West Indian whites failed to develop 'integrated, locally rooted societies, comparable with the North American colonies'.[7] As will be seen later, even Scottish migrants failed to leave the classic ethnic stamp of their schools and churches on the Caribbean islands where they settled.

This was not the only point of difference between the two colonial systems. Another was the dramatic difference in the treatment of blacks. Not for nothing was the Caribbean known as the graveyard of the slaves. Even by the standards of unfree labour in the North American plantation colonies of Virginia and Maryland, the suffering of the slaves in the West Indies was especially horrendous. About 1830, crude death rates in the USA and Jamaica were 20 and 26 per thousand. The differences in birth rates were even more dramatic – 50 and 23 per thousand respectively. It was reckoned in the 1750s that a quarter of all slaves died within three years of arrival. But averages often concealed: on the Codrington plantations in Barbados between 1741 and 1746, 43 per cent of all African negroes died within three years of arrival. Partly this was based on an inhumane calculation. Planters generally believed until the later eighteenth century that buying 'salt-water' blacks, straight off the slave ships, was 'cheaper' than encouraging family life and reproduction of the existing stock. Thus it was common practice for plantations to buy slaves at crop time and set them to work with little or no time spent on 'seasoning' (acclimatization). By definition, slavery was also an oppressive regime where work was only done under the threat of severe punishment. Some scholars have suggested that coercion reached especially rigorous and exacting levels in the Caribbean because the grossly skewed ratios of whites and blacks generated rancorous fear and paranoia among British planters about the menace of slave rebellions. Sir Hans Sloane saw the response in Jamaica:

The Punishments for Crimes of Slaves, are usually for Rebellions burning them, by nailing them down on the ground with crooked Sticks on every Limb, and then applying the Fire by degrees from the Feet and Hands, burning them gradually up to the Head, whereby their pains are extravagant.[8]

Crimes of a lesser nature were punished by 'Gelding, or chopping off half of the Foot with an Ax, while for trying to escape the slave was burdened with iron rings, chains, pottocks and spurs'. Thomas Thistlewood, a plantation overseer on the same island, made running away a capital offence. On 9 October 1751 he wrote in his journal that three runaways – 'Robin and two boys' – had been captured. To deter others from escaping, Robin was hanged and beheaded and his head put on a pole 'at ye Angle of ye Road in the home pasture'.[9]

Essentially, however, the high levels of slave mortality were caused by the unrelenting nature of the plantation regime. The slave gangs on the sugar estates toiled from dawn to dusk in land preparation, in harvesting the canes and in sugar boiling. In the Caribbean about 90 per cent of the slaves worked on these tasks. One scholar estimates that it was 'probably one of the highest labour participation rates anywhere in the world'.[10] The arduous toil helps to explain why about half British West Indies slave women never bore a child in the mid-eighteenth century. On the American mainland there was never the same intensity of work on a single crop. Tobacco cultivation, tending farms, cutting timber and domestic service were just some of the varied range of tasks undertaken there. Recent work by nutritionists and anthropologists on slave skeletal remains in Barbados burial grounds has added a new dimension to an understanding of slave mortality in the Caribbean. These results point unambiguously to malnutrition as a vital factor, reducing the immunity of the black population to the epidemic diseases which infested the low-lying plantations and their malignant environments.[11]

Nor should the human factor be neglected in this account. The Caribbean was notorious for planter absenteeism. In 1832, 540 (84 per cent) of a total of 646 sugar estates were owned by absentees or minors. Proprietors were normally keen to escape home (because of the low life expectancy in the tropics) as soon as they had managed to make enough for independent, leisured living in Britain. By 1800 it was their attorneys, managers and overseers who actually ran most plantations in the West Indies. This class was committed to maximizing production not simply to satisfy the expectations of their masters but because they also were determined to get rich quickly and return to spend their last years in more congenial surroundings at home. The pervasive culture of avarice engendered a regime of unrelenting and pitiless rigour on the slave plantations. Untold numbers of blacks were quite literally worked to death. It is hardly surprising, therefore, that modern scholarship has identified the islands of the British West Indies as the location of the most deadly and destructive systems of slavery in the New World. Only in the later decades of the eighteenth century, when the policy on most estates altered in favour of breeding new generations of black labour rather than simply purchasing 'salt-water' slaves, did a distinct trend develop towards amelioration. After 1807, when the slave trade to British territories was outlawed, that process became unstoppable.

2

The Scottish connection with the Caribbean colonies has, until very recently, rarely attracted much attention from Scottish historians. A striking example of this neglect is the recently published compendium of modern scholarship, *The Oxford Companion to Scottish History* (2001).[12] The index contains only one reference to the West Indies and that merely relates to the sale of Scottish coarse linen in the Caribbean. Slavery and the slave trade come off even worse. There is no index entry to 'slavery' and the single 'slave trade' reference is exclusively concerned with the campaigns of the Scottish missionary societies in the nineteenth century against the immoral commerce in human beings. The omission is surprising because, as will become apparent, the role of the Scots in the British Caribbean was deeply significant. The transience of the Scottish presence, which left little cultural trace compared with the long-term impact of the Scots in North America, may be one explanation for the neglect. Another may be that economic historians in particular have been bewitched by the extraordinary success story of Scottish merchants in the Chesapeake tobacco trade and have marginalized other key aspects of transatlantic commerce. The darker side of Scottish business in the slave economies could also have caused them to have been overlooked in the past, especially by Victorian writers who much preferred tales of heroism, achievement and genius in constructing their saga of the Scot abroad.

The truth is that the Scots were very active in the Caribbean from an early date and long before the union of 1707. The Edinburgh merchant John Watson thought that in the West Indies 'all you can expect is women, whores and boys under 14 or 15 years old'.[13] But the Scottish contingent was much more varied than this. Between 1648 and 1660 about 2,000 Scots left for the New World, and many settled in Barbados, Jamaica and Virginia.[14] The majority were exiled prisoners of war following Cromwell's victories. Another 7,000 or thereabouts went to the New World between 1660 and the Union of Parliaments. But at the time most (around two-thirds) were drawn to the West Indies rather than the mainland American colonies, though the Scots were still at that juncture in a minority in the Caribbean compared with the English, French, Irish and Sephardic Jews. They were a motley crew: transported criminals and vagabonds; indentured servants; militant Covenanters banished to the Caribbean by the vengeful policies of Charles II and later his brother, James VII and II; seamen; adventurers intent on making a quick fortune; respectable merchants, planters, clerks and bookeepers. They did not confine their wanderings to the English colonies, even though these territories had a special interest in recruiting Scots servants who were Protestant, served the same king and had an international reputation for their martial spirit. As an entry in the *Calendar of State Papers* noted: 'The Scotch were the general travaillers and soldiers in most foreign parts.'[15] They were apparently good men to have on your side when the English colonies were surrounded by French, Spanish and Dutch enemies. But the nomadic

Scots went their own way. In the last few decades of the seventeenth century they were also to be found in St Eustatius (some having lived in the Netherlands and from there settled in this Dutch colony), and in Montserrat, Florida and Mexico.

The strange world these Scots entered has been vividly brought to life in a searching portrayal of Barbados in the middle decades of the seventeenth century when the island was already growing rich through sugar cultivation.[16] It also had a more favourable climate than other colonies because of the gentle trade winds that crossed the island. In happy contrast to the homeland, Barbados was always warm and endowed with a rich variety of exotic fruits, flowers and trees. But it was far from being a tropical paradise. All newcomers dreaded the 'Contrey Diseas' (probably yellow fever) and other killers such as dysentery and various fevers. The beautiful island was lethal for Europeans. One contemporary observer, Richard Ligon, commented dryly: 'Black Ribbon, for mourning, is much worn here.'[17] Barbados's burgeoning wealth was also built on the exploitation of both free and slave labour. Even white servants were treated no better than 'galley slaves', fed as little as possible and housed in conditions 'scarcely fit for animals'.[18] The island produced great affluence for some planters; for servants and slaves, however, it was 'a place of torment'. But even the proprietors were vulnerable to disease and their property was easily destroyed by drought, hurricanes, slave revolts and losses at sea. They were 'reckless and competitive', willing to risk all in the obsessive pursuit of profit and indifferent to cultural or social amenities.[19] To them, Barbados was but a temporary domicile from which they would eagerly escape when they had made their fortunes. Ligon thought that there were few whose minds were 'not over-balanc'd with avarice and lucre' and who did 'not hanker after their own country'.[20] Barbadians had created a society 'extravagant, loose, morally and culturally debased and riddled with fear of social revolt'.[21] Drunkenness was endemic, the very 'custom of the country'; and fornication, adultery, incest and petty violence routine. It was hardly surprising that some settlers of more religious inclinations feared for the safety of the colony. Only rapid repentance and a rejection of the 'sins of Sodom' could save Barbados from the wrath of a vengeful God. This was life at the tropical edge of European civilization in the 1650s and 1660s.

The sporadic Scottish movement to the Caribbean continued in the first few decades after the union. The foundation of sugar houses in Glasgow before 1700 illustrated the relationship. Ayr had also sent out repeated ventures to Montserrat in the same period. Some authorities even suggest that the interest in the Caribbean by the Clyde ports was older than their more famous trade in tobacco with North America. Certainly, of the seventy-five fully recorded incoming voyages from the New World before the union, thirty-two were from the West Indies compared with forty-three from mainland America. But even this figure probably understates the Caribbean connection since so much of that trade was done through London and Bristol on Scottish account. The War of the Spanish Succession cemented the link. St Kitts was ceded to Britain in 1713, and when the land of the island was redistributed half the lots of 100 acres and above went to Scots. The most famous of the Scots purchasers were two officers who had served in the British army during the war. Colonel William MacDonald and Major James Milliken married the widow and daughter of the richest plantation owner on the island. They returned to Scotland flushed with financial success in the late 1720s, when they set up a direct trade in Caribbean sugar to Port Glasgow which cut out the British middlemen. This in turn eventually became Scotland's most powerful West India house of the eighteenth century, the giant syndicate of Alexander Houston and Company.[22]

Even Scottish disasters helped fashion the connection. Some of the few survivors of the ill-fated Darien expedition settled in Jamaica. One of the most prominent was Colonel John Campbell from Inveraray, who had been Captain of the troops at Darien. Before his death in 1740 Campbell rose to become a member of both the Jamaica Assembly and Council. He established an enormous network of Campbell relatives and associates in the west of the island which exerted a potent commercial and social influence on the area for the rest of the eighteenth century. The planter historian Edward Long noted in 1774: 'I have heard a computation made of no fewer than one hundred of the name Campbel [sic] only actually resident in it [Jamaica] all claiming alliance with the Argyle family.'[23] The destruction of Jacobitism after Culloden in 1746 also led to several hundred Scots Jacobites being transported to the Caribbean to be sold as indentured servants. The majority were from the Highland and northeastern counties. On 28 June 1747, the *Veteran* sailed from Liverpool bound for the Leeward Islands with 150 Jacobite prisoners on board.

The vessel, however, was attacked and captured by a French privateer off Antigua and the prisoners were taken to the French island of Martinique where they were released. It is known that a number of them spent the next few years serving in French regiments in the Caribbean rather than toiling in the fields of sugar plantations.

By the 1730s the distinctive pattern of Scottish migration to the West Indies had already emerged and salient differences with the North American experience were apparent. Immigrants to the mainland colonies came from virtually every level of Scottish society, from the younger sons of the gentry to poor servants and unemployed labourers. Most Scots who sailed to the mainland colonies also settled there permanently. In addition, immigration tended, especially from the 1760s and 1770s, to be in family and kindred units. Movement to the West Indies shared some of these features, notably in the significance of indentured servants. But in the main, Scots in the Caribbean were planters, merchants, colonial officials, attorneys, doctors, overseers and tradesmen, most of whom had no intention of spending the rest of their days in the tropics. The prevalence of slavery on the islands helps to account for this difference. Black slave labour carried out the unskilled and semi-skilled tasks which were often performed by white labour in several of the mainland colonies. There was also an enduring sexual imbalance in the West Indies. Most migrants were young men in their teens and early twenties. Entirely typical was the young poet and farmer Robert Burns who, in 1786, was seriously considering taking up an appointment as a book keeper on a Scottish-owned sugar estate in Port Antonio, Jamaica. Even more mature emigrants seem to have left their families at home rather than expose them to the risk of the malignant diseases of the West Indies. For the white population, at least, the Caribbean in the eighteenth century was very much a man's world.

This pattern of steady Scottish movement into the West Indies before c. 1750 fits the general picture of British imperial expansion. In the seventeenth and early eighteenth centuries the empire had been unambiguously English in its colonial populations, governance, language, law and traditions. It seemed that 'anglicisation swept all before it'.[24] By the 1750s, however, a remarkable change had taken place. Especially at élite level, the political and imperial bastions of empire were being overrun in numerical terms by settlers from the Celtic nations and immigrants of non-British origin. The officer corps of the army, the merchant communities, the governing élites and the professional cadres of the colonial hierarchies were all transformed and Scots, even more than the Irish or Welsh, were in the vanguard of the revolution.

Tentative estimates put Scottish emigration to the West Indies from the 1750s to 1800 at somewhere between 12,000 and 20,000.[25] When the islands of Dominica, Vincent, Grenada and Tobago were acquired by Great Britain in the Treaty of Paris (1763), they were mainly settled by Scotsmen. Sir William Forbes, the Edinburgh banker, recorded in his *Memoirs* that 'extensive speculations were entered by some Scotchmen for the purchase and cultivation of lands in the newly acquired West India Islands'.[26] Growing Scottish dominance can also be identified in Antigua. Only one of the leading gentry families on the island before 1680 was Scots. The vast majority were English but with significant elements of Dutch and Irish. The Scottish proportion hardly altered among newcomers between 1680 and 1706. However, of the eighteen members of the Antigua planter and merchant élite who became established between 1707 and 1775 no less than eleven were of Scottish origin. It was a similar story in Jamaica. Edward Long, the historian of the colony, waxed eloquent in 1774 on the impact of the Scots:

Jamaica, indeed, is greatly indebted to North Britain, as very nearly one third of the inhabitants are either natives of that country, or descendants from those who were. Many have come from the same quarter every year, less in quest of fame, than of fortunes . . . To say the truth, they are so clever and prudent in general, as, by an obliging behaviour, good sense, and zealous services to gain esteem, and make their way through every obstacle.[27]

In the period 1771–5 Scots accounted for nearly 45 per cent of all inventories at death valued above £1,000. In addition, in the same time-frame roughly two-fifths of personal property inventories belonged to Scots, with most of the rest to settlers of English, Welsh and Sephardic Jewish origin.[28] When Trinidad and Guyana were annexed during the Napoleonic Wars they too became fresh new fields for Scottish enterprise. Indeed, albeit on a lesser scale, even non-British territories such as St Eustatius (Dutch) and St Croix (Danish) attracted Scots settlement. They were to be found in almost every sizeable island in the West Indies apart from those governed by Spain.

Contemporaries were well aware of these Caledonian incursions and sought explanations. Edward Long thought the Scots had 'sounder constitutions' than the English and hence adapted more easily to the tropical climate. More convincingly, he praised the artisans, particularly the stonemasons and millwrights who were 'remarkably expert and, in general, are sober, frugal and civil'.[29] He also commented on the educational attainments of the Scots which meant they were better equipped to obtain posts as clerks and book-keepers, and then to progress to become attorneys who actually managed the estates of absentee planters.

But there was also a bigger picture to be considered. Scots from gentry backgrounds still sought opportunity at the imperial periphery because of the continuing difficulty of breaking into the network of patronage and professional employment in London and the limited career opportunities in their native country. Desperation as much as the search for opportunities explains why so many were willing to hazard their lives in the lethal environment of the West Indies. But in the decades after *c.* 1760 the British Caribbean did offer rich pickings because of the upward curve in European demand for sugar, and as a result of the spectacular conquests of foreign islands during the Seven Years and Napoleonic Wars. External events also impinged on the Scottish Caribbean diaspora. From the 1770s, the West Indies became the most dynamic sector of Scottish overseas commerce. After 1783 the Caribbean took over from the American tobacco trade as the leading sector. Already in 1775 Glasgow's exports to the West Indies were valued at twice as much as those to the mainland colonies. By 1790 the sugar islands had become the Clyde's premier overseas centre of trade. It was not simply a question of intelligent diversification after the tobacco business was undermined by the American War of Independence. The Caribbean now became a strategic factor in the whole process of Scottish industrialization. In the early years, raw sea-island cotton from the Caribbean plantations helped to power the mills of the western Lowlands. Equally, the boom in the export trade was partly dictated by demand for 'slave cloth', rough linen clothing produced in massive volume by the spinners and weavers of the eastern counties.

Scotland was also in an excellent position to respond to the Caribbean need for professional skills. Nowhere was this more evident than in the field of medicine. Not surprisingly, the islands had great need of doctors. Mortality rates were particularly high during the difficult period of 'seasoning'. The medical needs of the vast slave populations were originally less important, though this changed in the later decades of the century. A rapid rise in slave prices and the threat of an increasingly vocal anti-slavery agitation transformed attitudes. Partly as a matter of self-interest and as a counter to the anti-slavery critics, island Assemblies passed new laws for the health care of slaves. In 1788 the Assembly of Jamaica, for instance, enacted the *Code Noire* which required a doctor or a surgeon to submit annual reports on the extent and causes of slave mortality on each plantation. When similar legislation was passed elsewhere it became necessary for planters to employ more doctors. This was not always straightforward. European physicians had a wide choice of overseas employers, ranging from the army and navy to the great chartered companies such as the East India Company, the South Sea Company, the Royal African Company, together with their foreign counterparts. The supply of private practitioners in the colonies almost dried up during the American and Napoleonic Wars, though the medical labour market was flooded afterwards in years of peace. Scotland, above all other countries in the UK, was best able to serve this market. It was not simply a question of the renown of the great eighteenth-century medical schools of Edinburgh and Glasgow. The sheer volume of doctors produced by this small country was likely to yield a substantial surplus for export. Between 1751 and 1800, over 85 per cent of medical graduates in Britain were trained in the Scottish universities.[30]

The Scots, therefore, made an overwhelming impact on Caribbean medicine. In 1750, 60 per cent of the doctors in Antigua were Scots or Scottish-trained. There is no reason to believe that the pattern elsewhere was much different. Some were as much adventurers and speculators as medical practitioners. They adopted a firmly pragmatic and hard-headed approach. Education had an overtly utilitarian function as the essential means to greater wealth. Dr Robert Glasgow wrote from St Vincent in 1774: 'Education is a noble Position, it is a fortune sufficient of itself to carry a person, genteely through life with a small share of industry.'[31] As one scholar has put it: 'To Scots in all but the highest ranks, learning took the place of inherited money, property and status. It became a catalyst for the acquisition of a fortune.'[32]

Making money from other ventures was therefore central to the doctors' aim of rising in the world. Dr William Stephen in St Kitts made considerable gains by purchasing so-called 'refuse negroes', treating them and then reselling them when in a healthier condition as prices improved. Dr Alexander Johnston from Aberdeen set out for fame and fortune in Jamaica. He started by establishing a wealthy clientele (he was not much interested in badly-paid slave medicine), then moved into land speculation and cattle-ranching. Johnston confided to his brother in 1784: 'Now I have thoughts of entering into the slave trade and selling each year in the parish and the two neighbouring ones, *one* (or *two*) guineas – with perhaps 250 or 300 slaves in each and giving a security upon my whole property for one guinea man would come to near perhaps, 20,000 pounds value.'[33] Perhaps the best-documented example of the breed is that of Walter Tullideph who settled in Antigua in 1726. He had been apprenticed to a surgeon in Edinburgh and then practised medicine in Antigua, where several relatives and associates were already established as doctors, merchants and colonial officials. Through this family nexus he entered trade, then acquired a plantation through marriage to 'an agreeable young widow' who was also a rich heiress.[34] He became a shipowner and eventually developed trading connections in North America, Ireland, Scotland and the English outports. He even climbed the political ladder in the island to the office of assemblyman and councillor before retiring to the Scottish estate he purchased in 1757. It was this kind of success story, however unrepresentative, which seduced hordes of other ambitious young Scotsmen to try their luck in the tropics.

Scottish hegemony in the Caribbean was underpinned by complex networks of patronage, ethnic connection and family loyalty. Nowhere was this more obvious than in the virtual Caledonian monopoly of the major political offices in the Caribbean. The new governors appointed in 1763 at the end of the Seven Years War were all Scots: General Robert Melville in the Ceded Islands, General James Grant of Ballindalloch in East Florida and Sir Harry Erskine in West Florida. In the 1790s, Alexander Lindsay, Earl of Balcarres and Governor of Jamaica, was one of the most powerful figures in the empire. Patrick Crawford of Hisleside was Governor of the Leeward Islands in the 1730s. Below the gubernatorial ranks were clutches of Scots in the customs and treasury service, the legal bureaucracies and the higher echelons of the army.

The limited prospects in the homeland for minor Scottish peers and gentry made them more eager than their counterparts in England to seek posts at the other side of the world. But contemporaries had another explanation. Their imperial prominence was seen as further confirmation of the insidious growth of the power of the Scots at the very heart of government. The first manifestation of these sentiments came during the term of office in the early 1760s of John, Earl of Bute, the first Scottish-born Prime Minister after the union. His brief tenure coincided with a significant increase in the number of Scots who rose to positions of political influence. Only eight Scottish Members of Parliament held state office in the years 1747 to 1753; yet between 1761 and 1767, twenty-eight achieved high rank. Bute was seen to be favouring his own kind. English political cartoons of the time were savagely racist in tone, portraying the Scots as treacherous and greedy mendicants, growing rich at England's expense. Bute himself, usually represented as a jackboot in reference to his long legs and as a pun on his name, came in for some of the most scathing treatment. He was satirized in one ribald print after another as the well-endowed seducer of the mother of George III, explicit sexual symbolism for the intolerable penetration of England by the army of Scots swarming across the Border craving pensions and places:

> Friend and favourite of France-a,
> Ev'ry day may you advance-a,
> And ven dead by tomb be writon,
> 'Here lies von whom all must sh-t-on,
> Oh, the Great, the Great North Briton!'[35]

Though his tenure of office ended in 1763 Bute remained a significant political figure with forty-three MPs in his 'interest' in the later 1760s. As Prime Minister, and later through his personal networks and clientages, Bute exerted considerable influence on the appointment to key political and judicial posts in the Caribbean and elsewhere in the Empire.

Even his impact, however, paled in relation to the ascendancy of another Scot, Henry Dundas, in the managing of imperial patronage.

Dundas's rise to power was meteoric. He became Solicitor-General of Scotland in 1766 and Lord Advocate in 1775. Crucially, these posts were not simply confined to the law but extended to a whole range of other political and administrative duties. It was the senior law officers who ran Scotland in the later eighteenth century. However, control over patronage was the real key to power for Dundas. From 1779, as sole Keeper of the Signet, he became the decisive influence over appointment to government posts in Scotland and systematically used his position to build up a complex network of clients, voters and local interests who depended on him for favours, places, promotions and pensions. His ascendancy was further buttressed by his appointment first as a commissioner of the Board of Control of the East India Company in 1784 and later as its President from 1793 to 1801. Dundas was capable of serving many masters for his own ends, and indeed in 1782–3 he had been a member of three governments, each of a different political hue. But thereafter his loyal and close relationship with the younger Pitt (which included sharing in many heroic drinking sessions) put the seal on his rise to pre-eminence. His position in the final analysis rested not on conviviality but rather on his ability to deliver what has been termed 'the well-drilled phalanx in the north' for Pitt's interest. In 1780 Dundas personally controlled twelve of the forty-one Scottish constituencies contested; by 1784 this had risen to twenty-two, and in 1790 to thirty-four. 'King Harry the Ninth' was coming close to the zenith of his personal power in Scotland.[36]

His influence also needs to be seen in the context of post-union Scottish politics. The union ended the Parliament and, in due course, the incipient 'parties' that had started to develop within it before 1707 also withered on the vine. Scottish parliamentary politics as such disappeared. Westminster hardly ever spent time on Scottish business and, apart from a brief flurry of legislation after the '45, the London Parliament showed only occasional interest. So it was not a question of sending MPs south to defend or promote Scottish concerns, for these were rarely debated. Dundas's game was rather to maximize the number of his loyal supporters in the House of Commons, and by so doing to make himself indispensable to the government of the day and consolidate and, if possible, expand his sources of power and patronage. The number of places and sinecures in the navy and army, and in the colonial, excise and government service by Scots increased substantially during his period of hegemony. By 1800, Scotland had obtained more than a quarter of all official pensions and one-third of state sinecures, a much higher proportion than was warranted by her size of population (one-sixth of England's) or national wealth. Success on this scale eventually provoked outrage in London, and Parliament determined that the volume of patronage to the greedy Scots should be drastically curbed. But the number of requests for posts was still far in excess of the supply. For the years 1784–90 alone, there survives in the National Library of Scotland a bundle of almost 600 petitions for everything from university professorships to peerages and imperial appointments, and these are not by any means all received by Dundas during these years. As a result he was able to pick and choose, not simply ensuring rewards to political clients and associates, but also selecting to some extent on the basis of talent, ability and potential.[37]

More than any other political figure of the eighteenth century, Dundas symbolized the intimate connections between the empire, Scotland and British politics. Too often, because of his appointment to the Board of Control, he is exclusively associated with Scottish patronage in India. But because his political career spanned almost four decades, and as a result of his abiding connections with the highest levels of the British state, he was able to play a pivotal role in key appointments in every corner of the empire. In the West Indies, his most telling interventions were in the selection of fellow Scots as governors or lieutenant-governors of several of the islands. These in turn became the bases of elaborate layers of secondary patronage:

Important offices in the West Indies were granted by letters patent to men who had obligations or duties in England, who had no intention of leaving England, and who performed their colonial duties by deputy. Supported by fees, the offices were expected to earn sums sufficient to support both the deputies who were the functionaries in the colonies and the patentees who were generally absentees. Offices granted by letters patent included the secretary who was in charge of all public records, the provost marshal who was the chief constable, and the naval officer who enforced the Navigation Acts, and in Jamaica the lucrative post of Receiver General. Governors who were expected to perform their duties in person received salaries from the Crown which were generally supplemented by grants from colonial assemblies.[38]

Substantial incomes could be derived from the system. The Governor of Barbados in the 1720s reputedly made £10,000 a year. In the Leeward Islands, £600 was paid annually for the office of provost marshal, £800 to £1,000 for the secretaryship and £500 for the naval office. It was not uncommon for some of those salaries then to be used to buy into sugar plantations and other property.

The distribution of Scottish political patronage was only one side of the coin. The second was probably even more pervasive. Family and personal networks formed the complex interconnecting webs of association between Scots which could go a long way to explain their success in the Caribbean. The networks had several functions. They facilitated access to jobs, contacts and credit for new arrivals from Scotland. They helped to reduce some of the immense risks intrinsic to transoceanic commerce by entrusting key tasks in business or plantation management to trusted associates and family members. They were also a vital social mechanism cementing the ethnic links between Scottish sojourners and the homeland to which they sought to return one day. The network offered in addition a system of mutual support in a distant and sometimes hostile land. Scottish planters, for instance, would have attorneys, book-keepers, doctors, executors and trustees either from their kindred group or local area back in Scotland. As in other parts of the empire, the tight territorial relationship between small, well-defined areas in the colony and specific neighbourhoods in the Old Country is very striking. For instance, in Tobago a single coherent Scottish network operated in the later eighteenth century by migrants from a triangle bounded by the towns of Elgin, Huntly and Banff.

But kinship relationships were paramount and the enduring glue of these networks. The first essential step on a Caribbean career was an introduction through letters or recommendations into the 'interest' or circle of patronage and connections of an established member of the kindred group. Archibald Cameron from Lochaber noted when he landed in 1766:

I happened luckly to se Archy Torcastle and Jon Cameron a brother of Stronse upon my Arraivel. John desaired me to make his House my home.

I verry thankfully Accept his offer. Mr Gair the Gentleman I was recommended to by Doctor Gair was vastly keind to me Used all his endeavours to get me Provided. There bing no prospect of a Berth in town, I went up the Country with Archy to Mount Cameron.[39]

As another Scot wrote from Jamaica, recognizing that family connection was all-important in gaining a place:

Mr James Campbell was in this Island . . . I have not heard from him since (altho I have wrote him) and I believe I may give up all expectation of his doing any thing for me as he has too much Bussiness to remember such as me (as I am not a Campbell) when out of sight. Mr Maxwell . . . say'd he could be of little service to me, which I really believe to be the case, as he has a good many of his own Poor relations to provide for.[40]

The disappointed petitioner had come up hard against the huge network of Argyll Campbells and their affiliates, the Malcolms, reputedly at least a hundred strong, concentrated in the parishes of Hanover and Westmoreland in the west of Jamaica, with place-names such as Campleton, Argyle and Glen Islay scattered across the area. This was probably the most formidable Scottish dynasty in the Caribbean, founded by Colonel John Campbell, the survivor of the Darien expedition in 1700, though branches of the Grant family from the north-east Lowlands, through the Monymusk and Dalvey kindreds, were also prominent in Jamaica. The clan system in the Highlands may have been in its death throes at this time. But clanship was being reinvented in the colonies almost as a family corporation to deliver jobs, posts, sinecures and offices for its members. Even these powerful networks, however, could not always guarantee preferment for their young kinsmen. Indeed, the impression given in some of the correspondence of the time is that the imperial labour market was sometimes so saturated that even family loyalty failed to deliver. Patrons found themselves inundated with requests. James Baillie from Inverness had made a fortune in the West Indies and inevitably became the focus for relatives seeking posts in the Caribbean. He noted in 1770 that he wished 'the Rest of my ffamily well provided for but because places were so seldom to be got' and he had his 'hands so full of Relations', he did not really expect to 'provide for two of them'. Alexander Johnston, the doctor and speculator we have already met, became so frustrated with the constant stream of requests from home that he angrily retorted: 'Do not be plaguing me with recommendations and people. Let them stay where they are.'[41]

3

Some fascinating nuggets from private correspondence aside, little of the historical material allows us much insight into the human world of the Scots in the eighteenth-century Caribbean. Account books, legal records and trade ledgers are essential to build a general picture but they rarely cast light on the human story. Fortunately, there is one source which does introduce us to the world of Scottish communities in the Caribbean. As previously mentioned in Chapter 6, Janet Schaw sailed with her brother Alexander and other family members and servants on the Jamaica packet from Burntisland on the Firth of Forth bound for Antigua in October 1774. Alexander was going to the West Indies to take up an appointment as a customs official in St Kitts. Brother and sister were from a family of gentleman farmers near Edinburgh. Janet wrote home regularly and her letters were gathered in a volume and published eventually as the *Journal of a Lady of Quality being the Narrative of a Journey from Scotland to the West Indies, North Carolina and Portugal in the years 1774 to 1778*.[42] The transoceanic travels of this Scotswoman in her mid-thirties, encompassing as they did voyages to the Caribbean, North America and southern Europe in the 1770s, powerfully reinforces the idea that the Atlantic had now become a great human highway. The journals also provide important insights into the perceptions, assumptions and lifestyles of Scottish expatriates in the West Indies.

From first seeing Antigua from the deck of her ship, Janet Schaw was impressed: 'The beauty of the Island rises every moment as we advance towards the bay; the first plantations we observed were very high and rocky, but as we came further on, they appeared more improved, and when we got into the bay, which runs many miles up the Island, it is not of my power to paint the beauty and the Novelty of the scene.' The 'little paradise' reminded her of Scotland and especially the Highlands 'around Dunkeld' in its physical appearance. Even the tropical climate was not repellent because of the breezes that blew from the east and rendered the island 'healthy and agreeable'. On arrival she and her companions became engaged from the beginning of her brief visit to its end in the busy social life of Antigua. Sumptuous feasts, culminating in desserts with countless varieties of exotic fruit, frequent balls, and a continuous round of visiting and entertainment left the party almost exhausted before they left for St Kitts. Janet was also surprised at the ladies' fashions. London itself 'cannot boast of more elegant shops than you meet with at St Johns' (the capital of the island). Every six weeks the latest fashions were sent from Britain. The stores of St Kitts were also 'full of European commodities'. So enamoured was she of Caribbean society that she began to dread the arrival of the ship that would take her off on the next stage of her journey to the Carolinas: 'We live in constant fear of the arrival of our ship, which will hurray us away, and we have not less than twenty invitations, and we dance every night for several hours, from which no person is exempted.'

Yet even amid the continuous round of pleasure, Janet Schaw was also able to take note of some of the peculiar features of the society. A constant theme running through her journals was the Scottishness of Antigua. This was partly due to the sheer number of Scots she encountered, some known to her personally, others by repute. She even landed 'at a Wharf belonging to a Scotch Gentleman' and thereafter met many Duncans, Millikens, Blairs, Bairds, Hallidays, Tullidephs, Mackinnons and Malcolms. There were also 'mainy Scotch names' on the churchyard graves. In St Kitts, Janet was shown 'several fine plantations belonging to Scotch people who do not reside in them'. One evening, she was entertained to tea by 'a whole Company of Scotch people, our language, my manners, our circle of friends and connections, all the same'. They were all from a professional background and well educated. Their intention was as Henry Brougham put it, 'not to subsist in the colonies but to prepare for shining in the mother country'. A natural consequence was the affirmation of their Scottishness in the tropics. These sojourners were eager to maintain the connection with the homeland to which they wished to return. Janet Schaw and her companions were besieged with questions about life in Scotland. In the same way, Scots stuck together in the Caribbean and provided one another with mutual help. They gave their business primarily to Scottish merchant houses, in part because they supplied a secure connection with home. Mercantile correspondence with expatriates abound, with detailed information on parents, brothers, sister, aunts, uncles and cousins in Scotland. Schaw noted also the extent of planter absenteeism, that several resident planters left their families at home, and that children were always sent back to Scotland for education. Thus there were no Scottish schools or even Presbyterian churches. In Antigua, Janet had to attend an Anglican service on the Sabbath.

On occasion, some of the darker features of Caribbean life and society come through, despite Janet Schaw's euphoria and overall approval. She was conscious of the terrible human cost of living in this paradise. While 'those who live will not fail to make fortunes' the 'change of living more than Climate kills four out of five the first year'. She noted also how the single men who predominated as estate managers and overseers habitually took mistresses from among the younger slave women under their control. Ownership of women slaves implied possession of their bodies as well as their labour. Rape was not a legal offence because the rights of an owner to a slave's body were enshrined in colonial law. It was not simply those who worked on the plantations who kept coloured mistresses. Janet Schaw found her old friend Lady Isabella Hamilton keeping a mulatto girl as a 'pet'. She was probably the bastard child of her husband. Doctors also consorted across the races. When Dr Jonathen Troup arrived in Dominica in 1789, he discovered two of his new medical colleagues, both Scots, had six mulatto children each. It was not too long before Troup himself had a string of mistresses. The evidence suggests that men like these often bought the freedom of their off-spring or even left them money in their wills. Schaw, however, was not impressed:

. . . tho' children of the Sun, they are mortals, and as such must have their share of failings, the most conspicuous of which is the indulgence they give themselves in their licentious and even unnatural amours, which appear too plainly from the crouds of Mulattoes, which you meet in the streets, houses and indeed every where; a crime that seems to have gained sanction from custom, tho' attended with the great inconveniences not only to Individuals, but to the publick in general. The young black wenches lay themselves out for white lovers in which they are but too succesful.

The other Caribbean vice of white men, heavy drinking, also contrib-uted to the general licentiousness. Doctors commonly had to treat many suffering from gonorrhoea after drunken episodes had led to their seduction of slave girls. The aforementioned Dr Troup often attended to this infection but he himself also succumbed to 'virulent gonnorhea'. Despite this he confessed in his journal that he continued to 'make love to a number of Girls in [his] drunkenness'.[43]

Janet Schaw's response to the slave population of Antigua and St Kitts gives an intriguing insight into contemporary attitudes to slavery. Her first contact with blacks came soon after landing. A 'parcel of monkeys' ran in front of her party. She soon discovered, however, that these were not animals but 'negro children, naked as they were born'. The coercive nature of Antiguan society also soon became obvious. At Christmas, for instance, Janet noted the tradition that 'the crack of the inhuman whip must not be heard'. But the sense of profound insecurity felt by the small white minority living among a large majority of enslaved blacks also meant that the militia had to be especially alert at these times: 'It is necessary to keep a look out during this season of unbounded freedom; and every man on the Island is in arms and patrols go all round the different plantations as well as keep guard in the town.' Eventually, in St Kitts, she visited a plantation and saw the system of slave labour for herself. Every ten slaves had a driver, who walked behind them, holding in his hand a short and long whip. Because both men and women were naked 'down to the girdle' she could easily see the marks of the lash on their bodies. Each slave had a basket which was carried up the hill filled with manure and then brought back with sugar canes for the mill: 'They go up at a trot, and return at a gallop, and did you not know the cruel necessity of this alertness, you would believe them the merriest people in the world.'

Schaw's reaction to this scene of routine brutality is interesting. On the one hand, she admits that it must appear 'dreadful' to 'a humane European'. But there is another side to it. The blacks have to been seen as subhuman and therefore cannot suffer pain in the same way as whites. Cruelty therefore is more acceptable:

When one comes to be better acquainted with the nature of the Negroes, the horrour of it must wear off. It is the suffering of the human mind that constitutes the greatest misery of punishment, but with them it is merely corporal. As to the brutes it inflicts no wound on their mind, whose Natures seem made to bear it and whose sufferings are not attended with shame or pain beyond the present.

Janet Schaw's reaction was probably fairly typical of both her time and social class. Although anti-slavery doctrine was gaining a limited circulation by the 1760s, it was not really until the later 1780s that a major public movement was established for the abolition of the British slave trade from Africa. The historian of the abolitionist school in Scotland can state: 'At least until the 1760s there was almost total white acceptance of the use of black men and women as slaves.'[44] The Christian churches sanctioned enslavement until the eighteenth century. St Augustine had set out the accepted Christian doctrine in *De Civitate Dei* when he counselled those in bondage to accept their condition with patience and humility because their reward would come after death. Similarly, the schoolman John Mair reminded his readers of Aristotle's dictum that 'some men are by nature slaves, others by nature free'. Eminent Scots had little difficulty with slavery. James Bruce of Kinnaird, the famous explorer of Abyssinia, saw nothing wrong in accepting the gift of a white Irish slave from the Bey of Tunis. Archibald Dalzel, brother of the Professor of Greek at the University of Edinburgh, wrote one of the first scholarly treatises on Africa, his *History of Dahomey* (1793). But he was also a slave trader and vocal apologist for slavery. Even Robert Burns, the future author of that great egalitarian hymn, *A Man's a Man for a' That*, could contemplate taking a job as a book-keeper on a Jamaican slave plantation in 1786, until the income from the Kilmarnock edition of his poetry made it less necessary for him to leave Scotland.

The role of the Scots in the slave trade and the slave colonies remains controversial. Some Victorian commentators in the years after emancipation were keen to draw a contrast between the experience of Glasgow and the English ports of Liverpool and Bristol where commercial success was unambiguously founded on slaving. Liverpool, in particular, did not make any attempt to conceal the fact. The city's Exchange was decorated in style with a frieze of elephant and negro heads. Some asserted that Glasgow was different and had little to do with the transatlantic traffic in human beings. Certainly Scottish merchants did not take part in the trade on the scale of their counterparts elsewhere. Yet it is futile to deny the close link between the Scottish economy and slavery. Glasgow's success was built on tobacco, sugar and cotton, all commodities produced by slave labour. The slave markets across the Atlantic were also vital to Scottish herring fishermen and linen producers. Capital for the improvement of sugar and tobacco plantations came from Scottish banks and also from private investors, trusts and institutions. The Scots were also more involved than most in the management of the Caribbean economy as plantation owners, overseers, doctors and colonial officials, and profits from these posts were often repatriated to Scotland. Their record was not always creditable. Samuel Taylor Coleridge observed in 1812 that 'of the overseers of the slave plantations in the West Indies three out of four are Scotsmen, and the fourth is generally observed to have very suspicious cheekbones: and on the American Continent the . . . Whippers-in or Neger-Bishops are either Scotchmen or (monstro monstrosius!) the Americanised Descendants of Scotchmen'.[45] James Ramsay, himself a Scot, concluded from his long experience in St Kitts that 'adventurers from Europe are universally more cruel and morose towards slaves than Creoles or native West Indies'.[46] Mrs A. C. Carmichael, the wife of a Scottish planter in St Vincent, also took the view that the blacks regarded the Scots and English overseers differently: 'Scotchmen are proverbially active and economical . . . perhaps there are not two qualities which the majority of negroes dislike more thoroughly.' They were known as hard taskmasters. One of her own slaves described Scotsmen as 'all mean, hold-purse fellows . . . Dey go mean, me no like dem.'[47]

Modern research has also documented much greater direct Scottish involvement in the slave trade than previously assumed. Only a handful of direct slaving voyages from Glasgow and Edinburgh probably took place. But men in smaller towns like Dumfries and Kirkcudbright were more active. Expatriate Scots also participated in Bristol, Liverpool and London.[48] Robert Gordon from Moray was a leading Bristol slaver with ten or more vessels involved in the trade. At least five Scots managed Liverpool slaving syndicates. Their involvement in London was even greater. Around one in ten of all the capital's African traders were Scots in the 1750s, a figure which increased in subsequent decades. Many were also active in Africa, partly through their connections with the Company of Merchants Trading to Africa. Scots were factors and surgeons in the Company's forts and also private traders searching the coastal waters of Sierra Leone and the Gold Coast for their human cargoes. One of the most notable ventures came in 1748 when a consortium of five Scots led by Richard Oswald, Augustus Boyd and Alexander Grant acquired a slave 'trade castle' on the Sierra Leone River at Bance Island linked to a dozen 'outfactories' or slave-gathering posts further inland. The enterprise was mainly staffed with kinsmen and associates of the principals. Between 1748 and 1784 the firm and its satellites shipped nearly 13,000 slaves across the Atlantic.

The full and enthusiastic engagement of Scots at every level of the slave system is beyond doubt. But this is only part of the story. While their fellow countrymen found profit and employment through exploiting slavery, many of the great figures of the Scottish Enlightenment were building the intellectual case against it. Only Lord Kames in his *Sketches in the History of Man* (1774) dissented by attempting to prove that the negro was naturally inferior and only above the apes in intelligence. But he was virtually in a minority of one: 'In the latter half of the eighteenth century the anti-slavery idea ran along all the filaments of an Atlantic intellectual web, at the centre of which sat the philosophers of the Scottish Enlightenment.'[49]

The cream of Scotland's intelligentsia vigorously condemned the slave system on moral, philosophical and economic grounds. Scottish empirical philosophy, especially in the thinking of Francis Hutcheson, emphasized sympathy and fellow-feeling between individuals as the foundation of ethical behaviour. Reconciling this thesis of intrinsic 'benevolence' with the oppression of slavery was impossible. The great French *philosophe*, Montesquieu, is recognized as the father of the intellectual opposition to slavery, especially in his seminal *L'Esprit des Lois* (1748). But it was the intellectual élite of the Scottish Enlightenment who synthesized his work with their own thinking and had the most powerful impact throughout the British colonies. The influential *Encyclopedia* passage on slavery was taken mainly from the writings of the minor Scots jurist, George Wallace. Adam Smith offered a more pragmatic analysis by showing that 'the work done by slaves, though it appears to cost only their maintenance, is in the end dearest of all'.[50] The assumption of the economic advantage of slavery over free labour was therefore exploded by Europe's most influential thinker on economics. John Millar, a student of Smith's, in his *Observations Concerning the Distinction of Ranks* (1771), argued that slavery was a cancer in society, fomenting the rebellion of forced labour and inducing luxury among the governing classes in addition to indolence among free workers.

James Beattie, of the Chair of Moral Philosophy at Marischal College, Aberdeen, in his *Elements of Moral Science* (1790) summarized the indictment of his fellow literati against slavery and the growing critique from evangelical religion:

. . . that slavery is inconsistent with the dearest and most essential rights of man's nature; that it is detrimental to virtue and industry; that it hardens the heart to those tender sympathies which form the most lovely part of the human character; that it involves the innocent in hopeless misery, in order to produce wealth and pleasure for the author of that misery; that it seeks to degrade into brutes beings whom the Lord of heaven and earth endowed with rational souls, and created for immortality; in short, that it is utterly repugnant to every principle of reason, religion, humanity and conscience.[51]

Many of these views first sought the light of day in the many discussion clubs of Enlightenment Scotland, such as the Select Society, the Speculative Society and the Poker Club. They were also in a number of cases the published versions of lectures listened to by innumerable Scottish students, many of whom, ironically, later found employment in the slave societies of the empire. James Beattie, for instance, spent a lifetime in the crusade against slavery. As early as 1788 he was instrumental in promoting Aberdeen support for petitions against the slave trade. He taught at Marischal College in the city from 1760 until 1799 and hoped to influence his students against a system he regarded as barbaric and immoral:

I have been collecting material on the subject [slavery] for upwards of twenty-five years; and, as far as my poor voice could be heard, have laboured in pleading the cause of the poor Africans. This, at least, I can say with truth, that many of my pupils have gone to the West Indies and, I trust, have carried those principles with them and exemplified those principles in their conduct to their unfortunate brethern.[52]

But Beattie was naive. The Scottish intellectual attack on slavery seemed in the short run mainly insulated from the actual practice of countless Scots in the sugar plantations and the African trade, some of whom were doubtless Beattie's former students. The correspondence of these young Scots, many of respectable family and good education, reveals hardly any concern with the morality of slavery. The enormous vested interests integral to the slave economy won over abstract theory. But the penetrating censures of the Scottish intellectuals were far from irrelevant. In the longer term they contributed in a major way to the arsenal of ideas which, combining with the passions of evangelical religion and economic change, ended the slave trade in 1807 and led to final emancipation in the British Empire in 1833. Moreover, some Scots who had served in the Caribbean became key figures in the anti-slavery movement. Among these, the Reverend James Ramsay from St Kitts, and James Stephen and Zachary Macaulay from Jamaica, were of paramount importance. Appalled by their experiences in the West Indies, they drew on those horrors to provide the anti-slavery movement with practical information, guidance and leadership.

Against bitter opposition from planter interest, Ramsay was a robust opponent of slavery during the two decades he served as a clergyman in the West Indies. His publication of *The Essay on the Treatment and Conversion of African Slaves in the British Sugar Colonies* (1783) is regarded by one authority as 'the most important event in the early history of the antislavery movement'.[53]

Ramsay became an important source on the facts of slavery to such abolitionist leaders as William Wilberforce and William Pitt. Similarly, James Stephen's two-volume work on Caribbean slavery remains one of the seminal texts of emancipationist literature. Zachary Macaulay saw the slave system at close quarters. He was the younger son of a Presbyterian minister from Argyll and followed the classic route of a Scots lad in the plantations. Through the influence of an Argyll patron, Sir Archibald Campbell, a former Governor of Jamaica, he went out as a book-keeper, aged sixteen, to that island and then became an overseer on a sugar plantation. He later recalled 'the vexatious, tyrannical, pitiless and capricious conduct' of the Jamaican overseers.[54] Fired with outrage against the system, he eventually became Governor of the colony of liberated slaves in Sierra Leone and later played a prominent role in the Anti-Slavery Society. But men like these were unrepresentative. The vast majority of Scots in the West Indies in the eighteenth century not only favoured the slave system but worked it enthusiastically. One scholar has speculated on the reasons why the Scots made such very efficient middle-managers of empire: 'Their religious background must have been a factor. With its stern rules, invigilation and penances the Kirk had evolved a type of Scot uniquely fitted to serve the Empire as officer, or policeman, overseer, manager; a Scot with an inbred instinct for harrying the unregenerate poor, or Negroes, or natives, for their own good as well as his employer's.'[55] These were all recognizable features of the imperial Scot, not simply in the Caribbean but in all the colonial situations from the North American frontier to the Australian outback.

But it was not simply the middle cadres of the Scottish diaspora which had a distinctive attitude. One argument has it that Scots imperialists in general were more authoritarian than their English counterparts, that they 'found the business of presiding over thousands of unrepresented subjects in the colonies neither very uncongenial nor particularly unfamiliar'.[56] If this view is correct, it indicates a very specific Scottish contribution to empire. The Scots were indeed over-represented among the ranks of the new breed of colonial governors and their officials not only in the Caribbean but elsewhere in North America and the Antipodes. The Linda Colley comment quoted above is not original. It was part of the stock-in-trade of many Scottophobes in Westminster politics and London journalism. But the accusations cannot simply be dismissed because they came from such bigoted sources. A large number of the new imperial élite who were Scots were the sons of gentry families and hence members of a ruling class with unusually wide powers. Landownership in Scotland was and is more concentrated than in any other part of Europe. Feudal privileges lived on when they had disappeared elsewhere in the British Isles. In the later seventeenth century, ancient powers were buttressed by new legislation giving the landed classes wide authority to enforce change on their estates. As Sir John Sinclair had it: 'In no country in Europe are the rights of proprietors so well defined and carefully protected.'[57] Scottish landowners as a class were used to being obeyed and their tenants were long accustomed to the firm hand of proprietorial authority.[58] It would not be in the least surprising if these traditions were exported to all corners of the globe with Scottish governors in the vanguard of empire.

11

Colonizing the Indian Empire

I

Much ink has been spilt in the press, popular books and fictional accounts about the spectacular and dramatic failure of Scotland in the 1690s to establish a colony on the isthmus of Panama. It is hardly surprising, indeed, that the 'Darien Disaster' has entered Scottish historical consciousness. A visionary scheme to establish a vast emporium of trade linking the Atlantic and Pacific Oceans was fatally undermined by a combination of tropical disease, Spanish intervention, organizational incompetence and perfidious Albion. The Darien episode has all the colourful ingredients of a good story. But the more mundane origins of the adventure have often been overlooked amid the popular focus on the unfolding tale of courage, death, destruction, treachery and national catastrophe. In origin, the plan was far from being either romantic or quixotic but rather the product of discussions between hard-headed and very experienced merchants in the leading Scottish towns and some of their connections in the London business community. 'The Company of Scotland Trading to Africa and the Indies', which was then set up as a result of these deliberations, was originally designed to carve out a share of the English East India Company's (EIC) highly lucrative commercial empire. Only when the plan collapsed because of pressure from the EIC and the Westminster government, who feared a Scottish challenge to their hegemony in the East, was the Darien scheme eventually adopted.

Those Scots frustrated at the robust defence of English trade monopolies in the Indies in the years immediately before the union would doubtless have been amazed at the sheer scale of Scottish penetration of the EIC less than two generations later. In 1821 Sir

Walter Scott famously wrote to Lord Montagu that 'India is the corn chest for Scotland where we poor gentry must send our younger sons as we send our black cattle to the south'[1] Scott's description would have been true for any period from the early decades of the eighteenth century and beyond. John Riddy's invaluable figures are persuasive in this respect. Scotland had about one-tenth the population of the British Isles in the eighteenth century, so – all other things being equal – one might expect to find around one Scot in every ten in the army and civil service of the East India Company. The reality was quite different. In the richest of the EIC's provinces, Bengal, between 1774 and 1785, 47 per cent of the Writers appointed were Scots, as were 49 per cent of the officer cadets and more than 50 per cent of the assistant surgeon recruits. The Company also issued their much-prized free merchants' residence permits allowing trade within the east as long as goods were not exported to Britain. Between 1776 and 1785, 371 merchants were awarded this privilege and of these no less than 60 per cent were Scots.[2] By 1813 there were thirty-eight prominent private merchant houses in Calcutta. Of these, fourteen were dominated by Scots. One young Scot noted in a letter home in 1773 that his compatriots 'grow so numerous that I am afraid I shall not be able to enumerate them with that readiness I have hitherto done'.[3]

Precise figures are more elusive in the other EIC provinces, Bombay and Madras. Scottish influence seems to have been less in Bombay, the smaller and poorer of the two. But Madras was broadly similar to Bengal. From 1720 to 1757, for example, all the Principal Medical Officers there were Scots. Again, the Scottish officer class had a dominant position simply because of the high proportion of Scottish regiments serving in India. Fourteen royal regiments (in addition to those of the EIC itself) garrisoned the Indian provinces of the Company between 1754 and 1784. Seven had been raised in Scotland, amounting to some 4,000 to 5,000 men, with six alone defending Madras and the Malabar Coast in the early 1780s.[4] The martial contribution of some Scottish families in India was truly remarkable. So enormous was their involvement that Major Sir Duncan Campbell of Barcaldine, Bart. could pen a huge tome entitled *Records of Clan Campbell in the Military Service of the Honourable East India Company 1600–1858* with biographical details of many hundreds of the name who had held the rank of captain and above and who had seen active service on the subcontinent. Little wonder that Henry Dundas, the all-powerful figure in Indian appointments through his presidency of the Board of Control in the later eighteenth century, could write to Sir Archibald Campbell, his nominee as Governor of Madras: 'It is said that with a Scotchman at the Board of Control and a Scot at the Government of Madras all India will soon be in their hands, and that the county of Argyll will be depopulated by the emigrations of Campbells to be provided for at Madras.'[5]

This evidence prompts several comments. In some ways, the Scottish migration to India was not unlike that to the Caribbean. The West Indies movement was dominated by single males, younger sons of the landed gentry or the scions of middle-rank professional and mercantile families, who had limited prospects at home. They were an élite, numbering no more than 1,000 between 1750 and 1815, who served in India not to stay but to earn 'an independence' or 'a competence' as quickly as possible, then return home, buy a small landed property and live well on the income from rentals and investment in government securities and East India stock. A lad who went to Bengal at sixteen or seventeen, the basic age for entering EIC service, hoped to be back in Britain before he was forty, 'free and independent like a gentleman and able to enjoy myself, my family and friends in the manner I could wish'. One of the Dalrymple clan reported in similar vein to his family patron, Sir Hew Dalrymple, during the long voyage to Calcutta in 1752: 'I do expect it to be fifteen or twenty years at least. In that time I may be made Governour. If not that, I may make a fortune which will make me live like a gentleman.'[6] But, for reasons explored below, India differed from the West Indies in one crucial respect. Contemporary opinion had it that the fabulous riches of the East made it easier for a man to make money faster, and, if his luck was in, come home with an even more colossal pile than could be accumulated anywhere else in the empire. For this reason, competition for Indian places, especially in the second half of the eighteenth century, was much more intense than elsewhere. For the same reason, the Scots who ventured to the East, outside the rank and file of the military, were usually well-born, even if their family were of modest means. To a greater extent than in North America and the Caribbean, they were the sons of the gentry and even, on occasion, of the aristocracy.

The resounding success of some legendary figures did excite emulation among many others. John Johnstone of Westerhall returned to Scotland in 1765 with an estimated fortune of £300,000 which helped him to acquire three landed estates and a parliamentary interest. It was said of him that he pursued wealth with an enterprise and a dedicated ruthlessness second only to the victor of Plassey, the mighty Robert Clive himself. Equally celebrated was William Hamilton, arguably the most famous doctor to serve in India during the whole three centuries course of the empire. A cadet of the family of Hamilton of Dalziell in Lanarkshire, he first came to the East as a naval surgeon in 1711. His major claim to fame was his successful treatment of the Moghul emperor for venereal disease. Hamilton was showered with gifts including an elephant, 5,000 rifles, two diamond rings, a set of gold buttons and a presentation set of all his own surgical instruments fashioned in gold. He also brought untold benefits to the East India Company when its rights to free trade in Bengal, Bihar and Orissa were confirmed in consequence of Hamilton's cure of the royal patient. John Farquhar outdid both Johnstone and Hamilton in rapacity and parsimony. At his death in 1826 he was worth £1.5 million, making him one of the richest Britons of the nineteenth century. Farquhar's commercial drive was matched only by his eccentricity. On his return from India he was said to have offered to endow one of the Scottish universities with the immense sum of £100,000 to establish a Chair of Atheism, only to be disappointed when his generosity was summarily rejected. There were also the Scots who rose to the very top in Indian government. An extraordinary figure here was Sir John Malcolm, born in the Scottish Borders in 1769, one of seventeen children of a tenant farmer in Dumfriesshire. Tradition has it that he excelled in his interview with the Directors of the EIC in 1781. Aged twelve, he was asked by the assembled worthies, 'Why, little man, what would you do if you were to meet Hydar Ali, the Sultan of Mysore?' Hydar Ali was one of the most formidable territorial princes in India and a feared enemy of the British. The precocious Malcolm was said to have instantly replied, 'Do? Why, I'd oot wi' my sword and cut aff his heid.' This might have gained him acceptance for service in the army of the EIC. But 'Boy Malcolm', as he was known, also prospered under the patronage of the Johnstones and their networks. He rose irresistibly through the ranks to become a lieutenant-colonel, emissary to Persia on two crucial diplomatic missions and, eventually, to receive the crowning glory of the governorship of Bombay from 1827 to 1830, before returning home covered in honours.

Not even the tobacco and sugar princes of Glasgow could equal the colossal fortunes of men such as these. 'Nabobs' (a corruption of Nawab) became notorious when they returned to Britain for wealth beyond the dreams of avarice. But there was a much darker side to the Indian adventure. In simple terms, the risks of never returning home were very high. Many loathed the heat and the humidity and the sense of being overwhelmed by a vast and intimidating alien culture. One company officer in 1780 had not yet made enough to retire but he still intended to come back to Scotland rather than die 'in this vile country'. Thirty years before, a brother officer had voiced similar thoughts: 'I'd almost as soon live in Hell as in India,' he wrote with feeling.[7] For the homesick and maladjusted there was always some compensation in the solaces of hard drinking, Indian concubines, flamboyant socializing, and an endless round of feasts and bibulous dinners. But little could protect Europeans from the relentless ravages of disease. Success in India depended on many things – patronage, luck, ruthlessness and the nerve to take risks. Above all, however, it depended on the simple fact of survival.[8]

Mortality rates among the Company's men were often horrendous. Even on the outward-bound voyage to India disaster could occur. Highland regiments, usually famed for their sense of discipline and *esprit de corps*, were sometimes likely to mutiny when the dread news came through that they were to be posted to India. Episodes such as the fate of the Highlanders of the 78th Foot were long remembered. During the voyage to the East, the regiment lost 247 men, including its commander, the Earl of Seaforth, from fever and scurvy. While a single human catastrophe on this scale may have been unusual, more typical was the lethal impact of disease on Europeans in India itself. Over the period 1707 to 1775, 57 per cent of the EIC's civil servants died there. Before the 1760s about two-thirds of all the Writers, who had competed so eagerly to go to India and make their fortunes, never returned:

Grisly as an average mortality of 57 per cent for the whole period 1707 to 1775 undoubtedly is, the averages per decade tell an even more macabre story: 66 per cent of those who joined the civil service between 1707 and 1716 died in India; between 1717 and 1726 the rate was 60 per cent; it was

66 per cent between 1727 and 1736; 62 per cent from 1737 to 1746; and 74 per cent from 1747 to 1756. Thereafter the figures begin to improve . . .'[9]

Ironically this grim harvest took place at a time when mortality among the British upper classes at home was falling. A study of the British peerage shows that nearly 45 per cent died between fifteen and fifty, which was roughly the age of service in India.[10] Before the 1770s, however, around two-thirds of the civil service aged from seventeen to forty would die in Bengal: 'a man aged twenty in the sample who stayed in Britain could expect another forty years of life; a young man who went to Bengal could expect to die there'.[11] It has to be remembered also that the civil servants were the salaried élite of the EIC who lived in much more comfortable circumstances than the Company's servants as a body. The culling was even worse in the army. In the 1760s such was the death rate among the European regiments that an annual renewal of men of at least a quarter was necessary. One return of casualties among the officers and cadets of the Bengal army between 1770 and 1776 crystallizes the enormity of the problem. A mere six fell in action, nine died by drowning, but 208 were killed by disease. Manifestly, even if some did make their fortunes, the riches would often only be enjoyed by widows, father-less children and other family members back in Britain.

Yet the risks involved do not appear to have deterred. Influential patrons, EIC directors and government officials continued to be inundated with countless requests for places and posts in both the civil and military service. India was not seen as a death-trap but as a fabulously rich society with huge potential for plunder. In this sense, a fundamental distinction was made between India on the one hand and the West Indian and American colonies on the other. To make your pile in the plantation economies required investment of time, effort, money, steady application to business and the management of complex enterprises. Profits accumulated over long periods of time rather than through a few lucky windfalls. The perception about Bengal, Madras and Bombay was that the opportunities for massive gains were not only much more abundant, but great wealth could come very quickly indeed to the fortunate few.

To understand this mentality it is necessary to begin by briefly sketching the nature of the East India Company's presence in the subcontinent. The Company was first granted its exclusive right to conduct English trade with India and the East by a charter of Elizabeth I in 1600: Asian commerce was immensely attractive as a source of commodities and crops which were not easily available in Europe. Pepper and spices were at first the most desirable articles but they were joined in the eighteenth century by mass exports to the West of fine textiles, cotton cloth, silk, tea, coffee, porcelain and furniture. Trade was lucrative but also very costly, and capital was tied up for long periods because of the six-month voyage from Europe around the Cape of Good Hope and back again. Risks were also not inconsiderable. Thus commerce between Asia and Europe came to be dominated by huge corporations usually chartered by individual states. In addition to the EIC, Denmark, France, Holland and Sweden all had similar organizations which could raise substantial capital, plan strategies for the long term and spread risk among numerous shareholders. By the early eighteenth century, for instance, the EIC had stock of £3.2 million, a borrowing capacity of £6 million and 3,000 shareholders. By contemporary standards it was a commercial colossus and a huge international company, pulling ahead of both the Dutch and the French East India companies, especially in the key textile trades. To facilitate these, the EIC had acquired three bases, or 'factories', at Madras, Bombay and Calcutta. The Moghul empire in India was keen to foster trade and made available areas like these to foreign merchants where they were given protection, allowed certain privileges and some jurisdiction over their employees. Bengal, the territory which served Calcutta, soon became pre-eminent as a rich province and a centre of excellence for the production of cottons and silks.

From about the middle decades of the eighteenth century, the British moved to a much more aggressively expansionist policy in India. The reasons for this transformation in policy have long been debated by scholars and the detailed issues need not detain us here. In part it was the result of the long conflict with France being played out on the Asiatic stage. But, in addition, the decline of Moghul imperial power led to the emergence of more influential regional princedoms. Several of these became closely associated with the British as allies, partners in the struggle for spheres of influence, creditors and employers of the EIC's troops to advance their cause in local territorial disputes. This new instability, however, could also mean intermittent conflict between EIC and Indian interests. In 1756, for instance, relations broke down with the new Nawab of Bengal, Siraj-ud-Daule, who then annexed the settlement of Calcutta. A force from Madras under the leadership of Robert Clive took revenge on the Nawab by comprehensively defeating his army at Plassey in June 1757. This was a watershed victory. Successive Nawabs then became clients of the British and when one did attempt to break out of this dependency in 1763 he suffered defeat with his allies at the battle of Buxar the following year. By the Treaty of Allahabad of 1765, the EIC was granted the *diwani*, or the right, to administer and tax the whole of Bengal and its associated provinces. At a stroke, British rule was established over 20 million Indians. Even more crucially, from the perspective of the Company's servants, Plassey and Buxar became the key foundations for a veritable bonanza of pillage. The years 1757 to *c.* 1770 were the years in which the fame of India as a place of easy riches was built. As one authority has noted: 'For the Company civil servants these twelve years were the only time during the eighteenth century when survival in Bengal virtually guaranteed that a man would return home with a fortune.'[12]

It was not company salaries which provided the route to wealth. The formal hierarchy of the civil service consisted of Writers, then above them Factors, Junior Merchants and Senior Merchants. By the standards of the public administration at home they were well rewarded, partly to compensate them for the risks they ran, absence from their families and the high cost of living in Calcutta. But most of the Company's servants until the later eighteenth century did not accept that they were administrators. They regarded themselves also as merchants, trading not only for their employers, the EIC, but also for their own private benefit. During the halcyon years of the 1750s and 1760s there was plenty of scope for exploitation of their business talents. In a sense they could also behave as independent and often predatory entrepreneurs. The distances from the Company's head-quarters in Leadenhall Street, London, were simply too great to permit effective supervision. Servants were therefore allowed a remarkable freedom of action until the EIC reforms of the 1780s.

One of their key privileges was the right to private trade on their own account within Asia. This rather than their salaries was the primary source of income for civil servants, army officers, surgeons and even chaplains. This jealously guarded perquisite was incorporated in a Writer's covenant (or contract of employment) and was approved of by the Company until the 1760s and beyond. Sharp practice flourished. One common procedure was to use the Company's funds for private business, so avoiding high interest charges. Some servants sold their own goods to the EIC under assumed Indian names while others charged commission in their role as collectors of rents and dues from the native population living in the Company's settlement.

But all of this was for the small fry. The really spectacular gains were made by more senior figures in the civil and military services who were prepared to exploit the new British position of power in Bengal. They were now in a position to dictate who should become Nawabs and also fill the major provincial offices. Aspirants had to pay a very high price for British support and protection. 'Presents' became an integral part of the political relationships between clients and their imperial patrons. Even when an Indian ruler proved truculent, gain was still possible in the long run. Thus in 1763 Mir Kasim took up arms against the Company but was eventually defeated and deposed. His successor, Mir Jafir, was required to pay large sums in compensation for the losses experienced by the Company's private traders during the rebellion. When a Select Committee of the House of Commons investigated, it concluded that £2,169,665 had been distributed in the form of presents in Bengal between 1757 and 1765, a figure which some modern scholars consider to have been an underestimate. By the early 1780s the enormous flow of presents had slowed to a trickle but not before it had enriched many principal Company servants, including Robert Clive, who left for home with the greatest fortune of all, and such irrepressible Scots as John Johnstone.

Rapacity also pervaded the senior ranks of the EIC army. A favourite ploy was lending to Indian grandees at exorbitant rates of interest. Fighting a campaign was usually conditioned by the prospect of prize money or plunder. Prize money was collected from the spoils of battle and distributed according to a fixed scale. The greatest prizes of all could be expected to come from a siege, because the Indian rich traditionally hoarded their wealth and an assault on a besieged town or fortress held out the promise of spectacular gains. In 1799 the capital of Mysore, Seringapatam, was stormed by royal troops led by Lord Harris, the Commander-in-Chief at Madras, including battle-hardened Highlanders of the 73rd and 74th regiments, commanded by the Scot, General David Baird. The taking of Seringapatam with Scottish soldiers to the fore was immortalized in David Wilkie's epic painting which now hangs in the National Gallery of Scotland. It depicts Baird, the hero of the hour, standing triumphantly above the corpse of the Sultan of Mysore, Tipu Sahib. However, the canvas does not reveal either the terrible carnage of the battle when over 10,000 Mysoreans died, the atrocities which were committed the following day or the mass of booty eagerly seized by the victorious British troops. Harris, the overall commander of the operation, was reputed to have returned to England with £150,000 after the fall of Seringapatam.

Modern scholarship had shown that the 'annual plunder of Bengal' (to use Edmund Burke's phrase) lasted for a relatively short period of time and involved relatively few people. But systematic pillage on this scale made an enormous impact at home and acted as a powerful incentive to recruitment for the Indian service which more than counterbalanced the risks and hazards associated with life in Asia. An increase in the number of Writers began in the early 1760s. Twenty-eight were appointed in 1762. By 1770 this figure had reached forty-six. Numbers rose partly because of the expanding activity of the EIC. The main engine, however, as the Company confirmed, was the enormous pressure brought to bear on directors by patrons keen to sponsor many more young men to take advantage of the supposed riches of Bengal. To Warren Hastings, Governor of the province in the 1770s, it was 'the curse of patronage' above all else which accounted for the Company becoming dangerously bloated with additional servants. Ironically, this growing surplus of manpower also helped to signal an end to the golden years of predatory pillage. Not only had many of the richer seams been worked out but there were now too many players on the field. Competition for India jobs by the 1770s had never been more intense. This was hardly surprising. The Indian bonanza had attracted massive publicity at home. The story of the greatest nabob of all, Robert Clive, and his extraordinary rise from rags to riches, was enough in itself to generate interest. He and others of his kind were satirized on the London stage, notably in *The Nabob* by Samuel Foote, first performed in November 1773. Parliamentary investigations were being held to expose the chicanery and extortion by those who had come back to Britain with huge personal fortunes. What caused increasing concern was their penetration to the very heart of British political authority. The number of nabob MPs rose from five in 1767 to twenty-six by 1780. Some argued that in the process they were using the same corrupt and rapacious methods in Parliament which they had refined in Asia. Horace Walpole fumed in 1773: 'What is England now? A sink of Indian wealth, filled with nabobs and emptied by Macaronis! A senate sold and defused! A country overrun by horse-races! A gaming, robbing, wrangling, railing nation without principles, genius, character or allies.'[13] Public disquiet at how Bengal was governed then led to the 1773 Regulating Act to provide greater discipline on the Company's activities. This was then followed by the impeachment in 1786 of Warren Hastings over his methods and rewards, a process which then dragged on for a further nine years before ending in his acquittal.

All this gave the oxygen of publicity to Indian service and is the essential context for understanding the relentless clamour for Bengal jobs which characterized the period. It also begs a key question: how, against this background of intense competition, did the Scots manage to do so well in achieving Indian places?

2

The question is not easily answered. One theory has it that, on the model of the Roman Empire, the ambitious and talented from distant provinces came to positions of ascendancy in the metropolis. But Scottish success was not equalled by the other nations of the Celtic fringe, the Welsh and the Irish. The Welsh failed to make their mark in India. They were not an insignificant force in North America, but apart from figures like Sir William Jones, founder of the Asiatic Society of Bengal, their presence in the subcontinent was hardly noticed. It was a somewhat different story with the Irish. Traditionally, pride of place is given to the Highland regiments in the conquest of India. But this is an exaggeration. The Irish were much superior numerically. Indeed, in 1815 over 50 per cent of the crown forces were Irishmen. They were also well represented in the European levies of the East India Company. It would not be an exaggeration to say that the Irish rank and file were the real cutting edge of imperial expansion in India. However, enduring discrimination against

Catholics reduced the number of Irish officers. They were also notable by their virtual absence in the EIC civil service. One recent assessment has concluded:

Unlike the Scots, Irishmen were not welcomed as partners nor were they encouraged to regard it [the Empire] as a source of careers: they were seen as rivals and competitors. Very little Irish money was invested in the East India Company, and though there was a substantial Irish recruitment into the Company's army from the 1760s on, the number of Irish compared to the Scots in the administrative branch was negligible.[14]

Once upon a time it was believed that Henry Dundas, the leading Scottish politician of the day, Pitt's right-hand man and the key figure in Indian appointments from 1784, was ultimately responsible for Scottish success. The Earl of Rosebery, for instance, later in the nineteenth century memorably asserted that Dundas had 'Scotticised India and Orientalised Scotland'.[15] The facts, however, do not support the claim. There was no significant increase in the proportions of Scots appointed to Indian posts after the advent of Dundas in the 1780s. The boom times of the Scottish invasion of India had already taken place before he became an influential commissioner on the EIC Board of Control from 1784 and President of this body from 1793. Indeed, Dundas himself was wary of the widespread suspicion that he was advancing his fellow countrymen; hence Scottish appointments actually declined somewhat compared with the 1770s when the Governor, Warren Hastings, seemed intent on diverting most Indian patronage to his friends and associates north of the Border. Dundas did receive countless applications and recommendations for Indian appointments but he usually replied that he could only oblige a small number. As he observed in one response:

From the contents of your letter, I perceive that you are under great misapprehension on the subject of Writers to India, and it is necessary to put you right on the subject. The whole appointments belong exclusively to the Individual Directors except two which they annually give to the President of the Board of Control. In addition to these two I reckon that on an average, while I was at the head of India affairs, I received two more from individual Directors, whom I had occasion to oblige in the course of my Patronage in their Departments.[16]

As Dundas's letter stressed, the key to Indian appointments lay with the Company's directorate. For much of the eighteenth century, however, this London-based organization was dominated by the great English merchants of the capital, as were the ranks of the 3,000 shareholders who provided the Company's finance. Manifestly, this placed aspiring Scots at a disadvantage because these men were likely to favour their own associates in the London commercial fraternity. But there was more to it than this. Scottish Members of Parliament after the union were slow to obtain the kind of state offices that could have provided influence. Only three held such appointments before 1753 and none did so in the armed services. Many in the capital regarded the Scots, in the words of one historian, as 'poor and pushy relations, unwilling to pay their full share of taxation, yet constantly demanding access to English resources in terms of trades and jobs'.[17]

At times, this latent suspicion could explode into rampant Scottophobia. The '45 and its aftermath was one such occasion. The fact that a small force, drawn from the poorest region of Britain, was able to march almost to the very centre of power was not only unnerving but perceived as national humiliation. This was one reason why the government's post-Culloden strategy of 'pacification' in the Highlands was so draconian. The '45 also reminded many south of the Border that the Scots could still not be fully trusted. As previously discussed, national resentments came to the boil again with Bute's premiership. John Wilkes and his associates launched a xenophobic campaign against Scottish ambition, which was taken up by rioting crowds. Dundas recalled this frenzied Scottophobia when he counselled during the 1780s against advancing too many Scots to positions within the India service for fear of inciting yet another angry backlash.

However, amid these several constraints the Scots still retained some advantages which help to explain their rapid rise to power in the Indian empire. They were hungrier for imperial appointments not simply because of the comparative poverty and more limited opportunities within Scotland itself, but because breaking into the more lucrative political and administrative posts in London was exceedingly difficult until the later decades of the eighteenth century. They therefore were more willing to seek preferment far from home in conditions which would have repelled many patrician Englishmen. This was a tradition which generations of their families had followed in the past to Europe. The empire was simply a new frontier in the centuries-old migrations of the Scots. This might explain why more high-born Scots than Englishmen were to be found in the EIC's civil service. Of the 114 applications which survive from Scotsmen to join the Company's civil service between 1750 and 1795, a little over a third listed their fathers' occupations. Nearly half were gentry, with the rest from commerce and the professions. Unusually, however, blood relations of the Scottish aristocracy, including the third son of the Earl of Bute himself, the brother of the Earl of Strathmore, a son of the Earl of Dundonald and three Lindsays from the family of Lord Balcarres, also featured in the civil and military branches of the Company.

The Scots were also able to exploit the niche military market in India. Even in Britain the army was one area where they seem to have been able to penetrate the officer class with relative ease. By the mid-eighteenth century, for instance, one in four British army regimental officers was a Scot. The martial background of the Highland gentry and the fact that a commission in the Company's army was free, though less prestigious than similar positions in the royal regiments, made a military career in India attractive. A post in the army also required less use of patronage than the more desirable civil appointments. This may explain why there were proportionally more Scots, particularly Gaels, in the military than in the civil service. Yet, as already noted, officers did not simply depend on their salaries but stood to gain also from booty and profits from personal trade. Continuous hostilities in India during the later eighteenth century (four wars were fought against the sultanate of Mysore alone), together with the new dynamic towards territorial annexation, massively expanded the Company's forces. By 1800 it was one of the largest standing armies in the world with numbers rising from just over 18,000 men in 1763 to 154,500 by 1805. Most troops were native Indians (sepoys) but were officered by Europeans. Another niche career was medicine. As early as 1731 John Drummond of Quarrell, himself a major force in Scottish patronage in India, complained to one of his relatives: 'I have told you once again not to recommend any Surgeons to me, for all the East India Company ships have either Scots Surgeons or Surgeon's mates, and till some of them die I can, nor will look out for no more, for I am made the jest of mankind, plaguing all the Societys of England with Scots Surgeons . . .'[18]

Social standing, martial experience and educational background may indeed have given the Scots a cutting edge. But especially after 1760, the clamour for India posts was such that only the power of patronage could easily unlock them. As one senior army officer put it, though the Company was 'resolved to employ such as appears to have the most merit, at the same time there is no doubt but *interest will in the end prevail . . .*'.[19] Only in recent years has the story emerged in full detail of how Scottish outsiders colonized the jealously guarded citadels of India patronage. From modern researches a powerful link can be established between British politics in the post-union period and the increasing preferment of Scots to posts at the periphery of empire.

The crux of the matter was the volatility of the union relationship in the first few decades after 1707. The treaty had been born out of a marriage of convenience between the governing classes in Edinburgh and London, and its successful passage through the Scottish Parliament was a close-run thing, delivered in the teeth of a good deal of popular hostility outside the House. This was hardly the context for the stable and harmonious development of 'Great Britain'. Then again there was the continuing Jacobite threat, which was always more menacing in Scotland than in England, not least because the exiled House of Stuart could usually count on the military support of several of the strongest Highland clans. Jacobites were implacably opposed to the union since they viewed it – correctly – as a means of buttressing the Revolution of 1688–9 and so ensuring that the Stuarts would never again return to their rightful inheritance. Until Jacobitism was finally crushed (and this did not happen until after the '45), the union was always likely to be threatened to a greater or lesser extent. This was especially the case if France, with its enormous military and naval resources, chose to intervene on the Stuart side.

At first, the London strategy seems to have been to do as little as possible and so keep the Scots quiet. On the whole the policy succeeded at first, apart from the abolition of the Scottish Privy Council, the chief executive organ of government in Scotland, in 1708. The end of the Privy Council was a key development because it gravely weakened the ability of government to respond vigorously and decisively in crisis situations. The vacuum which it left at the centre of power could only give further comfort to the Jacobites. More provocative and serious were the inflammatory acts of the Tory government which replaced the Whig coalition at the elections of 1710. The High Church Tories seemed bent on a policy of cutting down the privileges of the Church of Scotland enshrined in the Treaty of Union. This was not so much hostility towards the Scots as such as a general campaign against Presbyterians in both England and Scotland by high Anglicans in the Tory Party. The initiative was enthusiastically supported by Scottish Tories, who were also noted for their Episcopalian loyalties. In 1711 James Greenshields, an Episcopalian minister, appealed to the House of Lords against his imprisonment by the magistrates of Edinburgh for defying the presbytery of the city and using the English liturgy. Recourse to the Lords was possible within the terms of the treaty of 1707, but the subsequent decision to allow the Anglican prayer book to be used for worship in an Episcopalian meeting-house enraged the capital's Presbyterians. This was then followed in 1712 by two more offensive measures, the Toleration Act and the Patronage Act. The former granted freedom of worship to Scottish Episcopalians as long as they agreed to pray for the reigning monarch, while the latter re-established the primary right of patrons, who were usually local landowners, to appoint to vacant parishes and church offices. Patronage had been abolished as part of the Presbyterian revolution of 1690 because it conflicted with the rights of the community itself to decide on a candidate to fill a parish vacancy.

All this outraged the Kirk and seemed to undermine the Act of Security guaranteeing Presbyterian rights in the event of union, an enactment central to the acceptance of the treaty itself. But in addition, the legislation of 1712 raised the issue of the nature of 1707 and the extent to which the treaty was an inviolate, fundamental law or subject to change at the whim of the sovereign legislature in Westminster. Perhaps of more direct impact on the Scottish people was the new taxation regime within the union. In the first few decades after 1707 there was a huge increase in customs and excise duties together with a significant extension in the range of commodities on which tax was paid. Partly, this was because the existing levels of taxation were simply not sufficient to cover the cost of Scottish civil government and administration, and London ministers were also soon appalled at the scale of smuggling and customs evasion. In addition, after the War of the Spanish Succession ended in 1713, the tax burden in Britain started to shift from the land tax to customs dues and excise payments on a whole range of commodities, including beer, salt, linen, soap and malt. These were all vital necessities of life for most people in Scotland. Salt, for instance, was the universal food preservative of the day and linen the most widely produced cloth. Equally, tax increases were likely to bite deeply because the Scottish economy was still in the doldrums in the first decade after union, and those pamphleteers who had optimistically predicted an economic miracle were now proven hopelessly wrong. Home salt, which had not been taxed before 1707, doubled in price when duties were imposed in 1713. That same year, the House of Commons voted to apply the malt tax to Scotland in direct defiance of the provisions of the treaty itself, a decision which would have significantly pushed up the price of ale, the most popular drink in Scotland at the time. The fury was such that the tax was never properly enforced.

To the Scots this was the climax of a whole stream of provocative actions which threatened to break the union. Scottish peers and members of the Commons came together in a series of meetings and agreed that the only solution was repeal of the treaty. What was remarkable was the unanimity of all parties on such a fundamental issue, a very rare occurrence indeed in the faction-ridden world of Scottish politics. The motion was put by the Earl of Findlater in the House of Lords in June 1713 and was only narrowly defeated by four proxy votes. The outcome demonstrated not only the disillusion of the Scottish nobility but also the fact that there was little enthusiasm in England for the union either. This alienation helped to feed the next great Jacobite rising, led by the Earl of Mar in 1715. Mar himself had been a crucial figure in helping the Court manage the votes for the treaty in 1706–7 and had then sat in the United Kingdom Parliament. But he was out of favour with the new Hanoverian monarch, George I, and changed sides to the Stuarts, thus living up to his nickname, 'Bobbing John'. In 1715 Mar was able to assemble an army of 10,000 men, which was more than double the force that the government levies under the Duke of Argyll were able to muster. After the collapse of the '15, the Earl of Stair, an ultra-loyal Whig and British ambassador to France, noted that there was a real danger of another rebellion unless the ruinous consequences of the union were addressed. This was an admission by a high-ranking friend of the Court that the survival of the union was not yet assured.

However, Stair's hopes for an improvement in Anglo-Scottish relationships were premature since there was a fundamental cause of friction which would not easily or quickly disappear. The view from Westminster was that the Scots were not paying their way through taxation because of the huge scale of smuggling and systematic revenue fraud said to be endemic in Scottish society. On the other hand, Scotland had been accustomed to low taxes and relaxed methods of gathering revenue before the union, so that the new impositions after 1707 were bitterly resented both on economic grounds and because they were seen as an attempt by London to force Scotland to contribute to the English National Debt, which had swollen hugely to finance the War of the Spanish Succession. Popular retribution both against revenue increases and against more rigorous methods of collection was exacted through violence against the hated customs officers. These local incidents were nothing, however, compared with the national outrage after the decision in 1724 by Sir Robert Walpole's government to apply the malt tax to Scotland with effect from June 1725. The earlier attempt in 1713 had brought about a vote in the House of Lords which nearly dissolved the union, and this latest initiative unleashed a wave of popular anger in the summer of 1725, with riots breaking out in Stirling, Dundee, Ayr, Elgin, Paisley and Glasgow. The disturbances in Glasgow were by far the most serious. The local Member of Parliament, Daniel Campbell of Shawfield, was suspected of supporting the hated Malt Tax Act. The mob took its revenge by burning and looting his impressive town-house, engaged in a pitched battle with the local garrison which resulted in eight fatalities, and then drove the retreating troops out of the city towards Dumbarton. It took the intervention of General Wade with a force of 400 dragoons and accompanying foot to restore order finally and bring to an end a dangerous challenge to the union state.[20]

Certainly the riots of 1725 concentrated the minds of Walpole's government on the Scottish problem. The insurrection itself was a serious matter, but of equal concern was the apparent impotence of the Scottish administration when confronted with such a major challenge to law and order. The Lord Advocate of Scotland, the country's senior law officer, Robert Dundas, had in fact opposed the Malt Tax and was dismissed as a result. The Secretary for Scotland, the Duke of Roxburgh, did little, and the vacuum in executive authority left by the abolition of the Privy Council was now obvious for all to see. The Earl of Islay, younger brother of the Duke of Argyll, who was sent to investigate the situation, reported to Walpole that there had been 'a long series of no administration' in Scotland; the 'mere letter of the law had little or no effect with the people'. This was tantamount to saying that Scotland was ungovernable within the union. It was not a situation which could be allowed to continue.[21]

Walpole's solution was to sack the incompetent Roxburgh and appoint Islay to manage Scottish affairs. The decision was a turning-point, not only in Anglo-Scottish relationships, but in the development of the Scottish connection with India. Islay, later third Duke of Argyll from 1743, became the dominant political figure in Scotland between the 1720s and his death in 1761, excepting the brief few years from to 1742 to 1746. Such was his power that he became known as the 'King of Scotland'. His influence rested on a solemn contract with Walpole: Islay would deliver political stability in Scotland and the votes of most Scottish MPs in return for the lion's share of patronage and the authority to govern north of the Border. The Walpole connection soon gave Islay immense sources of patronage which he deployed with great skill in alliance with his two principal agents, Andrew, Lord Milton, and Duncan Forbes of Culloden, 'King Duncan' as he was dubbed in the Highlands. The civil administration, law courts, army, church and universities were all penetrated as Islay relentlessly built up a formidable empire of clients and dependents. It was reckoned that two-thirds of the judges promoted to the Court of Session owed their position to his influence, and the Campbell interest was also paramount in the appointment of sheriffs who, it was alleged, were 'little more than a list of the sons, sons-in-law, and alliances' of Islay's clients. By the 1730s his power was such that even the monarch could describe him as 'Vice Roy in Scotland'. Fundamental to the operation of this new patronage machine was access to India posts.

There were never enough Scottish jobs available for use as bribes to the country's tiny electorate of around 4,000 individuals, their associates and dependants. Nor was it easy to surrender to the Scots the existing crown appointments in London, which were claimed by English interests. The rich vein of East India posts promised an attractive alternative. The Company was an independent corporation but ministers could always lean on it to provide a source of patronage in return for periodic renewal of its charter and the promise of commercial favours from the state in areas like government contracting for the army and navy. Thus it was that East India postings became the foundation for bringing more political stability to Scotland and forging a stronger union.[22] For Walpole's government it was a more effective and less costly strategy than military coercion, which could have been counterproductive. Its impact was quickly apparent. By 1750 there was already a marked influx of Scots into the Company. By that date they had taken three out of every eight Writers' posts in Bengal. A key figure in the deployment of this patronage between 1725 and 1742 was John Drummond of Quarrell, one of the few leading directors in the Company of Scottish birth. He linked the Argyll interest in the north with EIC contacts in London and the Walpole political connection which increasingly depended on an amenable phalanx of Scottish votes in the Commons for support. Jacobite families who had been 'out' in the '15 were given special attention for favour and reward in order to integrate them into the Whig establishment in Church and State. One reason for the steady haemorrhaging of Jacobite support between the two major rebellions of 1715 and 1745 may well have been this untold story of the impact of India patronage on traditional loyalties.

This early bedrock of Scottish success meant that when demand for India posts became insatiable after Plassey in 1757, Scottish interests and networks were firmly established. By that date more Scots than ever before had become members of the Company's directorate and major holders of stock. Some of the early eighteenth-century generation had also returned to Britain as rich men and maintained a strong interest in the Company's affairs. These men were important conduits for the distribution of patronage in later decades. Nevertheless it was an Englishman, Warren Hastings, who really drove the Caledonian gravy-train by the 1770s. Hastings was Governor of Bengal from 1772 to 1774 and subsequently Governor-General of India from 1774 to 1785. Impeached by Parliament for the alleged criminality of acts committed in these offices, his highly publicized trial lasted from 1788 to 1795. Less well known than this notoriety, however, was his role as 'Scotland's Benefactor'.[23] It was he rather than Henry Dundas who unashamedly promoted Scots and ensured that they attained a greater representation in the civil and military services than ever before or since. Hastings's policy was based on pragmatism and expediency. Surrounded by enemies in both London and India, he came to rely on the Scottish stockholders in the Company to maintain his position. They were never a majority but they proved their loyalty on several occasions. In return, Hastings was prepared to favour their kin and friends if they demonstrated ability. His 'Scotch Guardians', as he called them, were always selected for the most important and challenging missions of his governorship. They included Major Alex Hannay of Kirkcudbright who led the mission to the Moghul court in 1775, and Alexander Elliot, son of Sir Gilbert Elliot of Minto, Treasurer of the Navy, who was Hastings's emissary to the Bhonsla Raja of Berar (the Mahratta leader). The irony was that these Scots and others were fully implicated in Hastings's alleged crimes during his lengthy impeachment. But this was also confirmation of how close they had come to the very centre of power in the Indian empire.

12

Australian Foundations

I

The first British settlement on Australian soil was established in January 1788 when a fleet of eleven vessels under the command of Captain Arthur Phillip entered Port Arthur (later Sydney Harbour) in New South Wales. Their human cargo consisted of 736 male and female convicts. Thus began the largest forced exile of citizens ever undertaken by a British government. In the whole period of convict transportation to 1852, the Crown shipped more than 160,000 men, women and children in bondage to Australia. From the beginning the new settlement, first discovered by Captain James Cook seventeen years before the arrival of Phillip's force, was to be a colony with a difference. It was not created for reasons of trade, territorial expansion or in opposition to foreign powers. Instead, Botany Bay (to give its popular name) was designed to be a vast penitentiary on the edge of an unexplored continent half-way across the world. The concept had many attractions. Transportation was regarded as much cheaper than the building of yet more gaols. Advocates of the policy also viewed it as a potent deterrent, second only to capital punishment in its capacity to induce terror and dread among the criminal classes. A replacement for the Atlantic colonies, the traditional dumping-ground for undesirables, was also badly needed after the USA achieved independence in 1783. Canada, the East Indies, the Falkland Islands and West Africa were all considered. In the end, Botany Bay won out. Its remoteness in the far Pacific meant that even after a convict had served a sentence, return to the homeland would be difficult and costly. Permanent exile was doubly attractive to government at a time when the cancer of criminality was seen to be on the increase and when contemporaries believed in the existence of a corrupt class of unregenerate and persistent lawbreakers who continuously preyed on civilized society. As Jeremy Bentham put it in 1812, the 'thief colony' was an invaluable asset to the state because it contained 'a sort of exrementitious mass' which once convicted could be transported 'as far out of sight as possible' to a distant land where escape was virtually impossible.[1] Nevertheless, New South Wales was seen as something more than a convict colony. There was also the question of potential sources of timber for the Royal Navy and the strategic position of the settlement in relation to other rival encroaching empires.

There was a marked difference in Scottish and English perceptions of the value of transportation and the extent to which the courts in the two countries resorted to it. Transportation was more controversial in Scotland, partly because it had been much used by vengeful governments in the repression of political opponents from the days of Oliver Cromwell in the mid-seventeenth century to the sentences handed down to the Jacobites. The conviction of the Scottish radicals led by Thomas Muir in 1793 and their subsequent transportation to Botany Bay caused much anger at the time and led to a flood of pamphlets and broadsheets over the years condemning the punishment of enforced exile as cruel, unnatural and barbaric. Even distinguished members of the Scottish judiciary deplored transportation. Contrary to much received opinion, Francis Garden, Lord Gardenstone, bitterly attacked the system on the basis of cost. He regarded transportation to distant Australia 'the most absurd, prodigal and impracticable vision that ever intoxicated the mind of man'. In his view it left the country with a financial burden 'to the amount of ten times the loss incurred by the robbery and trial put together'. John McLaurin, Lord Dreghorn, another prominent Senator of the College of Justice, was critical of the punishment on humanitarian grounds, arguing that it was so abhorrent that transportation should not be imposed for any other than capital crimes.[2]

In fact there were relatively few Scots among the many convicts sent to Australia. In the first dozen years of the Botany Bay colony a mere seventy Scottish prisoners arrived and by 1823 the total had still only reached 855. In *per capita* terms, the English were four times more numerous. Over the period 1791 to 1817, 266 Scots were transported, but in some periods, such as 1795–9, the numbers fell to zero. By 1823, Scots accounted for but 3.5 per cent of all the convicts transported to Australia. The differences can be explained in terms of the English and Scottish legal traditions. In England, even petty criminals regularly received sentences of transportation. The Scots judiciary seem to have been more discriminating, convicting fewer people overall and sending a smaller number to Botany Bay. The saying went that 'A man is banished from Scotland for a great crime, from England for a small one, and from Ireland . . . morally speaking for no crime at all.'[3] The Scottish legal system was demonstrably more humane. The country's penal code never contained as many capital offences as the English and also provided only moderate punishment for theft, the most common crime, until the third offence. Figures from 1832, for example, suggest that only a fifth of those convicted north of the Border were transported, compared with over a third in England and Wales.[4]

However, because Scottish judges reserved the punishment for the worst offenders and the recidivists, those Scots convicts actually sentenced to transportation were often regarded as among the most feared, hardened and dangerous in the penal colony. When he surveyed the history of half a century of Scottish transportation, Archibald Alison concluded that 'the Scotch beyond all question, [were] the worst who arrived'. He noted that very few were sent to Australia 'who had not either committed some grave offence, or been four or five times, often eight or ten times, previously convicted or imprisoned'. Speaking as a distinguished lawyer, he asserted that the governing principle of Scots law in this regard was the transportation of 'persons only who are deemed irreclaimable in this country'.[5] Others agreed. The Reverend John West thought that the Scots were 'the most base and clever' of the convict population, while one observer in 1847 commented:

Both in New South Wales and Van Diemen's Land, Scotch convicts are considered the worst, and English the best. This seems to arise not so much from the laws of the two countries being so essentially different, as their being differentially administered; the punishment for minor crimes in particular, being infinitely more severe in England than in Scotland. Hence, hundreds are transported annually from England for offences which in Scotland would be punished by sixty days confinement in jail at Bridewell . . . In Scotland . . . they are mostly old offenders before they are transported.[6]

It may well be, however, that these claims were somewhat exaggerated. Increasingly, the Scots prisoners were sent to Van Diemen's Land (modern Tasmania) after 1812 rather than New South Wales. This penal colony soon developed an appalling reputation because the most recalcitrant convicts from elsewhere were often transferred there as a last resort. It could be, then, that the notorious reputation of the Scots reflected in part their location rather than their past record. Certainly, recent work on the age of Scottish convicts hardly suggests that the majority were hardened career criminals, inured to many years of transgression. Indeed, the average age was twenty-five and almost two-thirds of men and half the women were younger than that. Nearly 30 per cent of males were actually under twenty and a mere handful aged over thirty. This suggests that juvenile delinquency was becoming a growing problem in the cities. The typical Scottish criminal of both sexes was in the early twenties. The majority had committed one or more previous offences, with theft in particular and crimes against property in general drawing the most common convictions. A detailed analysis of male prisoners transported in 1830 shows that nearly three-quarters were unmarried and that most were born in Glasgow, Edinburgh, Aberdeen or Dundee and the rest in the rural counties; or they were Irishmen who had moved to Scotland.[7] A high proportion worked in the textile trades, especially in handloom weaving and cotton spinning. Members of the professional classes were notable by their absence. Only two were sentenced in that year, one a twenty-year-old medical student convicted of stealing money, and the other a 'surgeon' for trying to pass a forged note. Overwhelmingly, the transportees were drawn from the ranks of unskilled and semi-skilled labour. Interestingly, however, the famed Scottish educational tradition also permeated the ranks of the criminal classes. A mere 5 per cent of Scottish male convicts in that year were judged to be illiterate, a very much lower proportion than their English or Irish counterparts.

Transportation had a particular attraction for governments confronted with political radicalism in the era of the French Revolution which had spawned new ideas that seemed to provide an unprecedented challenge to the established order in the 1790s. But there was always the danger of making martyrs of radicals. Transportation eliminated political dissenters without making them heroes on the scaffold: the radical 'slipped off the map into a distant limbo, where his voice fell dead at his feet. There was nothing for his ideas to engage, if he were an intellectual, no machines to break or ricks to burn, if a labourer. He could preach sedition to the thieves and cockatoos, or to the wind. Nobody would care.'[8]

In the event, it was indeed Scottish agitators who first fell victim to the conservative backlash. In December 1792, events in France took a dramatic turn. The bloodbath of the French nobility and clergy in the 'September Massacres' attracted widespread coverage in the Scottish press, which did not spare its readers any of the gory details of the grislier executions by guillotine. From this point on, the Revolution was represented as a grave threat to the entire social order, a political force careering out of control and sliding rapidly into murderous anarchy. From the conservative perspective, worse was to follow when the Duke of Brunswick's mighty army of a coalition of the European powers, assembled to crush the Revolution with all speed, was itself roundly defeated by the citizens' army of France. The revolutionaries then proceeded to terrify the ruling classes across the Continent in their Decree of 19 November 1792 by offering military aid to all other peoples seeking liberty from oppression.

This transformed the political landscape in Scotland. The success of the French revolutionaries against all the odds convinced many who had never been part of the political nation that the *ancien régime* in Britain could also be destroyed by popular action and a new democratic order put in its place. It was this wave of unrestrained optimism and sheer political excitement which fuelled an explosive growth of reform societies all over Lowland Scotland between October and December 1792. By the end of that year, local societies of the Friends of the People had been founded in all the towns south of Aberdeen and in a large number of country villages in the central belt. But this was only one aspect of the popular response. The authorities were alarmed not so much by the rise of an essentially moderate and worthy parliamentary reform movement as by a series of spontaneous riots that erupted in several towns along the east coast. These were emphatically political in nature, with the planting of 'trees of liberty' and the usual ritual incineration of countless effigies of the hated Henry Dundas, the very personification of Old Corruption.

Conservative opinion in Scotland now firmly condemned the

Friends of the People, who were deemed guilty of the heinous crime of stirring up sedition among the common people. The combination of the terrible events in France and the threat of plebeian revolt at home rapidly closed the ranks of the propertied classes. Opposition Whig politicians who had previously dabbled in reform politics rallied to the cause of defending the constitution from 'the levelling spirit' which now menaced the whole social order and subverted the right of property to govern. Even before the first Convention of the Friends of the People met, the reform movement was already vulnerable to draconian government reprisals. Eighty of the reform societies sent delegates to the Convention, but many of the leading figures in the movement stayed away (apart from several Edinburgh advocates, including the eloquent and fiery Thomas Muir and William Dalrymple of Fordell). It was now plain that only an isolated minority of the upper-middle-class reformers were prepared to take the risk to promote the cause in the new circumstances. Indeed, much of the business of the Convention was devoted to a vain attempt to demonstrate loyalty to the established Constitution rather than the debating of reform proposals. From this point, the Friends of the People were on the defensive and they never recovered the initiative. During the Convention, Thomas Muir read out a fraternal address from the Society of United Irishmen which was branded seditious and treasonable and gave the government the opportunity to move against the reformers. Muir himself was arrested in January 1793, and his trial in August 1793 has been made notorious by the partiality of the presiding judge, Lord Braxfield, Lord Justice Clerk of Scotland. When it was pointed out that Christ himself had been a reformer, Braxfield snorted: 'Muckle he made o' that – *He* was hangit.'

The outcome after that was probably inevitable. Braxfield's charge to the jury asserted that the British Constitution could not possibly be improved and that the 'rabble' which had no property did not have the right of representation. The jury unanimously found Muir guilty and he was sentenced to fourteen years' transportation. Others followed, including Thomas Fyshe Palmer, a Unitarian minister of English birth and pastor in Dundee (seven years), two London radicals, Joseph Gerrald and Maurice Margarot (both fourteen years), and William Skirving, the Scottish secretary of the National Convention of the Friends of the People (another fourteen years). Muir,

Skirving, Palmer and Margarot were shipped to Australia together with eighty-three other less celebrated convicts in the *Surprize* in February 1794. From that point on, the legend of the 'Scottish Martyrs', condemned to many years of enforced exile in a penal colony at the ends of the earth, was born.

Their captivity started badly. Maurice Margarot seems to have suffered a mental collapse during the voyage and denounced his comrades to the captain as conspirators in a mutiny plot. As a result they spent five months in the brig on short rations. Conditions, however, improved dramatically when they landed. The acting governor, Francis Grose, promised Palmer 'every indulgence' provided that he 'avoid on all occasions a recital of those Politicks which have produced in you the miseries a man of your feelings and abilities must at this time undergo'.[9] As a result of this special status Gerrald was given a house on the harbour and Skirving granted a hundred acres of land. They even became involved in the rum trade, the staple of the convict economy. Nor is there any record of the 'Martyrs' being forced to work or suffering under the lash, the routine punishment in Botany Bay even for the tiniest breach of discipline. Transportation certainly did not destroy their political beliefs. Thomas Muir in *The Telegraph: A Consolotary Epistle*, a long poem to his friend Henry Erskine, began by describing the 'landscape of exile' where 'sullen Convicts drag the clanking chain and Desolation covers all the plain'. He then quickly goes on, however, to an undaunted reaffirmation of his radicalism:

> The best and noble privilege in Hell
> For souls like ours, is Nobly to rebell,
> To raise the standard of revolt and try
> The happy fruits of lov'd Democracy.[10]

Two of the radicals, Joseph Gerrald and William Skirving, did not survive long in Australia. Both died there in 1796. Maurice Margarot continued the life of duplicity he had started on the long voyage from Britain. A suspected informer and double agent who moved between the different colonial cliques, he returned to England in 1810 after seventeen years in exile and died a broken man five years later in London. The experiences of Palmer and Muir were much more exotic. Palmer, the Unitarian pastor, taught himself ship construction and, when his sentence was finished, bought and refitted an ancient

Spanish warship, *El Plumier*, which he tried to sail back to England via the East Indies. Near the Island of Guam in the Philippines the rotting shell of the vessel collapsed and the survivors, including Palmer, were imprisoned by the Spaniards. He died of cholera in gaol in 1802 and was buried among pirates in a common grave. Thomas Muir was the only member of the group to actually escape from captivity. His was a remarkable global odyssey. Early in 1796 he left Sydney Harbour concealed on an American fur-trading ship bound for Alaska where he transferred to a Spanish gunboat which took him south to California. He then made his way via the Caribbean and Cuba to Cadiz in Spain. During the voyage, the ship on which he was travelling was attacked by a Royal Navy squadron. In the ensuing battle, Muir's face was half shot away and he spent time in hospital on arrival in Spain. Word reached Paris of the extraordinary journey from captivity of the celebrated Scottish radical and he was brought to France as an honoured guest of the revolutionary government. However, his fame soon faded and he died alone and virtually penniless in 1799 at Chantilly. The final resting-place of the most renowned Scottish radical of all is unknown.

2

Before 1914 roughly a quarter of a million Scots emigrated to Australia, with particularly high levels of movement during the gold rushes of the 1850s. The colony never attracted the same numbers as Canada and the USA; nonetheless, the mark of the Scottish diaspora of the nineteenth century can still be seen in Australian place-names, churches, Caledonian and clan societies and professional bodies glorying in Scottish titles. Yet mass emigration to the Antipodes from Scotland developed relatively late and became truly significant only when assisted emigration from the Highlands started to increase from the 1830s. As already noted, the Scottish element among the convict population was a minor one. In the early nineteenth century it was a similar pattern for free migrants. The number of Scots in Australia in 1820 was almost negligible and virtually all of them were civil officials, soldiers, military officers and convicts. The return of land grants of more than 100 acres for the period 1812 to 1821 shows only thirty-four grants made to Scots (or one-tenth) out of a total of 380. In the 1820s the Scottish share started to expand, especially in Van Diemen's Land, where by 1828 there were 190 Scottish settlers, some with substantial holdings. At that date, Scots comprised one-sixth of the free settlers on the island.[11]

Before 1815 some influential Scottish voices were strongly opposed to Australia as an emigrant destination. The *Edinburgh Review* was the most prestigious journal of its day and one of its most persuasive contributors, Sydney Smith, was scathing. He predicted that the Australian settlement would provoke a costly war with other foreign powers: 'Endless blood and treasure will be exhausted to support a tax on Kangaroo skins.' Smith went further and roundly condemned the entire project as a 'pick-pocket quarter of the globe':

New South Wales is a sink of wickedness in which the majority of convicts of both sexes become infinitely more depraved than at the period of their arrival . . . As a mere colony it is too distant and too expensive, and in future will of course involve us in many of those just and necessary wars . . . For the first half century, the colony will make the convicts worse than they were before, and after that period they may probably begin to improve. A marsh, to be sure, may be drained, and cultivated; but no man who has his choice would select it in the mean-time for his dwelling place.[12]

Patrick Colquhoun, a man widely regarded as the nation's foremost expert on international commerce, joined the chorus of disapproval. He had been an American merchant, Lord Provost of Glasgow and a Police Commissioner in London. His *Treatise on the Wealth, Power and Resources of the British Empire in every Quarter of the World* was published in 1814 and was probably the most coherent work to be written on imperial matters to that date. Colquhoun was dismissive of the potential of New South Wales. Indeed, he argued that the infant colony should be abandoned in favour of the Cape of Good Hope, since it was too far away, had no strategic significance and had limited economic potential.

The reasons for his hostility to the Australian colonies and their virtual irrelevance as an emigrant destination before *c.* 1820 are not hard to seek. The 'tyranny of distance' was obviously one factor. New South Wales was at the ends of the earth and could only be reached after a long and hazardous sea journey of eight months across 15,000 miles of ocean. By contrast, North America was relatively familiar and accessible in a fraction of the time. Australia's original status as a penal colony also did little to attract settlement. Contemporaries depicted Botany Bay as a modern Gomorrha where drunkenness, sexual licence and immorality were practised enthusiastically and universally among convicts and custodians alike. To the Presbyterian minister John Dunmore Lang, it was 'the dunghill of the Empire'. Thomas Mitchell from Craigend in Stirlingshire, a major on half-pay, was appointed Assistant Surveyor-General of New South Wales in 1827. His mother reacted with a mixture of anger and incredulity at the news:

Your letter . . . has both astonished and distressed me very much . . . For my part *it is going out of the world altogether* [my italics]. How you and Mrs Mitchell and children will stand a sea voyage of six months is past my comprehension. I am well informed the country is in a deplorable state – no money in it . . . no person was sure of their lives or property – no society but the refuse of mankind . . . I have always looked upon this place with horror and pitied the families that went there.[13]

The reputation of the colony sank even further when news filtered through to Britain in 1808, on the twentieth anniversary of white settlement, that the officers of the New South Wales Corps had mutinied. Governor Bligh was deposed and the Corps then ran the colony for two years as a military junta. They had achieved a virtual monopoly over the importation of rum and were famously known as 'the Rum Corps'. Rum was 'the social anesthetic and real currency of early New South Wales . . . [it] was a drunken society from top to bottom. Men and women drank with a desperate addicted single-mindedness.'[14] Control over the importation and distribution of rum had given the Corps the economic muscle to launch the successful *coup d'état* against lawful authority.

Even government did little to encourage free settlement in the early days. Significantly, the first four governors of New South Wales were all naval officers: Captains Phillip and Hunter, Lieutenant King and Captain William Bligh (of *Bounty* notoriety). It was essentially a settlement which faced towards the sea rather than the land. Government regarded it as part of the maritime empire, most suitably governed by the navy, and not one designed to promote significant internal expansion. Colonial land policy was therefore deliberately exclusive. Until 1831, land was only granted in extensive holdings to men of sufficient capital. Governor Macquarie, the most powerful and influential colonial official of the period, strongly opposed emigrants without resources. They were, in his view, only a nuisance and an expense. Respectable men with 'at least Five Hundred Pounds' were, however, another matter.[15] They would not only be independent of civil support on arrival but could also bring substantial economic advantages to the penal colony by hiring convict labour which would then cease to be a charge on the state.

The Scottish connection with early Australia was therefore diluted by distance, the colony's reputation and the attraction of competing with longer-established imperial territories. At the same time, however, the impact should not be underestimated, especially as it rapidly became stronger. The effect would not be measured in numbers of emigrants until several decades later. Instead, it came about through Scottish penetration of the colonial service, landownership, merchanting and the military. Taken together this influence at élite level helped in the transformation of the colony from a penal settlement into a developing civil society. To a great extent new interest in the Antipodes reflected conditions in Scotland itself. The end of the Napoleonic Wars meant massive levels of redundancy for the officer classes of the British army and navy. Alternative posts had to be found. Now, even New South Wales had some attractions when the alternative was eking out a living as a half-pay officer at home. Soon applications began to pour into the Colonial Office for appointments within the administration, military and ancillary services. The Commissariat at New South Wales virtually became a Scottish preserve. As usual, the formidable Scottish network of clientage and patronage through Henry Dundas swung into action. Scots began to pack the offices of surgeons, secretaries, surveyors, engineers and the like. A key figure was Lachlan Macquarie, one of three Scottish Governors in the early years of the colony and by far the most able.[16] He himself came from a military background. Born on Mull in 1762, he was a younger son of the cousin of the chieftain of Clan Macquarie. He joined the army at fifteen, typical of many of his class of lesser Highland gentry who preferred service under the British crown in faraway places to financial ruin and loss of status at home. A career soldier with military experience in the West Indies, North America and India, he rose through the ranks to the command of the 73rd Highlanders. When he was appointed Governor in 1810, his entourage soon became dominated by Scots officials.

Other forces were also at work. By the early nineteenth century, Scotland was rapidly emerging as the world's second industrial nation. The economy had a cutting edge not simply in manufacturing but also in trade and agriculture. The new class of Lowland capitalist farmers had waxed rich on the booming profits of wartime. They were driven to look abroad not simply to invest capital but to escape the scarcity of rentable farms in Scotland and to secure opportunities for their non-inheriting younger sons. Flockmasters in the great sheep estates of the Highlands and the Lowlands quickly grasped the potential attractions of the vast stretches of cheap Australian land to establish an even greater pastoral empire in another hemisphere. Indeed, not only were huge land grants readily available after *c.* 1810, but government was also able to provide cheap labour to help run the sheep ranches by assigning convicts to substantial farmers through a system widely condemned by some as more akin to slavery. Soon Scottish pastoral princes emerged in the outback. They included men like Lachlan Macallister, who arrived in New South Wales in 1817 as an ensign in the 48th Regiment. He started with a land grant of 810 hectares and soon developed a ruthless paramilitary reputation for his relentless pursuit of any Aboriginal tribes and bush rangers who dared to stand in the way of his expanding empire. By 1838, he owned a property over eight times the size of his original land grant. Macallister named it 'Strathaird', after the family estate in Skye.

The story of Major Donald Macleod, a tacksman from Skye, reveals the same pattern of Highland background, military career and determined ambition in Australia. It also underscores the point made elsewhere in this book about the entrepreneurial energies of the Gaelic gentry and their ability to respond to the contraction of their position in the Highlands by seeking opportunities in the empire. Macleod served many years in the 56th Regiment before sailing with his family of nine to Van Diemen's Land. He was given a grant of 2,000 acres (which he named 'Talisker'), but the family's fortune was really made when they moved to Sydney and Port Phillip. Eventually, after a series of bloody battles with the Aborigines, which climaxed in the decimation of the local tribes, Macleod annexed over 20,000 acres for sheep farming. It was an even more draconian 'Highland Clearance', but this time perpetrated by the Gaels on the indigenous population of the Antipodes.

It was a similar story in commerce. Here the new Australian

connection was partly forged through the relationship with India described in the last chapter. Two of the most significant early Australian merchants, Robert Campbell and Alexander Berry, were both Scots and each had strong connections in the East Indies trade. The Campbell family were deeply involved in commerce between Glasgow and Calcutta, while Berry was a surgeon in the East India Company where he learnt the rudiments of commerce and left for Australia in 1808. Their careers show how India became a bridge between Scotland and the Antipodes. 'Merchant Campbell', as he is known to history, was able to demonstrate that Australia could have a mutually beneficial economic relationship with the rest of the empire through exportation of its staples to external markets. This vision was the key to the country's escape from its function as a penal colony. Campbell saw the immense potential of Australia's vast reserves of whales and seals. Every season countless numbers of black sperm whales came north from Antarctica to mate and calve along the coasts of south-eastern Australia and Van Diemen's Land. It was said in the early 1800s that the estuary around Hobart was too dangerous for small boats at these times because of the masses of pregnant and calving whales which gathered there. The kill rate by fishermen could easily rise to thousands a year. Despite the opposition of the East India Company, which held the monopoly, Campbell was exporting skins and whale oil directly to London from 1805. He defied the Company for another decade until free trade to and from Australia was eventually conceded in 1815. It was a major victory, signalling the economic potential of the colony and denying its familiar image as an infamous penitentiary for the worst criminality of British society.

The most influential figure of these early years in Australia's history was Lachlan Macquarie. His tombstone on the Isle of Mull reads:

He was appointed Governor of New South Wales AD 1809 and for 12 years fulfilled the duties of that situation, with eminent ability and success. His services in that capacity have justly attached a lasting honour to his name . . . the rapid improvement of the Colony under his auspices and the high estimation in which both his Character and Government were held, rendered him truly deserving of the appellation . . . The Father of Australia.

This was no idle boast, and not simply because Macquarie was the first colonial official to refer to the continent as 'Australia' in official despatches in the hope that it would became 'the Name given to this Country in future'. When he arrived in 1810 the previous governor, Bligh, had been deposed by the mutineers of the so-called Rum Rebellion. Administration was in a state of virtual collapse. Sydney was little more than an unplanned confusion of shacks and tents, and the whole settlement was in the grip of alcohol addiction. After twelve years, Macquarie could claim, 'I found New South Wales a jail and left it a colony.'[17] He made major improvements in the treatment of convicts, built churches, hospitals and public buildings, and encouraged the expansion across the hitherto impassable Blue Mountains to the west. When he left Australia in 1821, New South Wales had a white population of 30,000 and had plainly outgrown its original function as a penitentiary.

Macquarie had several advantages in his personal crusade to clean up the colony. His office as Governor gave him the powers of an autocrat, even more wide-ranging than elsewhere in the empire. He controlled political appointments and decisions, the distribution of land, the power to liberate or pardon, which religions were celebrated and who filled the posts in the bureaucracy and army. In addition, Macquarie arrived with military muscle. He was not only the Governor but also the commander of the battle-hardened 73rd Regiment of Highlanders who were more than a match for those who had challenged the previous administration. Macquarie also brought with him his own formidable experience and personality. He had served for nearly two decades as a career officer in India and the Middle East. He was self-righteous and vain, very fond of naming countless ports, towns, rivers and lakes after himself. But he also had a strong sense of moral duty born out of his Scottish Calvinism, and a well-developed sense of paternalistic fairness. Macquarie was well suited to running New South Wales as a military autocracy, 'a fine early example of that breed of Scottish administrators who kept the engine-room of Empire working through the nineteenth century'.[18]

On arrival he cancelled all land grants and civil and military appointments made since the outbreak of the Rum Rebellion. This was followed by a comprehensive attack on the vices of drink which he thought were poisoning the colony to death. Duties rose sharply on imported spirits, the number of licensed houses was drastically cut and then shut on the Sabbath. Convicts now had to attend mandatory church parades. Macquarie also started to build a new town based on his own memory of Georgian architecture at home, on an album of designs brought out by his wife, Elizabeth, and the professional skills of a convict architect, Francis Howard Greenway.

An ambitious plan of urban renewal was put in place. Macquarie laid out what is still the central grid of the city of Sydney. A hospital, known as the 'Rum Hospital' because it was paid for out of duties on rum, was constructed. Two convict barracks and other buildings followed in quick succession. Planned villages based on those he had seen in Scotland were founded. Craftsmen were selected on the docks from the convict ships as soon as they arrived. At the height of Macquarie's building schemes in 1819, four out of five convicts with artisan skills were labouring on government projects, to the immense frustration of free settlers bereft of these valued workers. An article in the *Edinburgh Review* scornfully referred to 'Ornamental Architecture on Botany Bay'. The great barrier of the Blue Mountains was breached by opening up the rich pasture lands beyond by a permanent way through the hill country. Macquarie promised a group of convicts conditional pardons if they completed the 126 miles of road in six months. They did so and were liberated.

He is best remembered for his radical policies towards the convict population. He sought their rehabilitation through work and saw emancipation as the key foundation of the colony's future development. As soon as a convict transport arrived, Macquarie personally welcomed the prisoners and pointed out to them that hard work and good behaviour would bring their own rewards. He liberally awarded good behaviour with pardons and, when prisoners had served their sentences, insisted that they should then enjoy full civil rights. 'Emancipists', as they were known, were appointed to the public service and even entertained on occasion in Government House. Macquarie saw clearly that since they so heavily outnumbered emigrant settlers, emancipists would be the future lifeblood of Australia.

There were many individual success stories, including those Scots who had been convicted of high treason during the 'Radical War' of 1820 for planning a national insurrection against the government. The authorities had then reacted with ruthless suppression. Three men, Wilson, Hardie and Baird, were executed for the crime of armed insurrection. Nineteen others who were convicted had their sentences commuted to transportation. Several of them prospered under the regime Macquarie had established. Allan Murchie, from Dunfermline, opened a public house named 'The Help me Thro' the World' in Sydney, John Anderson taught for thirty-four years in a Presbyterian school and Andrew Dawson from Stirlingshire became a Principal Overseer of Works in the government service. But Macquarie's enlightened methods did not always attract universal approval. Protests poured into the Colonial Office in London that he was making life easy for convicts at public expense. In 1819 the government sent Commissioner J. T. Bigge to New South Wales to investigate the accusations and report back. Bigge was bitterly critical and recommended that the colony once again become 'a place of dread' rather than rehabilitation. Macquarie resigned two years later and on his return to Britain received a pension but was denied recognition and a title. He died in 1824.

His successor was also a Scot and a career soldier, Sir Thomas Brisbane, from a landed family in Largs in Ayrshire. Brisbane did initially take a harder line in accordance with the Bigge recommendations, even reopening the notorious Norfolk Island as a place of secondary punishment, 'the *ne plus ultra*', as he put it, 'of convict degradation'.[19] But in essence he maintained Macquarie's policy towards the emancipists and, at the same time, introduced independent law courts and trial by jury in civil proceedings. Press censorship was also lifted. These were further steps in the ongoing metamorphosis of gaol to colony.

3

Until about 1845 there were probably more Aborigines in the Australian continent than whites. They had lived off the land and the sea as hunter-gatherers for more than eight millennia. Neither stock-rearing nor agriculture were practised but the Aborigines had developed such a remarkably intimate relationship with the land and its plants, animals and watercourses that they were able to survive even in the most hostile environments. At almost every point their culture and way of life were radically different from and therefore incomprehensible to the European settlers. The numerous tribes, who spoke many languages, had minimal material possessions. Even the territories where they hunted were considered accessible to all clan members in common. They saved nothing and lived entirely in the present. Men, women and children roamed the outback, apparently aimlessly, in search of food. They did not build houses or have recognizable forms of government. To Europeans they were not simply different but primitive, inferior and savage: 'No greater contrast could exist with the incessant digging, enclosing and building activities of the newcomers, determined to conquer their environment, and using military discipline and individual ownership as a means to that end.'[20] The relationship between settlers and natives was one of mutual incomprehension. The Aborigines were shocked by the white skins and pale eyes of Europeans, thinking at first they were the spirits of the dead. The newcomers in their turn were revolted by the rumours of cannibalism associated with the blacks, the ritual ornamentation of their bodies, their colour and their nakedness.

The first contacts seemed peaceable enough in and around Botany Bay. In addition, every governor from Phillip in 1788 to Brisbane in 1822 had instructions from London that the Aborigines were to be well treated. The aim in the relations between the races was to develop 'amity and kindness'. The Aborigines were even given the status of British subjects. Anyone who killed them or caused them 'any unnecessary interruption of their several occupations' merited punishment with the utmost severity of the law. The first Scottish Governor, John Hunter, in the course of his early explorations of New South Wales, noted in his *Historical Journal* that 'we wished to live with them on the most friendly footing, and . . . to promote, as such as might be in our power, their comfort and happiness'.[21] Macquarie hoped to encourage the Aborigines from their 'rambling Naked state' and transform them into farmers. In 1815 he experimented with sixteen native men cultivating a smallholding on Sydney Harbour. They soon wandered off into the bush. Sir Thomas Brisbane was at first equally solicitous. On his arrival as Governor he proclaimed his concern for 'these poor, distressed creatures' who, unless they were supported, would surely become extinct.

However, there was a vast difference between benevolent official policy, which itself abruptly changed in the later 1820s, and actual practice. Relations between the races rapidly deteriorated. European diseases quickly took a horrific toll of the Aboriginal populations. As early as 1789 a mysterious outbreak of smallpox carried off half the natives in the Sydney area. Convicts also became increasingly hostile to the Aborigines. They contrasted the cruel punishments meted out to prisoners who had committed even minor offences with the conciliatory treatment of the blacks by the penal authorities. Some often took their revenge when they completed their sentences and moved into the interior in the search for land. Between 1800 and 1830 settlement pushed outwards as the Australian wool economy, with its insatiable appetite for land, started to develop. Conflict between the white culture of private property and the black ethic of communal possession became inevitable. Recent research has shown how the Aboriginal clans did not accept the European invasion passively.[22] Instead, ferocious battles were fought across the expanding frontier with natives making devastating attacks on isolated homesteads and shepherds' huts in acts of reprisal and revenge. This in turn produced and justified genocidal retaliation to many whites, secure in the knowledge that in the outback they were safe from the distant powers of the colonial judiciary.

At the same time, intellectual arguments for the 'dispersal' of the Aborigines (as mass killing was euphemistically described) began to appear. When *Two Years in New South Wales* by the Scottish explorer, Allan Cunningham, appeared in 1828, the commentator in the *Quarterly Review* expressed the view emanating from the colony that the Aborigines were 'among the lowest, if not the very lowest, in the scale of human beings'. Others at the time considered them 'many degrees below even the worst of the Zealanders' and 'among the most hideous of all the living creatures of humanity'.[23] Horror stories also circulated of their appetite for cannibalism and human banquets. 'Scales of Civilization' put them near the bottom of the hierarchy of native peoples with American Indians at the top, followed by the Maoris and the Zulus. Not everyone agreed. Scottish explorers, such as Cunningham and later Sir Thomas Livingston Mitchell, praised the adaptability, ingenuity and skills of the Aborigines which they had encountered for themselves in many trips into the interior. Mitchell, who also had shot some blacks in his time, was largely responsible for retaining Aboriginal place-names in eastern Australia. But theirs were lonely voices among the growing chorus of racist propaganda.

During the long frontier war it is reckoned that perhaps 2,000 to 2,500 Europeans were killed and upwards of 20,000 Aborigines.

The overall death rate among the native population was, however, much higher because disease, malnutrition and the lethal effects of alcohol consumption, rather than violence, were the major killers. Scots, like other whites, were intimately involved in the multiple disasters which overwhelmed the Aboriginal tribes, including some of the bloodiest incidents. The murder by natives of one of their number, Ronald Macalister, in 1843 in Gippsland led to the formation of the so-called 'Highland Brigade' when 'every Scotchman who had a horse and gun gathered'.[24] They then carried out the notorious massacre of Warrigal Creek when over 100 Aboriginal men, women and children were killed. It was probably the biggest single act of butchery on the Australian frontier. The Aborigines in Van Diemen's Land were also driven to almost total extinction by successive settler raids. The east coast people in that territory were decimated in one protracted war in the 1820s. More research is required on the detail of these events but the participation of the Scots is certain. In the 1820s they constituted around one sixth of free settlers on the island and that proportion rose to one third in the following decade. Some of the newcomers were tenant farmers from the Lowlands, squeezed by falling produce prices after 1815 and high wartime rentals. But others were Highlanders, like the aforementioned Major Donald Macleod of Talisker in Skye who with his family of nine settled 2,000 acres in Van Diemen's Land in 1820. It was indeed a tragic irony that some of the worst atrocities committed against the Australian Aborigines were carried out by Gaels who had left Scotland as their own traditional world of clanship and tribalism disintegrated during the era of the Highland Clearances.

13

Warriors of Empire

I

The year 1815 was singularly important in the history of the British Empire. It is above all remembered for the battle of Waterloo, the final defeat of Napoleon and the end of the long European conflict which had begun in 1793. But from the British perspective 1815 was much more of an *annus mirabilis* than the victorious culmination of the Napoleonic Wars. By that date Britain had emerged as the leading world power which not only dominated the European stage but had also acquired an overseas empire of colossal scale and prodigious wealth. So extensive was this that around one in five of the inhabitants of the globe now owed allegiance to the British crown. The epic 'second Hundred Years War' with France for colonial hegemony, which had begun in the late seventeenth century, had now ended in comprehensive British victory both at sea and on land. Not only did Britannia rule the waves but the nation's military forces had achieved a global reach which no other European power could match. Even the disasters of the American War of Independence and the humiliating loss of the thirteen colonies in 1783 had failed to check the dynamic of expansion. The conflict with Revolutionary and Napoleonic France from 1793 to 1815 increased the number of imperial territories from twenty-six to forty-three. Huge stretches of India and Australia were annexed, as well as Malta and the Ionian Islands in the Mediterranean, the Cape, Gambia, the Gold Coast and Sierra Leone in Africa, and Trinidad, Tobago and St Lucia in the West Indies.

Those scholars who have considered the reasons for this remarkable saga of conquest and imperial expansion usually point to three fundamental factors. First, Britain had an immense economic advantage over France, its main rival for superpower status, by the end of the eighteenth century. Key regions in both Scotland and England were experiencing rapid economic growth powered by the engines of industrialization, urbanization and sustained increases in agricultural productivity. It was reckoned in 1800 that French productivity per head on the land was about one half that of the English.[1] Britain, therefore, had simply more resources to supply its armies, equip its navies and lend on a huge scale to its continental allies. Second, this growing wealth was more easily harnessed, managed and distributed for the purposes of war by the growth of the 'fiscal-military state'.[2] Britain was able to finance global conflicts and responsibilities because of a transformation in its public finances. This was achieved by a significant increase in taxation, which rose to levels as high as any in Europe, the development of a national debt, which revolutionized borrowing capacities, and the growth of an enlarged public administration concerned with the organization of military and fiscal activities. In this analysis it was financial muscle rather than great armies and navies which was at the root of British success. Third, the military factor ought not to be underestimated. Economic resources and financial innovation willed the means but the ends had to be achieved on many bloody battlefields across the world and by the unrelenting application of massive naval force on the high seas. As the example of Holland showed, it was possible to be a prosperous country and not be a great power. Economic resources were a necessary but not a sufficient cause of attaining that status. What was required in addition was the will and the capacity to deploy the state's military assets. Money, as Cicero had it, may be the sinews of war, but mobilization of wealth was not enough.[3] Only armies and navies could secure trade routes and protect colonies and bases against the predatory strategies of imperial rivals.

Thus it was that empire and militarism were linked together like Siamese twins. Between 1680 and 1783 Britain fought five major wars: King William's War, or the War of English Succession (1688–97); the War of the Spanish Succession (1702–13); The Wars of Jenkins' Ear and Austrian Succession (1739–48); the Seven Years War (1756–63); and the American War of Independence (1775–83). The last became a global confrontation between the British and the Americans, French and Spanish. In addition, between those conflicts, more low-level operations between the European powers in the colonial context were endemic. Not surprisingly, therefore, the British army and navy trebled in size over this hundred-year period. Average annual military expenditure stood at £5.4 million in the 1690s but had risen to £20.2 million during the American War of Independence. Behind these figures was a key change in imperial policy. For much of the first half of the eighteenth century the British Empire was depicted as an 'empire of the seas' in contrast to the territorial empires of conquest established by Rome and Spain.[4] Commerce, so it was argued, was the real basis of dominion, unlike the power attained either by 'Policy of Arms' which was 'but of short Continuance'.[5] Much of this was based on rhetoric rather than reality since Britain had already acquired several territorial prizes in the War of the Spanish Succession. Yet naval power before the Seven Years War was indeed concentrated on European waters rather than in the Atlantic, Asia or West Africa. The senior service was not at this time committed to an expansionist strategy. But international rivalry with France soon changed this. The age-old conflict between the two nations was rapidly taking on a global dimension. Both politicians and merchants feared the continuous threat posed by French incursions into the heart of the plantation economies of North America and the Caribbean. This aggression could have grave consequences because the flow of revenue from the overseas trades had become so vital to public finances that national bankruptcy might have been a real possibility if some key colonies had fallen to the French. In the event, the Seven Years War which began in 1756 in a spirit of defence was soon transformed, after a series of dazzling victories, into a campaign of conquest. By 1763 the British laid claim to lands throughout the world which were five times larger than a century before. The rich province of Bengal in India, Florida, Canada, and territories in the Caribbean and West Africa were now under British rule. One major consequence was a revolution in the global balance of the army and navy. In 1740, only three of the forty or so British army regiments had been stationed outside Europe. By the 1770s that position was being reversed.[6] The army of the East India Company also expanded. Despite its overwhelming dependence on native troops (sepoys) for rank and file, the Company also employed 10,000 white soldiers in the 1770s. They were outnumbered in a ratio of seven to one by the native levies.[7]

Even these increases in military manpower pale somewhat in comparison with the vast recruitment levels of the Revolutionary and Napoleonic Wars. This was a conflict with a difference. It lasted for many years, more than twice as long as the First and Second World Wars of the twentieth century added together. Major campaigns were fought throughout the world in Europe, Asia, North America, the Caribbean and Latin America. For the first time too in the eighteenth century, Britain faced the very real threat of foreign invasion. Napoleon's formidable Army of England was encamped menacingly a few miles across the Channel and from 1798 to 1805 the conquest of Britain was the prime strategic objective of France. Two major attempts were actually made to invade Ireland, one in 1796 and the other in 1798, to coincide with the mass insurrection of the '98 rebellion.

Confronted with such mortal dangers, Britain effectively became an armed nation in this period. Between the war of 1689–97 and the American War, the number of armed forces had doubled, if the militia is included. But the Revolutionary and Napoleonic Wars were of a different order of magnitude. Regular forces, the militia and the volunteers rose to three times the level of the American War. To finance this huge recruitment and support the armies of allies, government expenditure per annum rose from £16 million in 1786–90 to £97 million between 1811 and 1815.[8] This was national mobilization on a scale never known before in British history. The army which stood at around 40,000 men when hostilities began had expanded sixfold to around a quarter of a million by 1814. The Royal Navy's strength had grown even faster, from 16,000 in 1789 to 140,000 by 1812.[9] Whatever the significance of trade and emigration in the making of empire, overseas territory was acquired and defended in the final analysis by the musket and the cold steel of sword and bayonet. State-sponsored violence was at the heart of imperial expansion. This is the context in which the role of the Scottish military in the British Empire must be considered.

Each summer thousands of visitors crowd onto the Castle Esplanade in Edinburgh to witness one of the world's most famous military spectacles, the Edinburgh International Tattoo. The stars of the show are always the massed bands of the Highland regiments, the very incarnation of Scotland's long martial tradition, as they march past to the old tunes, splendidly dressed in sporran, kilt and tartan. For most Scots the Black Watch, the Argyll and Sutherland Highlanders and the others are the Scottish warrior élites with battle honours which stretch back to the eighteenth century. Their place as cultural icons of the nation has been established not simply by their distinguished service but by more than two centuries of publicity in books, music, poetry, song, dance, advertisement and film. As this chapter will demonstrate later, the role of the kilted battalions in the making of empire was indeed of paramount importance. Between 1777 and 1800 alone, the Highlands produced no fewer than twenty line regiments for the British army as well as many other fighting men for the fencible corps and the volunteers.[10] But this remarkable record has tended to overshadow and even marginalize the truly massive part played by Scots as a whole, and not simply Highlanders, in the imperial war machine, both at the level of the officer class and the rank and file.

The story goes back before the union as far as the officer élite is concerned. At the battle of Blenheim in 1704 the English held only seven of the sixteen regimental colonelcies in Marlborough's victorious army. Five Scots and four Irishmen had the rest. The Scottish presence was even more visible in the same campaign at Malplaquet in 1709. Then, of the twenty-five general officers, ten were Scots and three Irish. Remarkably, of the Scottish nobility in the last Scottish Parliament before the union, around a third were linked in some way to the British military establishment. Not surprisingly, they overwhelmingly voted in favour of the union treaty in the final crucial debates of 1706–7. Social and demographic influences motivated many landed families:

In the later sixteenth century the secularisation of church lands, the growing business potential of the legal profession, and after 1603 the increased patronage of the crown, all helped to maintain noble kindreds with the minimum of economic and social debasement among their junior ranks. However, by the third decade of union there was no more church land to go around, and the crown was soon to initiate moves to recover some of those lands already distributed; royal patronage was drying up due to economics and the fact that the Scots were increasingly unpopular in London; the legal profession was consolidating around established legal dynasties able to freeze out new-comers; merchant wealth was such that penurious younger sons could not possibly compete with the urban élite; and with the decline in feuding, noblemen were less inclined to support large retinues. In addition, noble finances in general were less secure than they had been for centuries. Military service at home or abroad was therefore one means by which an over-bloated and financially precarious nobility might avoid slipping into a kind of petty, debased nobility. This is not to say that an army career was always decided by push factors, for the military life continued to attract noblemen for more positive reasons, chiefly because it met their expectations of a martial nobility in a way that civil society no longer did, and because of the sheer excitement of war.[11]

To be in at the beginning, before the later huge expansion in the British military, was a decided Scottish (and Irish) advantage. Another was the intense engagement of scions of the Scottish aristocracy and gentry in the European wars of the mid-seventeenth century documented earlier in this book. The Scots élite continued to see themselves as a warrior class. By 1715 the military opportunities in Europe had declined in relation to the vast manpower demands of the Thirty Years War two generations before. But mercenary service in the armies of Holland (notably through the famous Scots Brigade) and France (especially for Jacobite families) remained possible and allowed for migration by experienced officers back and forth between the forces of the continental states and Britain. In consequence, a number of laird families in Scotland quite literally lived by the sword. Typical of the class were the Agnews of Lochnaw in Galloway. The third baronet, Sir James, had eight sons, all of whom became professional soldiers. The eldest, Andrew, the fourth baronet, died a lieutenant-general. His extended family were familiar figures to him in his campaigning days:

When Sir Andrew joined the 'Grey Dragoons' in Flanders during Marlborough's wars, as a young cornet, he found his brother-in-law and four kinsmen already with the regiment, and when he went again to Flanders in 1742 as lieutenant-colonel of the 21st regiment, his letters show that a large party of relatives, kinsmen and neighbours from his native Galloway used to meet each evening around the camp fires. These included Sir Andrew himself, his brother James Agnew who was major of the 7th Dragoons, and three younger brothers in the 6th Dragoons. Lord Stair, the British commander-in-chief, was himself a Galloway man, and a kinsman of the Agnews.[12]

The Agnews and their kindred were not untypical. By the 1750s something like one in four of all regimental officers in the army were Scots, a proportion far in excess of the Scottish share of the British population. Only the Anglo-Irish could come anywhere near these ratios. Similarly, between 1714 and 1763 just under one-fifth of all colonelcies went to Scottish officers.[13] Even this figure does not take account of the large numbers of their fellow countrymen who achieved officer status in the East India Company.[14] Historians offer conflicting reasons for the phenomenon. For some, it represented 'competitive provinciality' within the British state.[15] For others, the Scottish penetration of the officer cadres was inevitable: 'the stretching of the nation in war always offers opportunities for the fringes of the state'.[16] What is not in doubt, however, is either the extent or the long duration of the Scottish hegemony. The British military in the Seven Years War of 1755–63 is punctuated with Scottish names from the commanders-in-chief, John Campbell, Earl of Loudon and Sir Ralph Abercromby, to the officer class, a list replete with Donaldsons, Dundases, Eliotts, Forbes, Grants, Frasers, Scotts and innumerable others. In 1758, one English officer suggested with some exaggeration that the army in America was little more than a 'Scotes Expedition' which disadvantaged the English and Irish when it came to promotion.[17] Despite his hyperbole the critic might have had a point. The year before, the record shows that the ethnic composition of commissioned officers in British army units in North America was 31.5 per cent Scots, 31 per cent Irish, 12 per cent American and foreign and 24.5 per cent English.[18] All this adds up to something of deep significance. As explained earlier, the deployment of British military power abroad on an unprecedented scale would not have been possible without the vast sums raised by government through taxation and the more effective management of the National Debt. Much of this income stream came from the City of London and the richer south of England. Through their role in the British army Scots and Irish élites in effect colonized the fiscal-military state to the advantage of less favoured areas of the United Kingdom. In essence it was a form of resource transfer from the centre to the peripheries and one of the major but unacknowledged benefits of the union to Scotland.

Scottish soldiers, and not simply Highlanders, were also grossly over-represented in the armed forces during the titanic struggle of the Napoleonic Wars. Remarkably, despite the huge expansion in the military, they managed to retain about a quarter of all officer commissions, their traditional share since at least the 1740s. Since most came from small gentry, farming and professional backgrounds, the families of the Scottish middle classes must have generated a quite extraordinary number of officers in the later eighteenth and early nineteenth centuries. It was hardly surprising therefore that the martial ethos had such widespread popular appeal in Scotland during these decades.

Perhaps even more significant was mobilization for home defence. From the time of the Seven Years War home auxiliaries were crucial to the imperial strategy because they helped to release line regiments for overseas service. Thus besides the high proportion of Scots in the regular army, Scotland raised over 15,000 men as fencibles, recruited primarily for home defence in Great Britain and Ireland. This figure equated to nearly half the strength of the English militia and three-quarters of the strength of the Irish militia at the time.[19] The Scots, and to a lesser extent the Welsh, were also to the fore in the manning of the Volunteer regiments. These were local bodies established in 1798 on the suggestion of Henry Dundas. The Lord-Lieutenants in the counties were made responsible for the raising of these corps. They were sanctioned by the government but were funded by private subscription. No allowances were paid unless the volunteers were actually called up for duty. By the end of 1803 more than 52,000 Scots were serving as rank-and-file members of these regiments. With around 15 per cent of the British population, the nation provided 36 per cent of volunteers in 1797, 22 per cent in 1801 and 17 per cent in 1804.[20] Another striking feature of the Scottish enthusiasm for military service was the national commitment of the Volunteer regiments. English, and to a lesser extent Welsh, volunteers were only prepared to defend their local towns, villages and districts. But in 1798 nine out of ten of the Scottish Volunteer corps claimed a willingness to serve throughout all of Scotland.[21]

We can be much less certain about the Scottish role in the Royal Navy. Partly for this reason, the nation's military image has usually been defined by the army and particularly the distinctive Highland corps. But stray pieces of evidence also suggest that the recruitment of men to the navy should not be underestimated. In 1755 Scottish immunity to the press-gangs, the primary mechanism for manning the navy rapidly in time of war, was set aside. The Admiralty ordered local provosts and magistrates to give full support to the activities of the press in their areas. Even in the days of formal immunity, Scottish seamen had been taken offshore by press tenders. From the 1750s, however, and with the marked increase in the magnitude and global extent of naval warfare, they were much more at risk. Ironically, too, as the maritime economy of Scotland grew especially in the Atlantic and Irish trades, so the expanding Scottish fleet proved more attractive to the press. Between 1712 and 1759 the tonnage of Scottish merchantmen rose by 24 per cent, from 43,394 to 53,604 tons. By 1791 mercantile tonnage owned by the Scottish ports had risen even faster, to nearly 140,000 tons.[22] These were rich pickings for the press-gangs. During the American War of Independence the press was so 'hot' in the Clyde estuary that ordinary seamen's wages were driven up fourfold between 1775 and 1780 as crews were recruited into the navy, resulting in a serious scarcity of labour in the merchant marine.[23] By 1780 there were reckoned to be 13,000 sailors north of the Border who were prime targets for the press. At the local level the forced recruitment of seamen could have a considerable impact. This was especially the case in the Lowlands. Although Gaels were certainly not exempt, the press was much more active in and around the major ports. Significantly, the level of Greenwich pensions given to former sailors of the Royal Navy was higher in the Lowlands.[24] During the Seven Years War, for instance, the press took sixty-seven men from the Fife burgh of Kinghorn. This was around 14 per cent of all males in the town and neighbourhood. But, more interestingly, several of the unfortunate local victims were described as 'landmen' with no seafaring experience.[25]

Much more work certainly needs to be done on the full extent of naval recruitment in Scotland. However, there is already more than enough evidence from both the sea and the land to suggest that the Lowlands were far from being a demilitarized zone. The region may have lacked the martial profile of the Highlands but it still contributed very large numbers to the forces of empire. Indeed, it may well be that the Lowland military presence was substantially greater than that of the Highlands during the Napoleonic Wars. In 1795 eleven fencible regiments with Highland names and associations were half-filled with Lowlanders.[26] This pattern became even more apparent over time partly because of over-recruitment in some Highland districts. Thus in 1809, the 71st, 72nd, 74th, 75th, 91st and 94th were ordered out of the kilt and lost their designation as Highland regiments because the number of native-born Gaels had collapsed.[27] Even the most famous regiments were affected. Only 51 per cent of the recruits admitted to the Black Watch in 1798 were Highlanders.[28] For the Gordon Highlanders at their first recruitment in 1794, 40 per cent were drawn from the Highland counties.[29] The Volunteer regiments mobilized as the invasion scares intensified were overwhelmingly Lowland in composition. All this is in a sense hardly surprising. The vast majority of Scots lived east and south of the Highland line. The population base here was three to four times greater than the far north and west and the potential pool of recruitment much deeper. The Edinburgh recruiting district, which extended across the Lowlands from Stirling and Perth in the north to the English Borders, usually employed the largest number of officers and men in the recruiting parties.[30] It was clearly in this region that they hoped to achieve most success.

But the extent of Lowland militarization presents a paradox. Soldiering in the ranks was a low-status occupation in the eighteenth century. During the Seven Years War a private's pay before stoppages was 8*d*.a day, which placed the 'common soldier' at the very bottom of the social pile, below unskilled labourers and just above vagrants and paupers. Death or serious injury in battle were often the least of a soldier's worries. Colonial warfare could be even more threatening because it might mean being posted to the Caribbean islands or to India where lethal diseases were endemic and killed many more than fell in conflict. Despite the glamour invested in military glory, especially during the Napoleonic Wars, most people regarded soldiering as a last resort. In Robert Burns's *As Late By a Sodger I chanced to Pass*, a soldier's sweetheart turns down his offer of marriage:

> Gin I should follow you a poor sodger lad
> Ilk ane o' my cummers wad think I was mad.

The reaction of the Lowland population to the Militia Act of 1797 does not suggest that the majority of people were naturally inclined to the military life. Its terms suggested that conscription was to be enforced and the recruits would be sent to serve outside Scotland. The main target seemed to be young men of the labouring classes; others of higher rank could hire substitutes if selected. The legislation generated a furious response. Riotous protest spread from Berwick to Aberdeen. One serious confrontation in the mining village of Tranent in East Lothian left twelve people dead after a troop of dragoons, driven beyond endurance by the mob, finally ran amok.

In the past the ardour for a military life reflected the deep poverty and lack of opportunity in rural Scotland in the seventeenth century. But from the 1760s the Scottish economy began a rapid process of transformation. Urban growth was the fastest in Europe. The Scots achieved remarkable success in the Atlantic trades. Textile manufacturing boomed. Rural society was revolutionized by agricultural improvement. At least some of the gains filtered down, as recent research suggests that most people enjoyed a modest rise in living standards between c. 1780 and c. 1800. Detailed surveys of occupational groups ranging from farm servants to masons, from weavers to carpenters, indicate that while food prices were moving upwards in this period, money wages were rising faster still.[31] Curiously, these moderately better times coincided with huge levels of military recruitment.

Three possible explanations might help to solve the puzzle. First, despite some amelioration, Scottish wage levels still fell behind their equivalent in most of England. One investigation indicates that between 1765 and 1795 wrights in Aberdeen and Edinburgh never reached more than 40 to 50 per cent of wages of wrights in London and hardly two-thirds of their wages in Exeter or Manchester.[32] The fact that most soldiers were recruited from the poorer 'Celtic fringe' of Britain, Scotland, Ireland and Wales, suggests that the material factor remained relevant. Second, the long-term improvement, however limited, to c. 1800 concealed sharp differences over time in employment levels throughout the economy. Fluctuations in activity could be savage and prolonged and threw many thousands of workers into unemployment, as in 1778, 1782–3, 1793 and 1797–8. The recruiting parties were able to fish successfully in these pools of temporarily redundant labour. The pay might have been paltry but at least it was regular; there was food for the belly and a small pension on discharge. David Shaw, a Forfar weaver, ran away to join the army. He wanted to escape a life of poverty and was attracted by the pay and the colourful uniform. After one engagement with the French in Spain he lost a leg and recalled the heat of battle in verse:

When first the French cam' in my view,
My heart began to beat, sir;
But Forfar bluid was ever true,
An' how could I retreat, sir.
It's true I gat a wee bit fleg
But grumblin' I disdain, sir;
For tho' a ball gaed through my leg,
I fired an' load again, sir.

Burns seemed to have the same view that soldiering was an occupation of last resort for those who had fallen on hard times:

O, why the deuce should I repine
and be an ill foreboder?
I'm twenty-three and five feet nine,
I'll go and be a sodger.

I gat some gear wi' meikle care,
I held it weel the gither;
But now it's gane – and something mair:
I'll go and be a sodger.[33]

Third, the social transformation of the Lowlands may itself have been conducive to mass recruiting. As agricultural improvement spread throughout the region, farms were consolidated, subtenancies and cottar holdings removed and the terms of access to land became more rigorous and regulated. Fewer and fewer had legal rights to farms, and peasant proprietorship of the European type was virtually unknown. By the early nineteenth century most country folk in the Lowlands were non-inheriting children of farmers, servants, tradesmen, textile weavers and day labourers. It was a highly mobile population, the more so because the Scottish Poor Law was notoriously hostile to generous provision for the able-bodied unemployed. As numbers rose, mobility of people became inevitable. For full-time farm servants accommodation was an integral part of the wage reward. The unemployed worker who lost a job had no choice but to move. This was the rural context to the explosive rate of Scottish urban growth in this period. By the 1750s Scotland was seventh in a league table of European 'urbanized societies' (as indicated by the proportion of total population living in towns of 20,000 or over), fourth in 1800 and second only to England and Wales in 1850.[34] Some of the many thousands of urban dwellers did well; others eked out an existence close to the margins of destitution. All the large towns had armies of casual labourers who endured a life of poor wages, broken time and constant underemployment. The contemporary statistician James Cleland thought as much as a quarter of the labour force in Glasgow, the nation's largest city, fell into this category.[35] They were fair game for the recruiting parties which roamed the towns of Scotland in increasing numbers during the great conflict with France.

The same material factors governed the national passion for joining the ranks of the Volunteer corps which was not only greater than anywhere else in Britain but engendered such a flood of offers that government was forced to impose county quotas earlier than in England. The most recent students of the volunteering movement see the nation's 'military spirit' as a satisfactory explanation for such extensive mobilization.[36] One influence might have been that the east coast increasingly felt exposed to the threat of enemy raids from Holland and Germany. The Royal Navy had little presence north of the River Forth and the army's bases, which were mainly for recruitment, were confined to Aberdeen, Inverness and Fort William. Volunteering in the region was partly dependent on a need for collective self-defence based on fear of the French across the North Sea. But financial factors were still crucial. Half-pay and retired officers could achieve full salaries when commissioned into Volunteer regiments. This could make a big difference to experienced military men existing on modest pensions. Significantly, when the full-pay privilege was confined to one serving officer per company in 1803, the previously voracious demand for volunteer commissions fell away. The rank and file had a similar concern. The decision in 1798 to cut the weekly allowance by half from two shillings to one shilling caused massive discontent in the Scottish corps. It was pointed out these earnings were of importance to 'the lower and working classes of people', especially since many employers did not make deductions from normal pay when the volunteers were 'attending drill'.[37]

The motivations of individual recruits will probably always remain obscure. But the remarkable scale of Scottish Lowland recruitment for much of the second half of the eighteenth century is beyond dispute. So great was this that the military factor demands more attention than it has received in some wider assessments of Scottish history. So many men were absorbed, at a rate greater than anywhere else in Britain, especially in the long war between 1793 and 1815, that wage levels and the civilian labour market must have been powerfully affected, as well as sex ratios, in areas of intense recruitment. How far, for instance, was the relatively slow rate of Scottish population increase in the period c. 1750 to c. 1815, compared with England and Wales, conditioned by the absence of huge numbers of menfolk on military service as well as by the influence of differential rates of emigration? Certainly after post-war demobilization the annual rate of population increase moved up sharply in the 1820s.

Military service and volunteering ought also to be considered in discussions of Scottish radicalism. After a dramatic but brief response to the stirring events in France between 1792 and 1794, the Scottish Friends of the People Associations collapsed, with the leadership sentenced to transportation to Botany Bay and the membership cowed by a vengeful judiciary and repressive state apparatus. After 1794 Scotland was a nation of rock-solid stability. Even the years of high food prices in 1795 and 1796 failed to destroy the surface calm. The reasons for this are complex.[38] But among these the military factor again cannot be ignored. Henry Dundas enthused over the creation of an 'armed nation' because to him service which bound local communities to the command of their traditional leaders could only result in powerful reinforcement of the social hierarchy and the dilution of 'democratical' sentiments.[39] Other Tory observers were of a similar mind, arguing that the Volunteer corps after 1794 had banished sedition by uniting the classes in a common patriotism. Military service was seen to be the best counter-revolutionary antidote to the cancer of radicalism. Traditional authority, social order and patriotic feelings were all potential buttresses against anarchy. It is no coincidence that the proposal in 1816 to establish a national monument on Calton Hill in Edinburgh to commemorate the sacrifices and triumphs of the Napoleonic Wars should be so enthusiastically supported by these advocates of conservative militarism.

The balance of relationships between England and Scotland was also affected by the martial contribution of the Scots. Many of the nation's élite had been dismayed in the 1760s when the campaign to raise a Scottish militia for coastal defence had foundered on the rock of English distrust at the prospect of Scots being allowed to bear arms. Memories of the '45 lived on. Alex 'Jupiter' Carlyle, the minister of Inveresk, near Edinburgh, was appalled in 1760 because of the failure of the proposal. If the Scottish people were not allowed to defend themselves they would become 'silent and spiritless, like the effeminate inhabitants of a conquered nation'.[40] The notion of the union as a partnership of equals would then have little credibility. It was therefore the wars of the later eighteenth century which created a new equilibrium in the union connection. The Scottish contribution in blood was so great that it helped to reassert equality with England. In the period 1793–1815 the Scots had not only assumed responsibility for their own defence but had shown themselves capable in the mobilization of fencible and Volunteer corps of assisting England itself at its time of mortal danger. Crucially, the Scots were among the most ruthless and feared of the crown forces which routed the Irish rebellion of 1798. Thirteen of the twenty regiments stationed in Ireland on the eve of rebellion were Scots and later reinforcements drew heavily on Scottish reserves. A soldier's song from Midlothian recorded during the uprising conveys the sense of Protestant triumphalism when confronted by the Irish rebels:

> Ye Croppies of Wexford, I'd have you be wise,
> And not go to meddle with Mid-Lothian boys,
> For the Mid-Lothian boys, they vow and declare,
> They'll crop off your heads as well as your hair.
> Remember at Ross and at Vinegar Hill,
> How your heads flew about like chaff in a mill,
> For the Mid-Lothian boys, when a croppy they see,
> They blow out his daylights or tip him cut three.[41]

But the Scots military were not only valued for home defence. The Highland regiments especially had also shown themselves as the spearhead of empire on many a foreign field by 1815. We now turn to their story.

2

In the tradition of the Highland regiments of the British army, 1740 is a seminal date. In that year the six independent companies created by General Wade to police or 'watch' the disaffected Jacobite areas of the Highlands were embodied as the 43rd of Foot. The new regiment then became the 42nd of Foot, the 'Gallant Forty-Twa', in 1749, but is even more celebrated in fame, song and story as the Black Watch, 'Am Freiceadan Dubh', the name given because its characteristic dark colours of tartan set these Highland troops apart from the 'Saighdearan Dearg', the 'Red Soldiers', of the rest of the regular army. The early years of service were not auspicious. In March 1743 the regiment was sent to England, the intention being to transport it from there to Flanders. Discontent spread among the rank and file at being forced to leave the Highlands. This soon changed to anger and alienation when the rumour spread that they were to be shipped to the dreaded West Indies, known as the grave-yard of the ordinary soldier. One hundred and twenty men mutinied and deserted. Three were condemned to death and executed. The rest were then dispersed among other regiments, many of them ending up in the Caribbean and Georgia. False rumour for some had become awful fact. In time, however, the reorganized Black Watch served with great distinction in the War of the Austrian Succession, the Seven Years War and subsequent imperial conflicts. Its achievements did much to establish the image of the Highland soldier as the warrior of empire *par exellence*, courageous, loyal, steady under fire, hardy and adaptable, a new and admired icon of the ancient Scottish martial tradition. In 1758 it was decided to honour the corps with the title the Royal Highland Regiment and to raise a second battalion.

But Highland soldiers were no strangers to imperial warfare before 1740. By 1745 the Scots Brigade in Holland had risen to over 5,000 men and it was common for cadres there to move back and forth between the Low Countries and service in the British army. Highland officers served in the expedition in 1740 to the West Indies under the command of Lord Charles Cathcart. From the 1720s, too, East India Company military posts were being offered through the influence of the Company's Director and Scottish financier, John Drummond of Quarrell, to Jacobite families in Perthshire and Ross-shire to counter disaffection. Long before the concept of the 'Highland regiments' decked out in tartans and kilt became popular, the clan gentry were sending their sons into Lowland and English regiments. Even the first systematic use of Highland troops on the colonial frontier predated by a few years the foundation of the Black Watch. Clansmen from the central and northern Highlands were recruited to Georgia by

Scottish imperial officials in the 1730s, where they formed a defensive barrier against the incursion of Spanish forces on the bitterly contested frontier territories. One hundred and thirty Highlanders with another fifty women and children reached Savannah from Inverness in January, 1736:

They were not adventurers or men exiled by debt and want, but were men of good character, carefully selected for their military qualities. They were picked men, many of them from the Glen of Strathdean, and their officers were highly connected in the Highlands . . . These Highlanders did heroic service in defending Georgia from the Spaniards in the Battle of Bloody Marsh . . .[42]

Individual Highlanders also found their way into the far corners of empire where skills in the arts of violence were in demand, especially in colonies such as Virginia and Georgia which had a string of Scottish governors with military experience in the early decades of the eighteenth century. One such was a nameless Gael who is credited with decapitating the notorious Edward Teach, better known as Blackbeard the Pirate, at the Battle of Ockracoke Inlet, North Carolina, in 1719. As the *Boston Newletter* reported in grisly detail:

Rhode-Island . . . On the 12th [February] arrived here . . . Humphry Johnson in a Sloop from North Carolina, bound to Amboy who sailed the next Day, and informs that Governour Spotswood [a Scot] of Virginia fitted out two Sloops, well mann'd with Fifty pickt Men of His Majesty's Men of War lying there . . . under the Command of Lieutenant Robert Maynard of His Majesty's Ship Pearl, in pursuit of the Notorious and Arch Pirate Capt. Teach, who made his Escape from Virginia, when some of his Men were taken there; which Pirate Lieutenant Maynard came up with at North Carolina . . . [a bloody battle ensued] . . . both Companies ingaged in Maynard's Sloop, one of Maynard's Men being a Highlander, ingaged Teach with his broad Sword, who gave Teach a cut on the Neck, Teach saying well done Lad, the Highlander reply'd, if it be not well done, I'll do it better, with that he gave him a second stroke, which cut off his Head, laying it flat on his Shoulder, Teach's Men being about 20, and three of four Blacks were all killed in the Ingagement, excepting two carried to Virginia: Teach's body was thrown overboard, and his Head put on the top of the Bowsprit.[43]

But the boom time for the Highland regiments as such only really started after the defeat of the '45 rebellion and, in particular, during the Seven Years War, the American War of Independence and, most crucially of all, during the long years of conflict with France after 1793. Six regiments of the line were mobilized between 1753 and 1783, including Fraser's and Montgomery's regiments. A further ten were recruited during the American War. Around 12,000 men were involved during the Seven Years War, almost the same numbers as the Highland army of the biggest Jacobite uprising in 1715 and more than twice the level of the forces of Prince Charles Edward Stuart in the '45. It was indeed a great irony that after the death of clanship, Gaeldom became even more militarized than in the past. By the French Revolutionary and Napoleonic Wars the number of recruits was unprecedented. The most recent careful estimate suggests totals ranging from 37,000 to 48,000 men in regular, fencible and Volunteer units. This is quite an extraordinary figure, given that the population of the Highlands was around 250,000 to 300,000 during the second half of the eighteenth century.[44] The region had become the most intensively recruited region of the United Kingdom. Scotland had the highest density of those famous retired veterans, the Chelsea Pensioners, within the British Isles and the Highland counties had the biggest proportion of all.[45] In some areas recruitment reached massive levels. Between the years 1793 and 1805, 3,680 men were under arms from the Skye estates of Lord Macdonald, MacLeod of MacLeod and MacLeod of Raasay. From 1792 to 1837 the numbers included no less than 21 lieutenant-generals or major-generals, 48 lieutenant-colonels, 600 other officers and 120 pipers.[46] The west coast parish of Gairloch in 1799 was nearly stripped of its menfolk. A survey for the Lord-Lieutenant of Ross-shire concluded that the parish now mainly consisted of children, women and old men, so intensive had the recruitment of young men become. One other calculation suggests that on the vast territories of the Earl of Breadalbane which straddled Argyllshire and Perthshire, as many as three farm tenancies out of every five had experienced some level of recruitment in the 1790s.[47] It is therefore scarcely surprising to discover that Fort George at Ardersier, east of Inverness, the most formidable bastion fortress in Europe, built to control the clans after Culloden, quickly developed a different function. By the time of the American War after 1775 it had become 'the great drill square' where the

Highland levies were prepared for overseas duties.[48] Clanship had metamorphosed into imperial service. The Gaels now pioneered a role in the British military which was later to be assumed by conquered peoples of the empire with a martial tradition, such as the Ghurkas, Sikhs and Pathans. But the dramatic expansion of Highland recruitment was short-lived. By the later 1790s the manpower resources of the region were virtually exhausted, not only because of over-recruitment but also death in battle, disease, discharges and natural attrition. Even the most prestigious regiments were forced to extend their territorial range of recruitment. At least a third of the Black Watch who fought at Waterloo were drawn from the Lowlands, the Borders and England.[49] By the Victorian period Highland regiments comprised only a minority of Highlanders as mass emigration took its toll on the region, especially after the Great Famine of the 1840s which preceded the Crimean War by only a few years.[50]

Why the Highlands should supply so many soldiers for the British army for much of the second half of the eighteenth century is an intriguing question. After all, Gaeldom was portrayed in the 1740s as the very heartland of treachery, the region that had spawned the rebellion in 1745 which came close to overthrowing the Protestant succession itself. Loyal Whigs responded hysterically. 'Scoto-Britannicus' depicted Highlanders as being beyond the pale of civilization. Charles Edward Stuart had landed in the most remote and wild recesses of the kingdom 'amidst dens of barbarous and lawless ruffians' and 'a crew of ungrateful villains, savages and traitors'.[51] The Young Pretender was the agent of popery, the 'limb of Antichrist', and his clansmen 'a Hellish Band of Highland Thieves'.[52] With enormous relief Presbyterian Scotland celebrated the happy deliverance at Culloden from these pernicious forces of darkness. The *Glasgow Journal*, for instance, brought out a special large-print edition in honour of Cumberland's comprehensive victory and also to record 'the greatest rejoicings that have been known' in the city.[53] The forces of the crown then took a terrible revenge, unleashing a reign of terror throughout the disaffected areas of the north and west.

A huge regular army, supported by units of the Royal Navy, had been drawn into the very heart of the Highlands. Effectively the Jacobite areas were under military occupation. The missed opportunity after the 1715 rebellion and the policy of leniency of that period were not to be repeated. The clans had to be broken once and for all because only their fighting skills and loyalty to the Stuarts had brought Charles close to ultimate success. At first the Duke of Cumberland was attracted to a strategy of wholesale transportation of the clans to the colonies, but then he opted instead for a scorched-earth policy of burning, clearance and pillage. In May 1746 he moved to Fort Augustus in the Great Glen, to extract retribution from some of the most committed Jacobite areas of the surrounding region. Cumberland's explicit intention was to teach the people a lesson they would never forget. Numerous settlements throughout Glenelg, Kintail, Lochaber and Morvern were burnt, plundered and laid waste by four independent raiding parties, supported offshore by the Royal Navy. Even clans loyal to the crown were not immune from the relentless depredations which lasted for nearly a year after Culloden. Cattle, the main source of wealth in this pastoral society and the means of buying in grain from more agriculturally favoured areas, were confiscated on a massive scale. Fort Augustus, supplied from the booty plundered from the population of the surrounding districts, became for a time the largest cattle mart in Scotland. It was reckoned that in one year alone nearly 20,000 head of cattle were put up for sale, as well as numerous sheep, oxen, horses and goats. When the military onslaught ended, the legislative attack on clanship began. A Disarming Act stiffened previous legislation to prohibit the carrying of weapons of war. Highland dress was proscribed as the sartorial symbol of rebel militarism. The wearing of 'plaid, philibeg, trews, shoulder-belts . . . tartans or part-coloured plaid' was outlawed. One government minister memorably described the Act of Parliament as a bill for 'disarming and undressing those savages'.[54] The abolition of heritable jurisdictions (the private courts of landowners) and military land tenures were designed to destroy the power of the chiefs. Estates of rebel landowners were forfeited to the crown and the majority were sold off to pay creditors.

Against this background of ferocious and unyielding retribution, it might seem strange that the British state, a mere few years after Culloden, decided to deploy Highlanders as a military spearhead of imperial expansion. Not only that, but these former rebels were to be regimented in distinctive concentrated units, permitted to wear the banned Highland dress and encouraged to develop their own particular *esprit de corps*. These were privileges not afforded the

Irish (who vastly outnumbered the Scottish Gaels in the service of empire) or the Lowland battalions. In fact, the martial value of the Highlander was already being recognized some time before the Young Pretender landed in the Hebrides at the beginning of his ill-fated adventure. Just before the '45, prominent Whig politicians in the Highlands, such as Duncan Forbes of Culloden and the Duke of Argyll, had suggested raising regiments among the Jacobite clans. Military posts in the British army for the clan gentry would, it was argued, help to cure disaffection. Again, in 1739 one prophetic commentator had observed:

They [the Highlanders] are a numerous and prolifick People; and, if reformed in their Principles, and Manners, and usefully employ'd, might be made a considerable Accession of Power and Wealth to Great Britain. Some Clans of Highlanders, well instructed in the Arts of War, and well affected to the Government, would make as able and formidable a body for their Country's Defence, as Great Britain, or Switzerland, or any part of Europe was able to produce.[55]

But vengeance, subjugation and punishment were at first the preferred responses. Cumberland spoke for the victorious Hanoverians when he urged mass transportation of the rebels to the colonies rather than recruitment of the disaffected to the crown forces. The early history of the Black Watch, itself recruited from loyal clans, also suggested caution. True, the regiment had distinguished itself at Fontenoy but was kept south of the Thames during the '45 and then stationed in Ireland between 1749 and 1755. The mutiny of 1743 had not been forgotten, and in the immediate aftermath of rebellion most Highlanders were suspected of secret disloyalty. But the idea of recruiting Gaels did not die. It was advanced vigorously in 1754 and 1755 only to falter against the express opposition of the King and Cumberland. Then attitudes changed the following year. The arrival of a new Prime Minister, William Pitt, in 1756 signalled a more overt commitment to a 'blue water policy' which preferred colonial expansion to European commitments. A fresh and reliable military supply was now vital, not least because of the outbreak of the Seven Years War with France, a conflict which more than any other was to be fought in the colonial theatre. The catastrophic defeat inflicted by the French and their Indian allies on General Edward Braddock on the Monongahela River in Maryland with the loss of two-thirds of his command killed or wounded concentrated Pitt's mind. The 'Great War for Empire' was going very badly and the Prime Minister was also known for his resolute opposition to the use of foreign mercenaries. The only alternative was to expand domestic supply. By early 1757 even the Duke of Cumberland had given his agreement to employing Highland levies. Two additional battalions were sanctioned, commanded by Simon Fraser, son of the executed Jacobite, Lord Lovat, and Archibald Montgomery, later Earl of Eglinton. By the end of the war, ten more Highland regiments had been created. They were the first of many which served during the long American Revolutionary and Napoleonic campaigns. In 1766 Pitt looked back on his policy in a famous speech:

I sought for merit wherever it was to be found; it is my boast that I was the first minister who looked for it and found it in the mountains of the north. I called it forth and drew into your service a hardy and intrepid race of men, who, when left by your jealousy, became a prey to the artifice of your enemies, and had gone nigh to have overturned the state in the war before the last. These men in the last war were brought to combat on your side; they served with fidelity, as they fought with valour and conquered for you in every part of the world.[56]

Pitt had made the executive decision but Highland recruitment was hardly his own idea. The Secretary of War, Lord Barrington, had already told Parliament in 1751 that he was all for having 'as many Scottish soldiers as possible in the army' and '. . . of all the Scottish soldiers I should choose to have and keep in our army as many Highlanders as possible'.[57] A sea-change had taken place in government attitudes, in part because the destruction of the Jacobite threat was now recognized to be so complete. The menace of Stuart counter-revolution was removed. The Highlands, unlike Ireland, no longer posed an internal security threat. Mass recruitment to the crown forces could therefore proceed. At the same time, however, all of the ingrained fear of disaffection took time to dissipate. The solution was not to allow Highland troops to linger long in Scotland after training but to have them despatched overseas with all speed. Thus it was that the Highlanders became perforce the crack troops of imperial warfare, with wide experience in North America, the West Indies and India, encountering long and arduous tours of duty lasting for several years. In the view of Lord Barrington, they should be enlisted for life to prevent battle-hardened veterans causing trouble at home.[58] The perception of the '45 was also relevant. The Highlanders first impressed themselves on the British state as warriors, and formidable ones at that. The terrifying charge and slashing broadswords which routed Cope's regulars at Prestonpans were not easily forgotten. Even in the carnage of Culloden the following year much of the rebel army had performed with remarkable courage and an almost suicidal tenacity.

Over time the myth hardened and developed. It was argued that the Jacobite soldiers had followed the wrong cause but they had done so only at the behest of their chiefs. Throughout, they had displayed not only heroism in battle but undying loyalty. In such best-selling publications as *Young Juba or the History of the Young Chevalier* and *Ascanius or the Young Adventurer* attention was focused on the story of the 'Prince and the Heather' when the Young Pretender was never betrayed by his followers despite the high price on his head. The crown assumed that all these virtues were founded on the ethic of clanship, the martial society which had long disappeared from the rest of Britain. For this reason the government wished to keep Highlanders together in 'Highland regiments' under their 'natural' leaders. Fraser's Highlanders (the 71st of Foot) had no less than six chiefs of clans among its officers as well as many clan gentry. Ironically, while the state was bent on destroying clanship as a threat to the state, it was also at the same time committed to reinforcing clan allegiances through regimental recruitment. The intriguing feature was that the clan ethos was already dying rapidly in the 1750s through a cycle of inevitable decline which was soon to be accelerated in the later eighteenth century by commercialization of estates and clearance of people. But the state hardly doubted that the Highlander was nonetheless a natural warrior, not least because landowners seeking to establish family regiments constantly milked the glamorous image of clanship in order to gain a favourable response.

One of the reasons why Lowland and Border élites were much less successful in the business of eighteenth-century military entrepreneurship was that they lacked this key advantage in the bidding process. Another was that in the 1750s at least they did not benefit from the government's policy of using military patronage finally to draw the teeth of Jacobite disaffection. During the Seven Years

War this was overwhelmingly concentrated on recalcitrant Highland families. Thus Fraser's Regiment was not only headed by the son of an executed Jacobite but also included several kin of celebrated rebels. Among them was the brother of Ewen Macpherson of Cluny who had famously hidden in a specially designed cage on Ben Alder in Badenoch for seven years, where he set up the first casino in Gaeldom before escaping into permanent exile. Several supporters of the old cause successfully rehabilitated themselves in the eyes of the crown by their loyal service in the imperial war. While it would be wrong to exaggerate the number of former Jacobites in the kilted battalions, the presence of even a few gave an ironic twist to the campaign in America. Several of the line regiments who had fought against Highlanders during the '45 now found themselves allied with them against the French. Lascelle's 47th Foot had been shattered by the charge of the clans at Prestonpans. But on the Plains of Abraham outside Quebec they joined with Fraser's Highlanders to pursue the fleeing French in the decisive battle which won Canada for the British. General James Wolfe, the commander of the army that day, had himself faced the Jacobites on Culloden Moor as a junior officer in April 1746. Barrell's regiment, now known as Duroure's 4th Foot, had suffered the most intense and violent Highland attack on the left flank of the Hanoverian line at Culloden. During the Seven Years War, however, it successfully combined with Highland levies in the Caribbean campaigns.[59]

The foundation had been laid for a greater expansion of Highland recruitment between 1775 and 1783 and then on an even more colossal scale in the years 1793 to 1815. The higher echelons of the British military were increasingly influenced by German military concepts which stressed that the people of mountainous areas were especially suited to the martial life. David Stewart of Garth's *Sketches of the Character, Manners and Present State of the Highlands of Scotland, with Details of the Military Service of the Highland Regiments*, first published in 1822, was the most influential text on the Highland soldier in Victorian times. Stewart of Garth contended that 'nature' had produced the perfect warrior:

Nursed in poverty he acquired a hardihood which enabled him to sustain severe privations. As the simplicity of his life gave vigour to his body, so it fortified his mind. Possessing a frame and constitution thus hardened he was taught to consider courage as the most honourable virtue, cowardice the most disgraceful failing.[60]

In addition, the thought of the Enlightenment further fortified the legend. The 'stage' theory of the development of human civilization, propounded by such Scottish intellectuals as Adam Ferguson and John Miller, fitted perfectly with the stereotype of the Highlander as a soldier. The region was seen to be still located in the feudal period where militarism was a way of life. Ferguson, for instance, argued that the Gaels were not interested in the 'commercial arts' but were rather by their very nature disposed to making war.[61] The parallel notion soon also became popular that the Highlander could be spared from ordinary manual labour for military activity because the regional economy was so underdeveloped compared with other more advanced areas of the British Isles.[62]

There was more than enough actual evidence during 'the Great War for Empire' to justify beliefs like these. Statesmen who were accustomed to the slow, hard slog of army and navy recruitment were astonished at the speed with which the first Highland regiments were formed. Simon Fraser obtained his commission to raise a new battalion in January 1757. By March of that year he had recruited over 1,100 men. In the war itself the new formations performed with distinction. In another strange alliance Major Hector Munro won the battle of Buxar in India in October 1764 with the help of detachments of the 89th regiment. The battle effectively completed the British conquest of Bengal. Munro was no stranger to the Highlands, having once hunted Cluny Macpherson as a fugitive after Culloden. The Black Watch played a major role against the Indian nations in the brutal campaign known as Pontiac's War in America in 1763. Among other Highland battle honours were the capture of the great French fortress at Louisburgh on Cape Breton, the key to the St Lawrence river, and Wolfe's even more decisive victory over the French general, Montcalm, at Quebec.

By 1757, the number of Highlanders had reached 4,200 out of a total of 24,000 British regulars in North America. Despite their relative minority status, they managed to maintain a very high profile.[63] Colonial warfare was different from the formal ritual of the European theatre. Guerrilla actions were much more common. Raids, retreats and ambushes were the stock-in-trade of the Cherokees,

Micmacs and other tribal allies of the French in the wilderness. The Highlanders were not only among the most adept British troops at responding to these tactics but were also among the most ruthless in crushing the Indian enemy. By its nature wilderness warfare was ferocious, with prisoners and the wounded liable to be tomahawked and scalped. Highland soldiers used the same techniques of total war employed by 'Butcher' Cumberland's men after Culloden in genocidal campaigns against the Indian nations between 1760 and 1764. But it was not all a series of uninterrupted triumphs. Those battalions posted to Guadaloupe and Havana lost many men through yellow fever and malaria. The habit of using Highlanders as shock troops in battles of attrition could also have devastating consequences. At Ticonderoga on 7 July 1758, the Black Watch, which formed part of the British force, lost 8 officers, 9 sergeants and 299 other ranks killed, and 17 other officers, 10 sergeants and 306 other ranks wounded.[64] Yet by these bloody sacrifices the Gaels not only sealed their loyalty to the House of Hanover but ensured that the Highlands became the government's favourite recruiting ground in the imperial wars of the future. The Highland levies had come to be regarded as the expendable cannon-fodder of the empire with a feared reputation among the enemy. Stewart of Garth recalled that to the French they were the 'Sauvages d'Ecosse':

... they believed that they would neither take nor give quarter ... and that no man had a chance against their broadswords; and that with a ferocity natural to savages, they made no prisoners, and spared neither man, woman nor child ... they were always in the front of every action in which they were engaged.[65]

Not even their occasional resort to mutiny when denied bounties, suffered pay arrears or when their final military destinations were concealed sullied the warrior image.

3

A long tradition based largely on innumerable regimental histories has it that the Highland battalions of the later eighteenth century were the direct heirs of the clans. Their values were also said to be the intrinsic values of clanship: courage, loyalty, endurance and, above all, an innate capacity for making war. No one can deny, of course, that there was something distinctive about the Highland formations. For much of the century, most of Britain had strong cultural prejudices against soldiering. This did not seem to exist to the same extent in many parts of the Highlands. Joining the army was looked upon as a 'normal' occupation.[66] This may in part be accounted for by residual clanship. It is more likely, however, that the difference simply reflected the relative lack of employment opportunities in the poorest region of mainland Britain. Significantly, in better-off areas such as Highland Perthshire the Atholl Highlanders had difficulties recruiting during the American War. Of the parish of Blair Atholl in the county, it was said in the 1790s that 'many had learned to despise a soldier's pay and hate a life of servitude'.[67] The best areas for the recruiters were to be found in the north-west where economic conditions were less attractive. Even there, however, attitudes varied. In his *General View of the Agriculture of the Counties of Ross and Cromarty* (1813), Sir George Mackenzie concluded that by then it was 'notorious that the inhabitants have a strong aversion to military life'. When a battalion of the 78th Seaforth Highlanders, commanded by his own brother-in-law, was raised successfully, Mackenzie pointed out that the young recruits had joined the colours principally 'to save their parents being turned out of their farms'.[68]

But other apparent similarities existed between traditional clanship and British army service. There can be little doubt that the Highland battalions had a strong sense of identity based on their distinctive dress, language, common heritage and culture, and often on the same name. Imperial war was a godsend for the *Daoine-Uaisle*, the clan gentries, whose status on many Highland estates was being steadily undermined by rising rentals and the breaking-up of holdings to create crofting townships. The army became an escape route for many members of this class from the irresistible forces of agrarian modernization. In this period they virtually became a professional military class of full-pay and half-pay officers who only returned to farming in the years between wars.[69] Their traditional leadership role and influence on the localities where their regiments recruited must have been a factor of significance in enhancing *esprit de corps*. Indeed, the bond between a Highlander and his officer does seem to have been much closer than the relationship between English soldiers and their superiors.[70]

Yet when everything is considered, any close resemblance between the clans and the regiments was at best superficial, which was hardly surprising since recruitment boomed at the very time when the Highlands were being transformed from tribalism to capitalism. The mania for raising family regiments fits well into this prevailing context of rampant commercialism. Landowners were military entrepreneurs rather than patriarchal chieftains. They harvested the population of their estates for the army to make money, in the same way as they established sheepwalks, cattle ranches and kelp shores. But such profiteering had to be done behind the façade of clan loyalties and martial enthusiasm because it was these very attributes which gave the Highlands a competitive edge in the military labour market. Even sophisticated and experienced politicians like Henry Dundas were taken in. During the Napoleonic Wars he exuded praise for the clansmen and their 'chiefs', enthusiastically approved of the great scheme to embody even more of them in 1797 and applauded the Highland warriors for their hostility to the pernicious 'levelling and dangerous principles' of the urban radicals of the time.[71]

Successful recruitment could provide many benefits for the Highland élites. Raising a regiment not only provided commissions for a magnate's own kinsmen and associates, it also conferred influence and patronage in the neighbourhood among other impoverished minor gentry who desperately sought officerships and the secure incomes and pensions which came with them. Local power and standing were increased, but military service also consolidated connections with government. The rewards could be substantial. Sir James Grant, whose estates were heavily encumbered, was rewarded with a sinecure worth £3,000 a year and the lord-lieutenancy of Inverness in 1794. Mackenzie of Seaforth, who like most Highland landowners had financial difficulties, did even better. In quick succession he became Lord-Lieutenant of Ross in 1794, Lord Seaforth in the English peerage in the same year and, in 1800, Governor of Barbados. But there were also more direct and equally lucrative benefits to recruitment. Allocating lands to soldiers could provide an estate with more regular rentals than were likely to accrue from the small tenantry whose payments were notoriously volatile because of harvest failures and market fluctuations. The military had a secure income not only when on active service but also at a lower level through pensions when they retired. There is evidence that several proprietors showed a clear preference for such 'military' tenants as a result of this advantage.[72]

The Warrant or Beating Order issued by the Secretary of War, permitting the raising of a new corps, authorized the recruitment of officers and men, the numbers involved and the bounties to be paid to recruits. Bounties rose dramatically in the later eighteenth century as the army underwent continued expansion. Official levels for Highland recruits were £3 in 1757 but had spiralled to £21–£30 in 1794. Landlords in the north of Scotland were able to exploit these rising values because rather than paying full bounty money they used land on their estates in return for the supply of recruits. Tenants were expected to supply a family member or a 'purchased man' whose bounty was paid by the tenant himself.[73] Through this mechanism, landlords made huge profits which during wartime equalled and sometimes even surpassed the income from the agriculture of the estate. The human harvest was simply more lucrative. There was also an assumed expectation that men would be forthcoming from the ranks of the tenantry. When this was in doubt, systematic coercion was employed. Estate records teem with examples. Alexander Macdonnel of Glengarry ordered his agent to 'warn out' a list of small tenants from his Knoydart property, they 'having refused to serve me'. Similarly, MacLean of Lochbuie on the island of Mull threatened to remove seventy-one tenants, cottars and their families in 1795 because they had not provided sons for service. On several estates, the tradition of 'land for sons' was widespread. In the Lord Macdonald papers relating to his extensive lands in Skye, a document is headed '*List of Tenants who have been promised Lands and an exchange of lands for their sons*'.[74] These contracts were often very specific, indicating the length of leases and the tenurial arrangements as a result of sons traded for land. In the long run, however, they generated angry controversy. Many recruits did not return home but were buried in foreign graves through death in battle or, more likely, from disease. To the families, therefore, their holdings had often been acquired quite literally through the blood of their kinfolk. When these obligations were ended, for whatever cause, the people felt a sense of gross breach of trust. Recruitment was of immense profit to the landed classes of the Highlands. But its consequences brought down great opprobrium on their hapless successors and gave a special emotional edge to the contentious saga of the Highland Clearances.[75]

14

Empire and the Transformation of Scotland

I

By the middle decades of the eighteenth century the Scottish economy was on the move. Glasgow had become the leading tobacco entrepôt in Europe. Some 47 million lb. of American tobacco were imported in 1771 and the Glaswegian merchants had carved out a greater and greater share of the British trade at the expense of rivals in London, Liverpool, Whitehaven and Bristol. As late as 1738, the Scots accounted for only 10 per cent of the total British importation; but by 1765 this had risen to an astonishing 40 per cent of a UK trade which had itself expanded remarkably in the intervening decades. One of the most important aspects of this dazzling success story was that the new tobacco commerce renewed the old connections with Europe that had been eroded by sea war and economic nationalism earlier in the eighteenth century. Over 90 per cent of the tobacco imported was eventually re-exported to French, Dutch and German markets. The dynamic growth of linen manufacture, Scotland's premier industry, paralleled the remarkable achievements in overseas trade as output rose fourfold in value between the years 1736–40 and between 1768–72. At the last date, nearly 13 million yards were stamped for sale by the Board of Trustees, and the linen industry then employed around 20,000 handloom weavers and a much greater army of female spinners drawn from rural and urban households throughout the length and breadth of Scotland.[1]

There was also a series of landmark developments which seemed to signal a new age of prosperity and progress. The Royal Bank of Scotland was founded in 1727 and the British Linen Company in 1746. The establishment of the Royal soon led to the development of the 'cash accompt' in 1728, the world's first overdraft facility, while the Linen Company was the only British chartered bank in the eighteenth century devoted specifically to the encouragement of industry. Banking also flourished elsewhere, notably in Glasgow with the Arms, Ship and Thistle banks promoted vigorously by some of the city's wealthiest merchant princes. In 1759 came the foundation of Carron Iron Works, which was almost a symbol of economic modernity in Scotland. It was established to work and smelt iron on a large scale, using the latest techniques pioneered by the Coalbrookdale Company in England. The Prestonpans Vitriol Works had been set up ten years earlier and also developed an enviable reputation at the leading edge of the chemistry of textile finishing.

In less spectacular but equally important fashion, significant developments can also be identified in rural society. Commercial forces were now undeniably having a much greater impact both in the Highlands and the Lowland countryside. The black cattle trade from the central and western Highlands was one of the clear-cut success stories in the decades immediately following the union. By the 1750s, however, exports of timber, slate and fish from Gaeldom were also becoming significant. Similarly, in many parts of the Lowland countryside, market forces were becoming more dominant. This is confirmed by the evidence of changes in the rental structure, where payments in kind were tending to become less common and were being steadily replaced by cash rents. In addition, on a number of estates a radical change in tenure was under way as proprietors converted more and more smaller holdings into larger individual tenancies, which meant that the capitalist farming class of the Agricultural Revolution of later years was already emerging in embryonic form.[2]

Manifestly, therefore, the Scottish economy of the 1750s was more stable, dynamic and prosperous than at the time of the union. Equally, however, the scale and significance of the changes should be kept in perspective. There had been real advances *within* the existing structure of economy and society, but precious little indication yet that the *overall* social fabric of Scotland was being altered. Overwhelmingly the country remained a rural society with only one Scot in eight living in a town (defined as communities of 4,000 or more) in 1750. In a European league table of 'urbanized societies' using a different measure (of the proportion of the population living in towns of 10,000 inhabitants and above) Scotland was eleventh out of sixteen in 1650, tenth in 1700 and seventh in 1750. The proportion of town dwellers was increasing, but the overall Scottish distribution of population was still more akin to that of Ireland, the Scandinavian countries and Poland than to the more advanced European economies of England and Holland. In 1750, for instance, 17 per cent of the people of England lived in towns of 10,000 or more, compared with less than 9 per cent in Scotland at that date.[3]

Moreover, the life of the countryside, where most Scots lived and worked, was still based within traditional structures that would have been recognizable and familiar to earlier generations. Contemporary estate maps show that in most areas outside the progressive south-eastern counties, the landscape had hardly changed at all. Traditional rig cultivation and the scattered mosaic of irregular fields divided among different tenants were all visible. Enclosure had made little progress outside the advanced enclaves, and the 'improved' agricul-tural methods were rarely practised by most working farmers. As a result, average yields for oats and barley remained much the same as those of the later seventeenth century. The same pattern of continuity was also evident in social structure. Already by the early eighteenth century the three-tier social order of landlords, tenants and landless wage-labourers predominated in the midland and southern counties of England. In Scotland, however, the majority of the rural popu-lation maintained some connection with the land. Indeed, before the later eighteenth century, there were few entirely landless groups in the Scottish countryside. Cottar families with patches of land could still be found in large numbers in many parishes. Rural tradesmen, such as weavers, blacksmiths, tailors and masons, normally possessed a piece of land. All in all, therefore, Scotland's rural social structure had much more in common with that of most continental European societies than with its closest neighbour to the south.[4]

This traditional pattern, of basic continuity marked by some changes at the margin, abruptly came to an end in the 1760s. That decade seems to have been a defining watershed, because from then on Scotland began to experience a social and economic transforma-tion unparalleled among European societies of the time in its speed, scale and intensity. The currently favoured view of English moderni-zation as a process characterized by cumulative, protracted and evo-lutionary development does not fit the Scottish experience.[5] North of the Border there truly was an Industrial and Agricultural Revolution.

In fact, modern research on comparative urban development in Europe suggests that the explosive Scottish rate of town and city growth was the fastest of any region in Britain or the continent between 1750 and 1850.[6] In 1750, Scotland was seventh among European 'urbanized societies', fourth in 1800 but second only to England and Wales in 1850. By then, over one-third of Scots lived in towns of more than 5,000 inhabitants, a figure that does not include those who were being drawn in from the countryside to the small factory towns and planned villages which multiplied in this period. At the same time, a general reconfiguration of the demographic map of Scotland was taking place. Migration was under way on an unprecedented scale since the towns could grow rapidly only by inward movement from the country. In 1851, for instance, over half the inhabitants of the ten principal Scottish towns were migrants, not only from the Highlands and the rural Lowlands but increasingly also from the north of Ireland. The concentration of rapid urban growth in the Forth–Clyde valley, and particularly in the western towns, also had revolutionary effects. The Highlands and the Borders were losing people to the central Lowlands, which by the 1820s had absorbed more than half the Scottish population. The modern demographic structure of Scotland was now taking shape.[7]

The key engine of urbanization was industralization and, down to *c.* 1830, the main motors of growth were the textile industries of cotton, linen and wool. The omniscient contemporary economic commentator Sir John Sinclair suggested that the making of fabrics together with silk production employed over 257,000 individuals in the early 1800s, representing nearly 90 per cent of all those working in manufacturing.[8] The halcyon days of iron, engineering and shipbuilding were yet to come in the decades after 1830, and particularly from 1850. Despite the fame of Carron and the foundation of a further nine plants between 1779 and 1801, iron manufacture was much less successful than textiles before 1830. This sluggish performance was illustrated by the failure to build any additional works between 1798 and 1824 and by the recurrent financial difficulties experienced by existing companies. It was therefore the textile sector above all which sustained the first phase of the Scottish Industrial Revolution. There were at least four aspects to its significance.[9]

First, spinning was increasingly mechanized and production was concentrated in the mill complexes which, more than anything else, became the great physical symbols of the Industrial Revolution. Cotton achieved key technological advances with the adoption of the inventions from England of Hargreave's 'spinning jenny', Arkwright's water-frame and, above all, Crompton's 'mule'. When this last crucial innovation was linked to James Watt's steam engine, the cotton factories were liberated from the need to be close to sources of water power and could instead concentrate on a much bigger scale in towns and cities. By the 1820s, steam-powered flax spinning, after earlier difficulties, had transformed linen manufacture, while by the same decade all processes in the woollen industry, apart from weaving and knitting, could be mechanized. Second, there were enormous increases in production. The average annual output of linen stamped for sale stood at 3,488,232 yards between 1728 and 1731 but had multiplied almost tenfold, to reach 30,700,100 yards, in 1818–22. The record of cotton was even more spectacular but is least amenable to long-term statistical description. Third, within the textile sector there was a recognizable trend towards regional specialization. The heart of cotton manufacture was concentrated in Glasgow, Paisley and the western Lowlands; Dundee and the smaller towns of Angus and Fife became pre-eminent in linen; and the Borders increasingly achieved a reputation as a centre of excellence for the spinning and weaving of woollens. By 1844, for instance, over half of all Scotland's worsted frames were located in one Border town, Hawick. Fourth, textile finishing experienced extensive growth and investment not only in the development of the numerous bleachfields which operated throughout the textile areas but also in the technical advances made in printing and dyeing. Perhaps the pinnacle of achievement in this respect was the establishment of the St Rollox works in Glasgow in 1799 for the manufacture of bleaching powder. It was primarily because of this initiative that Scotland began to emerge as a world leader in industrial chemicals.[10]

Taken together, these diverse and mutually reinforcing activities of the textile industries generated a powerful dynamic for manufacturing growth at the heart of the Scottish economic system. Other activities, such as brewing, distilling and papermaking, also played a part, while recent research has demonstrated that coal-mining in Scotland was more developed than used to be believed and that it managed to achieve output levels between 1760 and 1800 that were significantly higher than the British average. But textiles remained crucial before 1830. In yet another of his many estimates, published in 1826, Sir John Sinclair thought that over a quarter of a million people worked in cotton, linen and wool, of whom no less than 60 per cent were occupied in cotton alone. He reckoned also that only 13,000 were employed in the iron trade and 19,000 in other manufactures.[11] It is also important to emphasize that there were significant continuities between the old economic order and the new. In cotton, the most technically advanced industry of the age, only spinning was fully mechanized before 1830. The number of handloom weavers servicing all the textile trades continued to rise to a peak of around 84,000 workers in 1840.[12] The machine was still far from triumphant. Even for those labouring in manufacturing, the typical working environment remained the home and the small workshop rather than the mill or the large factory complex. It was also the case that most Scots, perhaps as many as two out of every three, lived and died in rural communities rather than the tenements of the burgeoning cities and towns.

Yet the unprecedented industrial and urban expansion did have a transformational impact on Scottish society.[13] The effects of the new economic system were felt even in the most remote corners of the land. They embraced the islands of the Hebrides and Orkney and Shetland in the far west and north of the country, the innumerable farms and small villages of the rural Lowlands, as well as the booming urban areas. The voracious demands of industry and the towns for food, drink, raw materials and labour revolutionized economic and social relationships elsewhere in Scotland. The buoyant markets for kelp, fish, whisky, slate, cattle, timber and sheep to c. 1815 helped to transform Gaelic society, dissolved the traditional townships, encouraged land division into single crofts and subordinated ancient responsibilities of the landed classes to the new imperatives of profit. In parallel, customary relationships between clan élites and followers swiftly disintegrated as the entire fabric of society was recast in response to the new rigour of landlord demand, ideological fashion and, above all, the overwhelming force of market pressures emanating from the south. Over less than two generations Scottish Gaeldom had moved from tribalism to capitalism.[14]

The scale and speed of the revolution were no less remarkable in the rural Lowlands. There, too, the veritable explosion in grain and meat prices after c. 1780 as a result of urbanization has been identified as the basic dynamic in rapid commercialization.[15] It was in the two or three decades after *c.* 1760 that a recognizably modern landscape of enclosed fields, trim farms, separated holdings and new roads started to take shape in the countryside. The single farm under one master became the norm as holdings were united between 1760 and 1815. By 1830, most of those who toiled in Lowland agriculture were landless men and women servants. Their lives were often as much subject to the unrelenting pressures of labour discipline as those employed in the new industrial workshops and factories.[16] The market forces unleashed by industrialism spanned the length and breadth of Scotland. There had been a decisive break with the past and the country was set firmly on the path towards an industrial society.

2

Ever since Henry Hamilton's pioneering *The Industrial Revolution in Scotland*, first published in 1932, historians have pondered the origins of the country's economic transformation.[17] The imperial factor has often been mentioned, but no focused study of the relationship between empire and the eighteenth-century economy has yet been written. In part, this is because scholars are rightly suspicious of extracting one influence from a range of causes such as natural endowment, labour, enterprise, technology and others to explain industrialization. Historians are mentally tuned to avoid monocausal explanation like the plague. It may be also that there is a reluctance to consider in depth what can be regarded – in part at least – as a darker aspect of the Scottish past. Victorian writers liked to see the nation's industrial pre-eminence as the consequence of the Anglo-Scottish Union fortified by native talent, enterprise and ingenuity.[18] The notion that some of that success could possibly be due to the territorial subjugation of other lands and to plantation economies which depended on slave labour in North America and the West Indies had precious little appeal for a society which, in the nineteenth century, saw itself in the vanguard of the movement for slave emancipation. Some Victorian commentators took the moral high ground by suggesting that the Scots, unlike the merchants of Liverpool and Bristol, never contaminated themselves with the evils of the commerce in slaves. It was a view in overt conflict with the realities of the historical experience, as previous chapters in this book have shown. Malachy Postlethwayt pointed out in 1745 that Britain's commercial empire in the Americas rested on an African foundation. The 'African trade' was, in his words, 'the Great Pillar and Support of the British Plantation Trade' across the Atlantic.[19]

More sophisticated and more modern forms of denial have come from three sources. First, even those writers who grant the deep significance of Scottish involvement in empire have little to say about its connection with the economic revolution of the eighteenth century.[20] Second, when some commentators do ask the basic question, 'Where, after all, did the money go which was amassed in those phenomenal generations?', the answers are often sceptical.[21] Thus it is argued that the capital from empire was frittered away on 'dank pseudo-baronial castles built out of fortunes from Bengal to Manitoba which are no longer even considered fit to be used as mental hospitals'. The suggestion is that some colonial profits went into productive investment in Scotland but for the most part the tycoons of empire spent their wealth 'on themselves, granite palaces or Highland sporting estates'.[22] Third, it may be that Scottish historiography has been influenced indirectly by English thinking on empire and industrialization. The discussion south of the Border has tended, until recently at least, to be narrowly focused. It has mainly centred on the relationship between the profits from the slave trade and the Industrial Revolution rather than on the much bigger question of the likely connections between the empire in general and the domestic economy. Eric Williams's controversial work, *Capitalism and Slavery*, published more than fifty years ago, triggered the debate. He argued that the triangular trade between Britain, Africa and the West Indies made an 'enormous contribution' to Britain's industrial development through slave profits invested in the new manufacturing system.[23] Some scholars, however, have been able to demonstrate that there is little evidence for Williams's claims. One careful estimate suggests, for instance, that profits from the slave trade contributed under 1 per cent to total domestic investment in Britain in the later eighteenth century.[24] The Williams thesis still finds favour in some quarters, yet its patent exaggerations have meant that the whole topic of empire and economic growth has tended to become marginalized in English historical writing until very recently.[25] The topic has often become the special preserve of scholars working in the Marxist tradition who have long seen colonial plunder and profits as crucial to the birth of British industrial capitalism.[26]

The case of eighteenth-century Scotland is of special interest in this respect. There are good reasons for arguing that empire was more important for economic growth here than in most other regions of the British Isles. Markets are regarded by economic historians as a vital engine of growth, but in the eighteenth century mass demand for manufactured goods was slow to develop in Scotland. The national population was small, around 1.25 million in c. 1755. It also grew very slowly over the following decades, averaging only 0.6 per annum between 1755 and 1801, not much more than half the English rate and one third that of Ireland. Domestic demand was also circum-scribed by Scotland's relative poverty for most of the century. Until the 1760s wages over many occupations were no more than half those paid in England.[27] Families of rural labourers and unskilled workers in the towns for much of the first half of the century had a hard struggle to make ends meet.[28] Naturally, therefore, the country's manufactures increasingly relied on external markets to grow their businesses, not only in the colonies but also in England and Ireland as the old commercial ties with Europe contracted because of rising tariff barriers and the effects of war.

Furthermore, Scottish overseas commerce was dominated by Atlantic trade for most of the century after c. 1730. By 1762 just under half of Scottish imports and 52 per cent of exports were of colonial tobacco. Even when that lucrative trade declined after the American War imperial markets remained fundamental. The sugar and cotton trades from the West Indies became the new money-spinners. As late as 1814, nearly half of all the vessels leaving the Clyde ports sailed for the Caribbean, Jamaica, Grenada, Barbados, and the remaining British North American territories took double the Glasgow exports destined for the USA in that year.[29] The West Indian connection was also a key element in the development of Scottish cotton manufacture in the early decades of its expansion. Until near the end of the eighteenth century, the Caribbean was the great source of cheap and abundant sea-island cotton for the industry. Imports rose from 2.7 to 8.4 million lb. between 1790 and 1805 to supply the needs of the numerous spinning mules springing up across the western Lowlands.[30] The cotton revolution depended not only on new technology but also on falling raw material prices as production was stepped up. But for the Caribbean connection this critical advantage would have been much diminished.[31]

This empire of trade would not have existed but for the union of 1707, Scottish inclusion within the English system of tariff protection, the power of the Royal Navy, and the long series of wars fought successfully against France in the West Indies and the Caribbean for territorial and commercial hegemony. In the final analysis, the British markets in the Americas and India rested on the deployment of force backed by the massive financial resources of the state. One recent argument has it that there was a definable difference between the 'Scottish' and 'English' empires. The latter, it is suggested, was driven by the urge to conquer, while the former was more benign and was more concerned with making money and settling emigrants.[32] The supposed distinction is illusory. Even if the Scots were dedicated to profit rather than conquest (itself a highly questionable proposition), the colonies where they traded only remained British, and hence open markets for them, because of the muskets of the army and the fire-power of the navy. The governing assumption among all eighteenth-century European states was that global wealth was finite. Any increase in the share of one nation could only take place at the expense of another. Aggression, predatory behaviour and an obsession with protection of national interests by commercial regulation and armed force were inevitably built into these mercantilist beliefs. The trading communities were usually enthusiastic for colonial conflicts if they resulted in real commercial gains, hence the open letter of gratitude sent to the dying George II in 1760 by the Scottish Convention of Royal Burghs. Praise was heaped on the monarch for the military successes in the West Indies and Canada, culminating in the glorious capture of Quebec.[33] Scottish interests were quick to spot the opportunities opening up as a consequence of these victorious campaigns. As early as October 1759, Edinburgh publishers were already selling maps of Guadaloupe, Louisburg, Quebec and Montreal, all areas soon to attract Scottish adventurers when the Seven Years War came to an end.[34] They would have agreed with the famous aphorism, 'Trade is the source of finance and finance is the vital nerve of war.'[35]

Equally, the only effective guarantor of Scottish colonial commerce in such a hostile environment was the Royal Navy. That protection in turn depended on the Treaty of Union of 1707. A year before it was signed, the pro-unionist William Seton of Pitmedden recognized the harsh realities of an international world riven by mercantilist jealousies and mighty rivalries. The 'Course of Commerce' could only be exploited 'where there's force to protect it'. That force could not come from Scotland; the country was too poor and possessed tiny naval forces. Therefore only 'the Protection of some power Neighbour Nation' could provide the support necessary in a world of expansionist maritime powers.[36] These arguments soon became reality in the years after union. Scottish Atlantic traders then enjoyed the protection of a powerful Royal Navy founded on the fiscal-military resources of the English state. Coastal shipping was also better protected by the twelve cruisers despatched to 'North Britain' under the Cruiser and Convoy Act of 1708. However, it was only during the Seven Years War (1756–63) that the naval presence in home waters really became vital, as before then enemy privateers tended mainly to infest the English Channel and the Southern Approaches where there were richer pickings. In 1759 and early 1760, the formidable French Commodore Thurot sailed north into Scottish waters with three heavily armed frigates, two corvettes and 1,300 troops. Such a force could have created mayhem. However, thanks to the arrival of a substantial Royal Navy squadron, Thurot's expedition ended in disaster. His own flagship was sunk off Galloway and the Commodore's body, wrapped it was said in a silken shroud, was later washed up on the Kirkcudbright coast.[37] The whole affair was a striking demonstration of British naval power. It was this protection which enabled the Scottish merchant marine to expand dramatically from a tonnage of 47,751 in 1759 to 91,330 on the eve of the American War in 1775.[38]

3

Perhaps nowhere else in Scotland were the links between empire and the domestic economy more visible than in Glasgow and its hinterland, the major regional engine of Scottish industrialization. The tobacco lords and sugar princes did build impressive town mansions and spent vast sums on furnishings and paintings. But part of their fortunes also went on more productive investments. The success of their Atlantic enterprises depended largely on having suitable goods to sell to the colonists. But the underdeveloped Scottish economy was not always able to supply the required commodities on a sufficient scale. At first, then, the merchant houses were forced to look to England and Europe for much of the clothing, ironwork, glass, pottery, saddlery and other goods to export. As profits accumulated, however, the leading merchants started to finance their own sources of industrial supply. The result, as Table 6 confirms, was a quite remarkable transfer of capital from overseas trade to domestic manufacturing. This was limited before the mid-eighteenth century. Over the seventy years from 1660 to 1730, only nine 'manufactories' attracted colonial merchant funding. In the following seven decades, 1730 to 1815, no less than forty industrial partnerships were

Manufacture	Total number of units	Number outside Glasgow	Number outside West-Central Scotland
Textiles (silk, linen, wool)	23	2	–
Textiles (cotton-spinning)	12	10	1
Textiles (finishing processes)	9	4	1
Iron (malleable)	2	–	–
Iron (pig)	3	3	–
Mining (coal)	14	8	1
Mining (other minerals)	2	–	2
Sugar-houses	7	2	–
Rope/Sailcloth manufactories	3	2	–
Leather manufactories	4	–	–
Glassworks	3	2	–
Breweries	2	2	–
Soapworks	2	–	–
Tobacco – Spinners	1	–	–
Potteries and Delftworks	1	–	–
Total	88	35	5

Table 6. Gross total of industrial units with some element of Glasgow colonial merchant capital in stock, c. 1700–1815

Source: T. M. Devine, 'Colonial Commerce and the Scottish Economy, c. 1730–1815', in L. M. Cullen and T. C. Smout, eds., *Comparative Aspects of Scottish and Irish Economic and Social History, 1600–1900* (Edinburgh, 1977), p. 178.

established.[39] They ranged from coal mines to cotton mills, from sugar-houses to glassworks. The enterprises were of the 'factory' type, highly capitalized and often employing many dozens of people. They were quite different from the smaller workshops of the day and were designed to produce in large volume for the transatlantic markets or process the exotic commodities being shipped in from the colonies. The investments of these tycoons penetrated virtually all aspects of commercial activity. They financed the Monklands Canal to relieve Glasgow's incipient coal crisis by tapping into the immense mineral riches of Lanarkshire. The Forth and Clyde Canal, the city's route to the east, was related to the needs of the tobacco houses for a secure and speedy waterway link to their key European markets; between 1760 and 1800, at their behest, the work of Golborne, Smeaton and Rennie transformed the upper reaches of the Clyde from an un-navigable river into a superb ship canal. In addition, the colonial merchant élite founded Glasgow's first three banks, the Ship Bank (1750), the Arms Bank (1750) and the Thistle Bank (1761). Taken together all these developments had a transformational effect on the city's economic structure. The foundations for the great metamorphosis from trading port to international entrepôt and industrial giant had been laid.[40]

Tobacco and sugar money also seeped into the counties around Glasgow through rich merchants buying up landed estates. Their motives were many. Landownership not only provided social standing and the essential route to political prominence in the eighteenth century. It was also a secure asset, guaranteeing in most years a steady, passive and reliable income from rentals. This held a special allure for colonial merchants who were engaged in a very lucrative but also highly volatile international business. Many had also come as younger sons from gentry families and aspired to the foundation of their own dynasties.[41] For them to become landowners in their own right was the very apotheosis of worldly success. Money therefore poured from colonial trade into land in the hinterland of Glasgow. At least 44 per cent of the colonial merchant élite between c. 1770 and 1815 had managed to acquire a landed estate (see Table 7).[42] Several of the truly rich owned numerous properties in a number of counties. Huge sums were often involved. William McDowall of the mighty West India house of Alexander Houston and Company had landed assets valued at £287,000 in 1800. Alexander Speirs, the

Area	Number of merchant landowners	Number of estates
Barony of Glasgow	34	40
Lanarkshire	22	37
Renfrewshire	19	36
Dumbartonshire	11	11
Stirlingshire	6	10
Ayrshire	8	11

Table 7. Number and location of estates owned by Glasgow tobacco and West India merchants, c. 1770–1815
Source: T. M. Devine, 'Glasgow Colonial Merchants and Land, 1770–1815', in J. T. Ward and R. G. Wilson, eds., Land and Industry: the Landed Estate in the Industrial Revolution (Newton Abbott, 1971).

so-called 'mercantile god of Glasgow', who headed one of the three great syndicates in the tobacco trade, had by his death in 1783 secured estates in Renfrewshire and Stirlingshire worth over £174,000. James Dunlop, another famous Virginia tycoon, held £130,000 of property in land in 1793.[43]

Doubtless some of this opulent breed of merchant gentry were content to live out their lives at leisure, engaging in hunting, building mansions, entertaining and beautifying the grounds of their estates. But others were gripped by the contemporary mania for 'improvement' and were keen to see their properties as assets to be exploited for profit as effectively as their shares in cotton mills or in trading ventures.

Adam Smith in The Wealth of Nations certainly thought that merchants were 'generally the best of all improvers'. He noted that they were 'not afraid to lay out at once a large capital upon the improvement of lands' when there was 'a profitable prospect of raising the value of it in proportion to the expense'.[44] Sir John Sinclair, arguably the most knowledgeable commentator on matters agricultural in Scotland, was equally impressed by mercantile achievement: '. . . employing part of their capital in the purchase of land and improvement of the soil, [merchants] became most spirited cultivators'.[45] Sustained developments took place in some areas. The Monklands parishes in Lanarkshire were said to be 'in a huge degree of cultivation' in the 1790s because 'when a merchant has been successful, he purchases a piece of land, builds an elegant villa and improves his property at the dearest rates'.[46] Other enthusiastic comments came from Renfrewshire where the McDowall and Speirs families were very active. In Ayrshire the very wealthy Richard Oswald, who had made an immense fortune in arms contracting as well as slave-trading in Africa and merchanting in the Caribbean and Europe, poured many thousands of pounds into his estate of Auchencruive.[47] But he was only the most prominent of a number of wealthy traders who were doing the same thing throughout the county. The record also shows that few merchants gave up their commercial activities when estates were purchased. The profits from the colonial trades continued to be pumped into schemes of land improvement, the coal-mining ventures and factory villages which were often established on country properties.[48]

It would be a mistake, however, to conclude that only the Clyde ports and the western Lowlands felt the economic impact of empire. No region of Scotland was untouched. There were two reasons for this. First, as several previous chapters have shown at length, Scots of landed and mercantile background were remarkably successful in colonizing the military, administrative and professional offices of empire. Second, most of these adventurers saw themselves as sojourners, transient migrants who sailed half-way across the world to make their fortunes but then hoped to return home to live as independent gentlemen. Not all, or even the majority, managed to achieve this aim. Untold numbers succumbed to the lethal diseases which often made India and the Caribbean the graveyards of Europeans. Others fell in battle or failed to have little more than modest success. Still others, including some of the wealthiest, settled in London or the English shires rather than their native Scotland. No other city in Britain could match the capital for its financial, political and social attractions. Wealthy Scots who had made their money in the Caribbean sometimes also settled in the English south-west, with its close connections with the great Atlantic port of Bristol, and the fashionable spas of Bath and Bristol Hot Wells.[49] But many did come back, or at least repatriated some of their gains to Scotland. There could have been few gentry families in Scotland after c. 1760 which did not reap some benefit from the profits of empire, even if the precise scale of the gains made awaits much more detailed research.

In some cases imperial wealth meant the difference between extinction and survival. It was money from Indian service accumulated by the young George Bogle that saved the Bogles of Daldowie in Lanarkshire from financial disaster. The encumbered estates of the lairds of Brodie near Elgin in the north-east also escaped sequestration because of the investment of the Madras merchant Alexander Brodie, third son of the family, who came back from India with a fortune in 1784 which also enabled him to purchase Harris and improve its fisheries.[50] As in England at the same time, these successful servants of the East India Company caught the contemporary imagination and drew critical reactions. Their alleged corruption threatened to bring 'Asiatic principles of government' to undermine political stability in Britain. One estimate suggests that perhaps as many as 300 nabobs returned to Britain in the 1760s and 1770s.[51] The Scots were supposed to be conspicuous among them. Caledonian origins were depicted in the press as one of the more objectionable features of the breed. Thus the *Public Advertiser* in 1777 urged the root-and-branch reform of the East India Company on the grounds that 'the Scotch' were 'so deeply interested in our commerce, and great trading concerns'. A year earlier the same journal lamented the impact of the nabobs on England. The country was now at the mercy of 'needy, rapacious Scotch Adventurers' and 'wretched Scotch Politicians' who were part of a corrupt army of 'Calculators, Schemers, Speculators, Gamblers, Sharpers, Nabobs, Contractors' threatening the integrity of the English state.[52] Even in Scotland the nabob was often treated with some suspicion and hostility, though there was little of the hysterical reaction which occurred south of the Border. Many would have agreed with Horace Walpole's aphorism of 1783: 'No man ever went to the East Indies with good intentions.' In John Galt's novel, *The Last of the Lairds*, the appropriately named 'Mr Rupees', a 'Nabob' who 'came home from Indy' is seen as a rapacious figure who had bought up the lands of 'the right stock o' legitimate gentry, like sae mony ithers'.[53]

The irony was, however, that few of the nabobs were jumped-up *arrivistes* from humble backgrounds. The majority were the sons of minor landowners, military officers and city merchants, and so their fortunes often fortified the entrenched position of the traditional élites in Scotland rather than undermined it.[54] Moreover, contemporary alarm probably exaggerated their numbers. They were far fewer than the rabid abuse in the English press suggested. Nevertheless, the impact of the nabobs at the local level could sometimes be deeply significant. Sir Lawrence Dundas was said to have made £800,000 as an arms contractor during the Seven Years War and also became a proprietor and director of the East India Company. Dundas was able to purchase a goodly part of Orkney and Shetland and also substantial property in Stirlingshire.[55] The Forbes family had owned the estate of Newe in Aberdeenshire since the sixteenth century. Their fortunes changed for the better when John Forbes, who had founded the banking firm of the House of Forbes in Bombay, started to channel his wealth into the improvement of the family properties. Additional estates were purchased and sweeping changes on them continued under John's successor and nephew, Charles, who worked in the Bombay house until 1811.[56] John Johnstone, a scion of the Johnstone lairds in Dumfriesshire, was one of four brothers who became servants of the East India Company. One met his death in 1756 in the infamous 'Black Hole of Calcutta'. John Johnstone's career was spectacularly successful by comparison. He spent fourteen years in Bengal and 'pursued a fortune with an enterprise and ruthlessness which gave him one second only in size to Clive's'. When he finally came back to Scotland, Johnstone was reckoned to be worth £300,000, much of which he expended in buying three estates and building up a strong parliamentary interest.[57] At this stage of research only an interim judgement is possible on the overall impact of these adventurers on the national economy. However, since so much American, Indian and West India money went into Scottish land, the imperial factor may have been one reason why such a relatively poor society was able to find the resources to sustain a rapid programme of costly agricultural transformation in the later eighteenth century.[58]

Another vital engine of material progress was the linen industry. Its importance to the economy was undeniable. Linen was by any standards Scotland's largest manufacturing industry and biggest industrial employer in the eighteenth century. Between 1746 and the 1790s, output of cloth more than doubled in volume and trebled in value. Even after the 1780s, when the dramatic expansion of cotton captured attention, linen production continued apace. Official output again rose threefold to reach nearly 27 million yards annually in 1813-17. Work in linen spinning, weaving and finishing was critical to the way of life of countless families. Contemporary estimates suggest that about 40,000 weavers worked for the market in the 1780s and just under 170,000 women found their 'chief employment' in the spinning of linen yarn. When some of the finishing trades are included, full and part-time linen employment in that decade may have occupied more than 230,000 men, women and children.[59] Little wonder that John Naismith could remark in 1790: 'The linen manufacture has been the most universal source of wealth and happiness introduced into Scotland. To how many thousands has it afforded bread for these forty years past?'[60]

In broader terms, the industry was divided into two types of specialization. Most Scottish production concentrated on the cheaper and coarser lines which in turn were heavily geared to satisfying the needs of the export market. Fife, Angus and Perthshire were the dominant centres for these trades. Fine manufacture for lawns and cambrics tended to focus more on Glasgow and the western counties of Renfrewshire and Lanarkshire. The finer production was more oriented to the home market than in the regions of east-central Scotland. There the imperial factor was crucial in three ways. First, the industry enjoyed the protection of a high tariff wall against European competition. Second, the system of bounty payments set up by the state in 1743 to boost cloth exports to the colonies was vital. From 1745 bounties were also extended to low-priced cloth, which generated a dramatic increase in linen exports to the plantations across the Atlantic in the years that followed. Throughout the eighteenth century, 80 to 90 per cent of these exports were supported by the bounty and when it was temporarily withdrawn in 1754 the output of some of the coarser lines halved, only to recover vigorously when the subsidy was restored two years later.[61] Third, the colonial markets were critical to growth. European consumption was marginal and Ireland was of minor significance. Nine-tenths of all Scottish linen exported from Scotland went to North America and the West Indies. After the American War, the Caribbean became even more fundamental. In the last quarter of the eighteenth century, the standards of living of numerous working-class families in the eastern Lowlands of Scotland came to depend on the huge markets for cheap linen clothing among the slave populations of Jamaica and the Leeward Islands.[62]

4

There is an old, semi-discredited notion that Scottish Gaeldom was in some ways an 'internal colony' on the Celtic fringe of the British state.[63] In fact, the opposite was probably the case. Highland élites were as proactive as their Lowland counterparts in vigorously grasping imperial opportunities. Their families produced a whole stream of military commanders, merchant adventurers, slave traders, colonial officials and plantation owners. Many became apprenticed to Clyde commercial firms before moving into the American, Caribbean and Asian trades. Others made their mark from bases in the Highlands. Among the most notable were the Camerons of Lochiel at Fort William, who were not only involved in the domestic grain and cattle business but had commercial connections as far afield as the Caribbean, New York, Philadelphia and Boston. The McNeills of Taynish were slave traders, both in the islands of the West Indies and in the North Atlantic, while the Campbells of Ardchattan around Loch Etive promoted direct trade with the American colonies alongside a complex portfolio of other business interests.[64]

Like the Lowlands, the Highlands produced several colonial governors, including the formidable and effective Lachlan Macquarie (New South Wales), Sir Alexander Campbell of Inverneil (Madras) and James Murray (the first Governor of Canada). As elsewhere in Scotland, several Gaels who had made fortunes in the Empire returned to purchase landed estates and impress the neighbourhood with their wealth. James (later Sir James) Matheson, of the giant East India house of Jardine, Matheson and Company, made his pile in the China opium trade, and bought the island of Lewis in 1844. He is immortalized in Benjamin Disraeli's novel *Sybil* as a multimillionaire, 'richer than Croesus, one Macdrug, fresh from Canton with a million of opium in his pocket.'[65] His kinsman Sir Alexander Matheson, also a China trade tycoon, went on an even more spectacular spending spree, sinking a quarter of a million pounds in estates across Lochalsh, Kintail and Easter Ross. At the time of his death he owned even more territory than such flowers of the Highland aristocracy as the Dukes of Argyll and Atholl.[66] Another telling example was the Malcolms of Poltalloch. This Argyllshire family had made immense profits as Jamaica planters and slavers throughout the Caribbean.

Eventually their global trading domain stretched from the West Indies to Central and North America and to the shipping insurance business of the China Seas. Some of their repatriated wealth (reckoned to be already £40,000 per annum by the 1770s) was employed in the purchase of extensive property in Argyll.[67] One author has reminded us recently of the connection between the movement of these hard-bitten businessmen into Highland land-ownership and the Clearances: 'It is hardly surprising that the imperial classes who ruthlessly exploited the slave trade in the American South and the West Indies, where they regarded the naming of their slaves on a par with the naming of their livestock, should show limited sympathy in effecting the removal and relocation of erstwhile clansmen.'[68]

On this evidence, the Highland élites were no different from the Lowland gentry in their wholehearted embrace of empire. Indeed, one could go further and suggest that nowhere in Scotland was the link with the imperial project stronger than in Gaeldom. As shown in Chapter 13, the Highlands were the arsenal of empire after 1756. No other region in Scotland supplied as many rank and file and officers per head of population for the imperial regiments. Recruitment was not simply big business for landowners but also influenced the entire social and economic fabric of the area. The temporary migration of so many young men tempered demographic pressures in parishes balanced on the edge of fragile subsistence. The remittances sent home by the soldiers also sustained the incomes of numerous poor families.[69] The social structure of heavily recruited estates was transformed as larger farms were carved up to accommodate the smallholdings of volunteers who had been promised some land in return for service. Even the cycle of clearance was affected. Plans to lay arable land down to sheepwalks were put on hold in the Glengarry lands in Knoydart and the Kintail, Glensheil and Lochalsh estates of the Earl of Seaforth in the 1790s. These 'improvements' might have jeopardized the even more lucrative harvesting of men for the army.[70]

Above all, perhaps, recruitment was a key factor in Highland transatlantic emigration. For many soldiers, army service promised an economical route to the colonies at state expense. At the end of the Seven Years War and the American War some regiments clamoured to be disbanded and then receive the promised free land grants in America. These soldier settlements then became powerful magnets for streams of emigrants in future years. The Highlanders were also trusted imperial warriors. It was not just a question of the fame they had achieved in several celebrated feats of arms. Until recruitment started to dry up in the few years before 1800, the Highlands were also viewed as a dependable reservoir of rapidly mobilized manpower. This, as explained in Chapter 13, was because of the coercive methods of recruitment which operated there. These were unique in Britain and tantamount to a system of conscription. Another major factor was the supposed political reliability of the Highland levies. For a time, the British state feared the enemy within, the radical groups of the 1790s, almost as much as the menace of French military power across the Channel. But in official circles the Gaels were regarded as wholly uncontaminated by 'democratic principles'. They belonged to a hierarchical society where landlord authoritarianism was a routine fact of life. This explains the elaborate proposal by government to establish a Highland Corps in 1797. Not only was the force to be used in the event of invasion but also, significantly, in case of 'civil commotion'. As the proposer of the plan had it, 'at the moment they may be justly considered the only considerable Body of Men, in the whole Kingdom who are as yet absolutely Strangers to the levelling and dangerous principles of the present age, and they may be safely trusted indiscriminately with the knowledge and use of arms'.[71]

Government was prepared to go to extreme lengths in order to preserve this counter-revolutionary asset. This was an age of only modest state intervention in the economy. Yet the Highlands benefited with some very substantial funded projects to contain the emigration of a 'martial people'. It was believed that only a combination of economic development and legal controls could stem the haemorrhage. The latter were enshrined in the prohibition of emigration in 1775 and the Passenger Vessels Act of 1803. The former policy was affirmed in the decision to support a huge road, bridge and canal building project throughout the region in the nineteenth century. The monument to that enterprise was the Caledonian Canal, hewn through the Great Glen at enormous expense, an engineering marvel but a commercial white elephant. It is easy also to forget the link between the Highland fisheries and empire. As noted earlier, linen from the eastern Lowlands helped to clothe the teeming slave populations of the West Indies. In the 1790s there were around

465,000 slaves on the British islands. Scottish fish was also an important element in their diet. Cod and ling came from the coasts of Orkney and Shetland and the waters of the Minch. Both salted and smoked herring were exported in vast quantities from the sea lochs of the western Highlands. Most of the catch, when processed, was then sent to the port of Cork, in Ireland, where the transatlantic fleets were loaded with cheap foods for the slave islands.[72] Again, state support was important here. The fisheries fitted well with the prevailing principles of mercantilist practice. Subsidies would help to exclude foreign and especially Dutch competition from harvesting the British fishery while more boats augmented the pool of experienced seafarers who could be mobilized by the Royal Navy in time of war. From 1757 existing bounties rose to fifty shillings per ton for the mother-ships, or 'busses', which served the small open boats of the Highland townships. One measure of their impact was the increase in the tonnage of Scottish herring busses from seventy-seven in 1756 to 13,073 on the eve of the American War of Independence in 1775.[73]

Yet, the similarities between the two regions of Scotland and their imperial connections can be overstressed. The profits of empire helped to sustain economic transformation in parts of the Lowlands. In the Highlands the long-term effect was more ambiguous. There were some short-term gains during the so-called 'Age of Optimism' before 1815. But in the long run the Victorian Highlands became a 'problem' region, a byword for economic collapse, famine, mass emigration and social destitution.[74] A classic illustration of this is the case of James Matheson and the island of Lewis. When he purchased Lewis from the Earl of Seaforth, Matheson was reputed to be one of the richest men in Britain with a colossal fortune, largely built on the profits of the China opium trade, said to be worth over £1 billion at today's values. The construction of a huge Scotch-baronial mansion, Lewis Castle, to the design of the noted Glasgow architect Charles Wilson, cost £100,000. With money no object, the 600-acre grounds were transformed into a new wooded landscape with thousands of tons of earth shipped in from the mainland. But Matheson's spending was not confined to conspicuous consumption on the grand scale. He also invested heavily in the economic development of Lewis. Nearly £200,000 went on fishing, harbours, roads, schools and agricultural improvement. His investments included the creation of three large quays on the waterfront of Stornoway, a gasworks and a waterworks, and sixty miles of new roads to open up the interior of the island. However, partly due to the failure of the potato crop in 1846 and subsequent years, the great enterprise accomplished little in generating long-term development. Indeed, as early as the 1850s the Matheson strategy moved in a radically new direction. Between 1851 and 1855, over 2,300 of the island's inhabitants were 'assisted' to emigrate to Canada. Threats of eviction were used, famine relief was cut back and the cattle of those tenants in arrears of rent impounded in order to drive on the mass exodus. As a result, Matheson is remembered in Hebridean tradition not as a benevolent improver but as one of the villains of the Highland Clearances. By the end of the nineteenth century, the island on which he had lavished so much investment was in such an impoverished condition that it required state intervention to support the population.[75]

If, then, the imperial factor was one catalyst for sustained development in the south, why not also in the north and west? It is indeed intriguing that the areas of the Highlands least dependent on military recruiting, namely Perthshire, eastern Inverness-shire, and Easter Ross, emerged in the nineteenth century as the more prosperous parts of Gaeldom. They developed a structure of medium-sized farms rather than one dominated by small crofts; their crop regimes were varied and the potato, though significant, never established a virtual monoculture in the way it had done further north.

Of course, the Lowlands had a number of key advantages over the north-west which had nothing to do with the impact of empire. These included abundant reserves of coal and iron ore, a developed network of towns and cities, a more equable climate, much greater scope for intensive mixed agriculture and a widespread tradition of textile manufacturing which existed long before the transformation wrought by industrialization. We are not, therefore, comparing like with like. Different modes of development may well have taken place with or without the imperial influence. This was especially the case from 1815. After the Napoleonic Wars much of Gaeldom was locked into an economic vice that was inexorably contracting. The booming by-employments of the decades after c. 1770, kelping, illicit whisky-making, commercial fishing and seasonal migration, either stagnated or collapsed altogether, while at the same time regional population continued to increase. The future looked grim long before the final catastrophe of the potato famine in the 1840s. Only large-scale sheep farming, with all its sorry consequences of even more forced removals of communities, seemed to hold out much promise.

But the imperial factor was not irrelevant to this pessimistic scenario. Like kelp manufacture, most of the income from recruiting evaporated after 1815, with mass demobilization and the decades of peace which then followed until the Crimean War in the 1850s. Even in its heyday, one scholar has concluded that 'the evidence that imperial service made a significant contribution to improved land use is at best patchy'.[76] Some landed families preferred to invest their gains in more secure assets, such as stocks and shares in the East India Company, the Scottish banks, insurance companies and Consolidated Government Funds. Others frittered away fortunes in the pursuit of luxury. The MacLeods of Skye amassed imperial spoils of around £100,000, including £30,000 in prize money from the capture of an Indian island in 1783. But precious little found its way back to Skye.[77] The building of mansion houses, the restoration of ancestral seats to more elaborate styles and the reduction of family debt burdens were other common uses for imperial gains in the Highlands. The Malcolms of Poltalloch started a building programme in 1798 in Kilmartin parish, Argyll, which lasted, on and off, for forty years and culminated in 1848 with the huge expenditure of £100,000 on the spectacualr pile named Poltalloch House.[78]

Certainly imperial service did not save the hereditary Highland élite from disaster. At the end of his long career as engineer with the Scottish Fishery Board, in the course of which he had travelled far and wide in the Highlands, Joseph Mitchell noted that two-thirds of the estates in the Highlands had changed owners.[79] A more recent estimate suggests that by the 1880s, 'new' landlords from the south now owned around 70 per cent of the mainland and insular parishes of western Argyll, Inverness and Ross-shire. Land sales were a roll-call of some of the most renowned families in the Highlands. The Macdonalds of Clanranald, the Mackenzie Earls of Seaforth, the McNeills of Barra, the Macdonnels of Glengarry and many others all went to the wall. Grandees like the Dukes of Argyll, Sutherland, Gordon and Atholl survived but even they were forced to sell off parts of their territorial empires in the deep recession which hit the Highlands hard after 1815. For most of their class, however, imperial incomes had merely served to postpone the decline into the morass of spiralling debt, extended mortgages and interest charges which often ended in the forced sales of hereditary estates.[80]

But the years of intense recruitment of soldiers at the end of the eighteenth century also left their mark among the mass of the population of the region. Whereas the clan regiments of old had mobilized the entire male community, the approach of landowners to recruiting for the battalions of the British army was more selective. The tenantry were normally excluded, because that would not only have affected the regular payment of rent but also interrupted the entire cycle of work on the farms. Instead, estate papers show that the sons and brothers of tenants were targeted, together with those at the bottom of the social heap, the cottars and the landless poor. In return for service these groups were often promised patches of land which had to be divided up from larger farms. Some gained and others lost in the process, which inevitably stoked tensions between the landed and the landless. The policy of building up medium-sized tenancies on the Lowland model was abandoned on several properties. Instead the creation of small crofts was accelerated.[81]

The strategy proved disastrous. It anchored the people on patches of land where they eked out a bare living from potatoes, some seasonal work in the south and occasional fishing. But the real perils of subdivision only became evident over time. Two of the most telling examples come from the island territories of the Duke of Argyll on the Ross of Mull and Tiree. In 1806 approval was given on the Ross for the division of large farms to create crofts for the families of soldiers. A similar strategy was followed on the island of Tiree in 1801 in order to fulfil promises made to recruits. Profits from the kelp industry also encouraged the policy of fragmentation rather than consolidation of land. The disastrous long-term consequences were plain to see when the potatoes failed in 1846. Rising numbers and further subdivision resulted in what the estate described in the 1840s as 'a vast semi-pauper population'. Tiree and the Ross of Mull were among the areas of most acute destitution during the famine. This, too, was part of the balance sheet of empire. The Argyll estate had to pay out vast sums in famine relief and in 'assisted' emigration to Canada as the crisis deepened.[82]

Recruitment had another unhappy long-term consequence for the descendants of the military entrepreneurs of the eighteenth century. In the late-Victorian period landowners were accused of gross betrayal by breaking the solemn contracts to maintain recruits and their families in secure possession of tenancies. The historical realities of where the truth lies on such an emotive and contentious issue are inevitably mired in controversy. Estate records show that obligations were often confined to specified short-term periods, usually between five and seven years. There is also some evidence of these being honoured, even on properties like the Sutherland estate where some of the most notorious evictions took place. Equally, however, folk tradition was not always wrong. Lord Macdonald, for instance, manifestly failed to honour written promises made to recruits to the 76th Regiment which he raised for service in America in 1778.[83] More crucial, however, for the case against landlordism during both the crofting agitation of the 1880s and in the longer term was the widespread impact of the accusations. They became the stock-in-trade of some of the most influential anti-landlord tracts for the time, as, for instance, in Alexander Mackenzie's classic *History of the Highland Clearances*, first published in 1883:

... the children and nearest relations of those who sustained the honour of the British name in many a bloody field were ruined, trampled upon, dispersed, and compelled to seek an asylum across the Atlantic while those who remained from inability to emigrate, deprived of all the comforts of life, became paupers – beggars – a disgrace to the nation whose freedom and honour many of them had maintained by their honour and cemented with their blood.[84]

It was a powerful political message which left its mark on the whole course of Highland political and social history. Militarism in the service of empire had come back to haunt the landed classes.

15

Identities

I

By the end of the eighteenth century few could doubt the material benefits which empire had brought to Scotland. But even some staunch unionists were concerned that economic success had been achieved at considerable cultural cost. Specifically, they worried that Scotland's ancient identity as a nation was being rapidly eroded as the pressures of anglicization and assimilation accelerated in the wake of imperial achievement. In 1806 Sir Walter Scott, a celebrated friend of union, famously complained to one acquaintance who was an enthusiast for reforming Scots law along English lines that 'Little by little, whatever your wishes may be, you will destroy and undermine, until nothing of what makes Scotland, Scotland will remain.'[1] He saw that a real threat existed to the country's nationality, 'the lowering and grinding down of all those peculiarities which distinguished us as Scotsmen'.[2] Scott was not alone in his fears for national identity. Henry Cockburn, the great Whig lawyer, thought he was living through 'the last purely Scotch age'.[3] The omniscient Sir John Sinclair, editor of *The Statistical Account of Scotland*, was equally troubled about the loss of heritage and argued for the need to assert the nation's identity before it became 'North Britain' and 'completely confounded in England'[4]

On the face of it there seemed good reasons for alarm because the threat to 'Scottishness' came from an impressive array of powerful influences. The sheer speed and scale of economic modernization, itself fuelled to a significant extent by empire, created a huge discontinuity between an older Scotland and the new dynamic world of booming towns and cities, manufacturing industry and agricultural capitalism. To many observers urbanization also increasingly threatened to undermine two of the major foundations of Scottish identity, the Presbyterian church and Scots education, which had survived the union of 1707 and so gave a special distinctiveness to a stateless nation. The established church was ruptured by two secessions, in 1740 and 1782, and further weakened by continuous leakage to the dissenting congregations thereafter. When the church did finally split asunder in the Disruption of 1843 it was the culmination of these earlier cleavages. Religious leaders were also conscious that the parish system, designed for a rural society, no longer fitted the new world of the booming towns with teeming populations and burgeoning social problems. Not the least of their concerns was education, a source of great national pride in the eighteenth century, but now at risk through the supposed godlessness of the urban conurbations and their loss of the rural virtues of learning and piety. These fears were articulated in George Lewis's controversial pamphlet, *Scotland: a Half-Educated Nation*, published in 1834.[5]

Scottishness was also under sustained attack from the intellectuals of the Enlightenment. The nation's most gifted historian of the age, William Robertson, denounced everything before the Revolution of 1688 as feudal darkness, fanaticism and anarchy. He was joined in his denunciation by like-minded associates who rejoiced at the union of 1707 which, in their view, had liberated Scotland from centuries of obscurantism and set it on the path to improvement, stability and prosperity. In the first volume of his *Caledonia* (1807–24) George Chalmers celebrated the union as the 'freeing of the people of Scotland from their parliament' which had been riven by internecine faction and aristocratic jealousies.[6] As one modern author has put it, 'A country whose intellectuals believe their history is rubbish is surely at a disadvantage when it comes to producing convincing nationalist energy.'[7] These eighteenth-century thinkers all had an intense admiration of English political and economic achievements. Scottish progress to these ideals depended on more assimilation through 'completion of the union'. The 'bonfire of feudal controls' after the '45 rebellion, when military tenures and most heritable jurisdictions were swept away, was regarded as an important step towards a more civilized Scotland and a necessary precondition for fulfilling all the potential of the union.[8] In Robertson's words, 1707 'will render us one people'.

The intellectuals seemed to be in tune with the practical responses of the country's élite. Their colonization of government posts, army and naval commissions, East India jobs and trading opportunities throughout the empire unequivocally demonstrated their whole-hearted commitment to the imperial project. No class in Scotland had benefited more from the increasing global dominance of Britain. The ever-widening flow of imperial patronage rescued many a laird family from genteel poverty. It also provided a powerful bulwark which consolidated the existing political system. Jacobitism, the main counter-revolutionary threat, had been roundly defeated. On the face of it, this crushing victory had been won by Cumberland's redcoats at Culloden. But more subtle forces were also working over the longer term. Granting disaffected families generous access to the spoils of empire reconciled many to the Hanoverian state during the Seven Years War.[9] Popular radicalism inspired by the French Revolution arguably posed an even greater threat to the old regime than the exiled Stuarts had ever done. Scotland seemed especially ripe for reform. After the union there were forty-five parliamentary seats in the Scottish counties and fifteen elected from the burghs, each with 2,600 and 1,500 voters respectively. This tiny electorate was around 0.2 per cent of the Scottish population in the later eighteenth century. Even by the pre-democratic standards of the day this extraordinary concentration was unusual. Both England and Ireland had much larger franchises; Dublin's alone stood at 3,000 to 4,000 and by itself exceeded the total county electorate in Scotland.[10] Initial stirrings of reform came in the burghs during the 1780s, followed in the wake of events in France by the Scottish Friends of the People Associations which were first established in 1792. But the regime emerged unscathed from these challenges. Despite the enormous changes in Scottish society during these decades, no basic change in the country's structure of governance took place until the Reform Act of 1832.

The resilience of traditional landed authority can be variously explained.[11] The wars against France helped to close ranks in the face of a common enemy. Rising living standards until c. 1800 helped to defuse popular discontent. The state responded to the radical threat through the imposition of draconian legislation and savage punishments. But the rock-solid nature of Scottish political life was also related to empire. Access to imperial posts renewed the economic strength and resources of the old élite.[12] It also saved many landed families from demographic catastrophe. As population rose, so the system of primogeniture was likely to come under immense pressure. After *c.* 1750 there were a much larger number of non-inheriting younger sons than ever before. The opportunities of empire saved many of these men and their families from poverty and extinction. Political and social alienation which might have been stoked by frustrated ambition and downward social mobility was instead dissipated by imperial patronage and largesse. Here was a clear contrast with Irish Catholic élites who did not have the same good fortune as the Protestant Scots. Underemployed younger sons of Irish gentry families experienced particularly acute difficulties in the later eighteenth century when the numbers going abroad declined in both the European military service and trade. These 'restless spirits' then helped to fuel the social tensions which led to the great Irish rebellion of 1798.[13] It was a different story in Scotland, where a much higher proportion of young men from comfortable backgrounds made successful imperial careers. As Dr Johnson memorably put it, 'There are few ways in which a man can be more innocently employed than in getting money.'

The cement of political stability was patronage and a keystone of that system was the power of appointment to government and imperial posts. This was most famously seen in the career of Henry Dundas. By 1780 he controlled twelve of the forty-one Scottish constituencies which were contested. This number had risen to twenty-two in 1784, and by 1790 he had gained decisive influence over no less than thirty-four constituencies. Dundas had brought the distribution of patronage to a high state of refinement. Sydney Smith, cleric and famous wit, alleged that 'as long as he is in office, the Scotch may beget younger sons with the most perfect impunity. He sends them by loads to the East Indies and all over the world.'[14] But it is now clear that imperial patronage was successfully practised long before Dundas's day. It stretched back to Sir Robert Walpole's search for Scottish political stability in the 1720s and the regime of the Earl of Islay (later Duke of Argyll) from that decade until the 1760s.[15] Dundas certainly had a high profile as a political manager. The famous Gillray cartoon depicts him as a latter-day Oriental despot bestriding India, the City of London and Scotland.[16] But he also inherited a well-oiled machine which ultimately depended on the expansion of empire and the financial resources of the

British fiscal-military state for the smooth functioning of its many intricate parts.

Against this background it is hardly surprising that Scotland's élites were attracted to the idea of Britishness. As well as empire, historians have identified the several other factors helping to fashion this new, invented 'nationalism' out of the disparate peoples of the Isles. These included a common Protestantism linking Scotland, Wales and England, the impact of warfare with France, the Catholic 'other' against which all Britons could supposedly unite, domestic economic integration and the influence of a renewed British crown and monarchy.[17] Other social processes were at work, especially within the aristocracy. A formerly impoverished and indebted class were growing richer after c. 1750. Estate incomes rose because of agricultural improvement and the appetite of the industrial towns for food, drink and raw materials.[18] Many of the Scottish landed classes entered a new age of prosperity. In no other part of the British Isles was there anything like the same sensational increase in rental incomes as on the great aristocratic estates of Scotland. In England, rentals on most estates rose by around 70 to 90 per cent between 1750 and 1800. In Ireland, the increases were similar but closer to the 90 per cent mark. In Scotland, however, the gains were truly spectacular. Rental increases of 800 per cent and more were recorded between 1750 and 1815 on some estates.[19] This bonanza was in part a direct consequence of the transformation in demand for land products as a result of rapid industrialization. But it was also related to huge productivity gains in farming caused by the improved practices of fallowing, liming and new rotations. By the 1790s, oat yields (the Scottish staple grain) in counties such as Lanark and Angus were triple seventeenth-century averages. In England between 1750 and 1800, yields on oats rose by about 50 per cent. The figures so far gathered for Scotland suggest increases of 200 to 300 per cent.[20] Despite this huge increase in production, prices still continued to rise as population grew throughout Britain. During the Napoleonic Wars they sky-rocketed as foreign importation was interrupted. In the county of Fife, for instance, the market price for a boll of oats rose threefold, from £0.60 in 1790 to £1.70 a decade later.[21]

The new wealth had many effects. Conspicuous display became more fashionable. Many of the great houses of Scotland were either

built or extensively remodelled during the period. Culzean, Hopetoun, Mellerstain and Inveraray were only the most famous
examples. Internal furnishing aspired to standards of unprecedented
splendour, with gilded ornamentation, framed portraits, rich fabrics
and elaborate ceilings combining with the fashionable furnishings of
Chippendale, Sheraton and Hepplewhite.[22] More affluence also made
the Scottish nobility a better catch in the British marriage market
and, at the same time, provided the resources to live in greater style
in London and the English shires. There was, of course, little new
about Scottish lords marrying English ladies. But a 'romantic revolution' around the middle decades of the eighteenth century has been
well documented.[23] Of the sixteen representative Scottish peers in the
Westminster Parliament between 1747 and 1752, eight had English
wives.[24] Scottish ladies were also in demand by English aristocrats.
The most celebrated marriage took place in 1785 between Elizabeth,
Countess of Sutherland, possessor of an immense patrimony which
stretched across 800,000 acres of the north of Scotland, and George
Granville Leveson-Gower, soon to be Marquess of Stafford. The new
affluence of the Scottish aristocracy, not least in the provision of
attractive dowries, may have made marriage across the élites of
the two nations infinitely more attractive. But the Scots had also
something to gain. Marriage into the English élite promised more
career opportunity and political influence for future generations. The
cost, so some critics suggest, was that the Scottish patricians became
anglicized. They were 'strangers in their own lands, so much did they
succumb to English politics, English manners, English culture and
English spouses'.[25]

Whether all this amounted to the 'death of Scotland' as Walter
Scott and others feared is, however, more doubtful because the threat
of cultural assimilation was often more apparent than real. The
whole issue of Scottish and British identities was also more complex
than the pessimistic commentators of the early nineteenth century
were prepared to admit. Some scholars have argued, for instance,
that anglicizing tendencies were mainly confined to the élites.[26] The
vast majority of the Scottish people continued to speak in Scots or
Gaelic, attend the established and secession churches which, unlike
Anglicanism, stressed the separation of powers between church and
state, and take pride in the deeds of heroic Scottish icons like Bruce
and Wallace. The medieval verse accounts of John Barbour and Blind

Harry the Minstrel had wide appeal and were paralleled by such immensely popular new works as Jane Porter's *The Scottish Chiefs* (1810). Manifestations of 'Britishness' were certainly apparent at the annual celebrations of the King's birthday, and the radical movements of the 1790s were prepared to look to the Magna Carta of England as well as the Scottish Claim of Right of 1689 and the heroic struggle of the seventeenth-century Covenanters for their inspiration.[27] But no satisfactory study has yet been published on the extent of plebeian Britishness in Scotland. Close examination of the Highlands, the most militarized region in Scotland, has also failed to detect the widespread emergence of British patriotism despite the extent of service in line regiments, the militia and the volunteers. Above all the Gael was drawn to the armed forces for economic reasons. Local loyalties to family, kin and district tended to take precedence over national concerns.[28]

Nor would it be fair simply to describe the élites of Scottish society as uncritical anglicizers. Rather, they were developing a dual identity in which Scottishness and Britishness combined and interacted. One study of some key figures of the Enlightenment, including Hume, Boswell, Fergusson, Burns and the Adam brothers, has shown their hybrid loyalties both to Scotland and Britain. The balance of sympathy for one identity as opposed to the other varied considerably and subtly within the group.[29] This duality was even apparent among those intellectuals and politicians dubbed 'North Britons' because of their enthusiasm for reforming Scottish institutions along English lines. They were concerned to write correct English purged of Scotticisms and also commonly sought elocution training to refine their Scots accents to facilitate career advancement in the southern centres of power. At the same time, they showed much interest in the poetic and literary value of Scots. Nor did admiration for English laws, culture and institutions preclude the survival of Scottish national consciousness. At times of rampant Scottophobia in England, as when the Earl of Bute became the first Scots Prime Minister in the 1760s, the anglophile literati were provoked into angry responses. The reluctance of Westminster to extend the militia system to Scotland during the Seven Years War also caused outrage in these circles.[30] The union was essentially seen as a partnership between the two nations symbolized by the Union Jack with its combined saltire and the cross of St George.

Nowhere else was this joint endeavour more realized than in the Empire and in the imperial wars with France. It was in this arena that Scottish nationhood was reasserted and embellished. In the event, empire did not prove a threat to Scottish identity. Instead, the imperial project in the long run massively increased the nation's sense of self-esteem. By the Victorian era the contribution Scotland had made to the Empire was widely recognized. Through all the spheres of business, administration, settlement, soldiering, religion and education Scotland's role had been remarkably disproportionate. National pride was therefore roused not only by recognition of the imperial partnership with England but by the chronology of imperial expansion. After all, it was always described as 'the British Empire', never 'the English Empire', and most of its global development had taken place after the union between the two countries. Furthermore, key elements of the 'Scottish social ethic' were exported abroad and helped to fashion the imperial enterprise. Evidence of this has been given throughout this book. Higher education in many of the North American settlement colonies was more likely to be built on Scottish rather than English models. Senior Scottish officials in India, like Munro, Malcolm and Mountstuart Elphinstone, applied a whole range of ideas from the Scottish Enlightenment to issues of land tenure, governance and judicial systems on the subcontinent. Even in commerce, Scottish ethnicity was employed to gain a competitive edge over business rivals. Family networks and connections dominated the sugar and tobacco trades and the Scots drew bitter criticism from outsiders for their clannishness. If anything, however, hostility simply strengthened the bonds of ethnic loyalty.

2

The later eighteenth century also witnessed the reassertion and celebration of Scottish identity within the union through the development of the cult of tartanry. This too had strong links to empire and war through the crucial part played in its evolution by the fame of the imperial warriors of the Highland regiments. The adoption of tartan and the kilt as the national dress of a modernizing Scotland in the nineteenth century at first sight seems bizarre. For much of the period since medieval times Lowland society had regarded the Highlands as alien, hostile and barbarous. This antagonism hardened during the Jacobite rebellion of 1745–6 and its immediate aftermath. Presbyterian Scotland had been threatened with a Catholic counter-revolution spearheaded by a Highland army. There was rejoicing when it was annihilated at Culloden. Moreover, it was deeply ironic that as Scotland was transformed into an urban and industrial society, the élites of the nation looked towards the poorest and most underdeveloped rural region in the country as the source of some of the main symbols of cultural identity.[31]

On the other hand, this 'Highlandism', while curious, is not entirely incomprehensible. After all, Scotland was in a contradictory position within the imperial relationship with England. The Scottish economic miracle ultimately depended on the connection. But some feared that the massive political and material superiority of England could also lead to full-scale assimilation and the disappearance of the historic nation. In addition, this was a time when romantic nationalism was spreading throughout Europe. Scotland was unlikely to remain isolated. Yet any vigorous political assertion of national identity could undermine the imperial and union relationship on which Scottish economic success ultimately depended. Highlandism therefore answered the emotional need for a distinctive Scottish identity without in any way compromising the union. On the contrary, the indissoluble link between tartan, the deeds of the Highland warrior, patriotism and imperial service conferred a new cultural and emotional cohesion on the Anglo-Scottish connection. This is why an arch-unionist like Sir Walter Scott could be such an enthusiastic advocate of Highlandism. The tartan cult is also a reminder that Britishness is also a part of Scottishness. By the later eighteenth century one could not exist in the same form without the other. Arguably, then, Highlandism was in large part a direct response to the cultural implications of the union and empire. As one writer has put it, 'As Lowland Scotland becomes more and more like England, it turns to the Highlands for symbols and beliefs to maximize the difference.'[32] It was one of the many ironies in this story, however, that as the revolution in attitudes to Gaeldom was gathering speed, the traditional Highland world was being broken up by commercialization and clearance.

Walter Scott himself was the master impresario at what is often seen as the seminal event in the development of Highlandism. The visit of George IV to Edinburgh in August 1822 was an auspicious occasion, the first by a reigning monarch since Charles II in 1651. The King spent two weeks in the Scottish capital and a series of extraordinary pageants, all with a Celtic and Highland flavour, were stage-managed by Scott for His Majesty's delectation. What ensued was a 'plaided panorama' based on fake Highland regalia and the mythical customs and traditions of the clans. Scott had determined that Highlanders were what George would most like to see, and he therefore urged clan chiefs to bring 'followers' to Edinburgh suitably dressed for the occasion. Seven bodies of 'clansmen', MacGregors, Glengarry MacDonnels, Sutherlands and Campbells, paraded during the visit and His Majesty's generous figure was clad in kilt, plaid, bonnet and tartan coat for the occasion. The climax came with the procession from Holyroodhouse to Edinburgh Castle when the Honours of Scotland – crown, sceptre and sword of state – were solemnly paraded before the monarch with an escort led by the once-outlawed Clan Gregor. At the banquet in Parliament Hall, the King called for a toast to the clans and chieftains of Scotland, to which Sir Ewan MacGregor solemnly replied with one to 'The Chief of Chiefs – the King'.[33]

Scott had wished the royal visit to be 'a gathering of the Gael', but what his Celtic fantasy had in fact produced was a distortion of the Highland past and present and the projection of a national image in which the Lowlands had no part. The great ball in the Assembly Rooms during the royal visit in which full Highland regalia was worn has been seen as a key point in the acceptance of the kilt as the national dress of Scotland. With the exception of those in uniform, 'no Gentleman is to be allowed to appear in any thing but the ancient Highland costume'.[34] The head of state himself had now given tartan a bogus legitimacy. The Scottish ruling class was addressed as 'the chieftains and clans of Scotland' during the public events. More sceptical voices at the time were less impressed than the 'enthusiasts for the philabeg'. J. G. Lockhart, Scott's son-in-law and biographer, regarded the pageantry as a 'hallucination' in which the glorious traditions of Scotland were identified with a people which 'always constituted a small and always an unimportant part of the Scottish population'.[35] Even more appalled was Lord Macaulay. Looking back from the 1850s, he found it incredible that the monarch should show his respect for the historic Scottish nation 'by disguising himself in what, before the union, was considered by nine Scotchmen out of ten as the dress of a thief'.[36]

The 1822 visit was a significant milestone in the extraordinary history of Highlandism but its intrinsic importance may well have been exaggerated. Indeed, Scott's tartan fantasy can perhaps best be seen as the consequence of earlier developments which had already given Highland symbolism wide appeal. Essentially, therefore, Scott and his associates were providing George IV with what he expected to see on a visit to Scotland, a nation dressed in plaid and tartan. The year 1822 also saw an event with strong military overtones. Scotland was depicted as a martial society. For instance, in correspondence with Macleod of Macleod in July 1822 Scott wrote that 'the King is coming after all. Arms and men are the best thing we have to show him. Pray come and do not forget to bring the Bodyguard for the Credit of Old Scotland.'[37] Appropriate ceremonial garb for the ceremony included 'Gun . . . Broad Sword and Shoulder Belt . . . Target and Slinging Belt . . . a Brace of Highland Pistols . . . a "Chore Dubh" or Hose Knife called the "Skian" . . . a Powder Horn'.[38] It was an attempt to link the historic martial traditions of Scotland to tartan. A key factor in that important connection was the distinction, fame and honour which the kilted Highland regiments had brought to the nation during the imperial wars of the late eighteenth and early nineteenth centuries. During these conflicts the Highland soldier came to be defined as a proud symbol of Scotland's ancient nationhood and of her equal status with England in the creation of a British Empire.

This enduring association between militarism, Scottishness and Britishness came relatively late in the eighteenth century.[39] Highland levies, all exempt from the post-'45 ban on Highland dress, had fought with distinction during the Seven Years War and the American War of Independence. But they only became icons of national valour during the Revolutionary and Napoleonic Wars. Most of the regiments raised during the two previous wars were soon disbanded and, if not, were sent to remote imperial garrisons where they were unlikely to have much impact on the national consciousness.[40] It is striking that when David Stewart of Garth set about writing the history of the Black Watch around 1820 he was only able to compile a brief account because of the absence of a public record of its campaigns. This was scarcely surprising since this formation, soon to be celebrated as one of the most renowned Highland battalions, was stationed in Scotland for a mere four years between the 1740s and 1802.[41]

It was their role in three famous victories between 1799 and 1815 which transformed the Black Watch and the other Highland regiments into national celebrities. The first to catch the imagination was the successful storming of the capital of Tipu Sultan, ruler of Mysore, in 1799. This Indian prince had long been depicted as the very incarnation of Asiatic tyranny and cruelty. His overthrow, spearheaded by the 73rd and 74th Highlanders, under the command of the Scottish General David Baird, had a powerful impact at home. Wilkie's famous canvas of the victory of Seringapatam was the beginning of a long iconographic tradition in which the Highland soldier appeared during the nineteenth century in the visual record of empire, whether in paintings, prints, engravings, illustrations and children's books. After all, kilts and pipes were 'gifts to the painter' even in an era when military uniforms in general were becoming ever more ostentatious.[42]

The second triumph came soon after Seringapatam with the comprehensive defeat of the formerly invincible French at Alexandria in Egypt in 1800. This was a victory against the odds, restoring the prestige of the army after a succession of defeats in Flanders in 1794 and Holland in 1799. David Stewart of Garth himself fought in the campaign. He described how he and his comrades were 'opposed to a veteran enemy, greatly superior in numbers, elated with their victories and believed unconquerable, because hitherto unconquered'.[43] Once again, Highland soldiers were to the fore, in this case the Black Watch, the Gordon Highlanders (92nd) and the Cameron Highlanders (79th). The Black Watch in particular was given a rapturous public welcome when it returned to Edinburgh in triumph in 1802. The regiment had captured the standard of the Invincible Legion at Alexandria, the first seized from the French in battle. Finally, the Cameron Highlanders, the Gordon Highlanders and the Black Watch all distinguished themselves at Waterloo. *The Times* praised their bravery and élan while the three regiments also received the battle honour 'Waterloo' on their colours. The previous year (1814) Sir Walter Scott's best-seller, *Waverley*, had established the romantic image of the Gaels as a race of born warriors. The glorious exploits of the regiments on the field of battle seemed to confirm his

vision of the Highlanders as a martial race. At the end of the Napoleonic Wars their military prestige was never higher. The Highland
regiments took pride of place when the allies marched in triumph
into Paris. They then entered Edinburgh on returning home to a
tumultuous reception. The Quartermaster-Sergeant of the Black
Watch later recalled, 'we entered the city amidst the loud cheering
and congratulations of friends; while over our heads, from a thousand
windows, waved as many banners, plaided scarfs or other symbols
of courtly greetings'. They finally marched into Edinburgh Castle,
'proud of the most distinguished reception that ever a regiment had
met from a grateful country'.[44]

The popularity of the regiments breathed new life into the ancient
military tradition of the nation, fortifying the old belief of the Scots
as a brave warrior race who had never been conquered by more
powerful enemies like the Romans or the English. That dearly-won
independence was now threatened by the union with the Auld Enemy.
As Robert Burns had it in the 1780s:

> Farewell to a' our Scottish fame,
> Fareweel our ancient glory!
> Farewell ev'n to our Scottish name,
> Sae famed in martial story.[45]

The heroic deeds of the Highland regiments revived the old soldierly
tradition within the union and signalled that instead of falling to the
status of an English province, the Scots had fully contributed in blood
to the imperial cause. They therefore merited treatment as equals
and partners. Many more Lowlanders than Gaels served in the British
armed forces.[46] This was simply a reflection of the different size of
population in the two regions. But the tartan and the kilt conferred
a distinctive Scottishness on the Highland battalions which establish
an élite image as the expression of the nation's identity. A commission
in these regiments came to be regarded as a considerable prize.
Thomas Creevey, MP, the well-known diarist, wrote in 1828: 'We
have an event in our Family. Fergy [Sir Ronald Ferguson] has got a
regiment – a tip top crack one – one of these beautiful Highland
Regiments that were at Brussells, Quatre Bras and Waterloo.'[47]

The military cult was also linked to the sentimentalization of
Jacobitism. With the decisive nature of the Hanoverian victory at
Culloden in 1746 the scene was set for romanticizing the Jacobite

cause and the Highland warriors who had supported it. The rebels were effectively tamed, their martial power destroyed: hence the metamorphosis from faithless traitors to national heroes could proceed. Also influential was the outbreak of revolution in France. The famed military song, 'The Gathering of the Clans', a reinterpretation of 'The Campbells are Coming', set out a detailed list of Highland clans ready to take the field against Napoleon. This and other similar airs of the time expressed in popular form the transfer of loyalty from the Stuarts in the '45 to the Hanoverians in the later eighteenth century.[48] In this way Jacobitism was redefined as an ideology committed to monarchy in the abstract sense at a time when the institution in Britain was under attack from radical enemies both within and without. As such, it became politically acceptable, and wide dissemination of the Jacobite myth, with its potent mixture of themes of love, loyalty, exile and loss, was now possible. Jacobitism came to be regarded as representing the heroic Scottish past, the more seductive because it was so recent, and was of course seen as synonymous with the Highlands.[49]

Jacobitism and hence Highland 'tradition' entered the national consciousness through both music and literature. A powerful force in the process was Robert Burns, a prolific writer of Jacobite songs including the familiar 'Charlie's my Darling', 'Strathallan's Lament' and 'The White Cockade'. The fact that Burns himself was a poet of Jacobite sympathy who hailed from one of the traditional strongholds of Scottish Whiggism in Aryshire was itself a significant confirmation of the new perceptions. Burns sympathized with Jacobitism for patriotic reasons, seeing it as a movement that had fought for Scottish independence rather than for the restoration of an absolute monarchy, and his songs therefore associate the '45 with the heroic struggles of the Scottish past, from the Wars of Independence onwards. That great expression of nationalism, 'Scots wha hae', may itself have been inspired by the Jacobite rebellion. Burns's role was vital in placing Jacobitism, and so the Highlands, at the centre of the new national consciousness which was emerging in Scotland after the union. He was followed by James Hogg, who, in his *Jacobite Relics of Scotland*, published many examples of genuine early eighteenth-century Jacobite verse which – much to the chagrin of the Highland Society, which had commissioned the work – did not contain enough of the sentiment, pathos and nostalgia deemed essential in 'authentic' Jacobite verse. Much more acceptable were the songs of Carolina Oliphant, Lady Nairne, who composed 'Will ye no come back again?'. This famous lament for the exiled prince was written by the scion of an old Jacobite family who was born only twenty years after Charles had left Scotland for ever. Subsequently three major new collections appeared, *Songs of Scotland* (1825), *The Scottish Minstrel* (1824–8) and *The Scottish Songs* (1829). By the 1820s, melodies with a Jacobite theme were second only to love songs in number and quality in the popular Scottish canon.[50]

The prose writers added to this cultural momentum. David Stewart of Garth, Anne Grant of Laggan, Patrick Graham, and above all Sir Walter Scott, presented idealized images of heroic Highlanders who, despite following an unfortunate cause, had remained true and loyal. Scott's work, and in particular *Waverley*, more than any other single influence made Jacobitism acceptable – and, even more, it made it romantic and seductive, skilfully embedding the Jacobite movement firmly within a Highland context of chieftains, clans and tartans. With only some exaggeration, one Victorian writer asserted that as a result of Scott's novels 'the whole nation went over the water to Charlie'.[51] If the '45 put the Highlands on the map within the United Kingdom, Scott was mainly responsible for publicizing it widely to an appreciative reading public throughout the world. But Highlandism did not depend on his pen alone. In the final analysis it was founded on changes of Scottish identity which had been shaped by the new world of union and empire. That context powerfully influenced the sense of Scottishness which evolved in the nineteenth century. Yet, as this book has tried to demonstrate, virtually every other sphere of Scottish life, from economy to emigration, from rural transformation to political development, was fashioned in large part by engagement with empire. The new Scotland which was emerging in the later eighteenth century was grounded on the imperial project. The Scots were not only full partners in this grand design but were at the very cutting edge of British global expansion.

References

Introduction

1 P. J. Marshall, Introduction, in P. J. Marshall, ed., *The Oxford History of the British Empire*. Vol. 2, *The Eighteenth Century* (Oxford, 1998), p.5.
2 Rajat Kanta Ray, 'Indian Society and the Establishment of British Supremacy, 1763–1818', in Marshall, ed., *Oxford History*, pp.508–29.
3 Marshall, Introduction, pp.2–4.
4 Linda Colley, *Captives: Britain, Empire and the World 1600–1850* (London, 2002), p.4.
5 Sir G. Macartney, *An Account of Ireland in 1773 by a Late Club Secretary of that Kingdom* (London, 1773), quoted in Thomas Bartlett, ' "This famous island set in a Virginian sea": Ireland in the British Empire, 1690–1801', in Marshall, ed., *Oxford History*, p.262.
6 H. V. Bowen, *Elites, Enterprise and the Making of the British Overseas Empire, 1688–1775* (Basingstoke, 1996), p.150.
7 ibid., pp.151–2.
8 Bartlett, ' "This famous island" ', pp.273–4.
9 James Horn, 'British Diaspora: Emigration from Britain, 1680–1815', in Marshall, ed., *Oxford History*, pp.30–32.
10 See below, pp. 144–9.
11 David Allan, *Scotland in the Eighteenth Century* (Harlow, 2002), p.185.
12 John M. MacKenzie, Foreword, in S. Murdoch and A. Mackillop, eds., *Military Governors and Imperial Frontiers, c.1600–1800: A Study of Scotland and Empires* (Leyden, 2003), p.xvi.

Chapter 1

1 David Dobson, *Scottish Emigration to Colonial America, 1607–1785* (Athens, Georgia, 1994), p.26.

2 Eric J. Graham, *A Maritime History of Scotland, 1650–1790* (East Linton, 2002), pp.37–8.

3 Dobson, *Scottish Emigration*, p.33.

4 George Pratt Insh, *Scottish Colonial Schemes, 1620–1686* (Glasgow, 1922).

5 Robin Law, 'The First Scottish Guinea Company, 1634–9', *Scottish Historical Review*, LXXXVI (1997), pp.185–202.

6 Ned C. Landsman, 'Nation, Migration and the Province in the First British Empire: Scotland and the Americas, 1600–1800', *American Historical Review*, 104 (1999), p.465. See also essays on the Netherlands and France in N. Canny, ed., *Europeans on the Move. Studies on European Migration, 1500–1800* (Oxford, 1994), pp.153–91, 236–62.

7 David Ditchburn, *Scotland and Europe*. Vol. 1, *Religion, Culture and Commerce* (East Linton, 2000); J. A. Galloway and I. Murray, 'Scottish Migration to England, 1400–1560', *Scottish Geographical Magazine*, 112 (1996), pp.29–38.

8 S. Murdoch and A. Mackillop, eds., *Military Governors and Imperial Frontiers c.1600–1800: A Study of Scotland and Empires* (Leyden, 2003), pp.xxv, xxxi, xxxv.

9 Gordon Marshall, *Presbyteries and Profits: Calvinism and the Development of Capitalism in Scotland, 1560–1707* (Oxford, 1980).

10 Murdoch and Mackillop, eds., *Military Governors and Imperial Frontiers*, pp.xxv–li.

11 East New Jersey did become a permanent settlement, but did not achieve anything like the same level of success as the other Quaker colonies in West Jersey and Pennsylvania. See Ned C. Landsman, *Scotland and its First American Colony, 1680–1765* (Princeton, NJ, 1985).

12 T. C. Smout, N. C. Landsman and T. M. Devine, 'Scottish Emigration in the Seventeenth and Eighteenth Centuries', in Canny, ed., *Europeans on the Move*, pp.85–6.

13 Landsman, 'Nation, Migration and the Province', p.466.

14 Quoted in M. W. Flinn *et al.*, eds., *Scottish Population History from the Seventeenth Century to the 1930s* (Cambridge, 1977), p.459.

15 William Lithgow, *The Totall Discourse of the Rare Adventures and Painefull Peregrinations of Long Nineteen Yeares* (Glasgow, 1906).

16 This paragraph is largely based on Ditchburn, *Scotland and Europe*, pp.209–57, by far the most informative analysis of Scottish emigrant patterns in the medieval period.

17 J. F. Lydon, 'The Scottish Soldier in medieval Ireland: the Bruce invasion and the Galloglass', in G. G. Simpson, ed., *The Scottish Soldier Abroad, 1247–1967* (Edinburgh, 1992).

18 D. E. R. Watt, 'Scottish university men of the thirteenth and fourteenth

centuries', in T. C. Smout, ed., *Scotland and Europe, 1200–1850* (Edinburgh, 1986).

19 Ditchburn, *Scotland and Europe*, p.235.

20 T. M. Devine, *The Scottish Nation, 1700–2000* (Harmondsworth, 1999), p.71.

21 Allan I. Macinnes, Marjory-Ann D. Harper and Linda G. Fryer, eds., *Scotland and the Americas, c.1650–c.1939: A Documentary Source Book* (Edinburgh, 2002), p.139.

22 Murdoch and Mackillop, eds., *Military Governors and Imperial Frontiers*, pp.xxxii, xxxvii.

23 L. M. Cullen, 'Scotland and Ireland, 1600–1800: their role in the evolution of British society', in R. A. Houston and I. D. Whyte, eds., *Scottish Society 1500–1800* (Cambridge, 1989), p.227.

24 Keith M. Brown, 'Reformation to Union, 1560–1707', in R. A. Houston and W. W. J. Knox, eds., *The New Penguin History of Scotland* (London, 2001), p.204.

25 T. M. Devine and S. G. E. Lythe, 'The Economy of Scotland under James VI: a Revision Article', *Scottish Historical Review*, L (1971), pp.101–4.

26 Thomas Riis, *Should Auld Acquaintance Be Forgot . . . Scottish–Danish Relations c.1450–1707* (Odense, 1988), *passim*; see A. Biegański, 'Scottish Immigrants in Poland', *Scottish Slavonic Review*, 19 (Autumn 1991); T. C. Smout, ed., *Scotland and Europe 1200–1850* (Edinburgh, 1986). The forthcoming published proceedings of the symposium, 'The Scottish Community Abroad in the early Modern Period', AHRB Centre for Irish and Scottish Studies, University of Aberdeen, May 2002, will add a number of fresh perspectives on this aspect.

27 Essays by Nina Pedersen, Rimantas Zirgulis and Blanche Dahlberg, in S. Murdoch, ed., *Scottish Communities Abroad* (forthcoming 2003).

28 S. G. E. Lythe, *The Economy of Scotland in its European Setting, 1550–1625* (Edinburgh, 1960), pp.135–9.

29 Waldemar Kowalski, 'The Placement of Urbanised Scots in the Polish Crown during the 16th and 17th Centuries'. I am most grateful to Professor Kowalski for allowing me to read his innovative paper while he was resident as Caledonian Research Foundation Fellow, AHRB Centre for Irish and Scottish Studies, University of Aberdeen, 2003.

30 Smout, Landsman and Devine, 'Scottish Emigration', p.80.

31 A. F. Steuart, ed., *Papers relating to the Scots in Poland, 1576–1793* (Edinburgh, 1915), p.ix.

32 Lithgow, *Totall Discourse*, p.422.

33 Anna Biegańska, 'A Note on the Scots in Poland, 1550–1800', in Smout, ed., *Scotland and Europe*, pp.157–65.

34 T. A. Fischer, *The Scots in Eastern and Western Prussia* (Edinburgh, 1903).

35 Biegańska, 'Note on the Scots', pp.157–65. See also Anna Biegańska, 'In Search of Tolerance: Scottish Catholics and Presbyterians in Poland', *Scottish Slavonic Review* 17 (1991), and *idem*, 'James Murray, A Scot in the Making of the Polish Navy', *Scottish Slavonic Review*, 3 (1984).

36 Smout, Landsman and Devine, 'Scottish Emigration', p.82.

37 Jan de Vries, *European Urbanisation 1500–1800* (London, 1985), p.39.

38 I. D. Whyte, *Scotland before the Industrial Revolution* (Harlow, 1995), pp.172–9.

39 Michael Lynch, 'Urbanisation and Urban Networks in Seventeenth Century Scotland', *Scottish Economic and Social History*, 12 (1992).

40 Michael Lynch, 'Continuity and Change in Urban Society, 1500–1700; in R. A. Houston and I. D. Whyte, eds., *Scottish Society 1500–1800* (Cambridge, 1989), pp.85–117.

41 Kowalski, 'Urbanised Scots in the Polish Crown', *passim*.

42 Hugh Dunthorne, 'Scots in the Wars of the Low Countries, 1572–1648', in Grant G. Simpson, ed., *Scotland and the Low Countries, 1124–1994* (East Linton, 1996), pp.104–21.

43 Alexia N. L. Grosjean, 'Scots and the Swedish State: Diplomacy, Military Service and Ennoblement 1611–1660', unpublished Ph.D. thesis, University of Aberdeen, 1998, p.276.

44 Allan I. Macinnes, *Clanship, Commerce and the House of Stuart, 1603–1788* (East Linton, 1996), p.100.

45 Steve Murdoch, Introduction, in Steve Murdoch, ed., *Scotland and the Thirty Years War 1618–1648* (Leiden, 2001), p.19; Alf Åberg, 'Scottish Soldiers in the Swedish Armies in the Sixteenth and Seventeenth Centuries', in Grant G. Simpson, ed., *Scotland and Scandinavia, 800–1800* (Edinburgh, 1990), p.91.

46 John M. Mackenzie, Foreword, in Murdoch and Mackillop, eds., *Military Governors and Imperial Frontiers*, p.xvi.

47 G. Parker, *The Thirty Years War* (London, 1987), p.191.

48 L. M. Cullen, 'The Irish Diaspora of the Seventeenth and Eighteenth Centuries', in Canny, ed., *Europeans on the Move*, p.121.

49 ibid., pp.120–21.

50 Lythe, *Economy of Scotland*, p.151.

51 ibid.

52 A point made in discussion by Professor T. C. Smout at the Diaspora Research Programme Workshop, AHRB Centre for Irish and Scottish Studies, University of Aberdeen, January 2003.

53 Neal Ascherson, *Stone Voices. The Search for Scotland* (London, 2002), p.27.

54 Devine and Lythe, 'The Economy of Scotland under James VI', pp.92–106.

55 I. D. Whyte, 'Population Mobility in Early Modern Scotland', in Houston and Whyte, eds., *Scottish Society*, pp.54–7; A. J. S. Gibson and T. C. Smout, *Prices, Food and Wages in Scotland 1550–1780* (Cambridge, 1995), pp.225–60.

56 Flinn *et al*., eds., *Population History*, pp.117–20.

57 Christopher Smout, 'The Culture of Migration: Scots as Europeans, 1500–1800', *History Workshop Journal*, 40 (Autumn 1995), p.112.

58 For the Muscovy connection see Paul Dukes, 'Scottish Soldiers in Muscovy', in *The Caledonian Phalanx: Scots in Russia* (Edinburgh, 1987), pp.9–22.

59 S. Murdoch and A. Grosjean, *Scotland, Scandinavia and Northern Europe 1580–1707*, *http://www.abdn.ac.uk/ssne*

60 Steve Murdoch, *Britain, Denmark-Norway and the House of Stuart, 1603–1660* (East Linton, 2000), pp.208–13.

61 ibid., pp.212–15.

62 J. A. Fallon, 'Scottish Mercenaries in the Service of Denmark and Sweden, 1626–1632', unpublished Ph.D. thesis, University of Glasgow, pp.156ff.

63 My italics.

64 Jane Dawson, 'Two Kingdoms or Three? Ireland in Anglo-Scottish Relations in the Middle of the Sixteenth Century', in Roger A. Mason, ed., *Scotland and England 1286–1815* (Edinburgh, 1987), p.131; Marianne Elliott, *The Catholics of Ulster* (London, 2000), p.86.

65 Philip S. Robinson, *The Plantation of Ulster. British Settlement in an Irish Landscape, 1600–1670* (Dublin and New York, 1984), p.4.

66 Jane H. Ohlmeyer, *Civil War and Restoration in the Three Stuart Kingdoms: the Career of Randal MacDonnell, Marquis of Antrim 1609–1683* (Cambridge, 1993).

67 Robinson, *Plantation of Ulster*, p.85.

68 David Stevenson, *Scottish Covenanters and Irish Confederates. Scottish–Irish Relations in the mid-Seventeenth Century* (Belfast, 1981), pp.8–9.

69 J. C. Beckett, *The Making of Modern Ireland, 1603–1923* (London, 1966), p.47.

70 Jane H. Ohlmeyer, ' "Civilisinge of These Rude Partes": Colonisation within Britain and Ireland, 1580s–1640s', in Nicholas Canny, ed., *The Oxford History of the British Empire*. Vol. 1, *The Origins of Empire* (Oxford, 1998), pp.138–9.

71 Quoted in David Armitage, *The Ideological Origins of the British Empire* (Cambridge, 2000), p.56.

72 Macinnes, *Clanship, Commerce and the House of Stuart*, p.96.

73 David Armitage, 'Making the Empire British: Scotland in the Atlantic World, 1542–1717', *Past and Present*, 155 (May 1997), pp.35–61.

74 Quoted in Lythe, *Economy of Scotland*, pp.200–205.

75 Armitage, *Ideological Origins*, p.59.

76 Quoted in Robinson, *Plantation of Ulster*, p.1.

77 Elliott, *Catholics of Ulster*, pp.91–2.

78 M. Perceval-Maxwell, *The Scottish Migration to Ulster in the Reign of James I* (London, 1973), pp.257–60.

79 Raymond Gillespie, *Colonial Ulster: The Settlement of East Ulster, 1600–1641* (Cork, 1985), p.36.

80 ibid., pp.34–40.

81 Devine and Lythe, 'Economy of Scotland', pp.91–106.

82 Gillespie, *Colonial Ulster*, p.39.

83 Quoted in ibid., p.31.

84 ibid., p.30.

85 Nicholas Canny, *Making Ireland British, 1580–1650* (Oxford, 2001), p.230.

86 Douglas Catterall, *Community without Borders. Scots Migrants and the Changing Face of Power in the Dutch Republic, c. 1600–1700* (Leyden, 2002), pp.70–73.

87 Raymond Gillespie, 'The Presbyterian Revolution in Ulster, 1660–1690', in W. J. Shiels and Diana Wood, eds., *The Churches, Ireland and the Irish* (Oxford, 1989), pp.160–61; Stevenson, *Scottish Covenanters and Irish Confederates*, pp.12–42.

88 Perceval–Maxwell, *Scottish Migration to Ulster*, pp.228, 234.

89 Robinson, *Plantation of Ulster*, pp.91–108.

90 Armitage, 'Making the Empire British', p.46.

91 Canny, *Making Ireland British*, p.232.

Chapter 2

1 Alexander Broadie, ed., *The Scottish Enlightenment* (Edinburgh, 2001).

2 See below, pp.34–5 and, for example, Steve Murdoch, 'The Good, the Bad and the Anonymous: A Preliminary Survey of Scots in the Dutch East Indies 1612–1707', *Northern Scotland*, 22 (2002), pp.1–12.

3 S. Murdoch and A. Grosjean, *Scotland, Scandinavia and Northern Europe 1580–1707*, *www.abdn.ac.uk/ssne*

4 David Allan, *Scotland in the Eighteenth Century* (Harlow, 2002), pp.165–6.

5 David Dobson, *Scottish Emigration to Colonial America, 1607–1785* (Athens, Georgia, 1994), pp.33–6.

6 Allan I. Macinnes, Marjory-Ann D. Harper and Linda G. Fryer, eds., *Scotland and the Americas, c.1650–c.1939: A Documentary Source Book* (Edinburgh, 2002), pp.139,171.

7 Papers given at the symposium, 'The Scottish Community Abroad in the Early Modern Period', AHRB Centre for Irish and Scottish Studies, University of Aberdeen, May 2002, especially by Nina Pedersen (on Bergen) and Blanche Dahlberg (on Gothenburg). See also W. Kowalski, 'The Placement of Urbanised Scots in the Polish Crown during the Sixteenth and Seventeenth Centuries', unpublished paper, p.12, and N. Pedersen, 'Skotsk innvandring til Norge i tidlig moderne tid', unpublished M.Phil. thesis, University of Oslo, 2000, p.149.

8 R. E. Tyson, 'Famine in Aberdeenshire, 1695–99: Anatomy of a Crisis', in D. Stevenson, ed., *From Lairds to Louns* (Aberdeen, 1986), pp.49–50; ibid., 'The Population of Aberdeenshire 1695–1755: A New Approach', *Northern Scotland*, 6 (1984–5), pp.113–31; M. W. Flinn *et al.*, eds., *Scottish Population History from the Seventeenth Century to the 1930s* (Cambridge, 1977), pp.164–86.

9 P. Fitzgerald, '"Black '97": Reconsidering Scottish Migration to Ireland in the Seventeenth Century and the Scotch-Irish in America', in W. Kelly, ed., *The Irish, the Scottish and the Scotch-Irish: Connections and Comparisons* (forthcoming, 2003).

10 T. C. Smout, N. C. Landsman and T. M. Devine, 'Scottish Emigration in the Seventeenth and Eighteenth Centuries', in Nicholas Canny, ed., *Europeans on the Move* (Oxford, 1994), p.86.

11 Raymond Gillespie, 'The Presbyterian Revolution in Ulster, 1660–1690', in W. J. Sheils and Diana Wood, eds., *The Churches, Ireland and the Irish* (London, 1989), pp.159–70.

12 Fitzgerald, '"Black '97"', pp.7–8; L. M. Cullen, 'The Irish Diaspora of the Seventeenth and Eighteenth Centuries', in Canny, ed., *Europeans on the Move*, p.119.

13 Dobson, *Scottish Emigration, passim.*

14 James Horn, 'British Diaspora: Emigration from Britain, 1680–1815', in P. J. Marshall, ed., *The Oxford History of the British Empire*. Vol. 2, *The Eighteenth Century* (Oxford, 1998), pp.30–31.

15 Tyson, 'Population of Aberdeenshire', pp.113–31, and R. E. Tyson, 'Demographic Change', in T. M. Devine and J. R. Young, eds., *Eighteenth Century Scotland: New Perspectives* (East Linton, 1999), pp.199–202.

16 T. C. Smout, *Scottish Trade on the Eve of Union 1660–1707* (Edinburgh and London, 1963), p.245.

17 Eric J. Graham, *A Maritime History of Scotland 1650–1790* (East Linton, 2002), p.3.

18 Smout, *Scottish Trade*, pp.249–50.

19 ibid., pp.165–6.

20 Quoted in ibid., p.180.

21 T. M. Devine, 'Scotland' in P. Clark, ed., *The Cambridge Urban History of Britain*. Vol. 2 (Cambridge, 2000), pp.156–7.

22 Graham, *Maritime History*, pp.13–14.

23 Glasgow City Archives, Dunlop of Garnkirk Papers, D12/4, Correspondence of John Dunlop.

24 Graham, *Maritime History*, p.51.

25 T. M. Fortescue, ed., *Calendar of State Papers, America and the West Indies 1681–1697* (London, 1898–1904), 1696–97, p.71.

26 C. G. Headlam, ed., *Calendar of State Papers, America and the West Indies, 1701* (London, 1910), p.639.

27 Gordon Jackson, 'Glasgow in Transition, *c*.1660–*c*.1740', in T. M. Devine and G. Jackson, eds., *Glasgow*. Vol. 1, *Beginnings to 1830* (Manchester, 1995), pp.69, 72.

28 T. M. Devine, *The Tobacco Lords: a Study of the Tobacco Merchants of Glasgow and their Trading Activities, 1740–90* (Edinburgh, 1975), pp.56–7.

29 Douglas Catterall, *Community without Borders. Scots Migrants and the Changing Face of Power in the Dutch Republic, c.1600–1700* (Leyden, 2002), p.11.

30 Christopher Smout, 'The Culture of Migration: Scots as Europeans, 1500–1800', *History Workshop Journal*, 40 (Autumn 1995), p.113.

31 Murdoch, 'Good, Bad and Anonymous', pp.1–13.

32 T. M. Devine, 'The Scottish Merchant Community 1680–1740', in R. H. Campbell and A. S. Skinner, eds., *The Origin and Nature of the Scottish Enlightenment* (Edinburgh, 1982), pp.26–41.

33 Catterall, *Community without Borders*, pp.344–5.

34 Robert Feenstra, 'Scottish–Dutch Legal Relations in the Seventeenth and Eighteenth Centuries', in T. C. Smout, ed., *Scotland and Europe, 1200–1850* (Edinburgh, 1986), p.130; Smout, 'Culture of Migration', p.113.

35 Smout, 'Culture of Migration', p.114.

36 S. Schama, *Patriots and Liberators: Revolution in the Netherlands, 1780–1813* (London, 1977), pp.35, 167; T. C. Smout, 'Scottish–Dutch Contact 1600–1800', in *Dutch Art and Scotland* (Edinburgh, 1992), pp.24–5.

37 I. D. Whyte, *Scotland before the Industrial Revolution* (Harlow, 1995), p.288.

38 Macinnes, Harper and Fryer, eds., *Scotland and the Americas*, p.73.

39 ibid., p.2.

40 Linda G. Fryer, 'Documents relating to the Formation of the Carolina Company in Scotland, 1682', *South Carolina Historical Magazine*, 99 (April 1998), pp.110–34.

41 ibid., p.128.

42 George Pratt Insh, *Scottish Colonial Schemes, 1620–1686* (Glasgow, 1922), pp.186–228.

43 Ned C. Landsman, *Scotland and its First American Colony, 1683–1765* (Princeton, NJ, 1985). The remainder of the paragraph draws on this major study.

44 George Pratt Insh, *The Company of Scotland Trading to Africa and the Indies* (London, 1932), pp.20–21.

45 ibid., p.28.

46 David Armitage, *The Ideological Origins of the British Empire* (Cambridge, 2000), pp.158–9.

47 Eric J. Graham, 'In Defence of the Scottish Maritime Interest, 1681–1713', *Scottish Historical Review*, LXXI (1992).

48 Graham, *Maritime History*, pp.63–76; Jackson, 'Glasgow in Transition', in Devine and Jackson, eds., *Glasgow*, p.74.

49 David Armitage, 'Making the Empire British: Scotland in the Atlantic World, 1542–1707', *Past and Present*, 155 (May 1997), pp.61–2.

50 The details that follow come from W. Douglas Jones, '"The Bold Adventurers": A Quantitative Analysis of the Darien Subscription List (1696)', *Scottish Economic and Social History*, 21 (2001), pp.22–42.

51 Insh, *Company of Scotland*, pp.65–6.

52 ibid., pp.93–8.

53 David Armitage, 'The Scottish Vision of Empire: Intellectual Origins of the Darien Venture', in John Robertson, ed., *A Union for Empire: Political Thought and the British Union of 1707* (Cambridge, 1995), p.99.

54 Quoted in Insh, *Company of Scotland*, p.72.

55 Quoted in George Clarke, *The Later Stuarts, 1660–1714* (Oxford, 1955), p.285.

56 C. Storrs, 'Disaster at Darien (1698–1700?). The Persistence of Spanish Imperial Power on the Eve of the Demise of the Spanish Hapsburgs', *European History Quarterly*, XXIX (1999), pp.22–3.

57 ibid.

58 Quoted in Armitage, 'Scottish Vision of Empire', p.111.

59 Storrs, 'Disaster at Darien', p.27.

60 Anon., *Scotland's Lament for their Misfortunes* (Edinburgh, 1700).

61 Smout, *Scottish Trade*, p.252.

62 Armitage, 'Intellectual Origins of the Darien Venture', pp.109–10.

63 Jones, '"The Bold Adventurers"', pp.38–9.

Chapter 3

1 The major recent book-length studies on the origins of Union are: W. Ferguson, *Scotland's Relations with England: a Survey to 1707* (Edinburgh, 1977); B. Levack, *The Formation of the British State* (Oxford, 1987); P. W. J. Riley, *The Union of England and Scotland: A Study in Anglo-Scottish Politics in the Eighteenth Century* (Manchester, 1978); John Robertson, ed., *A Union for Empire: Political Thought and the British Union of 1707* (Cambridge, 1995); P. H. Scott, *1707: the Union of Scotland and England* (Edinburgh, 1979). Unless otherwise stated, the information in parts 1 and 2 of this chapter, though not necessarily the interpretations, comes from these works. The Economic and Social History Society of Scotland have also published a useful guide to the debate: Christopher A. Whatley, *'Bought and Sold for English Gold?' Explaining the Union of 1707* (Dundee, 1994).

2 Quoted in Ferguson, *Scotland's Relations with England*, p.201.

3 T. M. Gray, ed., *Memoirs of the Life of Sir John Clerk of Penicuik* (Edinburgh, 1892), p.41.

4 G. Burnet, *History of His Own Times* (Oxford, 1825), Vol. V, p.171.

5 G. Holmes and D. Szechi, *The Age of Oligarchy. Pre-industrial Britain 1722–1783* (London, 1993), p.71.

6 John R. Young, 'The Parliamentary Incorporating Union of 1707: Political Management, Anti-Unionism and Foreign Policy', in T. M. Devine and J. R. Young, eds., *Eighteenth Century Scotland: New Perspectives* (East Linton, 1999), pp.29–37.

7 Young, 'Parliamentary Incorporating Union', pp.29–37.

8 D. Duncan, ed., *History of the Union of Scotland and England by Sir John Clerk of Penicuik* (Edinburgh, 1993), p.118.

9 Young, 'Parliamentary Incorporating Union', pp.37–46.

10 ibid.

11 Duncan, ed., *History of the Union*, p.121.

12 Allan I. Macinnes, 'Studying the Scottish Estates and the Treaty of Union', *History Microcomputer Review*, 6 (1990).

13 Whatley, *'Bought and Sold'*, pp.15–22.

14 Macinnes, 'Studying the Scottish Estates', p.14.

15 George Lockhart of Carnwath, *Memoirs Concerning the Affairs of Scotland* (London, 1714), p.172.

16 David Armitage, 'The Scottish Vision of Empire: Intellectual Origins of the Darien Venture', in Robertson, ed., *Union for Empire*, pp.97–8.

17 There is an abbreviated version of Seton's speech in the Appendix to Whatley, *'Bought and Sold'*, pp.48–50.

18 Thomas Bartlett, ' "This Famous Island set in a Virginia Sea": Ireland in the British Empire, 1690–1801', in P. J. Marshall, ed., *The Oxford History of the British Empire*. Vol. 2, *The Eighteenth Century* (Oxford, 1998), pp.253–76.

19 Eric J. Graham, 'In Defence of the Scottish Maritime Interest, 1681– 1713', *Scottish Historical Review*, L (1971).

20 John Brewer, *The Sinews of Power: War, Money and the English State, 1688–1783* (London, 1989), p.xiv.

21 D. A. Baugh, 'Maritime Strength and Atlantic Commerce. The Uses of a "Grand Marine Empire" ', in Lawrence Stone, ed., *An Imperial State at War* (London, 1994), pp.185–223.

22 Brewer, *Sinews of Power*, p.xvii.

23 ibid., pp.40–41.

24 Baugh, 'Maritime Strength and Atlantic Commerce', p.186.

25 Brewer, *Sinews of Power, passim.*; Patrick K. O'Brien, 'Inseparable Connections: Trade, Economy, Fiscal State and the Expansion of Empire, 1688–1815', in Marshall, ed., *Oxford History of the British Empire*, pp.63–70; Patrick K. O'Brien, 'The Political Economy of British Taxation, 1660–1815', *Economic History Review*, 2nd Series, xli (1988), pp.1–32.

26 Reported in T. M. Devine, 'The Union of 1707 and Scottish Development', *Scottish Economic and Social History*, V (1985), pp.23–40.

27 Lawrence Stone, Introduction, in Stone, ed., *An Imperial State at War*, pp.9–10; O'Brien, 'Trade, Economy, State and Empire', p.68.

28 R. C. Nash, 'The English and Scottish Tobacco Trades in the Seventeenth and Eighteenth Centuries: Legal and Illegal Trade', *Economic History Review*, 2nd Series, XXXV (1982), pp.354–72.

29 Eric J. Graham, *A Maritime History of Scotland, 1650–1790* (East Linton, 2002), pp.101–16.

30 Ned C. Landsman, *Scotland and its First American Colony, 1683–1765* (Princeton, NJ, 1985), pp.107–8.

31 ibid., p.107.

32 T. H. Hollingsworth, 'A Demographic Study of the British Ducal Families', in D. V. Glass and D. E. C. Eversley, *Population in History* (London, 1965), pp.354–78.

33 L. Timperley, 'The Pattern of Landholding in Eighteenth Century Scotland', in M. L. Parry and T. R. Slater, *The Making of the Scottish Countryside* (London, 1980), pp.137–54.

34 Robin Fraser Callander, *A Pattern of Landownership in Scotland* (Finzean, 1987), pp.45–8.

35 ibid., p.58.

36 T. M. Devine, *The Transformation of Rural Scotland. Social Change and the Agrarian Economy 1660–1815* (Edinburgh, 1994), pp.19–35.

Chapter 4

1 C. Shammas, *The Pre-Industrial Consumer in England and America* (Oxford, 1990), p.78.

2 Jordan Goodman, *Tobacco in History* (London, 1993), p.90.

3 Quoted in Arthur Herman, *The Scottish Enlightenment* (London, 2002), p.138.

4 T. M. Devine, 'The Golden Age of Tobacco', in T. M. Devine and G. Jackson, eds., *Glasgow*. Vol. 1, *Beginnings to 1830* (Manchester, 1995), pp.140–41.

5 Ian Charles Cargill Graham, *Colonists from Scotland: Emigration to North America, 1707–1783* (Ithaca, NY, 1956), p.127.

6 Jacob M. Price, 'The Rise of Glasgow in the Chesapeake Tobacco Trade, 1707–1775', *William and Mary Quarterly*, 3rd Series, XI (1954), p.198.

7 Anon., *A Candid Enquiry into the Causes of the Late and Intended Migrations from Scotland*, quoted in Andrew Hook, *Scotland and America: A Study of Cultural Relations, 1750–1835* (Glasgow, 1975), p.10.

8 T. M. Devine, *The Tobacco Lords: a Study of the Tobacco Merchants of Glasgow and their Trading Activities, c.1740–90* (Edinburgh, 1990 edn.), p.114.

9 Herman, *Scottish Enlightenment*, p.140.

10 R. C. Nash, 'The English and Scottish Tobacco Trades in the Seventeenth and Eighteenth Centuries: Legal and Illegal Trade', *Economic History Review*, 2nd Series, XXXV (1982), pp.354–72; Jacob M. Price, 'Glasgow, the Tobacco Trade and the Scottish Customs, 1707–1730', *Scottish Historical Review*, LXIII (1984), p.9.

11 Price, 'Rise of Glasgow'.

12 Jacob M. Price, *France and the Chesapeake* (Ann Arbor, Mich., 1973), pp.519, 617.

13 C. B. Coulter, 'The Virginia Merchant', unpublished Ph.D. thesis, Princeton University, 1944, p.9.

14 Devine, *Tobacco Lords*, p.66.

15 A. C. Land, 'The Tobacco Staple and the Planter's Problems: Technology, Labour and Crops, *Agricultural History*, XLIII (1969), pp.79–81.

16 Glasgow City Archives (GCA), Alexander Henderson's Letterbook, Henderson to John Glassford and Co., 5 June 1759.

17 Jacob M. Price, 'The Economic Growth of the Chesapeake and the European Market', *Journal of Economic History*, XXIV (1964), pp.497–510.

18 Price, *France and the Chesapeake*, pp.594–604.

19 Devine, *Tobacco Lords*, p.67.

20 Quoted in Price, 'Rise of Glasgow', p.306.

21 R. F. Dell, 'The Operational Record of the Clyde Tobacco Fleet, 1747–1775', *Scottish Economic and Social History*, 2 (1982), p.7.

22 ibid., pp.1–15, for the data which follow in the next few paragraphs.

23 See, for example, H. Hamilton, *An Economic History of Scotland in the Eighteenth Century* (Oxford, 1963), p.260.

24 GCA, TD 161–1, Ship Bank Balance Book, 1752–61; Register of Deeds, B.10/15/8045; National Archive of Scotland (NAS), Currie Dal Sequestrations, B/1 (1777).

25 Jacob M. Price, 'What did Merchants Do? Reflections on British Overseas Trade, 1660–1790', *Journal of Economic History*, XLIX (1989), p.278.

26 Devine, *Tobacco Lords*, pp.4–7.

27 What follows is based on ibid., pp.72–80; Jacob M. Price, *Capital and Credit in British Overseas Trade: the View from the Chesapeake, 1700–1776* (Cambridge, Mass., 1980), pp.20–39; Jacob M. Price and Paul G. E. Clemens, 'A Revolution of Scale in Overseas Trade: British Firms in the Chesapeake Trade, 1767–1775', *Journal of Economic History*, 47 (1987), pp.39–40.

28 GCA, B.10/15/6653, Copartnery, Arch. Buchanan, Speirs, etc., 8 December 1759; Speirs Papers, TD 131/6/1A, State of the Private Affairs of Alexander Speirs.

29 Andrew Brown, *History of Glasgow* (Glasgow, 1795), II, p.143.

30 Price, *Capital and Credit*, p.55.

31 T. M. Devine, 'Sources of Capital for the Glasgow Tobacco Trade, c. 1740–80', *Business History*, 16 (1974), pp.113–29.

32 ibid.

33 T. C. Smout, 'Where had the Scottish Economy Got to by the Third Quarter of the Eighteenth Century?', in I. Hont and M. Ignatieff, eds., *Wealth and Virtue* (Cambridge, 1983); Christopher A. Whatley, *The Industrial Revolution in Scotland* (Cambridge, 1997), pp.17–23.

34 Unless otherwise stated all the material which is contained in the following paragraphs comes from Devine, *Tobacco Lords, passim.*

35 Price and Clemens, 'Revolution of Scale', pp.33, 39–40.

36 H. B. McCall, *Memoirs of my Ancestors* (Birmingham, 1884), p.10.

37 NAS, RA 15/1179, James Lawson Letterbook, Lawson to John Semple, 30 December 1762.

38 Alexander Carlyle, *Autobiography* (Edinburgh, 1861), p.9; W. A. Mathew, 'The Origin and Occupations of Glasgow Students, 1740–1839', *Past and Present*, 33 (1966), p.91.

39 W. J. Addison, ed., *A Roll of the Graduates of the University of Glasgow* (Glasgow, 1898). Few graduated, however, as the tradition of university

attendance in arts courses leading to graduation only became established in the following century. Instead, students attended 'classes' and the class 'ticket', signed by the professor, was therefore a kind of minor degree parchment.

40 NAS, RA 15/1179, James Lawson Letterbook, Lawson to John Semple, 20 February 1763.

41 GCA, TD 200/53, Indenture between Neil Campbell and Messrs. Archibald Ingram and John Glassford.

42 T. M. Devine, ed., *A Scottish Firm in Virginia, 1767–1777* (Edinburgh, 1984), pp.1–76.

43 ibid.

Chapter 5

1 D. Dobson, *Scottish Emigration to Colonial America, 1607–1785* (Athens, Georgia, 1994).

2 David Noel Doyle, 'Scots-Irish or Scotch-Irish', in Michael Glazier, ed., *The Encyclopedia of the Irish in America* (Indiana, 1999), pp.42, 47.

3 The comment is Ned Landsman's in T. C. Smout, N. C. Landsman and T. M. Devine, 'Scottish Emigration in the Seventeenth and Eighteenth Centuries', in N. Canny, ed., *Europeans on the Move* (Oxford, 1994), p.99.

4 Bernard Bailyn, *Voyagers to the West: Emigration from Britain to America on the Eve of the Revolution* (London, 1986), pp.7, 27.

5 Marianne S. Wockeck, *Trade in Strangers: the Beginnings of Mass Migration to North America* (Pennsylvania, 1999).

6 David Richardson, 'The British Empire and the Atlantic Slave Trade, 1660–1807', in P. J. Marshall, ed., *The Oxford History of the British Empire*. Vol. 2, *The Eighteenth Century* (Oxford, 1998), pp.440–64.

7 Bailyn, *Voyagers to the West*, p.27. See also Bernard Bailyn, *The Peopling of British North America* (London, 1986).

8 J. M. Bumstead, 'The Scottish Diaspora: Emigration to British North America, 1763–1815', in Ned C. Landsman, ed., *Nation and Province in the First British Empire* (London, 2001), pp.127–50.

9 Daniel K. Richter, 'Native Peoples of North America and the Eighteenth Century British Empire', in Marshall, ed., *Oxford History of the British Empire*, pp.347–71.

10 James Horn, 'British Diaspora: Emigration from Britain, 1680–1815', in ibid., p.35; D. W. Galenson, *White Servitude in Colonial America: an Economic Analysis* (Cambridge, 1981).

11 Quoted in Jacqueline A. Rinn, 'Factors in Scottish Emigration', unpublished Ph.D. thesis, University of Aberdeen, 1979, p.205.

12 L. M. Cullen, 'The Irish Diaspora of the Seventeenth and Eighteenth Centuries', in Canny, ed., *Europeans on the Move*, p.119.

13 *Aberdeen Journal*, 2 May 1749.

14 *Pennsylvania Gazette*, 7–14 October 1736, quoted in Rinn, 'Factors in Scottish Emigration', p.216.

15 ibid.

16 Elaine A. Mitchell, 'The Scot in the Fur Trade', in W. Stanford Reid, ed., *The Scottish Tradition in Canada* (Toronto, 1976), p.36.

17 Andrew Fletcher of Saltoun, *The Political Works of Andrew Fletcher Esq. of Saltoun* (Glasgow, 1749), pp.100–101.

18 Dobson, *Scottish Emigration to Colonial America*; Smout, Landsman and Devine, 'Scottish Emigration', p.98.

19 Wockeck, *Trade in Strangers*, pp.172–3.

20 ibid.

21 Robert E. Tyson, 'Demographic Change', in T. M. Devine and J. R. Young, eds., *Eighteenth Century Scotland: New Perspectives* (East Linton, 1999), pp.195–209.

22 Ian D. Whyte, 'Urbanisation in Eighteenth Century Scotland', in Devine and Young, eds., *New Perspectives*, pp.176–94.

23 Smout, Landsman and Devine, 'Scottish Emigration', pp.88–9.

24 Robert A. Dodgshon, 'Agricultural Change and its Social Consequences in the Southern Uplands of Scotland, 1600–1780', in T. M. Devine and D. Dickson, eds., *Ireland and Scotland 1600–1850* (Edinburgh, 1983), pp.55–6.

25 Smout, Landsman and Devine, 'Scottish Emigration', pp.90–100.

26 Bailyn, *Voyagers to the West, passim*.

27 ibid., part 4, *passim*.

28 Rinn, 'Factors in Scottish Emigration', p.161.

29 T. M. Devine, *The Scottish Nation, 1700–2000* (Harmondsworth, 1999), pp.105–23.

30 *Virginia Gazette*, 9 June 1774, quoted in Ian Charles Cargill Graham, *Colonists from Scotland: Emigration to North America, 1707–1783* (Ithaca, NY, 1956), p.28.

31 W. H. Fraser, *Conflict and Class* (Edinburgh, 1988).

32 Quoted in A. Durie, *The Scottish Linen Industry in the Eighteenth Century* (Edinburgh, 1979), p.60.

33 Malcolm Gray, 'The Social Impact of Agrarian Change in the Rural Lowlands', in T. M. Devine and R. Mitchison, eds., *People and Society in Scotland*. Vol. 1, *1760–1830* (Edinburgh, 1988), pp.53–7.

34 T. M. Devine, *The Transformation of Rural Scotland. Social Change and the Agrarian Economy 1660–1815* (Edinburgh, 1994).

35 ibid., p.107.

36 Bailyn, *Voyagers to the West*, pp.607–8.

37 Ned C. Landsman, 'The Provinces and the Empire. Scotland, the American colonies and the development of British provincial identity', in Lawrence Stone, ed., *An Imperial State at War* (London and New York, 1994), p.270.

38 ibid.

Chapter 6

1 W. A. Speck, *The Butcher: the Duke of Cumberland and the Suppression of the '45* (Oxford, 1981).

2 Allan I. Macinnes, *Clanship, Commerce and the House of Stuart, 1603–1788* (East Linton, 1996), pp.193–205.

3 T. M. Devine, 'Urbanisation', in Devine and Mitchison, eds., *People and Society in Scotland*, Vol. 1, *1760–1830* (Edinburgh, 1988), pp.27–52.

4 Allan I. Macinnes, 'Scottish Gaeldom: the First Phase of Clearance', in Devine and Mitchison, eds., *People and Society in Scotland*, pp.70–90.

5 Andrew Mackillop, *More Fruitful than the Soil. Army, Empire and the Scottish Highlands, 1715–1815* (East Linton, 2000).

6 T. M. Devine, *Clanship to Crofters' War. The Social Transformation of the Scottish Highlands* (Manchester, 1994), pp.43–5.

7 M. Gray, *The Highland Economy* (Edinburgh, 1957), pp.223–6; T. M. Devine, *The Great Highland Famine. Hunger, Emigration and the Scottish Highlands in the Nineteenth Century* (Edinburgh, 1988), pp.1–27.

8 Robert A. Dodgshon, *From Chiefs to Landlords. Social and Economic Change in the Western Highlands and Islands c. 1493–1820* (Edinburgh, 1998), pp.233–48.

9 Devine, *Great Highland Famine*, pp.1–4.

10 Macinnes, 'Scottish Gaeldom', p.72.

11 Andrew Mackillop, 'Highland Estate Change and Tenant Emigration', in T. M. Devine and J. R. Young, eds., *Eighteenth Century Scotland: New Perspectives* (East Linton, 1999), pp.237–58.

12 Marianne McLean, *The People of Glengarry: Highlanders in Transition, 1745–1820* (Toronto, 1991), pp.62–77.

13 The most recent overview is Eric Richards, *The Highland Clearances* (Edinburgh, 2000).

14 Anthony W. Parker, *Scottish Highlanders in Colonial Georgia. The Recruitment, Emigration and Settlement at Darien, 1735–1748* (Athens, Georgia and London, 1997).

15 Macinnes, *Clanship*, p.229; A. Murdoch, ed., 'A Scottish Document concerning Emigration to North Carolina in 1772', *The North Carolina Historical Review*, LXVII (1990), pp.438–49.

16 Duane Meyer, *The Highland Scots of North Carolina, 1732–1776* (Chapel Hill, NC, 1957, 1961).

17 Bernard Bailyn, *Voyagers to the West: Emigration from Britain to America on the Eve of the Revolution* (London, 1986).

18 McLean, *People of Glengarry*, pp.78–97.

19 Mackillop, *More Fruitful than the Soil*, pp.168–203.

20 *South Carolina Gazette*, April 1774.

21 I. Adams and M. Somerville, *Cargoes of Despair and Hope* (Edinburgh, 1993), p.172.

22 Bailyn, *Voyagers to the West*, p.322.

23 ibid., p.421.

24 Quoted in A. J. Youngson, *After the '45* (Edinburgh, 1973), p.146.

25 J. M. Bumsted, *The People's Clearance* (Edinburgh, 1982), p.12.

26 Christine Johnson, *Developments in the Roman Catholic Church in Scotland, 1789–1829* (Edinburgh, 1983), pp.21–2.

27 Bumsted, *People's Clearance*, p.63.

28 McLean, *People of Glengarry*, pp.62–77.

29 Mackillop, *More Fruitful than the Soil*, pp.130–67.

30 T. M. Devine, 'A Conservative People? Scottish Gaeldom in the Age of Improvement', in Devine and Young, eds., *Eighteenth Century Scotland*, pp.225–36.

Chapter 7

1 James Horn, 'British Diaspora: Emigration from Britain, 1680–1815', in P. J. Marshall, ed., *The Oxford History of the British Empire*. Vol. 2, *The Eighteenth Century* (Oxford, 1998), p.31. See also essays by L. M. Cullen, T. C. Smout, N. C. Landsman and T. M. Devine in N. Canny, ed., *Europeans on the Move. Studies on European Migration, 1500–1800* (Oxford, 1994), pp.76–152; Henry A. Gemery, 'European Emigration to North America, 1700–1820: Numbers and Quasi-Numbers', *Perspectives in American History*, I (1984), pp.283–342.

2 David Noel Doyle, 'Scots–Irish or Scotch–Irish', in Michael Glazier, ed., *The Encyclopedia of the Irish in America* (Indiana, 1999), pp.42, 47, summarizing the work of R. J. Dickson, L. M. Cullen, M. Wokeck and G. Kirkham.

3 Kerby A. Miller, *Emigrants and Exiles* (Oxford, 1985), p.169.

4 David N. Doyle, *Ireland, Irishmen and Revolutionary America, 1760–1820* (Dublin and Cork, 1981), p.51.

5 R. J. Dickson, with a new Introduction by G. E. Kirkham, *Ulster Emigration to Colonial America 1718–1775* (Belfast, 1997), pp.xvi–xvii.

6 T. L. Purvis, D. H. Akenson and F. and E. McDonald, 'The Population of the United States, 1790: A Symposium', *William and Mary Quarterly*, 3rd Series, XLI (1984), pp.85–135; D. Noel Doyle, 'The Irish in North America, 1776–1845', in W. E. Vaughan, ed., *A New History of Ireland*. Vol.5, *1801–1870* (Oxford, 1989), p.692.

7 Kevin Kenny, *The American Irish. A History* (Harlow, 2000), pp.23–5.

8 James G. Leyburn, *The Scotch–Irish. A Social History* (Chapel Hill, NC, 1962), pp.142–3, 327–8.

9 Maldwyn A. Jones, 'The Scotch–Irish in British America', in Bernard Bailyn and Philip D. Morgan, eds., *Strangers within the Realm: Cultural Margins of the First British Empire* (Chapel Hill, NC, 1991), p.284.

10 Arthur McKee, '"A Peculiar and Royal Race": Creating a Scotch–Irish Identity, 1889–1901', in P. Fitzgerald and S. Ickringill, eds., *Atlantic Crossroads. Historical Connections between Scotland, Ulster and North America* (Newtonards, 2001), pp.67–83.

11 Patrick Fitzgerald, 'The Scotch–Irish and the Eighteenth Century Irish Diaspora', *History Ireland* (Autumn 1999), pp.37–41.

12 Miller, *Emigrants and Exiles*, pp.137–68.

13 Doyle, 'Scots–Irish or Scotch–Irish', p.843.

14 Leyburn, *Scotch–Irish*, p.328.

15 Quoted in Fitzgerald, 'Scotch–Irish', pp.37–8.

16 Doyle, *Ireland, Irishmen and Revolutionary America*, p.57.

17 Philip S. Robinson, *The Plantation of Ulster. British Settlement in an Irish Landscape, 1600–1670* (Dublin and New York, 1984).

18 J. C. Beckett, 'Irish–Scottish Relations in the Seventeenth Century', in J. C. Beckett, *Confrontations. Studies in Irish History* (London, 1972), pp.26–46.

19 Smout, Landsman and Devine, 'Scottish Emigration', pp.87–8.

20 ibid.

21 David Hayton, *Ireland after the Glorious Revolution* (Belfast, 1976), pp.7–9.

22 Patrick Griffin, *The People with no Name* (Princeton, NJ, and Oxford, 2001), pp.19–20.

23 A. T. Q. Stewart, *The Narrow Ground: Aspects of Ulster, 1609–1969* (London, 1977), pp.96–9.

24 Jones, 'Scotch–Irish', p.289.

25 ibid., pp.289–90.

26 E. W. McFarland, *Ireland and Scotland in the Age of Revolution* (Edinburgh, 1994), pp.1–2.

27 S. J. Connolly, 'Ulster Presbyterians: Religion, Culture and Politics, 1660–1850', in H. Tyler Blethen and Curtis W. Wood, Jr., eds., *Ulster and*

North America. Transatlantic Perspectives on the Scotch–Irish (Tuscaloosa, 1997), pp.24–40.

28 H. Tyler Blethen and Curtis W. Wood, Jr., Introduction, in Blethen and Wood, eds., *Ulster and North America*, pp.5–6.

29 McFarland, *Ireland and Scotland*, p.1.

30 ibid., p.2.

31 T. M. Devine, *The Scottish Nation, 1700–2000* (Harmondsworth, 1999), pp.209–11.

32 Leyburn, *Scotch–Irish*, p.151.

33 Brenda Collins, 'The Origins of Irish Immigration to Scotland in the Nineteenth and Twentieth Centuries', in T. M. Devine, ed., *Irish Immigrants and Scottish Society in the Nineteenth and Twentieth Centuries* (Edinburgh, 1991), pp.5–7.

34 McFarland, *Ireland and Scotland*, p.5.

35 ibid.

36 R. D. Anderson, *Scottish Education since the Reformation* (Dundee, 1997), pp.12–19.

37 I. M. Bishop, 'The Education of Ulster Students at Glasgow University during the Eighteenth Century', unpublished M. A. thesis, Queen's University of Belfast, 1987, p.89.

38 W. R. Scott, *Francis Hutcheson: His Life, Teachings and Position in the History of Philosophy* (Cambridge, 1900).

39 McFarland, *Ireland and Scotland*, pp.19–25.

40 See below, pp.181–2.

41 J. R. R. Adams, *The Printed Word and the Common Man: Popular Culture in Ulster 1700–1900* (Belfast, 1987), pp.72–3.

42 Quoted in L. McIlvanney, *Burns the Radical: Poetry and Politics in Late Eighteenth-Century Scotland* (East Linton, 2001), p.226.

43 ibid., p.221.

44 Kenny, *American Irish*, p.14.

45 J. A. Froude, *The English in Ireland in the Eighteenth Century* (London, 1872), Vol. 1, p.392.

46 ibid.

47 Jones, 'Scotch–Irish', p.292.

48 D. W. Miller, 'Presbyterianism and "Modernisation" in Ulster', *Past and Present*, 80 (August 1978), p.73, quoted in ibid., p.292.

49 Doyle, 'Scots–Irish or Scotch–Irish', p.843.

50 Graeme Kirkham, 'Ulster Emigration to North America 1680–1720' in Blethen and Wood, eds., *Ulster and North America*, pp.76–117.

51 David Dickson, *Arctic Ireland: the Extraordinary Story of the Great Frost and Forgotten Famine of 1740–41* (Belfast, 1997).

52 Kirkham, 'Ulster Emigration', pp.76–117.

53 T. M. Devine, 'The English Connection and Irish and Scottish Development in the Eighteenth Century', in T. M. Devine and David Dickson, eds., *Ireland and Scotland 1600–1850* (Edinburgh, 1983), pp.12–30.

54 R. E. Tyson, 'Famine in Aberdeenshire, 1695–99: Anatomy of a Crisis', in D. Stevenson, ed., *From Lairds to Louns* (Aberdeen, 1986), pp.49–50.

55 David Dickson, *New Foundations. Ireland, 1660–1800* (Dublin, 1987).

56 Doyle, 'Scots–Irish and Scotch–Irish', p.847.

57 Cullen, 'The Irish Diaspora', *Europeans on the Move*, p.148.

58 ibid., pp.145–8.

59 Maldwyn A. Jones, 'Ulster Emigration, 1783–1815', in E. R. R. Green, ed., *Essays in Scotch–Irish History* (London and New York, 1969), p.54.

60 Marianne S. Wokeck, *Trade in Strangers. The Beginnings of Mass Migration to North America* (Pennsylvania, 1999), pp.192–8.

61 T. M. Truxes, *Irish–American Trade* (Cambridge, 1988), pp.128, 132.

62 Dickson, *Ulster Emigration*, pp.xiv–xv.

63 Kenny, *American Irish*, p.15.

64 William Macafee, 'The Demographic History of Ulster, 1750–1841', in Blethen and Wood, eds., *Ulster and North America*, pp.41–60.

65 Cullen, 'Irish Diaspora', *Europeans on the Move*, p.141.

66 Dickson, *Ulster Emigration*, p.xiii.

67 Miller, *Emigrants and Exiles*, pp.152–5.

68 Doyle, *Ireland, Irishmen and Revolutionary America*, p.53.

69 Griffin, *The People with No Name*, pp.1–2.

70 Jones, 'Ulster Emigration, 1783–1815', pp.46–68.

71 E. Estyn Evans, 'The Scotch–Irish: Their Cultural Adaptation and Heritage in the American Old West' in E. R. R. Green, ed., *Essays in Scotch–Irish History* (London and New York, 1969), pp.75–6.

72 Leyburn, *Scotch–Irish*, p.257.

73 Quoted in ibid, p.318.

74 Esmond Wright, 'Education in the American Colonies: the Impact of Scotland', in Green, ed., *Essays in Scotch–Irish History*, p.21.

75 ibid.

76 Quoted in Miller, *Emigrants and Exiles*, p.165.

77 Quoted in David Hackett Fischer, *Albion's Seed: Four British Folkways in America* (Oxford, 1989), p.813.

78 Richard J. Hooker, ed., *The Carolina Backcountry on the Eve of the Revolution: the Journal and other Writings of Charles Woodmason, Anglican Itinerant* (Chapel Hill, 1953), p.116.

79 Estyn Evans, 'The Scotch–Irish', p.76.

80 Jones, 'Scotch–Irish in British America', p.295.

81 Miller, *Emigrants and Exiles*, pp.159–60.

82 Kenny, *American Irish*, p.34.
83 Griffin, *The People with No Name*, p.114.
84 See below, pp. 181–2.
85 Estyn Evans, 'The Scotch–Irish', p.84.
86 ibid., p.80.
87 Wayland F. Dunaway, *The Scotch–Irish of Colonial Pennsylvania* (Chapel Hill, NC, 1944), pp.185–6.
88 Estyn Evans, 'The Scotch–Irish', p.82.
89 ibid. See also Daniel K. Richter, 'Native Peoples of North America and the Eighteenth-Century British Empire', in Marshall, ed., *Oxford History of the British Empire*, Vol. 3, pp.347–72.
90 Leyburn, *Scotch–Irish*, pp.223–4.
91 Quoted in Jones, 'Scotch–Irish in British America', p.296.
92 ibid., pp.295–6.
93 Quoted in Leyburn, *Scotch–Irish*, p.227.
94 Fischer, *Albion's Seed*, p.646.
95 Jones, 'Scotch–Irish in British America', p.296.
96 ibid., p.297.
97 Dunaway, *Scotch–Irish of Colonial Pennsylvania*, pp.119–29.
98 Leyburn, *Scotch–Irish*, pp.301–4.
99 ibid.
100 Arthur Herman, *The Scottish Enlightenment* (London, 2002), p.201.
101 Kenny, *American Irish*, p.39.
102 Leyburn, *Scotch–Irish*, pp.271–95.
103 Marilyn J. Westerkamp, *Triumph of the Laity: Scots–Irish Piety and the Great Awakening, 1625–1760* (Oxford, 1988).
104 Herman, *Scottish Enlightenment*, p.202.
105 Dunaway, *Scotch–Irish of Colonial Pennsylvania*, pp.213, 218–28.
106 Wright, 'Education in the American Colonies', p.25.

Chapter 8

1 Bernard Bailyn, *The Peopling of North America. An Introduction* (London, 1986), p.26.
2 Robert K. Donovan and Michael Fry, 'Religion in the Affairs of Scotland and America', in John Carter Brown Library, *Scotland and the Americas 1600–1800* (Providence, Rhode Island, 1995), p.53.
3 Ned C. Landsman, 'Nation, Migration and the Province in the First British Empire: Scotland and the Americas, 1600–1800', *American Historical Review*, 104 (April 1999), p.471, n.17.
4 Ned C. Landsman, 'The Legacy of British Union for the North American

Colonies: Provincial Elites and the Problem of Imperial Union', in John Robertson, ed., *A Union for Empire. Political Thought and the British Union of 1707* (Cambridge, 1995), p.302.

5 James McLachlan, 'Education', in *Scotland and the Americas*, pp.65–75. The figures which follow come mainly from this seminal piece.

6 W. R. Brock, *Scotus Americanus* (Edinburgh, 1982), pp.87–8, 96, 107.

7 Douglas Sloan, *The Scottish Enlightenment and the American College Ideal* (New York, 1971), pp.225–47.

8 Roger L. Emerson, 'The Scottish Literati and America, 1680–1800', in Ned C. Landsman, ed., *Nation and Province in the First British Empire. Scotland and the Americas, 1600–1800* (London, 2001), pp.183–220.

9 Dalphy I. Fagerstrom, 'Scottish Opinion and the American Revolution', *William and Mary Quarterly*, 3rd Series, XI (1954), pp.252–75.

10 Michael Fry, *The Scottish Empire* (Edinburgh, 2001), p.59.

11 Quoted in Andrew Hook, *Scotland and America. A Study of Cultural Relations, 1750–1835* (Glasgow, 1975), p.20.

12 Sloan, *Scottish Enlightenment and the American College Ideal*, p.226.

13 Landsman, 'Nation, Migration and the Province', p.473.

14 Mary L. Lustig, *Robert Hunter, 1660–1734: New York's Augustan Statesman* (Syracuse, N. Y., 1983).

15 B. Hundle, *The Pursuit of Science in Revolutionary America* (Chapel Hill, NC, 1956), pp.38, 48–50, 58–61.

16 Donovan and Fry, 'Religion in the Affairs of Scotland and America', pp.57, 62.

17 Susan O'Brien, 'A Transatlantic Community of Saints: The Great Awakening and the First Evangelical Network, 1735–1755', *American Historical Review*, 91, No.4 (October 1986), pp.811–32.

18 *Scots Magazine*, IX (1747), p.145.

19 Donovan and Fry, 'Religion in the Affairs of Scotland and America', p.54.

20 See above, pp.147–8 and Marilyn J. Westerkamp, *The Triumph of the Laity: Scots–Irish Piety and The Great Awakening, 1625–1760* (Oxford, 1988); A. Fawcett, *The Cambuslang Revival: the Scottish Evangelical Revival of the Eighteenth Century* (London, 1971).

21 Robert Kent Donovan, 'The Popular Party of the Church of Scotland and the American Revolution', in Richard B. Sher and Jeffrey R. Smitten, eds., *Scotland and America in the Age of the Enlightenment* (Edinburgh, 1990), pp.81–114.

22 George Shepperson, 'Writings in Scottish–American History: A Brief Survey', *William and Mary Quarterly*, 3rd Series, XI (October 1954), p.165.

23 ibid., p.163.

24 Andrew Hook, *From Goosecreek to Gandercleugh. Studies in Scottish–American Literary and Cultural History* (Edinburgh, 1999), p.10.

25 This problem is noted in several of the essays in Tom Devine and Paddy Logue, eds., *Being Scottish. Personal Reflections on Scottish Identity Today* (Edinburgh, 2002).

26 C. Duncan Rice, 'Scottish Enlightenment, American Revolution and Atlantic Reform', in Owen Dudley Edwards and George Shepperson, eds., *Scotland, Europe and the American Revolution* (Edinburgh, 1976).

27 ibid.

28 Ned C. Landsman, 'Witherspoon and the Problem of Provincial Identity in Scottish Evangelical Culture', in Sher and Smitten, eds., *Scotland and America*, pp.30–80.

29 Brock, *Scotus Americanus*, pp.92–3.

30 Dalphy I. Fagerstrom, 'The American Revolutionary Movement in Scottish Opinion, 1763–1783', unpublished Ph.D. thesis, University of Edinburgh, 1951, pp.103ff.

31 Varnum Collins, *President Witherspoon: A Biography* (Princeton, NJ, 1953). More recent studies include articles by Ned Landsman and Peter Diamond in Sher and Smitten, eds., *Scotland and America*, pp.30–43, 115–31.

32 Sloan, *Scottish Enlightenment and the American College Ideal*, pp.103–45.

33 W. M. Mathew, 'The Origins and Occupations of Glasgow Students, 1740–1839', *Past and Present*, 33 (1966).

34 Quoted in W. C. Lehmann, *Scottish and Scotch–Irish Contributions to Early American Life and Culture* (London, 1978), p.118.

35 Brock, *Scotus Americanus*, p.113.

36 ibid., pp.111–12.

37 Donald D'Elid, *Benjamin Rush: Philosopher of the American Revolution* (Philadelphia, 1979).

38 Jane Rendall, 'The Influence of the Edinburgh Medical School on America in the Eighteenth Century', in R. G. W. Anderson and A. D. C. Simpson, eds., *The Early Years of the Edinburgh Medical School* (Edinburgh, 1976), pp.95–124.

39 Sloan, *Scottish Enlightenment and the American College Ideal*, pp.238–9.

40 Rice, 'Scottish Enlightenment', pp.75–6.

41 For a gloss on the controversy see Hook, *Goosecreek to Gandercleugh*, pp.10–16.

42 Daniel Walker Howe, 'European Sources of Political Ideas in Jeffersonian America', *Reviews in American History*, 10, No. 4 (December 1982), pp.28–44.

43 John M. Mackenzie, 'Scots in South Africa: Problems of Sources and Methodology', paper presented to the Diaspora Programme Workshop, AHRB Centre for Irish and Scottish Studies, University of Aberdeen, January 2003.

44 Alexander Broadie, ed., *The Scottish Enlightenment. An Anthology* (Edinburgh, 1997).

45 Alexander Broadie, *The Scottish Enlightenment* (Edinburgh, 2001), pp.1–3.

46 C. J. Berry, *Social Theory of the Scottish Enlightenment* (Edinburgh, 1997).

47 Anand C. Chitnis, *The Scottish Enlightenment* (London, 1976), *passim*.

48 A. Broadie, *The Tradition of Scottish Philosophy* (Edinburgh, 1990); David Allan, *Virtue, Learning and the Scottish Enlightenment* (Edinburgh 1993); R. H. Campbell and Andrew S. Skinner, eds., *The Origins and Nature of the Scottish Enlightenment* (Edinburgh, 1982).

49 Broadie, *Scottish Enlightenment*, p.15.

50 Quoted in G. C. Mossner and I. S. Ross, eds., *The Correspondence of Adam Smith* (Oxford, 2nd edn., 1987), p.309.

51 Ned C. Landsman, 'The Provinces and the Empire. Scotland, the American Colonies and the Development of British Provincial Identity', in Laurence Stone, ed., *An Imperial State at War. Britain from 1689 to 1815* (London, 1994), pp.268–9.

52 Broadie, *Scottish Enlightenment*, pp.117–18.

53 Arthur Herman, *The Scottish Enlightenment* (London, 2002) is the most recent example of this tendency.

54 B. Bailyn, ed., *Pamphlets of the American Revolution*, Vol. 1 (Harvard, 1965), Introductory Essay, 'The Transforming Radicalism of the American Revolution'.

55 Howe, 'European Sources of Political Ideas', pp.29–30, 39, 42.

56 Raymond P. Stearns, *Science in the British Colonies of America* (Urbana, Ill., 1970).

57 Quoted in Rice, 'Scottish Enlightenment', p.76.

58 Morton White, *Philosophy of the American Revolution* (New York, 1978).

59 Caroline Robbins, 'When is it that Colonies may turn Independent: an Analysis of Environment and Politics of Francis Hutcheson, 1694–1746', *William and Mary Quarterly*, 3rd Series, XI (1954), pp.213–51.

60 Quoted in David Noel Doyle, *Ireland, Irishmen and Revolutionary America, 1760–1820* (Dublin and Cork, 1981), p.113.

61 ibid., p.112.

62 Gary Wills, *Explaining America* (New York, 1981); Brock, *Scotus Americanus*, pp.92–3.

63 McLachlan, 'Education', in *Scotland and the Americas*, p.74.

64 Quoted in Brock, *Scotus Americanus*, pp.92–3.

65 Richard B. Sher, 'Introduction: Scottish-American Cultural Studies, Past and Present', in Sher and Smitten, eds., *Scotland and America*, pp.10–12.

66 H. W. Schneider, *History of American Philosophy* (New York, 1947), p.246.

67 Gerald Stovrzh, *Alexander Hamilton and the Idea of Republican Government* (Stanford, 1970); Howe, 'European Sources of Political Ideas', p.37.

68 Howe, 'European Sources of Political Ideas', pp.36–7.

69 Herman, *Scottish Enlightenment*, pp.212–13.

70 See, *inter alia*, R. A. Ryerson, 'Political Mobilisation and the American Revolution: the Resistance Movement in Philadelphia, 1765–1776', *William and Mary Quarterly*, 3rd Series, XXXI (1974), pp.565–89; E. R. R. Green, 'The Scotch–Irish and the Coming of the Revolution in North Carolina', *Irish Historical Studies*, Vol. VII, 1950–51, pp.78–86; Doyle, *Ireland, Irishmen and Revolutionary America*, pp.109–37; Maldwyn A. Jones, 'The Scotch–Irish in British America', in Bernard Bailyn and Philip D. Morgan, eds., *Strangers within the Realm. Cultural Margins of the First British Empire* (Chapel Hill, NC, 1991), pp.309–11.

71 Michael Fry, *The Scottish Empire* (Edinburgh, 2001), p.58; B. G. Moss, 'The Roles of the Scots and Scotch–Irishmen in the Southern Campaigns in the War of American Independence, 1780–1783', unpublished Ph.D. thesis, University of St Andrews, 1979, pp.538–9.

72 Wallace Brown, *The King's Friends* (Providence, Rhode Island, 1965), p.215.

73 Quoted in Hook, *Scotland and America*, p.69.

74 See below, pp.210–11.

75 Julian P. Boyd, *The Declaration of Independence and the Evolution of the Text* (Princeton, N. J., 1945), pp.34–5.

76 Brown, *King's Friends*, p.260.

77 Hook, *Scotland and America*, p.51.

78 Wallace Brown, *The Good Americans. The Loyalists in the American Revolution* (New York, 1969), p.46.

79 Brown, *King's Friends*, p.259.

80 Brock, *Scotus Americanus*, p.129.

81 Fagerstrom, 'Scottish Opinion and the American Revolution', pp.255–6; Landsman, 'Provinces and the Empire', pp.268–9.

82 Fagerstrom, 'Scottish Opinion and the American Revolution', pp.258–62.

83 D. B. Swinfen, 'The American Revolution in the Scottish Press', in Edwards and Shepperson, eds., *Scotland, Europe and the American Revolution*, pp.66–74.

84 Fry, *Scottish Empire*, p.62.

85 Swinfen, 'American Revolution in the Scottish Press', pp.66–74.
86 Emory G. Evans, 'Planter Indebtedness and the Coming of Revolution in Virginia', *William and Mary Quarterly*, 3rd series, XIX (1962), pp.511–33.
87 Landsman, 'Legacy of British Union', pp.301–2.
88 Brown, *King's Friends*, pp.205–7.
89 Allan I. Macinnes, *Clanship, Commerce and the House of Stuart, 1603–1788* (East Linton, 1996), pp.159–81, 247.
90 Duane Meyer, *The Highland Scots of North Carolina* (Chapel Hill, NC, 1957,1961), pp.147–156.
91 Hook, *Scotland and America*, pp.51–64.
92 Quoted in ibid., p.62.

Chapter 9

1 Edward J. Cowan, 'The Myth of Scotch Canada', in Marjory Harper and Michael E. Vance, eds., *Myth, Migration and the Making of Memory. Scotia and Nova Scotia, c.1700–1990* (Halifax, 1999), p.66.
2 W. Stanford Reid, ed., *The Scottish Tradition in Canada* (Toronto, 1976), p.ix.
3 Quoted in Cowan, 'Myth', p.55.
4 ibid., p.58.
5 J. K. Johnson, *Becoming Prominent: Regional Leadership in Upper Canada, 1791–1841* (Kingston and Montreal, 1989), p.106.
6 J. M. Bumsted, 'The Scottish Diaspora: Emigration to British North America, 1763–1815', in Ned C. Landsman, ed., *Nation and Province in the First British Empire* (London, 2001), pp.145–6.
7 ibid., pp.143–4.
8 *Glasgow Journal*, 14 January 1760.
9 ibid., 28 January 1760.
10 D. S. Macmillan, 'The "New Men" in Action: Scottish Mercantile and Shipping Operations in the North American Colonies, 1760–1825', *Canadian Business History: Selected Studies, 1497–1971* (Toronto, 1972), pp.44–103.
11 ibid.
12 Peter C. Newman, *Company of Adventurers*, Vol. 1 (Toronto, 1985), p.47.
13 ibid.
14 ibid., p.49.
15 ibid., p.2.
16 Quoted in ibid., p.18.
17 ibid., p.16.

18 J. S. A. Brown, '"A Parcel of Upstart Scotchmen"', *The Beaver*, 68 (1988), p.4.

19 ibid.

20 Newman, *Company of Adventurers*, pp.179–80.

21 Quoted in ibid., p.203.

22 ibid., pp.203–4.

23 Brown, 'Parcel of Upstart Scotchmen', p.5.

24 Cowan, 'Myth', pp.58–9.

25 Brown, 'Parcel of Upstart Scotchmen', p.5.

26 D. Macpherson, *Annals of Commerce* (1805), Vol. 4, p.129.

27 Quoted in Elaine A. Mitchell, 'The Scot in the Fur Trade', in W. Stanford Reid, ed., *The Scottish Tradition in Canada* (Toronto, 1976), p.36.

28 ibid.

29 Bumsted, 'Scottish Diaspora', p.130.

30 Allan I. Macinnes, *Clanship, Commerce and the House of Stuart, 1603–1788* (East Linton, 1996), p.232.

31 J. M. Bumsted, *The People's Clearance* (Edinburgh, 1982), pp.188–212.

32 R. Hyam, 'Imperial Interests and the Peace of Paris', in R. Hyam and G. Martin, *Reappraisals in British Imperial History* (London, 1975), p.30, quoted in P. J. Marshall, ed., *The Oxford History of the British Empire*. Vol. 2, *The Eighteenth Century* (Oxford, 1998).

33 P. J. Marshall, 'British North America, 1760–1815' in Marshall, ed., *Oxford History of the British Empire*, Vol. 2, p.381.

34 Bumsted, 'Scottish Diaspora', pp.136–7.

35 Quoted in Marianne McLean, *The People of Glengarry: Highlanders in Transition, 1745–1820* (Toronto, 1991), p.97.

36 ibid., *passim*.

37 This connection was first made in the Introduction in Harper and Vance, eds., *Myth, Migration and the Making of Memory*, pp.16–17.

38 J. M. Bumsted, 'Settlement by Chance: Lord Selkirk and Prince Edward Island', *Canadian Historical Review*, LIX (1978), pp.170–88.

39 The poems which follow appear in Margaret Macdonnell, *The Emigrant Experience: Songs of Highland Emigrants in North America* (Buffalo and Toronto, 1982).

40 The remainder of this chapter is drawn mainly from McLean, *People of Glengarry, passim*.

Chapter 10

1 Adam Smith, *Wealth of Nations* (1776; London, 1937), p.366.
2 J. R. Ward, 'The British West Indies in the Age of Abolition, 1748–1815', in P. J. Marshall, ed., *The Oxford History of the British Empire*. Vol. 2, *The Eighteenth Century* (Oxford, 1998), p.427.
3 Richard B. Sheridan, *Sugar and Slavery. An Economic History of the British West Indies 1623–1775* (Barbados, 1974), p.11.
4 By Sidney W. Mintz, quoted in Richard B. Sheridan, *Doctors and Slaves. A Medical and Demographic History of Slavery in the British West Indies, 1680–1834* (Cambridge, 1985), p.127.
5 ibid., pp.127–8.
6 Quoted in R. B. Sheridan, 'The Formation of Caribbean Plantation Society, 1689–1748', in Marshall, ed., *Oxford History*, p.402.
7 Ward, 'British West Indies', p.433.
8 Quoted in Sheridan, *Doctors and Slaves*, p.190.
9 ibid.
10 Philip D. Morgan, 'The Black Experience in the British Empire, 1680–1810', in Marshall, ed., *Oxford History*, p.470.
11 See, *inter alia*, Michael Craton, *Testing the Chains: Resistance to Slavery in the British West Indies* (Ithaca, NY, 1982); Elsa V. Coreia, *Slave Society in the British Leeward Islands at the End of the Eighteenth Century* (New Haven, 1965); Jerome S. Handler and Frederick W. Lange, *Plantation Slavery in Barbados: An Archaeological and Historical Investigation* (Cambridge, Mass., 1978); Sheridan, *Doctors and Slaves, passim*; Morgan, 'The Black Experience', pp.467–73.
12 The subject is, however, being opened up in recent specialist studies. See Douglas J. Hamilton, 'Patronage and Profit: Scottish Networks in the British West Indies, *c.* 1763–1807', unpublished Ph.D. thesis, University of Aberdeen, 1999; T. M. Devine, 'An Eighteenth Century Business Elite: Glasgow West India Merchants, *c.* 1750–1815', *Scottish Historical Review*, LVII, 163 (April 1978), pp.40–65; Michael Fry, *The Scottish Empire* (Edinburgh, 2001), pp. 70–82; G. Jackson, 'New Horizons in Trade', in T. M. Devine and G. Jackson, eds., *Glasgow*. Vol. 1, *Beginnings to 1830* (Manchester, 1995), pp.214–21. Also important are the works of American scholars such as R. B. Sheridan (in the volumes cited above) and Alan L. Karras, *Sojourners in the Sun: Scottish Migrants in Jamaica and the Chesapeake, 1740–1800* (Ithaca, N. Y., and London, 1992).
13 Quoted in L. M. Cullen, 'The Irish Diaspora of the Seventeenth and Eighteenth Centuries', in N. Canny, ed., *Europeans on the Move. Studies on European Migration, 1500–1800* (Oxford, 1994), p.127.

14 David Dobson, *Scottish Emigration to Colonial America, 1607–1785* (Athens, Georgia, 1994), pp.66–80.

15 Quoted in ibid., p.69.

16 Jack P. Greene, 'Changing Identity in the British Caribbean: Barbados as a Case Study', in Nicholas Canny and Anthony Pagden, eds., *Colonial Identity in the Atlantic World, 1500–1800* (Princeton, N. J., 1987), pp.213–66.

17 R. Ligon, *A True and Exact History of the Island of Barbados* (London, 1673), p.117.

18 Greene, 'Changing Identity in the British Caribbean', p.221.

19 ibid., p.224.

20 Ligon, *True and Exact History*, p.117.

21 Greene, 'Changing Identity in the British Caribbean', p.225.

22 Eric J. Graham, *A Maritime History of Scotland 1650–1790* (East Linton, 2002), pp.37–44.

23 E. Long, *The History of Jamaica or General State of the Antient and Modern State of that Island*, II (1774), p.286.

24 H. V. Bowen, *Elites, Enterprise and the Making of the British Overseas Empire 1688–1775* (Basingstoke, 1996), pp.150–51.

25 Analysed in Hamilton, 'Patronage and Profit', pp.35–8.

26 Sir W. Forbes, *Memoirs of a Banking House* (London and Edinburgh, 1860), p.39.

27 Long, *History of Jamaica*, II, pp.286–7.

28 Sheridan, *Sugar and Slaves*, pp.369, 375.

29 Long, *History of Jamaica*, II, pp.286–92.

30 Sheridan, *Doctors and Slaves*.

31 Quoted in Karras, *Sojourners in the Sun*, p.51.

32 ibid.

33 Quoted in Allan Karras, 'The World of Alexander Johnston: the Creolisation of Ambition, 1762–1787', *Historical Journal*, XXX, No. 1, p.70.

34 R. B. Sheridan, 'The Rise of a Colonial Gentry: a Case Study of Antigua, 1730–1775', *Economic History Review*, 2nd series, XIII, No. 3 (April 1961), pp.350–51.

35 Quoted in Hamilton, 'Patronage and Profit', p.208. See also L. Colley, *Britons* (London, 1996 edn.), pp.120–22.

36 Michael Fry, *The Dundas Despotism* (Edinburgh, 1992), pp.111–13; T. M. Devine, *The Scottish Nation, 1700–2000* (Harmondsworth, 1999), pp.197–200.

37 Devine, *Scottish Nation*, p.200.

38 Sheridan, *Sugar and Slaves*, p.373.

39 Quoted in Hamilton, 'Patronage and Profit', p.79.

40 National Library of Scotland, MS 5030, Thomas Riddoach to Charles Stewart, 5 January 1777.

41 Quoted in Karras, 'World of Alexander Johnston', p.70.

42 All references below to this text, unless otherwise stated, are from the edition edited by E. W. Andrews and C. McL. Andrews (New Haven, 1939), pp.19–143; pp.259–76.

43 Aberdeen University Library, Special Collections, MS 2070, Journal of Jonathan Troup, folios 17, 19.

44 C. Duncan Rice, *The Rise and Fall of Black Slavery* (London, 1975), p.155.

45 Quoted in C. Duncan Rice, 'Controversies over Slavery in Eighteenth and Nineteenth Century Scotland' in Lewis Perry and Michael Fellman, eds., *Antislavery Reconsidered: New Perspectives on the Abolitionists* (Baton Rouge, La., and London, 1979), p.30.

46 Quoted in Richard B. Sheridan, 'The Role of the Scots in the Economy and Society of the West Indies', in Vera Rubin and Arthur Tuden, eds., *Annals of the New York Academy of Sciences*. Vol. 292, *Comparative Perspectives on Slavery in New World Plantation Societies* (New York, 1977), p.100.

47 ibid.

48 David Hancock, 'Scots in the Slave Trade', in Ned C. Landsman, ed., *Nation and Province in the First British Empire* (London, 2001), pp.60–93.

49 Rice, *Black Slavery*, p.167.

50 Adam Smith, *The Theory of Moral Sentiments* (London, 1804), I, p.345.

51 Quoted in Rice, *Black Slavery*, p.176.

52 Quoted in C. Duncan Rice, 'Abolitionists and abolutionism in Aberdeen: a test case for the nineteenth-century anti-slavery movement, *Northern Scotland*, I, No. 1 (December 1972), p.70.

53 Sheridan, 'The Role of the Scots in the Economy and Society of the West Indies', p.103.

54 Quoted in ibid.

55 Victor Kiernan, 'Scottish Soldiers and the Conquest of India', in Grant G. Simpson, ed., *The Scottish Soldier Abroad, 1247–1967* (Edinburgh, 1992), p.98.

56 Linda Colley, *Britons*, p.139.

57 Quoted in Robin Fraser Callander, *A Pattern of Landownership in Scotland* (Finzean, 1987), p.136.

58 T. M. Devine, *The Transformation of Rural Scotland. Social Change and the Agrarian Economy 1660–1815* (Edinburgh, 1994), pp.60–64.

Chapter 11

1 Quoted in Alex M. Cain, *The Cornchest for Scotland: Scots in India* (Edinburgh, 1986), p.7.

2 John Riddy, 'Warren Hastings: Scotland's Benefactor?' in Geoffrey Carnall and Colin Nicholson, eds., *The Impeachment of Warren Hastings* (Edinburgh, 1989), p.42.

3 Cain, *Cornchest*, p.13.

4 G. J. Bryant, 'Scots in India in the Eighteenth Century', *Scottish Historical Review*, LXIV, 1: No. 177 (April 1985), pp.23–4.

5 Sir Lewis Namier and J. Brooke, eds., *History of Parliament: The House of Commons, 1754–1790* (London, 1964), Vol. 1, p.168.

6 Quoted in P. J. Marshall, *East Indian Fortunes: the British in Bengal in the Eighteenth Century* (Oxford, 1976), p.215.

7 Quoted in Bryant, 'Scots in India', p.27.

8 Marshall, *East Indian Fortunes*, p.217. See also William Dalrymple, *White Mughals* (London, 2002), pp.37, 410–11.

9 ibid., pp.218–19.

10 T. H. Hollingsworth, 'A Demographic Study of British Ducal Families', in D. V. Glass and D. E. C. Eversley, eds., *Population in History* (London, 1965), pp.361–3.

11 Marshall, *East Indian Fortunes*, p.255.

12 ibid., p.234.

13 Quoted in Lawrence James, *Raj. The Making and Unmaking of British India* (London, 1998 edn.), pp.47–8.

14 Thomas Bartlett, ' "This Famous island set in a Virginia Sea": Ireland in the British Empire, 1690–1801', in P. J. Marshall, ed., *The Oxford History of the British Empire. Vol. 2, The Eighteenth Century* (Oxford, 1998), p.272.

15 Quoted in Michael Fry, *The Dundas Despotism* (Edinburgh, 1992), p.111.

16 Quoted in James G. Parker, 'Scottish Enterprise in India, 1750–1914', in R. A. Cage, ed., *The Scots Abroad* (London, 1985), pp.197–8.

17 Linda Colley, *Britons: Forging the Nation 1707–1837* (London, 1996 edn.), p.12.

18 J. Drummond to William Drummond, 18 March 1731, quoted in George Kirk McGilvary, 'East India Patronage and the Political Management of Scotland, 1720–1774', unpublished Ph.D. thesis, Open University, 1989, p.207.

19 My italics. General S. Fraser to William Campbell of Succoth, 25 November 1769, quoted in Bryant, 'Scots in India', pp.29–30.

20 T. M. Devine, *The Scottish Nation, 1700–2000* (Harmondsworth, 1999), pp.18–22.

21 ibid.

22 See McGilvary, 'East India Patronage', and George K. McGilvary, 'Post-Union Scotland and the Indian Connection', *Cencrastus*, 37 (Summer 1990), pp.30–33; Riddy, 'Warren Hastings', pp.30–57; James Gordon Parker, 'The Directors of the East India Company, 1754–1790', unpublished Ph.D. thesis, University of Edinburgh, 1977.

23 The phrase comes from Riddy's essay. See Riddy, 'Warren Hastings', pp.30–57.

Chapter 12

1 Jeremy Bentham, *Panopticon Versus New South Wales: Two Letters to Lord Pelham* (London, 1812), p.7.

2 Quoted in David S. Macmillan, *Scotland and Australia, 1788–1850* (Oxford, 1967), p.29.

3 Quoted in L. C. Robson, *The Convict Settlers of Australia* (Melbourne, 1976), p.10.

4 Ian Donnachie, 'Scottish Criminals and Transportation to Australia', *Scottish Economic and Social History*, 4 (1984), pp.21–38.

5 Quoted in L. Evans and P. Nicholls, *Convicts and Colonial Society 1788–1853* (Sydney, 1976), p.133.

6 A. Marjoribanks, quoted in ibid., p.132.

7 Ian Donnachie, 'Scottish Criminals and Transportation to Australia', pp.21–38.

8 Robert Hughes, *The Fatal Shore* (New York, 1988 edn.), pp.175–6.

9 Quoted in ibid., p.178.

10 ibid.

11 Macmillan, *Scotland and Australia, passim.*

12 *Edinburgh Review*, 32, No. 63, pp.46–7.

13 Quoted in Anon., 'It was a Vast Blank', in Eric Richards *et al.*, eds., *That Land of Exiles. Scots in Australia* (Edinburgh, 1988), p.57.

14 Hughes, *Fatal Shore*, p.110.

15 Quoted in A. G. L. Shaw, *Convicts and the Colonies* (London, 1966), p.93.

16 The others were John Hunter (1795–1800) and Sir Thomas Brisbane (1821–1825)

17 Quoted in *That Land of Exiles*, p.23.

18 Hughes, *Fatal Shore*, p.293.

19 Quoted in ibid., p.365.

20 Glyndwr Williams, 'The Pacific: Exploration and Exploitation', in P. J. Marshall, ed., *The Oxford History of the British Empire*. Vol. 2, *The Eighteenth Century* (Oxford, 1998), p.570.

21 Quoted in *That Land of Exiles*, p.52.

22 H. Reynolds, *The Other Side of the Frontier* (North Queensland, 1981); Richard Broome, *Aboriginal Australians: Black Response to White Dominance, 1788–1980* (Sydney, 1982).

23 Quoted in Don Watson, *Caledonia Australis. Scottish Highlanders on the Frontier of Australia* (Sydney, 1984), p.100.

24 ibid., p.166.

Chapter 13

1 Lawrence Stone, Introduction, in Lawrence Stone, ed., *An Imperial State at War* (London and New York, 1994), p.22.

2 John Brewer, *The Sinews of Power: War, Money and the English State, 1688–1783* (London, 1989).

3 ibid., p.42.

4 P. J. Marshall, 'Britain and the World in the Eighteenth Century: I, Reshaping the Empire', *Transactions of the Royal Historical Society*, 6th Series, VIII (1998), pp. 4–6.

5 Quoted in ibid., p.5.

6 Linda Colley, *Captives: Britain, Empire and the World 1600–1850* (London, 2002), pp.311–12.

7 Gerald Bryant, 'Officers of the East India Company's Army in the Days of Clive and Hastings', *Journal of Imperial and Commonwealth History*, VI, No. 3 (May 1978), pp.203–27.

8 J. E. Cookson, *The British Armed Nation 1793–1815* (Oxford, 1997), p.5.

9 Clive Emsley, *British Society and the French Wars 1793–1815* (London, 1979).

10 Heather Streets, 'Identity in the Highland Regiments in the Nineteenth Century: Soldier, Region, Nation', in Steve Murdoch and Andrew Mackillop, eds., *Fighting for Identity. Scottish Military Experience c.1550–1900* (Leiden and Boston, 2002), p.218.

11 Keith M. Brown, 'From Scottish Lords to British Officers: State Building, Elite Integration and the Army in the Seventeenth Century', in Norman Macdougall, ed., *Scotland and War AD 79–1918* (Edinburgh, 1991), p.143.

12 J. Hayes, 'Scottish Officers in the British Army, 1714–63', *Scottish Historical Review*, 37 (1958), p.24.

13 ibid., pp.24–5.

14 Bryant, 'Officers of the East India Company's Army', pp.203–27.

15 Eric Richards, 'Scotland and the Uses of the Atlantic Empire', in Bernard Bailyn and Philip D. Morgan, eds., *Strangers within the Realm: Cultural Margins of the First British Empire* (Chapel Hill, NC, and London, 1991), p.98.

16 John M. Mackenzie, 'Essay and Reflection: On Scotland and the Empire', *International History Review*, XV (1993), p.719.

17 Stephen Brumwell, *Redcoats. The British Soldier and War in the Americas 1755–1763* (Cambridge, 2002), p.88.

18 ibid., p.319.

19 Cookson, *British Armed Nation*, p.127.

20 ibid., p.128.

21 Linda Colley, *Britons. Forging the Nation 1707–1837* (London, 1996 edn.), pp. 310–11.

22 Eric J. Graham, *A Maritime History of Scotland, 1650–1790* (Edinburgh, 2002), pp.238, 296.

23 T. M. Devine, 'Transport Problems of Glasgow West India Merchants during the American War of Independence, 1775–83', *Transport History*, IV (1971), pp.266–304.

24 Steve Murdoch and Andrew Mackillop, Introduction, in Murdoch and Mackillop, eds., *Fighting for Identity*, p.xxxvi.

25 ibid.

26 Cookson, *British Armed Nation*, p.129.

27 D. M. Henderson, *Highland Soldier: A Social Study of the Highland Regiments 1820–1920* (Edinburgh, 1989), pp.7–8.

28 E. and A. Linklater, *The Black Watch: the History of the Royal Highland Regiment* (London, 1977), p.227.

29 J. M. Bulloch, *Territorial Soldiering in the North-East of Scotland during 1759–1814* (Aberdeen, 1914), p.230.

30 Cookson, *British Armed Nation*, p.130.

31 J. H. Treble, 'The Standard of Living of the Working Class', in T. M. Devine and R. Mitchison, eds., *People and Society in Scotland*. Vol. 1, 1760–1830 (Edinburgh, 1988), pp.188–226.

32 E. H. Hunt, 'Industrialisation and Regional Inequality: Wages in Britain, 1760–1914', *Journal of Economic History*, 46 (1986), pp.935–96. See also A. J. S. Gibson and T. C. Smout, *Prices, Food and Wages in Scotland 1550–1780* (Cambridge, 1995), pp.275–6.

33 Both verses quoted in Dauvit Horsbroch, 'Tae See Oursels as Ithers See Us: Scottish Military Identity from the Covenant to Victoria 1637–1837', in Murdoch and Mackillop, eds., *Fighting for Identity*, pp.119, 121–2.

34 Jan de Vries, *European Urbanisation, 1500–1800* (London, 1984), pp.39–48.

35 T. M. Devine, *The Scottish Nation, 1700–2000* (Harmondsworth, 1999), p.168.

36 Cookson, *British Armed Nation*, pp.141–3: A. Cunningham, *The Volunteer Force: A Social and Political History 1859–1908* (London, 1975).

37 Cookson, *British Armed Nation*, pp.142–3.

38 T. M. Devine, 'The Failure of Radical Reform in Scotland in the Late Eighteenth Century: The Social and Economic Context', in T. M. Devine, ed., *Conflict and Stability in Scottish Society 1700–1850* (Edinburgh, 1990), pp.51–64.

39 J. E. Cookson, 'The Napoleonic Wars, Military Scotland and Tory Highlandism in the Early Nineteenth Century', *Scottish Historical Review*, LXXVIII, 1: No. 205 (April 1999), pp.60–75.

40 Quoted in David Allan, *Scotland in the Eighteenth Century* (Harlow, 2002), p.38. See also John Robertson, *The Scottish Enlightenment and the Militia Issue* (Edinburgh, 1985).

41 E. W. McFarland, *Ireland and Scotland in the Age of Revolution* (Edinburgh, 1984), p.180.

42 W. C. Cooper, *The Story of Georgia* (New York, 1938), Vol. 1, p.1.

43 *Boston Newsletter*, 23 February to 2 March 1719, quoted in Allan I. Macinnes, Marjory-Ann D. Harper and Linda G. Fryer, eds., *Scotland and the Americas, c.1650– c.1939: A Documentary Source Book* (Edinburgh, 2002), p.103.

44 By Dr Andrew Mackillop. See his *More Fruitful than the Soil. Army, Empire and the Scottish Highlands, 1715–1815*, (East Linton, 2000), p.236.

45 ibid., p.150.

46 S. E. M. Carpenter, 'Patterns of Recruitment of the Highland Regiments of the British Army, 1756 to 1815', unpublished M.Litt. thesis, University of St Andrews, 1977, p.75.

47 Mackillop, *More Fruitful than the Soil*, p.115.

48 B. P. Lenman, *The Jacobite Clans of the Great Glen 1650–1784* (London, 1984), p.212.

49 Carpenter, 'Patterns of Recruitment', pp.103–4.

50 Heather Streets, 'Identity in the Highland Regiments in the Nineteenth Century: Soldier, Region, Nation', in Murdoch and Mackillop, ed., *Fighting for Identity*, p.222.

51 Quoted in William Donaldson, *The Jacobite Song* (Aberdeen, 1988), p.46.

52 ibid.

53 *Glasgow Journal*, 28 April 1746.

54 Quoted in W. A. Speck, *The Butcher: the Duke of Cumberland and the Suppression of the '45* (Oxford, 1981), p.174.

55 *Gentleman's Magazine*, IX (June 1739).

56 Quoted in Carpenter, 'Patterns of Recruitment', p.33.

57 W. Cobbett, *The Parliamentary History of England from the Earliest Period to 1803*, Vol. XIV, (1816), p.728.

58 Lenman, *Jacobite Clans*, p.190.

59 Brumwell, *Redcoats*, p.270.

60 New Edition (Inverness, 1885), p.288.

61 Mackillop, *More Fruitful than the Soil*, pp.216–17.

62 Robert Clyde, *From Rebel to Hero. The Image of the Highlander 1745–1830* (East Linton, 1995), p.161.

63 Brumwell, *Redcoats*, p.270.

64 Fryer, Harper and Macinnes, eds., *Scotland and the Americas*, p.108; Stephen Wood, *The Scottish Soldier* (Manchester, 1987), p.36.

65 D. Stewart, *Sketches of the Character, Manners and Present State of the Highlanders of Scotland* (repr. Edinburgh, 1877), Vol. 1, p.303.

66 Mackillop, 'For King, Country and Regiment? Motive and Identity in Highland Soldiering 1746–1815', in Murdoch and Mackillop, eds., *Fighting for Identity*, pp.185–212.

67 Quoted in Leah Leneman, *Living in Atholl, 1685–1785* (Edinburgh, 1986), p.140.

68 Sir George S. Mackenzie, *General View of the Agriculture of the Counties of Ross and Cromarty* (London, 1813), p.298.

69 Mackillop, *More Fruitful than the Soil*, pp.170, 177.

70 Brumwell, *Redcoats*, pp.281–2.

71 Cookson, *British Armed Nation*, pp.137–8.

72 ibid., pp.132–3.

73 Mackillop, *More Fruitful than the Soil*, p.144.

74 Eric Richards, *A History of the Highland Clearances: Agrarian Change and the Evictions, 1746–1886* (London, 1982), pp.152–3.

75 T. M. Devine, 'Social Responses to Agrarian Improvement: the Highland and Lowland Clearances in Scotland', in R. A. Houston and I. D. Whyte, eds., *Scottish Society, 1500–1800* (Cambridge, 1989), pp.160–61.

Chapter 14

1 I. D. Whyte, *Scotland before the Industrial Revolution* (Harlow, 1995), pp.291–309, 328–33; T. C. Smout, 'Where had the Scottish Economy Got to by the Third Quarter of the Eighteenth Century?' in I. Hont and M. Ignatieff, eds., *Wealth and Virtue* (Cambridge, 1983), pp.45–72.

2 T. M. Devine, *The Transformation of Rural Scotland. Social Change and the Agrarian Economy, 1660–1815* (Edinburgh, 1994), pp.19–35; Allan I.

Macinnes, *Clanship, Commerce and the House of Stuart, 1603–1788* (East Linton, 1996), pp.210–34.

3 T. M. Devine, 'Scotland', in P. Clark, ed., *The Cambridge Urban History of Britain*, Vol. 2 (Cambridge, 2000), pp.151–64.

4 Devine, *Transformation of Rural Scotland*, pp.19–35.

5 N. F. R. Crafts, *British Economic Growth during the Industrial Revolution* (Oxford, 1985).

6 Jan de Vries, *European Urbanisation, 1500–1800* (London, 1987).

7 M. Gray, 'Migration in the Rural Lowlands of Scotland, 1750–1850', in T. M. Devine and D. Dickson, eds., *Ireland and Scotland 1600–1850* (Edinburgh, 1983), pp.104–17.

8 Sir J. Sinclair, *Analysis of the Statistical Account of Scotland* (London, 1826), p.321.

9 John Butt, 'The Scottish Iron and Steel Industry before the Hot-Blast', *Journal of the West of Scotland Iron and Steel Institute*, 73 (1966).

10 Christopher A. Whatley, *The Industrial Revolution in Scotland* (Cambridge, 1997), pp.22–30.

11 Sinclair, *Analysis*, p.321.

12 Norman Murray, *The Scottish Handloom Weavers, 1790–1850. A Social History* (Edinburgh, 1978), pp.13–39.

13 The essays in T. M. Devine and R. Mitchison, eds., *People and Society in Scotland*. Vol. 1, *1760–1830* (Edinburgh, 1988) provide much detail on this point. See also Christopher A. Whatley, *Scottish Society 1707–1830* (Manchester, 2000), pp.219–300.

14 For the most recent interpretations of this process see T. M. Devine, *Clanship to Crofters' War. The Social Transformation of the Scottish Highlands* (Manchester, 1994), pp.32–53; Allan I. Macinnes, 'Highland Society in the Era of "Improvement"', in A. Cooke *et al.*, eds., *Modern Scottish History 1707 to the Present*. Vol. 1, *The Transformation of Scotland, 1707–1850* (East Linton, 1998), pp.177–202.

15 M. Gray, 'Scottish Emigration: the Social Impact of Agrarian Change in the Rural Lowlands, 1775–1875', *Perspectives in American History*, VII (1973), pp.112–31; Devine, *Transformation of Rural Scotland*, pp.36–59.

16 T. M. Devine, 'Scottish Farm Service in the Agricultural Revolution', in T. M. Devine, ed., *Farm Servants and Labour in Lowland Scotland 1770–1914* (Edinburgh, 1996 edn.), pp.1–8.

17 There is a full modern bibliography in Whatley, *Industrial Revolution in Scotland*, pp.92–103.

18 See, for example, James Pagan, *Sketches of the History of Glasgow* (Glasgow, 1847); Senex (J. M. Reid), *Glasgow Past and Present*, 3 vols. (Glasgow, 1884); George Stewart, *Progress of Glasgow* (Glasgow, 1883).

19 M. Postlethwayt, *The African Trade, the Great Pillar and Support of the British Plantation Trade in America* (London, 1745).

20 For example, Michael Fry, *The Scottish Empire* (Edinburgh, 2001) has little to say about the eighteenth-century linkages, though more about those in the Victorian era.

21 Neal Ascherson, *Stone Voices. The Search for Scotland* (London, 2002), p.259.

22 ibid., p.260.

23 Eric Williams, *Capitalism and Slavery* (1944; London, 1964), p.105.

24 David Richardson, 'The British Empire and the Atlantic Slave Trade, 1660–1807', in P. J. Marshall, ed., *The Oxford History of the British Empire*. Vol. 2, *The Eighteenth Century* (Oxford, 1998), p.461; C. H. Feinstein, 'Capital Accumulation and the Industrial Revolution', in R. Floud and D. McCluskey, eds., *The Economic History of Britain since 1700* (Cambridge, 1981), Vol. 1, p.131.

25 See, for example, William Darty, Jnr., 'British Industry and the West Indian Plantations', in J. E. Inikori and S. L. Engerman, eds., *The Atlantic Slave Trade* (Durham, NC, 1992), pp.253–79. For a recent more general and more positive assessment of the relationship between Empire and the British economy, see Jacob M. Price, 'The Imperial Economy, 1700–1776', in Marshall, ed., *Oxford History of the British Empire*, pp.97–9.

26 P. J. Marshall, introduction, in Marshall, ed., *Oxford History of the British Empire*, p.17.

27 Whatley, *Scottish Society*, p.77.

28 A. J. S. Gibson and T. C. Smout, *Prices, Food and Wages in Scotland 1550–1780* (Cambridge, 1995), pp.231–2, 343–56.

29 Gordon Jackson, 'New Horizons in Trade', in T. M. Devine and G. Jackson, eds., *Glasgow*. Vol. 1, *Beginnings to 1830* (Manchester, 1995), pp.216–17, 227.

30 ibid., p.227.

31 T. M. Devine, 'Colonial Commerce and the Scottish Economy, c. 1730–1815', in L. M. Cullen and T. C. Smout, eds., *Comparative Aspects of Scottish and Irish Economic and Social History, 1600–1900* (Edinburgh, 1977), p.181.

32 Michael Fry, 'A Commercial Empire: Scotland and British Expansion in the Eighteenth Century', in T. M. Devine and J. R. Young, eds., *Eighteenth Century Scotland. New Perspectives* (East Linton, 1999), pp.53–69.

33 T. Hunter, ed., *Extracts from the Records of the Convention of Royal Burghs 1759–1769* (Edinburgh, 1918), p.vi.

34 Eric J. Graham, *A Maritime History of Scotland, 1650–1790* (East Linton, 2002), p.229.

35 Quoted in ibid., p.3.

36 W. Seton of Pitmedden, *A Speech in Parliament on the First Article of the Treaty of Union* (Edinburgh, 1706).

37 Graham, *Maritime History*, pp.207–14.

38 ibid., p.296.

39 T. M. Devine, 'The Colonial Trades and Industrial Investment in Scotland, *c.* 1700–1815', in P. Emmer and F. Caastra, eds., *The Organisation of Interoceanic Trade in European Expansion, 1450–1800* (Aldershot, 1996).

40 Devine, 'Colonial Commerce and the Scottish Economy', pp.177–90.

41 T. M. Devine, *The Tobacco Lords: A Study of the Tobacco Merchants of Glasgow and their Trading Activities, 1740–90* (Edinburgh, 1990 repr.), pp.3–17.

42 T. M. Devine, 'Glasgow Colonial Merchants and Land 1770–1815', in J. T. Ward and R. G. Wilson, eds., *Land and Industry: the Landed Estate in the Industrial Revolution* (Newton Abbott, 1971).

43 ibid.

44 J. R. McCulloch, ed., Adam Smith, *An Inquiry into the Nature and Causes of the Wealth of Nations* (Edinburgh, 1863 edn.), Book III, p.181.

45 Sir John Sinclair, *General Report of the Agricultural State and Political Circumstances of Scotland* (Edinburgh, 1791–8), VII, pp.377–9.

46 Devine, 'Glasgow Colonial Merchants and Land'.

47 W. P. Robinson, 'Richard Oswald the Peacemaker', *Ayrshire Archaeological and Natural History Collections*, 2nd Series, III (1959), pp.119–35.

48 Devine, *Tobacco Lords*, p.26.

49 Douglas J. Hamilton, 'Patronage and Profit: Scottish Networks in the British West Indies, *c.* 1763–1807', unpublished Ph.D. thesis, University of Aberdeen, 1999, p.291; R. B. Sheridan, 'The Wealth of Jamaica in the Eighteenth Century', *Economic History Review*, 2nd Series, XVIII (1965), pp.309–10.

50 George Kirk McGilvary, 'East India Patronage and the Political Management of Scotland, 1720–1774, unpublished Ph.D. thesis, Open University (1989), pp.298–9.

51 P. Lawson and J. Phillips, ' "Our Execrable Banditti"; Perceptions of Nabobs in Mid-Eighteenth Century Britain', *Albion*, XVI (1984), p.227.

52 Quoted in ibid., pp.230, 236.

53 John Galt, *The Last of the Lairds* (Edinburgh, 1976 edn.), p.25.

54 George K. McGilvary, 'Post-Union Scotland and the Indian Connection', *Cencrastus*, 37 (Summer 1990), pp.30–33.

55 McGilvary, 'East India Patronage', pp.242–5.

56 Robin Fraser Callander, *A Pattern of Landownership in Scotland* (Finzean, 1987), p.75.

57 P. J. Marshall, *East Indian Fortunes: the British in Bengal in the Eighteenth Century* (Oxford, 1976), p.2237.

58 Devine, *Transformation of Rural Scotland*, pp.45–6, 59, 100.

59 Alastair J. Durie, *The Scottish Linen Industry in the Eighteenth Century* (Edinburgh, 1979), pp.158–60.

60 John Naismith, *Thoughts on Various Objects of Industry Pursued in Scotland* (Edinburgh, 1790), p.93.

61 Durie, *Scottish Linen Industry*, pp.151–2.

62 ibid., p.152.

63 Michael Hechter, *Internal Colonialism: the Celtic Fringe in British Natural Development* (London, 1975), pp.79–123.

64 Macinnes, *Clanship*, pp.226–33.

65 T. M. Devine, *The Great Highland Famine. Hunger, Emigration and the Scottish Highlands in the Nineteenth Century* (Edinburgh, 1988), p.212.

66 T. M. Devine, 'The Emergence of the New Elite in the Western Highlands and Islands, 1800–1860', in T. M. Devine, ed., *Improvement and Enlightenment* (Edinburgh, 1989, pp.130, 140–41.

67 Allan I. Macinnes, 'Landownership, Land Use and the Elite Enterprise in Scottish Gaeldom: From Clanship to Clearance in Argyllshire, 1688–1858', in T. M. Devine, ed., *Scottish Elites* (Edinburgh, 1994), pp.19, 25–8.

68 Macinnes, *Clanship*, p.233.

69 A. E. J. Cavendish, *An Reisimeid Chataich* (1928), pp.5, 49.

70 Marianne McLean, *The People of Glengarry: Highlanders in Transition, 1745–1820* (Toronto, 1991), pp.146–7.

71 Quoted in Robert Clyde, *From Rebel to Hero. The Image of the Highlander 1745–1830* (East Linton, 1995), p.187.

72 T. M. Truxes, *Irish-American Trade 1660–1783* (Cambridge, 1988), pp.34, 41, 164–5.

73 Graham, *Maritime History*, pp.240–47.

74 Devine, *Great Highland Famine*, pp.1–3.

75 ibid., pp.212–25.

76 Allan I. Macinnes, 'Highland Society in the Era of "Improvement"', in Cooke *et al.*, eds., *The Transformation of Scotland* p.195.

77 I. F. Grant, *The MacLeods, the History of a Clan* (London, 1959), pp.516–18.

78 Macinnes, 'Landownership, Land Use and The Elite Enterprise', p.19.

79 Devine, 'Emergence of the New Elite', pp.108–10.

80 ibid., pp.110–22.

81 For a full account see Andrew Mackillop, *More Fruitful than the Soil. Army, Empire and the Scottish Highlands, 1715–1815* (East Linton, 2000), pp.143–67.

82 ibid., pp.164–5; T. M. Devine, 'Highland Landowners and the Highland Potato Famine', in Leah Leneman, ed., *Perspectives in Scottish Social History* (Aberdeen, 1988), pp.141–62.

83 ibid., p.147; Eric Richards, *A History of the Highland Clearances: Agrarian Change and the Evictions, 1746–1886* (London, 1982), pp.150–54.

84 Alexander Mackenzie, *History of the Highland Clearances* (Inverness, 1883), p. 2, quoted Donald MacLeod's *Gloomy Memories of the Highlands* (1840–41).

Chapter 15

1 J. G. Lockhart, *Memoirs of the Life of Sir Walter Scott* (Edinburgh, 1837), Vol. 2, pp.110–11.

2 Quoted in John Prebble, *The King's Jaunt* (London, 1988), p.11.

3 P. H. Scott, 'The last purely Scotch Age', in D. Gifford, ed., *The History of Scottish literature. Vol. 3, The Nineteenth Century* (Aberdeen, 1988), p.11.

4 Quoted in Peter Womack, *Improvement and Romance* (London, 1989), p.80.

5 Richard J. Finlay, 'The Rise and Fall of Popular Imperialism in Scotland 1850–1950', *Scottish Geographical Magazine*, 113 (1997), pp.13–14.

6 Quoted in Colin Kidd, 'Sentiment, Race and Revival: Scottish Identities in the Aftermath of Enlightenment', in L. Brockliss and D. Eastwood, eds., *A Union of Multiple Identities* (Manchester, 1997), p.111.

7 T. C. Smout, 'Problems of Nationalism, Identity and Improvement in Later Eighteenth-Century Scotland', in T. M. Devine, ed., *Improvement and Enlightenment* (Edinburgh, 1989), p.13.

8 Kidd, 'Sentiment, Race and Revival', p.111; Colin Kidd, *Subverting Scotland's Past* (Cambridge, 1993), pp.208, 210, 213.

9 B. P. Lenman, *The Jacobite Clans of the Great Glen 1650–1784* (Edinburgh, 1984), pp.179, 202, 208.

10 L. M. Cullen, 'Scotland and Ireland, 1600–1800: their Role in the Evolution of British Society', in R. A. Houston and I. D. Whyte, eds., *Scottish Society 1500–1800* (Cambridge, 1989), pp.241–2.

11 T. M. Devine, *The Scottish Nation, 1700–2000* (Harmondsworth, 1999), pp.196–218; *idem*, 'The Failure of Radical Reform in Scotland in the late Eighteenth Century: the Social and Economic Context', in T. M. Devine, ed., *Conflict and Stability in Scottish Society 1700–1850* (Edinburgh, 1990), pp.51–64.

12 Devine, *Scottish Nation*, pp.144–5.

13 Cullen, 'Scotland and Ireland', pp.241–4.

14 Quoted in Michael Fry, *The Dundas Despotism* (Edinburgh, 1992), p.111.

15 George Kirk McGilvary, 'East India Patronage and the Political Management of Scotland, 1720–1774', unpublished Ph.D. thesis, Open University, 1989, *passim*.

16 John M. MacKenzie, 'Essay and Reflection: On Scotland and the Empire', *International History Review*, XV (1993), pp.717–18.

17 L. Colley, *Britons: Forging the Nation 1707–1837* (London, 1993); J. Brewer, *The Sinews of Power: War, Money and the English State, 1688–1783* (London, 1989); R. Samuel, ed., *Patriotism. The Making and Unmaking of British National Identity* (London, 1989).

18 T. M. Devine, *The Transformation of Rural Scotland. Social Change and the Agrarian Economy, 1660–1815* (Edinburgh, 1994), pp.36–110.

19 ibid.; Colley, *Britons*, p.168; B. A. Holderness, 'Prices, Productivity and Output', in G. E. Mingay, ed., *The Agrarian History of England and Wales*. Vol. 6, *1750–1850* (Cambridge, 1989), pp.179–83.

20 Devine, *Transformation of Rural Scotland*, pp.55–7.

21 ibid., pp.37–9.

22 M. Glendinning, Ranald Macinnes and Aonghus MacKechnie, *A History of Scottish Architecture* (Edinburgh, 1996), pp.147–61.

23 Colley, *Britons*, p.170.

24 John S. Shaw, *The Political History of Eighteenth Century Scotland* (London, 1999), p.63.

25 Colley, *Britons*, p.173. Colley, of course, does not assent to this view. Her position is that the Scottish nobility became more 'British' than 'English'. See also Shaw, *Political History*, p.37.

26 Richard J. Finlay, 'Keeping the Covenant: Scottish National Identity', in T. M. Devine and J. R. Young, eds., *Eighteenth Century Scotland. New Perspectives* (East Linton, 1999), pp.122–33.

27 C. A. Whatley, 'Royal Day, People's Day: the Monarch's Birthday in Scotland *c.* 1660–1860', in Roger Mason and Norman Macdougall, eds., *People and Power in Scotland* (Edinburgh, 1992), p.183; J. Brims, 'The Scottish "Jacobins", Scottish Nationalism and the British Union', in Roger A. Mason, ed., *Scotland and England, 1286–1815* (Edinburgh, 1987).

28 Andrew Mackillop, *More Fruitful than the Soil. Army, Empire and the Scottish Highlands, 1715–1815* (East Linton, 2000), pp.204–33.

29 J. A. Smith, 'Some Eighteenth Century Ideas of Scotland', in N. T. Phillipson and R. Mitchison, eds., *Scotland in the Age of Improvement* (Edinburgh, 1970), pp.107–24.

30 Colin Kidd, 'North Britishness and the Nature of Eighteenth-Century British Patriotisms', *Historical Journal*, 39, No. 2 (1996), pp.361–82.

31 T. M. Devine, *Clanship to Crofters' War. The Social Transformation of the Scottish Highlands* (Manchester, 1994), pp.84–8.

32 Peter Womack, *Improvement and Romance* (London, 1989), p.145.

33 John Prebble, *The King's Jaunt* (London, 1988).
34 ibid., p.103.
35 H. R. Trevor-Roper, 'The Invention of Tradition: the Highland Tradition of Scotland', in E. J. Hobsbawm and T. O. Ranger, eds., *The Invention of Tradition* (Oxford, 1983), p.24.
36 ibid., p.30.
37 Murray G. A. Pittock, 'The Jacobite Cult', in Edward J. Cowan and Richard J. Finlay, eds., *Scottish History. The Power of the Past* (Edinburgh, 2002), p.195.
38 ibid.
39 J. E. Cookson, *The British Armed Nation 1793–1815* (Oxford, 1997), p.149.
40 J. E. Cookson, 'The Napoleonic Wars, Military Scotland and Tory Highlandism in the Early Nineteenth Century', *Scottish Historical Review*, LXXVIII (April 1999), p.63.
41 D. Stewart, *Sketches of the Character, Manners and Present State of the Highlanders of Scotland* (2 vols., repr. Edinburgh, 1877), I, pp.vi–ix.
42 MacKenzie, 'Scotland and Empire', pp.726–7.
43 Stewart, *Sketches*, I, pp.446ff.
44 Quoted in William Donaldson, *The Jacobite Song* (Aberdeen, 1988), p.92.
45 J. Barke, *Poems and Songs of Robert Burns* (London, 1983), p.552.
46 Cookson, *British Armed Nation*, pp.128–9.
47 Quoted in Robert Clyde, *From Rebel to Hero. The Image of the Highlander 1745–1830* (East Linton, 1995), p.177.
48 Donaldson, *Jacobite Song*, p.94.
49 Leah Leneman, 'A New Role for a Lost Cause: Lowland Romantication of the Jacobite Highlander', in L. Leneman, ed., *Perspectives in Scottish Social History* (Aberdeen, 1988), pp.107–24.
50 Donaldson, *Jacobite Song, passim*.
51 ibid., p.94.

Bibliography

This contains works cited in the list of references and other texts which have proved helpful in developing the thinking behind the book as a whole and key themes within it.

Alf Åberg, 'Scottish Soldiers in the Swedish Armies in the Sixteenth and Seventeenth Centuries', in Grant G. Simpson, ed., *Scotland and Scandinavia, 800–1800* (Edinburgh, 1990).

I. H. Adams and M. Somerville, *Cargoes of Despair and Hope* (Edinburgh, 1993).

J. R. R. Adams, *The Printed Word and the Common Man: Popular Culture in Ulster 1700–1900* (Belfast, 1987).

William Forbes Adams, *Ireland and Irish Emigration to the New World from 1815 to the Famine* (Yale, 1832).

W. J. Addison, ed., *A Roll of the Graduates of the University of Glasgow* (Glasgow, 1898).

Sydney E. Ahlstrom, 'The Scottish Philosophy and American Theology', *Church History*, XXIV (1955).

Donald Harmen Akenson, 'Irish Migration to North America, 1800–1920', in Andy Bielenberg, ed., *The Irish Diaspora* (Harlow, 2000).

David Allan, *Virtue, Learning and the Scottish Enlightenment* (Edinburgh, 1993).

David Allan, *Scotland in the Eighteenth Century* (Harlow, 2002).

Ian G. Anderson, ed., *Scotsmen in the Service of the Czars* (Edinburgh, 1990).

Ian G. Anderson, 'The Scots Soldier of Fortune', in Ian G Anderson, ed., *Scotsmen in the Service of the Czars* (Edinburgh, 1990).

R. D. Anderson, *Scottish Education since the Reformation* (Dundee, 1997).

R. G. W. Anderson and A. D. C. Simpson, eds., *The Early Years of the Edinburgh Medical School* (Edinburgh, 1976).

Evangeline Walker Andrews and Charles McLean Andrews, eds., *Journal of a Lady of Quality; being the Narrative of a Journey from Scotland to the West Indies, North Carolina, and Portugal, in the years 1774 to 1776* (New Haven, 1939).

Anon., *Scotland's Lament for their Misfortunes* (Edinburgh, 1700).

Anon., *A Candid Enquiry into the Causes of the Late and Intended Migrations from Scotland* (n.d.).

Anon., 'It was a Vast Blank', in Eric Richards *et al.*, eds., *That Land of Exiles. Scots in Australia* (Edinburgh, 1988).

Anon., 'Scots Traders were the Envy of Europe', *Scotland's Story*, 18 (2000).

David Armitage, 'The Scottish Vision of Empire: Intellectual Origins of the Darien Venture', in John Robertson, ed., *A Union for Empire: Political Thought and the British Union of 1707* (Cambridge, 1995).

David Armitage, 'Making the Empire British: Scotland in the Atlantic World, 1542–1707', *Past and Present*, 155 (May 1997).

David Armitage, 'Greater Britain: A Useful Category of Historical Analysis?', *American Historical Review*, 104, No. 2 (April 1999).

David Armitage, *The Ideological Origins of the British Empire* (Cambridge, 2000).

Neal Ascherson, *Stone Voices. The Search for Scotland* (London, 2002).

B. Bailyn, ed., *Pamphlets of the American Revolution*, Vol. 1 (Harvard, 1965), Introductory Essay, 'The Transforming Radicalism of the American Revolution'.

Bernard Bailyn, *The Peopling of British North America. An Introduction* (London, 1986).

Bernard Bailyn, *Voyagers to the West: Emigration from Britain to America on the Eve of the Revolution* (London, 1986).

Bernard Bailyn and Philip D. Morgan, eds., *Strangers within the Realm: Cultural Margins of the First British Empire* (Chapel Hill, NC and London, 1991).

Dudley Baines, *Emigration from Europe 1815–1930* (Basingstoke, 1991).

J. Barke, *Poems and Songs of Robert Burns* (London, 1983).

J. W. Barnhill and Paul Dukes, 'North-east Scots in Muscovy in the Seventeenth Century', *Northern Scotland*, I, No. 1 (1972).

Thomas Bartlett, '"This famous island set in a Virginian sea": Ireland in the British Empire, 1690–1801', in P. J. Marshall, ed., *The Oxford History of the British Empire. Vol. 2, The Eighteenth Century* (Oxford, 1998).

D. A. Baugh, 'Maritime Strength and Atlantic Commerce. The Uses of a "Grand Marine Empire"', in Lawrence Stone, ed., *An Imperial State at War* (London, 1994).

Priscilla Bawcutt and Bridget Henisch, 'Scots Abroad in the Fifteenth Century: The Princesses Margaret, Isabella and Eleanor', in Elizabeth

Ewan and Maureen M. Meikle, eds., *Women in Scotland, c. 1100–c.1750* (East Linton, 1999).

C. A. Bayly, ed., *The New Cambridge History of India*. Vol. 2, 1, *Indian Society and the Making of the British Empire* (Cambridge, 1988).

C. A. Bayly, *Imperial Meridian: The British Empire and the World, 1780–1830* (London, 1989).

C. A. Bayly, ed., *The Raj: India and the British 1600–1947* (London, 1990).

C. A. Bayly, 'The British Military-Fiscal State and Indigenous Resistance: India 1750–1820', in Patrick Tuck, ed., *The East India Company: 1600–1858*, V: *Warfare, Expansion and Resistance* (London, 1998).

J. C. Beckett, *The Making of Modern Ireland, 1603–1923* (London, 1966).

J. C. Beckett, *Confrontations: Studies in Irish History* (London, 1972).

Göran Behre, 'Gothenburg in Stuart War Strategy 1649–1760', in Grant G. Simpson, ed., *Scotland and Scandinavia, 800–1800* (Edinburgh, 1990).

Jeremy Bentham, *Panopticon Versus New South Wales: Two Letters to Lord Pelham* (London, 1812).

Jonas Berg and Bo Lagercrantz, *Scots in Sweden* (Stockholm, 1962).

C. J. Berry, *Social Theory of the Scottish Enlightenment* (Edinburgh, 1997).

Rowland Berthoff, *British Immigrants in Industrial America, 1790–1950* (Cambridge, 1953).

Rowland Berthoff, 'Celtic Mist Over the South', *Journal of Southern History*, LII (1986).

Anna Biegańska, 'James Murray: A Scot in the Making of the Polish Navy', *Scottish Slavonic Review*, 3 (1984).

Anna Biegańska, 'A Note on the Scots in Poland, 1550–1800', in T. C. Smout, ed., *Scotland and Europe, 1200–1850* (Edinburgh, 1986).

Anna Biegańska, 'In Search of Tolerance: Scottish Catholics and Presbyterians in Poland', *Scottish Slavonic Review*, 17 (1991).

A. Biegańska, 'Scottish Immigrants in Poland', *Scottish Slavonic Review*, 19 (1991).

Andy Bielenberg, ed., *The Irish Diaspora* (Harlow, 2000).

Andy Bielenberg, 'Irish Emigration to the British Empire, 1700–1914', in Andy Bielenberg, ed., *The Irish Diaspora* (Harlow, 2000).

I. M. Bishop, 'The Education of Ulster Students at Glasgow University during the Eighteenth Century', unpublished M.A. thesis, Queen's University of Belfast, 1987.

H. Tyler Blethen and Curtis W. Wood, Jr., eds., *Ulster and North America: Transatlantic Perspectives on the Scotch-Irish* (Tuscaloosa, 1997).

H. Tyler Blethen and Curtis W. Wood, Jr., Introduction, in J. Tyler Blethen and Curtis W. Wood, Jr., eds., *Ulster and North America: Transatlantic Perspectives on the Scotch-Irish* (Tuscaloosa, 1997).

Elizabeth A. Bonner, 'Continuing the "Auld Alliance" in the Sixteenth

Century: Scots in France and French in Scotland', in Grant G. Simpson, ed., *The Scottish Soldier Abroad, 1247–1967* (Edinburgh, 1992).

H. V. Bowen, *Elites, Enterprise and the Making of the British Overseas Empire, 1688–1775* (Basingstoke, 1996).

Julian P. Boyd, *The Declaration of Independence and the Evolution of the Text* (Princeton, N. J., 1945).

Ciaran Brady, Mary O'Dowd and Brian Walker, eds., *Ulster: An Illustrated History* (London, 1989).

Ciaran Brady, 'Sixteenth-century Ulster and the Failure of Tudor Reform', in Ciaran Brady, Mary O'Dowd and Brian Walker, eds., *Ulster: An Illustrated History* (London, 1989).

John Brewer, *The Sinews of Power: War, Money and the English State, 1688–1783* (London, 1989).

Carl Bridge, ed., *New Perspectives in Australian History* (London, 1990).

J. Brims, 'The Scottish "Jacobins", Scottish Nationalism and the British Union', in Roger A. Mason, ed., *Scotland and England, 1286–1815* (Edinburgh, 1987).

A. Broadie, *The Tradition of Scottish Philosophy* (Edinburgh, 1990).

Alexander Broadie, ed., *The Scottish Enlightenment. An Anthology* (Edinburgh, 1997).

Alexander Broadie, *The Scottish Enlightenment.* (Edinburgh, 2001).

W. R. Brock, *Scotus Americanus* (Edinburgh, 1982).

L. Brockliss and D. Eastwood, eds., *A Union of Multiple Identities* (Manchester, 1997).

Tom Brooking, *Lands for the People?: The Highland Clearances and the Colonisation of New Zealand: A Biography of John McKenzie* (Dunedin, 1996).

Richard Broome, *Aboriginal Australians: Black Response to White Dominance, 1788–1980* (Sydney, 1982).

Andrew Brown, *History of Glasgow* (Glasgow, 1795).

J. S. A. Brown, ' "A Parcel of Upstart Scotchmen" ', *The Beaver*, 68 (1988).

Keith M. Brown, 'From Scottish Lords to British Officers: State Building, Elite Integration and the Army in the Seventeenth Century', in Norman Macdougall, ed., *Scotland and War AD 79–1918* (Edinburgh, 1991).

Keith M. Brown, 'Reformation to Union, 1560–1707', in R. A. Houston and W. W. J. Knox, eds., *The New Penguin History of Scotland* (London, 2001).

Wallace Brown, *The King's Friends* (Providence, Rhode Island, 1965).

Wallace Brown, *The Good Americans. The Loyalists in the American Revolution* (New York, 1969).

Stephen Brumwell, *Redcoats. The British Soldier and the War in the Americas 1755–1763* (Cambridge, 2002).

Deborah C. Brunton, 'The Transfer of Medical Education: Teaching at the Edinburgh and Philadelphia Medical Schools', in Richard B. Sher and Jeffrey R. Smitten, eds., *Scotland and America in the Age of the Enlightenment* (Edinburgh, 1990).

Gerald Bryant, 'Officers of the East India Company's Army in the Days of Clive and Hastings', *Journal of Imperial and Commonwealth History*, VI, 3 (May 1978).

G. J. Bryant, 'Scots in India in the Eighteenth Century', *Scottish Historical Review*, LXIV, 177, (April 1985).

J. M. Bulloch, *Territorial Soldiering in the North-East of Scotland during 1759–1814* (Aberdeen, 1914).

J. M. Bumsted, '"Things in the Womb of Time": Ideas of American Independence, 1633 to 1763', *William and Mary Quarterly*, 3rd Series, XXXI (1974).

J. M. Bumsted, 'Settlement by Chance: Lord Selkirk and Prince Edward Island', *Canadian Historical Review*, LIX (1978).

J. M. Bumsted, *The Scots in Canada* (Ottawa, 1982).

J. M. Bumsted, *The People's Clearance* (Edinburgh, 1982).

J. M. Bumsted, 'The Scottish Diaspora: Emigration to British North America, 1763–1815', in Ned C. Landsman, ed., *Nation and Province in the First British Empire* (London, 2001).

G. Burnet, *History of His Own Times* (Oxford, 1825).

John Hill Burton, *The Scot Abroad* (Edinburgh, 1864).

John Butt, 'The Scottish Iron and Steel Industry before the Hot-Blast', *Journal of the West of Scotland Iron and Steel Institute*, 73 (1966).

R. A. Cage, ed., *The Scots Abroad* (London, 1985).

Alex M. Cain, *The Cornchest for Scotland: Scots in India* (Edinburgh, 1986).

Angus Calder, *Revolutionary Empire: The Rise of the English-Speaking Empires from the Fifteenth Century to the 1780s* (London, 1981).

Raymond Callahan, 'The Company's Army, 1757–1798', in Patrick Tuck, ed., *The East India Company: 1600–1858*, V: *Warfare, Expansion and Resistance* (London, 1998).

Robin Fraser Callander, *A Pattern of Landownership in Scotland* (Finzean, 1987).

James K. Cameron, 'Some Scottish Students and Teachers at the University of Leiden in the Late Sixteenth and Early Seveneenth Centuries', in Grant G. Simpson, ed., *Scotland and the Low Countries, 1124–1994* (East Linton, 1996).

Major Sir Duncan Campbell of Barcaldine, *Records of Clan Campbell in the Military Service of the Honourable East India Company 1600–1858* (London, 1925).

R. H. Campbell and A. S. Skinner, eds., *The Origins and Nature of the Scottish Enlightenment* (Edinburgh, 1982).

David Cannadine, 'Review Article: The Empire Strikes Back', *Past and Present*, 147 (May 1995).

Nicholas Canny, 'Migration and Opportunity: Britain, Ireland and the New World', *Irish Economic and Social History*, XII (1985).

Nicholas Canny and Anthony Pagden, eds., *Colonial Identity in the Atlantic World, 1500–1800* (Princeton, N. J., 1987).

N. Canny, ed., *Europeans on the Move. Studies on European Migration, 1500–1800* (Oxford, 1994).

Nicholas Canny, ed., *The Oxford History of the British Empire*. Vol. 1, *The Origins of Empire* (Oxford, 1998).

Nicholas Canny, 'Writing Atlantic History; or, Reconfiguring the History of Colonial British America', *Journal of American History*, 86, No. 3 (December 1999).

Nicholas Canny, *Making Ireland British, 1580–1650* (Oxford, 2001).

Alexander Carlyle, *Autobiography* (Edinburgh, 1861).

Geoffrey Carnall and Colin Nicholson, eds., *The Impeachment of Warren Hastings* (Edinburgh, 1989).

S. E. M. Carpenter, 'Patterns of Recruitment of the Highland Regiments of the British Army, 1756 to 1815', unpublished M.Litt. thesis, University of St Andrews, 1977.

Lois Green Carr, Philip D. Morgan and Jean B. Russo, eds., *Colonial Chesapeake Society* (Chapel Hill, NC and London, 1988).

Douglas Catterall, *Community without Borders. Scots Migrants and the Changing Face of Power in the Dutch Republic, c. 1600–1700* (Leyden, 2002).

A. E. J. Cavendish, *An Reisimeid Chataich* (1928).

Anand C. Chitnis, *The Scottish Enlightenment* (London, 1976).

Thorkild Lyby Christensen, 'Scoto-Danish relations in the sixteenth century', *Scottish Historical Review* 48 (1969).

Thorkild Lyby Christensen, 'Scots in Denmark in the Sixteenth Century', *Scottish Historical Review*, 49 (1970).

J. C. D. Clark, 'English History's Forgotten Context: Scotland, Ireland, Wales', *Historical Journal*, 32, No. 1 (1989).

P. Clark, ed., *The Cambridge Urban History of Britain*, Vol. 2 (Cambridge, 2000).

George Clarke, *The Later Stuarts, 1660–1714* (Oxford, 1955).

John Clive and Bernard Bailyn, 'England's Cultural Provinces: Scotland and America', *William and Mary Quarterly*, 3rd Series, XI (1954).

Robert Clyde, *From Rebel to Hero. The Image of the Highlander 1745–1830* (East Linton, 1995).

W. Cobbett, *The Parliamentary History of England from the Earliest Period to 1803*, Vol. XIV (1816).

Trevor Colbourn, ed., *Fame and the Founding Fathers: Essays by Douglass Adair* (Williamsburg, 1974).

L. Colley, *Britons: Forging the Nation 1707–1837* (London, 1993, 1996).

Linda Colley, *Captives: Britain, Empire and the World 1600–1850* (London, 2002).

Brenda Collins, 'The Origins of Irish Immigration to Scotland in the Nineteenth and Twentieth Centuries', in T. M. Devine, ed., *Irish Immigrants and Scottish Society in the Nineteenth and Twentieth Centuries* (Edinburgh, 1991).

Varnum Collins, *President Witherspoon: A Biography* (Princeton, NJ, 1953).

S. J. Connolly, 'Ulster Presbyterians: Religion, Culture and Politics, 1660–1850', in H. Tyler Blethen and Curtis W. Wood, Jr., eds., *Ulster and North America: Transatlantic Perspectives on the Scotch-Irish* (Tuscaloosa, 1997).

Philippe Contamine, 'Scottish Soldiers in France in the Second Half of the Fifteenth Century: Mercenaries, Immigrants or Frenchmen in the Making?', in Grant G. Simpson, ed., *The Scottish Soldier Abroad, 1247–1967* (Edinburgh, 1992).

A. Cooke *et al.*, eds., *Modern Scottish History 1701 to the Present.* Vol. 1, *The Transformation of Scotland, 1707–1850* (East Linton, 1998).

J. E. Cookson, *The British Armed Nation 1793–1815* (Oxford, 1997).

J. E. Cookson, 'The Napoleonic Wars, Military Scotland and Tory Highlandism in the Early Nineteenth Century', *Scottish Historical Review*, LXXVIII (April 1999).

W. C. Cooper, *The Story of Georgia* (New York, 1938).

Elsa V. Coreia, *Slave Society in the British Leeward Islands at the End of the Eighteenth Century* (New Haven, 1965).

A. A. Cormack, *Scotsmen in the First Swedish East India Company, 1731–1745* (Banff, 1975).

C. B. Coulter, 'The Virginia Merchant', unpublished Ph.D. thesis, Princeton University, NJ, 1944.

Edward J. Cowan, 'The Myth of Scotch Canada', in Marjory Harper and Michael E. Vance, eds., *Myth, Migration and the Making of Memory. Scotia and Nova Scotia, c. 1700–1900* (Halifax, 1999).

Edward J. Cowan and Richard J. Finlay, eds., *Scottish History. The Power of the Past* (Edinburgh, 2002).

N. F. R. Crafts, *British Economic Growth during the Industrial Revolution* (Oxford, 1985).

Michael Craton, *Testing the Chains: Resistance to Slavery in the British West Indies* (Ithaca, NY, 1982).

L. M. Cullen and T. C. Smout, eds., *Comparative Aspects of Scottish and Irish Economic and Social History, 1600–1900* (Edinburgh, 1977).

L. M. Cullen, 'Scotland and Ireland, 1600–1800: their Role in the Evolution of British Society', in R. A. Houston and I. D. Whyte, eds., *Scottish Society 1500–1800* (Cambridge, 1989).

L. M. Cullen, 'The Irish Diaspora of the Seventeenth and Eighteenth Centuries' in N. Canny, ed., *Europeans on the Move. Studies on European Migration, 1500–1800* (Oxford, 1994).

A. Cunningham, *The Volunteer Force: A Social and Political History 1859–1908* (London, 1975).

William Dalrymple, *White Mughals* (London, 2002).

William Darty, Jnr., 'British Industry and the West Indian Plantations', in J. E. Inikori and S. L. Engerman, eds., *The Atlantic Slave Trade* (Durham, NC, 1992).

Martin Daunton and Rick Halpern, eds., *Empire and Others: British Encounters with Indigenous Peoples, 1600–1850* (Philadelphia, 1999).

Jane Dawson, 'Two Kingdoms or Three?: Ireland in Anglo-Scottish Relations in the Middle of the Sixteenth Century', in Roger A. Mason, ed., *Scotland and England, 1286–1815* (Edinburgh, 1987).

Jane Dawson, 'Anglo-Scottish Protestant Culture and Integration in Sixteenth-century Britain', in Steven G. Ellis and Sarah Barber, eds., *Conquest and Union: Fashioning a British State, 1485–1725* (London, 1995).

Donald D'Elid, *Benjamin Rush: Philosopher of the American Revolution* (Philadelphia, 1979).

R. F. Dell, 'The Operational Record of the Clyde Tobacco Fleet, 1747–1775', *Scottish Economic and Social History*, 2 (1982).

T. M. Devine, 'Transport Problems of Glasgow West India Merchants during the American War of Independence, 1775–83', *Transport History*, IV (1971).

T. M. Devine and S. G. E. Lythe, 'The Economy of Scotland under James VI: a Revision Article', *Scottish Historical Review*, L (1971).

T. M. Devine, 'Glasgow Colonial Merchants and Land, 1770–1815', in J. T. Ward and R. G. Wilson, eds., *Land and Industry: the Landed Estate in the Industrial Revolution* (Newton Abbott, 1971).

T. M. Devine, 'Sources of Capital for the Glasgow Tobacco Trade, *c.* 1740–80', *Business History*, 16 (1974).

T. M. Devine *The Tobacco Lords: a Study of the Tobacco Merchants of Glasgow and their Trading Activities, 1740–90* (Edinburgh, 1975).

T. M. Devine 'Colonial Commerce and the Scottish Economy, *c.* 1730–1815', in L. M. Cullen and T. C. Smout, eds., *Comparative Aspects of Scottish and Irish Economic and Social History, 1600–1900* (Edinburgh, 1977).

T. M. Devine, 'An Eighteenth Century Business Elite: Glasgow West India Merchants, *c.* 1750–1815', *Scottish Historical Review*, LVII, 163, (April 1978).

T. M. Devine, 'The Scottish Merchant Community 1680–1740', in R. H. Campbell and A. S. Skinner, eds., *The Origin and Nature of the Scottish Enlightenment* (Edinburgh, 1982).

T. M. Devine and D. Dickson, eds., *Ireland and Scotland 1600–1850* (Edinburgh, 1983).

T. M. Devine, 'The English Connection and Irish and Scottish Development in the Eighteenth Century', in T. M. Devine and David Dickson, eds., *Ireland and Scotland 1600–1850* (Edinburgh, 1983).

T. M. Devine, ed., *A Scottish Firm in Virginia, 1767–1777* (Edinburgh, 1984).

T. M. Devine, 'The Union of 1707 and Scottish Development', *Scottish Economic and Social History*, V (1985).

T. M. Devine, *The Great Highland Famine. Hunger, Emigration and the Scottish Highlands in the Nineteenth Century* (Edinburgh, 1988).

T. M. Devine, 'Highland Landowners and the Highland Potato Famine', in Leah Leneman, ed., *Perspectives in Scottish Social History* (Aberdeen, 1988).

T. M. Devine and R. Mitchison, eds., *People and Society in Scotland.* Vol. 1, *1760–1830* (Edinburgh, 1988).

T. M. Devine, 'Urbanisation', in T. M. Devine and R. Mitchison, eds., *People and Society in Scotland.* Vol. 1, *1760–1830* (Edinburgh, 1988).

T. M. Devine, ed., *Improvement and Enlightenment* (Edinburgh, 1989).

T. M. Devine, 'The Emergence of the New Elite in the Western Highlands and Islands, 1800–1860', in T. M. Devine, ed., *Improvement and Enlightenment* (Edinburgh, 1989).

T. M. Devine, 'Social Responses to Agrarian Improvement: the Highland and Lowland Clearances in Scotland', in R. A. Houston and I. D. Whyte, eds., *Scottish Society, 1500–1800* (Cambridge, 1989).

T. M. Devine, ed., *Conflict and Stability in Scottish Society 1700–1850* (Edinburgh, 1990).

T. M. Devine, 'The Failure of Radical Reform in Scotland in the late Eighteenth Century: the Social and Economic Context', in T. M. Devine, ed., *Conflict and Stability in Scottish Society 1700–1850* (Edinburgh, 1990).

T. M. Devine, ed., *Irish Immigrants and Scottish Society in the Nineteenth and Twentieth Centuries* (Edinburgh, 1991).

T. M. Devine, ed., *Scottish Elites* (Edinburgh, 1994).

T. M. Devine, *Clanship to Crofters' War. The Social Transformation of the Scottish Highlands* (Manchester, 1994).

T. M. Devine, *The Transformation of Rural Scotland. Social Change and the Agrarian Economy, 1660–1815* (Edinburgh, 1994).

T. M. Devine and G. Jackson, eds., *Glasgow*. Vol. 1, *Beginnings to 1830* (Manchester, 1995).

T. M. Devine, 'Scottish Farm Service in the Agricultural Revolution', in T. M. Devine, ed., *Farm Servants and Labour in Lowland Scotland 1770–1914* (Edinburgh, 1996 edn.).

T. M. Devine, 'The Colonial Trades and Industrial Investment in Scotland, c. 1700–1815', in P. Emmer and F. Caastra, eds., *The Organisation of Interoceanic Trade in European Expansion, 1450–1800* (Aldershot, 1996).

T. M. Devine, 'The Golden Age of Tobacco', in T. M. Devine and G. Jackson, eds., *Glasgow*. Vol. 1, *Beginnings to 1830* (Manchester, 1995).

T. M. Devine and J. R. Young, eds., *Eighteenth Century Scotland. New Perspectives* (East Linton, 1999).

T. M. Devine, 'A Conservative People? Scottish Gaeldom in the Age of Improvement', in T. M. Devine and J. R. Young, eds., *Eighteenth Century Scotland. New Perspectives* (East Linton, 1999).

T. M. Devine, *The Scottish Nation, 1700–2000* (Harmondsworth, 1999).

T. M. Devine, 'Scotland', in P. Clark, *The Cambridge Urban History of Britain*, Vol. 2 (Cambridge, 2000).

Tom Devine and Paddy Logue, eds., *Being Scottish. Personal Reflections on Scottish Identity Today* (Edinburgh, 2002).

Peter J. Diamond, 'Witherspoon, William Smith and the Scottish Philosophy in Revolutionary America', in Richard B. Sher and Jeffrey R. Smitten, eds., *Scotland and America in the Age of the Enlightenment* (Edinburgh, 1990).

David Dickson, *New Foundations. Ireland, 1660–1800* (Dublin, 1987).

David Dickson, *Arctic Ireland: the Extraordinary Story of the Great Frost and Forgotten Famine of 1740–41* (Belfast, 1997).

R. J. Dickson, *Ulster Emigration to Colonial America, 1718–1775* (Belfast, 1997).

Mark Dilworth, 'Beginnings 1600–1707', in Raymond McCluskey, ed., *The Scots College Rome, 1600–2000* (Edinburgh, 2000).

David Ditchburn, 'A Note on Scandinavian Trade with Scotland in the later Middle Ages', in Grant G. Simpson, ed., *Scotland and Scandinavia, 800–1800* (Edinburgh, 1990).

David Ditchburn, 'The Place of Guelders in Scottish Foreign Policy, c. 1449–c. 1542', in Grant G. Simpson, ed., *Scotland and the Low Countries, 1124–1994* (East Linton, 1996).

David Ditchburn, *Scotland and Europe*. Vol. 1, *Religion, Culture and Commerce* (East Linton, 2000).

David Dobson, *Scottish Emigration to Colonial America, 1607–1785* (Athens, Georgia, 1994).

Robert A. Dodgshon, 'Agricultural Change and its Social Consequences in the Southern Uplands of Scotland, 1600–1780', in T. M. Devine and D. Dickson, eds., *Ireland and Scotland 1600–1850* (Edinburgh, 1983).

Robert A. Dodgshon, *From Chiefs to Landlords. Social and Economic Change in the Western Highlands and Islands c. 1493–1820* (Edinburgh, 1998).

Gordon Donaldson, *The Scots Overseas* (London, 1966).

Gordon Donaldson, 'Introduction to Scotland and Scandinavia: Studies Commemorative of the Union of Orkney and Shetland with Scotland', *Scottish Historical Review*, XLVIII, 145 (April 1969).

Gordon Donaldson, 'Scots', in Stephan Thernstrom, ed., *Harvard Encyclopedia of American Ethnic Groups* (Cambridge, 1980).

William Donaldson, *The Jacobite Song* (Aberdeen, 1988).

Ian Donnachie, 'Scottish Criminals and Transportation to Australia', *Scottish Economic and Social History*, 4 (1984).

Robert Kent Donovan, 'The Popular Party of the Church of Scotland and the American Revolution', in Richard B. Sher and Jeffrey R. Smitten, eds., *Scotland and America in the Age of the Enlightenment* (Edinburgh, 1990).

Robert K. Donovan and Michael Fry, 'Religion in the Affairs of Scotland and America', in John Carter Brown Library, *Scotland and the Americas 1600–1800* (Providence, Rhode Island, 1995).

Derek A. Dow, ed., *The Influence of Scottish Medicine* (Carnforth and Park Ridge, NJ, 1988).

James Dow, '*Skotter* in Sixteenth-Century Scania', *Scottish Historical Review*, 44 (1965).

James Dow, 'Scottish Trade with Sweden 1512–80', *Scottish Historical Review*, 48 (1969).

James Dow, 'Scottish Trade with Sweden 1580–1622', *Scottish Historical Review*, 48 (1969).

David Noel Doyle, *Ireland, Irishmen and Revolutionary America, 1760–1820* (Dublin and Cork, 1981).

David Noel Doyle, 'The Irish in North America, 1776–1845', in W. E. Vaughan, ed., *A New History of Ireland*, V: *Ireland under the Union, 1* (Oxford, 1989).

David Noel Doyle, 'Review article; Cohesion and Diversity in the Irish Diaspora', *Irish Historical Studies*, XXXI, 123 (May 1999).

David Noel Doyle, 'Scots-Irish or Scotch-Irish', in Michael Glazier, ed., *The Encyclopedia of the Irish in America* (Indiana, 1999).

Paul Dukes, 'The Leslie Family in the Swedish Period (1630–5) of the Thirty Years War', *European Studies Review*, 12, 4 (1982).

Paul Dukes, 'Problems Concerning the Departure of Scottish Soldiers from Seventeenth-century Muscovy', in T. C. Smout, ed., *Scotland and Europe, 1200–1850* (Edinburgh, 1986).

Paul Dukes, 'Scottish Soldiers in Muscovy', in *The Caledonian Phalanx: Scots in Russia* (Edinburgh, 1987).

Paul Dukes, 'The First Scottish Soldiers in Russia', in Grant G. Simpson, ed., *The Scottish Soldier Abroad 1247–1967* (Edinburgh, 1992).

Wayland F. Dunaway, *The Scotch-Irish of Colonial Pennsylvania* (Chapel Hill, NC, 1985).

D. Duncan, ed., *History of the Union of Scotland and England by Sir John Clerk of Penicuik* (Edinburgh, 1993).

Richard S. Dunn, *Sugar and Slaves: The Rise of the Planter Class in the English West Indies, 1624–1713* (Chapel Hill, 1972).

Hugh Dunthorne, 'Scots in the Wars of the Low Countries, 1572–1648', in Grant G. Simpson, ed., *Scotland and the Low Countries, 1124–1994* (East Linton, 1996).

Alastair J. Durie, *The Scottish Linen Industry in the Eighteenth Century* (Edinburgh, 1979).

J. K. Eastham, ed., *Economic Essays in Commemoration of the Dundee School of Economics, 1931–1955* (Dundee, 1955).

Owen Dudley Edwards and George Shepperson, eds., *Scotland, Europe and the American Revolution* (Edinburgh, 1976).

Leroy V. Eid, 'Irish, Scotch and Scotch-Irish: A Reconsideration', *American Presbyterians*, LXIV (Winter 1986).

Leroy V. Eid, 'Scotch-Irish and American Politics', in Michael Glazier, ed., *The Encyclopedia of the Irish in America* (Indiana, 1999).

A. Roger Ekirch, 'The Transportation of Scottish Criminals to America during the Eighteenth Century', *Journal of British Studies*, 24 (1985).

Steven G. Ellis and Sarah Barber, ed., *Conquest and Union: Fashioning a British State, 1485–1725* (London, 1995).

Roger L. Emerson, 'Scottish Cultural Change 1660–1710 and the Union of 1707', in John Robertson, ed., *A Union for Empire: Political Thought and the British Union of 1707* (Cambridge, 1995).

Roger L. Emerson, 'The Scottish Literati and America, 1680–1800', in Ned C. Landsman, ed., *Nation and Province in the First British Empire. Scotland and the Americas, 1600–1800* (London, 2001).

P. Emmer and F. Caastra, eds., *The Organisation of Interoceanic Trade in European Expansion, 1450–1800* (Aldershot, 1996).

Clive Emsley, *British Society and the French Wars 1793–1815* (London, 1979).

E. Estyn Evans, 'The Scotch-Irish: Their Cultural Adaptation and Heritage in the American Old West', in E. R. R. Green, ed., *Essays in Scotch-Irish History* (London and New York, 1969).

Emory G. Evans, 'Planter Indebtedness and the Coming of Revolution in Virginia', *William and Mary Quarterly*, 3rd Series, XIX (1962).

L. Evans and P. Nicholls, *Convicts and Colonial Society 1788–1853* (Sydney, 1976).

Elizabeth Ewan and Maureen M. Meikle, eds., *Women in Scotland, c.1100–c.1750* (East Linton, 1999).

Dalphy I. Fagerstrom, 'The American Revolutionary Movement in Scottish Opinion, 1763–1783', unpublished Ph.D. thesis, University of Edinburgh, 1951.

Dalphy I. Fagerstrom, 'Scottish Opinion and the American Revolution', *William and Mary Quarterly*, XI, 3rd Series, (1954).

J. A. Fallon, 'Scottish Mercenaries in the Service of Denmark and Sweden, 1626–1632', unpublished Ph.D. thesis, University of Glasgow, 1972.

A. Fawcett, *The Cambuslang Revival: the Scottish Evangelical Revival of the Eighteenth Century* (London, 1971).

Dmitry G. Fedosov, 'The First Russian Bruces', in Grant G. Simpson, ed., *The Scottish Soldier Abroad 1247–1967* (Edinburgh, 1992).

Robert Feenstra, 'Scottish–Dutch Legal Relations in the Seventeenth and Eighteenth Centuries', in T. C. Smout, ed., *Scotland and Europe, 1200–1850* (Edinburgh, 1986).

C. H. Feinstein, 'Capital Accumulation and the Industrial Revolution', in R. Floud and D. McCluskey, eds., *The Economic History of Britain since 1700* (Cambridge, 1981).

W. Ferguson, *Scotland's Relations with England: a Survey to 1707* (Edinburgh, 1977).

Richard J. Finlay, 'The Rise and Fall of Popular Imperialism in Scotland 1850–1950', *Scottish Geographical Magazine*, 113 (1997).

Richard J. Finlay, 'Keeping the Covenant: Scottish National Identity', in T. M. Devine and J. R. Young, eds., *Eighteenth Century Scotland. New Perspectives* (East Linton, 1999).

T. A. Fischer, *The Scots in Germany* (Edinburgh, 1902).

T. A. Fischer, *The Scots in Eastern and Western Prussia* (Edinburgh, 1903).

T. A. Fischer, *The Scots in Sweden* (Edinburgh, 1907).

David Hackett Fischer, *Albion's Seed: Four British Folkways in America* (Oxford, 1989).

Patrick Fitzgerald, 'The Scotch-Irish and the Eighteenth Century Irish Diaspora', *History Ireland*, (Autumn 1999).

Patrick Fitzgerald and Steve Ickringill, eds., *Atlantic Crossroads. Historical Connections between Scotland, Ulster and North America* (Newtownards, 2001).

P. Fitzgerald, ' "Black '97": Reconsidering Scottish Migration to Ireland in the Seventeenth Century and the Scotch-Irish in America', in W. Kelly, ed., *The Irish, the Scottish and the Scotch-Irish: Connections and Comparisons* (forthcoming, 2003).

David Fitzpatrick, ' "A peculiar tramping people": the Irish in Britain, 1801–70', in W. E. Vaughan, ed., *A New History of Ireland*. V, *Ireland Under the Union, I, 1801–70* (Oxford, 1989).

Rory Fitzpatrick, *God's Frontiersmen: The Scots-Irish Epic* (London, 1989).

Donald Fleming and Bernard Bailyn, eds., *Perspectives in American History*. Vol. 7, *Dislocation and Emigration* (Cambridge, 1973).

Andrew Fletcher of Saltoun, *The Political Works of Andrew Fletcher Esq. of Saltoun* (Glasgow, 1749).

M. W. Flinn *et al.*, eds., *Scottish Population History from the Seventeenth Century to the 1930s* (Cambridge, 1977).

R. Floud and D. McCluskey, eds., *The Economic History of Britain since 1700* (Cambridge, 1981).

Aaron Fogleman, 'Migrations to the Thirteen British North American Colonies: New Estimates', *Journal of Interdisciplinary History*, XXII, 4 (Spring 1992).

Sir W. Forbes, *Memoirs of a Banking House* (London and Edinburgh, 1860).

T. M. Fortescue, ed., *Calendar of State Papers, America and the West Indies 1681–1697* (London, 1898–1904).

R. Foskett, 'Some Scottish Episcopalians in the North American Colonies, 1675–1750', *Records of the Scottish Church History Society*, XIV (1963).

W. H. Fraser, *Conflict and Class* (Edinburgh, 1988).

J. A. Froude, *The English in Ireland in the Eighteenth Century* (London, 1872).

Michael Fry, *The Dundas Despotism* (Edinburgh, 1992).

Michael Fry, 'A Commercial Empire: Scotland and British Expansion in the Eighteenth Century' in T. M. Devine and J. R. Young, eds., *Eighteenth Century Scotland. New Perspectives* (East Linton, 1999).

Michael Fry, *The Scottish Empire* (Edinburgh, 2001).

Linda G. Fryer, 'Documents relating to the Formation of the Carolina Company in Scotland, 1682', *South Carolina Historical Magazine*, 99 (April 1998).

John Kenneth Galbraith, *The Scotch* (New York, 1964).

D. W. Galenson, *White Servitude in Colonial America: an Economic Analysis* (Cambridge, 1981).

J. A. Galloway and I. Murray, 'Scottish Migration to England, 1400–1560', *Scottish Geographical Magazine*, 112 (1996).

John Galt, *The Last of the Lairds* (Edinburgh, 1976 edn.).

Alison Games, *Migration and the Origins of the English Atlantic World* (Cambridge, 1999).

Henry A. Gemery, 'European Emigration to North America, 1700–1820: Numbers and Quasi-Numbers', *Perspectives in American History*, I (1984).

A. J. S. Gibson and T. C. Smout, *Prices, Food and Wages in Scotland 1550–1780* (Cambridge, 1995).

Raymond Gillespie, *Colonial Ulster: The Settlement of East Ulster, 1600–1641* (Cork, 1985).

Raymond Gillespie, 'Continuity and Change: Ulster in the Seventeenth Century', in Ciaran Brady, Mary O'Dowd and Brian Walker, eds., *Ulster: An Illustrated History* (London, 1989).

Raymond Gillespie, 'The Presbyterian Revolution in Ulster, 1660–1690', in W. J. Shiels and Diana Wood, eds., *The Churches, Ireland and the Irish* (Oxford, 1989).

R. J. Girdwood, 'The Influence of Scotland on North American Medicine', in Derek A. Dow, ed., *The Influence of Scottish Medicine* (Carnforth and Park Ridge, NJ, 1988).

D. V. Glass and D. E. C. Eversley, eds., *Population in History* (London, 1965).

D. V. Glass and Roger Revelle, eds., *Population and Social Change* (London, 1972).

Michael Glazier, ed., *The Encyclopedia of the Irish in America* (Indiana, 1999).

M. Glendinning, Ranald Macinnes and Aonghus MacKechnie, *A History of Scottish Architecture* (Edinburgh, 1996).

Jordan Goodman, *Tobacco in History* (London, 1993).

Elsa–Britta Grage, 'Scottish Merchants in Gothenburg, 1621–1850', in T. C. Smout, ed., *Scotland and Europe 1200–1850* (Edinburgh, 1986).

Eric J. Graham, 'In Defence of the Scottish Maritime Interest, 1681–1713, *Scottish Historical Review*, L (1971).

Eric J. Graham, *A Maritime History of Scotland, 1650–1790* (East Linton, 2002).

Ian Charles Cargill Graham, *Colonists from Scotland: Emigration to North America, 1707–1783* (Ithaca, NY, 1956).

I. F. Grant, *The MacLeods, the History of a Clan* (London, 1959).

James Grant, *The Scottish Soldiers of Fortune: Their Adventures and Achievements in the Armies of Europe* (London, 1890).

M. Gray, *The Highland Economy* (Edinburgh, 1957).

M. Gray, 'Scottish Emigration: the Social Impact of Agrarian Change in the Rural Lowlands, 1775–1875', *Perspectives in American History*, VII (1973).

M. Gray, 'Migration in the Rural Lowlands of Scotland, 1750–1850', in T. M. Devine and D. Dickson, eds., *Ireland and Scotland 1600–1850* (Edinburgh, 1983).

Malcolm Gray, 'The Social Impact of Agrarian Change in the Rural Lowlands', in T. M. Devine and R. Mitchison, eds., *People and Society in Scotland*. Vol. 1, *1760–1830* (Edinburgh, 1988).

T. M. Gray, ed., *Memoirs of the Life of Sir John Clerk of Penicuik* (Edinburgh, 1892).

E. R. R. Green, 'The Scotch-Irish and the Coming of the Revolution in North Carolina', *Irish Historical Studies*, VII (1950–51).

E. R. R. Green, *Essays in Scotch-Irish History* (London and New York, 1969).

Jack P. Greene, *Peripheries and Center: Constitutional Development in the Extended Polities of the British Empire and the United States, 1607–1788* (Athens, Georgia, 1986).

Jack P. Greene, 'Changing Identity in the British Caribbean: Barbados as a Case Study', in Nicholas Canny and Anthony Pagden, eds., *Colonial Identity in the Atlantic World, 1500–1800* (Princeton, NJ, 1987).

Patrick Griffin, *The People with No Name* (Princeton NJ, and Oxford, 2001).

Patrick Griffin, 'The People with No Name: Ulster's Migrants and Identity Formation in Eighteenth-Century Pennsylvania', *William and Mary Quarterly*, 3rd Series, LVIII, 3 (July 2001).

N. E. S. Griffiths and John G. Reid, 'New Evidence on New Scotland, 1629', *William and Mary Quarterly*, 3rd Series, XLIX, 1 (January 1992).

Alexia N. L. Grosjean, 'Scots and the Swedish State: Diplomacy, Military Service and Ennoblement 1611–1660', unpublished Ph.D. thesis, University of Aberdeen, 1998.

Alan J. Guy and Peter B. Boyden, eds., *Soldiers of the Raj. The Indian Army 1600–1947* (Coventry, 1997).

Euan Hague, 'The Emigrant Experience: The Scottish Diaspora', *Scottish Affairs*, 31 (Spring 2000).

Paul Hallberg and Christian Koninckx, eds., 'A Passage to China: Colin Campbell's Diary of the First Swedish East India Company Expendition to Canton, 1732–33', *ACTA Humaniora*, 37.

D. Hamilton, 'The Scottish Enlightenment and Clinical Medicine', in Derek A. Dow, ed., *The Influence of Scottish Medicine* (Carnforth and Park Ridge, NJ, 1988).

Douglas J. Hamilton, 'Patronage and Profit: Scottish Networks in the British West Indies, *c.* 1763–1807', unpublished Ph.D. thesis, University of Aberdeen, 1999.

H. Hamilton, *An Economic History of Scotland in the Eighteenth Century* (Oxford, 1963).

Ronald Hamowy, 'Jefferson and the Scottish Enlightenment: A Critique of Garry Wills's *Inventing America: Jefferson's Declaration of Independence*', *William and Mary Quarterly*, 3rd Series, XXXVI (October 1979).

David Hancock, *Citizens of the World: London Merchants and the Integration of the British Atlantic Community, 1735–1785* (Cambridge, 1995).

David Hancock, 'Scots in the Slave Trade', in Ned C. Landsman, ed., *Nation and Province in the First British Empire* (London, 2001).

Jerome S. Handler and Frederick W. Lange, *Plantation Slavery in Barbados: An Archaeological and Historical Investigation* (Cambridge, Mass., 1978).

Marcus Lee Hansen, *The Atlantic Migration, 1607–1860: A History of the Continuing Settlement of the United States* (Cambridge, 1951).

John D. Hargreaves, *Aberdeenshire to Africa: Northeast Scots and British Overseas Expansion* (Aberdeen, 1981).

Marjory Harper and Michael E. Vance, eds., *Myth, Migration and the Making of Memory. Scotia and Nova Scotia, c. 1700–1990* (Halifax, 1999).

John Harrower, 'Diary of John Harrower, 1773–1776', *American Historical Review*, VI (October 1900 to July 1901).

Charles H. Haws, *Scots in the Old Dominion, 1685–1800* (Edinburgh, 1980).

J. Hayes, 'Scottish Officers in the British Army, 1714–63', *Scottish Historical Review*, 37 (1958).

David Hayton, *Ireland after the Glorious Revolution* (Belfast, 1976).

C. G. Headlam, ed., *Calendar of State Papers, America and the West Indies, 1701* (London, 1910).

Daniel R. Headrick, *The Tools of Empire: Technology and European Imperialism in the Nineteenth Century* (Oxford, 1981).

Michael Hechter, *Internal Colonialism: the Celtic Fringe in British Natural Development* (London, 1975).

D. M. Henderson, *Highland Soldier: A Social Study of the Highland Regiments 1820–1920* (Edinburgh, 1989).

Arthur Herman, *The Scottish Enlightenment* (London, 2002).

E. J. Hobsbawm and T. O. Ranger, eds., *The Invention of Tradition* (Oxford, 1983).

B. A. Holderness, 'Prices, Productivity and Output', in G. E. Mingay, ed., *The Agrarian History of England and Wales*. Vol. 6, *1750–1850* (Cambridge, 1989).

H. Hollingsworth, 'A Demographic Study of the British Ducal Families', in D. V. Glass and D. E. C. Eversley, eds., *Population in History* (London, 1965).

G. Holmes and D. Szechi, *The Age of Oligarchy. Pre-industrial Britain 1722–1783* (London, 1993).

Michael Holmes, 'The Irish and India: Imperialism, Nationalism and Internationalism', in Andy Bielenberg, ed., *The Irish Diaspora* (Harlow, 2000).

I. Hont and M. Ignatieff, eds., *Wealth and Virtue* (Cambridge, 1983).

Andrew Hook, *Scotland and America: A Study of Cultural Relations, 1750–1835* (Glasgow, 1975).

Andrew Hook, 'Philadelphia, Edinburgh and the Scottish Enlightenment', in Richard B. Sher and Jeffrey R. Smitten, eds., *Scotland and America in the Age of the Enlightenment* (Edinburgh, 1990).

Andrew Hook, *From Goosecreek to Gandercleugh. Studies in Scottish-American Literary and Cultural History* (Edinburgh, 1999).

Richard J. Hooker, ed., *The Carolina Backcountry on the Eve of the Revolution: The Journal and other Writings of Charles Woodmason, Anglican Itinerant* (Chapel Hill, NC, 1953).

A. G. Hopkins, *The Future of the Imperial Past* (Cambridge, 1997).

A. G. Hopkins, 'Viewpoint; Back to the Future: From National History to Imperial History', *Past and Present*, 164 (August 1999).

James Horn, 'British Diaspora: Emigration from Britain, 1680–1815', in P. J. Marshall, ed., *The Oxford History of the British Empire. Vol. 2, The Eighteenth Century* (Oxford, 1998).

Dauvit Horsbroch, 'Tae See Oursels as Ithers See Us: Scottish Military Identity from the Covenant to Victoria 1637–1837', in Steve Murdoch and Andrew Mackillop, eds., *Fighting for Identity: Scottish Military Experience c. 1550–1900* (Leiden and Boston, 2002).

Cecil J. Houston and William J. Smyth, *Irish Emigration and Canadian Settlement: Patterns, Links, and Letters* (Toronto, 1990).

R. A. Houston and I. D. Whyte, eds., *Scottish Society 1500–1800* (Cambridge, 1989).

R. A. Houston and W. W. J. Knox, eds., *The New Penguin History of Scotland* (London, 2001).

Daniel Walker Howe, 'European Sources of Political Ideas in Jeffersonian America', *Reviews in American History*, 10, 4 (December 1982).

Robert Hughes, *The Fatal Shore* (New York, 1988 edn.).

B. Hundle, *The Pursuit of Science in Revolutionary America* (Chapel Hill, NC, 1956).

E. H. Hunt, 'Industrialisation and Regional Inequality: Wages in Britain, 1760–1914', *Journal of Economic History*, 46 (1986).

T. Hunter, ed., *Extracts from the Records of the Convention of Royal Burghs 1759–1769* (Edinburgh, 1918).

R. Hyam and G. Martin eds., *Reappraisals in British Imperial History* (London, 1975).

R. Hyam, 'Imperial Interests and the Peace of Paris', in R. Hyam and G. Martin, *Reappraisals in British Imperial History* (London, 1975).

Edward Ingram, 'The Role of the Indian Army at the end of the Eighteenth Century', in Patrick Tuck, ed., *The East India Company: 1600–1858.* Vol. 5, *Warfare, Expansion and Resistance* (London and New York, 1998).

J. E. Inikori and S. L. Engerman, eds., *The Atlantic Slave Trade* (Durham, NC, 1992).

George Pratt Insh, *Scottish Colonial Schemes, 1620–1686* (Glasgow, 1922).

George Pratt Insh, *The Company of Scotland Trading to Africa and the Indies* (London, 1932).

George Pratt Insh, *The Darien Scheme* (London, 1947).

Gordon Jackson, 'Glasgow in Transition, c. 1660–c.1740', in T. M. Devine and G. Jackson, eds., *Glasgow*. Vol. 1, *Beginnings to 1830* (Manchester, 1995).

G. Jackson, 'New Horizons in Trade', in T. M. Devine and G. Jackson, eds., *Glasgow*. Vol. 1, *Beginnings to 1830* (Manchester, 1995).

Lawrence James, *The Rise and Fall of the British Empire* (London, 1994).

Lawrence James, *Raj. The Making and Unmaking of British India* (London, 1998 edn.).

Lawrence James, *Warrior Race. A History of the British at War* (London, 2001).

John Carter Brown Library, *Scotland and the Americas, 1600 to 1800* (Providence, Rhode Island, 1995).

Christine Johnson, *Developments in the Roman Catholic Church in Scotland, 1789–1829* (Edinburgh, 1983).

J. K. Johnson, *Becoming Prominent: Regional Leadership in Upper Canada, 1791–1841* (Kingston and Montreal, 1989).

Maldwyn A. Jones, 'Scotch-Irish', in Stephen Thernstrom, ed., *Harvard Encyclopedia of American Ethnic Groups* (Cambridge, 1980).

Maldwyn A. Jones, 'Ulster Emigration, 1783–1814', in E. R. R. Green, ed., *Essays in Scotch-Irish History* (London and New York, 1969).

Maldwyn A. Jones, 'The Background to Emigration from Great Britain in the Nineteenth Century', in Donald Fleming and Bernard Bailyn, eds., *Perspectives in American History*. Vol. 7, *Dislocation and Emigration* (Cambridge, 1973).

Maldwyn A. Jones, 'The Scotch-Irish in British America', in Bernard Bailyn and Philip D. Morgan, eds., *Strangers within the Realm: Cultural Margins of the First British Empire* (Chapel Hill, NC, 1991).

W. Douglas Jones, '"The Bold Adventurers": A Quantitative Analysis of the Darien Subscription List (1696)', *Scottish Economic and Social History*, 21 (2001).

Carol M. Judd and Arthur J. Ray, eds., *Old Trails and New Directions: Papers of the Third North American Fur Trade Conference* (Toronto, 1980).

Carol M. Judd, 'Mixt Bands of Many Nations: 1821–70', in Carol M. Judd and Arthur J. Ray, eds., *Old Trails and New Directions: Papers of the Third North American Fur Trade Conference* (Toronto, 1980).

Alan Karras, 'The World of Alexander Johnston: the Creolisation of Ambition, 1762–1787', *Historical Journal*, XXX, 1 (1987).

Alan L. Karras, *Sojourners in the Sun: Scottish Migrants in Jamaica and the Chesapeake, 1740–1800* (Ithaca, N. Y., and London, 1992).

Billy Kay, 'To Norroway o'er the foam', *Scotland's Story*, 27 (2000).

Billy Kay and Cailean Maclean, *Knee Deep in Claret: A Celebration of Wine and Scotland* (Edinburgh, 1983).

Hugh Kearney, *The British Isles: A History of Four Nations* (Cambridge, 1989).

Kevin Kenny, *The American Irish. A History* (Harlow, 2000).

Colin Kidd, *Subverting Scotland's Past* (Cambridge, 1993).

Colin Kidd, 'North Britishness and the Nature of Eighteenth-Century British Patriotisms', *Historical Journal*, 39, 2 (1996).

Colin Kidd, 'Sentiment, Race and Revival: Scottish Identities in the Aftermath of Englightenment', in L. Brockliss and D. Eastwood, eds., *A Union of Multiple Identities* (Manchester, 1997).

Victor Kiernan, 'Scottish Soldiers and the Conquest of India', in Grant G. Simpson, ed., *The Scottish Soldier Abroad, 1247–1967* (Edinburgh, 1992).

Graeme Kirkham, 'Ulster Emigration to North America 1680–1720', in J. Tyler Blethen and Curtis W. Wood, eds., *Ulster and North America: Transatlantic Perspectives on the Scotch-Irish* (Tuscaloosa, 1997).

A. C. Land, 'The Tobacco Staple and the Planter's Problems: Technology, Labour and Crops', *Agricultural History*, XLIII (1969).

Ned C. Landsman, *Scotland and its First American Colony, 1680–1765* (Princeton, NJ, 1985).

Ned C. Landsman, 'Religion and Revolution: The Two Worlds of John Witherspoon', in Richard B. Sher and Jeffrey R. Smitten, eds., *Scotland and America in the Age of the Enlightenment* (Edinburgh, 1990).

Ned C. Landsman, 'Witherspoon and the Problem of Provincial Identity in Scottish Evangelical Culture', in Richard B. Sher and Jeffrey R. Smitten, eds., *Scotland and America in the Age of the Enlightenment* (Edinburgh, 1990).

Ned C. Landsman, 'Border Cultures, the Backcountry, and "North British" Emigration to America', *William and Mary Quarterly*, 3rd Series, XLVIII, 1 (January 1991).

Ned C. Landsman, 'The Provinces and the Empire. Scotland, the American Colonies and the Development of British Provincial Identity', in Lawrence Stone, ed., *An Imperial State at War. Britain from 1689 to 1815* (London, 1994).

Ned C. Landsman, 'The Legacy of British Union for the North American Colonies: Provincial Elites and the Problem of Imperial Union', in John Robertson, ed., *A Union for Empire: Political Thought and the British Union of 1707* (Cambridge, 1995).

Ned C. Landsman, *From Colonials to Provincials: American Thought and Culture, 1680–1760* (Ithaca, NY, and London, 1997).

Ned C. Landsman, 'Nation, Migration and the Province in the First British Empire: Scotland and the Americas, 1600–1800', *American Historical Review*, 104 (April 1999).

Ned C. Landsman, ed., *Nation and Province in the First British Empire* (London, 2001).

Robin Law, 'The First Scottish Guinea Company, 1634–9', *Scottish Historical Review*, LXXVI, 2, No. 202 (October 1997).

P. Lawson and J. Phillips, ' "Our Execrable Banditti"; Perceptions of Nabobs in Mid-Eighteenth Century Britain', *Albion*, XVI (1984).

W. C. Lehmann, *Scottish and Scotch-Irish Contributions to Early American Life and Culture* (London, 1978).

Leah Leneman, *Living in Atholl, 1685–1785* (Edinburgh, 1986).

Leah Leneman, ed., *Perspectives in Scottish Social History* (Aberdeen, 1988).

Leah Leneman, 'A New Role for a Lost Cause: Lowland Romantication of the Jacobite Highlander', in L. Leneman, ed., *Perspectives in Scottish Social History* (Aberdeen, 1988).

B. P. Lenman, *The Jacobite Clans of the Great Glen 1650–1784* (Edinburgh, 1984).

Bruce P. Lenman, 'Aristocratic "Country" Whiggery in Scotland and the American Revolution', in Richard B. Sher and Jeffrey R. Smitten, eds., *Scotland and America in the Age of the Enlightenment* (Edinburgh, 1990).

James G. Leyburn, *The Scotch-Irish. A Social History* (Chapel Hill, NC, 1962).

B. Levack, *The Formation of the British State* (Oxford, 1987).

R. Ligon, *A True and Exact History of the Island of Barbados* (London, 1673).

Arnvid Lillehammer, 'The Scottish-Norwegian Timber Trade in the Stavanger Area in the Sixteenth and the Seventeenth Centuries', in T. C. Smout, ed., *Scotland and Europe 1200–1880* (Edinburgh, 1986).

Arnvid Lillehammer, 'Boards, Beams and Barrel-Hoops: Contacts Between Scotland and the Stavanger Area in the Seventeenth Century', in Grant G. Simpson, ed., *Scotland and Scandinavia, 800–1800* (Edinburgh, 1990).

E. and A. Linklater, *The Black Watch: the History of the Royal Highland Regiment* (London, 1977).

William Lithgow, *The Totall Discourse of the Rare Adventures and Painefull Peregrinations of Long Nineteen Years* (Glasgow, 1906).

George Lockhart of Carnwath, *Memoirs Concerning the Affairs of Scotland* (London, 1714).

J. G. Lockhart, *Memoirs of the Life of Sir Walter Scott* (Edinburgh, 1837).

E. Long, *The History of Jamaica or General State of the Antient and Modern State of that Island*, II (1774).

Mary L. Lustig, *Robert Hunter, 1660–1734: New York's Augustan Statesman* (Syracuse, NY, 1983).

R. J. Lyall, 'Scottish Students and Masters at the Universities of Cologne and Louvain in the Fifteenth Century', *Innes Review*, 36 (1985).

J. F. Lydon, 'The Scottish Soldier in Medieval Ireland: the Bruce Invasion and the Galloglass', in G. G. Simpson, ed., *The Scottish Soldier Abroad, 1247–1967* (Edinburgh, 1992).

Michael Lynch, 'Continuity and Change in Urban Society, 1500–1700', in R. A. Houston and I. D. Whyte, eds., *Scottish Society 1500–1800* (Cambridge, 1989).

Michael Lynch, 'Urbanisation and Urban Networks in Seventeenth Century Scotland', *Scottish Economic and Social History*, 12 (1992).

S. G. E. Lythe, 'Scottish Trade with the Baltic, 1550–1650', in J. K. Eastham, ed., *Economic Essays in Commemoration of the Dundee School of Economics, 1931–1955* (Dundee, 1955).

S. G. E. Lythe, *The Economy of Scotland in its European Setting, 1550–1625* (Edinburgh, 1960).

H. B. McCall, *Memoirs of my Ancestors* (Birmingham, 1884).

Sir G. Macartney, *An Account of Ireland in 1773 by a Late Club Secretary of that Kingdom* (London, 1773).

Raymond McCluskey, ed., *The Scots College Rome, 1600–2000* (Edinburgh, 2000).

Alister McCrae, *Scots in Burma: Golden Times in a Golden Land* (Kiscadale, 1990).

Mícheál Mac Craith, 'The Gaelic Reaction to the Reformation' in Steven G. Ellis and Sarah Barber, eds., *Conquest and Union: Fashioning a British State, 1485–1725* (London and New York, 1995).

J. R. McCulloch, ed., Adam Smith, *An Inquiry into the Nature and Causes of the Wealth of Nations* (Edinburgh, 1863 edn.).

James Roderick Macdonald, 'Cultural Retention and Adaptation among the Highland Scots of Carolina', unpublished Ph.D. thesis, University of Edinburgh, 1992.

Forest McDonald and Ellen Shapiro McDonald, 'The Ethnic Origins of the American People, 1790', *William and Mary Quarterly*, 3rd Series, XXXVII (1980).

Roderick A. McDonald, ed., *West Indies Accounts: Essays on the History of the British Caribbean and the Atlantic Economy* (Barbados, Jamaica, Trinidad and Tobago, 1996).

Margaret Macdonell, *The Emigrant Experience: Songs of Highland Emigrants in North America* (Toronto, Buffalo and London, 1982).

Norman Macdougall, ed., *Scotland and War AD 79–1918* (Edinburgh, 1991).

E. W. McFarland, *Ireland and Scotland in the Age of Revolution* (Edinburgh, 1994).

George Kirk McGilvary, 'East India Patronage and the Political Management of Scotland, 1720–1774', unpublished Ph.D. thesis, Open University, 1989.

George K. McGilvary, 'Post-Union Scotland and the Indian Connection', *Cencrastus*, 37 (Summer 1990).

L. McIlvanney, *Burns the Radical: Poetry and Politics in Late Eighteenth-Century Scotland* (East Linton, 2001).

Allan I. Macinnes, 'Scottish Gaeldom: the First Phase of Clearance', in T. M. Devine and R. Mitchison, eds., *People and Society in Scotland*. Vol. 1, *1760–1830* (Edinburgh, 1988).

Allan I. Macinnes, 'Studying the Scottish Estates and the Treaty of Union', *History Microcomputer Review*, 6 (1990).

Allan I. Macinnes, 'Landownership, Land Use and the Elite Enterprise in Scottish Gaeldom. From Clanship to Clearance in Argyllshire, 1688–1858', in T. M. Devine, ed., *Scottish Elites* (Edinburgh, 1994).

Allan I. Macinnes, *Clanship, Commerce and the House of Stuart, 1603–1788* (East Linton, 1996).

Allan I. Macinnes, 'Highland Society in the Era of "Improvement"', in A. Cooke *et al.*, eds., *Modern Scottish History 1707 to the Present*. Vol. 1, *The Transformation of Scotland, 1707–1850* (East Linton, 1998).

Allan I. Macinnes, Marjory-Ann D. Harper and Linda G. Fryer, eds., *Scotland and the Americas, c.1650–c. 1939: A Documentary Source Book* (Edinburgh, 2002).

Arthur McKee, '"A Peculiar and Royal Race": Creating a Scotch-Irish Identity, 1889–1901', in P. Fitzgerald and S. Ickringill, eds., *Atlantic*

Crossroads. Historical Connections between Scotland, Ulster and North America (Newtonards, 2001).

Alexander Mackenzie, *History of the Highland Clearances* (Inverness, 1883).

Sir George S. Mackenzie, *General View of the Agriculture of the Counties of Ross and Cromarty* (London, 1813).

John M. MacKenzie, ed., *Popular Imperialism and the Military 1850–1950* (Manchester and New York, 1992).

John M. MacKenzie, 'Essay and Reflection: On Scotland and the Empire', *International History Review*, XV (1993).

John M. MacKenzie, *Orientalism. History, Theory and the Arts* (Manchester and New York, 1995).

John M. MacKenzie, 'Scots in South Africa: Problems of Sources and Methodology', unpublished paper presented to the Diaspora Programme Workshop, University of Aberdeen, January 2003.

John M. MacKenzie, Foreword, in S. Murdoch and A. Mackillop, eds., *Military Governors and Imperial Frontiers, c.1600–1800: A Study of Scotland and Empires* (Leyden, 2003).

Andrew Mackillop, 'Highland Estate Change and Tenant Emigration', in T. M. Devine and J. R. Young, eds., *Eighteenth Century Scotland: New Perspectives* (East Linton, 1999).

Andrew Mackillop, 'At the Sharp End of Building the Empire', *Scotland's Story*, 45 (2000).

Andrew Mackillop, *More Fruitful than the Soil. Army, Empire and the Scottish Highlands, 1715–1815* (East Linton, 2000).

Andrew Mackillop, 'For King, Country and Regiment? Motive and Identity in Highland Soldiering 1746–1815', in Steve Murdoch and Andrew Mackillop, eds., *Fighting for Identity: Scottish Military Experience c.1550–1900* (Leiden and Boston, 2002).

James McLachlan, 'Education', in John Carter Brown Library, *Scotland and the Americas 1600–1800* (Providence, Rhode Island, 1995).

Martha McLaren, *British India and British Scotland 1780–1830* (Akron, Ohio, 2001).

Marianne McLean, *The People of Glengarry: Highlanders in Transition, 1745–1820* (Toronto, 1991).

Donald MacLeod, *Gloomy Memories of the Highlands* (1840–41).

Mona Kedslie McLeod, *Agents of Change: Scots in Poland, 1800–1918* (East Linton, 2000).

David S. Macmillan, *Scotland and Australia, 1788–1850* (Oxford, 1967).

D. S. Macmillan, 'The "New Men" in Action: Scottish Mercantile and Shipping Operations in the North American Colonies, 1760–1825', *Canadian Business History: Selected Studies, 1497–1971* (Toronto, 1972).

James F. McMillan, 'Development 1707–1820', in Raymond McCluskey, ed., *The Scots College Rome, 1600–2000* (Edinburgh, 2000).

T. E. McNeill, 'Lordships and Invasions: Ulster, 1177–1500', in Ciaran Brady, Mary O'Dowd and Brian Walker, eds., *Ulster: An Illustrated History* (London, 1989).

Bridget McPhail, 'Through a Glass, Darkly: Scots and Indians Converge at Darien', *Eighteenth-Century Life*, Vol. 18, n.s., 3 (November, 1994).

D. Macpherson, *Annals of Commerce (1805)*, Vol. 4 (London).

William Charles Macpherson, *Soldiering in India 1764–1787* (Edinburgh and London, 1928).

William Macafee, 'The Demographic History of Ulster, 1750–1841', in J. Tyler Blethen and Curtis W. Wood, Jr., eds., *Ulster and North America: Transatlantic Perspectives on the Scotch-Irish* (Tuscaloosa, 1997).

William L. Marr and Donald G. Paterson, *Canada: An Economic History* (Canada, 1980).

Gordon Marshall, *Presbyteries and Profits: Calvinism and the Development of Capitalism in Scotland, 1560–1707* (Oxford, 1980).

P. J. Marshall, 'British Expansion in India in the Eighteenth Century: A Historical Revision', *History*, 60 (1975).

P. J. Marshall, *East Indian Fortunes: the British in Bengal in the Eighteenth Century* (Oxford, 1976).

P. J. Marshall and Glyndwr Williams, *The Great Map of Mankind* (London, Melbourne and Toronto, 1982).

P. J. Marshall, 'Empire and Authority in the later Eighteenth Century', *Journal of Imperial and Commonwealth History*, XV, 2 (January 1987).

P. J. Marshall, 'The Seventeenth and Eighteenth Centuries' in C. A. Bayly, ed., *The Raj. India and the British 1600–1947* (London, 1990).

P. J. Marshall, 'Imperial Britain', *Journal of Imperial and Commonwealth History*, XXIII, 1 (January 1995).

P. J. Marshall, 'A nation defined by Empire, 1755–1776', in Alexander Grant and Keith J. Stringer, eds., *Uniting the Kingdom? The Making of British History* (London and New York, 1995).

P. J. Marshall, 'Britain and the World in the Eighteenth Century: I, Reshaping the Empire', *Transactions of the Royal Historical Society*, 6th Series, VII (1998).

P. J. Marshall, 'British Expansion in India in the Eighteenth Century: A Historical Revision', in Patrick Tuck, ed., *The East India Company: 1600–1858*. Vol. 5, *Warfare, Expansion and Resistance* (London and New York, 1998).

P. J. Marshall, 'Private British Trade in the Indian Ocean before 1800', and 'Private British Investment in Eighteenth-Century Bengal', in Patrick

Tuck, ed., *The East India Company: 1600–1858*. Vol. 4, *Trade, Finance and Power* (London and New York, 1998).

P. J. Marshall, ed., *The Oxford History of the British Empire*. Vol. 2, *The Eighteenth Century* (Oxford, 1998).

P. J. Marshall, Introduction, in P. J. Marshall, ed., *The Oxford History of the British Empire*. Vol. 2, *The Eighteenth Century* (Oxford, 1998).

P. J. Marshall; 'British North America, 1760–1815', in P. J. Marshall, ed., *The Oxford History of the British Empire*. Vol. 2, *The Eighteenth Century* (Oxford, 1998).

Terence Martin, *The Instructed Vision: Scottish Common Sense Philosophy and the Origins of American Fiction* (Bloomington, Indiana, 1961).

Roger A. Mason, ed., *Scotland and England, 1286–1815* (Edinburgh, 1987).

Roger Mason and Norman Macdougall, eds., *People and Power in Scotland* (Edinburgh, 1992).

W. M. Mathew, 'The Origins and Occupations of Glasgow Students, 1740–1839', *Past and Present*, 33 (1966).

M. Matowist, 'The Problem of Inequality of Economic Development in Europe in the Later Middle Ages', *Economic History Review*, 2nd Series, XIX, 1 (April 1966).

Henry F. May, *The Enlightenment in America* (New York, 1976).

Russell R. Menard, 'British Migration to the Chesapeake Colonies in the Seventeenth Century', in Lois Green Carr, Philip D. Morgan and Jean B. Russo, eds., *Colonial Chesapeake Society* (Chapel Hill, NC, and London, 1988).

R. R. Menard, 'Migration, Ethnicity and the Rise of an Atlantic Economy: The Re-Peopling of British America, 1600–1790', in Rudolph J. Vecoli and Suzanne M. Sinke, eds., *A Century of European Migrations, 1830–1930* (Urbana and Chicago, Ill., 1991).

Donald H. Meyer, *The Democratic Enlightenment* (New York, 1976).

Duane Meyer, *The Highland Scots of North Carolina, 1732–1776* (Chapel Hill, NC, 1957, 1961).

D. W. Miller, 'Presbyterianism and "Modernisation" in Ulster', *Past and Present*, 80 (August 1978).

Howard Miller, *The Revolutionary College. American Presbyterian Higher Education 1707–1837* (New York, 1976).

Kerby A. Miller, *Emigrants and Exiles* (Oxford, 1985).

Kerby A. Miller, ' "Scotch-Irish", "Black Irish" and "Real Irish": Emigrants and Identities in the Old South', in Andy Bielenberg, ed., *The Irish Diaspora* (London, 2000).

G. E. Mingay, ed., *The Agrarian History of England and Wales*. Vol. 6, *1750–1850* (Cambridge, 1989).

Elaine A. Mitchell, 'The Scot in the Fur Trade', in W. Stanford Reid, ed., *The Scottish Tradition in Canada* (Toronto, 1976).

Toby Morantz, 'The Fur Trade and the Cree of James Bay', in Carol M. Judd and Arthur J. Ray, eds., *Old Trails and New Directions: Papers of the Third North American Fur Trade Conference* (Toronto, Buffalo and London, 1980).

Philip D. Morgan, 'The Black Experience in the British Empire, 1680–1810', in P. J. Marshall, ed., *Oxford History of the British Empire*. Vol. 2, *The Eighteenth Century* (Oxford, 1998).

B. G. Moss, 'The Roles of the Scots and Scotch-Irishmen in the Southern Campaigns in the War of American Independence, 1780–1783', unpublished Ph.D. thesis, University of St Andrews, 1979.

G. C. Mossner and I. S. Ross, eds., *The Correspondence of Adam Smith* (Oxford, 2nd edn., 1987).

A. Murdoch, ed., 'A Scottish Document concerning Emigration to North Carolina in 1772', *The North Carolina History Review*, LXVII (1990).

A. J. Murdoch, Review article: 'The Rise and Fall of the Scottish Empire', *Scotland 2, 1* (1995).

Alexander Murdoch, *British History 1660–1832* (Houndsmills, 1998).

Steve Murdoch, 'Scotland, Denmark-Norway and the House of Stuart 1603–1660: A Diplomatic and Military Analysis', unpublished Ph.D. thesis, University of Aberdeen, 1998.

Steve Murdoch, 'Cape Breton, Canada's "Highland" Island?', *Northern Scotland*, 18 (1998).

Steve Murdoch, *Britain, Denmark-Norway and the House of Stuart, 1603–1660* (East Linton, 2000).

Steve Murdoch, 'Scottish soldiers who wandered far away', *Scotland's Story*, 25 (2000).

Steve Murdoch, ed., *Scotland and the Thirty Years War 1618–1648* (Leiden, 2001).

Steve Murdoch and Andrew Mackillop, eds., *Fighting for Identity. Scottish Military Experience c.1550–1900* (Leiden and Boston, 2002).

Steve Murdoch, 'The Good, the Bad, and the Anonymous: A Preliminary Survey of Scots in the Dutch East Indies 1612–1707', *Northern Scotland*, Vol. 22 (2002).

S. Murdoch and A. Grosjean, *Scotland, Scandinavia and Northern Europe 1580–1707, www.abdn.ac.uk/ssne.*

S. Murdoch and A. Mackillop, eds., *Military Governors and Imperial Frontiers, c.1600–1800: A Study of Scotland and Empires* (Leyden, 2003).

S. Murdoch, ed., *Scottish Communities Abroad* (forthcoming, 2003).

Norman Murray, *The Scottish Handloom Weavers, 1790–1850. A Social History* (Edinburgh, 1978).

John Naismith, *Thoughts on Various Objects of Industry Pursued in Scotland* (Edinburgh, 1790).

Sir Lewis Namier and J. Brooke, eds., *History of Parliament: The House of Commons, 1754–1790* Vol. 1 (London, 1964).

R. C. Nash, 'The English and Scottish Tobacco Trades in the Seventeenth and Eighteenth Centuries: Legal and Illegal Trade', *Economic History Review*, 2nd Series, XXXV (1982).

Gayl D. Ness and William Stahl, 'Western Imperialist Armies in Asia', in Patrick Tuck, ed., *The East India Company: 1600–1858*. Vol. 5, *Warfare, Expansion and Resistance* (London and New York, 1998).

Peter C. Newman, *Company of Adventurers*, Vol. 1 (Toronto, 1985).

John Nicks, 'Orkneymen in the HBC 1780–1821', in Carol M. Judd and Arthur J. Ray, eds., *Old Trails and New Directions: Papers of the Third North American Fur Trade Conference* (Toronto, Buffalo and London, 1980).

Mark Norton, 'A Voyage into the Unknown', *Scotland's Story*, 29 (2000).

Patrick K. O'Brien, 'The Political Economy of British Taxation, 1660–1815', *Economic History Review*, 2nd Series, XLI (1988).

Patrick K. O'Brien, 'Inseparable Connections: Trade, Economy, Fiscal State and the Expansion of Empire, 1688–1815', in P. J. Marshall, ed., *The Oxford History of the British Empire*, Vol. 2, *The Eighteenth Century* (Oxford, 1998).

Susan O'Brien, 'A Transatlantic Community of Saints: The Great Awakening and the First Evangelical Network, 1735–1755', *American Historical Review*, 91, 4 (October 1986).

Jane H. Ohlmeyer, *Civil War and Restoration in the Three Stuart Kingdoms: the Career of Randal MacDonnell, Marquis of Antrim 1609–1683* (Cambridge, 1993).

Jane H. Ohlmeyer, ' "Civilisinge of These Rude Partes": Colonisation within Britain and Ireland, 1580s–1640s', in Nicholas Canny, ed., *The Oxford History of the British Empire*. Vol. 1, *The Origins of Empire* (Oxford, 1998).

Conrad Ozóg, 'Scottish Merchants in Poland 1550–1750', *Journal of the Sydney Society for Scottish History*, 3 (June 1995).

James Pagan, *Sketches of the History of Glasgow* (Glasgow, 1847).

Anthony W. Parker, *Scottish Highlanders in Colonial Georgia. The Recruitment, Emigration and Settlement at Darien, 1735–1748* (Athens, Georgia, and London, 1997).

James G. Parker, 'Scottish Enterprise in India, 1750–1914', in R. A. Cage, ed., *The Scots Abroad* (London, 1985).

G. Parker, *The Thirty Years War* (London, 1987).

James Gordon Parker, 'The Directors of the East India Company', 1754–
1790, unpublished Ph.D. thesis, University of Edinburgh, 1977.

Trevor Parkhill, 'Emigration: 17th and 18th Centuries', in Michael Glazier,
ed., *The Encyclopedia of the Irish in America* (Indiana, 1999).

M. L. Parry and T. R. Slater, eds., *The Making of the Scottish Countryside*
(London, 1980).

G. L. Pearce, *The Scots of New Zealand* (Auckland and London, 1976).

Douglas M. Peers, ' "The Habitual Nobility of Being". British Officers and
the Social Construction of the Bengal Army in the Early Nineteenth
Century', *Modern Asian Studies*, 25, 3 (1991).

M. Perceval-Maxwell, *The Scottish Migration to Ulster in the Reign of
James I* (London, 1973).

Lewis Perry and Michael Fellman, eds., *Antislavery Reconsidered. New
Perspectives on the Abolitionists* (Baton Rouge, La., and London, 1979).

N. T. Phillipson and R. Mitchison, eds., *Scotland in the Age of Improvement*
(Edinburgh, 1970).

Murray G. A. Pittock, 'The Jacobite Cult', in Edward J. Cowan and Richard
J. Finlay, eds., *Scottish History. The Power of the Past* (Edinburgh, 2002).

J. G. A. Pocock, 'The Limits and Divisions of British History: In Search
of the Unknown Subject', *American Historical Review*, 87, 2 (April
1982).

Andrew Porter, ' "Gentlemanly Capitalism" and Empire: The British Experience since 1750', *Journal of Imperial and Commonwealth History*,
XVIII, 3 (October 1990).

M. Postlethwayt, *The African Trade, the Great Pillar and Support of the
British Plantation Trade in America* (London, 1745).

John Prebble, *The King's Jaunt* (London, 1988).

Malcolm D. Prentis, *The Scots in Australia. A Study of New South Wales,
Victoria and Queensland, 1788–1900* (Sydney, 1988).

Jacob M. Price, 'The Rise of Glasgow in the Chesapeake Tobacco Trade,
1707–1775', *William and Mary Quarterly*, 3rd Series, XI (1954).

Jacob M. Price, 'The Economic Growth of the Chesapeake and the European
Market', *Journal of Economic History*, XXIV (1964).

Jacob M. Price, *France and the Chesapeake* (Ann Arbor, Mich., 1973).

Jacob M. Price, *Capital and Credit in British Overseas Trade: the View
from the Chesapeake, 1700–1776* (Cambridge, Mass., 1980).

Jacob M. Price, 'Glasgow, the Tobacco Trade and the Scottish Customs,
1707–1730', *Scottish Historical Review*, LXIII (1984).

Jacob M. Price and Paul G. E. Clemens, 'A Revolution of Scale in Overseas
Trade: British Firms in the Chesapeake Trade, 1767–1775', *Journal of
Economic History*, 47 (1987).

433

Jacob M. Price, 'What did Merchants Do? Reflections on British Overseas Trade, 1660–1790', *Journal of Economic History*, XLIX (1989).

Jacob M. Price, 'The Imperial Economy, 1700–1776', in P. J. Marshall, ed., *The Oxford History of the British Empire*. Vol. 2, *The Eighteenth Century* (Oxford, 1998).

Thomas L. Purvis, 'The European Ancestry of the United States Population, 1790', *William and Mary Quarterly*, 3rd Series, XLI (1984).

T. L. Purvis, D. H. Akenson and F. and E. McDonald, 'The Population of the United States, 1790: A Symposium', *William and Mary Quarterly*, 3rd Series, XLI (1984).

W. J. Rattray, *The Scot in British North America*, Vols. 1 and 2 (Toronto, 1890).

Rajat Kanta Ray, 'Indian Society and the Establishment of British Supremacy, 1763–1818', in P. J. Marshall, ed., *The Oxford History of the British Empire*. Vol. 2, *The Eighteenth Century* (Oxford, 1998).

J. M. Reid (Senex), *Glasgow Past and Present* (Glasgow, 1884).

W. Stanford Reid, ed., *The Scottish Tradition in Canada* (Toronto, 1976).

Jane Rendall, 'The Influence of the Edinburgh Medical School on America in the Eighteenth Century', in R. G. W. Anderson and A. D. C. Simpson, eds., *The Early Years of the Edinburgh Medical School* (Edinburgh, 1976).

Jane Rendall, 'Scottish Orientalism: From Robertson to James Mill', *Historical Journal*, 25, 1 (1982).

H. Reynolds, *The Other Side of the Frontier* (North Queensland, 1981).

C. Duncan Rice, 'Abolitionists and Abolitionism in Aberdeen: a Test Case for the Nineteenth-century Anti-slavery Movement', *Northern Scotland*, Vol. 1, 1 (December 1972).

C. Duncan Rice, *The Rise and Fall of Black Slavery* (London, 1975).

C. Duncan Rice, 'Scottish Enlightenment, American Revolution and Atlantic Reform', in Owen Dudley Edwards and George Shepperson, eds., *Scotland, Europe and the American Revolution* (Edinburgh, 1976).

C. Duncan Rice, 'Controversies over Slavery in Eighteenth and Nineteenth Century Scotland', in Lewis Perry and Michael Fellman, eds., *Antislavery Reconsidered. New Perspectives on the Abolitionists* (Baton Rouge, La., and London, 1979).

C. Duncan Rice, *The Scots Abolitionists 1833–1861* (Baton Rouge La., and London, 1981).

Eric Richards, *A History of the Highland Clearances: Agrarian Change and the Evictions, 1746–1886* (London, 1982).

Eric Richards, ed., *The Flinders History of South Australia* (Netley, S. Australia, 1986).

Eric Richards, Alexia Howe, Ian Donnachie and Adrian Graves, *That Land of Exiles: Scots in Australia* (Edinburgh, 1988).

Eric Richards, 'Scotland and the Uses of Atlantic Empire', in Bernard Bailyn and Philip D. Morgan, eds., *Strangers within the Realm: Cultural Margins of the First British Empire* (Chapel Hill, NC, and London, 1991).

Eric Richards, *The Highland Clearances* (Edinburgh, 2000).

David Richardson, 'The British Empire and the Atlantic Slave Trade, 1660–1807', in P. J. Marshall, ed., *The Oxford History of the British Empire*. Vol. 2, *The Eighteenth Century* (Oxford, 1998).

Daniel K. Richter, 'Native Peoples of North America and the Eighteenth Century British Empire', in P. J. Marshall, ed., *The Oxford History of the British Empire*. Vol. 2, *The Eighteenth Century* (Oxford, 1998).

John Riddy, 'Warren Hastings: Scotland's Benefactor?', in Geoffrey Carnall and Colin Nicholson, eds., *The Impeachment of Warren Hastings* (Edinburgh, 1989).

Thomas Riis, *Should Auld Acquaintance Be Forgot . . . Scottish–Danish Relations c.1450–1707* (Odense, 1988).

P. W. J. Riley, *The Union of England and Scotland: A Study in Anglo-Scottish Politics in the Eighteenth Century* (Manchester, 1978).

Jacqueline A. Rinn, 'Factors in Scottish Emigration', unpublished Ph.D. thesis, University of Aberdeen, 1979.

Caroline Robbins, 'When is it that Colonies may Turn Independent: an Analysis of the Environment and Politics of Francis Hutcheson, 1694–1746', *William and Mary Quarterly*, 3rd Series, XI (1954).

John Robertson, *The Scottish Enlightenment and the Militia Issue* (Edinburgh, 1985).

John Robertson, ed., *A Union for Empire: Political Thought and the British Union of 1707* (Cambridge, 1995).

Philip S. Robinson, *The Plantation of Ulster. British Settlement in an Irish Landscape, 1600–1670* (Dublin and New York, 1984).

W. P. Robinson, 'Richard Oswald the Peacemaker', *Ayrshire Archaeological and Natural History Collections*, 2nd Series, III (1959).

L. C. Robson, *The Convict Settlers of Australia* (Melbourne, 1976).

Rosanne Rocher and Michael E. Scorgie, 'A Family Empire: The Alexander Hamilton Cousins, 1750–1830', *Journal of Imperial and Commonwealth History*, XXII, 1 (January 1995).

Peter Ross, *The Scot in America* (New York, 1896).

Vera Rubin and Arthur Tuden, eds., *Comparative Perspectives on Slavery in New World Plantation Societies. Annals of the New York Academy of Sciences, Vol. 292* (New York, 1977).

R. A. Ryerson, 'Political Mobilisation and the American Revolution: the Resistance Movement in Philadelphia, 1765–1776', *William and Mary Quarterly*, 3rd Series, XXXI (1974).

R. Samuel, ed., *Patriotism. The Making and Unmaking of British National Identity* (London, 1989).

Richard Saville, *Bank of Scotland: A History 1695–1995* (Edinburgh, 1996).

S. Schama, *Patriots and Liberators: Revolution in the Netherlands, 1780–1813* (London, 1977).

H. W. Schneider, *History of American Philosophy* (New York, 1947).

P. H. Scott, *1707: the Union of Scotland and England* (Edinburgh, 1979).

P. H. Scott, 'The Last Purely Scotch Age', in D. Gifford, ed., *The History of Scottish Literature*. Vol. 3, *The Nineteenth Century* (Aberdeen, 1988).

W. R. Scott, *Francis Hutcheson: His Life, Teachings and Position in the History of Philosophy* (Cambridge, 1900).

Stanislaw Seliga and Leon Koczy, *Scotland and Poland. A Chapter of Forgotten History* (Scotland, 1969).

W. Seton of Pitmedden, *A Speech in Parliament on the First Article of the Treaty of Union* (Edinburgh, 1706).

C. Shammas, *The Pre-Industrial Consumer in England and America* (Oxford, 1990).

A. G. L. Shaw, *Convicts and the Colonies* (London, 1966).

John S. Shaw, *The Political History of Eighteenth Century Scotland* (London, 1999).

George Shepperson, 'Writings in Scottish-American History: A Brief Survey', *William and Mary Quarterly*, 3rd Series, XI (October 1954).

Richard B. Sher and Jeffrey R. Smitten, eds., *Scotland and America in the Age of the Enlightenment* (Edinburgh, 1990).

Richard B. Sher, 'Introduction: Scottish-American Cultural Studies, Past and Present', in Richard B. Sher and Jeffrey R. Smitten, eds., *Scotland and America in the Age of the Enlightenment* (Edinburgh, 1990).

R. B. Sheridan, 'The Rise of a Colonial Gentry: a Case Study of Antigua, 1730–1775', *Economic History Review*, 2nd Series, XIII, 3, (April 1961).

R. B. Sheridan, 'The Wealth of Jamaica in the Eighteenth Century', *Economic History Review*, 2nd Series, XVIII (1965).

Richard B. Sheridan, *Sugar and Slavery. An Economic History of the British West Indies 1623–1775* (Barbados, 1974).

Richard B. Sheridan, 'The Role of the Scots in the Economy and Society of the West Indies', in Vera Rubin and Arthur Tuden, eds., *Comparative Perspectives on Slavery in New World Plantation Societies. Annals of the New York Academy of Sciences*, Vol. 292 (New York, 1977).

Richard B. Sheridan, *Doctors and Slaves. A Medical and Demographic*

History of Slavery in the British West Indies, 1680–1834 (Cambridge, 1985).

R. B. Sheridan, 'The Formation of Caribbean Plantation Society, 1689–1748', in P. J. Marshall, ed., *The Oxford History of the British Empire*. Vol. 2, *The Eighteenth Century* (Oxford, 1998).

J. Shiels and Diana Wood, eds., *The Churches, Ireland and the Irish* (Oxford, 1989).

Grant G. Simpson, ed., *Scotland and Scandinavia, 800–1800* (Edinburgh, 1990).

Grant G. Simpson, ed., *The Scottish Soldier Abroad, 1247–1967* (Edinburgh, 1992).

Grant G. Simpson, ed., *Scotland and the Low Countries, 1124–1994* (East Linton, 1996).

Sir John Sinclair, *General Report of the Agricultural State and Political Circumstances of Scotland* (Edinburgh, 1791–8).

Sir J. Sinclair, *Analysis of the Statistical Account of Scotland* (London, 1826).

Douglas Sloan, *The Scottish Enlightenment and the American College Ideal* (New York, 1971).

Adam Smith, *Wealth of Nations* (1776; London, 1937).

Adam Smith, *The Theory of Moral Sentiments* (London, 1804).

J. A. Smith, 'Some Eighteenth Century Ideas of Scotland', in N. T. Phillipson and R. Mitchison, eds., *Scotland in the Age of Improvement* (Edinburgh, 1970).

T. C. Smout, 'Scottish Commercial Factors in the Baltic at the End of the Seventeenth Century', *Scottish Historical Review*, XXXIX, 127 (1960).

T. C. Smout, *Scottish Trade on the Eve of Union 1660–1707* (Edinburgh and London, 1963).

T. C. Smout, ed., *Scotland and Europe, 1200–1850* (Edinburgh, 1986).

T. C. Smout, 'Problems of Nationalism, Identity and Improvement in Later Eighteenth-Century Scotland', in T. M. Devine, ed., *Improvement and Enlightenment* (Edinburgh, 1989).

T. C. Smout, 'Scottish–Dutch Contact 1600–1800', in Julia Lloyd Williams, ed., *Dutch Art and Scotland. A Reflection of Taste* (Edinburgh, 1992).

T. C. Smout, 'Perspectives on the Scottish Identity', *Scottish Affairs*, 6 (Winter 1994).

T. C. Smout, N. C. Landsman and T. M. Devine, 'Scottish Emigration in the Seventeenth and Eighteenth Centuries', in N. Canny, ed., *Europeans on the Move. Studies on European Migration, 1500–1800* (Oxford, 1994).

Christopher Smout, 'The Culture of Migration: Scots as Europeans, 1500–1800', *History Workshop Journal*, 40 (Autumn 1995).

T. C. Smout, 'Where had the Scottish Economy Got to by the Third Quarter of the Eighteenth Century?', in I. Hont and M. Ignatieff, eds., *Wealth and Virtue* (Cambridge, 1983).

W. A. Speck, *The Butcher: the Duke of Cumberland and the Suppression of the '45* (Oxford, 1981).

W. Stanford Reid, ed., *The Scottish Tradition in Canada* (Toronto, 1976).

Raymond P. Stearns, *Science in the British Colonies of America* (Urbana, Ill., 1970).

A. F. Steuart, ed., *Papers relating to the Scots in Poland, 1576–1793* (Edinburgh, 1915).

Alexander W. K. Stevenson, 'Trade Between Scotland and the Low Countries in the Later Middle Ages', unpublished Ph.D. thesis, University of Aberdeen, 1982.

Alexander Stevenson, 'Medieval Scottish Associations with Bruges', in T. Brotherston and D. Ditchburn, eds., *Freedom and Authority: Scotland c.1050–c.1650* (East Linton, 2000).

David Stevenson, *Scottish Covenanters and Irish Confederates. Scottish–Irish Relations in the mid-Seventeenth Century* (Belfast, 1981).

D. Stevenson, ed., *From Lairds to Louns* (Aberdeen, 1986).

Alasdair M. Stewart, ed., *Scots in the Baltic*. Proceedings of a Centre for Nordic Studies Seminar, University of Aberdeen, October 1977.

A. T. Q. Stewart, *The Narrow Ground: Aspects of Ulster, 1609–1969* (London, 1977).

D. Stewart, *Sketches of the Character, Manners and Present State of the Highlanders of Scotland* (2 vols., repr. Edinburgh, 1877).

George Stewart, *Progress of Glasgow* (Glasgow, 1883).

Lawrence Stone, ed., *An Imperial State at War* (London and New York, 1994).

Lawrence Stone, Introduction, in Lawrence Stone, ed., *An Imperial State at War* (London and New York, 1994).

C. Storrs, 'Disaster at Darien (1698–1700). The Persistence of Spanish Imperial Power on the Eve of the Demise of the Spanish Hapsburgs', *European History Quarterly*, XXIX (1999).

Gerald Stovrzh, *Alexander Hamilton and the Idea of Republican Government* (Stanford, 1970).

Heather Streets, 'Identity in the Highland Regiments in the Nineteenth Century: Soldier, Region, Nation', in Steve Murdoch and Andrew Mackillop, eds., *Fighting for Identity. Scottish Military Experience c.1550–1900* (Leiden and Boston, 2002).

D. B. Swinfen, 'The American Revolution in the Scottish Press', in Owen Dudley Edwards and George Shepperson, eds., *Scotland, Europe and the American Revolution* (Edinburgh, 1976).

Maurice Taylor, *The Scots College in Spain* (Valladolid, 1971).

Stephan Thernstrom, ed., *Harvard Encyclopedia of American Ethnic Groups* (Cambridge, 1980).

L. Timperley, 'The Pattern of Landholding in Eighteenth Century Scotland', in M. L. Parry and T. R. Slater, *The Making of the Scottish Countryside* (London, 1980).

Kathleen Toomey, 'Emigration from the Scottish Catholic Bounds, 1770–1810 and the Role of the Clergy', unpublished Ph.D. thesis, University of Edinburgh, 1991.

J. H. Treble, 'The Standard of Living of the Working Class', in T. M. Devine and R. Mitchison, eds., *People and Society in Scotland*. Vol. 1, *1760–1830* (Edinburgh, 1988).

H. R. Trevor-Roper, 'The Invention of Tradition: the Highland Tradition of Scotland', in E. J. Hobsbawm and T. O. Ranger, eds., *The Invention of Tradition* (Oxford, 1983).

Katie Trumpener, *Bardic Nationalism: The Romantic Novel and the British Empire* (Princeton, NJ, 1997)

T. M. Truxes, *Irish–American Trade 1660–1783* (Cambridge, 1988).

Patrick Tuck, ed., *The East India Company: 1600–1858*. Vol. 4, *Trade, Finance and Power* (London and New York, 1998).

Patrick Tuck, ed., *The East India Company: 1600–1858*. Vol. 5, *Warfare, Expansion and Resistance* (London, 1998).

R. E. Tyson, 'The Population of Aberdeenshire 1695–1755: A New Approach', *Northern Scotland*, 6 (1984–5).

R. E. Tyson, 'Famine in Aberdeenshire, 1695–99: Anatomy of a Crisis', in D. Stevenson, ed., *From Lairds to Louns* (Aberdeen, 1986).

R. E. Tyson, 'Demographic Change', in T. M. Devine and J. R. Young, eds., *Eighteenth Century Scotland: New Perspectives* (East Linton, 1999).

E. Ashworth Underwood, *Boerhaave's Men. At Leyden and After* (Edinburgh, 1977).

W. E. Vaughan, ed., *A New History of Ireland*. Vol. 5, *Ireland Under the Union, I, 1801–70* (Oxford, 1989).

Jan de Vries, *European Urbanisation, 1500–1800* (London, 1987).

J. R. Ward, 'The British West Indies in the Age of Abolition, 1748–1815', in P. J. Marshall, ed., *The Oxford History of the British Empire*. Vol. 2, *The Eighteenth Century* (Oxford, 1998).

J. T. Ward and R. G. Wilson, eds., *Land and Industry: the Landed Estate in the Industrial Revolution* (Newton Abbott, 1971).

Don Watson, *Caledonia Australis. Scottish Highlanders on the Frontier of Australia* (Sydney, 1984).

D. E. R. Watt, 'Scottish University Men of the Thirteenth and Fourteenth Centuries', in T. C. Smout, ed., *Scotland and Europe, 1200–1850* (Edinburgh, 1986).

Marilyn J. Westerkamp, *Triumph of the Laity: Scots-Irish Piety and the Great Awakening, 1625–1760* (Oxford, 1988).

C. A. Whatley, 'Royal Day, People's Day: the Monarch's Birthday in Scotland *c.* 1660–1860', in Roger Mason and Norman Macdougall, eds., *People and Power in Scotland* (Edinburgh, 1992).

Christopher A. Whatley, '*Bought and Sold for English Gold?' Explaining the Union of 1707* (Dundee, 1994).

Christopher A. Whatley, *The Industrial Revolution in Scotland* (Cambridge, 1997).

Christopher A. Whatley, *Scottish Society 1707–1830* (Manchester, 2000).

Morton White, *Philosophy of the American Revolution* (New York, 1978).

I. D. Whyte, 'Population Mobility in Early Modern Scotland', in R. A. Houston and I. D. Whyte, eds., *Scottish Society 1500–1800* (Cambridge, 1989).

I. D. Whyte, *Scotland before the Industrial Revolution* (Harlow, 1995).

I. D. Whyte, 'Urbanisation in Eighteenth Century Scotland' in T. M. Devine and J. R. Young, eds., *Eighteenth Century Scotland: New Perspectives* (East Linton, 1999).

Eric Williams, *Capitalism and Slavery* (1944; London, 1964).

Glyndwr Williams, 'The Pacific: Exploration and Exploitation', in P. J. Marshall, ed., *The Oxford History of the British Empire.* Vol. 2, *The Eighteenth Century* (Oxford, 1998).

Julia Lloyd Williams, ed., *Dutch Art and Scotland. A Reflection of Taste* (Edinburgh, 1992).

Garry Wills, *Inventing America. Jefferson's Declaration of Independence* (New York, 1978).

Gary Wills, *Explaining America* (New York, 1981).

David A. Wilson, *United Irishmen, United States* (Ithaca, NY, and London, 1998).

Marianne S. Wokeck, *Trade in Strangers. The Beginnings of Mass Migration to North America* (Pennsylvania, 1999).

Peter Womack, *Improvement and Romance* (London, 1989).

Stephen Wood, *The Scottish Soldier* (Manchester, 1987).

Esmond Wright, 'Education in the American Colonies: The Impact of Scotland', in E. R. R. Green, ed., *Essays in Scotch-Irish History* (London and New York, 1969).

John R. Young, 'The Parliamentary Incorporating Union of 1707: Political Management, Anti-Unionism and Foreign Policy', in T. M. Devine and J. R. Young, eds., *Eighteenth Century Scotland: New Perspectives* (East Linton, 1999).

A. J. Youngson, *After the '45* (Edinburgh, 1973).

Index

In this index, the term 'American colonies' is used for the period before the Revolutionary War and 'United States' for the period afterwards.

emigration to Canada 196–7, 209, 210–11, 218

Presbyterian church attitudes to 169, 184

Scottish Enlightenment, influence of 178–81, 183

Scottish immigrants in 179, 181–7; Highlanders 131, 184, 186; anti-Scottish feeling following 186–7

trade/commerce, effect on 184, 185, 232

Ulster Scots in 149, 154, 156, 157, 162, 181–2

American students
at European universities 166
at Scottish universities 166, 174, 177

American West 155–6, 157–62
farming communities 157–8
feuds/range wars 162
Indian Wars 159–61, 314–15
Ulster Scots in 158–61

Anderson, John 286

Anglicanism 351
in Ireland 143, 147, 149, 150, 156, 161
Presbyterian church, opposition to 265
see also Protestantism

Anne, Queen 49, 52
Protestant succession 52, 53, 61

Antigua see Leeward Islands

Anti-Slavery Society 248

Argyll, Dukes of 54, 59, 125, 266, 268, 310

Argyll, Earl of 22

Aristotle 244

Arkwright, Richard 324

armies/mercenaries
American Revolutionary militia 182, 184, 211
attrition rates 13, 14
British army see British army
colonial militia 28, 182, 184, 211, 243, 251, 256, 258–9, 261, 280
Continental Army (American Revolution) 182
desertion rates 14
Danish 17
Dutch 13, 26, 27, 295, 305
French 7, 26, 230, 293, 295, 357

Garde Ecossais (France) 7, 26

German 313

Indian native troops (sepoys) 263, 292

Irish soldiers xxvi, 260–61, 295; officer class 294

mutiny 254, 280

numbers of soldiers 14, 16

officer class 16, 261, 263

post-army life 14

prisoners of war 28, 30

recruitment 14, 17; pressed men 17

Russian 16

Scots 55–6, 354

Scots Brigade (Netherlands) 26

Scottish regiments see Scottish regiments

Scottish soldiers see Highland soldiers; Scottish soldiers

Swedish 13, 14, 15, 16, 17

arms trade 334, 336

Army Presbytery 145
see also Presbyterian church

artisans/tradesmen, as emigrants 113, 114, 232

Ascherson, Neal 15

Asiatic Society of Bengal 260

Atholl, Duke of 55

Atlantic Ocean 207

Atlantic trade 31–4, 36, 51, 64, 69, 88, 330, 332, 338, 341
importance of 328–9, 337
tobacco 32–3, 34, 70, 77–9, 81–3, 88, 320

St Augustine
De Civitate Dei 244

Australia, naming of 283–4

Australian colonies xxiv, 271–89
alcohol consumption in 280, 284
Bigge report on 286
Blue Mountains 284, 285
civil society, transition to 281, 282, 284–5, 286
colonial administrators 277, 280–81, 283–6, 287
colonial militia 280, 284
distance to, as a problem 279–80, 281
East India Company and 283
'emancipists' (ex-convicts) in 285
farming communities 282
gold rushes 278

industrial development – *cont.*
  raw materials 113, 120–21, 123, 128,
    130, 138, 222, 232, 321, 325, 342,
    343
  urban development and 323–6
  see also economic growth
industrial labour force 320, 324, 332,
  336–7
insurance premiums 64, 80
interest rates 43
Inuits (Canada) 194, 200
investment *see* capital investments/
  market
Ireland
  Act of Union (1800) xxvi
  British Empire and xxvi
  Catholicism in 24–5, 64, 142, 143,
    150, 152, 349
  England and xxvi, 17, 18, 20, 179
  the Flight of the Earls 18
  France and 293
  land ownership 18–23, 150
  land rents 150, 151, 154
  migrants from xxvi, 107–8, 140–63,
    231, 260; numbers of 140, 151
  political representation 348
  population levels 107, 140, 151
  Presbyterian church in 145
  Protestantism in 24, 141, 142, 143,
    145, 147, 149, 150, 152, 231, 260
  Scotland and 17, 20, 22, 31, 146–9
  Scottish immigrants xxvi, 4–5, 17–25,
    29, 96, 97, 144–5, 147; *see also*
    Ulster Scots *below*
  Scottish mercenaries in 6–7, 17–18
  Ulster Plantation 20, 21–5, 144
  Ulster Scots xxvi, 18, 19, 20, 22–4,
    96, 97, 100, 106, 140–63; *see also*
    Scottish immigrants *above*
  urban development 153
  see also Irish . . .
Ireland, John 7
Irish famines 107, 151
Irish radicalism 146, 148, 276
Irish Rebellion (1641) 24
Irish Society (USA) 144
Irish soldiers xxvi, 260–61, 295, 296,
  309–10
  numbers of 310
  officer class 294, 296

Irvine, Washington 205–6
Islay, Earl of (3rd Duke of Argyll) 268,
  349–50

Jackson, Andrew 162
Jacobite poetry 359–60
Jacobite rising (1715) 63, 98, 130, 307
  causes of 266
Jacobite rising (1745) 98, 119, 120, 130,
    138, 185, 307, 308, 310
  effects of 262, 264, 308–9, 354
  Prestonpans, battle of 312, 313
Jacobites 53–6, 60, 61, 65, 186, 264,
    348
  at Culloden 119; state retribution
    after 119–20, 229, 262, 263,
    308–9, 310
  East India Company and 269
  in Highland regiments 313
  transportation of 272
  see also Stuart, House of
Jamaica
  as a British colony xxiii, 222
  colonial administrators 229, 233,
    234–5, 248
  medical profession in 234
  Scottish immigrants 229, 231, 234,
    239
  slaves in 224, 248, 337
  sugar plantations 230
  see also Caribbean colonies
James VI of Scotland (James I of
    England) 1, 3, 19–20, 24, 49
James VII of Scotland (James II of
    England), Duke of York 37, 39, 41,
    53
James Edward Stuart (Old Pretender) 53
Jardine, Matheson and Company 338
Jeanie (merchant ship) 81
Jefferson, Thomas 179, 180
  American Declaration of
    Independence, draft of 174–5, 183
Jews
  Sephardic Jews in Caribbean 231
Johnson, Dr Samuel 108, 165, 349
Johnson, William 153
Johnston, Dr Alexander 234, 239–40
Johnstone, Gabriel 167
Johnstone, James 61
Johnstone, John 336

THE SCOTTISH NATION: 1700–2000   T. M. DEVINE

The Number One Scottish Bestseller

In 1999, for the fist time since 1707, a Scottish parliament took substantial control of the national destiny. And here, for the first time in a generation, is a trenchant single-volume overview of Scotland's last three centuries.

'One of the most significant Scottish books of the century' *Herald*

'Outstanding ... Scottish history has been waiting a long time for a counterpart to Roy Foster's masterpiece of revisionist synthesis, *Modern Ireland* ... Devine has written it' Niall Ferguson, *Sunday Times*

'Magnificent ... a high achievement, a history of modern Scotland which, rarely for the subject, endows with sweep and power the changes that have created the country we live in' Michael Fry, *Herald*

'The work of a compendious historical mind. In it, you can smell the stink of the nineteenth-century Glasgow slums ... hear the disputations of the Enlightenment scholars ... It is perhaps the first history of Scotland which both a nationalist and a unionist Scot can keep on their shelves with pride, and that is a large achievement in itself' John Lloyd, *Financial Times*

'A formidable work – a serious attempt to describe within one set of covers the complex and troubled history of modern Scotland ... the range of the book is quite remarkable' Donald Dewar

'A fiercely intelligent account of Scotland ... rich with detail and incident ... Devine is the country's most prominent historian, and from the evidence of this book, rightly so'
Rosemary Goring, *Scotland on Sunday* Books of the Year

MORE PENGUIN

EMPIRE: HOW BRITAIN MADE THE MODERN WORLD   NIALL FERGUSON

The British Empire was the biggest empire in all history. At its peak it governed a quarter of the world's land and people and dominated all its seas.

Though little now remains of the Empire as a political power, its legacy is all around us. It laid the foundation for the global triumph of capitalism. It gave the world its common language, English. It exported both Protestantism and parliaments. And it defeated a succession of rival empires from the Habsburgs' to Hitler's.

In the twenty-first century another English-speaking superpower seems to bestride the globe. But today's American empire was yesterday's British colony. For better and for worse, the world we now know is in large measure the product of Britain's Age of Empire.

How did a rainy island in the North Atlantic manage to achieve all this? What were the special factors that enabled Britain to make the modern world – and made the modern world so British? These are the crucial questions addressed by Niall Ferguson in *Empire*.

This was the first age of globalization. But it was, says Ferguson, globalization with gunboats. *Empire* shows how the British wrested power from their rivals by a combination of imitation and intimidation. It shows how mass migration from Britain turned the American and Australian continents white – and how the missionary movement sought to enlighten the 'dark' continents of Africa and Asia. Above all, *Empire* explains how the British Empire rose – and why it finally fell. Ferguson's answers are controversial but compelling.

There has never been a better time to reassess the achievements – both good and evil – of the British world order. With unrivalled verve and clarity, *Empire* unfolds the imperial story for a new generation of readers.

'Professor Ferguson is the most brilliant British historian of his generation' Andrew Roberts, *The Times*

'Marvellous' *The Sunday Times*

'Elegant and thoughtful' *Sunday Telegraph*

'Excellent' *FT Weekend*

read more   🐧

MORE PENGUIN

SPAIN'S ROAD TO EMPIRE: THE MAKING OF A WORLD POWER 1492–1763   HENRY KAMEN

How did an impoverished, thinly populated country, isolated from the rest of Europe, become the world's first superpower?

Henry Kamen's superb book sheds fascinating new light on Imperial Spain's journey to power, from the capture of Moorish Granada to the opening up of the frontiers in Texas and California. Drawing on extensive research and eye-witness accounts, he overturns our traditional view of the all-conquering enemy of Protestant Europe, demonstrating that the Spanish Empire was above all a global, collaborative venture, which depended as much on the cooperation (willing or otherwise) of native Americans, Africans and Asians as that of Europeans for its success. It was, he argues, this diversity of resources and peoples that made Spain's impact on world history so overwhelming.

'Brilliant . . . lucid, scholarly and perceptive . . . a revelation'
Peter Preston, *Observer*

'The best as well as the boldest existing book on the subject . . .This is salutary revisionism, which Kamen tackles with his usual virtues: forthright language, vigorous pace, vivid examples, resilient thinking, critical intelligence, robust scholarship, uninhibited audacity . . . At last Henry Kamen has given us a history which . . . looks at "the untold story"'
Felipe Fernandez-Armesto, *Literary Review*

'A splendid new book' Paul Kennedy, *Guardian*

'Kamen, an expert on imperial Spain ... pulls off a considerable achievement. He changes our perception of the Spanish empire'
Ann Wroe, *Daily Telegraph*

read more (penguin logo)

MORE PENGUIN

NEW PENGUIN HISTORY OF THE WORLD
J. M. ROBERTS

A book of breathtaking range by the pre-eminent giant-scale historian of our age. One of the most extraordinary history bestsellers on the Penguin list, John Roberts's book has now been completely updated to the end of the last century and revised throughout to make sure it keeps its amazing appeal to a new generation of readers. The entire text has been overhauled to take account of the great range of discoveries that have changed our views on early civilizations and to bring it fully up-to-date. The book has also been completely redesigned and reset. The result is a book that is both an essential work of reference for anyone with the slightest historical interest and a great reading experience.

'A stupendous achievement – the unrivalled World History for our day. It extends over all ages and all continents. It covers the forgotten experiences of ordinary people as well as chronicling the acts of those in power. It is unbelievably accurate in its facts and almost incontestable in its judgements' A. J. P. Taylor, *Observer*

'A work of outstanding breadth of scholarship and penetrating judgements. There is nothing better of its kind' Jonathan Sumption, *Sunday Telegraph*

'This is a book I would like to put into the hands of anyone interested in the past' Alan Bullock

'Anyone who wants an outline grasp of history, the core of all subjects, can grasp it here' *The Economist*

www.penguin.com

PENGUIN HISTORY

ENLIGHTENMENT: BRITAIN AND THE CREATION OF THE MODERN WORLD   ROY PORTER

Winner of a Wolfson Literary Award for History

'Provocative and illuminating ... a pulsing narrative, packed with redoubtable characters and laced with pithy quotations' *Sunday Times*

'This is a book which has understood the age ... and, a surprisingly rare virtue, loves and sympathizes with its dashing, dazzling spirit ... the most brilliant intellectual moment in European history ... has inspired a brilliant, lucid and admirable book' Philip Hensher, *Observer*

'Where once "the Enlightenment" served as shorthand for rigid self-regulation, Porter's Enlightened Britons display a delightful appetite for fun ... simply superb' Kathryn Hughes, *New Statesman*

'Porter's new book is exhilarating because it attempts to provide a coherent map of the jostling highways of ideas that drove through the century, tracking main routes and byways, from suicide and sex to children's books and landscape gardens ... a provocative and illuminating survey' Jenny Uglow, *Sunday Times*

'Roy Porter's sparkling exercise in cartography should help anybody who finds the quicksilver concept of the Enlightenment hard to grasp' Ben Pimlott, *Independent on Sunday*

'Highly readable ... Porter has shattered for ever the notion that the Enlightenment was a monopoly of French culture ... The century popularly associated with powdered periwigs, knee breeches, rapiers and snuff ... was also the century of scientific discovery, intellectual freedom and "modernization"' Robert Blake, *Literary Review*

'A sparkling compendium of eighteenth-century ideas-in-action, full of vivid mini-biographies and suggestive connections with our modern world of clubs, networking and spin' John Walsh, *Independent* Books of the Year

---

PENGUIN HISTORY

DISCOVERIES: THE VOYAGES OF CAPTAIN COOK
NICHOLAS THOMAS

Captain James Cook was one of the greatest sea explorers of all time. His epic voyages charted the islands of the Pacific, defined the coasts of New Zealand and eastern Australia, and ventured into both Arctic and Antarctic ice. His men suffered near shipwreck, were ravaged by tropical diseases and survived frozen oceans.

Cook's voyages are remarkable and enduringly controversial for their meetings with peoples. Aboriginal Australians, Maori, Hawaiians and many others encountered Europeans – often for the first time. These meetings were charged with mutual curiosity, animated by pleasure, and disturbed by violence. Contact meant mutual knowledge, but also trade, sex, and disease. Cook became steadily more intrigued by Islanders' lives, arts, and rituals, and at the same time more troubled by the consequences of his own voyages. He wrote copiously and sometimes passionately, trying to find the words for what was novel and curious, trying to define himself and his mission as essentially humane.

Nicholas Thomas draws on twenty years' research into Pacific art, culture and history to explore the drama of Cook's expeditions. Central to the story is Captain Cook's curiosity. A brilliant map-maker even before he entered the Pacific, Cook would journey emotionally and intellectually into unknown waters, and meet people on beaches who were used to voyaging themselves. Tahitians, Maori, and Hawaiians would position this enigmatic visitor on their own maps, in ways he could neither understand nor control. Their meetings would be sometimes rewarding, sometimes dangerous, always strangely rich and unpredictable. *Discoveries* re-imagines these encounters for a new audience, overturning the familiar images of Cook as both hero and as ruthless colonizer, and exploring the fascinating and far more ambiguous figure beneath.

'Rich, vivid and deeply provocative, Thomas's work combines premiere adventure story with thorough history and intensive sociology' *Publishers Weekly*

'A fabulous new book ... focuses on the extraordinary encounters between Cook's salt-encrusted mariners and the colourful Pacific islanders' Giles Milton, *Living History*

read more ⓟ

PENGUIN HISTORY

THE TRIAL OF THE CANNIBAL DOG: CAPTAIN COOK IN THE SOUTH SEAS ANNE SALMOND

Captain James Cook's three voyages to the South Seas are among the most astonishing expeditions in history – as he and his men circled the world, charting perilous tropical seas and icy Antarctic waters.

Cook forged strong, enlightened relationships with the peoples of the Pacific and outraged his crew by ignoring skirmishes ending in the murder and cannibalism of their comrades. And one day at Queen Charlotte Sound, New Zealand, sailors staged a bizarre ritual in defiance of their captain – the trial, execution and eating of a pet dog. But when Cook eventually began to mete out cruel punishments to the Islanders, the result was his own violent downfall in Hawai'i in 1779. Drawing on all contemporary accounts, Anne Salmond's vivid narrative weaves the stories of the European explorers and Pacific Islanders – and the lasting impact of their explosive collision.

'Masterly ... peppered with adventure, romance and treachery'
Giles Milton, *Daily Mail*

'Tremendous ... Few historical encounters are as gripping'
Anne Wroe, *Daily Telegraph*

'Triumphant' Michael King, *New Zealand Listener*

'Wonderful ... a brilliantly engaging book about one of the strangest tales of the British Empire ... read it with relish'
Kathryn Hughes, *Mail on Sunday*

'A magisterial, essential study of the most epic and poignant voyages in British maritime history' Roger Hutchinson, *Scotsman*

'Exemplary ... A record Homeric in its scope'
Min Wild, *Independent on Sunday*

read more ⬤

MORE PENGUIN

EMPIRE MADE ME: AN ENGLISHMAN ADRIFT IN SHANGHAI ROBERT BICKERS

The highly charged, evocative story of one ordinary man's life and death as a servant of the British Empire.

Shanghai in the wake of the First World War was one of the world's most dynamic, brutal and exciting cities, rivalled only by New York and Berlin. Its waterfront crammed with ocean freighters, gunboats, junks and a myriad coastal craft, it was the great focus for trade between China and the world creating, for Chinese and foreigner alike, immense if precarious opportunities. Shanghai's great panorama of nightclubs, opium-dens, brothels, racetracks and casinos was intertwined with this industrial powerhouse to create a uniquely seductive but also terrifying metropolis.

Into this maelstrom stepped a tough and resourceful ex-veteran Englishman to join the Shanghai police. It is his story, told in part through his rediscovered photo-albums and letters, that Robert Bickers tells here. Aggressive, bullying, racist, self-aggrandizing, Maurice Tinkler was in many ways a typical Briton-on-the-make in an empire world that gave authority to its citizens purely through their skin colour. But Tinkler was also very much more than this – for all his bravado, he could not know that the history that packed him off to Shanghai could just as readily crush him.

A detective story, a recreation of a lost world and a meditation on loss, *Empire Made Me* is both a moving account of one man's life and a fascinating insight into how the British Empire *really* worked.

'A fascinating and dispassionate portrait of how the British Empire kept afloat for so long. In the process he vividly brings to life the forgotten multitude of ordinary British who oiled its wheels, arrested its enemies, fed off its fat, and sometimes died for its cause' Matthew Kneale

'Bickers' detailed recovery of an obscure and "unimportant" policeman's life gives a valuable street-level view of a complex scene. A fascinating book' *FT Magazine*

'Superb' Giles Foden

read more

PENGUIN CLASSICS

THE WEALTH OF NATIONS   ADAM SMITH

Edited with an introduction and notes by Andrew Skinner

'It is not from the benevolence of the butcher, the brewer, or the baker that we expect our dinner, but from their regard to their own interest'

With this landmark treatise on political economy, Adam Smith paved the way for modern capitalism, arguing that a truly free market – fired by competition yet guided as if by an 'invisible hand' to ensure justice and equality – was the engine of a fair and productive society. *The Wealth of Nations* examines the 'division of labour as the key to economic growth, by ensuring the interdependence of individuals within society. Smith's work laid the foundations of economic theory in general and 'classical' economics in particular, but the real sophistication of his analysis derives from the fact that it also encompasses a combination of ethics, philosophy and history to create a vast panorama of society.

Published in two volumes (Books I–III and Books IV–V), this edition contains an in-depth discussion of Smith as an economist and social scientist, as well as a preface, further reading and explanatory notes.

read more (Penguin logo)

PENGUIN CLASSICS

SELECTED POEMS   ROBERT BURNS

Edited by Carol McGuirk

'What an antithetical mind! – tenderness, roughness – delicacy, coarseness – sentiment, sensuality – soaring and grovelling, dirt and deity – all mixed up in that one compound of inspired clay!' Byron on Burns

This important selection of the poems and songs of Robert Burns (1759–96) presents the texts arranged in probable order of composition and uses where possible their first published form. It thus gives modern readers a flavour of what it must have felt like for Burns's first audience encountering his work in the 1780s and 1790s. Unlike most modern editions this one gives equal weight to Burns the great song-writer as well as Burns the great poet, making his songs accessible by printing both lyric and tune. Other special features include a full glossary and a chronological sketch on Scottish history and literature.

'No lyric poet so exploits our capacity for imaginative sympathy. Shelley, who had some stakes in the matter, called poets the unacknowledged legislators of the world. If so, there is no amending law as given by Burns. With an entirely deceptive simplicity, he tells us who we are, by what we feel' Carol McGuirk

---